PRINCIPLES OF
PROPERTY LAW
THIRD EDITION

by

BRUCE ZIFF

Professor of Law

University of Alberta

CARSWELL
Thomson Professional Publishing

Canadian Cataloguing in Publication Data

Ziff, Bruce H.
   Principles of property law

3rd ed.
Includes index.
ISBN: 0-459-27675-1 (bound)   ISBN 0-459-27677-8 (pbk.)

1. Property - Canada.   I. Title.

KE618.Z54 2000   346.7104   C00-931001-0
KF561.Z54 2000

The acid-free paper used in this publication meets the minimum requirements of American National Standard for Information Science – Permanence of Paper for Printed Library Materials, ANSI Z39.48-1984.

CARSWELL
Thomson Professional Publishing

One Corporate Plaza, 2075 Kennedy Road, Scarborough, Ontario M1T 3V4
Customer Relations:
Toronto 1-416-609-3800; Fax 1-416-298-5082
Elsewhere in Canada/U.S. 1-800-387-5164; Fax 1-877-750-9041

For Barb, Hannah and Eli

PREFACE

This edition, as with the first two, is designed as a textbook for use in first-year property law courses in the common law jurisdictions in Canada. My aim is to establish a framework for understanding basic principles, as a first step in the process of coming to terms with the deep complexity that tends to characterize property law regimes. The primary values that I see as informing and guiding the law in this area are explored in Chapter 1. That discussion is intended to serve as a cohesive for the collection of rules and principles presented in the remaining chapters.

My focus is Canada. However, despite this general orientation, I have found it useful to canvass developments in other common law jurisdictions. Moreover, because the book deals with general principles, one should appreciate that there are copious provincial variations, that build on, or deviate from, the basic concepts presented here. This means that to understand Canadian property law it will always be necessary to examine local variations. When examples are called for, I have taken these mainly from Alberta law, although I have also occasionally referred to statutory provisions from other provinces.

I have tried to avoid an approach that presents an anthology of tales from the reported case law. A full account of the law of property cannot be derived by relying too heavily on what judges tell us about the law, either inferentially through the outcomes they arrive at, or more directly, by virtue of the language and lines of reasoning that the judgments adopt. So much more is available to us by looking, for instance, at those political theories that seem to inform the system; by presenting data on how the law operates; by assessing the worth of property doctrine on economic, social, psychological and moral grounds; or even by reflecting on the occasional stanza of poetry. These perspectives are presented here, not as mere plumage, but in the hope that they are useful heuristics.

Four years have passed since the second edition was published. Naturally, the law has changed somewhat. Various reforms, incremental in many instances, can be seen in evidence in all twelve chapters. The most notable juridical developments have been those concerning Aboriginal land rights. Among these, the Supreme Court of Canada decision in *Delgamuukw v. British Columbia*[1] stands out. This pronouncement, along with a host of Supreme Court decisions concerning other facets of the law governing Aboriginal rights decided since the second edition of this text was released,[2] prompted a root and branch revision of the discussion of Aboriginal property entitlements.

In addition to developments in the law, there has also been, to my mind, something of a renaissance in property law scholarship both in Canada and elsewhere. In the last few years valuable works on property theory, policy and

---

1 [1997] 3 S.C.R. 1010, [1998] 1 C.N.L.R. 14, 153 D.L.R. (4th) 193.
2 See, *e.g., R. v. Van der Peet*, [1996] 2 S.C.R. 507, [1996] 4 C.N.L.R. 177, 137 D.L.R. (4th) 289. See also the cases and materials referred to in Part 3(b), Chapter 2.

law (dealing with both real and personalty) have been published.[3] Two of these contributions strike me as especially significant. I have benefited greatly from James Harris's *Property and Justice*,[4] which is a thoughtful analysis and appraisal of the core idea of property and its place within liberal societies. The Ontario Law Reform Commission's *Report on Basic Principles of Land Law*,[5] which deals with a number of knotty legal problems that have been neglected for so long in Canada, should be placed among the most helpful of the recent publications concerning substantive law and the possibilities of reform. The works that have appeared over the span of the last four years can be added to an already impressive array of resources.[6] I draw extensively on this literature, both new and old. Given the expansive ways that one can define or imagine the idea of property in law, and the modest ambitions of this introductory treatment of the subject, the secondary source references are meant to provide a helping hand for those interested is going deep on specific topics.

Generally speaking, in preparing this edition I have used material available to me as of December 1, 1999.

Bruce Ziff
Edmonton
April 28, 2000

---

3 Here are some of the important new works, both Canadian and foreign: M.L. Benson & M.-A. Bowden, *Understanding Property: A Guide to Canada's Property Law* (Toronto: Carswell, 1997); M.J. Mossman & W.F. Flanagan, eds., *Property Law: Cases and Commentary* (Toronto: Emond Montgomery, 1998); Ontario Law Reform Commission, *infra*, note 5; R. Pipes, *Property and Freedom* (New York: A.A. Knopf, 1999); J.E. Penner, *The Idea of Property in Law* (Oxford: Clarendon Pr., 1997); Harris, *infra*, note 4; S. Fisher, *Commercial and Personal Property Law* (Sydney: Butterworths, 1997); S. Hepburn, *Principles of Property Law* (Sydney: Cavendish Pr., 1998); K. Gray & S.F. Gray, *Land Law* (London: Butterworths, 1999); P. Sparkes, *A New Land Law* (Oxford: Hart Pub., 1999).

4 (Oxford: Clarendon Pr., 1996).

5 (Toronto: A.G. (Ont.), 1996).

6 Such as P. Butt, *Land Law*, 3rd ed. (Sydney: Law Book, 1996), K. Gray, *Elements of Land Law*, 2nd ed. (London: Butterworths, 1993); A.H. Oosterhoff & W.B. Rayner, *Anger & Honsberger's Law of Real Property* (Aurora, Ont.: Canada Law Book, 1985).

ACKNOWLEDGMENTS

I received a good deal of help in the preparation of the third edition. As revisions were about to begin, I was fortunate to receive a grant from the Foundation for Legal Research. This allowed me to hire Alison Hayter, who served as the principal research assistant for the project. Ryan DuRussel and Rebecca Sober also worked on the manuscript, the funding for their contributions having been made available by the University of Alberta.

As ever, I benefited from the advice, in various forms, of colleagues and friends, especially David Schneiderman and Richard Bauman. Technical support was provided by Ann Wynn, who ensured that my computer behaved properly. I am also grateful for the assistance of Steve Hostetter and Todd Pinksy at Carswell.

Moral support, in abundance, was provided by my wife, Barb Strange, and by my two adorable children, Hannah and Eli.

Thank you all very much. Thanks also to those who helped with the first two editions of the book.

B.Z.

TABLE OF CONTENTS

TABLE OF CASES

1

THE NATURE OF PROPERTY

> Oh dear me,
> The warld's ill-divided.
> Them that work the hardest
> Are aye wi' least provided.
>
> Mary Brooksbank[1]

1. INTRODUCTION

In this chapter my goals are to introduce the idea of property as a legal concept, and to outline the main arguments that are raised to justify private property. Most of the chapter is devoted to a consideration of the philosophical foundations that are said to support that institution. Coming to terms with the ideologies behind private ownership rights is of some significance. As Richard Pipes has offered, "[o]ne of the major themes of Western political theory during the past 2,500 years has been controversy over the benefits and drawbacks of private ownership".[2] Just as bold is the suggestion that "[p]roperty has been at the core of most social upheavals in human history, including those of the recent past".[3]

Some fundamental propositions will be presented and assessed. What emerges from the examination of the rationales presented below is, perhaps predictably, a collage of different perspectives. Each commands a measure of respect, though none, in my view, offers a thoroughly compelling moral argument in favour of private property. The discussion that follows is of an introductory nature, and it will certainly not produce tidy solutions to the questions that are posed. It would be misleading to suggest that this could be easily accomplished. Instead, my objective here is to air some central issues that can then resonate throughout the remainder of the text. In the succeeding chapters I hope to show how the justifications considered here influence the composition of Canadian property law. The theoretical grounds for conferring ownership form threads that bind (or at least that might serve to bind) together the myriad property rules covered in this textbook.

---

1 The first two editions of this textbook implied that the author of this song was unknown. The words and music of "Oh Dear Me" can be found in N. Buchan & P. Hall, *The Scottish Folksinger* (Glasgow: Collins, 1978) at 33-4.

2 R. Pipes, *Property and Freedom* (New York: A.A. Knopf, 1999) at xi-xii.

3 R. Vogt, *Whose Property? The Deepening Conflict Between Private Property and Democracy in Canada* (Toronto: U. of T.Pr., 1999) at 3.

2.   THE 'PROPERTIES' OF PROPERTY

(a)   an introductory foray[4]

Property is sometimes referred to as a bundle of rights. This simple metaphor provides one helpful way to understand the core concept.[5] It reveals that property is not a thing, but a right, or better, a collection of rights (over things) enforceable against others.[6] Explained another way, the term property signifies a set of relationships among people that concern claims to tangible and intangible items. The reference to 'rights' reveals that property, to a legal positivist, means entitlements created by law. In Jeremy Bentham's words, "[p]roperty and law are born and die together. Before laws were made there was no property; take away laws and property ceases".[7] Under this conception, property is a legal construct, born and bred under a legal regime. However, there is no complete catalogue of the objects that are regarded as property. Likewise, the *subjects* of property, that is, those who may acquire ownership, are also part of a fluctuating class. In other words, we look to the juridical definition of property to tell us not only what may be owned, but who among the citizenry can qualify to be an owner.

Take a closer look at these ideas: first, at the notion of a bundle. This suggests that property is a collection of incidents. Professor A.M. Honoré, in a classic treatment of the nature of ownership, identified eleven elements that he claimed provided the most ample conception of property to be found within a mature legal system. He said this:

> Ownership comprises the right to possess, the right to use, the right to manage, the right to the income from the thing, the right to the capital, the right to security, the rights and incidents of transmissibility and absence of term, the duty to prevent harm, liability to execution, and the incident of residuarity.[8]

I see this list as describing rights to:

(i)   possession, management and control;
(ii)   income and capital;
(iii)   transfer *inter vivos*[9] and on death; and
(iv)   protection under law.

---

4 See further T.C. Grey, "The Disintegration of Property" in J. R. Pennock & J.W. Chapman, eds., *Property: Nomos XXII* (New York: N.Y.U.P., 1980) 69; K. Gray & S.F. Gray, "The Idea of Property in Land" in S. Bright & J. Dewar, eds., *Land Law: Themes and Perspectives* (Oxford: O.U.P., 1998) 15; J.E. Penner, *The Idea of Property in Law* (Oxford: Clarendon Pr., 1997).

5 *Cf.* Penner, *supra*, note 4. It has been argued that the bundle of rights description is a phallic metaphor: see J.L. Schroeder, "Chix Nix Bundle-O-Stix: A Feminist Critique of the Disaggregation of Property", 93 Mich.L.Rev. 239 (1994).

6 See C.B. Macpherson, "The Meaning of Property" in C.B. Macpherson, ed., *Property: Mainstream and Critical Positions* (Toronto: U. of T.Pr., 1978) at 2.

7 J. Bentham, *Theory of Legislation* (London: Kegan Paul ed., 1904, 1802) at 113.

8 A.M. Honoré, "Ownership" in A.G. Guest, ed., *Oxford Essays in Jurisprudence* (London: O.U.P., 1961) 107, at 113.

9 An *inter vivos* transfer is one made between living persons.

The "absence of [a] term", found in Honoré's list, means that these rights might last forever. Furthermore, Honoré saw property in its most fulsome sense as involving two additional facets:

(v) liability to seizure (which he calls "liability to execution"); and
(vi) prohibitions on harmful use.

The Honoré bundle contains a wide range of entitlements. Included are *claims* against others: the owner of a plot of land (which will be called 'Blackacre', following a long-standing tradition in writings about land law) has the right to ask a trespasser to leave, and the interloper has a reciprocal duty to comply. An owner holds *powers* of disposal. Some entitlements are *privileges* or *liberties*, in that the owner's use cannot be abridged by others. The right to destroy property is a privilege in the sense used here. The owner of Blackacre also enjoys *immunities*, including exemptions from certain types of expropriation.[10]

The inclusion of a liability to seizure and a prohibition against harmful use as components of a plenary description of property is a controversial move.[11] These are hardly *rights* enjoyed by an owner: they appear to be subtractions from, not elements of, the largest notion of ownership imaginable. Even if that is so, the identification of a *liability* and a *disability* (items (v) and (vi) respectively) exposes two significant features of property. First, ownership usually entails duties as well as rights: the bitter accompanies the sweet.[12] Responsibilities to the public are sometimes assumed by a property owner: a person owning firearms is duty-bound to take certain precautions; a landowner is typically required to keep noxious weeds under control, *etc.* Under property law regimes it is common to find a large number of ownership based duties, scattered though they may be throughout the law.

Some systems make the imposition of proprietary obligations quite patent. In Ukraine, for example, a new Land Code has been developed to regulate private, state and collective ownership.[13] While conferring fundamental rights of ownership over land (in this post-communist era), the Code also contains a list of responsibilities associated with ownership and use. Hence, owners and occupiers must "use the land efficiently", "employ environmentally safe production technology" and must not "allow economic activity to have an adverse effect on ecological conditions in the territory". Moreover, a landowner must not "infringe

---

10 These labels are taken from W.N. Hohfeld, "Some Fundamental Legal Conceptions as Applied in Judicial Reasoning", 23 Yale L.J. 16 (1913). A more detailed analysis of the interrelationship between the work of Hohfeld and Honoré can be found in L.C. Becker, "The Moral Basis of Property Rights" in *Nomos XXII, supra,* note 4, 187, at 190-1. *Cf.* S.R. Munzer, *A Theory of Property* (Cambridge: C.U.P., 1990) at 18.
11 See also A. Carter, *The Philosophical Foundations of Property Rights* (London: Harvester, Wheatsheaf, 1989) at 5-6; A. Ryan, *Property* (Minneapolis: U. of Minn.Pr., 1987) at 54-5.
12 See further D. Lametti, "Property and (Perhaps) Justice. A Review Article of James W. Harris, *Property and Justice* and James E. Penner, *The Idea of Property in Law*" (1998) 43 McGill L.J. 663.
13 *Land Code of Ukraine,* signed by President L. Kravchuk of Ukraine in Kiev on March 13, 1992.

the rights of owners of other parcels of land''.[14] In short, the Code identifies some fundamental duties of ownership. A pure rights-based definition of ownership obscures the duties that typically also apply, whatever their scope may be in a given locale.[15]

Second, Honoré's suggestion that the ''duty to prevent harm''[16] is actually to be found 'inside' the definition of property reminds us that not all rights of ownership involve absolute entitlements. Blackstone described property as ''that sole and despotic dominion which one man [sic] claims and exercises over the external things of the world, in total exclusion of the right of any other individual in the universe''.[17] This language conjures up some impressive images about property entitlements. However, Blackstone's broad assertion is not now, if it ever had been, an acceptable definition of the nature of property. The fact is that few of the components that make up the bundle are totally unfettered by some qualification or limitation. Blackstone knew this perfectly well, for his *Commentaries on the Laws of England* describe a host of restrictions on basic rights of ownership. Returning to Honoré's list, the right to security is not absolute, nor even is the liability to seizure; some goods are exempt. Likewise, the right to destroy one's own property may generally exist during the owner's life, though a testamentary direction (*i.e.*, one contained in a will) to destroy property may not be enforceable.[18] In general, pressing societal needs, or countervailing values, may result in the imposition of limits on the elements that are associated with ownership.

In addition, property rights can be aggregated in a host of ways. There are a variety of different bundles that the law might construct. Parliament and the courts can augment or reduce the number of incidents that apply to any particular kind of property interest. Going further, an object may be property for some purposes in the law but not for others: for example, confidential information may not be susceptible to theft according to the criminal law, even if it might be treated as property in the sphere of private law.[19] As well, it is sometimes fruitless to try to single out one person as *the* owner of a particular thing; this is not always the

---

14 Art. 40. See also *Land Code of the Azerbaijan Republic*, art. 49 [copy on file at the University of Alberta].

15 See further E. Freyfogle, ''Context and Accommodation in Modern Property Law'', 41 Stan.L.Rev. 1529 (1988-89).

16 *Supra*, note 8, at 113.

17 W. Blackstone, *Commentaries on the Laws of England* (Chicago: U. of Chi. ed. 1979, 1765-9) vol. 2, at 2.

18 See further the review of the law in *Re Wishart* (1992) 46 E.T.R. 311 (N.B.Q.B.). See also *Eyerman v. Mercantile Trust Co.*, N.A., 524 S.W. 2d 210 (Missouri C.A., 1975). *Cf. Matter of the Estate of Beck*, 676 N.Y.S.2d 838 (Surr.Ct., 1998). See also K. Mackie, ''Testamentary Conditions'' (1998) 20 U.Q.L.J. 38, at 50-1, where cases calling into question wills seeking to preserve property are canvassed.

19 *R. v. Stewart*, [1988] 1 S.C.R. 963, 63 C.R. (3d) 305, 50 D.L.R. (4th) 1. Even in a non-criminal law setting, ''the . . . characterization of confidential information as property is controversial'': *Cadbury Schweppes Inc. v. FBI Foods Ltd.*, [1999] 1 S.C.R. 142, 167 D.L.R. (4th) 577, 42 B.L.R. 159, at 169 S.C.R. (*per* Binnie J.). See further the analysis at 169 S.C.R.*ff*. Note also that title to property may pass under contract law, but not for the purposes of the criminal law: *R. v. Milne*, [1992] 1 S.C.R. 697, 85 Alta.L.R. (2d) 257, 12 C.R. (4th) 175.

case. The law accepts that two or more persons may co-own Blackacre; a tract of land belonging to A may be encumbered with a right of use held by B; both a landlord and a tenant have a proprietary interest in land that is held under a lease; and one person may have title to Blackacre for life, with others being entitled to possession once the life estate ends. Ownership is divisible.[20]

Pausing here, one sees that Honoré's list does not identify an irreducible core element.[21] It talks about the idea of property in its most robust sense, not its essential minimum element(s). Some suggest that no single attribute is required. On this account, it is all a matter of "nominalism"[22] – property is that which the law decides must bear that label. By contrast, some judicial decisions have suggested that certain features are essential. So, it has been said that a right cannot subsist as property unless it is "definable, identifiable by third parties, capable in its nature of assumption by third parties, and [has] some degree of permanence or stability".[23] Under another version, to count as property a right must be binding on third parties and capable of being assigned. Although this approach may find adherents, it is neither invariably accepted[24] nor universally true.[25] Take the ability to transfer property, for example. This power need not always form part of the bundle,[26] and may only be essential in the case of money or money-like holdings.[27]

Another view is that property implies a state-enforced right of exclusion over things, good (generally) against the world. Felix Cohen said that,

[p]rivate property is a relationship among human beings such that the so-called owner can exclude others from certain activities or permit others to engage in those activities and in either case secure the assistance of the law in carrying out [that] decision.[28]

---

20 See further J.W. Singer, "The Reliance Interest in Property", 40 Stan.L.Rev. 614 (1988) at 637*ff*.

21 But see Honoré, *supra*, note 8, at 113, where the feature of exclusivity is treated as central.

22 See further T.W. Merrill, "Property and the Right to Exclude", 77 Neb.L.Rev. 730 (1998).

23 *National Provincial Bank Ltd. v. Ainsworth*, [1965] A.C. 1175, [1965] 2 All E.R. 472 (H.L.) at 1248 (*per* Lord Wilberforce). See also *Halwood Corp. Ltd. v. Chief Commissioner of Stamp Duties* (1992) 33 N.S.W.L.R. 395 (S.C.). Merrill, *supra*, note 22, would characterize this approach as "multi-variable essentialism".

24 This will be apparent in the discussion of the modes of judicial analysis employed in analyzing novel claims to property rights: see Part 4(a), *infra*.

25 "An interest may qualify as 'property' for some purposes even though it lacks some attributes. For example, an individual can have a 'property' right in his job yet the job is not assignable, transferable, descendible, or devisable. The 'right to publicity' is transferable during life but may not be devisable": *First Victoria National Bank v. United States*, 620 F.2d 1096 (5th Cir., 1980) at 1104 (*per* Goldberg J.).

26 See *The Queen v. Toohey* (1982) 158 C.L.R. 327 (Aust.H.C.) at 342; *Dorman v. Rodgers* (1982) 148 C.L.R. 365 (Aust.H.C.) at 374.

27 J.W. Harris, *Property and Justice* (Oxford: Clarendon Pr., 1996) at 48.

28 See F. Cohen, "Dialogue on Private Property", 9 Rutgers L.Rev. 357 (1954) at 373. "Suppose we say, that is property to which the following label can be attached: To the World: Keep off X unless you have my permission, which I may grant or withhold. Signed: Private Citizen. Endorsed: The State.": *ibid.* at 374. See also K.J. Gray, "Property in Thin Air", [1991] C.L.J. 252, especially at 292*ff*. Merrill, *supra*, note 22, adopts this definition as the best one. He describes it as "single-variable essentialism".

This formulation goes a long way toward providing a helpful functional definition of property, one that emphasizes the right of exclusion as the essential part of the bundle. This power means more than the right of physical expulsion and includes the idea that an owner holds a *monopoly* over whatever rights of use, transfer, income, *etc.*, are recognized as part of a given proprietary package. It has been said that property law constructs not a wall but rather a gate, which an owner may open or shut according to his or her preferences.[29] This metaphor also reminds us that property creates power relationships among people, a feature of ownership that surfaces again below[30] and in various places throughout the text.[31]

Helpful as Cohen's boiler-plate definition is, its shortcomings should be recognized. If the right of exclusion is at the centre of property, it must still be appreciated that this may not always involve an absolute right to exclude. For instance, at common law, innkeepers and common carriers owe a duty of reasonable accommodation; they cannot deny service without just cause.[32] A finder of goods has rights against the whole world except the true owner or others with a superior right. That finder does have a property right even if those with an antecedent claim cannot be excluded.[33] A homeowner knows that the right of privacy may be curtailed in many ways, including through a lawful search and seizure of the premises. Human rights legislation prevents owners from engaging in discriminatory practices in renting, selling or in the provision of services. Under marital property law, a spouse who owns a home may be excluded from it, and exclusive occupation given to the other (non-owning) spouse. Remember, even the right of exclusivity can be circumscribed. In addition, it is hard to imagine a property entitlement that, in fact, included only the right to exclude (or include) others, and nothing else. Almost all (perhaps all) property rights confer more than this bare power.

The Cohen definition, as with the others presented, is only *descriptive* of what is regarded as property, not *prescriptive* as to the rights that should be placed within its embrace. Nor does it easily allow property to be distinguished from other entitlements. For example, we could say that I have a right not to be harmed by the tortious conduct of others, a 'right' that I may enforce by precluding (excluding) certain actions by others. I also have a right to work and I can prevent others in their efforts to stop me from doing so. Are these property rights? Certainly these examples represent rights against the world and the sole question is whether they can be said to convey the notion of exclusion of others in a meaningful way. Is the concept of property that all-consuming?

---

29 Penner, *supra*, note 4, at 74.

30 See Part 3(d), *infra*.

31 The notion of property as a power base forms a *leitmotif* in Chapter 7.

32 For an argument that this common law obligation extended to others who offered services to the public, see J.W. Singer, ''No Right to Exclude: Public Accommodations and Private Property'', 90 Nw.U.L.Rev. 1283 (1996) especially (for our present purposes) at 1304*ff.*

33 See the discussion of the law of finders in Part 4, Chapter 4.

(b) public and common property

Private property is often contrasted with notions of public and common property. For public property, it is the state that possesses the power of exclusion. However, the rights of enjoyment for public holdings are not entirely the same as those held by a private owner. In principle, the allocation of public goods should be predicated on an assessment of collective interests, which should mean that the obligations of good governance affect the way that the property is used. By and large private owners are not constrained in that way.[34] Public property is therefore subject to state control and is burdened with public obligations.

The label 'common property' is often used to refer to interests for which there is a shared right of use conferred on us all. Hence, there exists no corresponding ability to exclude others. If there is absolutely no element of exclusivity, the property right appears to be outside of the Cohen definition quoted earlier.[35] Indeed, common property in its purest form is the right *not* to be excluded. Whether something is common property or is seen simply as the property of no one may be inconsequential. The ambiguity inherent in these different analyses is sometimes reflected in the way the matter is discussed. The air we breathe may be thought of as the common property of all, but it is equally sensible to think of it as the antithesis of property.[36]

Some cultures are regarded as recognizing forms of *communal* or *collective* ownership. Just what these terms mean is not always clear. Often what is contemplated is that rights enure to those who fit within a certain class: one is entitled simply by being a member of that class. Similarly, a right might be regarded as collective because allocations must be made by the entire group (or a majority or super-majority), or because once one leaves the group, the right to share is lost.

Even with these conceptions in mind, I still find it difficult to see a difference between private and collective ownership (apart from the paradigm form of common property that I have described above). As we have already seen, private property does not always mean *individual* ownership: the law allows two or more people to share property as joint tenants or as tenants in common.[37] In either of these cases the co-owners are entitled to possession of the whole (unless they agree otherwise). Therefore, at the edges it might be fairly hard to distinguish between (say) a tenancy in common (*i.e.*, shared private ownership) and communal property. The members of a community might decide that all of their holdings will be 'communally owned'. Yet if the rights that they create apply only to those who are members of the community, then how, if at all, does this differ from a widely held tenancy in common? Once collective or communal title is used to describe a form of ownership in which some people are 'in' and some

---

34 See further J. Waldron, *The Right to Private Property* (Oxford: Clarendon Pr., 1988) at 40.

35 See the text accompanying note 28, *supra*.

36 *Colls v. Home & Colonial Stores Ltd.*, [1904] A.C. 179, [1904-07] All E.R.Rep. 5 (H.L.) at 182-3 A.C. (*per* Lord Halsbury L.C.) speaking of light and air. Light, air and water "unavoidably remain in common": Blackstone, *supra*, note 17, vol. 2, at 14. " 'Common property' means no property": Harris, *supra*, note 27, at 110.

37 These two types of concurrent ownership are described at length in Chapter 9.

'out', the rights of those on the inside start to look very much like a version of shared private property.[38]

What I hope this analysis illustrates, in part, is that conceptions of private and common property can overlap. Likewise, public and common property rights tend to merge in our consciousness. It is tempting to see public parks and roads, *etc.*, as common property, given that we are all presumptively allowed access; we seem to have the right not to be excluded from these places. But title to these lands is typically placed in public authorities, so therefore these areas are technically under public ownership. Even the private-public dividing line is rather obscure. A private landowner may hold title to Blackacre, but the 'ultimate' or 'radical' title remains in the state (in the 'Crown', as the quaint expression goes).[39] And in public parks, informal private property-like rules sprout up to order rights of use for such things as water fountains, swings and benches.[40]

3.   THE CASE FOR PRIVATE PROPERTY[41]

(a)   introduction

Laws about property reflect important social values. To illustrate, consider the well-known hypothetical referred to as 'the Heinz dilemma', invented by Lawrence Kohlberg to test levels of moral development among children. Heinz's wife is ill, but the couple cannot afford the drugs required for treatment of the malady; without this, the wife will die. In Kohlberg's work, the children-respondents were asked whether Heinz should steal the drug. Carol Gilligan used this test to demonstrate that young girls and boys reason through such problems differently, thereby undermining Kohlberg's research design and data.[42] My reason for raising it here is different again. For present purposes, what is important is that Kohlberg, Gilligan, and at least some of the respondents in the studies,

---

38 Harris uses the term "communitarian property" to describe widely held private ownership under which internal rules dictate the relations of the people who hold title. He gives as an example of this type of arrangement the interest recognized in *Mabo v. Queensland (No. 2)*, [1992] 5 C.N.L.R 1, 175 C.L.R. 1, 107 A.L.R. 1 (Aust.H.C.): Harris, *supra*, note 27, at 103-4.
39 See further Part 2(a), Chapter 2.
40 See further R.C. Ellickson, "Property in Land", 102 Yale L.J. 1315 (1993) at 1386-7, which considers usufructs that arise in relation to such things as the use of public basketball courts.
41 A very select number of Western thinkers are canvassed here, and only in an introductory way. For further reading, see Harris, *supra*, note 27 (which is especially valuable); L.C. Becker, *Property Rights: Philosophic Foundations* (London: Routledge & Kegan Paul, 1977); Carter, *supra*, note 11; *Nomos XXII*, *supra*, note 4; Macpherson, *supra*, note 6, Munzer, *supra*, note 10; Waldron, *supra*, note 34; A. Reeve, *Property* (London: MacMillan, 1986); C. Lewis, "The Right to Private Property in a New Political Dispensation in South Africa" (1992) 8 S.A.J.H.R. 389; E.F. Paul *et al.*, eds., *Property Rights* (New York: C.U.P., 1994). The discussion in this Part is intentionally ahistorical. It does not describe the emergence of modern concepts of property ownership through stages of development. Rather it seeks to present an array of arguments that are capable of being invoked to support the status quo in Canada. A historical treatment can be found in R. Schlatter, *Private Property: The History of an Idea* (New York: Russell & Russell, 1973). See also J. Brewer & S. Staves, eds., *Early Modern Conceptions of Property* (New York: Routledge, 1995).
42 C. Gilligan, *In a Different Voice: Psychological Theory and Women's Development* (Cambridge: H.U.P., 1982).

accepted that the law would place the pharmacist's rights to the property above the needs of Heinz's wife. (It probably would unless Heinz could successfully raise the defence of 'necessity' in response to a charge of theft.) Why, then, do we value property so highly?

Much has been written about the right to property as a human value, and naturally so: in the realm of political philosophy the search for acceptable social, legal and political institutions inevitably requires an assessment of the value of property and the role of the state in the creation and preservation of ownership rights. These questions are extremely important, because the main upshot of accepting a right of private ownership is that items that might otherwise fall under the direct control of the community are given over to private interests. It is possible that, under the distributions that result from privatizing the decision-making power over resources, some will do quite well (in material terms) and others not. There had better be good reasons for allowing that to happen.

I think most Canadians accept that private property is worthwhile. A poll conducted in 1987 indicated that 81% of Canadians considered it either 'important' or 'very important' that the *Canadian Charter of Rights and Freedoms* be amended to include entrenched protections for the right to property.[43] Less than a third of Canadians who were questioned in another survey felt that it was possible for society to be run effectively without the presence of a profit motive.[44]

While private property might seem as natural as the morning sun to most of us, that is just an illusion; in fact, it is a thoroughly contestable notion. Many Canadians might feel that enacting constitutional protections for property would improve our lives, but I find it intriguing that conceptions of perfect societies often involve the virtual elimination of private ownership, usually in the cause of advancing some notion of equality. This approach is evident in Plato's *Republic* and Thomas More's *Utopia*, two of the best-known examples of this type of theorizing. Another is Edward Bellamy's novel *Looking Backward*, released in 1888, but set in the year 2000.[45] In Bellamy's world, private property has been demoted to a subordinate role. Productive capital, profit, and land are all communally owned. By 2000, market dealings are disdained:

> People nowadays interchange gifts and favors out of friendship, but buying and selling is considered absolutely inconsistent with the mutual benevolence and disinterestedness which should prevail between citizens and the sense of community of interest which supports our social system. According to our ideas, buying and selling is essentially anti-social in all its tendencies. It is an education in self-seeking at the expense of others, and no society whose citizens are trained in such a school can possibly rise above a very low grade of civilization.[46]

As a forecast, we know how mistaken Bellamy turned out to be. Nevertheless, this failure does not detract from the idea that imagined communities such as

---

43 D. Johansen, ''Property Rights and the Constitution'' (Background Paper) (Ottawa: Library of Parliament, Research Branch, 1992) at 10.

44 W. Clement & J. Myles, *Relations of Ruling: Class and Gender in Postindustrial Societies* (Montreal: McGill-Queen's, 1994) at 95*ff*.

45 E. Bellamy, *Looking Backward 2000-1887* (Chicago: Packard & Co. ed., n.d.).

46 *Ibid.* at 60.

Bellamy's often promote sharing and co-operation, suggesting that what we settle for as optimal in the real world is based on a moral compromise.

All of the justifications that are outlined here – there are seven main categories of argument that will be considered – reflect the conviction that property provides a basis for enhancing the human condition. It is a vital ingredient in the process of human flourishing; or so it is claimed. Of course, such unsupported assertions about the goodness of property do not take us very far. An interesting feature of the various arguments relating to the need for private property is that they try to substantiate that conclusion in different ways. The theories presented below are therefore all versions of the goodness claim. If in some instances the lines of reasoning appear to intersect, it is probably because they do. Indeed, the extent to which each justification of property actually adds to the others is something that you might consider. So too is the question of whether or not the case for private property is made out.

Asking about the rationales of private ownership engages three discrete issues. The first relates to whether, as a general matter, private property should ever be recognized in preference over other possible regimes (such as public or common property). On the assumption that private property can at least sometimes be justified, a second-order issue arises concerning those occasions when private property should prevail over the other forms; to seek a solution here involves a right-by-right or item-by-item inquiry. For example, questions might arise as to whether or not the law should protect private property rights over airspace, genetic material, or ancient folklore practices.[47] Furthermore, in framing the law it is possible that we might decide that a select number of incidents of ownership might be granted, leaving some property holders with far less than all of the sticks in the bundle.

The third-order question focuses on the persons to whom privately ownable property should be allocated. This is still a general matter, because it goes only so far as to set the rules for ownership. This third question – who gets what? – becomes important only once we have determined that some form of private ownership should exist. We will see that there are a variety of rationales that promote private ownership. In answering the first two questions these theories tend to complement each other. This is because they all advance the idea of private property, and the cogency of any one of them will tend to expand the things that should be capable of being held as private property. That is true as long as one theory cannot be said to be morally superior to the other justifications of ownership. When one turns to rules for assigning rights (the third order), conflicts can more readily emerge, because the theories may point to different criteria as the proper bases of specific allocational rules. As I will try to show here and throughout the book, focusing on the 'why' of property law is useful at all of these three levels. One needs to be convinced that there is a defensible basis for the main framework of private property law. Also, understanding the functions served by property assists in understanding the proper scope of specific rules.

---

47 See Part 4(a), *infra*.

(b)   economic arguments

(i)   the basic law and economics stand[48]

The promotion of economic efficiency is commonly advanced as a justification for private property. 'Look around you', a Canadian entrepreneur might say, 'the wealth and abundance that you see is the product of the right of private property that encourages us to produce more and reap the rewards. This benefits everyone. Compare the deprivation found in the states of the former Soviet Union if you want to appreciate the importance of private property to our material well-being.' Indeed, the privatization of land in nations from the former Soviet bloc is largely premised on the theory that creating a market in land is economically sound. Law reformers in eastern Europe have thus turned to the property law regimes found in the West in an effort to understand how efficiency and ownership interact.[49]

Some economists treat the law, in its essence, as something akin to a colossal pricing mechanism[50] within which property and labour serve as the chief commodities of exchange. And according to the conventional economic position the principles governing property will tend toward efficiency and wealth maximization if several features are in place. First, the law should protect *exclusivity* of ownership, that is, it should effectively enforce my ownership rights and ensure that these exclusive rights cannot be infringed or exploited by anyone else without my say so. It is here that the related ideas of incentives and expectations come into the picture. There would be little reason for a farmer to tend to a carrot patch if, just prior to harvest, anyone else could abscond with the crop with impunity. Second, the law should allow entitlements to be *transferable*, so that they can circulate in the market. If this is done, property interests should eventually gravitate to those people who value them most. Third, the law should make a broad array of items available for exchange. Property should be as *universal* as is feasible.[51] In addition, the idea of universality suggests that the ownership rights should be tenable by as many people as possible. The more players the better. With these three elements in place, the market can work to shift resources efficiently, each trader being assumed to be a rational wealth maximizer – *homo economicus*. The operating assumption here is that 'value' is determined by ascertaining who is prepared to pay the most for a specific good. It is the 'almighty

48 See further R. Cooter & T. Ulen, *Law and Economics*, 2nd ed. (New York: Addison-Wesley, 1997) chs. 4 and 5.

49 See generally G.S. Alexander & G. Skapska, eds., *A Fourth Way? Privatization, Property, and the Emergence of New Market Economies* (London: Routledge, 1994); D.L. Weimer, ed. *The Political Economy of Property Rights: Institutional Change and Credibility in the Reform of Centrally Planned Economies* (Cambridge: C.U.P., 1997).

50 C. Veljanovski, *The Economics of Law: An Introductory Text* (London: Institute of Economic Affairs, 1990) at 15. See also R.A. Posner, *The Economics of Justice* (Cambridge: H.U.P., 1981) at 75: "The basic function of law from an economic and wealth-maximization perspective is to alter incentives."

51 R.A. Posner, *Economic Analysis of Law*, 5th ed. (New York: Aspen Law, 1998) at 36*ff*. See also H. Gensler, "Property Law as an Optimal Economic Foundation", 35 Washburn L.J. 50 (1995).

buck' (as my mother called it) that controls the measure of value, not need, and not some other measure of desire.

This outline, of course, is merely a rough-hewn depiction of the rudiments of a market economy. What is crude about this portrayal is that, in this unadorned form, it reflects a faith in the market that many modern economists do not appear to hold. But typically the economic argument in favour of private property is clothed with a recognition that the market can sometimes work rather imperfectly, and this means that a measure of legal regulation is occasionally needed to establish efficient allocations when bargaining in the marketplace is hampered or stifled.

(ii)   the tragedy of the commons

The economic case for individual ownership is sometimes made by reference to a parable known as the tragedy of the commons.[52] Consider a situation in which farmers share a pasture on which each may place as many cattle as they wish (or own). Under these circumstances, a given farmer, A, will be motivated to graze as many cattle as possible. The advantage to that farmer of adding each additional cow is its ultimate market value. The cost of doing so is the loss of the grazing space needed to sustain one cow. Yet, that is a loss which will be borne by all of those using the commons, so only a fraction of this extra burden affects A directly. Since the benefits of the extra cow are captured fully by A, but the costs spread widely, A must certainly come out ahead. But there's a catch. Every farmer should see the sense of spreading the cost in the same way as A; each should follow the logic that suggests more grazing. Given that the commons is finite, the inevitable result will be over-grazing and a degradation of the pasture lands, leading in the end to calamitous economic losses for all. The pattern of events described in the tragedy of the commons has been shown to occur in the exploitation of genetic plant resources[53] and when unregulated commercial fishing is allowed to take place.[54]

One lesson that might be gleaned from the story of the commons is that the use of private pastures would not lead to the same tragic result because the land would be more carefully conserved. Private property can operate to reduce the ability of an owner to shunt off costs onto others. In the language of economics, private ownership can reduce social costs or 'negative externalities'. Likewise, by protecting the exclusivity of the owner, private property tries to limit the

---

52 G. Hardin, "The Tragedy of the Commons", 162 Science 1243 (1968). "The 'Tragedy of the Commons' provides a powerful argument for the assignment of property rights": J.L. Harrison, *Law and Economics* (St. Paul: West Pub. Co., 1995) at 43. Michael Taylor does not share this enthusiasm. He claims that "in almost every detail Hardin goes wrong": M. Taylor, "The Economics and Politics of Property Rights and Common Pool Resources", 32 Nat. Resources J. 633 (1992) at 634.

53 R.A. Sedjo, "Property Rights, Genetic Resources, and Biotechnological Change", 32 J.L. & Econ. 199 (1992).

54 See further D.R. Mathews, *Controlling Common Property: Regulating Canada's East Coast Fishery* (Toronto: U. of T. Pr., 1993); "After the Collapse" (1995) 18(1) Dal.L.J. (Special Issue).

misappropriation of 'positive externalities' by others. When a sports event is viewed by spectators from a vantage point outside the stadium at no cost, positive externalities are being taken.[55] Private property tries to prevent these results. In short, "the main allocative function of property rights is the internalization of beneficial and harmful effects".[56] Put in other terms, private ownership is supposed to control (or capture) the benefits and burdens of exploitation.

Glenn Stevenson's review of styles of pasture management on the Swiss Alps (appropriately enough) showed that privately held lands were more productive than those held under various types of communal arrangements. However, Stevenson acknowledged that his findings did not take account of the costs generated by the different systems. Highly revealing, I think, is that some of the pasture lands had been run as commons for centuries without succumbing to the destruction through over-exploitation that the parable warns will inevitably ensue.[57] Given the Swiss experience it would seem that the tragedy of the commons story is not so much an argument in favour of private property as it is a manifestation of the perils of *unregulated* common property.[58] To avoid the ruination of the pasture one could establish rules for commons use that would promote proper management. Returning to the parable, the law might allow grazing of a limited number of cattle. Implementing a regulatory system would entail costs, of course. One would need to establish appropriate standards, and enforcement mechanisms would have to be put in place. But so what? All systems of property, even those involving private ownership, entail costs,[59] a reality that is becoming painfully clear as eastern bloc countries confront the difficulties inherent in establishing vibrant market economies. Consider the state resources that are devoted to the criminal justice system to protect property, and the enormous body of civil law directed essentially toward the same end. And think about the precautions you take, as well as the time and money you spend, to guard your possessions.

In addition, the contours of ownership rights must be carefully shaped. For instance, the fracturing of private property entitlements into small bits can wind up paralyzing resource use, producing what has been termed a tragedy of the anticommons. This kind of tragedy occurs when too many people have a right of exclusion (the converse of a commons), with no one person holding effective use privileges. It has been suggested that this kind of diffusion of rights explains a

---

55 For a discussion of externalities, see D.M. Hausman, "When Jack and Jill Make a Deal", 9 Social Phil. & Policy 95 (1992).

56 H. Demsetz, "Towards a Theory of Property Rights", 57 Am.Econ.Rev. 347 (1967) at 347. For an analysis of a sad example of the law's failure to internalize negative externalities, see D.N. Dewees & M. Halewood, "The Efficiency of the Common Law: Sulphur Dioxide Emissions in Sudbury" (1992) 42 U.T.L.J. 1.

57 G.G. Stevenson, *Common Property Economics: A General Theory of Land Use Applications* (New York: C.U.P., 1991).

58 Four responses to the tragedy are canvassed in M.J. Trebilcock, "Economic Analysis of Law" in R.F. Devlin, ed., *Canadian Perspectives on Legal Theory* (Toronto: Emond Montgomery, 1991) 103, at 114-5. See also Elenor Ostrom's account of the factors that can lead to the successful management of common pool resources in E. Ostrom, *Governing the Commons: The Evolution of Institutions for Collective Action* (New York: C.U.P., 1990).

59 Taylor, *supra*, note 52, at 635.

curious development in post-communist Moscow: storefronts remain empty while street-side kiosks are found everywhere. It has been argued, persuasively, that the excessive parsing of property rights in relation to store-ownership (the right to sell being held by one set of stakeholders; the right to lease, by another; the right to occupy, by a third, *etc.*) has bogged down development because these various owners find it hard to mount a co-operative effort.[60]

In brief, even if we accept that the commons may be destroyed in a husbandry free-for-all, the problem then becomes determining *which* regulatory system should be adopted instead. Robert Ellickson has maintained that private property rules will normally be cheaper than a communal property regime in at least one area, namely, boundary protection. For private property, methods have to be established to monitor wrongful entry. That may be difficult. Still, with common property the monitoring process is far more complex. This is because under a communal regime each user would be permitted to enter the shared lands, but would be required to refrain from over-consumption (to avoid the tragedy).[61] Ellickson's argument seems to be sound (even ingenious) at a theoretical level. However, the creation of private allotments creates more fences and boundaries, and this will increase the costs of fixing the boundaries and monitoring the borders (a point that Ellickson makes). Plus, problems of private property rights violations can be acute if it turns out that a given society gives too much land to too few (a factor that he does not address). The more people who are left out, the greater the danger of a breach of the boundaries. In Canada there are hundreds of thousands of thefts and B-and-Es each year,[62] which surely underscores the potential for private property systems to generate costs.

Moreover, the impression that Hardin's story of the commons concerns a pure-form of shared ownership is mistaken. What he describes is a mixed system in which common lands are combined with privately held livestock. What the tragedy suggests at first glance is that this hybrid system will not work, so the land, like the cattle, should be privatized. By the same token, the tragedy would not likely occur in a community in which the herds of cattle were also shared equally amongst all members.[63] The incentive to over-graze would (*ex hypothesi*) then be absent. Now, other problems, such as diminished production, might then arise; that is another matter altogether. At least there would be no tragedy of the commons.

In addition, the adoption of private property will not invariably prevent new tragedies from occurring. The foisting of burdens (described above as negative

---

60 M.A. Heller, ''The Tragedy of the Anticommons: Property in the Transition from Marx to Markets'', 111 Harv.L.Rev. 621 (1998).

61 Ellickson, *supra*, note 40, at 1327-9. ''Monitoring boundary crossings is easier than monitoring the behavior of persons situated inside boundaries. For this reason, managers are paid more than night [guards]'': *ibid*. at 1327-8.

62 In 1998, there were a total of 1,375,881 reported property crimes in Canada, including 350,176 incidents of breaking and entering. The property crime rate was 4,541 per 100,000 people: Statistics Canada, *The Daily*, July 21, 1999, reproduced at <www.statcan.ca>.

63 See further A. Carter, *The Philosophical Foundations of Property Rights* (London: Harvester, Wheatsheaf, 1989) at 68.

externalities) onto others can occur whenever more than one person has a legitimate claim to a share of property. As we will see throughout this book, there are many areas of the law where this is so.[64] The case of oil and gas exploration demonstrates how resources can suffer the fate of premature development through the pursuit of individual gain. Oil and natural gas are fugacious materials, that is, they have a migratory capacity. Under the common law, where there are oil and gas deposits below the lands of several people, the benefits of exploitation will be enjoyed by those who first capture (or win) the resource. This is an example of what will later be referred to as a principle of first occupancy.[65] As a result,

the owners of the common pool are of necessity placed in a furious competition with one another – [all], in effect, attempting to rob [their] neighbour before [their] neighbour robs [them]. *All operators favour the present over the future*, and none has an interest in the maximization of aggregate recoverable resources.[66]

Speaking more generally, there is a built-in social cost in allowing individual ownership: action based on personal gain is often driven by short-term goals. This is because "we are all brief tenants on this planet".[67] When people die their property passes to someone else; until then, there exists an incentive to exploit it to the hilt, spreading part of the costs over to the next generation. Some owners will still be induced to use their property wisely, improving its worth with a view to enhancing its market value.[68] But there is still a danger that self-interest will impel some owners to exhaust non-renewable property resources now, regardless of how this might affect others later on. This self-interest may be tempered for individuals who wish to ensure material well-being for their children, but that motive will not influence all of us to the same degree. Perhaps this explains why hundreds of properties in Canada have been spoiled through the dumping of heavy metals and toxic waste.[69] The tragedy of the commons implies that there is an unhealthy tendency to look only to the short-term, for a vital premise of the parable is that each farmer acts on the basis of a present self-interest. Indeed, accepting this, together with the assumptions that a common pasture is a finite commodity and the cows will take from it more than they return, there may be no logical solution to the tragedy. This is a disheartening conclusion given that this planet is no more than a 'commons' with limited resources.

---

64 Such as when land is shared sequentially or contemporaneously. These problems of commons management are considered below in Chapters 5 and 9, respectively.

65 See Part 3(g), *infra*.

66 J. Richards & L. Pratt, *Prairie Capitalism: Power and Influence in the West* (Toronto: McClelland & Stewart, 1979) at 48 (emphasis added). See also *Borys v. Canadian Pacific Railway*, [1953] A.C. 217, [1953] 1 All E.R. 451, [1953] 2 D.L.R. 65 (P.C.) where the Privy Council warned that the only safeguard against the loss of gas, oil or water was to take occupancy (first). For a further example, concerning the sharing of expenses for the common elements of a condominium, see *York Region Condominium Corp. No. 771 v. Year Full Investment (Canada) Inc.* (1992) 10 O.R. (3d) 670, 26 R.P.R. (2d) 164, 95 D.L.R. (4th) 327 (Gen.Div.) affirmed (1993) 30 R.P.R. (2d) 296, 12 O.R. (3d) 641, 100 D.L.R. (4th) 449 (C.A.).

67 S.L. Udall, *The Quiet Crisis and the Next Generation* (Salt Lake City: Gibbs Smith, 1988) at xviii.

68 See further Ellickson, *supra*, note 40, at 1368-70.

69 R. Matas, "Waste Site Cleanup in Limbo", *Globe & Mail*, December 28, 1995, A4.

(iii)   *other critiques*

The economic justification lacks persuasiveness to the extent that there is no benchmark with which to determine if the efficiency that results is actually better than that produced by other forms of ownership.[70] This problem plagues all arguments that are consequentialist in nature, and which accordingly set out to show that private property works best by pointing to its demonstrable superiority. I concede that comparisons with other polities that have endured command economies for decades seem to support efficiency-based claims. Still, the implosion of the communist regimes in eastern Europe is hardly proof of the virtues of the market, because those developments are integrally tied to the erosion of non-democratic institutions that have no necessary connection with public property and communist economies. This factor, the pre-existing economic regimes that the command systems supplanted, taken with all that has happened in Europe this century, hardly create laboratory conditions for the testing of alternative modes of distribution.

The economic theories about ownership also seem heavily reliant on the belief that most people are rational wealth maximizers at heart. If enough of us don't fit that description then this starting premise breaks down, at least to the extent that the theory assumes the naturalness of this aspect of the human condition. Carol Rose has challenged the assumption that such preferences are 'just there', and has raised the possibility that our images of *homo economicus* are constructions of a dominant discourse that now pervade our thinking on the subject.[71] These questions are addressed again below, when the psychological undercurrents of ownership are examined.[72]

In any event, an economic theory cannot serve as a comprehensive guide for answering the second-order question (what should count as property?). Although universality is a precondition of high efficiency (*i.e.*, as many goods as possible ought to be tradeable) that goal must sometimes take a back seat to other values or concerns. For example, it has been mooted that the market should serve as the basis for determining who should receive babies for adoption.[73] More realistically, it has been argued that the law should recognize a market-alienable right over human organs.[74] These proposals are of course objectionable on moral grounds,

---

70 See further D. Kennedy & F.I. Michelman, "Are Property and Contract Efficient?", 8 Hofstra L.Rev. 711 (1980).

71 C.M. Rose, "Property as Storytelling: Perspectives from Game Theory, Narrative Theory, Feminist Theory" in *Property and Persuasion: Essays on the History, Theory, and Rhetoric of Ownership* (Boulder: Westview Pr., 1994) ch. 2, at 39.

72 See Part 3(e), *infra*. See also C. Jolls *et al.*, "A Behavioral Approach to Law and Economics", 50 Stan.L.Rev. 1471 (1998) and the commentaries following this article.

73 See E.M. Landes & R.A. Posner, "The Economics of the Baby Shortage", 7 J.Leg.Stud. 323 (1978); R.A. Posner, "The Regulation of the Market in Adoptions", 67 B.U.L.Rev. 59 (1987) (the lead article in a symposium contained in vol. 67(1)); J.R.S. Prichard, "A Market for Babies?" (1984) 34 U.T.L.J. 341. See also M.J. Mossman & W.F. Flanagan, eds., *Property Law: Cases and Commentary* (Toronto: Emond Montgomery, 1998) at 63*ff*, and the authorities cited there.

74 See, *e.g.*, B.G. Hanneman, "Body Parts and Property Rights: A New Commodity for the 1990s", 22 Sw.U.L.Rev. 399 (1993).

even though they might accord with principles of wealth maximization.[75] The drive for prosperity is not the only concern to which the law, including the law of property, should respond.

Moreover, there may be times when it is obvious that economic development would be inhibited by too much private property. Picture a world in which all roads and rivers were in private hands. It is hard to visualize how an economy could function when the capricious acts of an owner of some important thoroughfare might bring the commercial sector to its knees. The touchstone of universality suggests that every single road (not just the occasional toll road) should be placed into individual ownership but, interestingly, in no market economy is that idea taken seriously. Some public or common holdings seem necessary to keep free enterprise on track.[76]

The final point about efficiency and property is perhaps an obvious one: private property rights that are built on an economic efficiency model produce inequalities of condition. Ralph Waldo Emerson said it well: "property has been compared to snow – if it all fell level today, it will be blown into drifts tomorrow". Even if all property were gathered in and equitably redistributed, and even if every transaction could improve one party without making the other worse off, the ability to bargain and trade would likely produce differences in wealth. Even in a mixed economy with high rates of taxation (such as Canada), there will always be winners and losers, determined as a result of skill, capacity and Providence. What is more, the *labour* market relies heavily on the fact that some people will have few assets (apart from their 'human capital'):

> Belying its pompous declarations about the sanctity of property, the market glorified in this ideology has always rested on the propertylessness of the direct producers. Until the working poor were divested of any significant means of production of their own, there could be no truly 'free' market in labour. The original market ideologists from early advocates of enclosure to hard-nosed opponents of poor relief understood this.[77]

In a society that allocates ownership in pursuit of economic efficiency there is also likely to be, as in fact there is, abject poverty at one end of the wealth continuum and abundance at the other.[78] Highly unequal property holdings are contemplated as a possible result of the economic basis of property rights. There is no ceiling on the amount of wealth one can amass under this rationale; nor is there one imposed under Canadian law.[79]

---

75 See also R.A. Posner, "Law and Economics *Is* Moral", 24 Val.U.L.Rev. 163 (1990) at 170. See generally M.J. Radin, *Contested Commodities* (Cambridge: H.U.P., 1996).

76 See further C.M. Rose, "The Comedy of the Commons: Custom, Commerce, and Inherently Public Property" in *Property and Persuasion, supra*, note 71, ch. 5.

77 D. McNally, *Against* the *Market: Political Economy, Marxist Socialism and the Marxist Critique* (New York: Verso, 1993) at 218.

78 See the brief review of income disparities in Canada, in Part 5, Chapter 2.

79 For a brief account of the alleged benefits of inequality, see D.P. Levine, *Wealth and Freedom: An Introduction to Political Economy* (Cambridge: C.U.P., 1995) at 83-5.

(c)   arguments drawn from utilitarianism

The economic argument is sometimes seen as a sub-category of utilitarianism, of the sort associated with John Stuart Mill or, even more commonly, Jeremy Bentham.[80] In Bentham's vision the base concept of utility meant this:

> the principle which approves or disapproves of every action whatsoever, according to the tendency which it appears to have to augment or diminish the happiness of the party whose interest is in question: or . . . in other words, to promote or to oppose that happiness.[81]

For Bentham, utility was determined through a calculation of pleasure and pain. This process of computation was influenced by the ability of a society to promote equality, security, subsistence and abundance.[82] These four goals are all bound up with material well-being. That being so, the logical next step, which Bentham took, was to argue that wealth was a measure of happiness. People have an acquisitive need that must be satisfied to achieve happiness, and this can be best accomplished in a society that provides a measure of security for property holdings. This, in turn, means that the legal protection of property is imperative.

The claim that there is a need for security is reminiscent of efficiency arguments directed at the importance of preventing the misappropriation of property. In the discussion of the economic theory this was referred to as the need to recognize and protect the exclusivity of ownership.[83] Additionally, Bentham seems to have regarded people as being roughly similar to those rational wealth maximizers who would ruin the commons and who trade entitlements in the marketplace. Some modern utilitarian thinkers have increasingly drawn on efficiency as a measure of utility largely because of the precision it can yield, moving away from the hedonic approach so evident in Bentham. In this way, efficiency and utility shade into each other.

However, one should appreciate that old-style utilitarianism and the economic arguments mentioned above are not identical.[84] The computation of pain and pleasure made under early utilitarianism will take account of economic concerns, probably to a very high degree, but it would also import much more into the equation. Some versions of utilitarianism allow such qualities as greed to influence policy formulation, if this emotional weakness nevertheless yields pleasure. According to Bentham's rather uncompromising version of utilitarianism,[85] any rule or conduct could potentially prove beneficial, even if it might lead

---

80 There are many forms of utilitarian thought. For a general treatment, see R.G. Frey, ed., *Utility and Rights* (Minneapolis: U. of Minn.Pr., 1984). See also A. Ryan, *Property and Political Theory* (Oxford: Basil Blackwell, 1984) ch. 4.

81 J. Bentham, *An Introduction to the Principles of Morals and Legislation* (Darien, Conn.: Hafner Pub.Co. ed., 1970, 1789) at 2.

82 J. Bentham, *Theory of Legislation* (London: Kegan Paul ed., 1904, 1802) at 96*ff.*

83 See Part 3(b), *supra.*

84 See further R.A. Posner, *The Economics of Justice* (Cambridge: H.U.P., 1981) ch. 3, *passim.*

85 There are versions of utilitarianism that are more moderate than Bentham's. Some utilitarians would place side restraints on what a political regime could do, where, for example, an analysis based on utility would produce an erosion of human rights. See generally A.K. Sen & B. Williams, eds., *Utilitarianism and Beyond* (Cambridge: C.U.P., 1982).

to extreme suffering for some. To fall back on a standard example, we might wish to tolerate the imposition of lawful slavery on a few unfortunate individuals, if society was the better for it. Public condemnation would undoubtedly count against such action in the calculus, and could turn the tide. But it might not. Nothing is necessarily ruled out no matter how much fundamental freedoms might be eroded or sacrificed under a utilitarian-based legal regime.

By the same token, a utilitarian *might* be agreeable to the idea of forced redistributions, for if taking property from the rich increases overall utility, then so be it. A utilitarian might want to know, for example, if taking a million dollars from the very wealthiest people in Canada and handing it to the poorest among us would produce a net gain in happiness. If it would, then the hardcore utilitarian should be in favour of such action. This raises a key point – applied utilitarianism can just as easily found an argument against, rather than in support of, private property.[86] Individual ownership should prevail *if* this produces optimal happiness; but other approaches might produce even more. (A pure economic approach would tolerate forced redistribution only in cases in which the market has broken down. When that happens the imposition of a different distributive system should then be based on a guess as to the result the market might produce if it could operate properly.)

Bentham acknowledged that those who are well-off obtain less marginal happiness from additional gains in wealth than would be enjoyed by the desperately poor to whom money was transferred. And he also regarded equality as a measure of a healthy society. The obvious conclusion to be drawn ought to be that this type of redistribution would mark an improvement in total societal happiness. Yet Bentham resisted this conclusion because he thought that it would undermine the security necessary for the useful ownership of property.[87] The idea of satisfying expectations is a central feature of Bentham's version of utility; and this is linked, of course, with the need for security of property holdings.[88] He was convinced that an extensive confiscation of property would deaden industry. Moreover, he appears to have assumed that modern prosperous societies would move towards equality in the long term.[89] Even if one can accept this assessment of the importance of security of tenure, the second hunch (as to the development of modern society) seems too sanguine given the world in which we live.[90]

Resort to the language of utility is fairly common, at least in the sense that policy-makers speak of weighing factors, and taking into account the overall benefits to society, in arriving at decisions. However, in my view the vagueness of the formula for measuring pros and cons, especially in its original hedonic form, exposes the weakness of the utilitarian project as a basis for explaining why

---

86 See A. Ryan, *Property* (Minneapolis: U. of Minn.Pr., 1987) at 59.

87 *Theory of Legislation, supra*, note 82, at 99, 102-5, 111*ff*, and especially 119*ff*.

88 *Ibid.* at 159. See further A. Ryan, *Property and Political Theory* (Oxford: Basil Blackwell, 1984) at 99. The protection of expectations is apparent in the law of adverse possession and, arguably, in the law governing the rights of finders of lost property: see Parts 3 and 4, Chapter 4.

89 *Theory of Legislation, supra*, note 82, at 123.

90 See the data on the distribution of income in Part 5, Chapter 2.

we have systems of private property. Benthamite rule-utilitarianism speaks of a computation and implies that there can be a level of precision in the decision-making process. However, it provides no real basis for computing, weighing, measuring or testing a given policy. Recent utilitarian works, which tie utility to demonstrated preferences, do attempt to respond to this problem of incommensurability. Yet conclusions that are then drawn about utility based on, say, market choices, do not seem to add to the efficiency arguments considered above.[91] Whether we are seeking to compute pleasure, desire, preferences, the enhancement of personal capacities, *etc.*, I have always felt unable to do the math necessary to measure one form of property regime against others. The single metric we need to measure utility in all its diverse forms eludes us still.[92] In consequence, I feel that theories built on notions of utility are the least persuasive and illuminating of those advanced to justify individual ownership, except to the extent that they identify values worth caring about.

(d)   the promotion of freedom[93]

Those who watch Canadian television know that lottery tickets are sometimes promoted through commercials that convey a clear, cheerful, and loud message about what your winning ticket can buy: FREEDOM! These ads, annoying as they may be, nonetheless make an important statement about property and wealth: private property is supposed to promote autonomy. Indeed, some have argued that property is (or should be) the guarantor of every other basic freedom. Without property, one might argue, the ability to participate in democracy, to exercise free speech, is diminished. Recently, the economist Amartya Sen has argued that the true measure of the success of markets in promoting development is the extent that freedom is enhanced in the process, not the degree to which material wealth is generated. As he put it, "[t]he usefulness of wealth lies in the things that it allows us to do – the substantive freedoms it helps us to achieve".[94] Moreover, Sen identified a symbiosis between development and freedom. The expansion of freedom should be seen as both the primary *end* of development and the principal *means* of achieving development.[95]

Another property-freedom advocate, Charles Reich, has maintained that one of the functions of property "is to draw a boundary around public and private power".[96] Inside this line the owner enjoys greater freedom than outside, since within it the state must justify and explain any interference. Likewise, "the owner may do what all or most of his [sic] neighbors decry"[97] even if it is based on whim or caprice. In sum, property performs the function of promoting independ-

91 See further A. Sen, *Development as Freedom* (New York: A.A. Knopf, 1999) at ch. 2, *passim*.

92 See further "Law and Incommensurability", 146(5) U.Penn.L.Rev. (1998) (Symposium).

93 See J.W. Harris, *Property and Justice* (Oxford: Clarendon Pr., 1996) especially at ch. 13; J.M. Buchanan, *Property as a Guarantor of Liberty* (Brookfield, Vt.: Edward Elgar, 1993); R. Pipes, *Property and Freedom* (New York: A.A. Knopf, 1999).

94 Sen, *supra*, note 91, at 14.

95 Showing this nexus is the principal aim of his book: see, *e.g.*, the discussion, *ibid.* at 36*ff*.

96 C.A. Reich, "The New Property", 73 Yale L.J. 733 (1964) at 771.

97 *Ibid.*

ence, dignity and pluralism.[98] Reich was speaking about freedom in two distinct forms, though he seems to have blended them together. The absence of government regulation as to how one may use property describes a classic kind of *negative* liberty. However, this type of freedom is not the result of property. In fact, the reverse is true: it is a condition required for private property. A line is drawn, to use Reich's metaphor, because the state chooses to allow it to be drawn, and not because the concept of property produces it. There is nothing in the notion of property itself that prevents the state from abolishing all rights of ownership. A protection against this would have to be introduced by some other means, such as through a constitutional protection.

Let me restate this point in another way: the recognition of the value of negative freedom gives rise to the need to deploy certain tools to implement that freedom, such as the institution of property. Property is merely the agency used by the state to allow the enjoyment of negative freedom. For those who value freedom from governmental interference (and liberals and libertarians certainly do) property is an ideal concept to adopt. Private property rights keep the prying eyes of the state away. The private property holder enjoys extensive (if not complete) protection from unwanted intrusions. Property allows for privacy to be enjoyed.

Reich also spoke of the freedom that property can confer in another way: the right to control one's destiny; the right not to be reliant on the state (except to the extent needed to ensure the enforcement of property rights). It also involves the right "to be a subject, not an object".[99] In short, property can be empowering or enabling. It can confer on owners a power to control their own lives; to pursue their conceptions of the good life; to chart their own course. In theory, it can also support democratic institutions. Private property works to disperse power widely. This, then, can serve as a check on totalitarian tendencies that might be harboured by those holding political office.[100]

Even so, this analysis reveals a dark side to the notion of property as a form of decentralized private power.[101] For one thing, while private wealth can serve as a counterbalance against government, democratic values may nevertheless be diminished if property is not distributed evenly. We know that propertied interests can have an enormous impact on government through lobbying practices and election financing. Moreover, property confers on some citizens an enormous power to control others. Today this is accomplished through the governance of

98 *Ibid.*
99 I. Berlin, *Four Essays on Liberty* (London: O.U.P., 1969) at 131. But the idea of positive freedom is more complex than first appears: see *ibid.* at 131*ff.*
100 See generally A.O. Hirschman, *The Passions and the Interests: Political Arguments for Capitalism Before Its Triumph* (Princeton, N.J.: Princeton U.P., 1977). See further M. Robertson, "Property and Ideology" (1995) 8 Can.J.L. & Juris. 275, at 291-2.
101 See also M. Cohen, "Property and Sovereignty" reproduced in C.B. Macpherson, ed., *Property: Mainstream and Critical Positions* (Toronto: U. of T.Pr., 1978); W. Clement & J. Myles, *Relations of Ruling: Class and Gender in Postindustrial Societies* (Montreal: McGill-Queen's, 1994) at 4-5.

large corporate empires[102] and in other ways. The ability of a shopping mall owner to prevent otherwise lawful picketing[103] also reveals how property creates a power dynamic and how the freedom of owners limits that of others. Yes, private property decentralizes power, but it can also promote the emergence of an economic oligarchy. Private property, far from enhancing democratic institutions, can skew them in favour of the wealthy, and so can undermine the realization of equal participation in the political process.

Some subtle manifestations of the use of property as a means of exercising power and control can arise within family relationships. As we will see in Chapter 7, it is possible for property to be transferred conditionally. Such a transfer might be constructed so as to allow the original owner (or that person's estate) to reclaim the property if the condition is broken. In the reported case law one can find examples of testamentary gifts of land, money or goods which are made subject to the requirement that the recipient, say, abstain from such 'vices' as card playing,[104] intoxicating liquors,[105] and smoking.[106] Gifts of property have also been made on the condition that the recipient remain a member of,[107] or marry within, a stated religious faith.[108]

Perhaps the most perverse (and pathetic) Canadian example of how property can be used as a tool of manipulation is to be found in the story surrounding the will of Charles Millar. He was a wealthy man, who died in 1926 with no dependants. His will provided that the bulk of his estate was to be left to accumulate for ten years, after which it would go to "the Mother who has since my death given birth in Toronto to the greatest number of children as shown by the Registrations under the Vital Statistics Act".[109] As the Depression engulfed the country, a number of families were actively seeking the bequest. The press played up the contest, calling it a 'baby race' or 'stork derby'. One reporter's melancholy assessment sums up the scene behind the stories: "Looking back, the things I remember most are the smell of many babies [and] the unnatural talk of big money by tired women living on relief".[110] If that were not enough, it was estimated that

---

102 See also Robertson, *supra*, note 100, at 279*ff.*

103 See *Harrison v. Carswell*, [1976] 2 S.C.R. 200, [1975] 6 W.W.R. 673, 62 D.L.R. (3d) 68. This issue is raised again in Part 3, Chapter 10.

104 *Jordan v. Dunn* (1888) 15 O.A.R. 744 (C.A.); *Re Kennedy Estate*, [1950] 1 W.W.R. 151 (Man. K.B.).

105 *Re Kennedy Estate, supra*, note 104; *Jordan v. Dunn, supra*, note 104. See also *Re Fox* (1884) 8 O.R. 489 (Ch. D.); *Re O'Grady* (1921) 19 O.W.N. 389 (H.C.).

106 *Re Kennedy Estate, supra*, note 104.

107 *Re Murley Estate* (1995) 130 Nfld. & P.E.I.R. 271 (Nfld. T.D.).

108 *Re Kennedy Estate, supra*, note 104; *Re Tepper's Will Trusts*, [1987] Ch. 358, [1987] 1 All E.R. 970. But see *Fox v. Fox Estate* (1996) 28 O.R. (3d) 496 (C.A.) leave to appeal to S.C.C. refused (1996) 207 N.R. 80 (note) (S.C.C.).

109 See M.M. Orkin, *The Great Stork Derby* (Don Mills: General Pub.Co., 1981) at 57-8, where this clause is set out.

110 *Ibid.* at 103. The reporter is not identified. In the end, four families shared in the residue, which was worth $750,000.00. The winning total was nine babies. Illegitimate and stillborn children, unregistered births, and a birth occurring just outside the city limits of Toronto, were not counted. The will provoked a good deal of litigation: see, *e.g.*, *Re Millar*, [1938] S.C.R. 1, [1938] 1 D.L.R. 65, a leading case on the doctrine of public policy.

the mortality rate among the Millar will babies was three to four times greater than the national average at the time.[111]

Transfers such as these are attempts (albeit not always successful ones) to harness the power of property in order to make the donee of a gift do the bidding of the donor. Indeed, it has been claimed that "[t]he control which the law still gives to a man over the disposal of his property is one of the most efficient means which he has in protracted life to command the attentions due to his infirmities".[112] In short, under Canadian property law all testators can become King Lear for a day! A study conducted in rural Ireland in the 1930s revealed forms of patriarchal control over sons who stood to inherit the family estate. Canadian research has shown how this pressure can be applied to influence the choice of marriage partners.[113]

These examples also suggest that the labels 'private power' and 'private property' are perhaps misleading. This is because they assume a distinction between the private and the public that is increasingly being doubted.[114] The power enjoyed by a testator is one with a public dimension, because it depends on state enforcement. When a homeowner succeeds in having a trespasser removed from the property by police action, state power is being invoked. Property is a delegation of that power, and only with this severe qualification in place is it helpful to speak of it as something private and not public.

Occasionally, the state harnesses the power of property as a way of pursuing public policy. This type of use has been evident throughout the course of non-indigenous settlement in Canada. For example, grants of land from the Crown were sometimes made on the condition that the property would be settled and cultivated. In 1765 a transfer of lands to several persons in and around Annapolis, Nova Scotia contained the following stipulation:

> if each and every of the said grantees shall not settle either themselves or a family on each of their respective shares or rights, with proper stock and materials for the improvement of the said lands, on or before the last day of November, 1767, then the grant shall be void.[115]

About one hundred years later the same strategy was used to promote migration to the west. The promise by the federal government of land for a pittance, conditioned on minimum periods of occupation and development, was the back-

---

111 Orkin, *supra*, note 109, at 193.

112 *Van Alst v. Hunter*, 5 Johnson N.Y.Ch.Rep.159 (*per* Chancellor Kent) quoted with approval in *Banks v. Goodfellow* (1870) L.R. 5 Q.B. 549, at 564, where Cockburn C.J. added that "for these reasons the power of disposing of property in anticipation of death has ever been regarded as one of the most valuable of the rights incidental to property, while there can be no doubt that it operates as a useful incentive to industry in the acquisition of wealth, and to thrift and frugality in the enjoyment of it".

113 See G. Allan, "Property and Family Solidarity" in P. Hollowell, ed., *Property and Social Relations* (London: Heinemann Educational, 1982) 164, at 167, and the studies referred to there.

114 See, *e.g.*, A.C. Hutchinson & A. Petter, "Private Rights/ Public Wrongs: The Liberal Lie of the Charter" (1988) 38 U.T.L.J. 278.

115 *Wheelock v. McKown* (1835) 1 N.S.R. 41 (S.C.) at 43.

bone of the policy of western settlement through homesteading (which is dealt with again below[116]). The transfer of Prince Rupert's Land in 1670 to the Hudson's Bay Company[117] also exposes this connection. The grant itself was conditioned on the discovery of a passage to the Pacific. By the middle of the nineteenth century the Company, which controlled Rupert's Land as a private fiefdom, developed a practice of conveying plots of land in return for the grantee's promise not to deal in furs, not to distribute or import liquor, to resist foreign invasion, and to further the religious institutions of the colony.[118]

Property promotes freedom, I agree. Yet the success of private property in pursuing such a goal is adversely affected where rights of ownership are not widely held. Property may yield freedom and power. If so, there are many Canadians who are effectively powerless and lack a viable sense of freedom because of differentials in wealth. If "the paramount argument for private property is that it best protects the rights of the individual",[119] then there are many for whom the consummate protective device of private property is of limited worth. This powerlessness is compounded by the fact that the poor often lack a sense of political efficacy and tend to abstain from participation in democratic processes. Moreover, the emergence of large corporations has resulted in a loss of individual economic independence for many workers.[120]

The law of property does not just deprive some people of positive freedom. Negative freedom is lost as well. This is because to the extent that owners may expel non-owners, these others are not free (in the negative sense) to go where they like. The protective fence of property law keeps them out. It is small wonder, then, that the homeless congregate in parks and on other sites of public property from which they are not so readily excluded. There they are 'free' to do whatever they wish, provided it is not something that the law has reserved for the privacy of one's home, or prohibited altogether.[121]

(e)   theories based on personhood, moral development and human nature

A claim is sometimes made that private property is connected with human and moral development. This is a basis of justification often associated with

---

116 See Part 3(g), *infra*.

117 See also Part 2(b), Chapter 2.

118 K.M. Bindon, "Hudson's Bay Company Law: Adam Thom and the Institution of Order in Rupert's Land 1839-54", in D.H. Flaherty, ed., *Essays in the History of Canadian Law*, vol. 1 (Toronto: Osgoode Society & U. of T.Pr., 1981) 43, at 65. It is unclear how often this type of grant was used: *ibid*.

119 J.E. Cribbet & C.W. Johnson, *Principles of the Law of Property*, 3rd ed. (Westbury, N.Y.: Foundation Pr., 1989) at 7.

120 See also C.A. Reich, "Beyond the New Property: An Ecological View of Due Process", 56 Brooklyn L.Rev. 731 (1990) at 733.

121 See further J. Waldron, "Homelessness and the Issue of Freedom", 39 U.C.L.A.L.Rev. 295 (1991).

Hegel,[122] though it has, in some formulations, Marxist overtones. The opening premise is that "to achieve proper self-development – to be a person – an individual needs some control over resources in the external environment".[123] Property allows the human will to develop and thrive, bestowing on people the capacity to demonstrate individuality and full self-expression. Hegel saw property as a dominant factor in the transformation of people from abstract entities into moral and political beings distinct from others. A liberation, a transcendental shift, results from projecting one's will into an external object. Such an object, having no end in itself, then becomes subservient to the will of the claimant. Hegel asserted that this accounted for a right of appropriation.[124]

Hegel's thesis concerns highly abstract conceptions of freedom and self-development. His view was that property was essential to the moulding of each human will (though his work was not directed at making the case for a system of private property). More recently, Margaret Jane Radin has developed an intuitive personhood theory,[125] one that dwells on the way people feel about where they live, how they dress, and, more generally, how they regard their belongings. We treat some items as representing facets of ourselves (such as clothing or jewellery) or as extensions of our character (one's home or car). People often view objects as being endowed with a special significance because they are spiritual, memory-laden, rare, mysterious, or for some other reason worth treasuring.[126] The disappointment felt by those who suffer the loss or theft of an object holding sentimental value is another demonstration of the personhood aspect of ownership. These notions about personhood are important, though one should understand that they differ from the Hegelian concept. The happiness derived from owning certain objects, or the inner calm that ownership can confer, is far removed from Hegel's view of property as a *sine qua non* of human individuality.

The supposition that property satisfies a basic need for personal growth and maturation finds support in some psychological writing. One view is that acquisitiveness is an innate human quality. In fact, our natural disposition for such things as sustenance, self-defence and self-worth can be seen as supporting a primordial need for some type of institution of property (though this may not mean that

---

122 The heart of his theory is presented in G.W.F. Hegel, *Philosophy of Right*, T.M. Knox, trans. (Oxford: Clarendon Pr. ed., 1952, 1821) at paras. 34 to 71. An analysis of Hegel's work about property can be found in P.G. Stillman, "Hegel's Analysis of Property in the Philosophy of Right", 10 Cardozo L.Rev. 1031 (1989).

123 M.J. Radin, "Property and Personhood", 34 Stan.L.Rev. 957 (1982) at 957.

124 *Philosophy of Right, supra*, note 122, at para. 44.

125 *Supra*, note 123. This essay and others which develop and apply the personhood theory can be found in M.J. Radin, *Reinterpreting Property* (Chicago: U. of Chi. Pr., 1993). See also S.J. Schnably, "Property and Pragmatism: A Critique of Radin's Theory of Property and Personhood", 45 Stan.L.Rev. 347 (1993) (and Professor Radin's response at 409); J.L. Schroeder, "Virgin Territory: Margaret Radin's Imagery of Personal Property and the Inviolate Feminine Body", 79 Minn.L.Rev. 55 (1994).

126 See further R.W. Belk, "The Ineluctable Mysteries of Possessions", 6 J.Soc. Behavior & Personality 17 (1991) where the reasons for this conduct are explored.

private property is required).[127] Freud, not surprisingly perhaps, associated the quest for acquisitions with early childhood practices of anal retention. A child's desire for possessions (a security blanket or a favourite stuffed animal) may arise from some impulse, whether for comfort, reassurance, or as a result of an intuitive need to possess. Furthermore, analyses of the possessory habits of children show that these traits develop at an early age.

However, whether these commonly found characteristics exist by virtue of genetics, or, in contrast, from the prompting of parents during nurturing and from processes of acculturation generally, is a contested issue.[128] These actions may be socially constructed, since variations can be seen across different communities.[129] And, of course, people are not all alike when it comes to feelings about property. An English study found a relationship between gender and ownership. The results suggested that "men were mainly concerned with the self-referring, activity-related and instrumental aspects"[130] of their property. Women in the study stressed "both the symbolic and other-oriented features of possessions".[131] They tended to emphasize connections with others in their property dealings.

The personhood theory stresses the importance, however spawned, that people seem to place on security and privacy. It also suggests that moral virtues are in some (hard to define) way associated with ownership. Property, one might contend, allows for and promotes acts of generosity and philanthropy,[132] and the development of self-esteem[133] and diligence. Aristotle thought that private property was preferable to shared ownership, in part, because the former led to less dissension.[134] As late as 1936, John Maynard Keynes, echoing an argument that had currency in the eighteenth century, claimed that commerce (and with it private property) served to divert attention away from more objectionable pursuits:

---

127 G. Trasler, "The Psychology of Ownership and Possessiveness" in P. Hollowell, ed., *Property and Social Relations* (London: Heinemann Educational, 1982) 32. See further L. Bloom, "People and Property: A Psychoanalytic View", 6 J.Soc. Behavior & Personality 427 (1991).

128 Trasler, *supra*, note 127, at 39.

129 *Ibid.* at 43. One study found that the practice of collecting items, such as stamps or rare coins, was more commonly found in families of higher socio-economic status: *ibid.* at 42. See further A.D. Olmsted, "Collecting: Leisure, Investment or Obsession?", 6 J.Soc. Behavior & Personality 287 (1991).

130 H. Dittmar, "Meanings of Material Possessions as Reflections of Identity: Gender and Social Material Position in Society", 6 J.Soc. Behavior & Personality 165 (1991) at 182.

131 *Ibid.* The study also considered the impact of class. See also F.W. Rudmin, "Gender Differences in the Semantics of Ownership: A Quantitative Phenomenological Survey Study", 15 J.Econ.Psych. 487 (1994); N.L. Kampter, "Personal Possessions and Their Meanings", 6 J.Soc. Behavior & Personality 209 (1991); S.M. Livingstone & P.K. Lunt, "Generational and Life Cycle Differences in Experiences of Ownership", 6 J.Soc. Behavior & Personality 229 (1991).

132 See further T.H. Irwin, "Aristotle's Defence of Private Property" in D. Keyt & F.D. Miller, eds., *Aristotle's Politics: A Critical Reader* (Oxford: Basil Blackwell, 1991) at 200, where this rationale is critiqued.

133 See D.P. Levine, *Wealth and Freedom: An Introduction to Political Economy* (Cambridge: C.U.P., 1995) at 22, drawing on Thorstein Veblen's *The Theory of the Leisure Class* (London: MacMillan, 1899) at 26.

134 Aristotle, *The Politics* (Chicago: U. of Chi. Pr. ed., 1984) at 60 (Book II, ch. 5, 1263al).

Dangerous human proclivities can be canalized into comparatively harmless channels by the existence of opportunity for money-making and private wealth, which, if they cannot be satisfied in this way, may find their outlet in cruelty, the reckless pursuit of personal power and authority, and other forms of self-aggrandizement. It is better that a man should tyrannize over his bank balance than over his fellow citizens; and whilst the former is sometimes denounced as being but a means to the latter, sometimes at least it is an alternative.[135]

Freud saw private ownership as a useful instrument for the expression of aggressive behaviour:

In abolishing private property we deprive the human love of aggression of one of its instruments, certainly a strong one, though certainly not the strongest; but we have in no way altered the differences in power and influence which are misused by aggressiveness, nor have we altered anything in its nature. Aggressiveness was not created by property.[136]

The advancement of the personality as a product of owning is an alluring notion that is closely associated with the idea that property is connected with freedom.[137] Property allows us to be ourselves, one might say. But the drawbacks of this rationale of ownership should also be apparent. It is not just that there are human needs that property cannot satisfy. There are some things that money can't buy, but that limitation applies to all property systems. More significantly, property-owning may not always be an enriching experience; at least that is what we may feel when excesses come to public attention. It seems as likely to foster traits of greed, avarice, selfishness, or quests for power as any countervailing virtues. At times it seems more a prescription, than a panacea, for immorality.

The angst of ownership, the fears and anxieties that owners develop about the chance of theft, and the expensive precautions that are taken in response, arise only because people have valued possessions. Furthermore, it has been suggested that a life of privilege can be psychologically damaging, especially for those who inherit wealth.[138] Also, theories premised on the development of personhood help to explain the feelings of alienation and anomie sometimes experienced by workers. A wage-labourer lacks a proprietary connection to his or her employment, which can have a detrimental effect on how such people view themselves and their work. And the various personality-based theories speak volumes about poverty and homelessness[139] as causes of unhappiness.

Personhood theories can (and do) influence the design of specific allocation rules (a third-order event)[140] when, let us say, an economic analysis might suggest

135 J.M. Keynes, *The General Theory of Employment Interest and Money* (London: MacMillan, 1936) at 374, quoted in Hirschman, *supra*, note 100, at 134.

136 S. Freud, *Civilization and Its Discontents* (New York: W.W. Norton ed., 1961, 1930) at 60.

137 It would also be relevant to a utilitarian calculation of happiness.

138 J. Bronfman, *The Experience of Wealth: A Social-Psychological Perspective*, Ph.D. Dissertation, Brandeis University, 1987 (Ann Arbor: University Microfilms Int., 1987).

139 See R.P. Hill, "Homeless Women, Special Possessions, and the Meaning of 'Home': An Ethnographic Case Study", 18 J. Consumer Res. 298 (1991); R.P. Hill & M. Stamey, "The Homeless in America: An Examination of Possessions and Consumption Behaviors", 17 J. Consumer Res. 303 (1990).

140 See Part 3(a), *supra*.

a different approach.[141] For example, the movement to protect residential tenants (such as by providing greater security of tenure) can be seen as a recognition of the special status of the home to the average Canadian. Similarly, on marriage breakdown spouses may seek a division of their property. In such cases, a court may order a distribution of assets, after which an award can be made to allocate the present holdings. At this stage, the judge can consider the degree of attachment to a given chattel in determining to whom it should be given.

Theories about attachment and ownership also provide insights into the significance of Aboriginal land claims. In this context, instead of referring to personhood values it might be better to speak of 'grouphood' interests being taken into account.[142] A study conducted in Australia sought to draw a link between the recognition (or non-recognition) of Aboriginal land rights and the general learning that exists on the psychological dimensions of property ownership. It was argued that because Aboriginal communities possess a strong spiritual relationship with the land, the loss of traditional lands can contribute to community strife and personal unhappiness. This analysis is consistent with research that demonstrates the "diminished sense of self after the loss of cherished possessions".[143] This reasoning should have implications for the ways in which Canadian courts conceive of and resolve Aboriginal property disputes. The Royal Commission on Aboriginal Peoples seems to have understood that idea. As the Commission acknowledged, "Aboriginal people have told us of their special relationship to the land and its resources. This relationship, they say, is both spiritual and material, not only one of livelihood but of community and indeed of the continuity of their cultures and societies."[144]

(f)   labour, desert and consent

Arguments in favour of private property are sometimes based on the assertion that individuals are entitled to those things over which they have laboured. John Locke,[145] the person most commonly associated with this theory in modern times, spoke of a natural right to property, a right that existed, precariously, in the state

---

141 See also A. Ryan, *Property* (Minneapolis: U. of Minn.Pr., 1987) at 72.

142 I believe this term was coined by J. Moustakas in "Group Rights in Cultural Property: Justifying Strict Inalienability", 74 Cornell L.Rev. 1179 (1989).

143 R.P. Hill, "Blackfellas and Whitefellas: Aboriginal Land Rights, the *Mabo* Decision, and the Meaning of Land", 17 Human Rights Q. 303 (1995) at 320. The research on the impact of the loss of possessions referred to in this article is R.W. Belk, "Possessions and the Extended Self", 15 J. Consumer Res. 139 (1988); Hill, *supra*, note 139; and Hill & Stamey, *supra*, note 139.

144 *Report of the Royal Commission on Aboriginal Peoples* (Ottawa: Canada Communications Group, 1996) vol. 2(2) at 448.

145 See generally A.J. Simmons, *The Lockean Theory of Rights* (Princeton, N.J.: Princeton U.P., 1992) and the references to other works on Locke mentioned there. See also G. Sreenivasan, *The Limits of Lockean Rights in Property* (New York: O.U.P., 1995). Matthew Kramer argues that John Locke was concerned with advancing collective interests and that "Locke's theses are communitarian through and through *because* they are individualistic through and through": M.H. Kramer, *John Locke and the Origins of Private Property* (Cambridge: C.U.P., 1997) at 93.

of nature.[146] Unlike the Benthamite view, for Locke the law was not regarded as the source of property rights. Rather, a primary function of a legal system and of civil society is to recognize and protect the pre-political right to private property.

Although the baseline idea of labour as a predicate to ownership is straightforward enough, Locke's argumentation is nevertheless intricate. This is because in Locke's state of nature we find that property was held in common. His self-assigned task was to demonstrate how ownership of land and goods came to be placed in private hands, despite the absence of universal agreement. He assumed (unlike some other early natural law thinkers who theorized about the origins of ownership[147]) that reaching a consensus was not possible.

Locke's analysis starts with the assumption that each of us owns our own bodies (or persons) and therefore our labour.[148] Moreover, he took it as faith that God had "commanded Man to labour".[149] Locke reasoned that through the mixing of our labour with material objects we are, in essence, putting something of ourselves into the material world. This act extends ourselves and hence our rights of ownership into those worldly goods. This is the Lockean 'mixing metaphor' on which a great deal of his theory rests.

The inherent difficulty with this line of argument, if it were to stop there, is that it fails to resolve doubts as to how this unilateral action of the labourer can serve as an acceptable justification for depriving others of the rights of common ownership conceded at the outset. Appreciating this, Locke placed two qualifications on the mixing metaphor and its transformative effects. First, the taking could be permitted only as long as there is "enough, and as good"[150] material worth left in common for others. Second, one should not take so much as would spoil.[151]

Through an "inferential leap"[152] Locke tried to show how these qualifications survived the progression from the acorn-gathering society with which he starts to the modern era. With the acceptance of exchange currency (he spoke of gold and silver), the concern about wastage was satisfied; money does not spoil. The productive use of land, he argued, increased wealth.[153] Even if all land were appropriated by some to the exclusion of others, he seemed confident that there would not be a reduction in the quality of life for those without land. What remains

---

146 See further S. Buckle, *Natural Law and the Theory of Property: Grotius to Hume* (Oxford: Clarendon Pr., 1991).

147 Hugo Grotius and Samuel Pufendorf developed consent-based natural law theories of property rights: see Buckle, *supra*, note 146, chs. 1 and 2.

148 See also D.R. Denman, *The Place of Property* (Berhamstead, Eng.: Geographical Pub. 1978) at 1.

149 J. Locke, *Two Treatises of Government* (New York: New American Library, Mentor ed., 1963, 1690) Second Treatise, at para. 32. All further references are to the Second Treatise.

150 *Ibid.* at para. 27.

151 *Ibid.* at para. 31. Spoilage offends the law of nature and is deserving of punishment: *ibid.* at para. 37.

152 M.J. Radin, "Property and Personhood", 34 Stan.L.Rev. 957 (1982) at 979. See also C.B. Macpherson, *The Political Theory of Possessive Individualism* (Oxford: Clarendon Pr., 1962) at 203*ff.*

153 See, *e.g.*, Locke, *supra*, note 149, at para. 37.

for them is the right to contract for one's labour as a means of obtaining sustenance and prosperity.

Some of the problems with this analysis should be apparent. The acceptance of money as a substitute for goods was said to be based on a supposed tacit social consensus.[154] How do we know that this occurred? Additionally, an appropriation is justified only so long as there is enough and as good left for the rest; Locke does not abandon that starting premise. But he describes a world – in its state of nature – in which there is no scarcity and therefore for which there is no compelling need for enforceable rights of property at all. And only if it can be shown that modern levels of production actually do leave society with "enough, and as good" can it be accepted that the proviso is not offended. Of course, we have no way of knowing whether or not this is the case.

It is important to appreciate that the Lockean hypothesis is not undermined merely because societies are rife with inequality.[155] Although it is rooted in a conception of natural rights, this theory does not mandate, bare subsistence aside, that every person hold some sort of natural right to property. Each person is merely a candidate for these natural rights. After performing the necessary legal alchemy on some item by mixing it with our labour, we can acquire a right worthy of protection. For this reason Locke's labour theory establishes what may be termed a *special* right. This differs from the arguments based on universal or *general* needs that underlie the theories derived from personhood and liberty.[156] However, even the special rights of candidacy accepted under this version of labour theory are severely restricted. Since some tangibles are finite, the acquisitions of earlier generations necessarily limit the opportunities of later ones.[157] The early bird catches the worm in the Lockean world.

Additionally, the right to property based on labour reduces equality of opportunity if the law allows gift-giving, especially on death. The labour theory must show that this is acceptable, because allowing inheritance perpetuates inequalities that are produced by the initial wave of labour-based acquisitions.[158] Locke considered inheritance to be a natural right of children, but made no concerted effort to connect a general power of bequest to his views on labour. We might assume however that the right to give away property on death was regarded as part and parcel of the labourer's right of use flowing from ownership.

Robert Nozick has challenged the conclusion that the mixing of labour produces a gain for the labourer, suggesting instead that it could lead equally to the donation of that labour to the community.[159] This dilemma strikes at the heart of the problem, because it demands a convincing explanation as to why the mixer

---

154 *Ibid.* at para. 36.

155 See also R. Zucker, "Preface to Social Theory of Property Rights" , 8 Ratio Juris 199 (1995).

156 The distinction between specific and general claim rights is explained in J. Waldron, *The Right to Private Property* (Oxford: Clarendon Pr., 1988).

157 See also H. Rashdall, "The Philosophical Theory of Property" in L.T. Hobhouse *et al.*, *Property: Its Duties and Rights* (London: MacMillan, 1915) at 45-6.

158 The justifications for inheritance are examined in M.L. Ascher, "Curtailing Inherited Wealth", 89 Mich.L.Rev. 69 (1990).

159 R. Nozick, *Anarchy, State and Utopia* (Oxford: Basil Blackwell, 1974) at 174-5.

deserves anything at all. The move from the proposition of self-ownership,[160] all the way to the right to own goods that have been infused with labour, is not self-evident, especially when labour has been applied to an existing entity (such as by making paper from wood), rather than in the creation of some new item (such as through the writing of a book).[161] The Lockean mixing metaphor is, after all, only a metaphor and does not lead to any inescapable conclusion about the moral basis of ownership.

A possible explanation for granting a proprietary interest may be that if people are not rewarded in this way they will not labour. If the answer goes no further than this, then Locke has merely anticipated (or influenced) the economic theorists. Presented in this way, Locke teaches us little more than that incentives are essential if productivity is to be promoted, or, put another way, that the failure to prevent the taking of positive externalities is economically unsound. One advantage of speaking of a theory of natural rights is that this has a more attractive ring when the right to private property is considered in a political context. Locke wrote within the political environment of his day, and it has been argued that his aim was to challenge monarchical absolutism.[162] His theory can be (and has been) paraded out when the question of providing constitutional protection for property is raised. It is shrewder to seek an entrenchment for property ownership when this position is premised on the law of nature rather than on the banal notion that it is economically efficient to do so. This may explain why Locke has been regarded by some as a major influence in the design of the American *Bill of Rights*,[163] In addition, it has been argued that Locke's work "legitimated the appropriation of the American wilderness as a right, and even as an imperative, under natural law".[164] In contrast, his impact on Canadian liberalism has been less apparent,[165] and pressures for the inclusion of an embracing property protection in Canada's constitution have so far not prevailed.[166]

---

160 The notion of self-ownership is doubted in J.W. Harris, *Property and Justice* (Oxford: Clarendon Pr., 1996) at 184*ff* (especially at 196-7).

161 See also F.G. Whelan, "Property as Artifice: Hume and Blackstone", in J.R. Pennock & J.W. Chapman, eds., *Property, Nomos XXII* (New York: N.Y.U.P., 1980) 101, at 103-4.

162 K.F. Minogue, "The Concept of Property and Its Contemporary Significance", in *Nomos XXII, supra*, note 161, 3, at 18.

163 See J.W. Ely, *The Guardian of Every Other Right: A Constitutional History of Property Rights*, 2nd ed. (New York: O.U.P., 1998). But see J.G.A. Pocock, *Machiavellian Moment: Florentine Political Thought and the Atlantic Republican Tradition* (Princeton, N.J.: Princeton U.P., 1975). See generally J. Nedelsky, *Private Property and the Limits of American Constitutionalism* (Chicago: U. of Chi. Pr., 1990).

164 R.A. Williams, Jr., *The American Indian in Western Legal Thought: The Discourses of Conquest* (New York: O.U.P., 1990) at 248. See also J. Tully, "Aboriginal Property and Western Theory: Recovering a Middle Ground" in E.F. Paul *et al.*, eds. *Property Rights* (New York: C.U.P., 1994) 153.

165 The impact of Locke's theories and other notions of productivity on the development of Canadian constitutional law is assessed in D. Schneiderman, *Constitutional Limits and Economic Interests: A Search for the Purposes of Canadian Constitutionalism* (LL.M. Thesis, Queen's University, 1993) [copy on file at the University of Alberta].

166 Property rights are protected in the unentrenched *Canadian Bill of Rights*, R.S.C. 1985, App. III, para. 1(a).

The labour justification is sometimes married with the idea of *desert*.[167] The gist of the claim is that even if we were to put aside the mixing metaphor we might still wish to grant ownership to the deserving labourer. Don't worry about the fact that certain rights must flow from the infusion of your own person into an object; rather look at the benefit that emerges from that work, and award this to the person who has brought it about. In short, the element of desert arises from the added value that labour contributes to our well-being. Fairness and justice demand that there be compensation.

Certainly, the adding of value through the investment of labour might provide a sufficient basis for allocating property to a particular individual over other claimants. But I do not think that desert is any more compelling than the pure labour theory as a way of justifying the carving out of private rights from the prior communal ownership. In other words, if we first assume that a system of private ownership exists, then it is easy to see why we might confer property on someone who deserves it for one reason or other. This is what I have described above as a third-order concern: in a universe in which private property exists, to whom should a given property interest be allocated? Once we have conceded that private property is justifiable (the first-order question), it is plausible to assert that distributions should be based on merit considerations including rewarding a person who, in all fairness, deserves some item. It might even be possible to allow labour and desert to determine if some new object should be treated as the property of the creator instead of being added to the common property (a second-order concern).

However, when addressing the first-order question, the theory of desert based on contributions of labour is not so obviously the correct approach. I believe that most people would think that those who take from a shared pool of goods should normally be accused of selfishness, not rewarded for their initiative. Consider this simple situation: Three people are sharing an island containing a copse of trees and some scrub land. Without the consent of the others, one of the owners chops down most of the trees and cuts them into lumber. Part of that wood is then used in some worthwhile way, say to build animal shelters. Most of the rest of the lumber is used to build a beautiful new home for the cutter on the scrub portion of the lot. A fence around the house is also built. On one plank is written 'no trespassers'. Despite these appropriations, the cutter continues to share the remainder of the commons with the other two occupants.

Let us accept for the sake of argument that the lumber has been put to good use, and that the scrub land has been improved. Would we really say that this person deserves to have the sole entitlement to the home, to the land around it,

---

167 See further L.C. Becker, *Property Rights: Philosophic Foundations* (London: Routledge, Chapman & Hall, Inc., 1977) at 32*ff*. For a different slant on the idea of property and justice (or 'propriety') see C.M. Rose, " 'Takings' and the Practices of Property: Property as Wealth, Property as 'Propriety' " in *Property and Persuasion: Essays on the History, Theory, and Rhetoric of Ownership* (Boulder: Westview Pr., 1994) ch. 3. See also G.S. Alexander, *Commodity & Propriety: Competing Visions of Property in American Legal Thought, 1776-1970* (Chicago: U. of Chi.Pr., 1997), or the abbreviated version: G.S. Alexander, "Property as Propriety", 77 Neb.L.Rev. 667 (1998).

and to all of the other objects that have been produced? Isn't it more likely that we would condemn this self-centred act and demand some compensation for the other two? If I am right in predicting that there would be censure not praise, then how does *desert* come into play?

One reply might be as follows: 'that is acceptable because we want to encourage the improvement of property and the productive use of resources.'[168] Of course, the other two inhabitants might not, on balance, benefit from the cutter's unilateral action. And as we will see, under the modern law of co-ownership it is highly probable that the cutter would be called upon to account for these acts.[169] It would be ironic in the extreme if a theory of desert could be used to explain the virtues of property as a whole for actions that the law would *not* regard as proper.

If we are supposed to approve of the cutter's actions because of some implicit understanding among the group, for instance, about the need to improve conditions on the island, then the basis of property rights is not really the desert theory at all. Rather it is the pre-existing consensus or edict that supports the claim that the cutter is entitled to keep everything that has been acquired.[170] This is, I believe, what James Harris means when he says that "[a]ll desert claims are hostage to convention".[171] Labour might be rewarded with a payment, or even a hearty round of applause, if that is the accepted practice, or if it has been so decreed in some authoritative way. For Harris there is no true natural right to property based on desert. In the absence of a convention, he sees a property award as "particularly problematic because of its distributional implications". Allocating property to some will limit the wealth available to others. Plus, property, as a reward for meritorious labour, competes with other justice claims, such as need, as the governing criterion.[172]

Despite this critique of the labour and desert justifications for private property, they appear to have an impact on the development of specific allocational rules. This is the third-order domain in which I think they can be of best use. In fact, the rhetorical force of the labour theory is sometimes present in the jurisprudence. Consider, for example, the American case of *International News Service v. Associated Press*.[173] There, the defendant copied news reports published by the plaintiff on the east coast, sending the stories to wire services in the west, in advance of the plaintiff's efforts to do the same. The United States Supreme Court held that the defendant's actions amounted to unfair competition. A majority accepted that it would be appropriate for a court to impose a restriction on the use of the stories by the defendant, to last for several hours after publication by the plaintiff. This embargo would allow the plaintiff that time to exploit the commercial value of its work. The defendant was enjoined because it was "endeav-

---

168 *Cf.* Locke, *supra*, note 149, at paras. 40-44.

169 See Part 5(b), Chapter 9.

170 As to consent-based theories of ownership, see Buckle, *supra*, note 146.

171 Harris, *supra*, note 160, at 207.

172 *Ibid.* at 208. The moral warrant of desert claims to income generated by property is challenged in J. Christman, *The Myth of Property: Toward an Egalitarian Theory of Ownership* (New York: O.U.P., 1994) at ch. 5.

173 248 U.S. 215 (1918).

oring to reap where it has not sown'' and was, as a result, ''appropriating to itself the harvest of those who have sown''.[174]

This all sounds like the labour or desert theories in action; but is it? The concept of reward for effort has already been seen as an element of economic efficiency and utilitarianism. Under those theories it is claimed that the failure to protect claims would adversely affect productivity. In the *I.N.S.* case it was the impact on efficiency and enterprise that was stressed: the plaintiff had expended considerable time and money to establish its news collection apparatus, only to have some of the benefits of these investments taken through the interloping acts of the defendant.[175]

There is no suggestion in *I.N.S.* that there is an inherent right to enjoy the fruits of one's labour. If there is, this right is honoured as much in breach as in observance, for there are many circumstances in which the law allows some people to reap blatantly where they have not sown. At other times, work is left unrewarded. For example, the reluctance of the law to reward labour evenly has been a source of grievance for those who engage in unpaid work in the home.[176] In Canada this remains mainly the job of women. Until recently, engaging in the Sisyphean chores of housework had not given rise to rights to the property over which one laboured or, for that matter, over other accumulations of the marriage partnership. Such claims tended to fail because there was no identifiable cash-nexus between the work and some tangible object. The lesson to be learned is obvious – it is economically irrational or perhaps contrary to the 'natural law' tenet of the labour theory to continue doing these household tasks if nothing is received in return.[177]

The problem of undervalued domestic labour has been dealt with, in part, through the introduction of matrimonial property laws that allow for the sharing of property on family breakdown, and which seek to recognize the contributions that both spouses make to the economic well-being of their household.[178] The doctrine of unjust enrichment, to be studied more fully later in the text,[179] has also emerged as a way of responding to this issue. Arguably, it provides a further instructive example of how notions of labour and desert can be seen in the development of legal doctrine. As a general principle, an unjust enrichment will be found when (i) one person has enjoyed an enrichment in circumstances in which (ii) another has experienced a corresponding deprivation, provided there is (iii) no juristic reason to deny relief. These principles emerged in Canada first as a means of compensating spouses who had contributed money or labour to the acquisition of family assets but who did not hold legal title. This idea of unjust enrichment is now most relevant to *de facto* marital relationships (which fall

---

174 *Ibid.* at 239-40 (*per* Pitney J.). Apart from this, news was regarded as common property: *ibid.* at 235.

175 See further R.A. Epstein, ''*International News Service v. Associated Press*: Custom and Law as Sources of Property Rights in News'', 78 Va.L.Rev. 85 (1992).

176 See Part 4(d), Chapter 6.

177 See also J.W. Singer, ''Re-Reading Property'', 26 New England L.Rev. 711 (1992) at 715.

178 These reforms are discussed in Part 7, Chapter 9.

179 See further Part 4(d), Chapter 6.

outside the scope of marital property law) and is of growing importance beyond the family context.

The undervaluation of housework was once the most pronounced contemporary example of how the law fails to reward some forms of labour. But the concern is a general one, often nowadays involving the use of information in various forms. The general nature of the problem can be shown by returning to *International News Service*. Plot that case in the middle of a time continuum. While the plaintiff may have developed its news collecting and distributing operation, it was not the first to conceive of doing so. That happened at some prior time and these earlier developments can be used, for free, by other news agencies. Nor did the plaintiff generate the news itself; it merely reported the events of the day. In both of these ways it was allowed to free-ride on the prior efforts of others.[180] Looking ahead, the injunction against the defendant was to last for only a few hours and no more. Afterwards, commercial use of the gathered news could be made by anyone. The plaintiff was not awarded a perpetual monopoly. It was allowed to draw on the earlier labours of others at no cost; in due course its work could be exploited in the same way.

Patent and copyright statutes strike a similar balance. These laws are designed to protect a creator from poaching or free-riding, but these laws do not protect all works for all time. Pure ideas, clever thoughts, no matter how brilliant they may be, are not amenable to copyright or patent protections.[181] In other words, the use of ideas contained in this book is not governed by the law of intellectual property, though the form in which they are presented is protected by my copyright. Moreover, these property law rights do not last forever. At a future point, we are all allowed to reap where others have sown.

(g)   entitlements derived from occupancy

Rights of property based on first occupancy – first in time is first in right – reflect an approach similar to the labour theory.[182] In this context, the act of taking possession is treated as the labour that merits the granting of a reward. This occupancy rule refers not only to original acquisitions in a state of nature; it has also been marshalled to justify the retention of profits, that is, the added value brought about through commercial dealings. On this view, profits are the 'discovered' value that belong to the occupier.[183]

However, 'occupancy' on its own cannot serve as a basis for the first-order inquiry of whether we should have private property at all. We cannot justify a

---

180 See further A.S. Weinrib, "Information and Property" (1988) 38 U.T.L.J. 117, especially at 122*ff.*
181 See further A. Beckerman-Rodau, "Are Ideas Within the Traditional Definition of Property? A Jurisprudential Analysis", 47 Ark.L.Rev. 603 (1994).
182 See R.A. Epstein, "Possession as the Root of Title", 13 Ga. L.J. 1221 (1979); L. Berger, "An Analysis of the Doctrine That 'First in Time is First in Right' ", 64 Neb.L.Rev. 349 (1985); C.M. Rose, "Possession as the Origin of Property", 52 U.Chi.L.Rev. 73 (1985).
183 See G. Pincione, "Can Capitalism Be Grounded on a Finders-Keepers Ethic?" , 5 Ratio Juris 202 (1992).

right of property simply because it encourages first occupancy; that is not a value that is comparable to the others that I have outlined so far (such as efficiency, liberty, self-development or justice). Although there is a common acceptance of the aphorism 'first come, first served', there is no convincing normative foundation for it, except perhaps that it fosters diligence, or that it would be wrong to disturb the first occupier. In fact, as a basic principle of fairness, which is how we sometimes seem to view first possession rules, it seems almost counterintuitive. How on earth could we justify a rule that gives everything to the first occupier if this leaves everyone else destitute?[184]

As in the case of labour and desert, the idea of first occupancy can serve as a way of resolving third-order issues (that is, designating the persons to whom privately ownable property should be distributed). The classic example is the law governing the capture of wild animals: the common law grants title to the first possessor.[185] Other allocations can also be made on such a basis. In 1996, the Government of Ontario decided to open up over 600,000 hectares of land to mineral claims in the northeastern part of the Province, and it used a first occupancy system to distribute the rights. Fleet-of-foot grubstakers (including high school track stars) were employed by mining companies to stake claims. Environmental groups also participated in the process.[186] To exert dominion over a parcel the runners were required to erect posts at the four corners of the claim, mark trees with axes, and inscribe the stakes to identify their holdings.[187]

Occupancy has also served as the basis for justifying the assertion of sovereignty under international law. It is a pivotal feature of the law affecting Aboriginal claims. For instance, until 1992 there was authority for the view that when the English 'First Fleet' reached Australia it found a country that was *terra nullius* (the land of no one). As a result, it was decided that English sovereignty was recognized from that point on, to the exclusion of Aboriginal claims.[188] This same ethnocentric notion of possession is reflected in Beamish Murdoch's *Epitome of the Laws of Nova Scotia*, published in the 1830s. His language is saturated with racist sentiment:

> [O]ur nation and that of France took possession of an uncultivated soil which was before filled with wild animals and hunters almost as wild. It might with almost as much justice be said that the land belonged to the bears and wild cats, the moose or the cariboo, that ranged over it in quest of food, as to the thin and scattered tribes of men, who were alternatively destroying each other or attacking the beasts of the forest. I do not think that they themselves had any idea of property (of an exclusive nature) in the soil, before their intercourse with Europeans.[189]

---

184 E. de Laveleye, "The Theory of Property" in J.H. Wigmore & A. Kocourek, eds., *The Rational Basis of Legal Institutions* (New York: MacMillan, 1923) 167, at 169.
185 See the brief discussion of the common law of capture, which governs the ownership of wild animals, in Part 3(a), Chapter 4.
186 "Environmental Groups Stake Claims", *Globe & Mail*, September 24, 1996, A4.
187 P. Brethour, "Rush for Riches in Temagami", *Globe & Mail*, September 18, 1996, B4.
188 See now *Mabo v. Queensland (No. 2)*, [1992] 5 C.N.L.R. 1, 175 C.L.R. 1, 107 A.L.R. 1 (Aust. H.C.) overruling *Milirrpum v. Nabalco Pty. Ltd.* (1971) 17 F.L.R. 141 (N.T.S.C.).
189 B. Murdoch, *Epitome of the Laws of Nova Scotia* (Halifax: Joseph Howe, 1832-3) vol. 2, at 57.

Fortunately, this characterization has not prevailed. Indeed, the application of the maxim 'first in time is first in right' can work to the advantage of indigenous groups (including Canada's First Nations). As will be seen, the basis of Aboriginal land rights under the common law is premised, in part, on prior occupancy.[190]

As with the ideas of Locke, the recognition of occupancy seems to do little more than smuggle in an argument based on economic benefits and incentives. If so, it is fair to question whether a system that promotes and rewards first occupancy is always the most prudent one, from an economic point of view. A recurring problem with rules based on occupancy is that they can work to impose costs on a party who seeks, but fails, to be the first taker.[191] Another concern is that they can promote the premature exploitation of resources.

The federal settlement policy for western Canada raises questions about the economic efficiency of first occupancy as a means of allocation. The Canadian homesteading policy that was in force from 1872 until 1930 was designed to promote settlement in the Canadian hinterland. (This area served, of course, as the ancestral home of a number of Aboriginal communities.) The *Dominion Lands Act*[192] allowed homesteaders to acquire 160 acres of land (a quarter section) on the payment of a nominal fee. A further quarter section of nearby land could also be acquired. To retain title, homesteaders were required to reside on and develop their plots. There is little doubt that the availability of land for homesteading generated the desired rush to settle in the west. Almost half of Prairie lands that passed into private hands were granted under the policy.[193] However, there is an ongoing debate as to whether this method of distribution made economic sense. One view is that the establishment of settlements beyond the reach of ready markets was ill-conceived and imposed hardships on the isolated homesteaders: "Since homesteads were allocated on a first-come, first-served basis, settlers were forced to claim them before they were economically viable."[194] And, in the prime locations, particularly those near railway lines, the land was doled out at prices that were undoubtedly below market value.[195]

---

190 See Part 3(b), Chapter 2.

191 Epstein, *supra*, note 175, at 114.

192 *An Act Respecting the Public Lands of the Dominion*, S.C. 1872, c. 23. See especially s. 33.

193 K. Norrie & D. Owram, *A History of the Canadian Economy*, 2nd ed. (Toronto: Harcourt Brace Canada, 1996) at 231.

194 *Ibid.* The authors regard the theory of premature settlement as elegant, but treat the matter as still open to debate.

195 See T.L. Anderson & P.J. Hill, "The Race for Property Rights", 33 J. Law & Econ. 177 (1990). Support for the American homesteading policy can be found in D.W. Allen, "Homesteading and Property Rights; Or, How the West was Really Won", 34 J. Law & Econ. 1 (1991). Allen attempts to demonstrate that the American approach provided an efficient means of securing control over carefully designated tracts of the American frontier. This justification is not equally applicable to the Canadian approach or context. For an economic defence of first occupancy as a means of property allocation, see D. Lueck, "The Rule of First Possession and the Design of the Law", 38 J. Law & Econ. 393 (1995).

(h)   a pluralist account

A principled system of property need not rely on a single strand of argument. Property law in Canada can be justified on a variety of different grounds. At the outset I suggested that the various grounds supporting a right of private property tend to reinforce each other. In a way, utilitarianism might be seen as a kind of pluralist defence of private property. When one defines 'utility' broadly, one might claim that, taking into account all of the reasons set out above, on balance private property is optimal.

Stephen Munzer's theory of property rights also demonstrates the linkage among existing property justifications.[196] His is a 'pluralist' account, based on principles of (i) utility and efficiency; (ii) justice and equality; and (iii) labour and desert. Munzer recognizes the cogency of preference-satisfaction models built on utilitarian and efficiency notions. These are blunted by the need to appreciate the equal moral worth of people, which would impede the operation of a hard-line kind of utilitarianism. Moreover, Munzer believes that material inequality is to be tolerated only if everyone possesses a minimum amount of property, and (more stringently) if the scale of inequality does not prevent full human development. At the same time, differences in merit demand rules of ownership that calibrate entitlements based on levels of desert flowing from labour. What emerges from Munzer's blend is a temperate system of private property.[197] The Canadian version of a mixed economy, at least that version which contains a meaningful social safety net, seems close to Munzer's model.

4.   THE FUNCTIONS OF MODERN PROPERTY LAW

(a)   resolving novel claims

The law of property performs a host of functions, including the determination of which items, tangible or otherwise, should be protected as property. We saw earlier in the chapter that there is no exhaustive list of what counts as property and no indisputably settled core of what must be contained within the bundle. Additionally, since property depends on whether the law will recognize and enforce entitlements (and non-property on the refusal to do so), it follows that novel claims of property may be validated or rejected by the courts and the legislatures. This is so: property is not a static concept, but rather is in a constant state of flux. This fluidity is apparent when disputes over new forms of property erupt. Here, on the cutting edge of developments, issues have arisen over such 'things' as the distinctive sound of a singer's voice,[198] an entertainment 'specta-

---

196 S.R. Munzer, *A Theory of Property* (New York: C.U.P., 1990).

197 *Ibid.* at 7.

198 Recognized in the American case of *Midler v. Ford Motor Co.*, 849 F.2d 460 (9th Cir., 1988). See E. Windholz, "Whose Voice is it Anyway?", 8 Cardozo Arts & Ent. J. 201 (1989). See also *Waits v. Frito-Lay Inc.*, 978 F.2d 1093 (9th Cir., 1992) cert. denied, 113 S.Ct. 1047 (1993); P. Buckley, "The Implications of Waits v. Frito-Lay for Advertisers Who Use Celebrity Sound-Alikes", 68 St. John's L.Rev. 241 (1994). See also the references in note 205, *infra*.

cle',[199] frozen sperm,[200] human pre-embryos,[201] cells extracted from a spleen,[202] genetic information,[203] the right of next-of-kin to a human brain preserved in paraffin,[204] and one's 'personality' or celebrity.[205] Two factors seem to have prompted recent developments in the juridical meaning of property. One relates to the rejection of the concept of property as thing-ownership in favour of the idea of property as a bundle of rights in which a broad array of abstractions are

---

199 Not recognized in *Victoria Park Racing & Recreation Grounds Ltd. v. Taylor* (1938) 58 C.L.R. 479 (Aust.H.C.).

200 *Hecht v. Superior Ct.*, 20 Cal. Rptr. 2d 275 (C.A. 2nd Dist., 1993) discussed in J.L. Collins, "Recognizing a Property Right in Reproductive Material", 33 U. Louisville J.Fam.L. 661 (1994-95).

201 *Davis v. Davis*, 842 S.W.2d 588 (Tenn., 1992) partial rehearing granted, No. 34, 1992 W.L. 341632 (Tenn., Nov. 23, 1992) cert. denied, 61 U.S.L.W. 3437 (U.S., Feb. 22, 1993). See further R.J. Muller, "*Davis v. Davis*: The Applicability of Privacy and Property Rights to the Disposition of Frozen Preembryos in Intrafamilial Disputes", 24 U.Toledo L.Rev. 763 (1993).

202 Not recognized in *Moore v. Regents of the University of California*, 271 Cal.Rep. 146 (S.C., 1990). See further W. Boulier, "Sperm, Spleens, and Other Valuables: The Need to Recognise Property Rights in Human Body Parts", 23 Hofstra L.Rev. 693 (1995). Canadian perspective on the *Moore* case can be found in J.M. Gilmour, " 'Our' Bodies: Property Rights in Human Tissue" (1993) 8 Can.J.L. & Soc. 113. See also E.R. Gold, *Body Parts: Property Rights and the Ownership of Human Biological Materials* (Washington, D.C.: Geo.U.P., 1996).

203 See further "Human Genetics and the Law: Regulating a Revolution" (1998) 61(5) Mod.L.Rev. (Special Issue); A.J. Stenson & T.S. Gray, *The Politics of Genetic Resource Control* (London: Macmillan, 1999); C.M. Valerio Barrad, "Genetic Information and Property Theory", 87 Nw.U.L.Rev. 1037 (1993). The United States government has obtained a patent covering the D.N.A. derived from a Hagahai tribesman living in Papua New Guinea: *Globe & Mail*, November 27, 1995, A22. See also Rural Advancement Foundation International (R.A.F.I.), "Indigenous Person from Papua New Guinea Claimed in U.S. Government Patent", Press Release: Oct. 4, 1995 [copy on file at the University of Alberta].

204 Not recognized in *Dobson v. North Tyneside Authority*, [1997] 1 W.L.R. 596, [1996] 4 All E.R. 474 (C.A.).

205 See *Athans v. Canadian Adventure Camps Ltd.* (1977) 17 O.R. (2d) 425, 4 C.C.L.T. 20, 34 C.P.R. (2d) 126, 80 D.L.R. (3d) 583 (H.C.) which draws on *Krouse v. Chrysler Canada Ltd.* (1974) 1 O.R. (2d) 225, 13 C.P.R. (2d) 28, 40 D.L.R. (3d) 15 (C.A.). See further E.M. Singer, "The Development of the Common Law Tort of Appropriation of Personality in Canada" (1998) 15 C.I.P.R. 65. *Cf. Gould Estate v. Stoddart Publishing Co.* (1996) 15 E.T.R. (2d) 167 (Gen.Div.) affirmed on different grounds (1998) 39 O.R. (3d) 545 (C.A.) leave to appeal to S.C.C. refused (1999) 236 N.R. 396 (note) (S.C.C.). The right to one's image was protected under Quebec law in *Aubry v. Éditions Vice-Versa inc.*, [1998] 1 S.C.R. 591, 45 C.C.L.T. (2d) 119, 78 C.P.R. (3d) 289 (*sub nom. Aubry v. Duclos*). See also B. St. M. Hylton & P. Goldson, "The New Tort of Appropriation of Personality: Protecting Bob Marley's Face", [1996] C.L.J. 56. For an account of the flourishing of this concept in America, see J.M. Left, "Not Just Another Pretty Face: Providing Full Protection Under the Right of Publicity", 11 U. Miami Ent. & Sports L.Rev. 321 (1994); M.F. Grady, "A Positive Economic Theory of the Right of Publicity", 1 U.C.L.A. Ent.L.Rev. 97 (1994). An argument that Canadian courts should reject the American approach is advanced in M.A. Flagg, "Star Crazy: Keeping the Right of Publicity Out of Canadian Law" (1999) 13 I.P.J. 179. For a recent American case, see *Parks v. Laface Records*, Unreported, November 18, 1999 (U.S. Dist.Ct., Mich.), which involved a claim by civil rights activist Rosa Parks against the rap group, Outkast. The Court "regrettably" dismissed the action, which alleged, *inter alia*, that there had been a breach of Parks' right of publicity. In British Columbia, Ron White, a Santa Claus look-alike, is suing a mall for the unauthorized use of his image: R. Matas, "West Coast Mall Has Been Naughty, Santa Claus Says", *Globe & Mail*, December 17, 1999, A3.

acknowledged as being amenable to protection as property.[206] The other involves advances in science and technology that have forced new issues into the legal arena, sometimes raising questions that cause the idea of property to totter on a legal and normative precipice.

In the assessment of innovative claims two distinct styles of judicial treatment seem to exist. Some courts adopt an 'attributes' approach. Here, the analysis hinges on whether the right being asserted looks like property: one searches for a strong 'family resemblance'.[207] As Craig Rotherham has argued, the quest is to find a normative basis for recognition internal to the law of property:

> According to one vision of the common law, in deciding a novel question, judges seek to draw upon and to extend traditionally the law's immanent normative resources. In this way, the common law is seen as developing by maintaining and improving its own internal coherence – growing where its internal normative principles dictate.[208]

A difficulty with this kind of judicial strategy has already been identified: it requires us to develop a firm conception of the necessary traits of property. It can also be circular, because the recognition of a right as proprietary can serve to endow it with features (such as transferability) that were not previously treated as being integral to that item or right.

A 'functional' approach, by contrast, looks first at the policy factors at play. It takes account of how property, as a tool of social life, should be used. This approach recognizes that property is not an acontextual entity that demands conceptual purity, but a purposive concept, to be used to meet social needs.[209] Here one sees that property is inseparably tied to social values. It is perhaps a truism that those things that are regarded as property – slaves,[210] trees, ideas, randomized palm-oil fat compositions for infant formulas,[211] *etc.* – provide us with an insight into the society in which we live. Of course, treating property as a tool to be used when appropriate can undermine the idea that the term has a defined content. An approach driven by policy to this extent often is aligned with a nominalist view of property, mentioned above.[212] If, under this analysis, property

---

206 This transition in the conceptualization of property is described in M.J. Horwitz, *The Transformation of American Law: 1870-1960* (New York: O.U.P., 1992) ch. 5, *passim.*

207 A. Carter, *The Philosophical Foundations of Property Rights* (London: Harvester, Wheatsheaf, 1989) at 5, drawing on the work of Ludwig Wittgenstein.

208 C. Rotherham, "Conceptions of Property in Common Law Discourse" (1998) 18 Leg.Stud. 41, at 48.

209 See also the analysis in K.J. Gray, "Property in Thin Air", [1991] C.L.J. 252, where it is argued that the question of whether or not a resource should be treated as private property (and therefore not held in common) depends on whether it should be thought of as 'excludable', from practical, legal and moral points of view.

210 As to the history of slavery in Canada, see W.R. Riddell, "The Slave in Canada", 5 J. Negro History 261 (1920); E.A. Bryce, *Slavery: United States and Canada*, M.A. Thesis, University of Pittsburgh (1932) [copy on file at the University of Alberta]; D.G. Bell, "Slavery and the Judges of Loyalist New Brunswick" (1982) 31 U.N.B.L.J. 9; B. Cahill, "Slavery and the Judges of Loyalist Nova Scotia" (1994) 43 U.N.B.L.J. 73.

211 Canadian Patent No. 2,006,136: *Globe & Mail*, December 28, 1995, A18.

212 See Part 2(a), *supra.*

is that which the law chooses to call property, the effect of such a declaration is not always easy to comprehend fully.

(i)   the university degree example

The controversy over whether university degrees are property has yielded helpful examples of the 'attributes' and 'functional' styles of judicial reasoning. This issue has arisen in cases concerning the division of marital property on divorce. In marriages of short duration a university degree may be the only asset of value, and so its divisibility under the marital property rules may become central to a divorce dispute. Typically, the term 'property' is not comprehensively defined in the governing legislation. Therefore, the task of determining whether a given item (such as a university degree) is marital property falls to the courts.

When this issue was considered in the Colorado case of *Graham v. Graham*[213] (in relation to an M.B.A.) the Court rejected a property-based claim. The degree was said to hold no resemblance to conventional forms of property: it has no market value; it is personal to the holder and so cannot be sold, inherited or given as security; it can be earned but it cannot be bought; it represents an intellectual achievement that may assist in the future acquisition of property, but "it has none of the attributes of property in the usual sense of that term".[214] This conclusion, it should be noted, is the prevailing view in Canadian family law.[215] University degrees are not regarded as property; other means have been found to recognize the contributions of those who assist their spouse through the travails of higher education.

The counterpoint is found in the Michigan case of *Woodworth v. Woodworth*,[216] which involved a claim for the division of the husband's law degree. The Court held that the recognition of the degree as property was an acceptable means of rectifying the enrichment enjoyed by the husband. The Court expressly rejected the attributes approach employed in *Graham*: whether the degree was property in a physical or metaphysical sense was said to be beside the point. It was held that the recognition of the degree as property (thereby bringing it within the purview of the marital property statute) was the only satisfactory means of providing compensation for the efforts of the non-student spouse. Alternatives, including the awarding of support, were regarded as imperfect mechanisms for responding to this form of enrichment. While the degree could not be transferred to that spouse, it could nevertheless be given a monetary value, and part of this value could be allocated to the non-student spouse.

---

213 574 P.2d 75 (Colo.S.C., 1978).

214 *Ibid.* at 77 (*per* Lee J.).

215 See *Caratun v. Caratun* (1992) 10 O.R. (3d) 385, 42 R.F.L. (3d) 113, 96 D.L.R. (4th) 404 (C.A.) leave to appeal to S.C.C. refused (1993) 46 R.F.L. (3d) 314 (note) (S.C.C.). See also *Samson v. Samson* (1996) 26 R.F.L. (4th) 333 (B.C.C.A.). See further M. McCallum, "*Caratun v. Caratun*: It Seems that We Are Not All Realists Yet" (1994) 7 C.J.W.L. 197; B. Hovius & T.G. Youdan, *The Law of Family Property* (Toronto: Carswell, 1991) at 269*ff.*

216 337 N.W.2d 332 (Mich. App., 1983). See also *O'Brien v. O'Brien*, 489 N.E.2d 712 (N.Y.C.A., 1985); K.R. Davis, "The Doctrine of *O'Brien v. O'Brien*: A Critical Analysis", 13 Pace L.Rev. 863 (1994). See *contra* the Canadian case of *Caratun v. Caratun*, *supra*, note 215.

(ii)   *the challenge of cultural appropriation*[217]

A controversy has emerged in Canada of late about something that has been called 'cultural appropriation'. According to one definition, this term means "the taking – from a culture that is not one's own – of intellectual property, cultural expressions or artifacts, history and ways of knowledge".[218] Concerns about misappropriation have underscored the complaints of some Aboriginal writers that non-Aboriginal novelists were, in effect, stealing their stories.[219] In some instances, this may involve the publishing of stories that had previously been part of an oral tradition. In other instances the claims have centred around novelists such as W.P. Kinsella, who write fictional accounts using native characters.[220] But the debate about cultural appropriation extends beyond the literary arts, and involves, among other things, recordings of traditional music,[221] works of visual art that use traditional motifs, symbols or designs,[222] and the use of ancient medicines as the basis of pharmaceutical patents.[223] Recently, some of these issues were joined (without much success) in a law suit brought by the descendants of Tasunke Witko (known as Crazy Horse) against the Hornell Brewing Company, distributors of a product called 'Crazy Horse Malt Liquor'.[224]

Cultural appropriation raises questions about the treatment of novel claims. The concerns that have been voiced about cultural appropriation centre on forms of 'taking' that tend to fall outside of the realm of the current law of property, or more specifically, the laws governing intellectual property law (the law of patents, trademarks, *etc.*). Consider, for example, the case of the recording of a traditional Aboriginal song. The law of copyright provides a limited protection for works of art: usually the right lasts for the life of the creator plus 50 years. After that, the work falls within the public domain. Moreover, to be amenable to protection the work must be recorded or 'fixed' in some way. And it must be possible to

---

217 See generally B. Ziff & P.V. Rao, eds., *Borrowed Power: Essays on Cultural Appropriation* (New Brunswick, N.J.: Rutgers U.P., 1997) [referred to below as "*Cultural Appropriation*"]. The discussion in this Part deals with the appropriation of intangible goods. Issues governing the restitution of tangible cultural property are raised, briefly, in Part 3(b), Chapter 2, and Part 4(b), Chapter 4.

218 Resolution of the Writers' Union of Canada, approved June, 1992.

219 See generally R.J. Coombe, "The Properties of Culture and the Possession of Identity: Post-colonial Struggle and Legal Imagination", in *Cultural Appropriation, supra*, note 217, 74.

220 See further R. Wiebe, "Proud Cree nation deserves much more than 'funny' stories", *Globe & Mail*, February 17, 1990, C3.

221 A. Seeger, "Ethnomusicology and Music Law", in *Cultural Appropriation, supra*, note 217, 52.

222 See further *Bulun Bulun v. R. & T. Textiles Pty. Ltd.* (1998) 157 A.L.R. 193 (F.C.) and the literature and case law referred to there. The *Bulun Bulun* case is discussed in A.T. Kenyon, "The 'Artist Fiduciary' – Australian Aboriginal Art and Copyright", [1999] Ent.L.R. 42. See generally J. Frow, "Public Domain and Collective Rights in Culture" (1998) 13 I.P.J. 39.

223 See N. Roht-Arriaza, "Of Seeds and Shamans: The Appropriation of Scientific and Technical Knowledge of Indigenous and Local Communities" in *Cultural Appropriation, supra*, note 217, 255.

224 See N. Jessup Newton, "Memory and Misrepresentation: Representing Crazy Horse in Tribal Court", in *Cultural Appropriation, supra*, note 217, 195. See further *Hornell Brewing Co. v. Rosebud Sioux Tribal Court*, 33 F.3d 1087 (C.A. 8th Cir., 1998). See also J. Cart, "A Culture Clash of Symbolism, Commercialism", *Los Angeles Times*, July 15, 1999, A2.

identify the creator(s) of the object, on whom the copyright can be conferred. A traditional song, then, would probably fall well outside of the ambit of the present law of copyright.[225] One wonders whether the law should be extended.

Some have suggested that complaints about appropriation are specious, at least when applied to the creation of fundamentally new works by authors and other artists. Robert Fulford's stern rebuke reflects contempt for the whole idea:

> The word 'appropriation' has lately become a rhetorical weapon in the hands of intellectuals claiming to speak for minority rights. Its power derives, oddly, from its very irrationality. In my experience, people hearing of it for the first time cannot believe that anyone would put forward so ludicrous an idea: even the most modest education in cultural history teaches us that art of all kinds has depended on the mixing of cultures.[226]

This cynical attitude fails to appreciate the values that support the critique of appropriation; some of those values are reflected in the general law of property. For example, it has been argued that cultural appropriation affects the development of cultural identity. In effect, this is a view based on personhood theory, as applied to communities, not individuals, and so reflects a type of grouphood analysis (a term that was used earlier in this chapter[227]). Others have invoked both labour theory and economic arguments, suggesting that the wrong people are benefiting from the cultural creations of the past. This view is often coupled with notions of communal ownership and collective rights. Another line of argument stresses the importance of the proper maintenance of cultural forms; this is an argument based on stewardship. Finally, some protagonists in the cultural appropriation debate have demonstrated that what is involved here is a conflict of 'sovereignties'. Lenore Keeshig-Tobias, a prominent Aboriginal writer, has said that

> . . . in our culture, people *own* stories. Individuals own stories. Families own stories. Tribes own stories. Nations own stories. And there is a protocol if you want to tell those stories: you go to the storyteller. And if you don't and you start telling those stories, then you are *stealing.*[228]

The problems posed by cultural appropriation are difficult to solve with property laws. This is because even if the values underlying the cultural appropriation debate are made out, finding an effective legal response remains problematic. For example, the ability of current artists to draw on the work of others raises questions about free speech and expression. Some artists might be silenced by rules that limit their creative fields of vision. Even if a balance can somehow be struck, attempting to create group rights means that definitional questions (Who is in? Who is out?) must be broached. Similarly, the potential forms of

---

225 See further K. Puri, "Cultural Ownership and Intellectual Property Rights Post-*Mabo*: Putting Ideas into Action" (1995) 9 I.P.J. 293.

226 R. Fulford, "The Trouble with Emily", Canadian Art (Winter, 1993) 33, at 38.

227 See Part 3(e), *supra*. See also J. Moustakas, "Group Rights in Cultural Property: Justifying Strict Inalienability", 74 Cornell L.Rev. 1179 (1989).

228 L. Keeshig-Tobias, in "The Public Face of the Cultural Appropriation Debate: Who Speaks for Whom?" Morningside (C.B.C. Radio), April 1, 1992, transcribed in (1992) 2 *Textual Studies in Canada* 30, at 42.

taking are numerous: how are these to be defined? Indeed, this may be an area in which the law of property simply fails to mediate conflicting claims adequately.

(iii)   *novel claims concerning land*

While the expansion of the notion of property over some goods, intangible or otherwise, has been robust, the same development is not apparent in relation to rights over land. Instead, the courts have adopted the cautious view that the categories of property rights should be carefully controlled. So, in the 1834 case of *Keppell v. Bailey*[229] it was said that courts should not permit the creation of various sorts of fancy interests in land. There was "no mischief" in allowing contractual rights over land of all shapes and sizes, to be binding on the contracting parties. However, "great detriment would arise and much confusion of rights [would ensue] if parties were allowed to invent new modes of holding and enjoying real property".[230] In an accordant way, in *Re Macleay* it was suggested that 1853 was "rather a modern time to alter the law of real property"![231] The creation of a closely guarded and limited number of categories of interests in land – the recognition of a *numerus clausus* policy for realty[232] – has slowed down (but not completely halted) the process of judicial reform of land law principles in Canada. Parliament, of course, is not limited in the same way.[233]

(b)   *other principal functions*

Property law serves not only as a means of determining the objects of ownership, it also allocates entitlements and provides a context in which those initial rights can be exchanged. The law balances the conflicting claims of property owners: conflicts that can arise, for example, between neighbours, concurrent or successive owners of the same property, or surface and subsurface owners. The law of property provides protection, through the criminal and civil law, against wrongful action by persons with no entitlements. It also serves as a mechanism to ascertain and facilitate the dispositional preferences of owners.[234]

---

229 (1834) 2 My. & K. 517, 39 E.R. 1042 (Ch.D.).

230 *Ibid.* at 1049 E.R. (*per* Brougham L.C.). A major concern here is that allowing land to be encumbered with fancy interests would fetter alienability.

231 (1875) L.R. 20 Eq. 186, at 191 (*per* Jessel M.R.).

232 See the exploration of this phenomenon in B. Rudden, "Economic Theory v. Property Law: The *Numerus Clausus* Problem" in J.M. Eekelaar & J. Bell, eds., *Oxford Essays in Jurisprudence*, 3rd series (Oxford: Clarendon Pr., 1987) 239. For a Canadian example of the doctrine in operation, see *Fairhill Developments Ltd. v. Aberdeen Properties Ltd.*, [1969] 2 O.R. 267, 5 D.L.R. (3d) 118 (H.C.). However, for a departure from these strictures, see *Freeborn v. Goodman*, [1969] S.C.R. 923, 6 D.L.R. (3d) 384, discussed in Part 8(c), Chapter 9. On the importance of precedent in the context of land law, see *Doe d. Evans v. Doyle* (1860) 4 Nfld.R. 432, at 436 (*per* Robinson J.): "surely nothing can be of greater importance to the peace of society than that rules which govern the disposition of property should be settled, and not fluctuating". See also *Re Hazell*, 57 O.L.R. 290, [1925] 3 D.L.R. 661 (C.A.) at 294 O.L.R.

233 See, *e.g.*, *Lunenburg (Town) v. Lunenburg (Municipality)*, 4 M.P.R. 181, [1932] 1 D.L.R. 386 (N.S.C.A.).

234 Issues relating to this function are broached in Part 2(a), Chapter 5.

These main functions are largely (but not solely) manifestations of attempts to promote economic efficiency through the reduction of transaction costs. As such, they draw on the economic arguments for private ownership canvassed above to a very high degree.[235] The term 'transaction costs' is used here to include expenses associated with market dealings, such as those that result from gathering information, bargaining, and resolving disputes. When these costs are low (or nil), market transactions are facilitated. When the reverse is true, bargaining and efficient allocations may be impeded, sometimes completely. One way of reducing transaction costs is to strive for clear ownership rules. As Carol Rose has suggested, 'crystal' rules are preferred to 'mud' rules because the former tend to reduce the costs of market dealings, though mud rules are sometimes needed to allow for flexibility in the pursuit of fairness.[236]

Land registration systems serve as a good illustration of an attempt to reduce transaction costs. Under the Torrens system of land registration (in use in several provinces in Canada) the government attempts to compile a record of all (or nearly all) interests that pertain to a given tract. Reliance on that title means that a historical search of the root of the vendor's title is normally not required when the land is sold. Absent fraud on the part of the purchaser, earlier defects in title are generally of no consequence to the present owner. Moreover, in a perfect Torrens system the register is a mirror of all interests affecting that tract. Ensuring entitlements (to a degree), and making the information about land ownership easily accessible, should facilitate the bargaining process and reduce the costs of sales.

As we have already seen, not all property law is, or should be, based on an efficiency rationale; other justifications and principles also vie for attention.[237] Some policies promote other interests and may have only an incidental connection with property. That is, non-property based issues can nonetheless affect the complexion of the law of property. Included here, for instance, are concerns about racial discrimination. Hence, the law no longer tolerates certain discriminatory practices in the renting of privately held premises. The lure of property can serve as a vehicle for social engineering in a variety of ways. The example of promoting settlement on the Prairies through homesteading incentives, which was considered above, serves also to illustrate this general point.[238] In a similar way, tax law is sometimes used to create incentives for investment, even though this may actually reduce tax revenues in the short-term. Hence, property law can be used as a way of giving effect to any number of public initiatives. Perhaps that is why understanding the law of property is so challenging: property rules can be affected by a wide spectrum of social goals.

Some interests have not significantly affected the composition of the law of property in the past. When I say this I am thinking specifically of the importance

235 See Part 3(b), *supra*.
236 See further C.M. Rose, "Crystals and Mud in Property Law", in *Property and Persuasion: Essays on the History, Theory, and Rhetoric of Ownership* (Boulder: Westview Pr., 1994) ch. 7.
237 See Part 3(a), *supra*.
238 See Part 3(g), *supra*.

of preserving our environment. All of the rationales of property reviewed above tend to promote the exploitation of resources. If one were to take stock of the range of property law doctrines, it would appear that the common law seems to care very little about conservation, except to the extent that principles have developed that seek to prevent natural resources from being depleted by one person, in order to protect the rights of other users. Even if private property regimes are less destructive of resources than common ownership systems (as the tragedy of the commons implies[239]), the driving force of economic theory is still efficient resource use. As a consequence, in the history of the development of private property one finds that other values have been subordinated.[240] Two cases provide graphic (if extreme) illustrations of what I mean.

In the 1881 case of *Ghen v. Rich*[241] a dispute arose over the ownership of a dead fin-back whale. The party who had lance bombed the whale prevailed over the person first taking physical possession. The Court concluded that were the whaler not allowed to claim ownership "this branch of industry must necessarily cease, for no person would engage in it if the fruits of his labor could be appropriated by any chance finder".[242] The view that whales should not be harvested or commodified was not considered. A few years later the Newfoundland Supreme Court was faced with a question of ownership rights to seals killed on the ice floes. In *Power v. Kennedy*[243] it was held that the indiscriminate killing of seals by a hunting party did not give rise to ownership of the carcasses left strewn behind. It was said that the killing must be accompanied by possession and that if someone discovers a body that contains no *indicia* of property, the person committing the killing "must be in a position then and there to assert his right of property, to point to the specific seals as his own or those of his fellows, and to exercise corporal control over them, unless he is resisted by force or deterred by threats of violence".[244] While this might seem to imply a conservationist posture that is absent in *Ghen v. Rich*, the rationale of the holding was efficiency-driven. The Court was concerned that this mode of hunting would prevent competition and pre-empt others from taking the "fruits of the ice-fields".[245]

These cases remind us of a point made at the outset, namely, that property is concerned with the allocation of rights as among individuals *over* objects. As matters now stand, it is rarely the function of the private law of property to protect property for its own sake.[246] That things cannot seek the law's protection comes

---

239 See Part 3(b)(ii), *supra*.
240 See further J. Sprankling, "The Antiwilderness Bias in American Property Law", 63 U.Chi.L.Rev. 519 (1996).
241 8 Fed. 159 (Mass.Dist.Ct., 1881).
242 *Ibid.* at 162 (*per* Nelson D.J.). The rules governing the capture of wild animals are discussed briefly in Part 3(a), Chapter 4.
243 (1884) 7 Nfld.R. 34 (S.C.).
244 *Ibid.* at 36 (*per* Pinsent J.).
245 *Ibid.* at 35.
246 In *Anderson v. Skender* (1992) 61 B.C.L.R. (2d) 292 (S.C.) reversed in part (1993) 84 B.C.L.R. (2d) 135, [1994] 1 W.W.R. 186, 17 C.C.L.T. (2d) 160 (C.A.) leave to appeal to S.C.C. refused [1994] 2 W.W.R. lxiv (note) (S.C.C.) McKenzie J. (at 297 of the trial judgment) made a valiant

to the surface in cases involving the right to sue (or have 'standing') in environmental litigation. Take, for instance, the case of *Sierra Club v. Morton*,[247] where an action was launched by an environmental organization seeking to prevent development in a wilderness area in California. No special interest beyond that of the community at large having been pleaded, the group's attempt to be given standing was rejected by the United States Supreme Court. In dissent, Douglas J. took the unorthodox position that the natural environment itself should have standing and could speak through a human instrumentality. If this seems remarkable, remember that some artificial and inanimate entities, such as corporations, have legal and constitutional rights both in Canada and the United States. If that is the case,

> [s]o it should be as respects valleys, alpine meadows, rivers, lakes, estuaries, beaches, ridges, groves of trees, swampland, or even air that feels the destructive pressures of modern technology and modern life. The river, for example, is the living symbol of all life it sustains or nourishes – fish, aquatic insects, water ouzels, otter, fisher, deer, elk, bear, and all other animals, including man, who are dependent on it or who enjoy it for its sight, its sound, or its life. The river as plaintiff speaks for the ecological unit of life that is part of it. Those people who have a meaningful relation to that body of water – whether it be a fisherman, a canoeist, a zoologist, or a logger – must be able to speak for the values which the river represents. The voice of the inanimate object, therefore, should not be stilled.[248]

Canadian law has not moved this far, though some success has been achieved by environmental groups seeking standing in comparable circumstances.[249] Generally, property law has now drifted away from the resource-utilization credo that is so marked in the common law. By and large, these changes have not been based on private law responses to pollution and other threats to the environment, but instead have taken the form of regulatory regimes involving licensing and criminal (including quasi-criminal) sanctions.[250] Perhaps the next stage will be the introduction of a general obligation of 'stewardship', that is, a duty that compels owners to respect the environment. This strategy can be pursued not only by imposing restrictions on the way the land can be exploited (there are now many laws that do this), but also through the introduction of a broadly cast *positive* duty

---

attempt to resolve a dispute over the destruction of trees along a boundary line by assessing the problem "from the tree's point of view".

247 405 U.S. 727 (1972).

248 *Ibid.* at 752. See further J.M. Caragher, "The Wilderness Ethic of Justice William O. Douglas", 1986 U.Ill.L.Rev. 645, at 650*ff*; C. Stone, "Should Trees Have Standing? Toward Legal Rights for Natural Objects", 45 S.Cal.L.Rev. 450 (1972). As to animal rights and property law, see G.L. Francione, *Animals, Property and the Law* (Philadelphia: Temple U.P., 1995). See generally E. Hughes *et al.*, eds., *Environmental Law and Policy*, 2nd ed. (Toronto: Emond Montgomery, 1998) at 424*ff*.

249 See, *e.g.*, *Sierra Club of Canada v. Canada (Minister of Finance)* (1998) 157 F.T.R. 123 (T.D.). *Cf. Society for the Preservation of the Englishman River Estuary v. Nanaimo (Regional District)* (1999) 28 C.E.L.R. (N.S.) 253 (B.C.S.C.).

250 See generally J.E. Cribbet, "Concepts in Transition: The Search for a New Definition of Property", 1986 U.Ill.L.Rev. 1.

of environmental care.[251] Bear in mind that such a development is entirely consistent with the complementary notions that ownership rights are always subject to restrictions,[252] and that property is a legal construct that is composed of both rights and obligations.

---

251 For a very robust conception of the idea of stewardship of land see W.N.R. Lucy, "Replacing Private Property: The Case for Stewardship", [1996] C.L.J. 566. See also the literature reviewed there.
252 See further E.T. Freyfogle, "The Construction of Ownership", 1996 U.Ill.L.Rev. 173.

2

THE INSTITUTION OF PROPERTY IN CONTEXT

> The things that lawyers know about
> Are property and land.
> But why the leaves are on the trees,
> And why the waves disturb the seas,
> Why honey is the food of bees,
> Why horses have such tender knees,
> Why winters come when rivers freeze,
> Why faith is more than what one sees,
> And hope survives the worst disease,
> And charity is more than these,
> They do not understand.
>
> H.D.C. Pepler, *The Devil's Dream*

1. INTRODUCTION

This chapter deals with three introductory topics that share the function of providing a setting for the study of principles of property. First, the historical development of the laws that are now found in the common law provinces and territories will be examined. Canadian property law grew mainly from a cutting of English law and the process of transplantation will be explained. The second part of the chapter concerns what I have termed the 'doctrinal' context. Here the main divisions, groupings and types of property rights will be described. The existing entitlements are closely intertwined with the origins of the law and so are intelligible only by looking initially to the past. Some legal terms, including a few which are a part of our normal vocabulary, reflect this strong association with the past: consider what might be the etymology of the words 'landlord' and 'tenant'.

In the final section of this chapter the analysis moves to the present – to the social setting in which property doctrines now operate. The nature of ownership in Canadian society and the impact of disparities in wealth will be addressed. This is a topic of enormous breadth and complexity, but only a brief overview is attempted. The presentation tries to identify those aspects of private property that are important to ordinary Canadians. It also seeks to show how property helps to define Canadian society.

2. SOURCES OF CANADIAN PROPERTY LAW

Modern Canadian law possesses many legal artifacts that reflect a colourful and engaging history that happened somewhere else. At the rock-bottom of Canadian law one discovers the elements of an English feudal ancestry. Revolutionary changes in the forms of social organization have eroded much of the practical impact of the feudal property regime, but the structures remain standing. This can be understood through an analysis of the main features of the system as it once operated. It is typical to draw back to the period immediately following the Norman Conquest of what is now England. Here one finds two main principles of feudal land law: the doctrines of tenures and estates. Both continue to serve as critical components of Canadian real property law.

(a)   feudal structures: tenures and estates

The label 'feudalism' is a modern, or at least retrospective invention, designed to describe the legal and social framework that endured in many parts of the world throughout the Middle Ages. The work of Littleton in the fifteenth century described the living organism of feudal property law as a fairly coherent set of principles. Such characterizations, even if they obscure a far more complex and ever-evolving legal order, nevertheless allow us to cull from the past the vestiges that still exist in England and, more miraculously, in most of Canada.[1]

Under the English system of tenures, land was (and still is) held of a lord, not owned outright by a subject.[2] The recipients do not obtain absolute (sometimes referred to as 'allodial') ownership of land. The function of the tenurial arrangement was to create an economic and social network. This was accomplished through the devolution of land from the Crown in return for allegiance, revenues and other benefits. Tenurial systems existed in England and elsewhere in Europe before the Norman Conquest, but landholding under the regime put in place following 1066 had many features that differed from most of its continental counterparts. For one thing, the imposition of tenure in England seems to have been universal, covering "[e]very acre of English soil".[3]

The first grants were from the Crown to the tenants in chief (or *tenants in capite ut de corona*). In large measure, these tenant-recipients were able to exercise rights of ownership. However, the notion that tenure initially created a property right has been doubted by modern scholars. Tenure created a bond of reciprocal obligations between tenant and lord; it was more akin to a contractual right than one of property. In essence, the grant involved oaths of loyalty sworn by the tenant, and undertakings of security of tenure given by the lord.[4] In time, the tenant apparently was able (subject to meeting certain requirements) to pass the lands to someone else. That might be done by the alienation of the tenant's full interest in the lands to a purchaser or donee, who would then assume the very

---

1 As Michael Stuckey has observed, the diminished importance of feudalism has led, over the centuries, to a decreasing need for detailed treatment of the legal aspects of the concept: M. Stuckey, "Feudalism and Australian Land Law: 'A Shadowy Ghostlike Survival?' " (1994) 13 U.Tas.L.Rev. 102. Hence this brief overview.

2 The doctrine of tenures describes the relationship between tenant and lord, not that which exists between the tenant and the land possessed: see *Ontario (Attorney General) v. Mercer* (1883) 8 App.Cas. 767 (P.C.) at 771-2.

3 F. Pollock & F.W. Maitland, *The History of English Law*, 2nd ed. (Cambridge: C.U.P. ed. 1911, 1898) vol. 1, at 232.

4 See generally S.F.C. Milsom, *The Legal Framework of English Feudalism* (Cambridge: C.U.P., 1976); R.C. Palmer, "The Origins of Property in England", 3 Law & Hist.Rev. 1 (1985) and the copious references cited there.

position occupied by the original tenant; this produced what is sometimes called a 'substitution'. Quite simply, a conventional sale of residential property today works in this way, with the purchaser assuming the tenure formerly held by the vendor.

In this early period of Norman feudalism a transfer by a tenant could also be undertaken in a way that created a further layer of tenure. This type of dealing is described as 'subinfeudation', the result of which was to place the granting tenant in the role of lord of the grantee. The new tenant (a tenant in demesne) held the land of the immediate overlord. The tenant in chief of the Crown thereby assumed the additional role of being a lord (termed a mesne lord). The tenant in demesne could create a further tenurial relationship. In theory, there was no limit on the extent of fragmentation of holdings through subinfeudation that could occur, and for over two centuries following the Conquest the process of subinfeudation continued apace. In this way a social and economic pyramid grew, with the sovereign at the apex, and with the tenants *in capite* and the various other sub-ordinate owners below. Each tenant held property of an overlord. To liken it to a pyramid can be misleading, since pyramids are usually soundly built and simple in design; English feudal land arrangements and hierarchies were not so rationally constructed.

As a central feature of these arrangements, a tenant was compelled to provide tenurial services to the immediate lord. An elaborate variety of services emerged, each involving different responsibilities and incidents. In a compendious way, Cribbet and Johnson have described the matrix of service obligations as being designed to satisfy four basic needs: (i) security; (ii) spirituality; (iii) splendour; and (iv) sustenance.[5]

Persons holding property directly of the Crown typically received grants under military tenure, 'knight service' being a common form. The prime obliga-tion was the provision of military aid, such as the supplying of knights for a period each year ('security'). Sound in principle as a means of raising a standing army, it proved unworkable in practice, and once the inefficiency of this method of conscription was recognized the obligation was commonly commuted into a money payment (known as scutage). Religious-based tenures, the main ones being called 'frankalmoign' and 'divine service', were granted to ecclesiastical bodies and the services provided in return related to sacred matters (spirituality). Tenures under grand serjeanty, held by tenants *in capite*, were used to provide various forms of personal service to the Crown (splendour). A comparable tenure, often held of a tenant *in capite* (as mesne lord), was described as petty serjeanty. Some of the duties that emerged under this category were peculiar, to put it mildly. For example, records from these times show that one owner was required to train a hare-dog belonging to the King; another tenant was required to find two white cups on the day of the coronation.[6]

---

5 J.E. Cribbet & C.W. Johnson, *Principles of the Law of Property*, 3rd ed. (Westbury, N.Y.: Foundation Pr., 1989) at 31*ff*.

6 See T. Blount, *Fragmenta Antiquitatis; Ancient Tenures of Land and Jocular Customs of Some Manors* (London: n.p., 1679) at 10, 67.

A key type of tenure was that known as 'free and common socage'; this was mainly agrarian based, and as such was designed to meet sustenance requirements. It also served as a form of residual tenure, encompassing a host of obligations that did not fall within the other kinds. Like the idiosyncratic features of serjeanty, some of the required services were rather curious. The grant of Rupert's Land to the Hudson's Bay Company in 1670 was in socage; in return the Company was obliged to provide "two Elcks and two black beavers when and so often as Wee our heirs and successors shall happen to enter" Rupert's Land.[7] This example illustrates a further point, that is, that while some of the required services were meaningful and extensive, others were purely nominal. Moreover, the inefficiency of knight service foreshadowed the eventual obsolescence of most of the services of tenure. From the very broad array that once existed, only free and common socage came to Canada.

Services were not the only obligations/entitlements that attached to land. There were also rights that were incidental elements of tenure. These 'incidents' (as they are now called) varied depending on the type of holding. The main ones were as follows: oaths of allegiance given by the tenant to the lord (homage and fealty); a right of the lord to call for financial contributions in certain circumstances (aids); transfer taxes (fines); death duties payable on the descent of land to an heir (relief and primer seisin); the power to recover the land when the tenurial term had expired or was forfeited (escheat and forfeiture); control over both (a) lands held by a minor, and (b) the marriage of the heir of the estate (wardship and marriage); and other local tax-like levies (customary dues).

Of these, it is escheat that remains important today. This incident allowed the lord to regain the land once the tenure that had been granted had ended:

> What is meant is that, when there is no longer any tenant, the land returns, by reason of tenure, to the lord by whom, or by whose predecessors in title, the tenure was created. [Some] writers speak of the lord as taking it by way of succession or inheritance, as if from the tenant, which is certainly not accurate. The tenant's estate (subject to any charges upon it which he may have created) has come to an end, and the lord is in by . . . right.[8]

Although the doctrine of tenures embodies the rules for allocating land rights and corresponding obligations, it does not describe their duration. That is the function of the doctrine of estates. It is under that doctrine that the time span of an interest in land is defined. By the beginning of the fourteenth century the common law recognized three types of freehold estates: the fee simple, the fee tail and the life estate. The meaning of these terms will be explored in depth in Chapter 5, but they may be briefly introduced here. The fee simple represents the

---

7 The full grant is reproduced in P.C. Newman, *Company of Adventurers: The Story of Hudson's Bay Company* (Markham: Viking, 1985) vol. 1, at 320*ff*. For an assortment of other unusual tenures, see R.E. Megarry, *Miscellany-at-Law: A Diversion for Lawyers and Others* (London: Sweet & Maxwell, 1955) at 154*ff*.

8 *Ontario (Attorney General) v. Mercer, supra*, note 2, at 772 (*per* Lord Selborne L.C.). See further *Sandhurst Trustees Ltd. v. 72 Seventh Street Nominees Pty. Ltd. (in Liq.)* (1998) 45 N.S.W.L.R. 556 (Eq.D.) at 563*ff*.

largest possible tenurial holding and fee simple ownership is, for all practical purposes, the same as absolute ownership; most land in common law Canada in private hands is held in fee simple. An estate in fee tail would subsist as long as there were lineal descendants (children, their children, *etc.*) who could inherit the land. The life estate, as the name implies, continues for the duration of a life or lives.[9]

The landholding rights described above all fell within the realm of free tenures, a prime attribute of which was that the obligations that were imposed had to be certain, or at least capable of ascertainment. At the base of the pyramid, propping it up on their shoulders, were vassal-labourers who initially held under unfree or villeinage tenures. These holdings were typically within manors, those internal fiefdoms that pervaded post-Conquest England. In many parts of England the manor was the locus of communal life. Within it were to be found a lord (usually a tenant *in capite*), others holding in demesne under free tenures, land held by labourers, and common pastures and wastelands.

The rights of ownership of the villein were initially enjoyed at the sufferance of the lord, with responsibilities that could be varied at whim. The only certainty here was that whatever was exacted would be onerous. The arduous toil of the vassal labourers made the decorous and comfortable existence inside the manor house possible. In stages, some internal constraints on the arbitrary powers of the lords developed. The governing rules were drawn from the custom of the manor, administered first through a Court Customary, and eventually under the watchful eye of the common law. The principles governing the entitlements of these tenures evolved into a form of tenure described as 'copyhold', a term derived from the methods of conveyancing and recording that were used. Labour shortages may have led to the improvement of the legal position of copyhold tenants. Whatever the impetus, by the sixteenth century "[c]opyhold lost its taint of servility, and became merely a form – indeed, one of the commonest forms – of tenure".[10] However, that was never true in Canada: copyhold does not appear to have ever been part of the common law of this country.[11]

The feudal network, simplified, can be pictured in this way:

---

9 These freehold estates share two common elements. First, given the manner in which their duration is determined, the time period during which a given freehold estate will last is always uncertain. Second, only the holder of a freehold estate can be said to be 'seised' of the land. To be seised is to be in possession as a freeholder and the person so designated enjoys certain legal protections. At the same time, it was the tenant holding seisin to whom the lord could look to exact the services and incidents of tenure. The concept of seisin is taken up again, briefly, in Part 5(a), Chapter 4, and in Part 4(a)(i), Chapter 7.

10 R.E. Megarry & H.W.R. Wade, *The Law of Real Property*, 2nd ed. (London: Stevens & Sons, 1959) at 28.

11 But copyhold has, arguably, been influential in the development of other areas of law: see Part 2, Chapter 10 (easements), and Part 3(c), Chapter 12 (land titles registration).

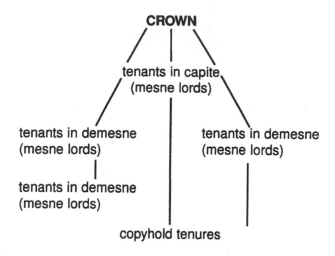

Tenures and estates still form the basis of land law in the common law provinces and territories of Canada, although most of the accompanying feudal trappings have long since disappeared. The process of disintegration began from within. As a means of generating a stable economic order, the establishment of tenures and the development of manorial control may have been effective to a degree; however, the system of services proved to be unsatisfactory. As a result, by the early thirteenth century many of these obligations were not enforced. The system of buying services in return for land gradually became obsolete.[12] A period of intense inflation in England at the end of the twelfth century had devalued the fixed obligations of tenure. Despite this, several of the *incidents* of tenure remained economically viable and were still lucrative enough that a litany of conflicts arose over the nature and extent of these entitlements. Those controversies shaped much of real property law until the seventeenth century, as the Crown sought to impose, and tenants endeavoured to avoid, tax-like claims in the form of these feudal dues. Restrictions on the right of the Crown to invoke the incident called 'aids' was a matter of sharp political debate and became one of the grievances dealt with in the *Magna Carta*.[13] Major reforms were introduced under Henry VIII in the sixteenth century, aimed at the preservation of revenues generated by incidents; these measures still have an afterimage in Canadian law.[14]

---

12 J.H. Baker, *An Introduction to English Legal History*, 3rd ed. (London: Butterworths, 1990) at 272.

13 Clause 15 of *Magna Carta*, 1215, provided that: ''Henceforth we will not grant anyone that he may take an aid from his free men, except to ransom his person, to make his eldest son a knight and to marry his eldest daughter once; and for these purposes only a reasonable aid is to be levied.'' This clause was not included in the 1216 re-issue, nor did it appear in the *confirmatio cartarum* of 1297 (25 Edw. 1): see M. Evans & R.I. Jack, eds., *Sources of English Legal and Constitutional History* (Sydney: Butterworths, 1984) at 50*ff*.

14 See Part 3, Chapter 6.

Two statutory reforms altered the shape of feudalism dramatically. The first of these highlighted the importance of the incidents of tenure in the thirteenth and fourteenth centuries. The second reflected the demise of this form of revenue collection by the seventeenth century. In the aftermath of these two changes only trace elements of the once vibrant feudal system remained.

The first of these developments was the enactment of *Statute Quia Emptores Terrarum* in 1290.[15] As early as the mid-thirteenth century the feudal pyramid looked more like a maze, for subinfeudation had become so common that the enjoyment of incidents had been seriously undermined. It had become difficult to determine the state of title to many parcels of land. This concern was described in the preamble of the statute, which spoke of the loss of escheats, marriages and wardships arising from the proliferation of tenures through subinfeudation.[16] *Quia Emptores* was designed to reduce these problems by prohibiting further subinfeudation; it did not abolish existing tenures. It was expected that as escheats and forfeitures occurred the pyramid would truncate until the Crown assumed again the position of immediate lord to all tenants of freehold land. This has come to pass almost completely in England, and no doubt the catastrophic decline in population brought on by the Black Death expedited the process. Once the pyramid had collapsed virtually all lands in the hands of tenants were held directly of the Crown.

After the Statute, a transfer of the fee simple estate from A to B could not be accompanied by obligations of continuing tenurial services or incidents owed by B to A. The transfer would produce a substitution, not a subinfeudation. The loss of the right to subinfeudate was momentous, but something was provided in return. Prior to 1290, there were doubts as to the right of a tenant to alienate land without the consent of the immediate lord; by the middle of the thirteenth century the lord's power to prevent a transfer seems to have been worn down.[17] Whatever control that remained was abolished by *Quia Emptores*: it allowed transfers to take place without the need to seek consent. That this was also true for the tenants *in capite* was confirmed by statute in 1327.[18] These measures are now treated as providing the first legislative manifestations of the policy of promoting free alienability, an idea that influences much of the contemporary law of property.[19]

Quia Emptores is not binding on the Crown and therefore the granting of new lands, or reconveying properties reclaimed through escheat, has continued. Additionally, while full subinfeudation was abolished, some grants can still be

---

15 18 Edw. 1, c. 3 (meaning, essentially, 'about purchasers').

16 The preamble states as follows: "Because purchasers of lands and tenements belonging to the fees of magnates and others have often in times past entered into their fees to the prejudice of those magnates and others, in that their free tenants have sold their lands and tenements to the purchaser to be held in fee by them and their heirs of their feoffors and not of the chief lords of the fees, whereby the same chief lords have very often lost escheats, marriages and wardships of lands and tenements belonging to their fees, a thing which seemed to those magnates and other lords exceedingly hard and hard to bear and tantamount in this case to manifest disinheritance . . .".

17 A.W.B. Simpson, *A History of the Land Law*, 2nd ed. (Oxford: Clarendon Pr., 1986) at 54.

18 1 Edw. 3, cc. 12, 13. The Crown was able to levy a reasonable fine in the event of an alienation.

19 Alienability is considered in detail in Part 3(e), Chapter 7.

made that come close to, but do not cross, the line drawn by the Statute. A private owner might grant a long term lease, say for 999 years, exacting a rent and retaining a reversion, as the landlord, to be enjoyed in possession once the period of the lease is over. In fact, the use of leases for agricultural purposes emerged in the wake of the Statute and eventually large areas of farmland in England were tilled and harvested by tenant farmers. In a similar way, the owner of the largest conceivable estate interest, the fee simple, is still entitled to carve from this some lesser entitlement, such as a life interest, at the expiration of which the fee simple owner is once again entitled to assume possession of the land.[20]

It was not until the seventeenth century that the enforcement and collection of incidents became outmoded. This prompted the introduction of the *Statute of Tenures, 1660*,[21] which was designed to reduce significantly the available tenurial forms. Steps toward this end had already been taken during the interregnum period over a decade earlier.[22] The 1660 Act had retrospective and prospective effects. It converted all tenures by knight service and serjeanty into socage and removed some of the onerous incidents of tenure. Also, the new law decreed that all future grants were to be in free and common socage. Henceforth the feudal system was merely a shell, a spent force as a means of economic organization, the revenue-raising function having been taken over by other modes of taxation. The way was now opened for the emergence of capitalism in which labour and land were commodified in a fashion far beyond that which had previously existed. Marx's observations are apposite: "The economic structure of capitalist society has grown out of the economic structure of feudal society. The dissolution of the latter set free the elements of the former."[23]

The legal framework of feudalism still serves a descriptive function and the old forms of tenures and estates are now employed to meet modern needs. Of the standard incidents, escheat or some close counterpart is required, because it is still possible that the estate in fee simple can come to an end with no person entitled to assume ownership. In effect, this means that ownerless land reverts to the Crown. Under the statutory regime in Alberta, for example, the Crown is regarded as the ultimate (or last) heir.[24] So entrenched are the pillars of tenure that in 1832, long after the full functioning of tenures as originally conceived had ceased, a parliamentary real property reform commission in England advised against a dismantling of the feudal structure on the basis that this would unsettle long-established principles and would be "an innovation too dangerous to be prudently hazarded".[25] A concern raised was that it would be necessary to provide for the statutory replacement of all of the rules derived from tenure, a task of immeasurable difficulty and entailing considerable cost. Likewise, in the Austra-

---

20 See further Part 2, Chapter 7.
21 12 Cha. 2, c. 24.
22 Simpson, *supra*, note 17, at 2.
23 K. Marx, *Capital* (Moscow: Foreign Language Publishing, n.d., 1867) vol. 1, at 715.
24 *Ultimate Heir Act*, R.S.A. 1980, c. U-1.
25 *Third Report of the Real Property Commissioners Appointed to Inquire Into the Law of England Respecting Real Property* (London: s.n., 1832) at 4. See further J.E. Hogg, "The Effect of Tenure on Real Property Law" (1909) 25 L.Q.R. 178.

lian state of Queensland, as part of major reforms to the law of real property, the gist of *Quia Emptores* was embodied in the new law.[26] In New Zealand it has been recommended that the law be modernized, though the proposed legislation bears the unmistakable stamp of thirteenth century English doctrine:[27]

s. 20 – *Feudal incidents of an estate in fee simple abolished*

It is declared that

(a) a Crown grant of land, or a certificate of title having the force and effect of a Crown grant of land, issued before or after this Act comes into force for an estate in fee simple confers on the person named in the Crown grant or the certificate of title a right of freehold tenure (free and common socage) without any incident of tenure for the benefit of the Crown;

(b) an estate in fee simple is transferable, and has always been transferable, without the permission of the Crown or the need to make any payment to the Crown;

(c) an instrument purporting to create, transfer or assign an estate in fee simple in any land subject to the reservation to the person executing the instrument of an estate in fee simple (subinfeudation) continues to create, transfer or assign an estate in fee simple without any such reservation.

(b)   the adoption of English law[28]

The incorporation of English property law principles into Canada was accomplished through the general laws of reception. There are several modes of reception and the applicable system mainly depends on how a British colony was acquired. Colonies obtained through conquest or cession from another imperial power retain the pre-existing foreign law until this is altered. The Province of Quebec is governed by the rules for conquest, and its system of property law, cloned from the civil law of France, differs in form and substance from that found in the rest of Canada. In settled colonies, the incoming waves of settlers are regarded as having brought the applicable English law to the new territories in their pockets. This characterization overlooks of course the Aboriginal presence and therefore assumes that the appropriation of Aboriginal lands was not a conquest.[29] The Maritime provinces are treated as settled colonies for these purposes, although they were in fact acquired by cession from France. In some jurisdictions,

---

26 *Property Law Act 1974*, No. 76, s. 21, provides: "Alienation in fee simple. [N.S.W. No. 30 of 1969, s. 36; *cf.* 18 Edw. 1 . . . (Quia Emptores)]. Land held of the Crown in fee simple may be assured in fee simple without licence and without fine and the person taking under the assurance shall hold the land of the Crown in the same manner as the land was held before the assurance took effect."

27 Law Commission (N.Z.), *A New Property Law Act* (Wellington: L.C.N.Z., 1994) at 55.

28 See generally P.W. Hogg, *Constitutional Law of Canada*, 4th ed. (Toronto: Carswell, 1998) ch. 2; J.E. Côté, "The Reception of English Law" (1977) 15 Alta.L.Rev. 29. See also J.C. Bouck, "Introducing English Statute Law into the Provinces: Time for a Change?" (1979) 57 Can.B.Rev. 74.

29 See generally B. Slattery, "Aboriginal Sovereignty and Imperial Claims" (1991) 29 Osgoode Hall L.J. 681.

including Ontario, the territories and the western provinces, a reception date is now fixed by statute. In Alberta, for example, that date is July 15, 1870.[30]

Reception does not constitute the only means through which the colonies acquired a legal regime. The laws incorporated by reception are in addition to those Imperial laws that are meant to apply directly to the colonies by their own force (*ex proprio vigore*). And Canadian law continues to be influenced by the absorption of English case law. Moreover, the reception of English domestic law provides just the first version of the colonial statute book and does not of itself preclude changes being introduced through subsequent enactments of the colonial (or post-colonial) governments.

Reception rules can either adopt the totality of the laws of the Imperial state, or attempt to determine which laws should be applied and which should be left behind. Under the governing provision in Alberta, for example, reception is selective: the received law must be applicable to conditions in the receiving jurisdiction as of the reception date. If it is, then the old law is received, no matter how much local conditions may change afterwards. The benchmark of applicability injects a measure of uncertainty into the reception process. Accordingly, the courts have had to grapple with the problem of determining which of the legal antiques designed for the social order of feudal society in that small, damp place that is England can be treated as relevant to the expansive, sparsely populated colonial holdings in (what is now) Canada, which were once populated by remittance men, clerics, farmers, Empire Loyalists, and others.

The application of reception principles to the law of property is exemplified by the extraordinary case of *Huggard Assets* (circa 1950),[31] where the question was whether the laws governing tenure by free and common socage were in force in Alberta. Remarkably, that matter had not previously been resolved. The case involved an attempt by the Province of Alberta to levy royalties against a company drilling in northern Alberta during the period of intense oil exploration in the Province that followed the discovery of major reserves in 1947. The company's interest in the fields was derived from a federal grant made in 1913, which reserved to the government a right to such royalties as might be prescribed from time to time by regulation. The Province of Alberta, which had acquired the federal government's rights under that grant in 1930, attempted to impose royalties on Huggard Assets.

In the Supreme Court of Canada a question was raised (by the Court itself) as to whether or not the levying of a royalty was in substance a kind of tenurial service which, because of its uncertainty, was invalid. This in turn raised the issue of whether or not free and common socage formed part of the received law of Alberta. The Supreme Court held (i) that the *Statute of Tenures* (of 1660) applied; (ii) that the grant of 1913 was in socage; and (iii) that the royalty was uncertain and, therefore, an invalid service.

---

30 *North-West Territories Amendment Act*, S.C. 1886, c. 25, s. 3.
31 *Alberta (Attorney General) v. Huggard Assets Ltd.*, [1953] A.C. 420, 8 W.W.R. (N.S.) 561, [1953] 3 D.L.R. 225 (P.C.).

On appeal to the Judicial Committee of the Privy Council it was accepted that tenure by socage had been received into Alberta, but not by virtue of the adoption of the *Statute of Tenures*, which was said to be aimed at the abolition of forms of tenure (namely knight service and serjeanty) that had never existed in the North American colonies. Instead, the Privy Council focused on the Charter of 1670 through which the Hudson's Bay Company had received Rupert's Land. The Charter granted the lands in free and common socage, so it could not be said that this type of tenure had not taken hold in Rupert's Land. Presumably, the Privy Council intended the ruling to apply to areas not strictly within the Hudson's Bay Charter, since substantial parts of Canada are not covered by the 1670 grant. On the main point, the Privy Council found that even if the royalties were uncertain under principles governing socage (an issue that was not decided), these requirements had been overridden by subsequent legislation. Therefore, the royalties were validly imposed.

Given that the *Statute of Tenures* provided not only that military tenures were abolished, but also that future tenures were to be in socage, one might have assumed that the Statute was received into Canadian law. The Privy Council seems to have been influenced by the state of affairs in British North America in 1660 and by the fact that the Statute was not intended to apply to colonial holdings. This, however, is not germane. While an Imperial statute may apply to the colonies by its own terms, the test in the case of reception is the applicability of the laws extant on the reception date, including those initially enacted only for domestic (*i.e.*, non-colonial) purposes.

A reception law, in some form, has an obvious and virtually irreplaceable function, but it is bound to produce some unevenness. The snapshot of laws on the reception date has captured only portions of some English reforms, while leaving out later developments.[32] Moreover, several important cornerstones of property law have not been the subject of judicial scrutiny, so it remains unresolved as to whether they have been received. *Quia Emptores* is among these, though several recent Canadian cases have (sensibly) referred to that statute as if its applicability were beyond doubt.[33] In some provinces, the matter has been dealt with by the explicit incorporation of *Quia Emptores* into the local law.[34]

---

32 See, *e.g.*, the discussion of settled estates in Part 4(c)(iv), Chapter 5.

33 See, *e.g.*, *Royal Bank v. Freeborn* (1974) 22 Alta.L.R. (2d) 279, 39 A.R. 380 (Q.B.); *Fuji Builders Ltd. v. Tresoor* (1984) 33 R.P.R. 78, [1984] 5 W.W.R. 80, 28 Man.R. (2d) 115 (Q.B.). See also *Hongkong Bank of Canada v. Wheeler Holdings Ltd.* (1990) 77 Alta.L.R. (2d) 149, 111 A.R. 42, (*sub nom. Canada Mortgage & Housing Corp. v. Hongkong Bank of Canada*) 75 D.L.R. (4th) 307 (C.A.) additional reasons at (1991) 78 Alta.L.R. (2d) 236, 112 A.R. 85, 75 D.L.R. (4th) 561 (C.A.) reversed in part [1993] 1 S.C.R 167, 100 D.L.R. (4th) 40, 6 Alta.L.R. (3d) 337. For a catalogue of received law as of 1964, see J.E. Côté, "The Introduction of English Law into Alberta" (1964) 3 Alta.L.Rev. 262. See also Law Reform Commission of Saskatchewan, *The Status of English Statute Law in Saskatchewan* (Saskatoon: L.R.C.S., 1990).

34 See, *e.g.*, R.S.O. 1980, Appendix A, reprinting *An Act Respecting Real Property*, R.S.O. 1897, c. 330. In the 1990 Revised Statutes of Ontario, the 1897 Act is listed among the Table of Unconsolidated and Unrepealed Acts (vol. 12, at 286). See also R.S.B.C. 1897, vol. 1, at xliii. In Australia, it has been said that "[i]f the slate were clean, there would be something to be said for the view that the English system of land law was not, in 1788, appropriate for application

To recap, the position today is as follows: Canadian landholding in the common law jurisdictions is not allodial but tenurial, all land in private hands being held of the Crown in the form of an estate. Within the common law jurisdictions the tenure under which land is held is free and common socage. The services and incidents of socage are of little or no practical importance except for the incident of escheat, which exists typically in some modified statutory form.[35] The fee simple estate is the interest enjoyed in most privately held lands. The modern law of property is comprised of doctrines that were received and are still in force, together with the interstitial reforms that have been introduced in each jurisdiction.

A striking feature of all of this is that the nature of life in English-speaking Canada and the needs of the economy there were far removed from those that gave rise to the development of the feudal principles in England. Drawn from the pages of history, one sees just small bits of doctrine, not the social setting in which the whole scheme arose. The complex rules concerning conveyancing, for example, were developed to serve the aims of the Crown and an aristocratic class. While there were propertied elites in Canada, their needs were of a wholly different nature. At the same time, some of these concepts seem quite suitable to the Canadian socio-economic setting, and the fiscal clashes of this feudal past seem to arise again in new dress. For instance, Medieval conveyancing devices designed to reduce liability under the incidents of tenure are today deployed as integral elements of tax avoidance schemes.[36]

At least as startling is that in part of British-held North America, namely Lower Canada (later part of Quebec), feudalism was still in operation long after the feudal principles of property law described above had fallen into disuse in England. Almost 200 years after the *Statute of Tenures* and some 60 years after the French Revolution, Lower Canada was still trapped within the confines of a seigneurial tenure system as oppressive and rigid as any that had existed in England. In 1843, a report commissioned by the Legislative Assembly in Quebec described a system that was vicious and injurious. The principles of landholding inhibited improvement and exchange, for the conditions of tenure were restrictive and the transaction costs, in terms of feudal fines applicable to transfers, were prohibitively high. A sale gave rise to a fine (a *mutation*), which could range as high as one-quarter of the purchase price; and taxes were levied on tenant's improvements.[37] These rights were neither merely symbolic nor moribund and were in fact vigorously enforced.[38]

---

to the circumstances of a British penal colony'', but that it was now too late to deny reception: *Mabo v. Queensland (No. 2)*, [1992] 5 C.N.L.R. 1, 175 C.L.R. 1, 107 A.L.R. 1 (Aust.H.C.) at 66 C.N.L.R. (*per* Deane and Gaudron JJ.).

35 See, *e.g.*, *Escheats Act*, R.S.O. 1990, c. E.20.

36 See Part 4(b), Chapter 6.

37 *Report of the Commissioners Appointed to Inquire into the State of the Laws and Other Circumstances Connected with the Seignorial Tenure* (1843), quoted in G. Meyers, *A History of Canadian Wealth* (Chicago: C.H. Kerr & Co., 1914) at 111. All further references are to the Myers text.

38 *Ibid.* at 112.

The result of these principles was the development of a custom economy in which the landowner was virtually unable to escape from these tenurial bonds.[39] Aspects of the regime resembled the worst excesses of copyhold tenure. Through the *corvée*, forced labour could be exacted, a result that the Commissioners regarded as "odious, and humiliating to man, a badge of servitude".[40] Such was the state of the law that "all progressive improvement in the country is checked; its resources for advancement in the arts of civilized life are in the hands of the seigneur, and they may alone reap the advantage".[41] By 1854, reform of the system had begun. In the other colonies in British North America the process of industrialization was already well under way.

3.   OTHER HISTORICAL FEATURES

It is true that feudal law forms the foundation of contemporary law, especially that relating to land. Still, to consider merely the introduction of a few select English doctrines is too limited a perspective. English law, like the English language, has drawn from Nordic, Germanic and Roman influences, among others. While Norman feudalism was the predominant source of law after the Conquest, some pre-existing institutions, such as a married woman's claim to dower,[42] existed in England before 1066. Post-reception reforms have come from a number of sources: the Torrens system of land registration and the basic elements of condominium (or strata) title were taken from Australian law; western Canadian homestead laws are based on American inventions; current matrimonial property laws adopt facets of European property regimes. Influences can emerge from many quarters.

(a)   the doctrine of marital unity

The received law of property involves far more than just tenures and estates. Consider, for example, the impact of the doctrine of marital unity on property ownership. At common law, on marriage the legal personality of husband and wife merged, the result of which was, in the context of property law, to deprive married women of a host of rights of ownership. The doctrine was sexist, giving husband and wife reciprocal but highly different rights and obligations. The wife was described by William Blackstone as being under the husband's "wing, protection and *cover*"[43] (hence the term coverture to describe the marriage relationship). Blackstone saw the doctrine as resulting from beneficence, owing to the fact that "[s]o great a favourite is the female sex of the laws of England".[44] Lori Chambers has offered a different assessment. With the doctrine in mind, she

---

39 *Ibid.* at 111.
40 *Ibid.*
41 *Ibid.*
42 This term is explained in Part 5(a), Chapter 5.
43 W. Blackstone, *Commentaries on the Laws of England* (Chicago: U. of Chi. ed., 1979, 1765-9) vol. 1, at 430 (emphasis in the original).
44 *Ibid.* at 433.

has suggested that "[i]n all common law jurisdictions, marriage, for women, represented civil death".[45]

Under the doctrine of marital unity, the husband assumed a duty of support that, in effect, survived into the wife's widowhood. She could also pledge her husband's credit to purchase necessaries. In addition, by the thirteenth century it had become established that the wife's property came under the husband's control on marriage. All chattels vested absolutely in him, subject to the wife's right to retain her personal paraphernalia. The spouses shared control over transfers of (the wife's) real estate, but the husband could collect any income that the land might yield. On death, the widower would receive a life interest known as 'curtesy'.[46]

Some insulation from the operation of these rules was available by placing the legal title of the wife's property in the hands of trustees, who would be given instructions to hold the settled property for her benefit. If transferred in this way, the property remained outside of the grasp of the husband. However, if the trust allowed the wife to acquire legal title from the trustees, any property that she obtained by exercising that power fell under the doctrine of marital unity.[47] Moreover, given that such a trust arrangement could be exploited by a coercive husband, mechanisms designed to limit the wife's right to call for the trust property (called restraints on anticipation) were often inserted into trust documents; these protective measures were eventually countenanced by the courts. Generally, these trust arrangements were of benefit only to those of means; in England these instruments commonly took the form of marriage settlements and were used primarily by wealthy families. It is not clear how frequently settlements were used in Canada. However, research into the practices that were followed in Nova Scotia does suggest that settlements were used there, even in relation to relatively small property holdings.[48]

This briefly presented tableau serves to show how rules of ownership can create or reinforce patterns of behaviour. The rules that denied married women full property rights worked to exclude them from the public domain – from the external working world. As a result, women were rendered reliant on their husbands for sustenance. At the same time, the gravitational pull of the doctrine took men out of the house and into the public realm, where they sought to provide for the family whom they were duty-bound to maintain. Economic realities, artificially altered by the doctrine, have helped to ingrain the gender-role stereotypes with which we are all familiar.[49]

---

45 L. Chambers, *Married Women and Property Law in Victorian Ontario* (Toronto: U. of T.Pr. & Osgoode Society, 1997) at 3.

46 This concept is explained in Part 5(b), Chapter 5. The right to curtesy was the only realty interest that the husband could unilaterally transfer.

47 See, *e.g.*, *Brittlebank v. Gray-Jones* (1887) 1 N.W.T.L.R. 70 (Man.Q.B.).

48 P. Girard & S. Veinot, "Married Women's Property Law in Nova Scotia, 1850-1910" in J. Guildford & S. Morton, eds., *Separate Spheres: Women's Worlds in the 19th-Century Maritimes* (Fredericton: Acadiensis Pr., 1994) 67, at 72-3.

49 See further J.C. Williams, "Married Women and Property", 1 Va.J.Soc.Pol. & L. 383 (1994).

The demise of the doctrine of marital unity, as it related to property, began in the middle of the nineteenth century,[50] with some Canadian provinces acting earlier than England and influencing the reforms there. The process involved a piecemeal dismantling. Initially, women were given increased control over their possessions in the throes of marriage breakdown. This was followed by legislation of more general application that conferred on married women the same rights and liabilities as unmarried women. In Ontario, the process of proprietary emancipation was impeded by a judicial response that undercut and confined the reforms and that clung to the common law rules. A similar pattern of reticence can be discerned in the case law emanating out of western Canada during the same period.[51] However, this resistance was eventually overcome by amendments that made the new order too clear to deny.[52] Though the doctrine was substantially abolished, small remnants lingered. As a result, as part of the major reforms of family law that occurred in Ontario in 1978 it was declared (out of an abundance of caution) that the doctrine of marital unity was dead for all matters within the competence of that Province.[53]

(b)   the overlay of English law on Aboriginal property rights

The tracing of English law from 1066 uses a convenient, but artificial, starting point. There was landholding in place before that date: what happened to the existing interests? When William I assumed sovereignty he acquired only ultimate or radical title; all rights previously enjoyed by landholders were not obliterated. The lands of those who opposed the Conquest were forfeited by operation of law and later granted to others. Blackstone suggests that the remaining lands were surrendered to the Crown, to be granted under the newly created tenures. Even if this was largely effectuated through a fictional surrender and regrant, the central point is that the Conquest did not automatically destroy all prior rights. The Crown's acquisition of radical title to land does not mean that it obtains absolute beneficial ownership to the exclusion of the indigenous inhabitants.

Similar issues arise in the interplay of native title and Canadian sovereignty. In Canada, European settlement and the reception of English law overlays the pre-existing property rights of Aboriginal communities. Since sovereignty works only as a potential trump over prior claims, the previous landholders, the Aboriginal peoples of what is now Canada, retain their property until these are taken away by a legitimate act of the state. For this reason, Canadian law recognizes land rights that were in existence before colonial acquisition. Since the early 1970s Canadian courts have defined and then refined the law's understanding of

50 See further L. Holcombe, *Wives & Property: Reform of the Married Women's Property Law in Nineteenth-Century England* (Toronto: U. of T.Pr., 1982).

51 See S. Allen, "One Hundred Years of Solicitude – Judicial Resistance to Reform of Married Women's Property Law in the West" (1995) 4 Dal.J.Leg.Stud. 175.

52 See further C.B. Backhouse, "Married Women's Property Law in Nineteenth-Century Canada", 6 Law & Hist.Rev. 211 (1988).

53 *Family Law Reform Act*, R.S.O 1980, c. 152, s. 65. See now *Family Law Act*, R.S.O. 1990, c. F.3, s. 64.

Aboriginal title.[54] Although the contours of the law seem increasingly to be coming into focus, there remains some conceptual uncertainty. What follows is an outline of basic principles.[55]

(i)   *the nature and sources of Aboriginal title*

Early authorities described Aboriginal title as a personal and usufructuary right.[56] When speaking of Aboriginal title, this characterization has now been rejected. Some Aboriginal rights, such as the right to fish or hunt in a certain locale, may be purely usufructuary, meaning that these entitlements are ones of use, and, therefore, are non-possessory. However, when speaking of Aboriginal *title*, a right to exclusive possession is being contemplated. At the same time, this kind of title is not, strictly, a fee simple estate. Both in legal and functional terms, Aboriginal title is *sui generis* (of its own class or kind).[57] In other words, that property holding is unique, so much so that it is unwise to assume that any particular rule of property law (drawn, say, from the array of rules contained in this text) applies to land that is held under Aboriginal title. In short, Aboriginal land rights cannot be placed into any conventional pigeonhole. You will see that in the categorization of property rights under Canadian law presented below,

---

54 The starting point of the contemporary jurisprudence is *Calder v. British Columbia (Attorney General)*, [1973] S.C.R. 313, [1973] 4 W.W.R. 1, 34 D.L.R. (3d) 145. Since that case, the Supreme Court has dealt with Aboriginal rights issues on numerous occasions. Among the leading cases are *Guerin v. The Queen*, [1984] 2 S.C.R. 335, [1985] 1 C.N.L.R. 120, 13 D.L.R. (4th) 321; *R. v. Sparrow*, [1990] 1 S.C.R. 1075, [1990] 3 C.N.L.R. 160, 70 D.L.R. (4th) 385, and *Delgamuukw v. British Columbia*, [1997] 3 S.C.R. 1010, [1998] 1 C.N.L.R. 14, 153 D.L.R. (4th) 193. In *Delgamuukw*, a general review of the basic features of Aboriginal title was undertaken. Lamer C.J.C. wrote the majority judgment (which was adopted by Cory and Major JJ.). La Forest J. wrote a separate concurring judgment (which was adopted by L'Heureux-Dubé J.). McLachlin J. (as she then was) concurred with Lamer C.J.C., adding that she was also in substantial agreement with the judgment of La Forest J. In the end, it was decided that no final determination on the merits was possible. The matter was remitted back to trial, with the Supreme Court providing a statement of principles to serve as a guide for the trial judge. See further D.W. Elliott, "*Delgamuukw*: Back to Court?" (1998) 26 Man.L.J. 97; W.F. Flanagan, "Piercing the Veil of Real Property Law: *Delgamuukw v. British Columbia*" (1998) 24 Queen's L.J. 279. A political scientist's perspective on *Delgamuukw* and other landmark Aboriginal cases decided in Canada and elsewhere is provided in P.H. Russell, "High Courts and the Rights of Aboriginal Peoples: The Limits of Judicial Independence" (1998) 61 Sask.L.Rev. 247. See also *Report of the Royal Commission on Aboriginal Peoples* (Ottawa: Canada Communications Group, 1996) especially vol. 2(2).

55 See further M. Asch, ed., *Aboriginal and Treaty Rights in Canada: Essays on Law, Equality, and Respect for Difference* (Vancouver: U.B.C.Pr., 1997); C.E. Bell, "New Directions in the Law of Aboriginal Rights" (1998) 77 Can.B.Rev. 36; "Symposium on Aboriginal Legal Issues" (1997) 36(1) Alta.L.Rev. (Special Issue); K. McNeil, *Common Law Aboriginal Title* (Oxford: Clarendon Pr., 1989).

56 *St. Catharines Milling & Lumber Co. v. The Queen* (1888) 14 App.Cas. 46 (P.C.) at 54.

57 *Delgamuukw v. British Columbia*, supra, note 54, at 1081*ff* S.C.R. See also *Guerin v. The Queen*, supra, note 54, at 389 S.C.R. (*per* Dickson J., as he then was); *St Mary's Indian Band v. Cranbrook (City)*, [1997] 2 S.C.R. 657, [1997] 8 W.W.R. 332, 147 D.L.R. (4th) 385. The relevance of the *sui generis* nature of Aboriginal title in the *St. Mary's Indian Band* case is discussed in Part 2(b), Chapter 7. See also J. Borrows & L.I. Rotman, "The *Sui Generis* Nature of Aboriginal Rights: Does It Make a Difference?" (1997) 36 Alta.L.Rev. 9.

Aboriginal rights are placed apart from the standard categories of real and personal property as a way of respecting this difference.[58]

Several features have been identified by the Supreme Court of Canada as marking out the unique elements of Aboriginal title.[59] First, it is inalienable except to the Crown. It cannot be sold, transferred or surrendered to any other party. Second, title is held communally by the members of an Aboriginal nation. Third, Aboriginal title also differs from other kinds of holdings by virtue of its source. In 1763 a Royal Proclamation was issued.[60] In part, it reserved to the indigenous population all land not within the established colonies in British North America and outside of the land granted to the Hudson's Bay Company. Aboriginal title is not contingent on this decree. Instead, the Proclamation is today viewed as having affirmed or declared the existence of a right that *preceded* the assumption of British sovereignty. By contrast, generic common law estates in land arise from grants made *after* sovereignty had been established.[61]

Apart from the built-in restraint on alienation mentioned above, there is a further limit on the rights enjoyed under Aboriginal title. As a general matter, the right to the exclusive use and occupation of the affected lands is within the bundle of rights conferred by this kind of title. This parallels fee simple ownership. Moreover, use of the lands is not limited by traditional practices that are integral to the Aboriginal society. Any number of non-traditional activities are permissible. However – and here is the distinctive ingredient – the use to which the land is put must be consistent with the nature of the group's attachment to that land. In *Delgamuukw v. British Columbia*, Lamer C.J.C. explained the rationale of this limitation:

> Implicit in the protection of historic patterns of occupation is a recognition of the importance of the continuity of the relationship of the aboriginal community to its land over time.
>
> . . . The relevance of the continuity of the relationship of an aboriginal community with its land . . . is that it applies not only to the past, but to the future as well. That relationship should not be prevented from continuing into the future. As a result, uses of the lands that would threaten that future relationship are, by their very nature, excluded from the content of aboriginal title.[62]

So, for example, Aboriginal title normally includes mineral rights, and these may be exploited for commercial gain, whether or not mining fits with the customary practices of the nation. However, when, for instance, the land has historically been used as a hunting ground, despoliation caused by strip mining might well offend the restriction on use. So might creating a paved parking lot at a place

---

58 See Part 4(a), *infra*.

59 *Delgamuukw v. British Columbia, supra*, note 54, at 1081*ff* S.C.R.

60 *Royal Proclamation of 1763*, reproduced in R.S.C. 1985, App. II, No. 1.

61 Title to lands in Canada granted by France also pre-dates the assumption of British sovereignty and survived its onset. See further *Drulard v. Welsh* (1906) 11 O.L.R. 647 (Div.Ct.) reversed (1907) 14 O.L.R. 54n (C.A.). However, such titles are premised on a grant by an imperial power; Aboriginal title is not.

62 *Supra*, note 54, at 1088-9 S.C.R.

of ceremonial or cultural significance. (The consequences for title resulting from a failure to abide by this principle have not been spelled out.[63])

One sees in this analysis merely an adumbration of the meaning of Aboriginal title: our understanding of the concept remains incomplete. As suggested above, proving the existence of an Aboriginal land right does not transform it into a traditional type of Anglo-Canadian landholding tenure. Rather, Aboriginal ownership rules – whatever these may be – are preserved, creating pockets of territory in Canada within which the English concepts of estates, tenures, *etc.*, do not apply.[64]

(ii)   *recognition of Aboriginal title and other rights*

In the *Delgamuukw* decision, a majority of the Supreme Court clarified the basic rules for establishing Aboriginal title.[65] To succeed it must be shown that the land was occupied prior to the assertion of British sovereignty. If present occupation is relied upon as proof that occupation existed prior to the assumption of sovereignty, continuity between present and pre-sovereignty occupation must be shown. Proof of an unbroken chain is not mandated; occupation may have been disrupted from time to time, for example, by settlers who failed to recognize or respect Aboriginal entitlements. Occupation will have been made out if it is proven that a connection with the land has been substantially maintained; this is an intentionally flexible standard. In any event, the occupation relied upon must have been exclusive.

The requirement that occupation be exclusive for land claims was justified by the Supreme Court on two grounds. One is the idea that the proof of title (*i.e.*, exclusive occupation) should be consistent with the property interest acquired (which includes a comparable right). Second, the requirement of exclusivity prevents the chance of conflicting and adverse claims being recognized in favour of different Aboriginal communities. Just what amounts to exclusive possession of land is not always easy to determine. As will be seen in Chapter 4, which deals with the concept of possession, that term does not have a single cognate meaning capable of application across the board. Possession (or occupation) is context-bound. Its meaning in the realm of Aboriginal land claims will be developed in that chapter, alongside other legal settings in which possession is germane.[66]

These requirements apply only to assertions of native *title*, which, as we have just seen, involves a protected right to exclusive possession. There are other kinds of Aboriginal rights capable of legal recognition. The range of possible entitlements can be placed along a spectrum in accordance with their degree of connection to the land. So, for example, some claims based on customs, practices

---

63 See further Flanagan, *supra*, note 54, at 316.

64 See further J.(S.)Y. Henderson *et al.*, *Aboriginal Tenure in the Constitution of Canada* (Toronto: Carswell, 2000).

65 *Delgamuukw v. British Columbia, supra*, note 54, at 1097 S.C.R. *Cf. Baker Lake (Hamlet) v. Canada (Minister of Indian Affairs and Northern Development)*, [1980] 1 F.C. 518, [1979] 3 C.N.L.R. 17, 107 D.L.R. (3d) 513 (T.D.), additional reasons at [1981] 1 F.C. 266 (T.D.).

66 See Part 6, Chapter 4.

and traditions may not entail occupancy rights over land, or indeed, involve the use of land in any way. Or, the right might involve a site-specific activity, such as a ceremony conducted at a sacred place, or a hunting right tenable in a given area. Such rights are not dependent on proof of Aboriginal title, and they are governed by different recognition criteria. Exclusive occupation does not have to be shown. However, it must be demonstrated that the practice, custom or tradition for which recognition is sought was a central and significant part of the Aboriginal group's culture at the time of first European contact.[67] In essence, one asks whether, absent this distinctive element, the culture of the community would be fundamentally altered. For land claims, proof of possession demonstrates, on its own, the centrality of the land to the group.

(iii)   *loss or alteration*

In general, then, Aboriginal land rights recognized under the common law are founded on the historical occupation of tribal lands. However, even if established, such rights are not immutable. In general, there are two ways in which they may be lost. The first is through surrender, such as where lands are ceded to the Crown under a treaty.[68] (Note, however, that a treaty need not include a surrender, and when it does it is also possible that the terms of the accord confer land or other Aboriginal rights on the contracting First Nation as part of the pact.) Second, an extinguishment can result from a valid, yet unilateral, sovereign act. At common law, this type of expropriation will be found only when it is shown that Parliament's intention is 'clear and plain'. The onus of proof lies on the party asserting extinguishment.[69]

A clear and plain intention to extinguish does not arise when a legislative scheme is created that merely allows for the granting of ancestral lands to non-Aboriginals. That the state remains poised to alter beneficial entitlements does not on its own, from that moment, destroy existing land rights. However, it has been contended that an extinguishment can be demonstrated through the granting of title to new settlers. Therefore, in the *Hamlet of Baker Lake* case it was suggested that "[t]he coexistence of an aboriginal title with the estate of the ordinary private land holder is readily recognized as an absurdity".[70] Even so, in that case it was also said that the grant of Rupert's Land to the Hudson's Bay Company did not extinguish Aboriginal title over those lands. For the most part,

---

67 *Delgamuukw v. British Columbia, supra*, note 54, at 1097-8 S.C.R. See also *R. v. Van der Peet*, [1996] 2 S.C.R. 507, [1996] 4 C.N.L.R. 177, 137 D.L.R. (4th) 289; *R. v. Gladstone*, [1996] 2 S.C.R. 723, [1996] 4 C.N.L.R. 65, 137 D.L.R. (4th) 648; *R. v. N.T.C. Smokehouse Ltd.*, [1996] 2 S.C.R. 672, [1996] 4 C.N.L.R. 130, 137 D.L.R. (4th) 528. The requirement that the claimed right must have existed at the time of contact has been the subject of extensive criticism in the literature: see, *e.g.*, Bell, *supra*, note 55, at 47*ff* and the other references cited there. See also G. Christie, "Aboriginal Rights, Aboriginal Culture, and Protection" (1998) 36 Osgoode Hall L.J. 507.

68 See, *e.g.*, *R. v. Howard*, [1994] 2 S.C.R. 299, [1994] 3 C.N.L.R. 146, 115 D.L.R. (4th) 312.

69 *Guerin v. The Queen, supra*, note 54; *Calder v. British Columbia (Attorney General), supra*, note 54.

70 *Supra*, note 65, at 565 F.C. (*per* Mahoney J.).

the Company's presence on the land was nominal; it was treated as in a position analogous to that of the Crown; its notional presence was not seen as inconsistent with the continuation of Aboriginal title.[71]

The effect of an inconsistent grant in Canadian law remains uncertain. It has been argued that a Crown grant arising from the purported exercise of the Crown's prerogative power cannot validly result in an extinguishment.[72] And, as will be seen below, there are severe constitutional constraints on the ability of the provinces to expunge Aboriginal rights.[73] Then, there is the clear and plain hurdle mentioned above. Some grants, such as leases, might only suspend, but not terminate, Aboriginal title. Moreover, it is possible that a grant of a fee simple has no effect on rights that are not based on title *per se*, on the ground that no inconsistency arises. It may even be the case that inconsistent grants in fee simple are subordinate to Aboriginal title.[74] On the other hand, it has been established in Australia that grants in fee simple, true leases, and other dispositions that are inconsistent with the continuance of native title, will extinguish that title.[75] Furthermore, if the land is later re-acquired by the Crown, native title is not revived.[76] We await a definitive ruling on these matters under Canadian law.[77]

The manner in which the state can affect Aboriginal rights is bracketed in two key ways. First, the Crown owes fiduciary obligations to Aboriginal peoples;[78] as a result, "in dealings between the government and aboriginals the honour of the Crown is at stake".[79] Providing a crystal clear generic definition of a fiduciary is hard enough. And, as with Aboriginal title, the fiduciary obligations that are imposed are unique, arising as they do from the Crown's historical obligation to

---

71 An even more controversial approach was taken in the American case of *State v. Elliot*, 616 A.2d 210 (Vt.S.C., 1993) where it was held that "the increasing weight of history" can produce an extinguishment of title. More precisely, the Vermont Court decided that title had been extinguished by a series of sovereign acts, none of which was directed at the matter of Aboriginal title; nor were any of them necessarily inconsistent with that title. See the critiques of this holding in J.P. Lowndes, "When History Outweighs Law: Extinguishment of Abenaki Aboriginal Title", 42 Buff.L.Rev. 77 (1994) and J.W. Singer, "Well Settled?: The Increasing Weight of History in American Indian Land Claims", 28 Ga.L.Rev. 481 (1994).

72 See further K. McNeil, "Racial Discrimination and Unilateral Extinguishment of Native Title" (1996) 1 A.I.L.R. 181; K. McNeil, "Aboriginal Title and the Division of Powers: Rethinking Federal and Provincial Jurisdiction" (1998) 61 Sask.L.Rev. 431, at 444.

73 See the text accompanying note 82, *infra*.

74 See McNeil, "Aboriginal Title and the Division of Powers", *supra*, note 72, at 444, n. 57, and the references cited there.

75 See *Mabo v. Queensland (No. 2)*, *infra*, note 96; *Wik Peoples v. Queensland*, *infra*, note 98, and *Ward v. Western Australia*, *infra*, note 98.

76 *Fejo v. Northern Territory* (1998) 195 C.L.R. 96 (Aust.H.C.).

77 See further K. McNeil, "Co-Existence of Indigenous Rights and Other Interests in Land in Australia and Canada", [1997] 3 C.N.L.R. 1.

78 *Guerin v. The Queen*, *supra*, note 54; *R. v. Sparrow*, *supra*, note 54. See further L.I. Rotman, *Parallel Paths: Fiduciary Doctrine and the Crown-Native Relationship in Canada* (Toronto: U. of T.Pr., 1996).

79 *R. v. Van der Peet*, *supra*, note 67, at 537 S.C.R. (*per* Lamer C.J.C.).

protect the interests of First Nations peoples.[80] As a rule, we require a fiduciary to subordinate his or her interests to the other party. Applied in the present setting, this core idea has led to the view that the Crown must act in good faith in all dealings and negotiations. The fiduciary element also influences the interpretation of statutory and constitutional provisions: protective provisions must be given a generous and liberal interpretation, and ambiguities should be resolved in favour of Aboriginal peoples.[81] Beyond this outline it is difficult to generalize; the duties vary with the nature of the issues at hand. As will be seen below, this becomes apparent when the state is called upon to justify action that is detrimental to Aboriginal interests.

Second, the state's ability to alter Aboriginal rights is subject to constitutional constraints. For one thing, subsection 91(24) of the *Constitution Act, 1867* confers on the federal government legislative competence over "Indians, and lands reserved for the Indians". This means that provincial laws directed at extinguishing native title are *ultra vires* and therefore void. Moreover, the Supreme Court has said that (otherwise valid) provincial laws of general application cannot produce an extinguishment, because they cannot, by definition, manifest a clear and plain intention to do so. The reasoning is that any law so framed would necessarily amount to an attempt to exercise the federal power concerning Aboriginal people.[82] Yet the possibility that provincial law can infringe – short of extinguishment – an Aboriginal right has nonetheless been recognized.[83]

In addition, and more critically, section 35 of the *Constitution Act, 1982*[84] provides that "existing Aboriginal and treaty rights of the Aboriginal peoples of Canada are hereby recognized and affirmed". This provision is designed to provide entrenched protections, good against even the federal government acting under its power to legislate in relation to Aboriginal peoples. This protection is very similar to the guarantees contained in the *Canadian Charter of Rights and Freedoms*, which also forms part of the *Constitution Act, 1982*. Protected by section 35 are a host of Aboriginal entitlements, including land rights in existence in 1982.

Section 35 recognizes the fact that prior to the advent of European settlement in North America, the continent was already occupied by a host of nations. In short, the section serves as the principal means through which that prior occupation is to be reconciled with the assertion of sovereignty by the Crown. The effect of this provision appears to be dramatic: in *R. v. Van der Peet*, Lamer C.J.C.

---

80 As to the general law of fiduciary obligations, see further *LAC Minerals Ltd. v. International Corona Resources Ltd.*, [1989] 2 S.C.R. 574, 35 E.T.R. 1, 61 D.L.R. (4th) 14, and *Hodgkinson v. Simms*, [1994] 3 S.C.R. 377, 5 E.T.R. (2d) 1, 117 D.L.R. (4th) 161; D.W. Elliott, "Aboriginal Peoples in Canada and the United States and the Scope of the Special Fiduciary Relationship" (1996) 24 Man.L.J. 137, and the references cited throughout.

81 *R. v. Van der Peet, supra*, note 67, at 537 S.C.R.

82 *Delgamuukw v. British Columbia, supra*, note 54, at 1120 S.C.R.

83 *Ibid.* at 1107 S.C.R. See also *R. v. Côté*, [1996] 3 S.C.R. 139, at 185. But see McNeil, "Aboriginal Title and the Division of Powers", *supra*, note 72, at 448*ff*, especially at 453.

84 Enacted by the *Canada Act, 1982* (U.K.) c. 11, s. 1. The text of the *Constitution Act, 1982* can be found in R.S.C. 1985, Appendix II, No. 44. See also *Canadian Charter of Rights and Freedoms*, s. 25.

declared that ''[s]ubsequent to s. 35(1) Aboriginal rights cannot be extinguished and can only be regulated or infringed consistent with the justificatory test laid out by this Court in *Sparrow* . . .''.[85] (This declaration, general as it appears, must be tempered by the suggestion in *R. v. Sparrow* that a valid expropriation *is* possible.[86])

If it can be shown that the effect of a given law is to infringe an Aboriginal right, then there is a *prima facie* violation of section 35. At that point issues of justification arise.[87] The state bears the burden of proving that its action should stand in the face of the guarantees found in section 35. Two tests must be satisfied. First, the state action must be in furtherance of a compelling and substantial objective. The recognition of the pre-existing occupation of Aboriginal peoples can satisfy this criterion. Another acceptable goal, which for practical purposes is likely to be more salient, is the *"reconciliation* of aboriginal prior occupation of North America . . . with the assertion of Crown sovereignty''.[88] In essence, this latter ground means that Aboriginal interests must be balanced against the needs of other communities, whether these groups are defined in social, political, economic or other terms. Action taken in the name of environmental conservation has been advanced as an example; such measures might be justified for the sake of enhancing Aboriginal rights in the long run, and/or as a means of addressing values important to a broader constituency.

However, proving the worth of a legislative project is not enough. The language of recognition and affirmation, as used in section 35, imports the fiduciary element mentioned earlier. As a consequence, the justificatory analysis must entail a consideration of whether the state action conforms with the fiduciary obligations owed to Aboriginal peoples. These duties can affect the second test in the justification analysis in different ways. For one thing, it should be determined whether there has been as little infringement of the right as possible. When an expropriation is involved, one factor in assessing the constitutional acceptability of the action is whether fair compensation can be provided. Another factor is whether a proper consultative process with the affected Aboriginal group(s) has taken place. It has also been said that a notion of priority applies here: state action must be respectful of the fact that Aboriginal rights are to be regarded, at least at the outset of the inquiry, as having priority over later stakeholders. In a sense, this seems to mean that the first occupancy of Aboriginal groups (the essence of the right) must be recognized. Of course, this cannot always be the trumping factor, for if it were, no justification under section 35 could ever be found. Priority does not always translate into constitutional superiority.

---

85 *Supra*, note 67, at 534 S.C.R.
86 *Supra*, note 54, at 1119 S.C.R., quoted in *Delgamuukw v. British Columbia, supra*, note 54, at 1109 S.C.R.
87 *Delgamuukw v. British Columbia, supra*, note 54, at 1107*ff* S.C.R., which develops further the analysis of justification introduced in *R. v. Sparrow, supra*, note 54. See also *R. v. Nikal*, [1996] 1 S.C.R. 1013, [1996] 3 C.N.L.R. 178, 133 D.L.R. (4th) 658; *R. v. Gladstone, supra*, note 67.
88 *Delgamuukw v. British Columbia, supra*, note 54, at 1111 S.C.R. (*per* Lamer C.J.C.) (emphasis in original).

The fiduciary duties to be imposed at this stage are influenced by the type of Aboriginal entitlement at issue. When a land claim is involved one might expect that if, say, the land is to be developed, the state's duty might include: accommodating Aboriginal peoples in the development of the resources; granting rights to others in a fashion that reflects the prior occupation of Aboriginal peoples; or minimizing economic barriers to Aboriginal participation. Moreover, "[t]here is always a duty of consultation".[89] Accordingly, the presence or absence of a dialogue will be germane in deciding whether a *prima facie* infringement of section 35 has been justified. The extent of the consultation that is expected will vary depending on the circumstances of the proposed infringement. In some cases, a minimal level of discussion will suffice. At the other extreme, the consent of the Aboriginal nation may be required.[90] At all events, consultation must be undertaken in good faith and with a view to addressing the concerns of the Aboriginal group. Furthermore, a cause of action arises when a breach of fiduciary principles is found. In addition, in light of the Crown's good faith obligation, fair compensation will ordinarily be expected to flow from an infringement of Aboriginal title. Naturally, the quantum of the award will turn on case-specific factors.

Contemporary property law and policy have been altered by the recognition of Aboriginal rights in at least five ways. First, of course, there are areas in Canada in which common law Aboriginal land rights remain contentious, or have been established. Second, a number of treaties, covering vast expanses of Canada, have been entered into over the past several centuries.[91] Treaty negotiations concerning other regions are underway. These negotiations take place in the shadow of the law as it is presently understood. Third, assertions of Aboriginal rights of all sorts frequently surface in criminal and quasi-criminal cases relating to such matters as hunting and fishing, where these rights are advanced as defences to charges laid under the general law. Fourth, the *sui generis* nature of Aboriginal title has meant that the applicability of general property law doctrine is sometimes called into question when land held under native title is involved. Several examples will surface from time to time in the text.[92] Fifth, in addition to land-based property rights, attention has turned in recent years to Aboriginal claims to sacred objects and other kinds of cultural property, including artifacts on display in museums

---

89 *Ibid.* at 1113 S.C.R. (*per* Lamer C.J.C.).
90 *Ibid.* The example given of a case in which consent may be required involves the proposed enactment of provincial regulations affecting hunting or fishing.
91 The coverage of the major treaties is depicted in T. Isaac, ed., *Aboriginal Law: Cases, Materials and Commentary*, 2nd ed. (Saskatoon: Purich Pub., 1995) at *xxix*. The areas affected by recent land claim settlements are shown at *xxx*.
92 A prime example relates to the place of Aboriginal title within the land registration systems: see Part 5(f), Chapter 12.

across Canada.[93] Related to this are concerns over the protection of Aboriginal intellectual property, an issue touched on in Chapter 1.[94]

Similar developments have been occurring elsewhere,[95] and some of these have been deeply influenced by the Canadian experience. In 1992, the landmark case of *Mabo v. Queensland (No. 2)*[96] was rendered by the High Court of Australia. The case was of profound importance because of the absence of treaty arrangements in that country. For the first time, common law Aboriginal land rights were recognized, under principles that resemble somewhat those worked out by the Canadian courts. In fact, Canadian case law is cited in the *Mabo* judgments. *Mabo* precipitated public debate,[97] a torrent of scholarly writing, legislative action at the federal and state levels, and a wealth of case law,[98] all of which have shaped the law of Aboriginal rights in Australia. That body of material has produced a boomerang effect. Just as the Canadian jurisprudence affected the reasoning in *Mabo*, that ruling, along with other Australian cases, are sometimes referred to (though not always adopted) by Canadian courts.[99]

---

93 There is now a large body of literature on this issue. In Canada, see "Material Culture in Flux: Law and Policy of Repatriation of Cultural Property" (1995) 29 U.B.C.L.Rev. (Special Issue). See also C.E. Bell & R.K. Paterson, "Aboriginal Rights to Cultural Property in Canada" (1999) 8 I.J.C.P. 167. As to the American position, see J. Nason, "Beyond Repatriation: Cultural Policy and Practice for the 21st Century" in B. Ziff & P.V. Rao, eds., *Borrowed Power: Essays on Cultural Appropriation* (New Brunswick, N.J.: Rutgers U.P., 1997) 291; P. Gerstenblith, "Identity and Cultural Property: The Protection of Cultural Property in the United States", 75 B.U.L.Rev. 559 (1995). I deal briefly with the rights of finders to retain Aboriginal artifacts in Part 4(b), Chapter 4.

94 See Part 4(a)(ii), Chapter 1.

95 For an analysis of the complex issues in South Africa, see T.W. Bennett, "Redistribution of Land and the Doctrine of Aboriginal Title in South Africa" (1993) 9 S.A.J.H.R. 443.

96 [1992] 5 C.N.L.R. 1, 175 C.L.R. 1, 107 A.L.R. 1 (Aust.H.C.). Here is a sampling: L. Berhrendt, "White Picket Fences: Recognizing Aboriginal Property Rights in Australia's Terra Nullius" (1999) 10 Constit.Forum 50; M.A. Stephenson & S. Ratnapala, eds., *Mabo: A Judicial Revolution* (St. Lucia, Qd.: U. of Qld.Pr.,1993); various articles contained in "Indigenous Peoples: Issues for the Nineties" (1993) 16 N.S.W.L.J. (special issue); various articles contained in (1993) 15 Syd.L.Rev. (special issue); J. Webber, "The Jurisprudence of Regret: The Search for Standards of Justice in *Mabo*" (1995) 17 Syd.L.Rev. 5; B.A. Keon-Cohen, "Mabo, Native Title and Compensation: Or How to Eat Your Porridge" (1995) 21 Monash U.L.Rev. 84. See generally the review in P. Butt, *Land Law*, 3rd ed. (Sydney: Law Book Co., 1996) ch. 25, and the references cited there. See also P. Butt & R. Eagleson, *Mabo, Wik & Native Title*, 3rd ed. (Sydney: Federation Pr., 1998); G. Triggs, "Australia's Indigenous Peoples and International Law: Validity of the *Native Title Amendment Act* (Cth)" (1999) 23 Melb.U.L.Rev. 372.

97 A brief review of some of the public backlash that followed the *Mabo* ruling is contained in R.P. Hill, "Blackfellas and Whitefellas: Aboriginal Land Rights, the *Mabo* Decision, and the Meaning of Land" (1995) 17 Human Rights Q. 303.

98 The most important post-*Mabo* decision is probably *Wik Peoples v. Queensland* (1996) 187 C.L.R. 1, 141 A.L.R. 129 (Aust.H.C.), in which the High Court of Australia held (by a 4:3 majority), among other things, that native title was not necessarily extinguished by the granting of pastoral leases (where these do not confer exclusive possession) from the Crown to private parties. See further F. Brennan, *The Wik Debate: Its Impact on Aborigines, Pastoralists and Miners* (Sydney: U.N.S.W.Pr., 1998). See also *Ward v. Western Australia* (1998) 159 A.L.R. 483 (F.C.) which further elaborates upon the effect of the granting and exercising of rights claimed to be inconsistent with the continuance of native title.

99 See, *e.g.*, *Delgamuukw v. British Columbia*, *supra*, note 54, at 1041 S.C.R. and 1103 S.C.R.

4.   BASIC DIVISIONS IN THE LAW OF PROPERTY

(a)   real and personal property

Property law may be divided into a number of components. The central distinction that is drawn is between real property (meaning, mainly, rights in relation to land) and personal property (things other than land). This distinction owes its origins to the rules of civil procedure that governed litigation at common law during the Middle Ages. In the words of Sir Henry Maine, "substantive law has at first the look of being gradually secreted in the interstices of procedure".[100] In the twelfth century rules of procedure developed, and these gave rise to a complex thicket of writs and forms of action, each with a limited purpose. In the case of property disputes, the system recognized two main actions: real and personal. The real action gave to the successful plaintiff an order for the return of property (the *res*), while in the case of personalty (or 'chattels'), the plaintiff could count on only compensation through an award of damages. In time, it was settled that the only property that could be pursued through a real action was land. The reason for this position relates to the relative unimportance of chattels in the Medieval mind-set. In his Blackstone-styled compendium of the laws of colonial Nova Scotia (circa 1832-3), Beamish Murdoch suggested that "[p]ersonal property, in the middle ages of Europe, was of small value compared with what it is now, and was rarely noticed in the earlier laws or writers on the subject".[101] The early common law did recognize a mixed action, arising from the wrongful detention of goods (an action in detinue), through which a court could order return of the goods or their value, but this did not guarantee the recovery of the items, since the defendant was able to satisfy such a judgment by paying the damages award. In the argot of the modern law and economics movement, realty was protected by a 'property rule' and chattels by a 'liability rule',[102] since, in the latter case, the plaintiff's right was principally an entitlement to a monetary payment.

The lease of land falls somewhere between the two main types of property. This is exemplified by the characterization of the lease (to this day) as a 'chattel real'. The leasehold developed initially as a contractual right and was used as a form of loan-security. The ousted tenant, at these early stages of development, was left with a personal claim, and the real actions *per se* were never made available to protect the tenant's interests. The functional transformation of the lease from a security interest into a method of agrarian landholding had become

---

"Despite . . . relevant differences, the analysis of the basis of aboriginal title in the landmark decision of the High Court in *Mabo v. Queensland [No. 2]* . . . is persuasive in the Canadian context": *R. v. Van der Peet, supra,* note 67, at 544 S.C.R. (*per* Lamer C.J.C.).

100 H. Maine, *Dissertation on Early Law and Custom* (London: J. Murray, 1883) at 389.

101 B. Murdoch, *Epitome of the Laws of Nova Scotia* (Halifax: Joseph Howe, 1832-3) vol. 3, at 1.

102 These terms are coined in G. Calabresi & A.D. Melamed, "Property Rules, Liability Rules, and Inalienability: One View of the Cathedral", 85 Harv.L.Rev. 1089 (1972). See further "Symposium: Property Rules, Liability Rules, and Inalienability: A Twenty-Five Year Retrospective", 106 Yale L.J. 2081 (1997) at 2081*ff.* But see B. Rudden, "Economic Theory v. Property Law: The *Numerus Clausus* Problem" in J.M. Eekelaar & J. Bell, eds., *Oxford Essays in Jurisprudence,* 3rd series (Oxford: O.U.P., 1987) 239, at 240, n. 1.

increasingly common by the fourteenth century. The tenant was now working the land. The grant of a term of years on this basis resembled the normal arrangements of tenurial holding to such a degree that the modern epithets of 'landlord' and 'tenant' became an appropriate way of describing the parties to this relationship. More important, the action of ejectment developed as a means of restoring possession to an ousted leaseholder. While not a real action in the strict sense, ejectment nevertheless adequately served the function of giving the tenant legal protection against wrongful dispossession. So, while the lease remained personalty, security of tenure was nevertheless recognized.

Differences in the law governing realty and personalty went beyond the available actions for wrongful dealings, and included separate rules for the methods of transfer of title, and rules concerning the devolution of property on the death of the owner. When a property owner died without leaving a will (that is, intestate), land devolved directly to the lawful heir. The heir was determined in accordance with the detailed rules of primogeniture under which the pre-eminent status of heir apparent to all lands was accorded to the eldest male child. (Absent such a child, daughters would share equally, comprising together the equivalent of one heir!) In the early common law, personalty initially passed to the personal representative for distribution. A third of this went to the widow, a third to the children, with the final portion, the 'dead man's part', being available for religious offices or for distribution to the poor. This was replaced by a statutory scheme of distribution in 1670 which, among other things, abolished the dead man's part and created rules for division that gave one-third to the widow and two-thirds to the children.[103]

The forms of action at common law have long been abolished, but they continue to "rule us from their graves"[104] and perhaps more so in Canada than in England. Minimally the labels remain: we still speak of realty and personalty, and the lease of land can still be described as a chattel real. Building on these original terms, a right against the world at large is referred to as a right *in rem*. A right against an individual is described as being *in personam*. It is no longer true that actionable conduct in relation to chattels is compensable only through an award of damages, for there is now a discretionary power to order specific restitution. The right to seek recovery of chattels recognizes that they may hold intrinsic and special worth for the owner. In other words, the modern law acknowledges that there is a personhood element to personal property that may justify an order for the return of some objects.[105]

Admittedly, there are differences in the nature of land and chattels that can account for the continuance of some distinct rules for each. Land is a permanent, fixed and finite commodity; most personalty is not. Still, for many legal purposes the boundary between these categories is fading. The rationale of separate treatment of land – its supreme economic and social importance – no longer seems

---

103 Statute of Distributions, 22 & 23 Cha. 2, c. 10. For a detailed account, see T.F.T. Plucknett, *A Concise History of the Common Law*, 5th ed. (Boston: Little, Brown & Co., 1956) at 729*ff*.
104 F.W. Maitland, *Forms of Action at Common Law* (Cambridge: C.U.P., 1936) at 1.
105 Recall the discussion of the personhood theory in Part 3(e), Chapter 1.

convincing. While as late as the eighteenth century it could be said that wealth consisted of landholdings, this seems no longer the case. Things such as contractual promises, stocks, bonds, human capital, patents, copyrights and the like, account for much more material wealth than real estate. As we move ever more swiftly into the information age, the sources of wealth are again in transition. We see this in the increased prominence of intellectual property and through the emergence of financial empires founded, in essence, on ownership of a piece of cyberspace. As the priority given to land has diminished over time, some distinctions in law based on the real-personal dichotomy have been abandoned. To return to an earlier example, on an intestacy all property, real and personal, now devolves on the personal representative and is distributed in accordance with modern statutory formulae.[106] Other lingering distinctions have been increasingly subjected to challenge.[107]

The merging of the laws governing real and personal property has given rise to some truly enigmatic statutory provisions. In Newfoundland, under the *Chattels Real Act*,[108] all realty is to be treated as chattels real. A narrow reading of the Act suggests that the change in characterization is designed solely to affect the devolution of property on death. However, if viewed more broadly it appears to abolish the concept of real property altogether.[109] Equally puzzling, though less encompassing, is subsection 7(3) of Alberta's *Law of Property Act*, which states as follows: "[a]ny words of limitation used in a transfer, conveyance or devise of land have the like force and meaning as the same words used by way of [a] limitation of personal estate".[110] The attempt to create parity of treatment is clear. What is confounding is that there is no developed concept of words of limitation relating to personal property. These pertain to the creation of estates, which is a land law concept that has never, strictly speaking, applied to chattels.[111]

(b)   other categories

Real property may be divided up into two further groups, corporeal and incorporeal hereditaments. Corporeal hereditaments (a term rarely used) include those interests capable of being held in possession: essentially freehold estates. Incorporeal hereditaments include a variety of interests which, among other things, are non-possessory in nature. Principal among these are easements, *profits*

---

106 In Alberta, see the *Devolution of Real Property Act*, R.S.A. 1980, c. D-34; *Intestate Succession Act*, R.S.A. 1980, c. I-9.

107 In some matters, namely in relation to private international law (also called 'conflict of laws'), the common law borrows the civilian distinction between movables and immovables. As to the function of this area of law and the rationale for adopting the civil law, see J.-G. Castel, *Introduction to Conflict of Laws*, 4th ed. (Markham, Ont.: Butterworths, 1997).

108 4 & 5 Will. 4, c. 18. See now *Chattels Real Act*, R.S.N. 1990, c. C-11.

109 *Cahill v. Caines* (1952) 120 Nfld. & P.E.I.R. 84 (Nfld.S.C.) at 87. Although decided in 1952, the case was not reported until 1994. See also *Doe d. Evans v. Doyle* (1860) 4 Nfld.R. 432 (S.C.). See further R. Gushue, "The Law of Real Property in Newfoundland" (1926) 4 Can.B.Rev. 310.

110 R.S.A. 1980, c. L-8.

111 See Part 8, Chapter 5.

à prendre and probably restrictive covenants, in addition to interests of less current importance, such as rentcharges.[112]

Chattels personal can be either 'choses in possession' (tangibles) or 'choses in action' (intangibles). A chose in action, by definition, cannot be reduced into possession. It is an abstract entity, enforceable solely by court action – hence the name. Initially, this applied only to a right to enforce a debt, including rights under promissory notes or other negotiable instruments. Eventually the scope of the category was extended to include a wide range of other intangibles, including copyrights, trademarks, patents, bonds and corporate shares. It would seem now that any assignable right counts as a chose in action in modern legal parlance. Transferability is conventionally regarded as the key,[113] but whether this remains true can be debated.[114] Some choses in action are represented by physical symbols: the abstract right to a share in a company is embodied in a share certificate. These sometimes tend to obscure the distinction between things in possession and those in action, for there is a tendency to regard the paper as the right itself. But the right to a corporate share is, strictly, a chose in action.

The following diagram provides a reprise of the discussion of categories presented so far:

A CLASSIFICATION OF PROPERTY INTERESTS

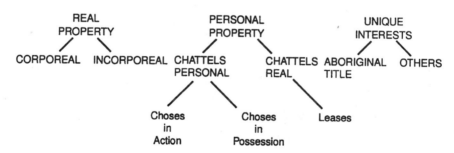

There are many other ways to slice the property law pie. Under the functional analysis employed by Andrew Bell,[115] property interests can be described in one of four ways. Some are *beneficial* rights, the holder of which has the embracing rights of use we normally associate with ownership. Others are *security* rights, designed to ensure that some principal obligation is performed. For instance, a

---

112 These concepts are defined in Chapter 10.

113 F. Lawson & B. Rudden, *The Law of Property*, 2nd ed. (Oxford: Clarendon Pr., 1982) at 26. Not all rights are assignable. As to the basic principles governing contractual assignments, see G.H.L. Fridman, *The Law of Contract*, 4th ed. (Toronto: Carswell, 1999) at 723*ff.*

114 See *Herchuk v. Herchuk* (1983) 27 Alta.L.R. (2d) 276, 35 R.F.L. (2d) 327, [1983] 6 W.W.R. 474 (C.A.).

115 A.P. Bell, *The Modern Law of Personal Property in England and Ireland* (London: Butterworths, 1989) at 4*ff.*

person who lends money that is secured by being granted a mortgage over property has a security interest. Property rights may be purely *managerial*, meaning that the holder has control (as a beneficial owner might) but no general entitlement to exploit the object. A trustee holding property for the benefit of others is in this position. Finally, one may hold a bare *remedial* right, a power to apply to the court for some form of relief, such as the right to seek the rescission of a contract or the rectification of a flawed deed.

Most of this book is about *private* property. There is also a *public* dimension to property law that concerns such things as zoning and other controls on the use of private lands, constitutional authority[116] and the use of public property. Additionally, the law of crime is intensely concerned with the protection of property. In 1998, some 1.375 million (non-violent) property crimes were committed. The property crime rate was 4,541 per 100,000 people.[117]

Hiving off the rules of property from the body of law as a whole is an artificial exercise (sometimes reinforced by law school curricula). The law is a seamless web and the connections with other discrete areas are often important. Treating property as the creation of law means that it is defined by those laws that can be used to provide enforcement. The law of torts can be invoked for this purpose: the law of trespass protects people, goods and land; conversion, detinue and nuisance are also concerned with tortious conduct affecting property interests. As mentioned above, the criminal law has a part to play in protecting and, therefore, helping to define, property.

One further division of property rights should also be introduced here, even if only in an elementary way. Property rights may be *legal* or *equitable* (or both). This distinction is one of overwhelming importance and emerges as a product of the historical development of two parallel court structures, one administering the common law, the other (the Court of Chancery) applying what came to be called rules of 'equity'. From a purely procedural standpoint these separate systems have been merged; however, the substantive doctrines developed in each realm remain separate. As a result, under the law, a trustee of property is regarded as the full owner. Under equity, the legal title of that trustee is recognized, but it is treated as creating only a managerial right. The beneficiaries of that trust are considered to be holding an equitable interest in the trust property. This is not a hollow concession; it does not place the trustee under a mere moral obligation to hold the property for the beneficiaries. Equity provides enforceable rights that can bind the trustee and the legal estate, and which can be used to compel the trustee to carry out the terms of the trust. But this is just a cursory explanation of this pivotal concept. It will be dealt with in more depth in Chapter 6 and intermittently elsewhere in the text.

---

116 See generally P.W. Hogg, *Constitutional Law of Canada*, 4th ed. (Toronto: Carswell, 1998) ch. 21.

117 Statistics Canada, *The Daily*, July 21, 1999, as reproduced at <www.statcan.ca>.

5.   THE SOCIAL CONTEXT: ISSUES OF WEALTH, CLASS AND POVERTY

The terminology of an 'estate' in land derives from the word 'status' and was originally used to describe the tenant and not the property held. Property still serves as a badge of status. Moreover, the manner in which property is distributed can be used to describe societies as a whole. From an international perspective, Canada is regarded as an economically developed nation of great wealth, standing first in the United Nations' *Human Development Report.*[118]

Just look at the statistical picture. As of 1997, about 65% of Canadians lived in owner-occupied dwellings. Less than half of these homes are currently encumbered by a mortgage.[119] More than 98% of all households have colour TVs, radios and telephones; 99.8% have refrigerators. A peek inside Canadian homes is also likely to reveal automatic washing machines (79.7%), dryers (76.7%), microwave ovens (86.3%), cable television (73.7%), VCRs (84.7%), dishwashers (48.5%), compact disc players (58.1%) and personal computers (36%). Over 83% of all households will have at least one vehicle parked outside.[120]

However, an examination of the overall distribution of this bounty should leave one more concerned about the state of material well-being in Canada. For one thing, the statistics presented above leave out the homeless altogether. In some Canadian cities, problems of homelessness have escalated in recent years. Plus, in March, 1998 (alone), over 700,000 Canadians, 2.4% of the population, were assisted with emergency food hampers from food banks.[121] These phenomena are especially disturbing given the levels of opulence enjoyed in so many households. The impact of economic hard times is obviously a factor in the rate of homelessness. And the relationship between homelessness and the destruction of the social safety net in Canada seems undeniable.

A Toronto-based survey of homeless people found *inter alia* these characteristics:

1. Aboriginals and blacks were over-represented, in relation to the city's general population;
2. Only 4% of the people in the sample were married; 72.3% were single; 8.7% were separated; 14.3% were divorced; and 0.7% were widowed.
3. 41% of the respondents had children; one-third of that group had shared custody of minor children.
4. 37.7% of the sample reported having no income. Income reported by others included welfare (20%), family benefits (11%) and full or part-time work (14%).

---

118 United Nations Development Program, *Human Development Report* (New York: O.U.P., 1998).
119 Statistics Canada, *Households by Dwelling Characteristics*, as reproduced at <www.statcan.ca>.
120 Statistics Canada, *Household Facilities and Equipment, ibid.*
121 *HungerCount 98*, as reproduced at <www.icomm.ca/cafb/hunger_count.html>.

5. Within the survey group, 42% were experiencing their first episode of homelessness; 14% had been homeless twice; 44% demonstrated patterns of chronic homelessness.
6. The rate of childhood sexual and physical abuse experienced by these people was higher than that reported in the general population.
7. Approximately 66% of the homeless population have been diagnosed as having some form of mental illness; this is 2-3 times the prevalence rate in the general population.[122]

Moreover, significant disparities of wealth exist. Canada is a stratified society in which wealth (and ergo power) are held by a fairly small elite, and where poverty for the nation's underclass is a lamentable fact of life. The path-breaking work of John Porter,[123] pursued further by Wallace Clement,[124] provides an insight into the monied elites in Canada, although this research is now somewhat dated. Porter was able to describe the high concentration of corporate power and control in Canada in the two decades following World War II. Clement's study of corporate concentration in the 1970s yielded comparable results.[125]

In *The Growing Gap*, released in 1998, Armine Yalnizyan showed how the differential in income between Canada's wealthiest and poorest was widening. In brief, her study found that the bottom half of the Canadian population holds less than 6% of our wealth. The top 10% holds 51.3%. Here is a more detailed breakdown:[126]

---

122 *Mental Illness and Pathways into Homelessness: Findings and Implications, Proceedings and Recommendations* (Toronto: Clarke Institute, 1998). See also Mayor's Homelessness Action Task Force, *Taking Responsibility for Homelessness: An Action Plan for Toronto* (Toronto: City of Toronto, 1999) (Golden Report); N. Klos, "Research Note: Aboriginal Peoples and Homelessness: Interviews with Service Providers" (1997) 6 Can.J.Urban Res. 40.

123 J. Porter, *The Vertical Mosaic: An Analysis of Social Class and Power in Canada* (Toronto: U. of T.Pr., 1965).

124 W. Clement, *The Canadian Corporate Elite* (Toronto: McClelland & Stewart, 1975); W. Clement, *Class, Power and Property: Essays on Canadian Property* (Toronto: Methuen, 1983).

125 *Class, Power and Property, ibid.* at 35.

126 A. Yalnizyan, *The Growing Gap* (Toronto: Centre for Social Justice, 1998) at 10.

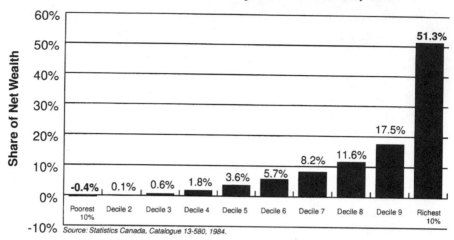

**Who holds the wealth in Canada?
All Households by Wealth Decile, 1984**

Source: Statistics Canada, Catalogue 13-580, 1984.

**The richest 10% of households held more than half the country's
net wealth.**

The income gap is again growing:[127]

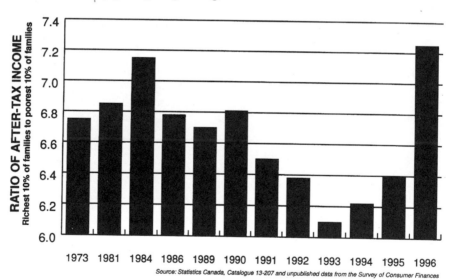

Source: Statistics Canada, Catalogue 13-207 and unpublished data from the Survey of Consumer Finances

---

127 *Ibid.* at 64. *Cf.* M.C. Wolfson & B.B. Murphy, "New Views on Inequality Trends in Canada
  and the United States", 121(4) Monthly Labor Review 3 (April, 1998).

Gender disparities in the upper echelons of the business world were reported by Wallace Clement. He found that a mere six out of a total of 946 economic elite positions were held by women.[128] This has changed *somewhat* over the last 25 years. While women account for almost half of the labour force in Canada, they hold 22% of the highest paying jobs.[129] Based on the 1996 census, Statistics Canada reported that women had an average annual income of $19,208 (a drop of 2.1% from 1990). The average annual income of men was $31,117 (down 7.8% from 1990).[130] Although women "have acquired real economic powers in the public sphere to an extent unprecedented in Western history",[131] there still seems to be a 'glass ceiling', which has impeded advancement within corporate structures.

Earnings of young people have declined during the course of the 1990s. And despite the federal government's declaration in 1989 that it would strive to eradicate child poverty by the year 2000, at the time of the publication of this book about 20% of Canada's children are living in families which have an income that falls below what Statistics Canada calls the low-income cut-off (LICO).[132] The overall national rate for all families is 17.5%.[133] The rate for seniors is slightly above the national average (18.7%).[134] Of all female single-parent families, 56% are considered low income;[135] for male single-parent families, the incidence of low income is 23.9%.

Poverty among Canada's Aboriginal peoples remains a dispiriting and disgraceful fact. In 1995, the average annual employment income of Aboriginal people was $17,382, which is 34% below the national average (of $26,474). In 1995, 44% of the Aboriginal population was living below the low-income cut-off point. Among Aboriginal children aged 6 to 14, the incidence of low income was 48%, which is more than double the national average (relative to both children and the general population).[136]

---

128 W. Clement, *The Challenge of Class Analysis* (Ottawa: Carleton U.P., 1988) at 11.

129 See also W. Clement & J. Myles, *Relations of Ruling: Class and Gender in Postindustrial Societies* (Montreal: McGill-Queen's, 1994) at 129; E. Church, "Women Hold Just 12% of Power Jobs, Survey Finds", *Globe & Mail*, Feb. 9, 2000, A1.

130 Unless otherwise noted, the data presented below are drawn from Statistics Canada, *The Daily*, May 12, 1998, as reproduced at <www.statcan.ca>.

131 Clement and Myles, *supra*, note 122, at 139.

132 Statistics Canada, *The Daily*, April 14, 1999, as reproduced at <www.statcan.ca>. The LICO is based on the premise that families below this line are likely to spend more than 54.7% of their income on food, shelter and clothing. They are therefore treated as living in straitened circumstances. Statistics Canada does *not* use LICO as a measure of poverty.

133 Statistics Canada, *Persons in Low Income*, as reproduced at <www.statcan.ca>.

134 *Ibid*. See further D. Cheal & K. Kampen, "Poor and Dependent Seniors in Canada" (1998) 18 Ageing & Society 147.

135 *The Daily*, *supra*, note 125.

136 Yet, according to Christopher Sarlo, even though in 1988 there were 1 million Canadians who reported income too low to afford the basic requirements of living, poverty is not a major problem in Canada: C.A. Sarlo, *Poverty in Canada*, 2nd ed. (Vancouver: Fraser Institute, 1996). *Cf.* M. Hurtig, *Pay the Rent or Feed the Kids: The Tragedy and Disgrace of Poverty in Canada* (Toronto: McClelland & Stewart, 1999).

These numbers tell just a fraction of the story. They do not reveal, for example, the degree to which wealth is distributed through inheritance. The stark figures reproduced above do serve to remind us, however, that for Canada's impoverished most of the coverage of this textbook is beside the point. Granted, for those who live in rental accommodations, the law of landlord and tenant will be relevant to a point, while those in rooming houses are, in some provinces, in the perilous position of having to rely on the limited rights of licensees.[137] And the law of mortgages and foreclosures may also be of some importance, especially in recessionary times. Still, the rest of the topics covered offer little to the poor.

Income derived from government benefits, including government pensions, welfare, unemployment insurance, and disability payments accounts for 11.3% of all income.[138] For those at the lower end of the income scale, these entitlements account for a much higher portion of income (just over half). The right to receive government-provided payments, as opposed to the money once in hand, has not conventionally been subjected to a property analysis. However, it has been suggested that these benefits constitute a type of 'new property', a term coined by Charles Reich.[139] His principal thesis is that employment and government benefits constitute a new and substantial wealth source and deserve constitutional protection in league with other established property interests. Reich's work has been influential in America. In *Goldberg v. Kelly*[140] the United States Supreme Court decided that the right to receive welfare payments was protected by the due process requirements of the Constitution. In that case it meant that hearings must be held before welfare payments could be terminated. However, that ruling has not made much of an imprint, leading Reich and others to doubt whether the procedural due process protections afforded in relation to some kinds of new property have made a meaningful difference.[141]

The idea of new property has been somewhat useful outside of the constitutional context. It has supported the view that university degrees and similar qualifications should be regarded as property under matrimonial property statutes.[142] However, absent a constitutional dimension, the concept of new property loses much of its impact. Use that label and the less fortunate in Canada are no better off. Accordingly, it might be considered advantageous to entrench a pro-

---

137 See the discussion in Part 6, Chapter 8.
138 *The Daily, supra*, note 125.
139 C.A. Reich, ''The New Property'', 73 Yale L.J. 733 (1964).
140 397 U.S. 254 (1970).
141 C.A. Reich, ''Beyond the New Property: An Ecological Review of Due Process'', 56 Brooklyn L.Rev. 731 (1990). This piece is part of a symposium issue, entitled ''The Legacy of *Goldberg v. Kelly*'', 56 Brooklyn L.Rev. 729-1105 (1990). For an evaluation of the early impact of Reich's work in the United States, see W. van Alstyne, ''Cracks in the 'New Property' '', 62 Cornell L.Rev. 445 (1977).
142 See *Caratun v. Caratun* (1987) 61 O.R. (2d) 359, 28 E.T.R. 59, 43 D.L.R. (4th) 398 (H.C.) affirmed (although reversed on this point) (1992) 10 O.R. (3d) 385, 42 R.F.L. (3d) 113, 96 D.L.R. (4th) 404 (C.A.) leave to appeal to S.C.C. refused (1993) 46 R.F.L. (3d) 314 (note) (S.C.C.). For a more general discussion, see M.A. Glendon, *The New Family and the New Property* (Toronto: Butterworths, 1981). (The question of whether or not university degrees are property is broached briefly in Part 4(a)(i), Chapter 1.)

tection of property within the *Canadian Charter of Rights and Freedoms*. Of course, the American experience reminds us that this may be fruitless. Additionally, the constitutional protection of property can cut in two directions. This type of guarantee can inhibit the expropriation of property, of the new and old varieties, by government. That being so, the possibility exists that it would impede the redistributive efforts of the state and work against the validity of some social programs. Generally, constitutional rights for property protect those who have property.[143] Indeed, under NAFTA provision is made to protect American investment from state expropriations that would violate the American constitutional standards concerning takings.[144] Whether this is of benefit to Canada in the long run is questionable, to put it mildly.

The *Canadian Charter of Rights and Freedoms* of 1982 protects negative liberties, constraining state action seen as jeopardizing individual freedom. A society that is seriously committed to a greater measure of equality of condition can pursue that goal in only a limited way with such constitutional guarantees. A more ambitious approach would be to place positive obligations on government. This idea lies at the heart of the proposals for the introduction of a social charter that were being floated in the early 1990s. Consider, for example, a constitutional reform which provides that:

> Governments have obligations to improve the conditions of life of children and youth and to take positive measures to ameliorate the historical and social disadvantage of groups facing discrimination.[145]

A social charter containing that provision does not deny the value of property. On the contrary, it implicitly adopts as a central premise the personhood theory of ownership described in Chapter 1.[146] The assumption is that for each Canadian to thrive it is necessary for the state to provide the material advantages that would allow all of us to exist as autonomous persons. Whether a social charter can make up for the failings of the *Charter* of 1982 in helping the nation's poor is by no means clear. So much would depend on factors such as the form it would take, its interrelationship with other elements of the Constitution, and the ability of unintended beneficiaries of the charter to hijack the protections and use these for other purposes.[147] The arrogation of rights for the benefit of powerful interests (such as major corporations) has been part of the history of the *Canadian Charter*

---

143 See further R.W. Bauman, "Living in a Material World: Property Rights in the Charter" (1992) 3 Constit.Forum 49.

144 See further D. Schneiderman, "NAFTA's Takings Rule: American Constitutionalism Comes to Canada" (1996) 46 U.T.L.J. 499.

145 *Draft Social Charter*, released by the National Anti-Poverty Organization (March 27, 1992) cl. 4. Other proposals for social charters, including those released by the federal and Ontario governments are included and analyzed in G. Brodsky, "Social Charter Issues After Beaudoin-Dobbie", *Points of View/Points de Vue* (Edmonton: Centre for Constitutional Studies, 1992).

146 See Part 3(e), Chapter 1.

147 These and other concerns about the efficacy of a social charter are raised in J. Bakan, "What's Wrong With Social Rights?" in J. Bakan & D. Schneiderman, eds., *Social Justice and the Constitution: Perspectives on a Social Union for Canada* (Ottawa: Carleton U.P., 1992) 85.

of Rights and Freedoms. Even if these problems were not to materialize, it must be acknowledged that a social charter can carry just so much freight. It might be able to produce a minimum level of sustenance, and it might lead to certain redistributions of wealth, but the market would remain the dominant organizing instrument.

3

THE PHYSICAL DIMENSIONS OF OWNERSHIP

> We till a corner of this earth to-day,
> And call it ours, because we do not see
> That it belongs to those who led the way,
> And to the men and women yet to be.
>
> For every acre of these fertile lands
> Lies monumental to the buried past;
> A heritage from half forgotten hands,
> We hold for those who follow us at last.[1]

1. INTRODUCTION

What rules govern the location of the boundaries that separate my property from yours? That is the principal question posed in this chapter.

The first part of the chapter deals with real estate. It can be readily appreciated that a tract of land carries with it more than a right to the horizontal plane of area which is described in some title document. Land ownership includes rights above and below the surface. The rules that govern these matters will be examined and assessed on the basis of the economic rationale of private ownership.[2] This discussion is intended to act as a vehicle for a consideration of the impact of efficiency on the composition of property rules generally.

Determining the extent of the surface of a given tract of land involves mainly a question of proper boundary description. Sometimes this is not a simple matter, such as when the forces of nature alter the pre-existing landscape; when land is bounded by water such changes are common. The law governing both land and water boundaries will be considered here.

Problems concerning the physical extent of ownership do not arise in the same way when chattels are involved. There is no counterpart to the airspace and subsurface rights that affect the range of land ownership. Moreover, a chose in action, even if represented by some tangible entity (such as a promissory note), has no physical matter whatsoever. (Mind you, the commingling of money in a bank account and other problems concerning the tracing of funds can arise.[3]) In contrast, a chose in *possession* has, by definition, a tangible quality, and issues of delimitation can arise in relation to this type of personalty. For example, a chattel may become attached to the land, thereby falling under the title of the landowner. The rules governing this transformation are furnished by the law of

---

1 Mary Gates, ''Freehold'', reproduced in (1924) 32 Queen's Quarterly 103.
2 See also Part 3(b), Chapter 1.
3 See further, L.D. Smith, *The Law of Tracing* (Oxford: Clarendon Pr., 1997).

fixtures. Similarly, the chattels of A may undergo an intermixture or accession with those of B, or be physically transformed into some new object by C. If these events occur a change in ownership may result. In the final part of the chapter we will address these situations.

2. THE TRADITIONAL STARTING POINT: *CUJUS EST SOLUM EJUS EST USQUE AD COELUM ET AD INFEROS*[4]

(a) introduction

The maxim *cujus est solum ejus est usque ad coelum et ad inferos* means (roughly) whoever owns the soil, holds title all the way up to the heavens and down to the depths of the earth.[5] Imagine the location of Blackacre on the globe. Below its surface the rights of ownership taper down until they come to a point at the nadir of the planet. Above the ground the boundaries rise at an angle extending from the surface. Given this, one might surmise that the owner of land acquires a great deal of space, from top to bottom, in a standard conveyance, even if the lateral dimensions of the parcel are quite modest. However, that is not so. The courts have resisted applying the maxim literally. *Cujus est solum* may be a useful point of departure in examining the scope of ownership rights, but it is so permeated with qualifications that it is best regarded as a "fanciful phrase"[6] of limited validity. This can be seen through an examination of the law governing the upper limits of land ownership.

(b) airspace

Ownership of a tract of land usually also confers rights in the airspace above the surface; most land would be perfectly useless if this were not so. Furthermore, rights to airspace may be severed from the surface and alienated separately. This was the position at common law[7] and it forms the basis of the strata titles enjoyed under modern condominium legislation.[8] The owner of a condo unit, as with the tenant in an apartment building, possesses a slice of the stratosphere.

However, contrary to the maxim, the property rights to a column of air do not reach forever upwards; far from it. Instead they are limited in a way that

---

4 See generally J.C. Cooper, "Roman Law and the Maxim '*Cuius est Solum*' in International Air Law" (1952) 1 McGill L.J. 23; A.J. Bradbrook, "The Relevance of the *Cuius Est Solum* Doctrine to the Surface Landowner's Claim to Natural Resources Located Above and Beneath the Land" (1988) 11 Adel.L.Rev. 462. See also F.O. Leger, "Air Rights and the Air Space Act" (1985) 34 U.N.B.L.J. 39. For a review of the American literature and authorities, see C. Cahoon, "Low Altitude Airspace: A Property Rights No-Man's Land", 56 J. Air L. & Com. 157 (1990).

5 Another version is '*a coelo usque ad centrum (terrae)*': *Abell v. York (County)* (1920) 61 S.C.R. 345, 57 D.L.R. 81, at 351 S.C.R.

6 *Wandsworth Board of Works v. United Telephone Co.* (1884) 13 Q.B.D. 904 (C.A.) at 915 (*per* Brett M.R.).

7 See *Iredale v. Loudon* (1908) 40 S.C.R. 313. See also Part 8(a), Chapter 9.

8 See, *e.g.*, *Condominium Property Act*, R.S.A. 1980, c. C-22. See also *Land Titles Act*, R.S.A. 1980, c. L-5, s. 87, which allows for the registration of "strata space".

strikes a balance between the realistic needs of landowners and those of the public, for whom the air is common property. The owner of the surface holds an entitlement to the airspace up to a certain height above the ground – that which can be used or occupied. Some courts speak of a standard based on ordinary use, or define the limits on the basis that an intrusion must not interfere with actual or potential use and enjoyment.[9]

The imprecision of this balancing approach can hamper land transactions because, without a crystal rule,[10] it may be difficult to know whether it is necessary to bargain with a landowner over the use of airspace.[11] Some measure of certainty emerges, however, from the rule applied in cases such as *Anchor Brewhouse v. Berkeley House.*[12] There, the plaintiff obtained an interim injunction to prevent the oversailing of the defendant's construction cranes. The plaintiff had no present use for the airspace being invaded, though there were long-term plans for development. It was argued that no invasion had occurred because the plaintiff could not otherwise have used the space, at least not at the time of the action. However, the Court in *Anchor* held that an intrusion by a structure located on the defendant's land constituted a trespass to the plaintiff's airspace. This ruling has the virtue of certainty, since it would seem to apply to any building or land-based object that intruded into neighbouring land.[13] That the outcome of the case allowed the plaintiff to be a "dog in a manger",[14] by capriciously withholding access if it wished to do so, was regarded by the Court as a regrettable result, but one which the judge felt unable to prevent. The defendant's only recourse would be to persuade the plaintiff to sell it a right to oversail.[15] Moreover, to award damages instead of issuing an injunction would mean, in effect, that the defendant would be purchasing, or unilaterally expropriating, the right to trespass simply by paying the amount ordered. To prevent that result, an interim injunction was issued.[16]

---

9 *Bernstein of Leigh (Baron) v. Skyviews & General Ltd.*, [1978] Q.B. 479, [1977] 2 All E.R. 902. See also *Didow v. Alberta Power Ltd.* (1988) 60 Alta.L.R. (2d) 212, 45 C.C.L.T. 231, [1988] 5 W.W.R. 606 (C.A.) leave to appeal to S.C.C. refused (1989) 94 A.R. 320n (S.C.C.). See also *Manitoba v. Air Canada*, [1980] 2 S.C.R. 303, 111 D.L.R. (3d) 513, 4 Man.R. (2d) 278, affirming [1978] 2 W.W.R. 694, [1978] C.T.C. 812, 86 D.L.R. (3d) 631 (Man.C.A.). *Cf. Lacroix v. The Queen*, [1954] Ex.C.R. 69, [1954] 4 D.L.R. 470. As to ownership in outer space, see K.A. Baca, "Property Rights in Outer Space", 58 J.Air Law & Com. 1041 (1993).

10 See C.M. Rose, "Crystals and Mud in Property Law", in *Property and Persuasion* (Boulder: Westview Pr., 1994) ch. 7.

11 See also S.E. Sterk, "Neighbors in American Land Law", 87 Colum.L.Rev. 55 (1987) at 55.

12 *Anchor Brewhouse Developments Ltd. v. Berkeley House (Docklands Developments) Ltd.*, [1987] 2 E.G.L.R. 173 (Ch.D.). See also *Lewvest Ltd. v. Scotia Towers Ltd.* (1981) 19 R.P.R. 192, 10 C.E.L.R. 139, 126 D.L.R. (3d) 239 (Nfld.T.D.). See further S. Gratton, "Judicial Reasoning and the Adjudication of Airspace Trespass" (1996) 4 Aust.Prop.L.J. 128.

13 Support for this approach can be found in *obiter* comments of Griffiths J. in *Bernstein v. Skyviews & General Ltd.*, *supra*, note 9, at 486 Q.B.

14 *Supra*, note 12, at 178 (*per* Scott J.).

15 See also *Fountainbleu Hotel Corp. v. Forty-Five Twenty-Five, Inc.*, 114 So.2d 357 (Fla.C.A., 1959) briefly but usefully treated in D.W. Barnes & L.A. Stout, eds., *Cases and Materials on Law and Economics* (St. Paul: West Pub.Co., 1992) at 43-4.

16 See further Gratton, *supra*, note 12. But see *Boomer v. Atlantic Cement Co.*, 257 N.E.2d 870 (N.Y.C.A., 1970) (where damages, not an injunction, were awarded for the nuisance caused by

The rule based on reasonable use and occupation tries to balance the needs of the community against those of the landowner. Does it do so fairly? Using the example of aerial remote sensing for minerals, Susan Morgan has argued for a different approach under which two considerations would predominate. First, the law should provide that an entry into airspace that does not interfere with actual or potential uses of the landowner and does not exploit that person's interests is not wrongful. Second – and here is Morgan's main point – an unauthorized entry that results in the appropriation of a benefit from the plaintiff should be actionable. This approach would allow a landowner to recover for an invasion of airspace if remote sensing mineral exploration was being undertaken by the defendant. However, most air traffic would not normally be treated as constituting a trespass.[17] Notice that the proposed standard would not be based simply on height. Rather, the objectives of the invasion and its impact on the landowner would become critical factors.[18]

Establishing boundaries for the geometric area above the surface is distinct from the question of the nature of the rights enjoyed within that area. It might be that these rights are possessory; or they might amount to something less, such as rights of use (termed 'usufructuary' rights). That classification will determine which remedies are available. A trespass to land can be maintained to protect only a direct interference with *possession* and is actionable without proof of damage. A claim based on interference with a mere right of use is, obviously, not based on the disruption of possession, and so trespass should not lie. In the case of the disruption of a usufructuary right, it would seem that an action in 'nuisance' can be brought, under which it must be proven that there has been an unreasonable interference with the enjoyment of the plaintiff's property.[19] The prevailing approach is to treat airspace rights as possessory (and therefore amenable to protection through an action in trespass).[20]

---

the defendant). For more on this important American decision, see "Symposium on Nuisance Law: Twenty Years After *Boomer v. Atlantic Cement Co.*", 54 Alb.L.Rev. 169-399 (1990).

17 S.M. Morgan, "The Law Relating to the Use of Remote Sensing Techniques in Mineral Exploration" (1982) 56 A.L.J. 30.

18 On the question of trespass and mineral exploration conducted through seismic testing emanating from nearby land, see H.L. Blomquist, "Geophysical Trespass? The Guessing Game Created by the Awkward Combination of Outmoded Laws and Soaring Technology", 48 Baylor L.Rev. 21 (1996). See also V.P. Goldberg, "The Gold Ring Problem" (1997) 47 U.T.L.J. 469.

19 This point appears to have been missed in *Didow, supra*, note 9, where it was concluded that as a general matter the appropriate action is trespass, but that temporary invasions, such as by oversailing cranes, should be treated as being actionable in nuisance. See also A.M. Linden & L.N. Klar, eds., *Canadian Tort Law: Cases, Notes and Materials*, 11th ed. (Toronto: Butterworths, 1999) at 78-9. *Cf.* L.N. Klar, *Tort Law*, 2nd ed. (Toronto: Carswell, 1996) at 90-1, especially n. 413.

20 See also *Trizec Manitoba Ltd. v. City Assessor for Winnipeg (City)* (1986) 25 D.L.R. (4th) 444, 41 Man.R. (2d) 42 (*sub nom. Trizec Manitoba Ltd. v. Winnipeg (City)*) (Q.B.) affirmed [1986] 5 W.W.R. 97, 28 D.L.R. (4th) 161, 42 Man.R. (2d) 98 (C.A.) leave to appeal to S.C.C. refused [1987] 1 W.W.R. lxviii (note) (S.C.C.). In the *Trizec* case it was found that airspace was part of the land for the purposes of municipal tax law. The Court left up in the air the question of whether it was correct "to categorize the right of a landowner to use the air space above his land as a right of ownership, as opposed to a right of possession": *per* Morse J. in 25 D.L.R. (4th) at 449. Is this a meaningful distinction?

(c) below the surface

The law governing rights to the lower stratum has attracted little case law analysis, and the few authorities that exist are in conflict.[21]

It might seem that there is no reason to treat subterranean ownership differently from airspace. If so, subsurface ownership should be limited to that which can be reached by the surface owner or which can be reasonably used by that person. There is support for this viewpoint.[22] Yet maybe there is a distinction worth drawing between the extent of rights enjoyed above and below the ground. The uses made of airspace by landowners and the public are largely different, and there is an obvious need to accommodate both constituencies, particularly today. Above the ground there is a notional competition between air travel and construction on the land. The competing interests below the surface are not perfectly analogous to these. Granted, some governmental agency may wish or need to have access to the subsurface to build a subway or to lay cable, *etc.*, but this would justify a claim for the resumption of *public* property through expropriation and would not require the recognition of a form of *common* property that would create a general right of access.[23] Moreover, the means of access to the subsurface are the same for the owner of the surface and a non-owner. Accordingly, there is no difference in the technologies used by these competing claimants as there is in connection with airspace, where landowners and the public pursue their respective interests literally from two different directions.[24]

The argument that subsurface rights are absolute, as the *cujus est solum* maxim suggests, held sway in the celebrated decision in *Edwards v. Sims*,[25] the Great Onyx Cave case. There, A, the owner of the surface, was held to be entitled to seek to prevent a neighbour, B, from using parts of the caves (those parts that could be proven by a land survey to lie below A's land) as a tourist attraction.[26] The caves were inaccessible from A's property, but there were openings on B's land. One member of the Court, Mr. Justice Logan, dissented. His rejection of the holding that A held absolute rights does not conceal his sense of disdain. He saw the majority ruling as creating "incalculable injury"[27] to B without benefiting the surface owner. Adopting the view that "any ruling that brings great and irreparable harm to a party is erroneous",[28] he maintained that the owner of the opening should own the caves and that this title should extend "even to the utmost reaches if he [or she] has explored and connected these reaches with the en-

21 Accord L.D. Griggs & R. Snell, "Property Boundaries and Incidental Rights Attached to the Ownership of Land in Tasmania" (1991) 10 U.Tas.L.Rev. 256.

22 *Boehringer v. Montalto*, 254 N.Y.S. 276 (S.C., 1931) noted in 30 Mich.L.Rev. 1126 (1932).

23 Recall the definitions of public and common property in Part 2(b), Chapter 1.

24 See also Note, "Ownership of Subjacent Land", 18 Iowa L.Rev. 67 (1932).

25 *Edwards v. Sims*, 24 S.W.2d 619 (Kentucky C.A., 1929). See also *Marengo Cave Co. v. Ross*, 10 N.E.2d 917 (Ind.S.C., 1937).

26 In *Edwards v. Lee's Administrators*, 96 S.W. 2d 1028 (Kentucky C.A., 1936) damages were awarded to the plaintiff (A, above).

27 *Edwards v. Sims*, *supra*, note 25, at 621.

28 *Ibid.* at 623.

trance''.[29] B's entitlements, the dissent claimed, arose by virtue of "discovery, exploration, development, advertising, exhibition and conquest".[30]

(d)   an economic perspective

As you can see, the dissenting opinion in *Edwards v. Sims* draws heavily on rhetoric that is used in relation to the 'economic', 'labour' and 'occupancy' justifications for private property.[31] Given the significance that these arguments seem to have in the formulation of property laws, one might be tempted to treat the minority position as the better view. Yet I doubt whether that conclusion is warranted. Even if sound in relation to the unique caves dispute before the Court, it is more difficult to see how the rule proposed in the dissenting opinion would apply in the ordinary case. Would the minority rule have been applicable if neither party had easy access to the caverns? If so, ownership would be based on a race to the subsurface, perhaps even at the expense of that geological treasure around which the litigation swirled.

Logan J.'s complaint about the outcome in *Edwards v. Sims* (like the Court's lament in *Anchor Brewhouse*[32]) arises because owners are permitted by our laws to hoard their property to their heart's content. As a rule, the fact that B has a better use for some specific item of property than A, the owner, will not affect their respective rights. One cannot steal a drug just because it would be worth more to a needy but impecunious patient than its retail sale value to a pharmacist.[33] Private property permits an owner to be pointlessly greedy.

There is another way to look at the majority ruling, one which shows that the case is not just a ringing endorsement of proprietary selfishness. A less cynical viewpoint is that the right of control over land (or other property) is one of the aspects of freedom that private property generates. On this reading, the conferring of entitlements over airspace and land "suggests a society that places a premium on individualism and autonomy".[34] Moreover, it might be assumed that most people will, by and large, act rationally in pursuing their self-interest. If that is so, then the owner of the caves should be willing to allow others to use them if the incentive to do so is high enough. In other words, it may be that the majority holding, which gives the owner of the surface absolute rights of ownership, can itself be supported on the basis of economic efficiency. The premise is that we all have our price.

---

29 *Ibid.* at 622.
30 *Ibid.* He also suggested that "[t]he rule should be that he who owns the surface is the owner of everything that may be taken from the earth and used for his [sic] profit or happiness". The suggestion here is that minerals would belong to the surface owner because they could be extracted from the earth; the cave could not.
31 See Parts 3(b), (f) and (g), Chapter 1.
32 See the text accompanying note 14, *supra*.
33 Recall the discussion of the Heinz dilemma in Part 3(a), Chapter 1.
34 Sterk, *supra*, note 11, at 95.

As we have seen,[35] the three touchstones of an efficient property law system are exclusivity, universality and transferability. These are well served by the majority rule: (i) the surface owner has clear and legally protectable control inside the boundary line (exclusivity is accorded); (ii) by extending rights to the depths of the earth the greatest possible area of land is made ownable (universality); and (iii) the clearness of the rule reduces the transaction costs that might be produced by the need to determine who has title to what lands. This kind of certainty facilitates exchange (transferability). This last point is especially salient here. A rule that is based on exploration is more vague than one which vests absolute rights in the surface owner. Moreover, some landowners would presumably wish to preserve their rights by being the first occupier of their subsurface. The staking of that claim would normally entail some expenditures. A law conferring absolute rights erects a line of ownership from the outset.

If the majority rule is an efficient one, then the harm to the cave operator (B) should not be as irreparable as the dissent claims. After all, B can buy the right to use the caves from A in the same way that the unsuccessful party in *Anchor* could have purchased a right to swing its construction cranes over the neighbouring property. Indeed, according to one theory, from an efficiency perspective, the determination of whether or not the caves will be used as a tourist attraction depends on the respective financial interests of A and B, and not on the initial legal allocation established through the litigation. Assuming that the parties can bargain without incurring significant transaction costs, the right to the caves will go to the party who values it most, and the legal allocation will affect merely who pays whom and how much. This is the essence of a theory developed by the Nobel laureate, Ronald Coase.[36] Adding a few facts to *Edwards v. Sims* will help to illustrate what is commonly called the 'Coase theorem'.

Assume that B, the tour operator, can make a net profit of $5,000 a month running tours over the full length and breadth of the cavern, including those parts that are owned by A. Without full access B estimates that profits would fall off to about $1,000 a month. Using the cave for touring is about the only way B has to make use of the property. Likewise, A's section of the cave has no other use. Assume also that a court would again uphold A's claim. Given these facts, the cave is valueless to A, apart from the fact that the right of use can be sold to B. In theory, A should be willing to sell, because any deal would make A financially better off. B should be willing to pay any amount up to $3,999.99, because B is better off by paying that price than using only her own portion of the cave. There is an overlap of self-interest here, so that if the parties can put aside their enmity an agreement might well be reached. Likewise, if B were to win in court, caving would also take place. B would then presumably be making $5,000 and would demand an amount more than $5,000 to stop altogether. From an efficiency point of view there is no reason why A would offer that much, since presumably he could never recoup more than B does ($5,000) by running tours himself.

---

35 See Part 3(b)(i), Chapter 1.
36 R.H. Coase, ''The Problem of Social Cost'', 3 J.L. & Econ. 1 (1960). See further P. Schlag, ''The Problem of Transaction Costs'', 62 S.Cal.L.Rev. 1661 (1989).

Let us alter the facts in one minor way. Assume now that A discovers an easy access to the cave and because of his low overhead costs he can make $6,000 a month over and above any other use to which he could put this property. If he prevails in a claim to the cave (by virtue of *cujus est solum*) he would be well advised to start spelunking. B could try to buy rights over A's portion of the cave, but this is bound to be futile. B would have to offer more than $6,000 and in return would acquire the right to make a mere $5,000. Any rational wealth maximizer would know that accepting such a deal would be absurd. Consider finally what would happen if B were to win in court. A would be better off by buying the rights to the caves and carrying on the business. He would be willing to offer any amount up to $5,999.99 because, even at that figure, he is better off than if he used the land for something else. B should be happy to receive any amount above $5,000, because then she would make more money than through her own touring operations, without having to feel damp in the process.

In sum, the Coase theorem demonstrates that the economic function of law is, in general terms, to influence the prices that are paid for various commodities. This might be taken to suggest that the legal rules of ownership are essentially irrelevant. If the ultimate use to which property is put is determined by the relative financial gains of the competing players, then why should it matter at all what the law says about ownership?

There are at least three reasons why property rules are critical. First, the law must make some initial allocation.[37] We need to know at the outset to whom a property right has been given so that the bargaining process can begin. Therefore, far from being irrelevant, Coase reminds us that a legal regime concerning property is indispensable. Second, in the promotion of deal-making the law should strive to facilitate the bargaining process; this it can do by reducing transaction costs. If legal doctrine gets in the way of transactions then the allocative potential of deal-making is obviously compromised. Remember, Coase's theorem presumes a world of nil (or very low) transaction costs. Once we factor in those costs we can see that difficulties in actually applying the theorem will emerge. The lesson, therefore, is that the lower the costs the more likely it is that trades will occur.

Third, when the market doesn't function as it should the law must try to determine which initial ownership rule is optimal. Some say that the law's role here is to be a "market mimicker".[38] This means that the law should establish rules of ownership that reflect the likely outcome of market transactions if the market were able to work efficiently. If we cannot count on the market to hammer out the best allocation through the process of exchange, then the initial allocation under law becomes a fairly significant matter. Moreover, it has been suggested that the party given an initial allocation is likely to value that entitlement more than had it been given to someone else in the first place. This is sometimes referred

---

37 As to the ways in which economic actors seek to influence this initial allocation, see C. Jung *et al.*, "The Coase Theorem in a Rent-Seeking Society", 15 Int.Rev.L. & Econ. 259 (1995).
38 J. Coleman, "The Normative Basis of Economic Analysis: A Critical Review of Richard Posner's *The Economics of Justice*", 34 Stan.L.Rev. 1105 (1982) at 1108.

to as the endowment effect; there is some empirical evidence suggesting that the phenomenon does occur.[39] Consequently, an inertia exists that can reduce the chances of a bargain in which that right is surrendered. In fact, far from under-mining the importance of property doctrine, Coase seems to be warning us that in the real world of transaction costs the establishment of legal entitlements will dictate who will ultimately hold the property a good deal of the time. Therefore ownership rules must be carefully drawn.

If the Coase theorem is allowed to play out in a perfect environment for exchange, then we might see the results that were contained in the various hy-pothetical situations discussed a few paragraphs above. The right to use the cave would move to the party that valued this most. Now let us assume that bargaining is problematic. The ability to resolve disputes through negotiation is sometimes difficult when there are only two possible bargainers, who are thereby forced to deal either with each other or with no one at all (economists sometimes refer to this as a 'bilateral monopoly'). If, for this reason, or owing to some other snag, we can't count on a negotiated solution, one must then ask what initial allocation would seem to be optimal.

Returning to *Edwards v. Sims*, we might conclude that B, the unsuccessful litigant, is the person who valued the cave most and so perhaps title should be placed in B. But it is not enough to try to resolve this distributional question in each individual case. This *ad hoc* approach creates too much uncertainty about what should be done in other situations. It would be better to devise a rule of general application.

There are a variety of possible solutions.[40] The law could give title to the cave to the landowner who owns its mouth. This rule might unify ownership of the caves in one owner and eliminate the need for agreements among all those owners under whose lands caverns might be found.[41] Of course, that solution would not be quite so tidy if there were several openings on several different properties. Plus, it might mean that a surface owner who wished to dig on his or her land would have to try to ascertain who had the subsurface rights. In other words, this approach still raises the possibility of conflicting claims resulting from divided ownership. Another solution, the one which I prefer, is found in the majority holding in *Edwards*: one simply applies the *cujus est solum* maxim. This creates certainty of entitlements and allows the general rule to apply without

---

39 See J.J. Rachlinski & F. Jourden, "Remedies and the Psychology of Ownership", 51 Vand.L.Rev. 1541 (1998) and the literature cited there. See generally D. Cohen & J.L. Knetsch, "Judicial Choice and Disparities Between Measures of Economic Values" (1992) 30 Osgoode Hall L.J. 737.

40 Six outcomes are discussed in R.A. Epstein, "Holdouts, Externalities, and the Single Owner: One More Salute to Ronald Coase", 36 J.L. & Econ. 553 (1993) at 563-7: These are: (i) the surface owners should own the cave below their parts of the surface; (ii) ownership should go to the owner of the cave entrance; (iii) ownership should be based on discovery or first occu-pancy; (iv) there should be shared ownership; (v) one party should be allowed to buy the other out by paying compensation (perhaps set by a third party); and (vi) the state should assume ownership through expropriation.

41 Epstein prefers this approach: *ibid.* at 565.

encrusting it with an exception. The assumption would therefore be that the owner of the surface is likely to value the use of the subsurface most, cave or no cave.

(e)   mines and minerals

Ownership of the surface may or may not include the right to mines and minerals found below; this depends on the nature of the initial grant of the land in question. At common law a grant of Blackacre by the Crown into private hands carried with it an estate in all mines and minerals, except gold and silver.[42] Other minerals might also be specifically reserved. The position in Canada is quite varied.[43] At one time the natural resources policy in the Northwest Territories (before the creation of the Provinces of Alberta and Saskatchewan and the present borders of Manitoba) allowed for the sale of mineral rights. This general policy was discontinued in the 1880s, and estimates are that approximately 10% of the titles issued in Alberta contain some rights to mines and minerals. Under current Alberta law, a Crown grant is taken to reserve mines and minerals impliedly.[44] The present approach is to confer limited mineral rights which are regulated under highly elaborate statutory frameworks.

Generally, once ownership of a mineral estate has been granted, a sale between private individuals passes mines and minerals automatically, unless those interests are expressly reserved.[45] As with airspace, title to a mineral estate can be severed from surface ownership. The sale of the right to work the mines and minerals gives rise to an implied right at common law to enter onto the surface lands as a means of access. In some jurisdictions this has been replaced by a statutory regime under which rights of mineral exploitation are carefully balanced against the need to allow other activities (such as farming) to be carried out on the surface. In Alberta, the general rule is that a right of entry must be expressly granted and the consideration paid for that right must be explicitly and separately set out in the transfer document; otherwise an order must be obtained from an administrative tribunal. That body has powers to set terms and conditions, and can order that compensation be paid to the surface owner.[46]

---

42 *Case of Mines* (1567) 1 Plowd. 310, 75 E.R. 472 (Exch.).

43 See further B.J. Barton, *Canadian Law of Mining* (Calgary: Canadian Institute for Resources Law, 1993) at 65*ff.*

44 *Public Lands Act*, R.S.A. 1980, c. P-30, s. 34.

45 Absent statutory guidance, the question of what counts as a mineral is determined by the parties' intentions on the date of the grant. The phrase 'mines and minerals' is not a definite term, but one capable of having a wide variety of meanings. In general, a reference to mines and minerals in a grant adopts the vernacular of the mining world, the commercial world and landowners at the time the grant was made: *Seymour Management Ltd. v. Kendrick*, [1978] 3 W.W.R. 202 (B.C.S.C.) at 204. *Cf. Western Industrial Clay Products Ltd. v. Keeping* (1997) 31 B.C.L.R. (3d) 86, 143 D.L.R. (4th) 302 (C.A.). The range of meanings available in a given context is surveyed in *Lonsdale (Earl) v. Attorney-General*, [1982] 1 W.L.R. 887, [1982] 3 All E.R. 579 (Ch.D.). See generally Barton, *supra*, note 43, at 40*ff.*

46 *Surface Rights Act*, R.S.A. 1980, c. S-27.1 [as am.] (especially s. 12).

3.   LATERAL BOUNDARIES

(a)   land bounded by land[47]

Determining the borders of the surface of a plot of land is often a simple matter. The vagueness of the *cujus est solum* maxim creates no confusion along the horizontal plane. And putting aside extraordinary events such as massive physical ruptures and avulsions, it is rare for the make-up of boundaries to change greatly over time. So, lateral boundary lines are usually clear and stable.

However, the existence of a fixed boundary is one matter; its adequate description is another. From a legal perspective a boundary is no more than an imaginary line. In Canada, government surveys have been used to divide large areas into smaller sections; many of these have then been divided into further subdivisions and lots. In Alberta, for example, the location of most land is described by a system of township surveys. The Province is divided by three vertical 'meridians' and within each meridian there are a number of vertical 'ranges'. Perpendicular to the ranges are a series of horizontal lines (township lines) that create box-like 'townships'. These are further divided into sections (36 for each township) and quarter sections. Smaller divisions are also possible. The following diagrams illustrate these basic units:[48]

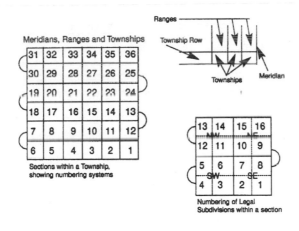

Some locales, including central parts of Edmonton, are described by Settlement Plans, under which less regular tracts are laid out. Additionally, where land has been made subject to a plan of subdivision, a parcel may be described by reference to Plan, Block and Lot numbers. Here is the description of my present house:

---

47 See generally Canadian Institute of Surveying and Mapping, *Survey Law in Canada* (Toronto: Carswell, 1989).

48 Attorney General (Alberta), *An Introduction to Land Titles* (Edmonton: Queen's Printer, 1989) at 4-5.

AT THE TIME OF THIS CERTIFICATION

Bruce Hamish Ziff
of 10912-125 Street
Edmonton, Alberta

is the owner of an estate in fee simple of and in
Plan RN41B (XXIXB)
Block Fifty Five (55)
The most northerly thirty six (36) feet
and seven (7) inches throughout of Lot Two (2)

When the land does not fit into any of these neat units, another form of description, such as a 'metes and bounds' delineation of the boundaries, may be necessary. This involves a detailed recitation of the perimeter of the land, starting typically at one corner of the tract (say, at the south east) and describing, from that vantage point, various physical lengths and markers. Here is an example:[49]

Part of Lot 24, Concession 3, in the Township of Kira in the County of Weir, and being more particularly described as follows:

PREMISING that the westerly limit of the road allowance between Lots 23 and 24 is a bearing of North 20° 13' 46" West and relating all other bearings thereto;

COMMENCING at a point in the westerly limit of the said road allowance a distance of 800.24' bearing North 20° 13' 46" West along the westerly limit of the road allowance from the southeast angle of Lot 24;

Thence South 63° 12' 31" West a distance of 214.62' to a point;

Thence North 20° 13' 46" West a distance of 123.03' to a point;

Thence North 65° 17' 30" East a distance of 245.7' to a point;

Thence South 20° 13' 46" East a distance of 125.15,' more or less, to the point of commencement.

The property described by this search would appear on a plan in this way:

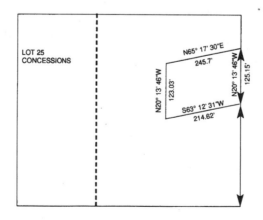

---

49 This legal description is drawn from D. Haden, *Ontario Title Searching Handbook 1992* (Toronto: Carswell, 1991) at 13. The diagram appears at 45.

The intended boundary lines applicable in the sale of property are usually clearly stated in the transfer document. However, when the property is sold it is common for the purchaser to obtain a survey of the lands. One purpose of this is to determine if the boundary markers are in the proper locations. Likewise, the agreement for sale may specify the size of the lot and a survey may be sought to ascertain whether this description is accurate. Or, it may be necessary for the purchaser (and the mortgage lender) to know that all zoning and planning requirements have been met, including those which require that structures be set a certain distance back from the boundaries.

A lack of clarity can occasionally be a problem. A deed may contain mixed signals. Imagine that a transfer contains a metes and bounds description of the circumference of the property, and also a reference to a neighbour's property line. What if these descriptors are inconsistent with each other? The short answer is that the true intentions of the parties will govern, but this is often difficult to ascertain. It has been suggested that in the case of such ambiguous legal descriptions, the following elements are ranked (in descending order of importance): (i) natural monuments; (ii) lines actually run and corners actually marked at the time of the grant (*i.e.*, artificial monuments); (iii) abutting established boundaries if referred to in the grant; (iv) courses and distances.[50] Statements of area may also be stated in the grant, but these are generally accorded the least evidential weight.[51] So, in the example presented here, the description of the neighbouring boundary (item (iii)) would trump the metes and bounds description (item (iv)).

When the parties are unsure of the boundary, it may be settled by agreement under a principle known as the conventional line doctrine. Such an agreement is capable of running with the land, and so is binding on successors.[52] Moreover, even absent an agreement, when the parties have assumed, wrongly, that a fence marks the boundary between two plots, the law of adverse possession may alter title. As we will see in Chapter 4, if a party has occupied land belonging to another for a requisite period of time (it is 10 years in Alberta), the adverse possessor may be entitled to retain the land.[53] And when one party mistakenly builds on land that belongs to a neighbour, title to the improved land may be affected. Alberta statute law provides that when a person has made lasting improvements on land under the belief that the land was hers (or his), that person (or any assigns) may be entitled to a lien on the land to the extent of its increased value. Alternatively,

---

50 *McPherson v. Cameron* (1868) 7 N.S.R. 208 (C.A.) at 212-3, cited with approval in *Clarissa Developments Inc. v. Richmond Hill Furriers Ltd.* (1996) 31 O.R. (3d) 529, 141 D.L.R. (4th) 536, 7 R.P.R. (3d) 54 (Div. Ct.) affirmed (March 10, 1997) Doc. CA M19742 (Ont. C.A.).

51 See T.W. Mapp, *Torrens' Elusive Title* (Edmonton: Alta.L.Rev., 1978) at 79; *Munroe v. Pinder Lumber & Milling Co.* (1926) 53 N.B.R. 236, [1927] 1 D.L.R. 1200 (C.A.) affirmed (without reference to this point) [1928] S.C.R. 177, [1927] 3 D.L.R. 1180. See also *Doyle v. MacDonald* (1999) 178 Nfld. & P.E.I.R. 287, [1999] P.E.I.J. No. 57 (S.C.) and the references cited there.

52 See, *e.g.*, *Gully Fish & Food Products Co. v. Duguay* (1998) 202 N.B.R. (2d) 156, 516 A.P.R. 156 (Q.B.). A detailed examination of the doctrine can be found in N. Siebrasse, "The Doctrine of Conventional Lines" (1995) 44 U.N.B.L.J. 229. But see *Bea v. Robinson* (1977) 18 O.R. (2d) 12 (H.C.) criticized by Professor Siebrasse at 259*ff.*

53 See Part 3, Chapter 4.

the improver may be entitled to – or may be required to – retain the land if a court considers that this would be just.[54]

Good fences make good neighbours, it is sometimes said, but the erection of a fence may itself spark a dispute. Even assuming that a fence is properly placed, that it does not amount to an actionable nuisance, and that it conforms with whatever planning codes apply, difficulties can still ensue, say, over expenses. Alberta's *Line Fence Act* provides that when two owners or occupiers want to build a fence for their common advantage, the cost of construction, maintenance and repair is to be shared equally.[55] Moreover, if the owner or occupier of Lot A erects a line fence, the owner of Lot B is required to pay a "just proportion of the value of the then value" of the fence, once the owner or occupier of Lot B "receives any benefit or advantage" from that fence.[56] Thereafter maintenance and repairs are to be borne in equal shares. The Act provides that any disputes arising from these rules are to be referred to arbitration.[57]

Natural encroachments – I am thinking mainly of trees – can also pose a threat to neighbourly harmony. It is well-established that the owner of Lot B may remove branches and roots from a tree planted on Lot A, apparently even if the health of the tree is thereby jeopardized.[58] When straddle trees are involved (the trunk straddling the boundary), whether consensually planted or otherwise, the law is less settled. Some cases have held that such trees are to be regarded as common property. If so, consent would be required before the tree could be removed altogether. That line of authorities was reviewed and rejected in a recent Saskatchewan decision, *Koenig v. Goebel*.[59] There, it was concluded that common ownership obtains when trees are planted by consent. For non-consensual straddle trees, it was suggested if the person who planted the tree can be ascertained, that person is to be treated as the sole owner. Failing that, it was said that the *Land Titles Act*, which defines land to include trees, should be applied. In such an

---

54 *Law of Property Act*, R.S.A. 1980, c. L-8, s. 60 (formerly s. 183 of the *Land Titles Act*). See, e.g., *Sel-Rite Realty Ltd. v. Miller* (1994) 20 Alta.L.R. (3d) 58, [1994] 8 W.W.R. 172, 39 R.P.R. (2d) 177 (Q.B.). See generally W.H. Hurlburt, "Improvements Under Mistake of Ownership: Section 183 of the Land Titles Act" (1978) 16 Alta.L.Rev. 107; K.H. Dickinson, "Mistaken Improvers of Real Estate", 64 N.C.L.Rev. 37 (1985). See also *Conveyancing and Law of Property Act*, R.S.O. 1990, c. C.34, sub. 37(1). *Cf. Property Law Act*, R.S.B.C. 1996, c. 399, sub. 36(2). The doctrine of proprietary estoppel may also be pertinent: see P. Butt, *Land Law*, 3rd ed. (Sydney: Law Book Co., 1996) at 33*ff.*

55 *Line Fence Act*, R.S.A. 1980, c. L-16, sub. 2(1). See further *Terrigno v. Wood* (1995) 33 Alta.L.R. (3d) 198 (Prov.Ct.). Not all fencing statutes adopt the same solution: see, *e.g.*, *Fences Act*, R.S.N.B. 1973, c. F-10.

56 Sub. 2(3).

57 S. 3.

58 The question of whether the person abating should be required to adopt the least harmful method was left open in *Anderson v. Skender* (1993) 84 B.C.L.R. (2d) 135, [1994] 1 W.W.R. 186, 17 C.C.L.T. (2d) 160 (C.A.), leave to appeal to S.C.C. refused [1994] 2 W.W.R. lxiv (note) (S.C.C.).

59 [1998] 6 W.W.R. 56, 162 Sask.R. 81 (Q.B.). See further the conflicting and accordant authorities reviewed in the judgment. See also *Trees Act*, R.S.O. 1990, c. T.20, ss. 2, 3.

instance, it seems that each person would be treated as owning the portion of the tree found on their property.[60]

(b) land bounded by water: basics[61]

The locations of bodies of water can sometimes have implications for land boundaries. The common law distinguishes among water formations depending on whether these are navigable and/or tidal. At common law, a presumption arises that the boundary of land that is adjacent to a non-tidal and non-navigable river extends to the middle of that river (*ad medium filum aquae*) unless the documents of title state otherwise. This presumption in favour of ownership is, according to the authorities, "not easily overcome".[62] When the body of water is tidal and navigable, ownership extends only to the high water mark.[63] Below that line, and outward to the centre, the Crown holds title. The strip between the high and low marks, the foreshore, also belongs to the state (unless it is granted away).

There are two other permutations: rivers may either be (i) tidal but non-navigable, or (ii) navigable but non-tidal. Determining the governing rules here is not plain sailing because the case law across the country is not uniform. The traditional English common law rule is that ownership of the beds of non-tidal streams and rivers is governed by the *ad medium* presumption. That approach has been applied by some courts in Canada.[64] However, it has also been maintained that the English approach is not suitable "to the great rivers of [North America]",[65] with the result that the beds of rivers that are navigable *in fact* are vested

---

60 Should the provisions of the *Land Titles Act* trump the claim of the tree planter? Does the law of fixtures have a role to play? It was also held in *Koenig* that the defendant was not permitted to trespass on the plaintiff's land to abate the nuisance: *supra*, note 59, at 61 and 64. See *contra* J. G. Fleming, *The Law of Torts*, 9th ed. (Sydney: Law Book Co., 1998) at 496-7 and the authorities cited there.

61 See generally D.W. Lambden & I. de Rijcke, eds., *Legal Aspects of Surveying Water Boundaries* (Toronto: Carswell, 1996).

62 *Derro v. Dube*, [1948] O.R. 52, [1948] 1 D.L.R. 565 (H.C.) affirmed [1948] O.W.N.758, [1948] 4 D.L.R. 876 (C.A.) at 59 O.R. (*per* McRuer C.J.H.C.) relying on *Keewatin Power Co. v. Kenora (Town)* (1908) 16 O.L.R. 184 (C.A.) at 192. See also *Massawippi Valley Railway Co. v. Reed* (1903) 33 S.C.R. 457. The owner of a river island would hold title from the shore to the centre of the beds on both sides of the island: *Re Byrne* (1981) 33 N.B.R. (2d) 429, 80 A.P.R. 429 (Q.B.).

63 *Turnbull v. Saunders* (1921) 48 N.B.R. 502, 60 D.L.R. 666 (C.A.).

64 In G.V. La Forest, *Water Law in Canada: The Atlantic Provinces* (Ottawa: Information Canada, 1973) at 244, after a review of the authorities, it was concluded that "[t]he probabilities are that in the few places in the Atlantic Provinces where rivers may be navigable in fact, though not tidal, the *ad medium filum* rule would apply". As to the position for lakes, see La Forest, *ibid.* at 245-6.

65 *R. v. Robertson* (1882) 6 S.C.R. 52, at 129 (*per* Strong J.). See also the judgment of Hall J. in *Lefaivre v. Quebec (Attorney General)* (1905) 14 Que.K.B. 115 (C.A.) at 124-5 [reversed on other grounds (1906) 37 S.C.R. 577, affirmed [1911] A.C. 489 (P.C.)]: "The condition of 'tidal' which is accepted in English jurisprudence, as the test of a navigable river, was at first attempted to be enforced on this continent, in regard to the rivers discharging directly into the sea, but as settlements advanced and great inland rivers were discovered and utilised for practical and profitable and useful navigation that condition was abandoned by common consent, and those rivers were held as navigable, which could be and were actually navigated for public purposes

in the Crown, even if they are not tidal.[66] On this reading of the law, everything turns on navigability, the basic test of which is whether the watercourse can be used as a public highway.[67] Some interruptions in navigability, caused for instance by rapids, will not normally mean that the river is non-navigable; nor can it be said that title for the impassable sections will be governed by the *ad medium* presumption.[68]

An approach centred on navigability seems sensible: placing title in the Crown for navigable watercourses assists the state in constructing wharves, docks and other structures designed to facilitate public thoroughfare. Still, whether this is *the* common law rule in Canada is debatable. Some light on this matter has been shed by two 1996 decisions involving Aboriginal fishing rights in British Columbia. In both instances, the Supreme Court of Canada adopted navigability as the test to determine whether or not title to the bed passes.[69] The reasoning of the Court relies heavily on the rules for the reception of English law, which vary across the county.[70] Moreover, the idea that a different approach should, perhaps, obtain in the Maritimes, was mentioned in the course of one of the judgments.[71] So, the rule conferring title to the beds of non-tidal navigable rivers may not have been completely repudiated.[72] Of course, legislation may alter these basic rules. In Alberta, for example, the title to the beds and shores of all permanently occurring natural bodies of water is vested in the Crown unless expressly conveyed away.[73]

---

and in the public interest, a sensible and acceptable definition, although not free from occasional difficulty in application.''

66 *Barthel v. Scotten* (1895) 24 S.C.R. 367; *Re Provincial Fisheries* (1895) 26 S.C.R. 444, affirmed [1898] A.C. 700 (P.C.).

67 See further *Welsh v. Marantette* (1983) 44 O.R. (2d) 137, 30 R.P.R. 111, 3 D.L.R. (4th) 401 (H.C.) affirmed on other grounds (1985) 52 O.R. (2d) 37, 36 R.P.R. 286, 21 D.L.R. (4th) 276 (C.A.) leave to appeal to S.C.C. refused (1986) 54 O.R. (2d) 800n (S.C.C.). See also *Coleman v. Ontario (Attorney General)* (1983) 27 R.P.R. 107, 12 C.E.L.R. 104, 143 D.L.R. (3d) 608 (Ont. H.C.) at 613-5 D.L.R.

68 *R. v. Nikal*, [1996] 1 S.C.R. 1013, [1996] 3 C.N.L.R. 178, 133 D.L.R. (4th) 658.

69 *R. v. Nikal, ibid.; R. v. Lewis*, [1996] 1 S.C.R. 921, [1996] 3 C.N.L.R. 131, 133 D.L.R. (4th) 700. On the subject of Aboriginal water rights, see R.H. Bartlett, *Aboriginal Water Rights in Canada: A Study of Aboriginal Title to Water and Indian Water Rights* (Calgary: Canadian Institute of Resources Law, 1988).

70 *R. v. Nikal, supra*, note 68, at 1046*ff* S.C.R. In *R. v. Lewis, supra*, note 69, at 952 S.C.R., Iacobucci J. seems to suggest that his conclusion that navigability is the standard is not based solely on the language of the reception statutes.

71 In *Friends of the Oldman River Society v. Canada (Minister of Transport)*, [1992] 1 S.C.R. 3, 3 Admin.L.R. (2d) 1, 88 D.L.R. (4th) 1, at 54 S.C.R., La Forest J. said this: "Except in the Atlantic provinces, *where different considerations may well apply*, in Canada the distinction between tidal and non-tidal waters was abandoned long ago . . . '' (emphasis added). This passage was cited, with apparent approval, by Cory J. in *R. v. Nikal, supra*, note 68, at 1049 S.C.R.

72 In *Swazey v. King* (1997) 186 N.B.R. (2d) 169, 476 A.P.R. 169 (C.A.), the *ad medium* presumption was applied, without any reference to the two recent Supreme Court of Canada decisions, or the other case law from outside the Maritimes doubting the applicability of the rule.

73 *Public Lands Act*, R.S.A. 1980, c. P-30, sub. 3(1) [as am.]. In Ontario, title for navigable waters

(c) *riparian rights*

At common law, ownership of lands abutting water carries with it usufructuary entitlements known as 'riparian rights'. These include a right of access to the water[74] and the right to take emergency measures to prevent flooding.[75] A riparian owner may appropriate an unlimited amount of water for 'ordinary' uses, a term that includes the husbandry of animals and domestic needs. Water may also be drawn for 'extraordinary' purposes, such as manufacturing or crop irrigation.[76] When the use is extraordinary, usage is limited in order to conserve water for the riparian tenements that are downstream. Specifically, the law provides that the flow of the river cannot be diminished as to its quality or quantity.[77] At common law, the majority rule is that downstream owners are entitled to receive the natural flow of the stream, though under another version of the rule the test is whether the extraction unreasonably interferes with the rights of downstream owners.[78] Under either approach, the rules create a simple form of local environmental control.

In many places, the common law riparian rules have been altered by legislation designed to control water resources in a more sophisticated fashion. Some of the new control systems build on the original riparian concepts. So, under recent reforms in Alberta, there is a general right of a riparian owner or occupier (as well as the owner or occupier of land under which there is groundwater) to divert water for "household purposes".[79] This term is roughly comparable to the definition of ordinary uses at common law. In Alberta, a household purpose refers to water diverted for human consumption, sanitation, fire prevention and for watering animals, gardens, lawns and trees. No permit is required to divert water for these purposes, and this right enjoys priority over rights granted under the legislation.[80]

However, unlike the common law, there is a cap placed on what may be taken: a maximum of 1250 cubic metres of water per year per household may be drawn for the designated household purposes.[81] Generally speaking, for other uses, namely those that fit within the common law category of extraordinary uses, a person holding common law riparian rights (along with everyone else) may not divert water unless authorized by virtue of the statutory scheme.[82] So complex is

is retained in the Crown: *Beds of Navigable Waters Act*, R.S.O. 1990, c. B.4. This change was introduced in the *Beds of Navigable Waters Act*, S.O. 1911, c. 6.

74 See *Corkum v. Nash* (1990) 71 D.L.R. (4th) 390, 98 N.S.R. (2d) 364, 263 A.P.R. 364 (T.D.) affirmed (1991) 87 D.L.R. (4th) 127, 109 N.S.R. (2d) 331, 297 A.P.R. 331 (C.A.).

75 *Tottrup v. Alberta* (1979) 10 Alta.L.R. (2d) 117, 17 A.R. 563, 102 D.L.R. (3d) 42 (C.A.) leave to appeal to S.C.C. refused (1979) 19 A.R. 188n (S.C.C.).

76 *Watson v. Jackson* (1914) 31 O.L.R. 481, 19 D.L.R. 733 (C.A.) at 744 D.L.R.

77 See *Gauthier v. Naneff*, [1971] 1 O.R. 97, 14 D.L.R. (3d) 513 (H.C.).

78 D.R. Percy, *The Framework of Water Rights Legislation in Canada* (Calgary: Canadian Institute of Resources Law, 1988) at 4.

79 *Water Act*, R.S.A. 1980, c. W-3.5, in force as of January 1, 1999, s. 21. See the qualifications noted in sub. 21(1).

80 S. 27.

81 Para. 1(1)(y).

82 Sub. 22(1). Special provisions pertain to some agricultural uses: see ss. 19, 24.

the modern balance of conservation and efficiency interests that the common law regime, defined by a few broad principles, has been replaced by detailed legislation (177 sections in all) which, among other things, creates an extensive administrative regulatory infrastructure.

Importantly, current legislative regimes typically do not completely replace the common law of riparian rights. Unless abrogated by statute, those rights remain in force.[83] This is consistent with the canon of statutory interpretation that presumes that legislative reforms do not adversely affect existing property rights unless those rights have been limited expressly or by necessary implication.[84]

(d)   accretion

As the contours of a body of water change, so does the configuration of the adjoining land. The legal effects of this inevitable process of transformation are regulated by the law of accretion, an element of common law riparian rights.[85] Erosion can diminish the size of the freehold; so can the encroaching advance of the water's edge (which is called diluvian).[86] Conversely, an accretion to the land, or a recession (dereliction) of the water, will work to the benefit of a riparian owner,[87] *if* certain conditions are satisfied.

In order for a landowner to acquire the benefit of an accretion, the process of transformation must be slow and imperceptible in action.[88] Hence, a rapid avulsion will not augment the riparian tenement. An accretion will be treated as being imperceptible even if the accreted area is composed of soil of a different quality or hue than that previously comprising the riparian land, so that the added area is quite noticeable. It is the progress of accretion that must be imperceptible, not the result.[89] Additionally, it does not matter that the soil deposits have built up partly as a result of the combined action of water and wind. Accretion may even occur through non-natural forces[90] (such as by the building of a dam upstream), provided, of course, that it is not the landowner who has brought about that result.

---

83 See *Johnson v. Anderson* (1936) 51 B.C.R. 413, [1937] 1 W.W.R. 245, [1937] 1 D.L.R. 762 (S.C.). See further *Water Act*, R.S.A. 1980, c. W-3.5, subs. 22(2), (3) and s. 153.

84 See generally *Canada (Attorney General) v. Nolan*, [1952] 3 D.L.R. 433 (P.C.).

85 See generally W. Howarth, "The Doctrine of Accretion: Qualifications Ancient and Modern", [1986] Conv. 247; P. Jackson, "Alluvio and the Common Law" (1983) 99 L.Q.R. 412. See also *Re Darrach* (1995) 135 Nfld. & P.E.I.R. 153, 420 A.P.R. 153 (P.E.I.S.C.) and the authorities cited there.

86 See, *e.g.*, *McCormick v. Pelée (Township)* (1890) 20 O.R. 288 (Ch.D.).

87 This may include minerals: see, *e.g.*, *Eliason v. Alberta (Registrar, Northern Alberta Land Registration District)*, [1980] 6 W.W.R. 361, 15 R.P.R. 232 (*sub nom. Re Eliason and Registrar, Northern Alberta Land Registration District*) 115 D.L.R. (3d) 360 (Alta.Q.B.).

88 See *Southern Centre of Theosophy Inc. v. State of South Australia*, [1982] A.C. 706, [1982] 1 All E.R. 283 (P.C.).

89 *Clarke v. Edmonton (City)*, [1930] S.C.R. 137, [1929] 4 D.L.R. 1010.

90 *Throop v. Cobourg & Peterboro Railway Co.* (1856) 5 U.C.C.P. 509, affirmed (1859) 2 O.A.R. 212n (C.A.); *Clarke v. Edmonton (City), supra*, note 89; *Standly v. Perry* (1879) 3 S.C.R. 356.

Why the law mandates that the process be slow and imperceptible is not altogether clear. It may be based on the idea that the law does not concern itself with trifling matters (*de minimis non curat lex*). If the accretion is slow then each minuscule change is so slight that it is ignored or regarded as non-existent. If the law were otherwise, the building-up of a slender deposit of silt (say, a quarter of an inch) along the boundary line would mean, possibly, that the land ceased to be a riparian tenement. Another theory is that the rule is one required for the permanent protection of property and is in "recognition of the fact that a riparian owner may lose as well as gain from changes in the water boundary or level".[91] It is by no means evident why this supposedly "more realistic"[92] explanation supports the imperceptibility requirement. If anything, it argues against it, since a rapid loss of riparian status is no less unfair and inconvenient. I think the reason has to do with the notion that the change should be permanent. We know that no alteration in the landscape is truly permanent; change is inevitable and continuous. However, only transformations that are likely to last for a period of time are worth caring about, as far as title is concerned. A slow transition resulting in an increase of land is likely to revert slowly as well (if at all). In other words, the need for gradual change is a factual proxy for the requirement that the build-up be an enduring development.

Accretion is a natural or inherent right associated with riparian tenements, but its operation may be excluded in the granting document, either expressly or by necessary implication. Furthermore, the doctrine applies whether or not the transfer document describes the boundary by reference to the water's edge, by a metes and bounds description, or in relation to some other land-based reference points, as long as the land so described is in fact contiguous with the water.[93]

4. SOME IMPLICATIONS OF OWNERSHIP: EXTERNALITIES

(a) generally

What does it really mean to draw a line around a tract of land and allocate that spot (and some space above and below it) to a private owner? The short answer is that the line marks out a region within which that owner enjoys a measure of control to exclude others. In Chapter 1 we saw that the property holder does not acquire an absolute power of exclusion just because he or she owns a bit of land. We know, for example, that the police may sometimes enter your home

---

91 *Southern Centre of Theosophy Inc. v. State of South Australia, supra,* note 88, at 721 A.C. (*per* Lord Wilberforce).

92 *Ibid.*

93 *Chuckry v. The Queen,* [1973] S.C.R. 694, [1973] 5 W.W.R. 339, 35 D.L.R. (3d) 607, adopting the dissenting opinion of Dickson J.A. in [1972] 3 W.W.R. 561, 27 D.L.R. (3d) 164 (Man.C.A.). *Cf. Monashee Enterprises Ltd. v. British Columbia (Minister of Recreation & Conservation)* (1981) 28 B.C.L.R. 260, 124 D.L.R. (3d) 372, 23 L.C.R. 19 (C.A.); *Nastajus v. North Alberta Land Registration District* (1989) 64 Alta.L.R. (2d) 300 (*sub nom. Nastajus v. Edmonton Beach (Summer Village)*) 92 A.R. 363 (C.A.).

regardless of what you may wish.[94] It is equally clear that the criminal law and other laws apply even in your personal fiefdom of Blackacre. You cannot do whatever you like inside the line.

However, if rights within the boundary line are not absolute, neither are the incidents of ownership limited merely to those *internal* entitlements. Ownership also has extraterritorial implications. Voting rights, the obligation to pay property taxes, rights relating to school attendance, *etc.*, all tend to be connected to occupation or ownership of a given property. Furthermore, the owner of Blackacre may be in a position to control the use of neighbouring land through a property law device called a restrictive covenant.[95] Attached to Blackacre may be a right of access (an easement) over a neighbouring property.[96] The tort of nuisance can be used to limit conduct that unreasonably interferes with activity on nearby lands. The benefits accorded to a riparian owner, including the ability to control the water uses of an upstream owner, can be seen as a right to prevent negative externalities (such as water pollution) from affecting nearby land. In sum, rights exist inside and outside the boundary line.

(b)   support of land

The owner of Blackacre enjoys a right of support for land in its natural state and at its normal level, a right that must be respected by the owners of neighbouring properties (who, by the same token, have a right of support for their land).[97] This right exists because the removal of soil on one property reduces the lateral pressures imposed against adjoining lands. A reduction in this lateral thrust can cause soil subsidence which, in turn, can result in considerable structural damage to buildings on the land. As a result, a purchaser of land is entitled to the level of support that existed at the time the land was acquired.[98] Excavation on Whiteacre that leads to subsidence on Blackacre is actionable and liability is strict: it does not matter that the work was undertaken with the utmost care.[99] This obligation extends to any land that may be affected by actions of some other property owner, not just contiguous properties. Moreover, the right to support applies both vertically and horizontally, so that subsidence that occurs through (say) mining operations beneath Blackacre may also be actionable. The right to

---

94 "[T]here are occasions when the interest of a private individual in the security of his house must yield to the public interest, when the public at large has an interest in the process to be executed": *Eccles v. Bourque*, [1975] 2 S.C.R. 739, 19 C.C.C. (2d) 129, 50 D.L.R. (3d) 753, at 743 S.C.R. (*per* Dickson J., as he then was). See also *R. v. Godoy*, [1999] 1 S.C.R. 311, 21 C.R. (5th) 205, 168 D.L.R. (4th) 257.

95 Covenants are addressed in Chapter 10.

96 These are described in detail in Chapter 10.

97 See, *e.g.*, *Cleland v. Berberick* (1916) 36 O.L.R. 357, 29 D.L.R. 72 (C.A.); *Bamlett v. Osterling* (1964) 47 D.L.R. (2d) 61 (Alta.T.D.). See also *Holbeck Hall Hotel Ltd. v. Scarborough Borough Council*, [1997] 2 E.G.L.R. 213 (Official Referee). Support may be provided through artificial means: *Snarr v. Granite Curling & Skating Co.* (1882) 1 O.R. 102 (Ch.D.).

98 See *McGillivray v. Dominion Coal Co.* (1962) 35 D.L.R. (2d) 345 (N.S.T.D.).

99 In Australia, it has been recommended that a standard of negligence be applied in cases involving a loss of support: New South Wales Law Reform Commission, *The Right to Support from Adjoining Land*, Report No. 84 (Sydney: N.S.W.L.R.C., 1997).

support may be waived by express language or by necessary implication. This is, of course, a question of construction, and one which is of particular importance when mining rights are granted by a party who also owns the surface.[100]

The natural right of support does not extend, directly, to buildings on the land.[101] In addition, the downward pressures imposed by buildings may cause subsidence of the very land on which they are situated. Nonetheless, if subsidence does occur on Blackacre, and if it can be shown that it would have occurred even absent the buildings on that parcel, then the loss of support caused by the owner of Whiteacre is actionable.[102] Furthermore, when subsidence arises from the loss of vertical support, the necessary causal connection is normally presumed to be present. If the case for the loss of support to lands is made out, consequential damages for structural or other injury to buildings may be recovered.[103] However, recovery will not extend to all losses, such as relocation expenses. Nor will damages be assessed on the basis of a depreciation in value of the injured land arising from apprehended *future* soil subsidence.[104]

5.   ON THE CUSP OF LAND AND CHATTELS: FIXTURES AND CONVERSION

(a)   the test for fixtures

A chattel that becomes sufficiently attached to land may be transformed into a 'fixture', thereby forming part of the realty.[105] This metamorphosis can be of great significance: a gift, devise, sale, mortgage, or lease of Blackacre carries with it all fixtures on that property, except those that are specifically excluded Following the termination of a lease, a landlord may become entitled to fixtures placed on the premises by a tenant; and, to use a time-honoured example, the unlawful building of a house by A, with the bricks of B, on the land of C, results in title to the bricks, as fixtures, residing in C, the owner of the land.[106]

The determination of whether a chattel has been transformed into a fixture is a matter of intention, objectively determined. This intention is ascertained by examining the 'degree' and 'object' (sometimes called 'purpose') of the annexation. When a chattel is attached to the land, however slightly, a rebuttable presumption is raised that the item has become a fixture. The extent of the attachment affects the strength of that presumption. The presumption is reversed

---

100 See further B.J. Barton, *Canadian Law of Mining* (Calgary: Canadian Institute for Resources Law, 1993) at 59*ff.*

101 See *contra Capilano Bungalow Court Ltd. v. Kitson* (1961) 29 D.L.R. (2d) 625 (B.C.S.C.).

102 *Boyd v. Toronto (City)* (1911) 23 O.L.R. 421 (Div.Ct.). See also *Bullock Holdings v. Jerema* (1998) 15 R.P.R. (3d) 185 (B.C.S.C.) at 188.

103 A right to support for buildings may be obtained through the acquisition of an easement: see Part 3, Chapter 10.

104 *Petrofina Canada Ltd. v. Moneta Porcupine Mines Ltd.*, [1970] 1 O.R. 643, 9 D.L.R. (3d) 225 (C.A.).

105 The appropriate Latin phrase for this is ''*quicquid plantatur solo, solo cedit*'' (whatsoever is attached to the land forms part of the land).

106 See, *e.g., Gough v. Wood & Co.*, [1894] 1 Q.B. 713 (C.A.) at 719.

if the chattel is resting on its own weight; here, it will be presumed to remain a chattel. The sole ground for the rebuttal of these two presumptions is the object/purpose of annexation. The test is whether the purpose of the attachment was (a) to enhance the land (which leads to the conclusion that a fixture exists); or (b) for the better use of the chattel as a chattel.[107]

These rules suggest that chattels that are attached to the realty to some degree may nevertheless be found to have remained chattels (such as underground gas tanks[108]), just as items not physically attached will sometimes be treated as fixtures. These outcomes are possible. The category of 'unattached' fixtures includes house keys, tools associated with fixtures,[109] dwellings resting on the ground,[110] and ornaments that are integral to the architectural design of the property.[111] Along the same lines, a microwave oven that is only slightly attached to the freehold might count as a fixture if it is part of a matched set of kitchen appliances. Under those circumstances ''[a]ny potential purchaser might conclude that it represented a fixed part of the kitchen''.[112]

Any attempt to reconcile the case law relating to the application of the law of fixtures seems destined to fail miserably.[113] Part of the difficulty must surely be due to the umpteen factual permutations that can arise. The variables in the tests relate to the purposes of attachment (of which there may be many) and also to the physical manifestations of affixing (the range of which may also be wide). In addition, the purpose-of-annexation test is hard to apply. For example, heavy machinery that is attached to the floor may enhance the factory, but equally, the attachment may be necessary for the proper functioning of the equipment. Yet the ultimate status of that machinery as a fixture or a chattel rests on resolving this issue.[114] The structurally equivocal dwelling known as a 'mobile home' illustrates this indeterminacy, since the case law on whether mobile homes are fixtures divides into two camps.[115] None of the mobile home rulings is necessarily wrong; so much depends on the facts.

---

107 See *Stack v. T. Eaton Co.* (1902) 4 O.L.R. 335 (Div.Ct.). For an assessment of the American test, see R.W. Polston, ''The Fixtures Doctrine: Was It Ever Really the Law?'', 16 Whittier L.Rev. 455 (1995).

108 *Salmonier Service Station Ltd. v. Imperial Oil* (1998) 169 Nfld. & P.E.I.R. 227, 521 A.P.R. 227 (Nfld.T.D.).

109 *Gooderham v. Denholm* (1859) 18 U.C.Q.B. 203 (C.A.); *L. & R. Canadian Enterprises Ltd. v. Nuform Industries Ltd.* (1984) 58 B.C.L.R. 79 (S.C.).

110 See *Elitestone Ltd. v. Morris*, [1997] 1 W.L.R. 687, [1997] 2 All E.R. 513 (H.L.) discussed in H. Conway, Note, [1998] Conv. 418.

111 *D'Eyncourt v. Gregory* (1866) L.R. 3 Eq. 382.

112 *Young v. McKinlay* (1994) 126 Sask.R. 69 (Q.B.) at 71 (*per* Noble J.).

113 Accord M. Haley, ''The Law of Fixtures: An Unprincipled Metamorphosis?'' [1998] Conv. 137, at 144; *Keefer v. Merrill* (1881) 6 O.A.R. 121 (C.A.) at 136: ''I am inclined to think that the task to bring all the decisions into harmony would be a hopeless one'' (*per* Patterson J.A.).

114 See further *Alberta v. Hansen* (1998) 21 R.P.R. (3d) 126 (Alta.Q.B.).

115 A mobile home was found to be a *CHATTEL* in: *Lichty v. Voigt* (1977) 80 D.L.R. (3d) 757 (Ont.Co.Ct.); *Royal Bank v. Beyak* (1981) 119 D.L.R. (3d) 505, 8 Sask.R. 145 (Q.B.); *Dunwoody Ltd. v. Farm Credit Corp.*, [1982] 1 W.W.R. 190, 41 C.B.R. (N.S.) 209, 15 Man.R. (2d) 208 (*sub nom. Re Plett & Plett*) (Q.B.); *Burlington Administration Group Ltd. v. Nikkel* (1979) 17 B.C.L.R. 229 (S.C.); *Canadian Imperial Bank of Commerce v. Nault* (1985) 66 A.R.

Whether or not a chattel becomes a fixture cannot be conclusively controlled by contract. In other words, an agreement that provides that a chattel 'shall not by attachment or otherwise be deemed a fixture' will not resolve the issue of characterization.[116] This is because the purpose of annexation must be patent for all to see: it must be such that, by reference to the external manifestations of annexation, the treatment of an item as a chattel or a fixture can be ascertained.[117] The *objective* test of intention found in the law of fixtures is mainly aimed at protecting third parties who may be dealing with the land at some future point. In theory, by relying on external factors, third parties, who may be unaware of some existing contractual arrangements, can 'know' whether a given item is a chattel or a fixture.

Even if a contract cannot resolve the legal classification of a chattel or fixture, it can affect the rights of the contracting parties *inter se*. An agreement may operate between the parties to allow one of them to restore a fixture to its chattel status and remove it. Likewise, identifying in a contract of sale those fixtures or chattels that are supposed to pass on the purchase of real property is by far the most sensible way of minimizing controversy between vendor and purchaser as to what forms part of the deal. Nevertheless, to repeat the initial point, these provisions cannot on their own bind third parties such that the contractual labeling of an item as a chattel or a fixture will govern.

(b)   tenant's fixtures

Special rules regulate fixtures attached by leaseholders. When a tenant attaches items to the leasehold property, these can become part of the land under the principles outlined above. The fact that it is the *tenant* who has affixed some item is not necessarily a determinative factor on the question of characterization, because, as we have just seen, intention is determined objectively. Indeed, if the function of the objective approach is to provide some external and visible evidence about the nature of affixation,[118] it would seem to follow that attachments by a tenant should be assessed on precisely the same footing as those of a freeholder. The possibility that a tenant might lose property through the application of the

---

313 (Master); *Atlin Air Ltd. v. Milikovic*, [1976] 4 W.W.R. 329 (B.C.S.C.); *Alberta Agricultural Development Corp. v. Corey Livestock Ltd.* (1992) 2 Alta.L.R. (3d) 65, [1992] 4 W.W.R. 571, 130 A.R. 50 (Master). It was held to be a *FIXTURE* in: *Dolan v. Bank of Montreal* (1985) 5 P.P.S.A.C. 196, 42 Sask.R. 202 (C.A.); *Berger v. Royal Bank*, [1991] A.J. No. 782 (Master); *Plaza Equities Ltd. v. Bank of Nova Scotia*, [1978] 3 W.W.R. 385, 11 A.R. 480, 84 D.L.R. (3d) 609 (T.D.); *Alberta Agricultural Development Corp. v. Lefebvre* (1992) 124 A.R. 42 (Master).

116 See, *e.g.*, *Diamond Neon (Manufacturing) Ltd. v. Toronto-Dominion Realty Co.*, [1976] 4 W.W.R. 664 (B.C.C.A.); *Lucky Venture Holdings Ltd. v. Dorge* (1992) 21 R.P.R. (2d) 157, 79 Man.R. (2d) 47 (Q.B.) additional reasons at (1992) 79 Man.R. (2d) 158 (Q.B.). As to the early Canadian authorities on this point, see H.E. Manning, "Fixtures", [1927] 1 D.L.R. 289. But see *Publishers Holdings Ltd. v. Industrial Development Bank*, [1974] 4 W.W.R. 440 (Man.Q.B.).

117 See also *Amic Mortgage Investment Corp. v. Investors Group Trust Co.* (1985) 40 Alta.L.R. (2d) 71, 37 R.P.R. 56, 62 A.R. 174 (C.A.).

118 *Hobson v. Gorringe*, [1897] 1 Ch. 182 (C.A.).

law of fixtures would, logically, inhibit development by leaseholders. Accordingly, it is well established that 'tenant's fixtures' are subject to special rules for detachment. Generally, a tenant may reclaim fixtures, that is, restore them to their chattel status. This right is subject to four considerations. First, at common law, the items must fall within a set of protected fixtures. This group includes items attached for purposes of (i) trade, (ii) ornamentation, or (iii) domestic convenience. These are wide categories, but the common law does not regard agricultural fixtures as being for trade, except apparently those used for market gardening.[119] Second, removal may be precluded if it will cause very serious damage to the property.[120] (Incidental damage caused by a proper removal must be remedied by the tenant.) Third, this implied right of detachment may be abridged by contract. Such a waiver should, on principle, be strictly construed against the landlord.[121] Fourth, there must be timely removal.[122] Normally this means that the tenant must act before the tenancy ends, at least when a fixed term lease has run its course.[123] In the case of a periodic lease, a sensible rule would be that the tenant should have a right of removal within a reasonable time after the tenancy is actually brought to an end. When the term has ended because there has been a forfeiture by the tenant, the law governing removal is a bit unclear. A strict approach suggests that the tenant loses the right of removal because of the forfeiture, but it has been held that the right to remove continues for a reasonable period afterwards.[124]

---

119 R.E. Megarry & H.W.R. Wade, *The Law of Real Property*, 5th ed. (London: Stevens & Sons, 1984) at 736. This was remedied by statute in England: *Landlord and Tenant Act, 1851*, c. 25. In *Carscallen v. Leeson* (1927) 23 Alta.L.R. 19, [1927] 3 W.W.R. 425, [1927] 4 D.L.R. 797 (C.A.) this Act was assumed to have been received into Alberta law, though it was held to be inapplicable in the *Leeson* case.

120 Some cases speak of irreparable damage; others of substantial or material damage. The standard may vary with the sub-class of tenant's fixture at issue. See further *Homestar Holdings Ltd. v. Old Country Inn Ltd.* (1986) 8 B.C.L.R. (2d) 211 (S.C.). *Cf.* H.N. Bennett, "Attachment of Chattels to Land" in N. Palmer & E. McKendrick, eds., *Interests in Goods*, 2nd ed. (London: L.L.P., 1998) ch. 11, at 277-8.

121 See, *e.g., 335426 Alberta Ltd. v. Westmount Village Equities* (1997) 201 A.R. 173 (Master). However, an implied relinquishment was found where the fixtures, which complemented the freehold, were added to the premises under a long-term lease: *Lévesque v. J. Clark & Son Ltd.* (1972) 7 N.B.R. (2d) 478 (Q.B.) at 484.

122 See generally G. Kodilinye, "Time for Removal of Tenant's Fixtures", [1987] Conv. 253.

123 *National Trust Co. v. Palace Theatre Ltd.* (1928) 23 Alta.L.R. 427, [1928] 1 W.W.R. 805, [1928] 2 D.L.R. 739 (C.A.).

124 See *Argles v. McMath* (1896) 23 O.A.R. 44 (C.A.) affirming (1894) 26 O.R. 224 (H.C.). See also *Sawridge Manor Inc. v. Selkirk Springs International Corp.* (1995) 8 B.C.L.R. (3d) 201 (C.A.). The requirement of timely removal has produced some questionable results, at least when a surrender of the lease occurs, either by operation of law (such as when the tenant abandons the premises and possession is taken by the landlord), or when there is a surrender by express agreement. In the former case, the requirement of removal before surrender has been applied. This may be justifiable given that this type of surrender is initiated by the tenant, who prompts the termination of the leasehold by abandoning the premises. However, when the tenant surrenders a lease in order that a new lease between the same parties may be entered into, the failure to reserve the fixtures installed during the first term means, in theory, that they will pass to the landlord and cannot be removed at the end of the second tenancy: see *Cullen v. McPherson* (1900) 40 N.S.R. 241 (S.C.). (The result is different if there is an extension of

(c)   the clash of security interests

The transition from chattel to fixture can affect more than just the landholder and the owner of the personalty. For example, a chattel may be sold subject to a security interest under which the vendor enjoys a right of repossession in the event of a default in payment.[125] When that chattel becomes attached to land that is also encumbered with a charge or mortgage, priority rules are needed to determine which of the two secured creditors will prevail in the event of a default in the obligations. Should the holder of the chattel security be entitled to seize the fixture? Should the lender under the land mortgage be entitled to claim the fixture as an addition to the land? Under the common law the general rule is that when the chattel becomes affixed it falls under the land security. This means that the security holder of the chattel loses the right of repossession and is left only with an action on the debt against the purchaser.

The ability of the mortgagee to augment the land security through the absorption of fixtures, even after the mortgage is granted over the realty, creates no great injustice as between the debtor/mortgagor and the lender/mortgagee. They can always agree that a different result will flow. But, as between the two lenders, the land mortgagee appears to receive a windfall. And as we have seen, the ability to prevent this result is limited since any attempt by contract to provide that a chattel shall not become a fixture would be fruitless.

Despite this, a shrewdly drafted contract *might* be able to provide some help to the chattel security holder, as long as the timing is right. English[126] and Australian[127] courts have held that a contractual right to enter and seize a fixture can create a real property interest. By registering this interest in land under the governing land registry system, notice of that right is thereby given to subsequent mortgagees and purchasers. The precise nature of this right-of-entry interest has never been thoroughly explained; admittedly, it has an awkward fit with established land law categories.[128] Whatever its legitimacy, the right of entry will not prevail over a mortgage interest in the land registered *before* the arrival of the fixture; here the land mortgagee will have priority.

---

the existing term: *Carscallen v. Leeson, supra*, note 119.) The loss of the right of removal following a surrender seems likely to produce unfair and unintended results. English law has now rejected the idea that the right of removal is inevitably lost when the term is surrendered on consent: *New Zealand Government Property Corp. v. H.M.& S. Ltd.*, [1982] Q.B. 1145, [1982] 1 All E.R. 624 (C.A.). Some Canadian cases seem inclined to accept an accordant view, for it has been held that the acceptance of a new term following the expiration of the old one will not necessarily destroy the right of removal: see *Badalato v. Trebilcock* (1923) 53 O.L.R. 359, [1924] 1 D.L.R. 465 (C.A.).

125 See Part 6(b), Chapter 11.

126 See, *e.g.*, *Re Morrison, Jones & Taylor, Ltd.*, [1914] 1 Ch. 50, relying on *Re Samuel Allen & Sons Ltd.*, [1907] 1 Ch. 575.

127 *Kay's Leasing Corp. Pty. Ltd. v. C.S.R. Provident Fund Nominees Pty. Ltd.*, [1962] V.R. 429 (S.C.).

128 D. Cooper, ''Retaining Title to Fixtures'' (1991) 6 Auck.U.L.Rev. 477, at 496*ff*. The right of entry is endorsed in H.N. Bennett & C.J. Davis, ''Fixtures, Purchase Money Security Interests and Dispositions of Interests in Land'', [1994] Conv. 448.

The current trend in Canada is to regulate these disputes by statute. At one time, in Alberta, a chattel sold subject to a security interest would (after due registration) be deemed to remain a chattel. A mortgagee of the land could prevent removal of that item from the land by paying the amount due under the chattel security.[129] This was a straightforward approach, but it left some matters unresolved, such as the liability, if any, that should result from damage to buildings caused by the removal of the fixture.

Modern personal property security legislation contains more elaborate principles for the balancing of the interests of the two types of security holders. In Alberta, a security interest in a chattel will normally enjoy priority over a subsequent land mortgage if that (chattel) security interest is taken before the item becomes a fixture.[130] Generally speaking, no registration of this interest is required to protect the chattel security against the prior mortgage, but the failure to register it in the land titles office will lead to a loss of priority over those who deal subsequently with the landowner. Included in this latter category are those who acquire an interest in the land, including, of course, a mortgagee.[131] If a security interest in goods is acquired after those goods have already become fixtures, generally priority will be enjoyed by those holding existing land mortgages, because in this case the goods have already become part of the land.

In those instances in which the chattel security has priority, a right of removal in the event of default (assuming this has been reserved) can be exercised, subject to certain restrictions as to how the repossession is carried out. A notice must be given to those having an interest in the land, and a party who is subordinate in priority to the chattel security holder is entitled to pay off the chattel security holder to prevent removal.[132] The process of detachment must be undertaken in a way that minimizes damage and inconvenience. An action may be launched by any person who has an interest in the land (other than the debtor) for damage resulting from the removal.[133]

---

129 *Conditional Sales Act*, R.S.A. 1980, c. C-21, s. 16 [repealed].

130 *Personal Property Security Act*, S.A. 1988, c. P-4.05, s. 36 [as am.]. See further R.C.C. Cuming & R.J. Wood, *Alberta Personal Property Security Act Handbook*, 4th ed. (Toronto: Carswell, 1998) at 341*ff*. For a critique of the *P.P.S.A.* solution, see B. MacDougall, ''Fixtures and the P.P.S.A.: Of the Wooden Horse of Troy, Creditors in the Weeds and Statutory Ambush'' (1993) 72 Can.B.Rev. 496. See also Law Reform Commission of British Columbia, *Report on Land-Related Interests and the Personal Property Security Act* (Vancouver: L.R.C.B.C., Report No. 143, 1995).

131 Also protected are *prior* mortgagees who have advanced money *after* the fixture is attached (for the amount of that advance), or who have obtained an order confirming sale or a vesting order in a (land) foreclosure action: sub. 36(3). See also subs. 33(5), (6) and s. 30.

132 The price to be paid is the lesser of the amount secured or the present market value of the goods if they are removed: sub. 36(11) [as am.].

133 *Personal Property Security Act*, S.A. 1988, c. P-4.05, subs. 36(7) - (14). The debtor may not be without a remedy if the property is damaged by removal: see ss. 66, 67 (taken together with sub. 36(7)).

(d)   conceptual metamorphosis: the equitable doctrine of conversion

Under the doctrine of conversion, an interest in realty may be deemed to be one of personality, or *vice versa*, even if no exchange or physical transformation has taken place. At the bottom of this idea is a maxim that reads: 'equity regards as done that which ought to be done'.[134] When there is a legal obligation to convert realty into personality, a court of equity will regard this as having been accomplished from the very moment that the obligation comes into force. The chief ingredient needed to produce this result is the duty to convert.[135] Therefore, when a trustee is required to sell land and hold the proceeds of sale on trust, the rights under the trust will be treated as personal property even before the sale takes place. Once a court order is made for the sale of land, the property is treated immediately as being personalty in the hands of the person entitled to the proceeds.[136] The doctrine of conversion contemplates that a future exchange will occur, as through a sale, and not a physical alteration of the item. However, it is conceivable that an obligation to affix a chattel, or to detach a fixture, could trigger the doctrine.

Given that the bright line that once existed between the law of real and personal property has been dimming, the question of whether a certain property should be regarded as being in one category or the other is often immaterial. One area in which it remains important is in connection with testamentary gifts, where, for example, the decedent's realty has been devised to A, and the personalty bequeathed to B. Here, entitlements may turn on whether or not some of the property in the estate is subject to an obligation to convert.

6.   THE TRANSFORMATION OF CHATTEL OWNERSHIP[137]

(a)   introduction

Title to chattels may be affected (i) by the intermixture of the chattels of two or more people; (ii) through the accession (or joining) of goods; or (iii) through an alteration under which an entirely new object is created.[138] In resolving such disputes, it has been said that "[t]he question of title is subverted in favour of the achievement of substantial justice between the parties".[139] What this means is

---

134 This maxim is considered in several places in the text: see, *e.g.*, Part 4(c), Chapter 9.

135 *Re Woods*, [1947] O.R. 753 (H.C.) (no duty to convert found on the facts).

136 See, *e.g.*, *Re Silva*, [1929] 2 Ch. 198, [1929] All E.R.Rep. 546.

137 See further L.D. Smith, *The Law of Tracing* (Oxford: Clarendon Pr., 1997) ch. 2, *passim*; P.D. Maddaugh & J.D. McCamus, *The Law of Restitution* (Aurora, Ont.: Canada Law Book, 1990) at 110*ff*; S. Fisher, *Commercial and Personal Property Law* (Sydney: Butterworths, 1997) at 102*ff*.

138 But take caution: the nomenclature is not used uniformly. Some of the variations are explained in G. McCormack, "Mixture of Goods" (1990) 10 Leg.Stud. 293, at 293-4.

139 R.B. Slater, "Accessio, Specificatio and Confusio: Three Skeletons in the Closet" (1959) 37 Can.B.Rev. 597, at 607.

that elements of intention, negligence and innocent action can affect the ultimate state of ownership under current Canadian law.

(b)   confusion (or commingling or intermixture)

Confusion occurs when fungible items are inseparably combined. Roman law (which has greatly influenced the English and Canadian law in this area) distinguished between the admixture of liquids (*confusio*) and dry goods (*commixtio*). Sometimes it is said that *confusio* refers to the combination of items that are incapable of separation (like liquids), while *commixtio* applies when separation is *theoretically* possible (such as in the case of combined dry goods).[140] Under Roman law the classification affected both the rights of ownership and the available legal remedies. In the case of *confusio*, a mixing would always have implications for the state of title; that was not invariably true for cases of *commixtio*. In theory, separate ownership survived the non-consensual combination of dry goods. But Roman law, ever practical, would not necessarily go to the length of requiring that individual grains (or whatever) be drawn from the combined mass. Sometimes all that the owner could claim was a proportionate share of the goods.

The tests for *confusio* and *commixtio* both refer "to an objective quality of the subject-matter, not to the practical possibility of re-establishing the status quo".[141] However, the Roman approach does not seem at all sensible (to me) if the law is proposing to draw meaningful distinctions between these two types of events. For all practical purposes, a full-blown mixing, whether of liquids or grains, creates an inseparable mass.

By the same token, the Romans were undoubtedly right in seeking to distinguish between cases of separable and non-separable mixing. If items belonging to two or more people become mixed, but it is possible to segregate them, we do not seem to have much of a problem of ownership. So, if branded cows belonging to two farmers roam and mingle together in a field no real issue of confusion arises. If, on the other hand, fungible solids become combined it seems sensible to discount the idea that separate titles to each unit continue (for whatever juristic reason) just because we think that the molecular integrity of every item remains intact. So when do we have a case of 'true' confusion under the current law? To my mind, the test under modern law should be whether it is "impracticable, and for all business purposes therefore impossible, to distinguish the particles, in respect of ownership".[142] If separation is not possible under this test, then something must be done to ascertain the proprietary entitlements of the various claimants.

It was once the accepted wisdom that if a confusion occurred through intentional wrongdoing or perhaps even out of negligence,[143] the person at fault would

---

140 *Indian Oil Corp. v. Greenstone Shipping S.A. (Panama)*, [1988] Q.B. 345, [1987] 3 All E.R. 893. See also P. Birks, "Mixtures" in N. Palmer & E. McKendrick, eds., *Interests in Goods*, 2nd ed. (London: L.L.P., 1998) ch. 9.

141 P. Birks, "Mixing and Tracing: Property and Restitution", [1992] C.L.P. 69, at 72.

142 *Spence v. Union Marine Insurance Co. Ltd.* (1868) L.R. 3 C.P. 427, at 438 (*per* Bovill C.J.).

143 But see *Lawrie v. Rathbun* (1876) 38 U.C.Q.B. 255, at 281.

suffer the loss, and title to the lot would pass to the innocent party. So, in a nineteenth century case it was declared that "[i]f a man puts corn into my bag, in which there is before some corn, the whole is mine, because it is impossible to distinguish what was mine from what was his".[144] When, in contrast, there is an accidental (*i.e.*, innocent) intermixture, or in cases of consent, the parties share the combined mass as co-owners, their portions being based on their relative contributions if this can be determined; otherwise, they share equally.

By holding that a wrongful intermixture results in the loss of title to everything, the law is erring on the side of the innocent party, principally, it would appear, because of the difficulties sometimes associated with determining the true state of affairs. In effect, though, the result is punitive in nature, because the wrongdoer loses everything including property he or she rightfully held. There are times when such an approach can produce too harsh a result. A rogue who adds a small portion of stolen grain to his own large, legitimately owned mass should not be required to forfeit everything. Therefore, it has been doubted that the general rule should be applied if to do so would lead to substantive injustice.[145] The function of the private (or civil) law of property is not to punish but to compensate. If acts of theft have occurred and deserve punishment, the criminal law is available as a means of pursuing that end.

In the early Canadian case of *McDonald v. Lane*[146] a question arose as to the title to logs that had been intentionally commingled by the defendant. A majority of the Supreme Court of Canada regarded it as well-settled that the plaintiff could retrieve from the confused mass only the amount that had been wrongfully taken. This seems to constitute a departure from the rule for wrongful confusion. This decision accords with recent English authority that serves to de-emphasize the punitive impact of the intermixture rules. In *Indian Oil v. Greenstone Shipping*[147] the defendant combined its own oil with oil of roughly equal grade belonging to the plaintiff. A claim by the plaintiff to the entire shipment failed. Instead, the Court held that the plaintiff was entitled to its initial share. As an aid to the plaintiff, however, the onus of determining the ratio of the contributions lay on the defendant. In resolving that issue the defendant would be put to the strict proof of its entitlement, with allowances and assumptions being drawn against it. (One would think that this rule of fair play should apply whenever one party is shown to be more at fault in causing the unplanned commingling.) The solution that would have been adopted had the oil been of different quality was left open by the Court in *Indian Oil*. One potential approach to that situation would be to

---

144 *Colwill v. Reeves* (1811) 2 Camp. 575, at 576, 170 E.R. 1257 (*per* Lord Ellenborough). See also B. Murdoch, *Epitome of the Laws of Nova Scotia* (Halifax: Joseph Howe, 1832-3) vol. 3, at 5-6.

145 *Sandeman & Sons v. Tyzack & Branfoot Steamship Co.*, [1913] A.C. 680, [1911-13] All E.R. Rep. 1013 (H.L.).

146 (1881-2) 7 S.C.R. 462. See also *The "Polar Star" v. Arsenault* (1964) 43 D.L.R. (2d) 354 (P.E.I.S.C.) affirmed (1965) 51 M.P.R. 152 (*sub nom. Louis Denber Inc. v. "Polar Star" (The)*) (C.A.); *Gilmour v. Buck* (1874) 24 U.C.C.P. 187 (C.A.).

147 *Indian Oil Corp. v. Greenstone Shipping S.A. (Panama)*, *supra*, note 140. See also *Coleman v. Harvey*, [1989] 1 N.Z.L.R. 723 (C.A.) and Note (1990) 106 L.Q.R. 552.

allocate to the plaintiff that part of the pool that is equal to the value of the plaintiff's initial share (or damages), while all the time resolving any factual uncertainties that might arise in these calculations against the defendant.

(c) accession

The doctrine of accession is designed primarily to resolve disputes in which two or more chattels become attached, such as when A's paint is applied to B's car. In addition, a natural accession occurs when an animal gives birth to offspring. Here, the general rule is that the owner of the mother acquires title to the progeny.[148]

As in the law of fixtures, when an accession has occurred through the fusion of two chattels, the title of one of the chattels is subsumed in the other. However, with fixtures it is axiomatic that it is the title to the personalty that is lost. The correct result is less obvious when two chattels are involved. Here, the law appears to prescribe that an accession is made to the 'principal' or dominant chattel which, generally speaking, has been taken to mean the item that has the greatest (market) value. However, doubts have been raised as to whether monetary worth should be the exclusive criterion. One can imagine a case in which one item is auxiliary or subordinate to the other, such as where an expensive engine is installed into a car that is valued at a lower price. The engine may well be worth more, but it would seem anomalous to say that the car has acceded to it. In brief, a test based on the relationship between the objects might sometimes be the best way to determine which is to be treated as the principal chattel.[149]

As with the law of fixtures, the difficulties that can occur in applying the rules for accession are manifold. The case of *McKeown v. Cavalier Yachts Pty.*[150] provides a stunning case in point. The plaintiff owned the hull of a sail boat to which the defendant – *arguably* unaware that title was in the plaintiff – had added substantial improvements. The value of the hull before the work was $1,777; the cost of the improvements was $24,409. On these facts, one would expect that the defendant would acquire title, having added the greatest element of value to the boat. However, the Court held otherwise. The additions to the hull occurred gradually. The first applications, being of less value than the original hull, accrued to the owner of the hull and increased the value of the original chattel. Each subsequent application produced the same result; each time the hull increased marginally in value. As a result, even though the total cost of the work exceeded the original cost of the hull, at no time was this true of any single affixing of new materials. In the end, the hull was found to be the principal chattel. If this reasoning is correct, disputes may be determined by whether and how one divides the process of accession, something that can be influenced by an act as simple and seemingly irrelevant as a coffee break![151]

---

148 See *Dillaree v. Doyle* (1878) 43 U.C.Q.B. 442. *Cf. Tucker v. Farm & General Investment Trust Ltd.*, [1966] 2 Q.B. 421 (C.A); *Case of Swans* (1592) 7 Co.Rep. 15b, 77 E.R. 435.

149 See also McCormack, *supra*, note 138; Smith, *supra*, note 137, at 105-6.

150 (1988) 13 N.S.W.L.R. 303 (S.C.).

151 *Cf. Capitol Chevrolet v. Earheart*, 627 S.W.2d 369 (Tenn.C.A., 1981); *Gidney v. Shank* (1995) 107 Man.R. (2d) 208, [1996] 2 W.W.R. 383 (C.A.).

In *Cavalier* there was no apparent dispute that the work undertaken on the hull produced an accession of materials: the items of the defendant and plaintiff were assumed to be inseparable. That determination can be more difficult in other fact situations, so, as with fixtures disputes, a test is required. Four have been advanced:

1. the 'injurious removal' test: can the items be removed without serious physical injury to the principal chattel?
2. the 'separate existence' test: has the separate identity of the acceded chattel been lost (as when a plank is added to a ship)?
3. the 'destruction of utility' test: would removal of the combined items destroy the utility of the principal chattel (such as by the taking of tires from a truck)?
4. the 'fixtures' test: looking at the degree and purpose of annexation, has an accession occurred?[152]

There is no sure guide as to which approach should govern when disputes arise. In fact, the proper approach may depend on the nature of the dispute. In *Firestone Tire v. Industrial Acceptance Corp.*[153] a contest arose between a conditional vendor of tires and the holder of a comparable security over the truck on which the tires had been installed. The purchaser of the truck and tires having defaulted under both obligations, the secured lenders each claimed a right to retake the goods covered by their respective security agreements. The vendor of the truck claimed that the title to the tires had merged in the truck (which was obviously the principal chattel) through accession. If correct, this would have extinguished the tire vendor's security interest. An application of the 'destruction of utility' test would probably have led to that conclusion. But instead, the Supreme Court of Canada adopted the injurious removal standard. A factor pointing to that approach was the desire to prevent a windfall from being gained by the truck vendor.

The Supreme Court did not reject the other approaches altogether, guardedly leaving open the possibility that another result should obtain when, for example, the goods had been improved by the conditional purchaser.[154] It would seem, however, that (perhaps) apart from the situation of a good faith purchaser acquiring title to what is believed to be property of the vendor, there is merit in a general

---

152 These tests are set out in *Thomas v. Robinson*, [1977] 1 N.Z.L.R. 385 (H.C.). See also *Paziuk v. Frank Dunn Trailer Sales Ltd.* (1994) 127 Sask.R. 303 (Q.B.); A. Alston, ''Chattels Attached to Chattels'' (1996) 4 Aust.Prop.L.J. 120.

153 *Firestone Tire & Rubber Co. v. Industrial Acceptance Corp.*, [1971] S.C.R. 357, 75 W.W.R. 621, 17 D.L.R. (3d) 229.

154 *Ibid.* at 359 S.C.R. (*per* Laskin J., as he then was). Compare *Regina Chevrolet Sales Ltd. v. Riddell*, [1942] 2 W.W.R. 357, [1942] 3 D.L.R. 159 (Sask.C.A.), which appears at first glance to adopt the 'utility' test to reach a different result from that arrived at in *Firestone*. However, in the *Riddell* case the tires fell under the conditional sales agreement for the car (which covered after-acquired attachments) *before* a separate security was given (via a chattel mortgage) over the tires. That being so, the car vendor had a better claim by virtue of its priority in time, without the need to argue that an accession of the tires had occurred.

rule that finds an accession only when absolutely necessary, and allows for detachment in all other instances. There is no need to encourage a fight over one piece of property when it is possible to conceive of it as, in reality, two pieces. This points to the general suitability of the injurious removal test, which normally is the hardest test to meet.[155]

As matters now stand in Alberta, the tires in *Firestone* would be regarded as an integral part of the truck. Under the *Personal Property Security Act* (the *P.P.S.A.*),[156] even a minimal attachment falls within the statutory definition of an accession.[157] The rationale of this low-threshold test for accession is to allow such security contests to be resolved by the detailed rules of the Act and not by the common law. This statutory scheme resembles that applied to fixtures.[158] Under the *P.P.S.A.*, the tire vendor would retain the right of removal as long as that security attached before the tires fell under the security of the truck vendor. Such was the case in *Firestone* (therefore the same solution would be arrived at under modern Alberta law through different means).

The determination of *whether* an accession has occurred is distinct from the ultimate remedy that a court might impose once an accession is found. The solution adopted in the *Indian Oil* case in the context of intermixture – treating the parties as entitled to a share, even if the confusion was wrongful – is unsuitable for cases of accession. After an accession there is, by definition, only one chattel, and treating the contestants as co-owners solves one problem but invites others. Imagine the disputes that might arise between these court-designated co-owners. To make matters worse, in most jurisdictions there is no established judicial power to order partition or sale for personalty to cure ongoing disputes between co-owners. Shared ownership would create a proprietary marriage of inconvenience without the ability to resort to a judicial order of 'divorce'.

What else can be done?[159] If the plaintiff seeks only damages (under the torts of trespass, conversion or detinue[160]) problems of locating the current title do not arise. However, when there is a dispute as to future ownership, a number of factors may come into play. The main reason for resolving which chattel is the principal one is to determine who should keep the acceded materials. If there has been an accession the title of the acceded goods is lost, just as in the law of fixtures. There is something quite convenient about this type of rule, but it might not always lead to a fair result.

---

155 See also *Thomas v. Robinson, supra*, note 152. McCormack suggests that judicial support has coalesced around the injurious removal test as the preferable standard: *supra*, note 138, at 295.
156 S.A. 1988, c. P-4.05, s. 38 [as am.].
157 Para. 1(1)(a).
158 See Part 5(c), *supra*. Notice also the finer points of determining priority in subs. 38(3), (4). See also s. 30.
159 See generally E. McKendrick, ''Restitution and the Misuse of Chattels – The Need for a Principled Approach'' in Palmer & McKendrick, *supra*, note 140, ch. 35, and the authorities cited there; and N. Palmer & A. Hudson, ''Improving Stolen Chattels'', *ibid.*, ch. 36.
160 See J.G. Fleming, *The Law of Torts,* 9th ed. (Sydney: Law Book Co., 1998) ch. 4, where these torts are discussed.

My view is that Canadian courts should adopt a highly flexible approach. In the case of an accession, three orders seem plausible. A court might (i) allow the wrongdoer to keep the goods, but order that person to pay damages; (ii) confer the new item on the fully innocent party; or (iii) allow the innocent party to regain the goods if a payment is made to the wrongful improver as a form of compensation for the added value.[161] In determining which order should be granted one approach would be to focus on the answers to two questions: (i) was the defendant (affixer) the owner of the principal chattel?; (ii) if so, was that person acting innocently, negligently or intentionally? Now, it must be understood that the degree of fault may be of no consequence when determining if there is liability in tort for a wrongful interference with chattels. The general rule is that the honest belief of the defendant that he or she has title to the goods will afford no defence to the torts of detinue, conversion and trespass. However, liability in tort should be distinct from the question of title to the transformed objects.

Following the lead of the intermixture case of *Indian Oil*, which I think adopts a sensible approach, it is possible to conceive of a range of outcomes that attempt to balance the interests of the parties. For example, an innocent accession by a person who does not own the principal chattel might result in the return of the chattel to the plaintiff, coupled with a compensatory payment to the defendant based on the value of the attached item. This is a controversial idea: it may not be fair to ask an owner to pay for improvements that she never sought. And it may appear peculiar to order a plaintiff to make a payment to a tortfeasor. There is precedent supporting this approach,[162] though there is some disagreement[163] as to what – beyond the fact of an innocent improvement having taken place – will suffice to prompt a restitutionary payment. If the improvement was something that was necessary in any event, there is a case for permitting compensation. That might occur when, for instance, broken car parts are replaced with new ones. Another case for compensation might arise when the goods are, or have been, sold, in which case at least some of the increase in value might be given to the innocent improver. Or, a payment might make sense when the owner wanted the improvements to be made, albeit by someone else.[164] Still, any compensation paid should be set off against whatever consequential damages result from changes to the plaintiff's chattel. Moreover, no recompense seems warranted when the defendant has intentionally added to the plaintiff's principal chattel. Otherwise the

---

161 See *Thomas v. Robinson*, *supra*, note 152.

162 See the cases referred to in *Thomas v. Robinson*, *ibid*.

163 See further the discussion of these restitutionary ideas of 'free acceptance' and 'incontrovertible benefit' in McKendrick, *supra*, note 159. See also the authorities and references considered there.

164 These are, arguably, examples of an incontrovertible benefit. See further *Peel (Regional Municipality) v. Canada*, [1992] 3 S.C.R. 762, 12 M.P.L.R. (2d) 229, 98 D.L.R. (4th) 140, where McLachlin J., as she then was, defined that term (at 795 S.C.R.) as follows: "[a]n incontrovertible benefit is an unquestionable benefit, a benefit which is demonstrably apparent and not subject to debate and conjecture. Where the benefit is not clear and manifest, it would be wrong to make the defendant pay, since he or she might have preferred to decline the benefit given the choice". See also M. McInnes, "The Canadian Principle of Unjust Enrichment: Comparative Insights in the Law of Restitution" (1999) 37 Alta.L.Rev. 1, at 32*ff.*

order would result in a forced sale of (acceded) goods from the defendant to the plaintiff.

Of course, none of these solutions should apply automatically. The flexibility to make orders that would avoid injustice should not be tightly bracketed. For instance, the personhood interests of the parties might sometimes be relevant. It may be appropriate in some cases of accession that the psychological attachment of a party to some item should be at least as important as the physical attachment that gave rise to the problem of accession in the first place.

(d)   alteration (or specificatio)

The alteration of an item, produced by A transforming a chattel owned by B into some new item, dealt with in Roman law under the doctrine of *specificatio*, conjures up images of the Lockean mixing metaphor and the labour justification of property ownership.[165] However, whereas in Locke's world this spawned a right to private property for goods that had previously been held in common, the problem posed here involves work done on property that has a prior private owner.

Title will be affected by an alteration only when the goods are substantially transformed, though the degree of change required is not well-articulated in the jurisprudence. Some authorities suggest that it depends on whether a new species of goods has been created, such as when corn is made into corn liquor,[166] or perhaps when a statue is carved from marble. Other approaches, based on reversibility of the effect of the work or the continued identification of the altered chattel, have also been advanced.[167] Such factors are quite similar to those applied to determine if an accession has occurred. Indeed, the similarities between accession and alteration should become apparent by reconsidering *Cavalier Yacht*, where the claim of the yacht builder was based, in part, on the value of the goods *and services* involved in the process of completing the yacht.[168] Likewise, in the Canadian case of *Jones v. De Marchant*[169] a successful claim was made to a fur coat that contained 18 pelts wrongfully taken from the plaintiff that were later combined with four others to complete the coat. The case involved elements of confusion (the plaintiff's pelts were mixed with the others), accession (the pelts had been inseparably merged), and alteration (the work performed to produce the coat was significant, and the pelts were changed into something new). Once an alteration occurs, the problems that emerge resemble those that affect accessions. Similar principles should apply to resolve disputes as to who should own this newly created item.

---

165 See Part 3(f), Chapter 1.

166 See *Silsbury v. McCoon et al.*, 3 N.Y. 379 (C.A., 1850).

167 See P. Mathews, "*Specificatio* and the Common Law" (1981) 10 Anglo-Am.L.Rev. 121. For a discussion of the early state of the law, see J.H. Baker, "Introduction to the Reports of Sir John Spelman" (1977) 94 Seld.Soc. 1, at 212*ff.*

168 *Supra*, note 150.

169 (1916) 26 Man.R. 445, 10 W.W.R. 841, 28 D.L.R. 561 (C.A.).

4

THE CONCEPT OF POSSESSION

Possession is very strong; rather more than nine points of the law.

Lord Mansfield (1774)[1]

1. INTRODUCTION

This chapter considers the place of possession in the law of property. The meaning of that term and the functions it serves will be focal.

We often hear it said, akin to Lord Mansfield's *dictum* quoted above, that 'possession is nine-tenths of the law'. The mathematics behind this adage may be off (how can such a thing be calculated?), but the sentiment underlying it is quite sound. Possession is a concept that is ubiquitous in the law of property, especially in relation to personalty, where its importance can be seen in the law of bailment, gifts, liens, and the sale of goods. Possession or the right to possession, not ownership or title *per se*, determines the ability of an owner (or other aggrieved person) to sue in tort in response to a wrongful interference with chattels.[2] Possession is sometimes relevant in other areas of the law, including such diverse fields as criminal law, international law and civil procedure.

In this chapter we will look at several loosely connected areas of law. The unifying thread is that they all help to explain something about the nature of possession as a juridical concept. So, the role played by possession in the *acquisition* and *extinguishment* of property rights will be demonstrated through the law of adverse possession. The law governing gifts demonstrates the place of possession in regulating the *transfer* of title. The law of finders will be used to show the *relative* nature of property rights. Possession as the basis for the *recognition* and *preservation* of common law Aboriginal title will also be considered. I hope to demonstrate the idea that possession is a flexible and chameleon-like concept, and one that is capable of providing a vital ingredient in the analysis and determination of property rights.

The importance of possession will surface from time to time in the remainder of the text. In Chapter 8 we will see that possession is relevant in determining whether a lease of land has been created. It is also an essential element in the creation of bailments. Some interests, such as easements, cannot be validly created if they involve a transfer of possession (as we will observe in Chapter 10).

It has been cautioned that "English law has never worked out a completely logical and exhaustive definition of 'possession' ".[3] Likewise, Canadian law

---

1 *Corp. of Kingston upon Hull v. Horner* (1774) Lofft. 576, at 591, 98 E.R. 807, at 815.
2 See generally J.G. Fleming, *The Law of Torts*, 9th ed. (Sydney: Law Book Co., 1998) ch. 4.
3 *United States of America v. Dollfus Mieg & Cie. S.A.*, [1952] A.C. 582, [1952] 1 All E.R. 572 (H.L.) at 605 A.C. (*per* Earl Jowitt).

"does not recognize the existence of a single concept of possession applicable for all purposes".[4] This is because the term becomes moulded by its various applications and as a result it assumes somewhat unique forms in the areas in which it is invoked. Therefore, the various meanings of possession are best understood in the legal and factual contexts in which they operate, at least once some rudimentary ideas are first explained.

2. SOME BASIC DEFINITIONS[5]

Few terms of property law are as readily found in common parlance as the word possession, and its meaning in everyday affairs is probably clear most of the time. At its core are two components: *animus possidendi* (an intention to possess) and *factum* (physical control). Yet if one can accept that the thickest conception of possession involves total and unshakeable physical dominion, coupled with full knowledge of the property and a resolute determination to exclude others, it must also be understood that the law does not always demand that such a perfect pattern exist. The accepted level often amounts to less than full manual control. Some items, land being the prime example, cannot be held in that way.

Samuel Pufendorf, a seventeenth century philosopher who wrote about occupancy theory and ownership rights, said that "as a rule, movable things are occupied with the hands and land with the feet – along with the intention to cultivate it and the establishment of exact or rough boundaries".[6] As we will see, these 'rules' are subject to a variety of qualifications. No simple formula, not even Pufendorf's, can indicate just what will suffice for possession in all situations. Among the relevant considerations are whether the acts of control can be seen as sufficient to exclude others, and the kind of dominion that is possible from a practical point of view.[7] Context counts, because the circumstances in which possession might arise are so varied. In an early Newfoundland case, for example, the determination of what constitutes first occupancy of a fishing ground fell to be considered. It was held that "it was not sufficient for the grapnel [*i.e.,* the anchor] to be overboard, but that it [must] take ground to entitle the party claiming the prior right of occupancy".[8] Such logistical matters are by no means the only relevant concerns. In addition, the degree of possession that the law will

---

4 *Lifestyles Kitchen & Bath v. Danbury Sales Inc.*, [1999] O.J. No. 3097 (S.C.J.) at para. 12 (*per* Cullity J.).

5 For an extensive analysis, see D.R. Harris, "The Concept of Possession in English Law" in A.G. Guest, ed., *Oxford Essays in Jurisprudence* (London: O.U.P., 1961) 69. The classic treatise is F. Pollock & R.S. Wright, *An Essay on Possession in the Common Law* (Oxford: Clarendon Pr., 1888). See also J.M. Lightwood, *A Treatise on Possession of Land* (London: Stevens & Sons, 1894). For a comparative analysis of the idea of possession in common law and civil law systems, see J. Gordley & U. Mattei, "Protecting Possession" , 44 Am.J.Comp.L. 293 (1996). See also N. Palmer, "Possessory Title" in N. Palmer & E. McKendrick, eds., *Interests in Goods*, 2nd ed. (London: L.L.P., 1998) ch. 3.

6 C.L. Carr, ed., *The Political Writings of Samuel Pufendorf* (New York: O.U.P., 1994) at 188, para. 8.

7 See *The "Tubantia"*, [1924] P. 78, [1924] All E.R.Rep. 615. *Cf. Eads v. Brazelton*, 79 Am.Dec. 88 (Ark.S.C., 1861).

8 *Arnold v. Whiteway* (1883) 6 Nfld.R. 518 (S.C.) at 519 (*per* Pinsent J.).

demand will depend on the *function* that the concept of possession is designed to serve. This purposive element is the most dynamic component in the definition. Put another way, the legal context in which the question of possession emerges will inform the factual requirements.

Just as the physical element may vary, so too may the cerebral element. An intention to possess may be found even without the holder having that high degree of subjective awareness composed of perfect knowledge and an absolute resolve to exert exclusive control. For example, it is sensible to assume that a person grabbing hold of a receptacle intends to possess those items that might normally be found inside of it. The finder of a locked box can be taken to intend to possess its contents, even if there is no actual knowledge of precisely what is inside.[9] In the same way, an owner of land may be taken to intend to possess items on the premises despite being unaware of all that might be there.

In instances when either the physical or mental elements are watered down, a type of legal fiction is created, sometimes described as constructive possession. As a general matter, when this extended meaning applies, possession and its constructive counterpart are equated. Indeed, the dividing line between these two images of possession is often difficult to discern: is there constructive or actual possession of all articles on a table at which you are sitting? The key here is that the concept of possession is broader than one might otherwise suppose. There is a distinction "between sensuous and juridical possession, the latter dependent on the former but striving to transcend its limitations".[10] It is the inherent elasticity of the concept of possession that allows courts to use that concept as a short-hand means of deciding who among competing claimants should, as a matter of justice, prevail.

Possession is sometimes contrasted with custody.[11] For example, an employee holding goods belonging to the employer is generally regarded as having custody only, with legal possession remaining in the employer.[12] This rule stems from the arcane view that a servant is no more than a conduit or functionary of his or her superior. This may be a tolerable approach when the employer is in actual, direct and immediate control of the employee's actions. That should be equally true of any owner/holder relationship.[13] Perhaps a better description would be that the employee is capable of taking possession (and not mere custody), and

---

9 See *Graftstein v. Holme*, [1958] O.R. 296, 12 D.L.R. (2d) 727 (C.A.) discussed in S.F. Sommerfeld, Note (1958) 36 Can.B.Rev. 558.

10 A. Brudner, *The Unity of the Common Law* (Berkeley: U.of Calif.Pr., 1995) at 46.

11 In 1888, Pollock and Wright cautioned that "[t]he whole terminology of the subject is still very loose and unsettled in the books, and the reader cannot be too strongly warned that careful attention must in every case be paid to the context": *supra*, note 5, at 28. Lamentably, this remains sage advice. For example, the terms possession and custody are sometimes treated as synonyms (and sometimes not).

12 See, *e.g.*, *Wiebe v. Lepp* (1974) 46 D.L.R. (3d) 441 (Man.C.A.). See further N.E. Palmer, *Bailment*, 2nd ed. (Sydney: Law Book Co., 1991) ch. 7, especially at 458*ff*, where exceptions to this general rule are discussed.

13 Therefore, it should be possible to apply this reasoning to an independent contractor, over whom the hirer maintains supervision: see *Allison Concrete Ltd. v. Canadian Pacific Ltd.* (1973) 40 D.L.R. (3d) 237 (B.C.S.C.).

that the employer then has an immediate right to possession. This interpretation would normally apply if a chattel were handed over to an independent contractor, say, for repair. Furthermore, a transfer for a fixed term (as in the case of a six-month car lease) reserves in the owner, not possession, but a postponed right to possession. I think that these descriptions accord more with common sense than does the adoption of the confusing custody-possession dichotomy.

3. ACQUISITION OF TITLE BY POSSESSION: SQUATTERS

(a)   introduction

In the introductory chapter it was noted that first occupancy can serve as a basis for allocating private property rights among rival claimants.[14] For example, the common law provides that title to wild animals vests in those taking possession; even hot pursuit is insufficient to confer ownership rights.[15] As a means of promoting the control of animals, the right conferred is qualified, for title is lost if the animal escapes. (Incidentally, for domestic animals, title is absolute, as it is for other chattels.) An *apparent* exception to the idea of qualified title to wild animals is made in the case of animals that have *animus revertendi* (literally, the intention to return), which is assumed to exist when the animal shows a habit of returning. Beamish Murdoch explained the basic rule and this refinement as follows:

> If an animal naturally wild, has been partly tamed, or has been restrained or imprisoned, and regain its natural liberty and habits, the right of property in it ceases. But although it leave its place of confinement or rest, and wander abroad, yet if it is in the habit of returning periodically to its master, it is regarded as . . . property still.[16]

In fact, in my view the *animus revertendi* concept is fully consistent with the general rule, because an animal with a propensity to return can be thought of as remaining in the constructive possession of the capturer. This aspect of the rule, like the main principle, is designed to induce owners to tame and control.[17]

Possession may also serve as a source of title to realty through the law of adverse possession, sometimes referred to colloquially as squatters' rights. Under these principles the right of the true owner (or the paper title holder) to sue may be statute-barred against a person who has been in adverse possession of that land for a specified period. In Alberta, for example, the period is ten years.[18] In most jurisdictions, the effect of the running of the full time is to extinguish the title of

---

14 See Part 3(g), Chapter 1.

15 *Pierson v. Post*, 3 Caines 175 (S.C.N.Y., 1805). Compare the special rules that developed in Newfoundland in relation to the seal hunt, as described in *Power v. Kennedy* (1884) 7 Nfld.R. 34 (S.C.). See generally B. Welling, *Property in Things in the Common Law Tradition* (Gold Coast, Qd.: Scribblers Pub., 1996) at 59*ff.*

16 B. Murdoch, *Epitome of the Laws of Nova Scotia* (Halifax: Joseph Howe, 1832-3) vol. 3, at 3.

17 Accord Welling, *supra*, note 15, at 76-7. See *contra* Note, 12 Minn.L.Rev. 172 (1927-8).

18 *Limitations Act*, S.A. 1996, c. L-15.1, subs. 3(1), (4). In some jurisdictions the period is longer: see, *e.g.*, *Statute of Limitations*, R.S.P.E.I. 1988, c. S-7, s. 16 (20-year period required).

the paper title holder, giving the adverse possessor the best claim to the land. Even before the full expiration of the period the squatter's interest is not merely incipient: it can found an action in trespass against a subsequent possessor, and it can be transferred.[19] The basis for such a rule is a proposition that echoes throughout the general law of property: as against a wrongdoer, possession is title.[20] Therefore, in an action for the recovery of land the plaintiff may rely on his or her prior possession as the basis for the suit, even if that possession was wrongfully acquired.

Extraordinary as the notion of title acquisition through long periods of occupancy may seem, it has a long pedigree in the common law and it is alive and well in most of Canada. One of its curious features is that it protects not first occupancy, but *last*: it provides a means of eradicating antecedent claims in favour of recent possessors. As a result, a person who has paid handsomely for a parcel of real estate may forfeit title to an interloper. So dramatic – even subversive – a result seems to demand a compelling rationale.

(b) the stated functions of adverse possession

The purpose of the law of adverse possession has been explained on a number of grounds. At root, it is merely one aspect of the basic rules concerning the limitation of actions that work to bar the initiation of stale legal claims. Adverse possession arises when no action has been commenced against a trespasser during the statutory period of time allowed for a suit to be filed. The policy is straightforward: delays can prejudice the preparation of a defence (witnesses may die, evidence may no longer be available, *etc.*). Therefore, a limit is placed on the right to commence legal proceedings. The loss of the right to sue is tied to the existence of a proprietary entitlement. This is because, as Jeremy Bentham maintained, without the law, property rights vanish.[21] Similarly, the laying to rest of old disputes can serve as a means of proving that a vendor holds good title. This 'quieting of titles' function can be performed because an owner who has enjoyed possession for an extended time can sell a plot of land knowing that defects in the paper title can be cured by the assertion of possessory rights against any unknown prior owners.[22]

A justification sometimes advanced is that a paper title holder is prompted to take positive action to work or occupy the lands in order to limit the risk that the property might be lost to an adverse claimant. Therefore, the rules of adverse possession reward the squatter who uses the property, and penalize the holder of the paper title for his or her failure to have done so. I have never found this to be

---

19 See *Asher v. Whitlock* (1865) L.R. 1 Q.B. 1.

20 *Freeman v. Allen* (1866) 6 N.S.R. 293 (S.C. *in banco*).

21 See Part 2(a), Chapter 1.

22 The comfort is only partial, however, since adverse possession is not necessarily inconsistent with the continuation of some property rights, such as easements and future interests. See M. Dockray, ''Why Do We Need Adverse Possession?'', [1985] Conv. 272, at 281, n. 30, and *Midanic v. Gross*, [1957] O.W.N. 35 (C.A.); *Teis v. Ancaster (Town), infra*, note 52. *Cf. Johnston v. Jones* (1975) 10 N.B.R. (2d) 520 (S.C.). Easements are discussed in Chapter 10; future interests are dealt with in Chapter 7.

a satisfactory explanation. If this is a rationale of adverse possession then it can be seen as promoting exploitation at the expense of resource preservation. Is this still a sound policy objective? Fears that the law of adverse possession can undermine private conservationist practices by rewarding the exploitive interloper have prompted at least one call for a rule that excludes the operation of the doctrine for wilderness holdings.[23]

Moreover, the reward-penalty explanation seems at once a harsh and ineffective mechanism to invoke to further the aim of promoting productivity. It is harsh because the penalty for non-use is tantamount to private expropriation, by a squatter, without compensation.[24] At the same time, the means of avoidance are quite minimal, since all that one must do to prevent a loss is to sue the squatter or occasionally assert title in some appropriate way. Therefore, the goal of promoting land use may not be achieved.[25] And the premise that this rationale promotes efficiency may be misguided: "the presumption that land left idle by its owner is not being used optimally is not valid, given that the value of land is often maximized by waiting for the optimal time to develop".[26] Whether the rules encourage development by squatters is also a dubious proposition. Charles Callahan has doubted that the law of adverse possession would prompt development:

> Of course I don't *know*, and, I suggest neither do you; but my hunch is that it will not do so. If we suppose a person with an urge to use someone else's land, and who is deterred from doing so by the possible consequences, will [this] reluctance be overcome by the knowledge that, if [she] gets away with it for a sufficiently long period, [she] will be in the clear?[27]

Slightly more convincing, from my point of view, than the promotion-of-productivity reasoning *per se*, is the idea that the rule protects the settled expectations of an adverse possessor who has acted on the assumption that her occupation will not be disturbed. The crux of this argument is that "[l]ong dormant claims have often more of cruelty than of justice in them".[28] This may be a fitting rationale when the possessor has made lasting improvements mistakenly believing that she holds the paper title. That might occur when a sale is made under a

---

23 J.G. Sprankling, "An Environmental Critique of Adverse Possession", 79 Cornell L.Rev. 816 (1994).

24 The idea that the law of adverse possession should be reformed to provide that the adverse claimant would be required to make a compensatory payment to the true owner before being awarded title is assessed in T.W. Merrill, "Property Rules, Liability Rules, and Adverse Possession", 79 Nw.U.L.Rev. 1122 (1984-5).

25 If this is a reason for the rule, it is severely undermined by the test of inconsistent use, discussed in Part 3(c), *infra*. It has also been suggested that the promotion of the productive use of the land has rarely influenced the application of the doctrine of adverse possession: Dockray, *supra*, note 22, at 276-7. See also C.C. Callahan, *Adverse Possession* (Columbus: Ohio St.U.P., 1961) at 92.

26 A.J. Miceli & C.F. Sirmans, "An Economic Theory of Adverse Possession", 15 Int.Rev.L. & Econ. 161 (1995) at 161. *Cf.* H. Gensler, "Property Law as an Optimal Economic Foundation", 35 Washburn L.J. 50 (1995) at 56-6.

27 Callahan, *supra*, note 25, at 92.

28 *A'Court v. Cross* (1825) 3 Bing. 329, at 332-3, 130 E.R. 540, at 541 (*per* Best C.J.). See also J.W. Singer, "The Reliance Interest in Property", 40 Stan.L.Rev. 611 (1988) at 665*ff*; M.J. Radin, "Time, Possession, and Alienation", 64 Wash.U.L.Q. 739 (1987) at 746.

fraudulent document of title, or when a fence is wrongly placed, so that the owner of Blackacre has been enjoying a strip of land that is actually part of Whiteacre.[29] Here, the law of adverse possession allows the *de jure* (legal) and *de facto* (actual) positions to be aligned. This type of situation, *i.e.*, squatting based on an honest mistake as to one's rights, still seems to occur. This explanation of the law of adverse possession comports with the efficiency-based theory that the law should protect good faith reliance on boundary errors. By fixing a period of time (say, ten years), the law encourages the would-be squatter to take precautions before investing in the property, while also limiting the true owner's ability to take advantage of any improvements that the adverse possessor might have made to the property:

> According to this theory, the objective of the doctrine is, first, to induce landowners to avoid boundary errors prior to making nonsalvageable investments in their land, and second, to induce 'victims' of errors, when they occur, to correct them in a timely fashion.[30]

In some jurisdictions the law of adverse possession has been abolished for lands under Torrens (or land titles) registration.[31] Torrens and similar land titles systems endeavour to provide a government-created record of all (or nearly all) interests over a given parcel of land. It is thought that allowing possessory claims to accrue tarnishes the principle that the register should be a mirror of all existing rights. Moreover, it might seem that the existence of Torrens registration removes some of the concerns that adverse possession addresses, such as the fear of stale claims being launched after evidence has disappeared. The register is supposed to tell the full story of who owns what.

But disputes may still occur under a land titles system. Some Torrens systems do not guarantee that the physical description in the certificate of title is accurate. Therefore a registered owner of misdescribed land may lose title to the wrongly described portion. One way for a registered owner to retain title despite the presence of a mistake as to the boundary is for that person to demonstrate that the disputed land was adversely possessed. In sum, for boundary errors adverse possession can still serve to quiet titles.[32] As a result, in certain jurisdictions the doctrine of adverse possession has been integrated into the Torrens system. This can be accomplished by allowing a squatter to acquire title by long-standing

---

29 See *Beaudoin v. Aubin* (1981) 33 O.R. (2d) 604, 21 R.P.R. 78, 125 D.L.R. (3d) 277 (H.C.); *Lutz v. Kawa* (1980) 13 Alta.L.R. (2d) 8, 15 R.P.R. 40, 112 D.L.R. (3d) 271 (C.A.). See also *Wood v. Gateway of Uxbridge Properties Inc.* (1990) 75 O.R. (2d) 769, 14 R.P.R. (2d) 262 (Gen.Div.) and the authorities cited there. See *contra Kosman v. Lapointe* (1977) 1 R.P.R. 119 (Ont.H.C.), criticized in A. Knox, Annotation (1977) 1 R.P.R. 120. In some jurisdictions, there is an alternative remedy for cases in which improvements are made on the land of another: see Part 3(a), Chapter 3.

30 Miceli & Sirmans, *supra*, note 26, at 170.

31 See, *e.g.*, *Land Titles Act*, R.S.O. 1990, c. L.5, sub. 51(1).

32 Adverse possession can put to rest other claims that Torrens will not. In Alberta, a person who obtains an imperfect title by gift may be defeated by a prior unregistered interest holder under the Torrens rules. Also, a purchaser who fraudulently acquires title under Torrens will not have an indefeasible interest under that system, but could nevertheless, in time, run out the clock against the defrauded owner.

occupation, while recognizing at the same time that such an interest will not bind a *bona fide* purchase for value without notice of the adverse claim. If, for example, after a period of possession has continued for nine years, the property is sold and the new owner registers, the accumulated period is wiped out. The squatter is therefore obliged to file a caveat to protect his or her possessory claim to preserve that interest against new owners. Of course, this act is likely to provoke a response, once notice of the caveat is sent to the paper title owner.[33]

(c)   the basic doctrinal elements[34]

A person asserting a squatter's right must have an intention to possess (*animus possidendi*) and must demonstrate the requisite *factum*. The degree of physical control needed to maintain an adverse claim reveals the malleability of the possession concept and the manner in which its definition is informed by policy considerations. To succeed, the acts of possession must be open and notorious, adverse, exclusive, peaceful (not by force), actual (generally[35]), and continuous. If any one of these elements is missing, at any stage during the statutory period, no rights against the paper owner can be successfully asserted. The precise nature of the required acts will depend on the type of property, so that the demanded level of control will be different for scrub land, farmlands, cottage property, or a residential lot.

In general, the squatter must use the property as an owner might.[36] Looked at another way, the adverse use must be such as to put the paper owner on notice that a cause of action has arisen. After all, the doctrine is based on the failure to take action within the limitation period, and therefore time should not run unless it is fair to hold a delay against the owner. This is reflected in the requirement that the occupation must be open and notorious, and not clandestine.[37] The adverse possessor must send out a clarion call to the owner, who, if listening, should realize that something is awry. If the adverse possession continues, the owner must commence an action within the limitation period to avoid being statute-

---

33 See further *Boulding v. Grove* (1998) 235 A.R. 72 (Q.B.) applying, with some reticence (at 75-6), the decision in *Lutz v. Kawa, supra*, note 29. The Australian State of New South Wales originally did not allow adverse possession over Torrens land, effective as against the registered proprietor, but the law was reversed in 1979: see now *Real Property Act, 1900*, ss. 45b-45k. See further P. Butt, *Land Law*, 3rd ed. (Sydney: Law Book, 1996) at 835*ff*. In Alberta, the *Land Titles Act*, R.S.A. 1980, c. L-5, allows for squatters' claims, but it has been recommended that this be abolished: Alberta Institute of Law Research & Reform, *Limitations* (Edmonton: A.I.L.R.R., 1986). This proposal was withdrawn from the final report; a separate study of the question was suggested: Alberta Law Reform Institute, *Limitations* (Edmonton: A.L.R.I., 1989) at 39.

34 See further S. Petersson, "Something for Nothing: The Law of Adverse Possession in Alberta" (1992) 30 Alta.L.Rev. 1291.

35 In some circumstances, constructive possession will suffice: see the text accompanying note 41, *infra*.

36 *Powell v. McFarlane* (1977) 38 P. & C.R. 452 (Ch.D.). See also *Taylor v. Willigar* (1979) 99 D.L.R. (3d) 118, 32 N.S.R. (2d) 11, 54 A.P.R. 11 (C.A.) referring to *Elliott v. Jardine* (1960) 45 M.P.R. 104 (N.S.C.A.).

37 The element of openness was missing in *Lundrigans Ltd. v. Prosper* (1982) 132 D.L.R. (3d) 727, 38 Nfld. & P.E.I.R. 10, 108 A.P.R. 10 (Nfld.C.A.).

barred. The criterion of notoriety, which means that the possession was known in the locale, does not appear to be a separate element. Instead, it seems that possession which is notorious serves to support a conclusion that the presence of the squatter was sufficiently 'open'.[38] One must bear in mind that the owner need not actually be aware that an adverse claim is afoot. Constructive notice will suffice. To use language now found in relation to the law governing limitations generally, the acts of the squatter must be discoverable. By the same token, if the owner does know of the presence of the squatter, this too should be enough to start the clock, even if in some objective sense the open or notorious aspects are disputable on the facts.

In appropriate circumstances intermittent use will be treated as meeting the requirement of continuity.[39] One would not normally expect that a non-winterized cottage in northern Alberta would be used by its owner year-round. Moreover, the continuity requirement is not breached if squatter A sells the inchoate possessory title to B, who then runs out the remainder of the period. In fact, curiously, this passing of the possession baton need not be consensual. If A is displaced by B, or (it seems) if B merely enters the land on A's departure, B can enjoy the time previously accumulated. A's time may be 'tacked' onto the continuing possession of B.[40]

When the squatter has entered without a paper title to back up his or her right to be there, only actual or pedal possession (*pedis possessio*) will suffice. Therefore, possession of a portion of the property will not confer rights over the whole parcel. However, when entry is made under colour of right, typically under a defective grant, actual possession of only a part will be enough to put the squatter into constructive possession of the entire tract covered by the faulty document.[41] Taken at face value, the requirement of pedal or actual possession means very little; at best it begs the question of what amounts — ever — to actual possession of land. There always seems to be some element of fiction when the core idea of possession is applied to realty. Still, the distinction between pedal and constructive possession, however fuzzy its borders, at least demonstrates that some significantly different quality of occupation is demanded in these two circumstances.

---

38 See *Newfoundland v. Collingwood* (1996) 1 R.P.R. (3d) 233 (Nfld.C.A.) at 240, where Cameron J.A. considered whether the possession was ''so notorious as to affect the level of openness required''.

39 See, *e.g.*, *Smith Estate v. Beals* (1990) 14 R.P.R. (2d) 34, 99 N.S.R. (2d) 67, 270 A.P.R. 67 (T.D.). But compare the finding in *Corkum v. Nash* (1990) 71 D.L.R. (4th) 390, 98 N.S.R. (2d) 364, 263 A.P.R. 364 (T.D.) affirmed (1991), 87 D.L.R. (4th) 127, 109 N.S.R. (2d) 331, 297 A.P.R. 331 (C.A.).

40 *Mulcahy v. Curramore Pty. Ltd.*, [1974] 2 N.S.W.L.R. 464 (C.A.).

41 See further *Mason v. Mason Estate* (1999) 176 N.S.R. (2d) 321, 538 A.P.R. 321 (C.A.). *Conrad v. Nova Scotia (Attorney-General)* (1994) 136 N.S.R. (2d) 170 (C.A.). But see *Re Ellis* (1997) 154 Nfld. & P.E.I.R. 271, 479 A.P.R. 271 (Nfld.T.D.). Apparently, actual possession of the surface does not give rise to constructive possession of the mines and minerals below, even if the faulty title purports to embrace both: see *Kaup v. Imperial Oil Ltd.*, [1962] S.C.R. 170, 32 D.L.R. (2d) 112, 37 W.W.R. 193. Note, however, that the authorities relating to constructive possession under a colour of right were not addressed in *Kaup*.

The requirement of adversity means the squatter must not be in possession with the permission of the owner.[42] And occupation cannot be adverse if the superior right of the true owner is acknowledged. However, an adverse claim may germinate out of a previously permitted presence, such as where a grant of a non-possessory right-of-way is so overused as to amount to an assumption of full control. Even a person entitled to be on the land as a co-owner may acquire a claim, as an adverse possessor, against other persons with whom the right to possession is shared. However, a heavy onus rests with the claimant to prove that the acts being relied upon are not referable to the permitted use, or, in the case of co-owners, that the person in possession intends to exclude the other co-owner(s).[43]

There must also be a dispossession of, or a discontinuance of occupation by, the true owner: the squatter must have *exclusive* possession. This element emphasizes not only the actions of the claimant but also those of the true owner, and it is patent that the degree of control demanded from an owner is far less than that which is needed, in the main, to found an adverse claim. The holder of paper title is regarded as being in constructive possession of the entire property when in actual possession of merely one part. Minor acts of dominion by an owner will usually suffice. The exclusivity component also relates to the exercising of control against others on the land. If a parcel is used freely by a variety of individuals, with no apparent control over access, one party might not be able to assert title by adverse possession. Still, if the circumstances suggest that one dominant party allowed others onto the land as an act of hospitality, this may not stand in the way of a claim of exclusive possession.[44] Obviously, the precise facts are crucial in such cases.

The next element is perhaps the most controversial and perplexing feature of the modern law in this area. It has been held that possessory title does not arise unless the squatter is using the land in a way that is inconsistent with the rights of the true owner and with the uses that the owner intends to make of the land. The specific defect in the squatter's position that is produced by the application of this 'test of inconsistent use' (or 'user') is not clear. In England it has been decided that (at common law) when the owner has only an intended future use, the squatter is to be regarded as being on the land under an implied licence, so that the adversity and exclusivity elements are absent.[45] In other words, in the presence of the licence it could not be said that the true owner had either been dispossessed or had discontinued occupation. Criticism of the implied licence theory prompted statutory reform in England, and the governing legislation now

---

42 See further *Robertson v. King Estate* (1999) 243 A.R. 201, [1999] A.J. No. 228 (Q.B.) affirmed (1999) 244 A.R. 379, 209 W.A.C. 379 (C.A.).
43 See *Gorman v. Gorman* (1998) 16 R.P.R. (3d) 173 (Ont.C.A.). See also *Friolet v. Friolet* (1998) 201 N.B.R. (2d) 118, 514 A.P.R. 118 (C.A.).
44 See *Nome 2000 v. Fagerstrom*, 799 P.2d 304 (Alaska S.C., 1990) critiqued in G.M. Clapacs, "When in Nome: Custom, Culture and the Objective Standard in Alaskan Adverse Possession Law", 11 Alaska L.Rev. 301 (1994).
45 *Wallis's Cayton Bay Holiday Camp Ltd. v. Shell-Mex & B.P. Ltd.*, [1975] Q.B. 94, [1974] 3 All E.R. 575, 29 P. & C.R. 214 (C.A.). *Cf. Powell v. McFarlane, supra*, note 36.

provides that a licence is not to be implied merely because the adverse possession does not conflict with the true owner's present or future enjoyment of the land. However, it leaves open the possibility of a finding that a permission was, in fact, given.[46]

This English reform, and the proper scope of the inconsistency test, were considered in *Buckinghamshire County Council v. Moran*,[47] where a narrow view of that test was adopted. At issue was the validity of a claim against a local authority over a vacant lot adjacent to the defendant's home. The defendant and his predecessor in title had used part of the lot as a garden, with full knowledge of the authority's rights. The claim to the lot by the defendant succeeded. The Court rejected the suggestion that an owner who holds land only for a special purpose in the future could never be treated as dispossessed, however drastic the acts of the squatter. However, it was said that the intentions of the owner as to the future, if known to the squatter, can affect the *animus* and place a heavy onus on the squatter to prove an intention to exclude the world at large (including the owner).

The test of inconsistent use has taken root in Canada through the Ontario case of *Keefer v. Arillotta*.[48] There, the claimant failed to demonstrate that land over which he had been granted an easement had been taken through adverse possession. He did succeed in acquiring title to a portion of the disputed land on which a garage had been placed. The element of inconsistent use was viewed as relevant to the *animus possidendi*: it must be shown that there was "an intention to exclude the owner from such uses as the owner wants to make of his property".[49] The owner's intentions were also considered relevant to the determination of the *factum* of adverse possession: the "[a]cts relied on as dispossessing the true owner must be inconsistent with the form of enjoyment of the property intended by the true owner".[50]

The *Keefer* ruling gives a wider application to the test than now exists under English law, as represented by the statutory reform and the holding in *Moran*. Indeed, it might appear, in view of *Keefer,* that time does not run against an owner who leaves land fallow with a view to future development or sale.[51] If taken

---

46 *Limitation Act, 1980*, Sch. 1, para. 8(4).

47 [1989] 2 All E.R. 225 (C.A.).

48 (1976) 13 O.R. (2d) 680, 72 D.L.R. (3d) 182 (C.A.). See also *Leigh v. Jack* (1879) 5 Ex.D. 264 (C.A.); *Williams Brothers Direct Supply Ltd. v. Raftery*, [1958] 1 Q.B. 159, [1957] 3 All E.R. 593 (C.A.); *Wallis's Cayton Bay Holiday Camp Ltd. v. Shell-Mex & B.P. Ltd., supra*, note 45. But see *Teis v. Ancaster (Town), infra*, note 52.

49 *Supra*, note 48, at 193 D.L.R. (*per* Wilson J.A., as she then was).

50 *Ibid.* See also *Wood v. Gateway of Uxbridge Properties Inc., supra*, note 29, which treats the requirement of inconsistent user as (a) based on an implied licence; and (b) negativing the requisite intention. Compare *Masidon Investments Ltd. v. Ham* (1984) 45 O.R. (2d) 563, 31 R.P.R. 200 (C.A.) where the Court treats the test as affecting the requirement that the true owner be dispossessed (and therefore relating to the *factum* of possession). Laskin J.A. suggested in *Teis. v. Ancaster (Town), infra*, note 52, at 224 O.R., that "[t]he test of inconsistent use focuses on the intention of the owner or paper title holder, not on the intention of the claimant".

51 See also B. Bucknall, "Two Roads Diverged: Recent Decisions on Possessory Title" (1984) 22 Osgoode Hall L.J. 375.

seriously, this element constricts the ambit of the doctrine of adverse possession severely, given that landowners could claim such a use for virtually all land held. As an asset that almost inevitably appreciates in the long run, this type of future use is often, if not invariably, present.

However, this precondition has not, seemingly, been read that broadly. Not all claims will fail in the face of the test of inconsistent use, because in *Keefer* itself an adverse possession claim succeeded in relation to the area on which the garage was situated. Furthermore, it has been held that the test does not apply if there is a mutual mistake as to the correct location of the boundary line. This is because:

> It makes no sense to apply the test of inconsistent use when both the paper title holder and the claimant are mistaken about their respective rights. The application of the test would defeat adverse possession claims in cases of mutual mistake, yet permit such claims to succeed in cases of knowing trespass. Thus applied, the test would reward the deliberate squatter and punish the innocent trespasser. Policy considerations support a contrary conclusion. The law should protect good faith reliance on boundary errors or at least the settled expectations of innocent adverse possessors who have acted on the assumption that their occupation will not be disturbed. Conversely, the law has always been less generous when a knowing trespasser seeks its aid to dispossess the rightful owner.[52]

In the end, then, the test of inconsistent use can serve to "strengthen the hand of the true owner in the face of an adverse possession claim by a knowing trespasser",[53] while allowing for the doctrine of adverse possession to apply in the case of an honest error. An analysis of reported American jurisprudence suggests that a belief in the *bona fides* of the occupancy was the common denominator of most successful squatters' claims.[54] Canadian law may be heading in the same direction.

Alberta has recently revised its law of adverse possession, as part of a general reform of its limitations rules. The ten-year rule for commencing an action to recover land has been retained, but two curious changes have been made. First, the repealed statute declared that the title of the true owner was *extinguished* after ten years.[55] There is no counterpart under the new law. It was once the case in English law that the effect of the running of the period was to destroy remedies but not rights, so that if one were able to reclaim the land peaceably, title could be reasserted.[56] Is this now the law in Alberta? Until an amendment is introduced, it is possible, and preferable, to imply that an extinguishment results. Second, the

---

52 *Teis v. Ancaster (Town)* (1997) 13 R.P.R. (3d) 55, 35 O.R. (3d) 216 (C.A.) at 225 O.R. (*per* Laskin J.A.). See further B. Bucknall, "*Teis v. Ancaster*: Knowledge, the Lack of Knowledge and the Running of the Possessory Title Period" (1997) 13 R.P.R. (3d) 68.

53 *Teis v. Ancaster, supra,* note 52, at 226 O.R.

54 R. Hemholz, "Adverse Possession and Subjective Intent", 61 Wash.U.L.Q. 331 (1983). This article set off a debate between Professors Hemholz and Cunningham: see, *e.g.*, R.A. Cunningham, "More on Adverse Possession: A Rejoinder to Professor Hemholz", 64 Wash.U.L.Q. 1167 (1986) and the other articles cited there.

55 *Limitation of Actions Act,* R.S.A. 1980, c. L-15, s. 44 [repealed].

56 See further R. Megarry & H.W.R. Wade, *The Law of Real Property,* 5th ed. (London: Stevens & Sons, 1984) at 1050.

new Act provides that in all situations to which the law applies (not just those pertaining to land), fraudulent concealment *suspends* the operation of the limitation period.[57] Under general principles of adverse possession, concealment would negative the openness criterion, and as a result would serve to *snap*, not suspend, the running of the period. I am not convinced that these changes are beneficial.

(d)   chattels

Imagine that your precious A.Y. Jackson landscape was stolen years ago, only to reappear in a local art gallery. The right to sue for the recovery of personal property may be barred through the passage of time. Some jurisdictions have provided explicitly that title is extinguished once time has completely run.[58] However, in others, including Alberta, there is no express provision for the extinguishment of title at the end of the period. As we saw in relation to the new law in Alberta concerning land, this suggests that though an action may not be brought, a legally recognized right of recaption or self-help may still exist. If so, even though the right to sue has been barred, the true owner retains the ability to recover the goods.[59] Alternatively, one might imply that title is extinguished, even absent a statutory provision declaring that result. There is American case law which holds that title is lost once the period has expired.[60]

Alberta's law now provides a general two-year period, which is applicable to action for the recovery of personal property, and which is triggered by the discoverability of the cause of action. This is subject to a sunset clause. generally, even absent discoverability, the action must be launched within ten years of the wrongdoing.[61] In relation to personalty, some problems of application can arise. For example, consider a case in which goods are wrongfully taken by A, but later acquired (somehow) by B. Assume that any action against A is now statute-barred, but not against B (but that title is not totally extinguished). One might even assume that B came upon the property after the right to sue A had expired. The original owner arguably retains the right to immediate possession of the goods *vis-à-vis* B, and so can sue, even though no remedy exists against A. If that is so, the chance to bring an action is never totally lost. This situation is contemplated by Manitoba's statute of limitations: an action against B would be barred after six years dating from the conversion by A.[62] Alberta's law is silent on the issue. Such a *lacuna* need not preclude the possibility that a court would recognize the tacking of consecutive periods of possession by parties in privity, such that time is calculated as from the initial taking (as in Manitoba).[63]

---

57 *Limitations Act*, S.A. 1996, c. L-15.1, sub. 4(1).

58 See, *e.g.*, *Limitation Act*, R.S.B.C. 1996, c. 266, sub. 9(2) in relation to an action for the conversion or detention of goods.

59 Consistent with this view is *Barberree v. Bilo* (1991) 84 Alta.L.R. (2d) 216, 126 A.R. 121 (Q.B.). See also *Miller v. Dell*, [1891] 1 Q.B. 468 (C.A.).

60 See, *e.g.*, *O'Keeffe v. Snyder*, 416 A.2d 862 (N.J.S.C., 1980).

61 *Limitations Act*, S.A. 1996, c. L-15.1, sub. 3(1).

62 *Limitations of Actions Act*, R.S.M. 1987, c. L150, sub. 54(2).

63 See, *e.g.*, *O'Keeffe v. Snyder*, *supra*, note 60. As to other aspects of the American law on this

It might be sensible to have different rules for realty and personalty. Land does not disappear, but chattels can, and so the failure to bring suit or regain possession of a stolen chattel might have been beyond the control of the true owner, who may well have been continuously searching for the missing or purloined item. However, the problems of permitting litigation after lengthy delays apply equally to disputes over chattels, and there is value in quieting title to personal property after the passage of some stated time, just as there is for land. It is perhaps even more necessary to have such a mechanism for chattels since there is no general registry of ownership of chattels that can be examined to determine whether or not the property is subject to a superior ownership claim. The full extinguishment of title would also serve to prevent the vigilantist action of self-help. When the ability to sue is lost, self-help is the owner's last hope if the goods are ever to be recouped. It is doubtful whether it is a sound policy to allow this right to endure forever.[64]

4.   THE RELATIVE NATURE OF TITLE: FINDERS[65]

(a)   generally

The law of finding is not an area of pressing practical concern.[66] Nonetheless, it provides a useful setting in which to explore the meaning of possession and the general nature of title to property. Prior to the advent of systems of land registration and recording, possession served as the primary basis for demonstrating title. The law protected the proven prior possession of a claimant (or the prior possession of those through whom this party had derived title). Apart from cases that fall within the province of the law of adverse possession, that evidentiary function has been largely eclipsed for land in Canada, given that every tract of patented land appears on some form of register. However, prior possession still serves as the principal mode of proving title to personal property. There is no general registry for personalty; and a register would not be feasible, or desirable, given the transaction costs inherent in attempting to keep that system current. The law of finders demonstrates the relative nature of title in Canadian property law[67] and the extent to which the law will protect prior possession, even when wrongfully acquired.

---

topic, see P. Gerstenblith, ''The Adverse Possession of Personal Property'', 37 Buff.L.Rev. 119 (1988-89).

64   See also J.E. Côté, ''Prescription of Title to Chattels'' (1968-69) 7 Alta.L.Rev. 93. The restrictions imposed on the right of self-help are addressed in Ontario Law Reform Commission, *Study Paper on Wrongful Interference With Goods* (Toronto: A.G. (Ont.), 1989) at ch. 8, *passim*.

65   See further E.R. Cohen, ''The Finders Cases Revisited'', 48 Tex.L.Rev. 1001 (1970); Welling, *supra*, note 15, at Part III.

66   But see D.C. Hoath, ''Some Conveyancing Implications of 'Finding' Disputes'', [1990] Conv. 348; J.W.A. Thornley, ''Vendor's Title to Chattels Found on Land After its Sale to Purchaser'', [1969] C.L.J. 28. See also R. Matas, ''Officer Can Keep $1-Million Windfall'', *Globe & Mail*, December 21, 1999, A1.

67   ''The English law of ownership and possession, unlike that of Roman law, is not a system of identifying absolute entitlement but of priority of entitlement'': *Waverley Borough Council v. Fletcher*, [1996] Q.B. 334 (C.A.) at 345 (*per* Auld L.J.). Canadian law follows the English approach.

Orthodoxy has it that the finder of a chattel acquires a title that is good against the entire world except for the true owner.[68] This statement is a little misleading. Not all found property is necessarily presently owned. A recovered item may have been abandoned by a previous owner. An abandonment involves the converse of possession-taking: there must be an intention to relinquish title, that is, an indifference as to the fate of a chattel, coupled with sufficient acts of divestment.[69] It is self-evident that a finder of ownerless property can face no superior claim. In addition, it is not only the true owner who may assert a prior right, but anyone with a valid and subsisting entitlement, including, theoretically, some previous finder.[70] Therefore, a more accurate general proposition is that a finder acquires title good against the world, except for those with a continuing antecedent claim.[71] This is a general statement about the relative rights of possessors and owners.

Conferring property rights on a person lucky enough to find an object that belongs to someone else may seem odd. It might be suggested that giving title to a finder rewards those who have brought found goods back into social use. It can also facilitate the return of an object to its rightful owner because the finder assumes a responsibility to take reasonable steps to try to return the item.[72] Looked at from a very different perspective, one can see that it might be problematic *not* to confer title. The failure to treat a finder as an 'owner' would presumably mean that no civil or even criminal wrong would be committed by taking the object *from* a finder. Such a rule would encourage the trespassing of found goods – a "free-for-all", to quote from a relatively recent case.[73] Moreover, if a finder obtains no rights, the chain of title thereafter would be equally precarious. Generally, a person without title can confer no greater right.[74] This problem is aggravated by the fact that there is no means of ensuring that any item obtained was not previously lost. These concerns have led to the odd-sounding proposition that even a trespassing or felonious finder has a title that the law will protect. Hence, in *Bird v. Fort Francis*[75] a young boy found money that had been secreted under

---

68 "[T]he finder of a jewel, though he does not by such finding acquire an absolute property or ownership has such a property as will enable him to keep it against all but the rightful owner": *Armory v. Delamirie* (1722) 1 Stra. 505, 93 E.R. 664 (*per* Pratt C.J.).

69 See generally *Stewart v. Gustafson* (1998) 171 Sask.R. 27, [1999] 4 W.W.R. 695 (Q.B.) and the literature and cases referred to there. See also A. Hudson, "Abandonment" in N. Palmer & E. McKendrick, eds., *Interests in Goods*, 2nd ed. (London: L.L.P., 1998) ch. 23. It has been held that garbage placed near the road for pick up and disposal is not abandoned property: *Williams v. Phillips* (1957) 41 C.A.R. 5 (Div.Ct.).

70 See, *e.g.*, *Clark v. Maloney*, 3 Har. 68 (Del.S.C., 1940) reproduced in E. Fraser, ed., *Cases and Readings on Property* (Chicago: Foundation Pr., 1944) vol. 2, at 52.

71 *Trachuk v. Olinek*, [1996] 4 W.W.R. 137, 36 Alta.L.R. (3d) 225, 177 A.R. 225 (Q.B.).

72 This and other duties are discussed in *Parker v. British Airways Board*, [1982] Q.B. 1004, [1982] 1 All E.R. 834 (C.A.).

73 *Ibid.* at 1010 Q.B. (*per* Donaldson L.J., as he then was) citing the Ontario decision in *Bird v. Fort Francis (Town)*, [1949] O.R. 292, [1949] 2 D.L.R. 791 (H.C.). The Court in *Parker* described the title of the dishonest taker as a 'frail' one, but did not explain the nature of this frailty.

74 See also Part 1, Chapter 12.

75 *Supra*, note 73.

a house. He had been trespassing at the time of the find. No 'true owner' having come forward, the boy claimed the money. His right to the property was upheld.

Precisely how far the law will go to protect the wrongful finder is not very clear. The Australian High Court has rejected the idea that an action lies for the failure to return contraband goods, the possession of which is itself a crime.[76] Similarly, in the British Columbia case of *Baird*[77] the right of the police to refuse to return money and travellers cheques that had been lawfully seized from the plaintiff was upheld. In that instance, no prosecution was ever launched, though the plaintiff admitted to having obtained the items illegally. The Court of Appeal applied the maxim *ex turpi causa non oritur actio* (an action cannot be founded on wrongdoing) to deny relief to the plaintiff. While the case did not involve a finding as such, the Court recognized that analogous issues arose. In fact, *Bird v. Fort Francis* was distinguished on the ground that "it was a kind of finders keepers case where there was not that degree of criminality or culpable immorality necessary to support an *ex turpi causa* plea".[78] Just where the dividing line between these two cases actually is to be found was not explained.

Putting to one side the problems associated with claims tinged by wrong-doing, some basic principles can be described. A finder is placed in a position inferior to that of subsisting prior claims, but superior to those arising afterwards. Timing is central and the jurisprudence on this subject has been largely concerned with settling priority questions of this type. The most notorious examples of competing claims concern chattels found by A on the land of B. In these contests, the owner of the land may claim antecedent *constructive* possession of the lost item by virtue of occupation of the property on which some item was found. The person discovering the item obviously relies on his or her *actual* possession of the object. In an area of the law that is notorious for its doctrinal uncertainty, there seems to be little doubt that only one of these two claims will succeed in a given case. A rule of equitable sharing has not been embraced.[79]

If the chattel is imbedded in the soil, the occupier of the premises will normally prevail over the finder. One way to explain this result is to treat the object as a fixture, and, therefore, as part of the realty itself.[80] However, the fixtures test is useful only as an analogue, because in the case of lost items lodged in the ground, the application of the test of objective intention that is used in the analysis of fixtures is totally artificial.[81] Moreover, if we accept that the law of fixtures should nevertheless govern, the result is especially drastic. The effect of finding that a chattel has become a fixture is to treat the title to the goods as having

---

76 See *Gollan v. Nugent* (1988) 166 C.L.R. 18 (Aust.H.C.). See also *R. v. MacEwen*, [1947] 2 D.L.R. 62, 87 C.C.C. 401, 19 M.P.R. 171 (P.E.I.S.C.).

77 *Baird v. British Columbia* (1992) 77 C.C.C. (3d) 365 (B.C.C.A.).

78 *Ibid.* at 369 (*per* Gibbs J.A.).

79 For the view that joint finders should share ownership, see R.H. Hemholz, "Equitable Division and the Law of Finders", 52 Fordham L.Rev. 313 (1983). Children shared money that they had found stuffed inside a sock in *Keron v. Cashman*, 33 A. 1055 (N.J.Ch., 1896). See also *Edmonds v. Ronella*, 342 N.Y.S.2d. 408 (S.C., 1973).

80 See *Elwes v. Brigg Gas Co.* (1886) 33 Ch.D. 562, [1886-90] All E.R. Rep. 559, at 567 Ch.D.

81 See Part 5(a), Chapter 3.

been subsumed under the title to the realty. If that occurs in the cases of embedded goods, then, on principle, the title of the true owner is lost, at least until, and if, the item is severed.

A second way of supporting the landowner's claim is to think of it as no more than an application of the *cujus est solum* maxim (which was described in Chapter 3[82]). Accordingly, a found object falls within the territorial zone of ownership defined by the maxim. However, this reasoning is a little *too* straight-forward: it does not explain those instances (to be considered shortly) in which items found on the surface of the land go to the finder. One would think that these items would also fall within the maxim's purview. Moreover, it must be shown that the landowner was in occupation of the land at some point during which the item was on the premises if that owner is to be able to show constructive possession of the found object. Ownership alone will not suffice.[83] Perhaps the reason the law favours the landowner when goods are attached to the soil is that in such an instance the finder would often have to disrupt the land in some way that violates the landowner's rights (albeit in some cases these acts of intrusion may be triv-ial). Yet even here the reasoning is not perfect. Presumably the landowner is still to be favoured even when the goods are found by someone who is digging with the blessing of the occupier.[84]

If a chattel is mislaid, not lost, it is said to be in the custody of the owner of the *locus in quo* (the land). This rule appears to draw a distinction between the absent-minded misplacement of an article (mislaid), as opposed to unwittingly dropping it (lost). The operating assumption here is that the rightful owner will retrace his or her steps to that location to look for the mislaid item.[85] Admittedly, the logic of this rule is transparent, given (i) that the determination of whether a chattel is lost or mislaid is often going be difficult; and (ii) the fact that there is no reason to think that the true owner would be more likely to embark on a search when the goods have been placed down rather than dropped. Likewise, when the goods have been cached, not lost, the occupier of the land is generally preferred over the finder.[86]

---

82 See Part 2(a), Chapter 3.

83 *Hannah v. Peel*, [1945] 1 K.B. 509, [1945] 2 All E.R. 288.

84 See *South Staffordshire Water Co. v. Sharman*, [1896] 2 Q.B. 44 [1895-99] All E.R.Rep. 259 (C.A.) where rings were found embedded in mud at the bottom of a pool; the landowner was held to be entitled. Yet another explanation for this rule is advanced in *Waverley Borough Council v. Fletcher*, *supra*, note 67, at 345 (*per* Auld L.J.): "[P]utting aside the borderline case of a recently lost article which has worked its way just under the surface, in the case of an object in the ground its original owner is unlikely in most cases to be there to claim it. The law, therefore, looks for a substitute owner, the possessor of the land in which it is lodged." However, this explanation merely begs the question as to why the owner of the land is the best surrogate owner.

85 *Bridges v. Hawkesworth* (1851) 21 L.J.Q.B. 75, [1843-60] All E.R.Rep. 122.

86 Compare *Kowal v. Ellis*, [1977] 2 W.W.R. 761, 76 D.L.R. (3d) 546 (Man.C.A.) where the finder won despite the conclusion that the found object (a pump) had been cached on the land of the plaintiff. For a brief critique, see S.K. McCallum, "*Kowal v. Ellis*: A Comment" (1979) 28 U.N.B.L.J. 202.

What of the case of a chattel found by A lying unattached on the surface of land occupied by B? This was the situation in the leading case of *Bridges v. Hawkesworth*,[87] where a packet of bills was discovered by a customer on the floor of a shop. The finder succeeded, but the exact basis for this ruling has been the subject of considerable debate.[88] One view is that, as the shopkeeper was unaware of the presence of the bills, the *animus* could not have been formed. Others have suggested that it was the absence of an intention to control the area of the shop where the bills were found that was central. A third position maintains that the lack of actual control over the public area of the shop was the determining factor. The judgment is somewhat opaque on this last point. The Court concluded that "[t]he notes never were in the custody of the [shopkeeper], nor within the protection of his house before they were found, as they would have been had they been intentionally deposited there".[89]

The main principles governing finding were reviewed in *Parker v. British Airways Board*.[90] That concerned a contest over rights to the proceeds from the sale of a gold bracelet found in a boarding lounge at Heathrow Airport. Without directly confronting the conflicting interpretations of *Bridges v. Hawkesworth*, the *ratio decidendi* of that earlier case was taken to be that the unknown presence of the notes could not, alone, confer rights on the landowner.[91] The Airways Board (which had leased the space from Heathrow) did not know of the bracelet, but the decision in *Parker* was not based on that fact alone. Instead it was held that the occupier will prevail when a chattel is discovered in an area over which there is a 'manifest intention' to exercise control over chattels that might be found there. Although airport authorities and their tenants tend to be vigilant about parcels that appear to have been left unattended (especially in Britain), it was found on the facts that the Board lacked the necessary manifest intention to control the lounge area, which was a place of regular public access. Accordingly, the finder won.[92]

The lead judgment in *Parker* dealt with a further permutation. In passing, it was said that when the finder is a trespasser, the landowner will normally be preferred, even if the landowner shows no manifest intention to control.[93] Here, miraculously, the landowner appears to have sufficient possession as against a

---

87 *Supra*, note 85.

88 Several theories as to what the case stands for are canvassed in A.L. Goodhart, "Three Cases on Possession", [1928] C.L.J. 195. Goodhart suggested that the *Hawkesworth* case was wrongly decided. For a critique of Goodhart, and an American realist analysis of the law of finders and the meaning of possession, see J.F. Francis, "Three Cases on Possession – Some Further Observations", 14 St.Louis L.Rev. 11 (1928).

89 *Supra*, note 85, at 124 All E.R.Rep. (*per* Patteson J.).

90 *Supra*, note 72, criticized in S. Roberts, "More Lost Than Found" (1982) 45 Mod.L.Rev. 683.

91 *Supra*, note 72, at 1012 Q.B.

92 See also *Grafstein v. Holme*, [1958] O.R. 296, 12 D.L.R. (2d) 727 (C.A.). Compare *Kowal v. Ellis*, *supra*, note 86, where it was held that a landowner did not have title to a pump found on his land since he did not know of its existence. Is actual knowledge required?

93 *Parker v. British Airways Board, supra*, note 72, at 1009 Q.B. (*per* Donaldson L.J.). The other members of the Court expressed no view on this issue. See further *Webb v. Ireland*, [1988] I.R. 353, where a majority of the Irish Supreme Court endorsed, in *obiter*, the views of Donaldson L.J.

trespasser (but not necessarily against someone else such as the lawful finder in *Parker*). This difference in outcome can be explained by regarding the trespasser rule as postponing possessory rights as a matter of policy. As in all other areas, concepts like possession are purposive instruments and do not demand mechanical application. In the area of finders law, prior possession serves as a convenient way of determining who should prevail – most of the time.

(b)   public lands and historical resources

In general, the basic rules governing finders apply to the state.[94] But there are notable qualifications. Legislation may require that goods found on public property be handed over to the appropriate authorities. Moreover, in England (and probably in Canada) the Crown may claim 'treasure trove' wherever it may be found. Put briefly, treasure trove consists of cached gold and silver in coin, bullion, or manufactured form, the ownership of which is unknown.[95] Though the initial rationale of the Crown prerogative over treasure trove was financial (or at least for the purpose of supplying metals for coinage), this no longer guides how such claims are treated. Prior to 1996, the practice in England was to pay a reward to the finder based on the value of the treasure. Most of these goods were destined for museums. If there was no curatorial interest shown in the items found, they were normally returned to the finder and no reward was offered.[96] The basic approach reflected in these protocols has now been given legislative sanction. Under the English *Treasure Act 1996*,[97] if found treasure has vested in the Crown, and if it is decided that the objects are to be transferred to a museum, the Secretary of State is empowered to provide a reward. The monies may be payable to (a) the finder or any other person involved in the find; (b) the occupier of the land at the time of the find; (c) any person who had an interest in the land at the time, or who has had such an interest at any time since then.[98] I suspect that (contrary to the common law) shared rewards will be granted under the Act.

Obviously, some items that do not fall within the embrace of the treasure trove doctrine may nevertheless be important as cherished and valuable *historical resources* and so should arguably be governed by special finding rules. Sometimes

---

94 *Waverley Borough Council v. Fletcher*, *supra*, note 67.

95 See generally N.E. Palmer, "Treasure Trove and Title to Discovered Antiquities" in N. Palmer & E. McKendrick, eds., *Interests in Goods* (London: L.L.P., 1993) 305, for a discussion of the law and practice prior to the introduction of reforms in 1996. At common law, the treasure must be made substantially of gold or silver: see *Attorney General of the Duchy of Lancaster v. G.E. Overton (Farms) Ltd.*, [1982] Ch. 277 (C.A.). A number of American states have departed from the English rule, and instead favour the treasure hunter: see generally L. Izuel, "Property Owners' Constructive Possession of Treasure Trove: Rethinking the Finders Keepers Rule", 38 U.C.L.A.L.Rev. 1659 (1991). The Crown is also entitled by prerogative to unclaimed shipwrecks: see *Ontario v. Mar-Dive Corp.* (1996) 141 D.L.R. (4th) 577, [1996] O.J. No. 4471 (Gen.Div.).

96 Palmer, "Treasure Trove and Title to Discovered Antiquities", *supra*, note 95, at 314*ff*.

97 C. 24. For an overview of the new law, see J. Marston & L. Ross, "Treasure and Portable Antiquities in the 1990s – Still Chained to the Ghosts of the Past: The Treasure Act 1996", [1997] Conv. 273.

98 S. 10.

historical cultural property might be best held by the state.[99] In the case of Aboriginal treasures perhaps the law should provide that these items belong to an appropriate Aboriginal claimant, whether that be a Band or an individual.[100] Such a claim might succeed anyway under the general law of finders if it can be shown that the claimant is the 'true' owner, or derived title from that owner. However, one can imagine how difficult these claims might be to prove: questions as to whether the goods were abandoned,[101] or whether the standard limitation periods had run their course, would normally arise. It may be that these general rules impede the implementation of a public policy designed to preserve historical treasures. Likewise, the basic finders principles may stand in the way of the restitution of cultural property. As I argued earlier on, these forms of property can advance the 'grouphood' interests of Aboriginal communities in Canada.[102] This is an area of the law that is in dire need of reform.

(c)   the jus tertii defence[103]

In disputes over property, the law is concerned with ascertaining the relative rights of the parties to the contest. This means that a better claim residing in some third person (a *jus tertii*) is, generally speaking, immaterial.[104] In the finders cases it is commonly assumed that there remains a true owner out there somewhere who could trump the claims of the litigants. In a dispute between other rival claimants this is not relevant. As far as the finder is concerned, mere possession is title as against a subsequent wrongful taker. This rule extends beyond finders: it applies to any right founded on possession, such as that of a bailee of goods[105] or an adverse possessor of land. Also, though it is accepted law that a person finding in the course of employment does so for the benefit of the employer, the latter's claim is irrelevant if it is not asserted. This is well illustrated by the case of *Hannah v. Peel*,[106] where a soldier found a brooch stashed on top of a window frame in a house that had been requisitioned during the war. His claim succeeded over the landowner, who had never actually occupied the house. Whether the

---

99 See, *e.g.*, *Historical Resources Act*, R.S.A. 1980, c. H-8 [as am.]. See also P.-L. Tan, "Finders Keepers? Heritage Protection of Found Objects in Queensland" (1994) 11 Environ. & Plan. L.J. 507; M. Lieboff, "Treasure, Objects and Items: Legal Protection of the Archaeological Heritage in England" (1996) 14 Law in Context 91 (part of a special issue entitled "Law and Cultural Heritage").

100 See generally C.E. Bell, "Limitations, Legislation and Domestic Repatriation" (1995) 29 U.B.C.L.Rev. 149. See also *Indian Act*, R.S.C. 1985, c. I-5, s. 91; M.J. Harris, "Who Owns the Pot of Gold at the End of the Rainbow? A Review of the Impact of Cultural Property on Finders and Salvage Laws", 14 Ariz.J.Int. & Comp.L. 223 (1997).

101 See, *e.g.*, *Charrier v. Bell*, 496 So.2d 601 (La.App., 1986).

102 See Part 3(e), Chapter 1.

103 See generally G. Battersby, "The Present Status of the *Jus Tertii* Principle", [1992] Conv. 100; C.D. Baker, "The *Jus Tertii*: a Restatement" (1990) 16 U.Q.L.J. 46; P.S. Atiyah, "A Re-examination of the *Jus Tertii* in Conversion" (1955) 18 Mod.L.Rev. 97; A. Jolly, "The *Jus Tertii* and the Third Man" (1955) 18 Mod.L.Rev. 371.

104 See, *e.g.*, *McDougal v. Smith* (1871) 30 U.C.Q.B. 607.

105 See, *e.g.*, *Thorne v. MacGregor*, [1973] 3 O.R. 54, 35 D.L.R. (3d) 687 (H.C.).

106 *Supra*, note 83.

finding was in the soldier's course of employment (he was on duty at the time) was not considered because the military advanced no claim.[107]

Yet the existence of a *jus tertii* is sometimes germane. When the defendant is a superior claimant,[108] or has acted on the authority of such a person,[109] the tables are turned, for the defendant's rights are then clearly better than those of the plaintiff-finder. Also, if the plaintiff is suing not on the basis of a disruption of possession, but rather by virtue of *a right to possession*, an apparently broader *jus tertii* defence may be available. If the defendant is able to show that this asserted right resides not in the plaintiff but in some third party, the *jus tertii* plea should succeed. While there is some controversy as to the scope of this rule, it is only plausible to accept the plea here if it serves to show that the alleged right of possession on which the plaintiff's action is founded is illusory and cannot stand on its own two feet in the presence of the proved rights of some other party.[110] If, for example, the plaintiff has sold the goods before the lawsuit, the defendant can point to this sale as showing that the plaintiff's right to possession, though once in existence, has been transferred to someone else. The defence should not be available to the defendant who asserts only that some higher right resides with someone – somewhere. Nor should it make any difference that a named third party has a right to possession in addition to the plaintiff,[111] because it is possible for the defendant's misconduct to give rise to a cause of action in favour of both of these parties.

5. TRANSFER OF TITLE THROUGH DELIVERY: GIFTS

(a) introduction

Possession can be central to the passing of title for both land and chattels. In the early common law, land was transferred through a ceremony known as 'livery of seisin' (delivery of possession), which was designed to give notoriety to the transaction.[112] Because land cannot be physically transferred, delivery was accomplished symbolically by the handing over of a twig or a clod of earth on or near the land, ideally in the presence of witnesses. Absent this, legal title did not pass.[113] While the transaction would customarily be recorded in a charter of

---

107 As to what counts as finding in the course of employment, see *White v. Alton-Lewis Ltd.* (1974) 4 O.R. (2d) 741, 49 D.L.R. (3d) 189 (Co.Ct.).

108 See, *e.g.*, *Eastern Construction Co. v. National Trust Co.*, [1914] A.C. 197 (P.C.).

109 See, *e.g.*, *Great Western Ry. Co. v. McEwan* (1871) 30 U.C.Q.B. 559.

110 This defence cannot be raised by a bailee, who is estopped from denying the title of his or her bailor. However, the bailee may allege that (s)he acted on the authority of a person holding a paramount title: see *White v. Brown* (1855) 12 U.C.Q.B. 477. As to the nature of bailment, see Part 8, Chapter 8.

111 English law now allows a plea of *jus tertii*: a defendant is permitted to show that a third person has a better right than the plaintiff in order to avoid the possibility of a second claim being launched: see *Torts (Interference with Goods) Act, 1977*, c. 32, s. 8; see also s. 7. See further the reforms recommended in Ontario Law Reform Commission, *Study Paper on Wrongful Interference With Goods* (Toronto: A.G. (Ont.), 1989) at ch. 12, *passim* and 161-2, 172-3.

112 For an analysis of livery of seisin, see further *Weaver v. Burgess* (1871) 22 U.C.C.P. 104 (C.A.). See also F.W. Maitland, "The Mystery of Seisin" (1886) 2 L.Q.R. 481.

113 See generally S.E. Thorne, "Livery of Seisin" (1936) 52 L.Q.R. 345.

feoffment (a document describing the transfer), the dispositive act was the ceremony and the charter served principally as a record of the event.[114] When livery of seisin gave way to transfers by deed, in theory a fully effective deed had to be signed, sealed[115] and *delivered*.[116] The passing of possession was required to transfer title to chattels, and in the Middle Ages the idea of seisin was applied "as freely to a pig's ham as to a manor or a field".[117] The modern law of gifts illustrates the continuing importance of possession in the process of transferring title, especially in transactions involving personalty.

As a general rule, there are three elements of a perfectly constituted gift: (i) an intention to donate; (ii) an acceptance; and (iii) a sufficient act of delivery.[118] Unless and until all three elements exist, no gift passes, and any action undertaken by the donor may be undone. But once all of these elements are in place, the resulting gift of property is (as between the parties to the transaction[119]) as irrevocable as if the recipient had obtained title by virtue of a contract.

The intentional element is comprised of the desire to divest oneself of title voluntarily. This requires that the donor have the mental capacity to appreciate

---

114 See further *Butt v. Humber* (1976) 6 R.P.R. 207, 17 Nfld. & P.E.I.R. 92, 46 A.P.R. 92 (Nfld.T.D.); *Berry v. Berry* (1882) 16 N.S.R. 66 (S.C.). In *Bouris v. Button* (1975) 9 O.R. (2d) 305, 60 D.L.R. (3d) 233 (H.C.) it was held that livery of seisin was still operative in Ontario. (*Cf. Bea v. Robinson* (1977) 18 O.R. (2d) 12, 3 R.P.R. 154, 81 D.L.R. (3d) 423 (H.C.).) The Court in *Bouris* relied on s. 2 of Ontario's *Conveyancing and Law of Property Act*, R.S.O. 1970, c. 85, which provides that "[a]ll corporeal tenements and hereditaments, as regards the conveyance of the immediate freehold thereof, lie in grant as well as in livery". However, apparently overlooked was s. 3 of that Act, which provides that "[a] feoffment, otherwise than by deed, is void". See now *Conveyancing and Law of Property Act*, R.S.O. 1990, c. C.34, s. 3. The relationship between these two sections is puzzling. The precursors of the Ontario provisions are to be found in the English *Real Property Act*, 1845, 8 & 9 Vict., c. 106. There, the equivalent of Ontario's s. 3 states that "a Feoffment shall be void at Law, unless *evidenced* by Deed" (emphasis added). Does the difference in the Ontario Act reflect a drafting error, or a change of policy?

115 The printed word 'seal' on a document has been held to suffice: *Bank of Nova Scotia v. Hooper* (1994) 150 N.B.R. (2d) 111, 385 A.P.R. 111 (Q.B.) affirmed (1994) 155 N.B.R. (2d) 132, 398 A.P.R. 132 (C.A.).

116 *Goddard's Case* (1584) 2 Co.Rep. 4, at 5, 76 E.R. 396. See generally T.G. Youdan, "The Formal Requirements of a Deed" (1979) 5 B.L.R. 71; D.E.C. Yale, "The Delivery of a Deed", [1970] C.L.J. 52. The requirement of a change of possession was, in time, attenuated: the intention of the donor to be bound by the act of execution can suffice: see Youdan, *ibid.* at 81*ff*. See also *Re Sammon* (1979) 22 O.R. (2d) 721, 94 D.L.R. (3d) 594 (C.A.) at 597*ff* D.L.R.; *Re Deeley Estate* (1995) 10 E.T.R. (2d) 30 (Ont.Gen.Div.).

117 *Cochrane v. Moore* (1890) 25 Q.B.D. 57 (C.A.) at 65 (*per* Fry L.J.). See also F.W. Maitland, "The Seisin of Chattels" (1885) 1 L.Q.R. 324.

118 But see *The Queen v. Carter* (1863) 13 U.C.C.P. 611. Additional elements, such as a requirement of registration, may be imposed by statute. For a case in which this affected the completion of a gift of a motorcycle, see *Hoiland v. Brown* (1979) 19 B.C.L.R. 4 (Co.Ct.). But was this case correctly decided on the facts?

119 In certain contexts, such as where it is alleged that a transaction is fraudulent, a voluntary transfer is more vulnerable to attack than one for which value is given. Likewise, under land registration principles, a purchaser for value is typically placed in a better position than a person who acquires title by means of a gift: see Part 5(g), Chapter 12.

the nature of the transaction.[120] Acceptance of a gift involves an understanding of the transaction and a desire to assume title. This is a requirement that is treated with little rigour: in the ordinary case acceptance is presumed to exist.[121] The donee may rebut that presumption by rejecting or disclaiming the interest.[122]

The third basic requisite for a gift deals with the organizing concept of this chapter, namely, possession. There must be an effective delivery of the gifted property or some accepted substitute.[123] As a rule, the gift must literally be *given* away. If we compare the law of gifts with basic principles of contract law, we see that the delivery element marks an important point of difference between the two. Generally speaking, a contract involves an exchange of promises; a gift does not. Delivery is normally required for a gift; this is not an indispensable part of a binding contract. In the realm of contract law, there are those who advocate that consideration (the exchange) should be eliminated as a requirement – the promise to be bound should be enough.[124] In essence, this stance is based on the importance, in terms of both deontological and utilitarian criteria, in holding people to their promises. Were that position to prevail, then the juridical idea of a gift (and with it the delivery requirement) would become otiose: the promise to be bound would be enough to make a contract. The great divide between these two kinds of transactions would disappear.

For now, delivery is still part of the picture. Under the present law, it serves a reflective function. The requirement of a transfer is a check on impulse, reminding the donor that what is being contemplated will in the end produce a divesting of title. To explain in a contemporary way, it recognizes that there is a difference (often subtle and subconscious) between the willingness of people to indulge in frivolous purchases when they are using a credit card instead of cash. This requirement explains why a jubilant declaration in the presence of numerous witnesses that a wedding present is being made will not suffice if there is no act of delivery, before, during or after the declaration.[125] The maxim that courts will not perfect an imperfect gift, such as by ignoring the delivery requirement, is well-established.[126]

Explained in another way, the delivery element allows donors to change their minds without, in the normal case, facing legal consequences. Thomas Mayhew explains why he thinks that this is an appropriate protection:

> We use gifts to indicate our favorites – if we choose to withdraw our affections, then we should not be forced into making the transfer nevertheless. The forced transfer is no longer an indication of our feelings – it is a redistribution without social meaning. The enforcement

---

120 See *Re Beaney*, [1978] 1 W.L.R. 770, [1978] 2 All E.R. 595 (Ch.D.). See further G.B. Robertson, *Mental Disability and the Law in Canada*, 2nd ed. (Toronto: Carswell, 1994) at 209-10, and the additional authorities cited there.
121 See *Wilson v. Hicks* (1910) 21 O.L.R. 623 (Div.Ct.) affirmed (1911) 23 O.L.R. 496 (C.A.).
122 See generally N. Crago, ''Principles of Disclaimer of Gifts'' (1999) 28 U.W.Aust.L.Rev. 65.
123 *Irons v. Smallpiece* (1819) 2 B. & Ald. 551, 106 E.R. 467.
124 See further M.A. Eisenberg, ''The World of Contract and the World of Gift'', 85 Cal.L.Rev. 821 (1997) and the references cited there. Eisenberg does not subscribe to this point of view.
125 See, *e.g.*, *Waite v. Waite* (1953) 9 W.W.R. (N.S.) 569, [1953] 3 D.L.R. 142 (B.C.S.C.).
126 The classic authority is *Milroy v. Lord* (1862) 4 De.G.F. & J. 264, 45 E.R. 1185.

(against the will of the giver) of a gift removes all characteristics of 'gift-ness' except the transfer of ownership.[127]

Now, one might argue that the same reasoning can be applied even after delivery. If the donor loses the desire to confer a benefit, here too the gift has been drained of social significance. The difference is that in the case of an already-transferred gift, undoing the transaction is itself problematic and may require unpleasant judicial or extra-judicial action. In addition, there is more likely to be some element of detrimental reliance after the gift is given than beforehand. And we would surely want to know just when – there has to be some point – it is too late to respect and respond to a change of heart.

The act of transfer also serves the purpose of providing tangible proof of a gift.[128] In the absence of consideration, delivery of the gifted item is the main way that the necessary donative intention can be shown concretely. The requirement of proper delivery is therefore the functional counterpart of the ancient ceremony of livery of seisin. Words alone are insufficient as proof of delivery because there is a "facility with which words may be distorted".[129] Put another way, the delivery of a gift is treated as a demonstration that the donor intends to be bound by the act of giving.

I think that the basic delivery requirement, and the doctrines which soften that requirement, reflect a curious ambivalence about gifts. The stress placed on the transfer of possession is a symptom of a cynical society which assumes bargains and not gifts, so much that when the trappings of a contract are missing, tangible proof of donative action is demanded. In a 1965 English decision, Lord Harman asserted that "the law of the transfer of property, dominated as it has always been by the doctrine of consideration, has always been chary of the recognition of gifts".[130] Likewise, it has been argued that gifts are inefficient, because the price paid for a gift by a donor is often higher than the economic value that the donee places upon it.[131] In addition, a donee might not be willing to reinsert the gift into the market and allow it to be bought by some rational wealth maximizer, out of a sense of fidelity to the donor. It is regarded as impolite to turn around and sell a gift. Yet, one would think that the law would want to encourage acts of generosity. It does so for gifts to charities, by providing tax relief to the donor and donee. Moreover, freedom, including the freedom to confer a gift, counts as a factor in the development of property rules; efficiency is not the 'be all and end all' of the law.

In any event, delivery is too blunt an instrument to perform its functions perfectly. A transfer, on its own, is an equivocal act. A temporary loan of a chattel

---

127 Quoted in Eisenberg, *supra*, note 124, at 848.
128 Compare the analysis in M. Pickard, "The Goodness of Giving, The Justice of Gifts and Trusts" (1983) 33 U.T.L.J. 381, at 385*ff*.
129 *Kingsmill v. Kingsmill* (1917) 41 O.L.R. 238 (H.C.) at 241 (*per* Middleton J.).
130 *Re Cole (a Bankrupt)*, [1964] 1 Ch. 175, [1963] 3 All E.R. 433 (C.A.) at 185 Ch.
131 J. Waldfogel, "The Deadweight Loss of Christmas", 83 Am.Econ.Rev. 1328 (1993) critiqued in Eisenberg, *supra*, note 124, at 845-6, in part on the ground that Waldfogel's study used only economic and not sentimental (or what I call personhood) measures of value.

(a bailment) also involves a transfer of possession; likewise a sale of goods will inevitably involve a parting with possession. And rashness is not necessarily prevented by insisting on a transfer. Conversely, the delivery element may be over-protective. Other means of proof might well exist and a deliberate intention to give a gift might be foiled only by the failure to show delivery. These concerns as to over-breadth have led courts to shape the contours of the delivery requirement in some remarkable ways. Perfect delivery of a gift involves a physical transfer of possession of the chattel from donor to donee. As a general matter, the donor must have done everything that can be done to perfect the gift.[132] However, one finds copious examples of some lesser form of transfer sufficing, the courts straining to find a sufficient delivery when the evidence of a desire to make a gift is irrefutable. Taking a broad view, there are two kinds of exception: (i) when some form of alternative mode of transfer has been recognized; and (ii) where a factual concession seems warranted. Additionally, there is a third category, involving gifts made in contemplation of death (*donationes mortis causa*), in which some special features of the delivery requirement can be discerned.

(b) doctrinal exceptions

Occasionally a purported gift will be recognized as valid even absent a transfer of possession. A declaration by the donor that the property will henceforth be held on trust for the donee will be binding. Following the declaration, the continued possession of the donor will be in his or her capacity as a trustee for the recipient, the latter being treated as the beneficial owner of the trust property. This notion sits uncomfortably close to the maxim that the courts will not perfect an imperfect gift. The line between statements by a donor such as 'I am giving you my car' and 'I will hold my car (on trust) for you' is not a very vivid one, especially if it is recognized that these utterances can have a greater impact than the declarant might appreciate. Despite this, the first situation looks like an imperfect gift and the second may amount to an effective declaration of trust. Even here one must be cautious, because the courts have not always demanded that the declarations invoke the explicit language of trust law.

Under the rule in *Strong v. Bird*[133] a purported gift, left unfulfilled, will be treated as complete if the donee is named (and later becomes) an executor under the will of the donor. As long as the intention to make a gift can be found to have continued until the death of the donor, by administering the estate the donee assumes control of the decedent's property. This is treated as being functionally equivalent to delivery. The rule, originally applicable only to a release of a debt,[134] has been applied to a broad range of gifts, even those involving land.[135] Furthermore, the promise of a gift, when relied on to the detriment of the putative donee, may support an estoppel or the imposition of a constructive trust. In this indirect

---

132 *Milroy v. Lord* (1862) 4 De G.F. & J. 264, 45 E.R. 1185, discussed in *Corin v. Patton* (1990) 169 C.L.R. 540 (Aust.H.C.).

133 (1874) L.R. 18 Eq. 315, [1874-80] All E.R.Rep. 230.

134 See, *e.g.*, *Rennick v. Rennick* (1962) 33 D.L.R. (2d) 649 (Sask.C.A.).

135 *Benjamin v. Leicher* (1998) 45 N.S.W.L.R. 389 (Eq.D.).

way, a gift is treated as perfected, assuming that the granting of an interest in the property is the most suitable means of responding to the detrimental reliance that has transpired.[136]

(c) *factual concessions*

The transfer of possession does not need to be contemporaneous with the expression of the intention to donate. Delivery may follow the formation or expression of this intention,[137] or precede it,[138] and it can be effective even if the donee was initially holding the property in some other capacity (for example, as an employee).[139] Additionally, the courts have acknowledged that *constructive* delivery will sometimes be enough. If the goods are unwieldy, or if the donor is unable to deliver the item (say, due to illness), something less than actual delivery has been found to suffice. If goods are delivered to some person acting as the agent or trustee of the donee, this too might be acceptable.[140] Even if the holder is not strictly an agent of the donee, delivery may be found if that person takes possession on behalf of the ultimate recipient.[141] In any of these situations, the acid tests appear to be whether or not (i) the donor has retained the means of control; or (ii) all that can be done has been done to divest title in favour of the donee.[142] The transfer of keys (say) to a safe will often meet this test, although it is more equivocal as a form of transfer if the donor retains a duplicate, because in that latter case there is no real relinquishment of control.[143] Whether such methods would be treated as sufficient when used simply out of convenience is by no means certain.

The delivery requirement poses special evidential problems for gift-giving between cohabiting family members, because both parties may have actual control of the premises on which the subject property is located.[144] Two such cases illustrate the problem. In *Re Cole*[145] a husband had taken his wife to a new home, which had been fully furnished. After a tour the husband grandly declared "it's all yours". The parties lived in the home and it appeared that they regarded the

---

136 See, *e.g.*, *McCormick v. McCormick*, [1987] 3 W.W.R. 286, 57 Sask.R. 32 (C.A.). See also *Brogden v. Brogden* (1920) 15 Alta.L.R. 499, [1920] 2 W.W.R. 803, 53 D.L.R. 362 (C.A.); *Le Compte v. Public Trustee*, [1983] 2 N.S.W.L.R. 109 (Eq.D.).

137 *Thomas v. Times Book Co.*, [1966] 1 W.L.R. 911, [1966] 2 All E.R. 241 (Ch.D.) noted in 53 Iowa L.Rev. 243 (1967).

138 See, *e.g.*, *Woodward v. Woodward*, [1995] 3 All E.R. 980 (C.A.).

139 The same is true when the donee has control over the property by virtue of a power of attorney: *MacDonald v. Lobsinger Estate* (1987) 27 E.T.R. 88 (Sask.Q.B.).

140 See, *e.g.*, *Tancred v. O'Mullin* (1866) 6 N.S.R. 145 (C.A.).

141 *Walker v. Foster* (1900) 30 S.C.R. 299.

142 This was not the case in *Kooner v. Kooner* (1979) 100 D.L.R. (3d) 76 (B.C.S.C.).

143 See, *e.g.*, *Watt v. Watt Estate* (1987) 28 E.T.R. 9, [1988] 1 W.W.R. 534, 49 Man.R. (2d) 317 (C.A.). See generally A.C.H. Barlow, "Gift *Inter Vivos* of a Chose in Possession by Delivery of a Key" (1956) 19 Mod.L.Rev. 394.

144 The policy balance is discussed in B. Hovius & T.G. Youdan, *The Law of Family Property* (Toronto: Carswell, 1991) at 23-5. The authors believe that a gift by words alone should be possible in these situations, although they accept that such gifts should be evaluated with great care.

145 *Supra*, note 130.

furnishings as belonging solely to the wife. However, the Court of Appeal found otherwise. The Court felt that there was no special concessionary rule that could be invoked, and nothing in the facts suggested that a transfer of dominion had occurred, given that the spouses were both in possession of the premises as a whole. The acts undertaken were seen as equally consistent with an intention to pass title as they were indicative of a desire to allow mere use and enjoyment to be shared. Expressly rejected was the notion that a showing of the chattels coupled with words that reflect the desire to confer a present gift would be adequate to pass title.[146] (Whether the husband's announcement could have been treated as a declaration of trust was not addressed.)

Langer v. McTavish Brothers Ltd.,[147] a case of remarkable similarity, provides a contrasting approach. There, a man brought his fiancee to a new home, showed her an array of furniture and declared: " . . . it's all yours". Soon afterwards the furniture and house were purchased and the couple moved into the home. A gift was found. It was said that to hold otherwise would be purely artificial, given the nature of the property and the circumstances of the parties.[148]

Physical delivery can be replaced with a transfer by deed. This is a sensible qualification since a deed will normally serve the probative and reflective functions performed by a transfer of possession, perhaps even more effectively than a mere delivery of the object. Documentary evidence can be less ambiguous than an act of delivery which, standing on its own, is as consistent with an intention to loan some item as to donate it. However, a document amounting to something less than a deed may not suffice to complete a gift.[149] Since choses in action cannot be delivered (because they are intangible), some other method must be found; the easiest means is by deed, or at least by means of a writing drawn and delivered in conformity with the general rules governing the assignment of a chose in action.[150] When a chose in action is represented by its own specific form of paper title, such as bonds or stocks, a gift of these by deed may not be sufficient. Here title may not pass under an *inter vivos* gift unless there has been compliance with any special rules that apply to the transfer of these rights.[151] The gift of a cheque is problematic for other reasons. A cheque is neither money nor a representation of money; it is only a direction to the drawer's bank, which can be

---

146 See also *Kellas v. Chapman* (1972) 9 R.F.L. 54, [1972] 5 W.W.R. 99, 27 D.L.R. (3d) 121 (Alta.C.A.) affirmed 11 R.F.L. 392, [1973] 3 W.W.R. 192, 33 D.L.R (3d) 128 (S.C.C.); *Kingsmill v. Kingsmill, supra*, note 129. *Cf. Smith v. Smith* (1733) 2 Stra. 956, 93 E.R. 965.

147 45 B.C.R. 494, [1932] 4 D.L.R. 90 (C.A.).

148 See also *Tellier v. Dujardin* (1906) 16 Man.L.R. 423, 6 W.L.R. 1 (C.A.); *Standard Trusts Co. v. Hill*, [1922] 2 W.W.R. 1003, 68 D.L.R. 722 (Alta.C.A.). See generally J.W.A. Thornley, "Transfer of Choses on Possession Between Members of a Common Household", [1953] C.L.J. 355.

149 See *Re Jones; Jones v. Rushford* (1979) 5 E.T.R. 252, 6 Sask.R. 27 (Q.B.). *Cf. MacDonald v. Lobsinger Estate, supra*, note 139.

150 See, *e.g., Judicature Act*, R.S.A. 1980, c. J-1, s. 21. See further L.A. Sheridan, "Informal Gifts of Choses in Action" (1955) 33 Can.B.Rev. 284. Can a gift of a part interest in a chattel (*e.g.*, a 25% share in a horse) be transferred by delivery? See *Cochrane v. Moore, supra*, note 117, where the issue was raised, though the case was decided on the basis that there was a valid declaration of trust.

151 See also *Re Loipersbeck Estate* (1999) 27 E.T.R. (2d) 159 (Man.Q.B.).

countermanded (by the drawer) before it is presented for payment. Therefore, a gift by cheque is not complete until presented,[152] and the intervening death of the donor should ruin the gift: at that point it can no longer be a simple *inter vivos* transaction.[153]

A gift of land involves a further wrinkle. In some provinces a transfer of the legal title to land can be accomplished only by registration on title, so it might follow that a gift is not complete until registration occurs. However, another view is that a gift is perfected (in equity) if the donor has done all that can be done to permit the transfer and render it binding. These elements may be satisfied when the donee has been given all the requisite documents, including a valid transfer, so as to allow registration to take place.[154]

It is sometimes suggested that *symbolic* delivery will do, for example, when the goods are heavy or unwieldy and hence virtually incapable of being transferred manually. Indeed, there may be occasions in which such symbolism serves the purposes of the delivery requirement; after all, that is what the *ceremony* of livery of seisin was all about. In theory, delivery is symbolic (as opposed to constructive) when some representation of the goods is handed over, rather than the effective means of control. This might be the case when a room full of furniture is purportedly transferred by the delivery of one article,[155] or when a photograph of the item is delivered. However, if one were to pore over the case law it would eventually become apparent that there is little authority on which to base the view that symbolic delivery is enough to complete a gift.[156]

(d)   *donationes mortis causa: gifts made in contemplation of death*

A *donatio mortis causa* (sometimes referred to below simply as a D.M.C.) has been described as having an amphibious nature,[157] meaning that it has elements that resemble both an *inter vivos* donation and a testamentary bequest. Like a gift

---

152 As in *Campbell v. Fenwick*, [1934] O.R. 692, [1934] 4 D.L.R. 787 (C.A.).

153 *Re Swinburne*, [1926] Ch. 38, [1925] All E.R. Rep. 313 (C.A.); *Re Owen*, [1949] 1 All E.R. 901 (Ch.D.). See also *Peden v. Gear* (1921) 50 O.L.R. 384, 64 D.L.R. 439 (H.C.).

154 See *Macleod v. Canada Trust Co.*, [1980] 2 W.W.R. 303, 20 A.R. 350 (*sub nom. Macleod v. Montgomery*), 108 D.L.R. (3d) 424 (C.A.) leave to appeal to S.C.C. refused (1980) 22 A.R. 360n (S.C.C.), where (at 311 W.W.R.) the principle that a gift is effective in such a case was recognized, though the facts to support its application were not found to be present. See also *Corin v. Patton, supra*, note 132; *Macedo v. Stroud*, [1922] 2 A.C. 330 (P.C.); *Costin v. Costin* (1997) N.S.W. Conv. R. 55-811 (C.A.).

155 *Lock v. Heath* (1892) 8 T.L.R. 295 (Dist.Ct.).

156 In the decision in *Rawlinson v. Mort* (1905) 21 T.L.R. 774 (K.B.) the language of symbolic delivery is used. However, the case may have been decided on the basis that there had been either a constructive delivery of the item (an organ) by a handing over of the keys, or an act of delivery when the donor placed his hand on the instrument and uttered sufficient words of gift. In *White v. Canadian Guarantee Trust Co.* (1916) 31 D.L.R. 560 (Man.K.B.) the handing over of an order for a car and the cheque to pay for it was regarded as effective symbolic delivery. Can this too be described as constructive delivery? Overall, "the predominant view is that symbolic delivery will not be sufficient to make a gift": B. Hovius & T.G. Youdan, *supra*, note 144, at 18-9.

157 See *McDonald v. McDonald* (1903) 33 S.C.R. 145, at 161 (*per* Mills J.) quoting "Story".

inter vivos, delivery is required. Moreover, it is not necessary that a D.M.C. comply with the formalities established for the execution of wills. Yet, like a will, a D.M.C. is ambulatory and does not become absolute until the death of the donor. It sits in a middle ground between the two, serving the purpose of allowing a conditional gift to be made in the face of apprehended death.[158]

A *donatio mortis causa* must be made in contemplation, but not necessarily with the expectation, of impending death.[159] This motivating element does not have to be made explicit by the donor and will be implied when the circumstances warrant the conclusion that the finality of the gift hinges on the death of the donor. The gift becomes absolute only when the donor has died. Until then, it is revocable and will be assumed to have been revoked once the peril passes.

Several features of the law governing D.M.C.s are subject to divided authority. This probably reflects the presence of conflicting judicial attitudes concerning the wisdom of allowing the D.M.C. to take effect as a type of informal will. First, in Canada[160] the traditional rule precluding a D.M.C. of land prevails, although it has been rejected in England as groundless.[161] However, there is at least one Canadian case upholding a D.M.C. of land.[162] (In my view, there is no compelling policy reason to justify a distinction here between realty and personalty.) Second, it has been held that a D.M.C. is available only if the donor is *in extremis*,[163] that is, under a sudden peril. This position seeks to confine the use of the D.M.C. to those occasions in which the drawing of a valid will is not realistically possible. However, to restrict the D.M.C. in this way serves to penalize delay and carelessness. Therefore, the majority view is that as long as there is an apprehension of death the donor need not be in a state of *extremis*.[164] Third, it has been said that the peril must be substantial; the everyday risks and dangers which life holds for us all are not enough.[165] A different view is that a subjective belief of danger should suffice, with the absence of a substantial basis for that fear

---

158 "*Donationes mortis causa* may be said to have been an anomaly in our law, both for their immunity to the Statute of Frauds 1677 and the Wills Act 1837 and as exceptions to the rule that there is no equity to perfect an imperfect gift": *Sen v. Headley*, [1991] Ch. 425, [1991] 2 All E.R. 636 (C.A.) at 430 Ch. (*per* Nourse L.J.).

159 See *Re Kuyat* (1962) 33 D.L.R. (2d) 153 (B.C.S.C.). See also *Sen v. Headley, supra*, note 158.

160 See, *e.g., Dyck v. Cardon* (1984) 17 E.T.R. 54, (*sub nom. Dyck v. Shingles*) 54 A.R. 382 (C.A.). See also the Australian case of *Bayliss v. Public Trustee* (1988) 12 N.S.W.L.R. 540 (S.C.).

161 *Sen v. Headley, supra*, note 158, at 440: "[a] *donatio mortis causa* of land is neither more nor less anomalous than any other" (*per* Nourse L.J.). See also C.E.F. Rickett, "No *Donatio Mortis Causa* of Real Property – A Rule in Search of a Justification?", [1989] Conv. 184. The *Sen* decision is criticized in P. Sparkes, "Death-Bed Gifts of Land" (1992) 43 N.I.L.Q. 35, but welcomed in J.W.A. Thornley, Note, [1991] C.L.J. 404.

162 *Cooper v. Severson* (1955) 1 D.L.R. (2d) 161 (B.C.S.C.).

163 *Thompson v. Mechan*, [1958] O.R. 357, 13 D.L.R. (2d) 103 (C.A.); *Canada Trust Co. v. Labadie*, [1962] O.R. 151, 31 D.L.R. (2d) 252 (C.A.). These decisions are criticized in R.E. Megarry, Note (1965) 81 L.Q.R. 21.

164 See, *e.g., Saulnier v. Anderson* (1987) 43 D.L.R. (4th) 19, 83 N.B.R. (2d) 1, 212 A.P.R. 1 (Q.B.); *Lumsden v. Miller*, [1980] 4 W.W.R. 143, 110 D.L.R. (3d) 226, 25 A.R. 359 (Q.B.).

165 *Thompson v. Mechan, supra*, note 163.

merely affording evidence as to whether or not that belief was actually held.[166] Fourth, it is debatable whether the donor must die of the very peril feared,[167] or whether some other cause will do, if death occurs before the initial threat has fully passed.[168] Fifth, when death is certain, it has been said that the gift must either be sustained as a valid *inter vivos* transfer or as a will. The reason for this stance is that there is no need for a gift that is revocable on survival if that possibility does not exist. This point remains contentious.[169]

Delivery is now required in order to complete a *donatio mortis causa*, though the requirement was not firmly established until the eighteenth century.[170] One might assume that because a dispute over this will-like transfer may erupt only after the donor has died (the time at which the gift becomes irrevocable), the need for a clear demonstration of intention through a change of possession would be demanded, even more so than for a transfer *inter vivos*.[171] Despite this, some decisions have, in fact, diluted the delivery requirement to take account of the circumstances (the impending peril, *etc.*) out of which a D.M.C. might emerge.[172] Plus, after death there would be no way to rectify a deficiency as to delivery; relaxing the rules (to a point) allows otherwise good gifts to be upheld.

The same types of factual concessions are accorded in the case of a D.M.C. as are made for an ordinary gift, and sometimes the standard has been relaxed even further.[173] Delivery of property under a D.M.C. will be sufficient as long as the evidence of title has been handed over, if that evidence would allow the donee to prove ownership and gain control.[174] As a result, a D.M.C. of money in an account made by the handing over of a bank book has been found to be valid.[175] Although this seems to provide support for the effectiveness of symbolic delivery,

---

166 See further *Re Craven's Estate*, [1937] Ch. 422, [1937] 3 All E.R. 33. *Cf. Rosenberger v. Volz Estate* (1945) 12 I.L.R. 34 (Ont.H.C.).

167 *Ward v. Bradley* (1901) 1 O.L.R. 118 (C.A.) at 125 (*per* Lister J.A.): "One essential of such a gift is that it is to take effect only in the event of the donor's death from [the] then existing disorder."

168 *Re Richards*, [1921] 1 Ch. 513; *Wilkes v. Allington*, [1931] 2 Ch. 104. See further H.E. Read, Note (1931) 9 Can.B.Rev. 663. In *Rosenberger v. Volz, supra*, note 166, a D.M.C. was found even though the donor died before he was thrust into the apprehended peril (the war).

169 See further *Re Lillingston*, [1952] 2 All E.R. 184 (Ch.D.).

170 See further M.J. Mossman & W.F. Flanagan, eds., *Property Law: Cases and Commentary* (Toronto: Emond Montgomery, 1997) at 477, and the references cited there.

171 See *Hall v. Hall* (1891) 20 O.R. 684 (H.C.) affirmed (1892) 19 O.A.R. 292 (C.A.).

172 In some jurisdictions there is a requirement of corroboration in an action against the estate of a donor: see, *e.g.*, *Alberta Evidence Act*, R.S.A. 1980, c. A-21, s. 12. As to the nature of the corroboration required in this context, see *Re Murphy Estate* (1998) 24 E.T.R. (2d) 53, 169 N.S.R. (2d) 284 (S.C.). Even where corroboration is not required by statute, rigorous scrutiny will be given: see *Dell'Aquilla v. Mellof* (1996) 143 Sask.R. 8 (Q.B.) at 15.

173 See *In re Wasserberg*, [1915] 1 Ch. 195, [1914-15] All E.R.Rep. 217. See also *Re Rosemergey* (1934) 49 B.C.R. 93 (S.C.). *Cf. Cain v. Moon*, [1896] 2 Q.B. 283, at 289; and *Kingsmill v. Kingsmill* (1917) 41 O.L.R. 238 (H.C.) at 244 (*per* Middleton J.): "I can see no reason for drawing an arbitrary distinction between what is necessary in the one case and the other". See further R.G. Murray, Note (1953) 31 Can.B.Rev. 935.

174 See *Chevrier v. Ontario (Public Trustee)* (1984) 16 E.T.R. 152 (Ont.Dist.Ct.).

175 *Re Kuyat, supra*, note 159. *Cf. Re Smith Estate* (1995) 9 E.T.R. (2d) 127, 132 Nfld. & P.E.I.R. 316 (Nfld.T.D.).

the pass book cases seem to turn on whether it is necessary to produce the book in order to gain access to the account. If so, these are instances of constructive delivery.[176]

The transfer of partial control may be sufficient to complete a D.M.C. In the case of *Re Lillingston*,[177] for instance, delivery of jewellery that had been stored in a safety deposit box was found to have occurred even though the donee required, but did not have, a password and a written authorization to open the box. The donee did have the key, however, and this was found to be enough to satisfy the delivery element, given that parting with that key had deprived the donor of any further direct access.[178]

6. RECOGNITION AND PRESERVATION OF RIGHTS THROUGH POSSESSION: COMMON LAW ABORIGINAL TITLE

In Chapter 2, we saw that common law Aboriginal title is predicated upon proof of possession. While subordinate to the Crown, which holds ultimate or radical title by virtue of its sovereign power, Aboriginal title is amenable to recognition and protection under law unless and until that right is lawfully erased.[179] Although the cases speak of *occupation*, a factual matter, this is tantamount to the idea that there must be sufficient legal *possession*, to the extent required by the common law of Aboriginal rights. In the discussion below, I use these two terms interchangeably.[180]

For the sake of convenience, the basic requirements to found Aboriginal title are repeated here. In *Delgamuukw v. British Columbia*,[181] a majority of the Supreme Court of Canada laid down a three-part test: (i) the land must have been occupied prior to sovereignty; (ii) when present occupation is relied upon as a way of proving pre-sovereignty occupation, a continuity between present and pre-sovereignty occupation must be shown; (iii) at the time of the assertion of sovereignty, the occupation must have been exclusive.

We have seen throughout this chapter how extraordinarily flexible the concept of possession in law is, and the variety of roles it plays in fixing entitlements. It can assume various meanings, even when claims over the same piece of property are involved. Hence, the legally recognized possession of a squatter differs from that which will be demanded of the holder of the paper title. In analyzing the

---

176 See *McMillan v. Brown* (1957) 12 D.L.R. (2d) 306 (N.S.S.C.) at 319.

177 *Supra*, note 169, relying on *In re Wasserberg, supra*, note 173.

178 As in the case of an *inter vivos* gift, possession of a cheque written by the donor will probably not amount to delivery: *Re Bernard* (1911) 18 O.W.R. 525, 2 O.W.N. 716 (Div.Ct.). However, in *Kendrick v. Dominion Bank* (1920) 48 O.L.R. 539, 58 D.L.R. 309 (C.A.) there was a valid D.M.C. involving the delivery of a cheque and a pass book. See also *Re Barnes*, [1950] O.W.N. 401 (Master) where a cheque returned N.S.F. was nevertheless held, on the peculiar facts of the case, to support a valid *donatio mortis causa*.

179 See Part 3(b), Chapter 2.

180 See also K. McNeil, *Common Law Aboriginal Title* (Oxford: Clarendon Pr., 1989) at 197.

181 [1997] 3 S.C.R. 1010, [1998] 1 C.N.L.R. 14, 153 D.L.R. (4th) 193.

elements of native title one searches for a suitable analogy among the forms of possession discussed above (or any other conception of possession) to help characterize the degree of occupation needed here. Should it be that required of an adverse possessor, the paper title holder, or some other type of claimant?[182] Principles of international law governing the acquisition of sovereignty over land may also be of assistance.

The choice of approach can be critical. However, at the risk of sounding trite, it must be remembered that the rights being considered here are unique. Accordingly, analogies are useful only as a starting point for analysis and should not dictate conclusions. At bottom, we are assessing questions of policy; this should shape our notions of Aboriginal occupation. In other words, the meaning of occupation or possession that is applied must respond to the specific context in which the issue arises. Here the dominant policy is the fair recognition of ancient land rights. This, in turn, is affected by what I have called personhood (or grouphood) values: the connection between ancestral lands and Aboriginal conceptions of self and spirituality should be front and centre.

The *Delgamuukw* case contains an analysis of the ways in which we might define occupation. There it was said that the rules for proof of occupancy must be grounded both in common law notions and Aboriginal perspectives on land. The Aboriginal landholding legal regime in place at the time of sovereignty forms part of this latter perspective. Canadian law is supposed to give equal weight to both of these points of view. In addition, it has been warned that the common law concept of exclusive occupation should be applied to Aboriginal land claims "with caution".[183]

In the case of a claim based on first occupancy, when there is no rival Aboriginal claimant, one would think that minimal control is all that should be demanded. The position is close to that of the true owner in an adverse possession dispute, who must show minor acts of ownership to support a plea that possession was not discontinued. Granted, it cannot be said that the Aboriginal community is in constructive possession of the whole lands initially, because that begs a question as to where the boundaries should be drawn. However, once it is accepted that some form of actual possession is enjoyed, in my opinion, a significant physical presence need not be shown for the group to retain rights over those lands. Stated another way, a court should be slow to find that land once occupied has been subsequently abandoned.

Furthermore, when faced with issues concerning the requisite quality of possession, courts should adopt a standard that recognizes and accommodates differences in geography, cultural norms, needs, technologies and so on. Again, this type of flexibility is evident in the cases on adverse possession, where account is taken of customs relating to the assertion of title that are found in a given locality. This means that among tribal groups who are hunters and gatherers, the form of control should reflect those practices, so that hunting grounds can be in occupation as much as settled villages or cultivated fields. The situation of Can-

---

182 Other analogies are canvassed in McNeil, *supra*, note 180, at 197*ff*.
183 *Delgamuukw v. British Columbia, supra*, note 181, at 1104 S.C.R. (*per* Lamer C.J.C.).

ada's Inuit nations demonstrates well the need for this type of definitional accommodation. When Inuit claims were addressed in the *Hamlet of Baker Lake* case it was found that the required degree of occupation existed. It was concluded that "to the extent the barrens lent themselves to human occupation, the Inuit occupied them".[184]

Proving occupation dating back centuries can be a difficult task. The evidential hurdles can be daunting. In response, it has been held that present occupation can serve as proof of pre-sovereignty occupation, provided a measure of continuity can be shown. This does not mean that an unbroken chain of possession is required, since showing that level of continuity is tantamount to simply requiring full proof of prior possession, from then until now. Occupation may have been disrupted, for example, by the non-extinguishing action of European colonizers. Instead, what must be proven is a substantial maintenance of the connection. Moreover, the nature of the possession may have changed over time without detrimentally affecting an occupancy-based claim.

The requirement that occupation must be *exclusive* is of particular importance when Aboriginal title is being asserted. This requirement arises from the fact that those holding this title have the right to exclusive possession: the proof required matches the entitlement being sought. Moreover, the exclusivity element serves to eliminate the possibility of inconsistent Aboriginal claims to the same territories.

Exclusivity does not, of course, mean that outsiders were invariably barred from entering the territory. The presence of other nations can, in fact, reinforce a claim to exclusivity when it is shown that these groups were permitted, following a request, to enter on the lands. Treaties may also support the idea that occupation was claimed, especially when the terms of the treaty confer a permission to enter. The presence of a legal conception of trespass would also, naturally, provide proof that exclusivity was contemplated and asserted. Intermittent trespasses are not enough to discount exclusivity. To require that the right of exclusion was enforced in all cases and at all times would be to set an unrealistic standard.

Importantly, shared arrangements among First Nations may still satisfy the requirement of exclusivity; shared exclusivity is possible.[185] Despite first appearances, this is not an oxymoron. As we will see in Chapter 9, any number of co-owners may share title to Blackacre. Each one has a full and unrestricted right of possession; no one owner may lawfully unilaterally exclude the other(s). Yet collectively, their title is good against the rest of the world. Similar ideas are applicable to shared Aboriginal land claims, remembering always, however, that the nature of the shared title need not resemble in any other way the forms of

---

184 *Baker Lake (Hamlet) v. Canada (Minister of Indian Affairs & Northern Development)*, [1980] 1 F.C. 518, [1979] 3 C.N.L.R. 17, 107 D.L.R. (3d) 513 (T.D.) at 561 F.C. (*per* Mahoney J.). See also *Mabo v. Queensland (No. 2)*, [1992] 5 C.N.L.R. 1, 175 C.L.R. 1, 107 A.L.R. 1, at 152 C.N.L.R. (*per* Toohey J.): "a nomadic lifestyle is not inconsistent with occupancy".

185 *Supra*, note 181, at 1105 S.C.R., relying on *United States v. Santa Fe Pacific Railroad Co.*, 314 U.S. 339 (1941). *Cf.* B. Slattery, "Understanding Aboriginal Title" (1987) 66 Can.B.Rev. 727, at 758.

co-ownership recognized by the Canadian law of real property applicable to non-Aboriginal rights.

5

THE DOCTRINE OF ESTATES

[A]n estate in the land is a time in the land, or land for a time,
and there are diversities of estates, which are no more than
diversities of time, for he who has a fee-simple in land has a time
in the land without end, or the land for a time without end, and
he who has land in tail has a time in the land or the land for a
time as long as he has issues of his body, and he who has an
estate in land for life has no time in it longer than his own life,
and so of him who has an estate in land for the life of another, or
for years.

Walsingham's Case

1. INTRODUCTION

This chapter examines the temporal limits of property ownership, as imposed
through the doctrine of estates. Under tenurial landholding, in which absolute
ownership is not recognized, rules for setting the duration of property rights are
needed. Those rules are supplied by the doctrine of estates.

An estate confers a segment of ownership, as measured by time. In the florid
prose of *Walsingham's Case*, "an estate is a time in the land, or land for a time".[1]
Another way to convey the idea is to say that "rights of property in land are four-
dimensional. They are defined not only by reference to the physical boundaries
of the property, but also by reference to the time for which the interest will
endure".[2] And there may be a series of consecutive estate owners, all holding a
legitimate right over the same tract of realty. Think of a time continuum from
here to eternity. That line may be broken into any number of segments. To take
a straightforward example, G may grant Blackacre to A for life, after which the
land is to pass to B. If two or more people can own portions of the continuum, as
in this example, their respective rights to exploit and encumber the property must
be co-ordinated. The law concerning estates is designed in part to balance the
rights of the segment-holders. The rules relating to the balancing of rights will be
addressed below as part of the analysis of life estates.

Canadian law distinguishes between freehold and leasehold estates. Freeholds will be considered in this chapter, with most attention being paid to the 'fee
simple' and the 'life estate'. A third member of this grouping, the 'fee tail', long
since regarded as a dinosaur in Canada, will receive only passing mention. Leaseholds are examined in Chapter 8.

---

1 *Walsingham's Case* (1573) 2 Plowd. 547, at 555, 75 E.R. 805, at 816-7.
2 *Newlon Housing Trust v. Alsulaimen*, [1999] 1 A.C. 313, [1998] 4 All E.R. 1 (H.L.) at 317 A.C.
(*per* Lord Hoffmann).

The doctrine of estates is a concept associated chiefly with possessory interests in land. Its application to personal property is less straightforward and this chapter contains an examination of that often overlooked area of law. Also considered are (i) the estate-like notion of timesharing, found today mainly in relation to vacation condominiums; and (ii) the forms of ownership held on behalf of, or by, Aboriginal peoples in Canada.

2.   THE ESTATE IN FEE SIMPLE: A TIME IN THE LAND WITHOUT END?

(a)   generally

The fee simple estate is the closest approximation to absolute ownership found in the Anglo-Canadian system of landholding. Although it may endure for only a second, and may relate to a small scrap of ground, it is commonly recited that the fee simple is the largest estate known to the law. This is true in conceptual terms: it is of potentially infinite duration and confers upon the holder a larger bundle of proprietary rights than those attaching to other estates, freehold or non-freehold.

A look at the nomenclature reveals something about the nature of this estate. The word 'fee' means that the interest is one of inheritance; and 'simple' signifies that the property can descend to the largest range of heirs contemplated by law. In modern terms, an estate in fee simple will continue after the death of the current holder, provided that it is passed to someone by will, or through intestacy (*i.e.*, to those entitled under statute to receive property not disposed of under a will). If there are no takers under these routes, the estate ends; an escheat occurs.

Under the common law, great precision is needed in the drafting of a transfer of a fee simple. To convey the fee, the incantation 'to A and his (or her) heirs' is required. Virtually nothing else will suffice and a failure to employ the proper language means (generally[3]) that only a life estate will pass to A.[4] So strict is this requirement that even transfer 'to A in fee simple'[5] or 'to A forever'[6] passes just a life interest. What is there in this phrase that points to the grant of a fee simple, and why this preoccupation with formalism? The translation of this language is as follows: 'To A' describes the recipient of the property. These are described as 'words of purchase'. A better label (but not one in current legal parlance) would be words of *receipt*, because the term 'words of purchase' is applied whether or not the property has been acquired by A through a sale or by gift.

The second half of the granting phrase – the words 'and her/his heirs' – contains 'words of limitation'. These denote the duration of the estate granted.

---

3 Several exceptions to this principle have been recognized. Of these, the most significant is the rule in *Shelley's Case*, which is discussed in Part 2(b), *infra*.

4 See, *e.g.*, *Millard v. Gregoire* (1913) 47 N.S.R. 78, 11 D.L.R. 539 (C.A.). See also *McDonnell Estate v. Scott World Wide Inc.* (1997) 149 D.L.R. (4th) 645, 160 N.S.R. (2d) 349, 11 R.P.R. (3d) 186 (C.A.).

5 See *Gold v. Rowe* (1913) 23 O.W.R. 794, 9 D.L.R. 26 (H.C.).

6 *Jack v. Lyons* (1879) 19 N.B.R. 336 (C.A.).

The heirs of the owner of the fee simple for the time being serve as a measuring device, indicating that the fee will endure at least as long as the current holder has some person to whom the land can devolve. On a subsequent transfer from A to 'B and his heirs', the line of heirs associated with B is the new basis of measurement. The distinction between words of purchase and limitation is important. Among other things, it serves to highlight that the heirs receive no entitlements under this grant. In an earlier time the heirs of the owner did enjoy a veto over transfers, but by the thirteenth century this power had evanesced,[7] leaving the heirs with only a *spes successionis*[8] – a mere hope of succeeding to the land.

The need to invoke just the right phrase is indicative of the ritualism of early English land law. In a world in which property holdings served as the quintessential social and economic status symbols, the demand for certainty in the solemn act of property transfer is perhaps understandable. Yet, if so, it might seem that the rule was relaxed when it was needed most, namely, in testamentary dispositions. The common law provides that the magic words are not essential in a will, so long as the devise shows in some convincing way that there was an intention to create a fee simple; otherwise only a life interest would be created as in the case of an *inter vivos* grant.[9] In truth, there is no real anomaly here. The more flexible attitude that developed for gifts in wills is a sensible indulgence, especially for the will-maker who has acted without legal advice and who therefore might not have appreciated the significance that the common law sometimes places on specific word recipes. Furthermore, a defect in a will might not come to light until the testator had passed away, at which time rectification would not be possible.

Beginning in the first half of the nineteenth century, the common law position governing the fee simple was modified in most jurisdictions.[10] Turning the old rule on its head, the reforms treat a transfer without words of limitation as conferring a fee simple (or at least the largest estate held by the transferor), unless the instrument suggests a contrary intention.[11] For example, Alberta law now provides as follows:

> No words of limitation are necessary in a transfer or conveyance of land in order to transfer all or any title in it, but every instrument transferring land operates as an absolute transfer of all right and title that the transferor has in the land at the time of its execution, unless a contrary intention is expressed in the transfer or conveyance.[12]

---

7 W.F. Walsh, *Commentaries on the Law of Real Property* (Albany: Matthew Bender, 1947) vol. 1, at 523. For a review of the various explanations of this development, see J.L. Barton, "The Rise of the Fee Simple" (1976) 92 L.Q.R. 108.

8 For more on this concept, see A.H. Oosterhoff, "Great Expectations: Spes Successionis" (1998) 17 Est., Tr. & Pen. J. 181.

9 See, *e.g.*, *Doe d. Ford v. Bell* (1850) 6 U.C.Q.B. 527 (C.A.). See also *Hamilton v. Dennis* (1866) 12 Gr. 325 (U.C.Ch.D.).

10 The first Canadian enactment appears to be *An Act to Amend the Law Respecting Real Property*, S.U.C. 1834, c. 1, s. 50.

11 See *Re Airey* (1921) 21 O.W.N. 190 (H.C.); *Chandler v. Gibson* (1901) 2 O.L.R. 442 (C.A.).

12 *Law of Property Act*, R.S.A. 1980, c. L-8, sub. 7(1).

This provision creates a 'rule of construction'. It provides a presumed interpretation that can be rebutted by showing that the grantor held a contrary intention. This can be contrasted with a 'rule of law', which prescribes a result that will apply even if it is inconsistent with the intention of the person making the transfer.[13] The strict common law requirement as to the language needed to transfer a fee simple provides a convenient illustration of a rule of law.

The modern rule of construction, under which the grant of a fee simple is presumed, is premised on the (logical but untested) assumption that the meaning contained in the statute actually accords with the intentions of landowners. This presumption yields to a contrary intention: this holds a key to understanding the merit of the legislative change. If, say, a donor wishes to confer an interest for life only (contrary to the current presumption), there is likely to be some positive evidence in the document, such as a further gift of the same property to someone else.

(b)   the enigma known as Shelley's rule

Among the few exceptions to the required use of the magic words in the conveyance of a fee simple estate, none has been more celebrated than the rule in *Shelley's Case*.[14] It is a rule of law (as defined above) under which a gift 'to A for life, remainder to A's heirs' works to place the fee simple in A, not the life estate that appears to have been given. Notice that the gift, as drafted, seems to provide that after A's death the heirs are to be recipients of the remainder of the estate: the second gift is a direct one, *to* the heirs. The effect of *Shelley's* rule is to leave the heirs with absolutely nothing. Put another way, the rule treats the words '*to* the heirs', not as words of purchase, as they appear to be, but as words of limitation, denoting the extent of the estate granted to A, and therefore equivalent to the phrase '*and* his heirs'. The rule is invoked when two interests in land are of the same quality (either both equitable or legal[15]) and are granted or devised in the same instrument.[16]

Within the body of this rule of law lies a preliminary question of construction. Before *Shelley* is triggered it must first be shown that the grantor intended to use the word 'heirs' in a particular way. For the rule to be invoked, the use of 'heirs' in the second half of the limitation must have been intended to refer to the whole line of inheritable issue over the generations, and not just those heirs who are

---

13 See further *Re Cutter* (1916) 37 O.L.R. 42, 31 D.L.R. 382 (H.C.) at 388 D.L.R.

14 *Shelley's Case*; *Wolfe v. Shelley* (1581) 1 Co.Rep. 93b, 76 E.R. 206. For a more detailed treatment of the rule and a brief look at some of its colourful history, see B. Ziff & M.M. Litman, ''Shelley's Rule in a Modern Context: Clearing the 'Heir' '' (1984) 34 U.T.L.J. 170. This article also contains a critique of the judgment in *Re Rynard* (1980) 31 O.R. (2d) 257, 118 D.L.R. (3d) 530 (C.A.). See also J.V. Orth, ''Requiem for the Rule in Shelley's Case'', 67 N.C.L.Rev. 681 (1989) at 686, in which the rule is described as being part of the ''prized arcana of the law''.

15 Equitable interests are discussed in Chapter 6.

16 And the rule applies even if an interest is inserted in between the gift to A and the remainder to A's heirs, such as where land is transferred 'to A for life, remainder to B for life, remainder to A's heirs'. Moreover, it applies when the remainder is stated as 'to the heirs of the body of A' or other words denoting a fee tail. As to the attributes of the estate in fee tail, see Part 3, *infra*.

alive at the death of A (whom we might call the immediate heirs). If the indefinite line from generation to generation is found to be the proper construction of the gift, and assuming all of the other conditions are met (the property is land, the two gifts appear in the same instrument, *etc.*), the rule applies. It confers the fee simple on A, no matter how much the donor might have wanted to avoid that result. Again, such is the nature of a rule of law that it may fly in the face of the objectives of the grantor.

The basic rule may actually pre-date *Shelley's Case*, although in that case one finds the most authoritative articulation of this doctrine. Its rationale is lost in history and several theories have emerged that seek to explain its original function.[17] According to the conventional wisdom the rule arose in the Middle Ages as an attempt to close a loophole used for the avoidance of the feudal incidents of relief, wardship and primer seisin. Payments under these heads fell due when property passed by descent from the ancestor (A, in the above example) to an heir.[18] No payments were due if two separate gifts, first to the ancestor (A), then to the heirs, were made. That is what appears to happen if G grants first 'to A', and then transfers the remainder 'to A's heirs'. By merging these two gifts in the ancestor through the operation of *Shelley's* rule the probability that title to the lands would ultimately pass through to the heirs by descent on the death of A (the taxable event) was increased.[19]

An alternative theory is that the rule was not aimed at frustrating donative intent (as it would do under this first explanation), but, on the contrary, that it endeavoured to perfect that intention. At common law, a gift 'to A's heirs', that is, a gift to heirs *in the plural*, was a nonsense. Under the principles of descent by primogeniture there could be only one heir on A's death. Owing to the rules of primogeniture, a gift to heirs (plural) could only have meant a gift to heirs from generation to generation. However, a simultaneous gift to persons over many generations could not be comprehended as a valid transfer if couched in words such as 'remainder to A's heirs'. Given these juristic strictures, the rule in *Shelley's Case* might have been designed to be curative: by giving the fee to A it was possible that the property might eventually pass to the line of heirs as initially intended. Converting the phrase 'to the heirs' from words of purchase to words of limitation was a means of reconstituting a flawed transfer, even though this meant deviating somewhat from the wording of the original gift.[20]

Don't despair – *Shelley's* rule doesn't crop up that often any more. It is discussed here as a means of flagging certain property law issues. It illustrates (on one view) the impact of feudal politics on the development of property doctrine. It demonstrates the interaction of rules of construction and rules of law and the difference between words of purchase and limitation. Furthermore, it

---

17 See Ziff & Litman, *supra*, note 14, where five theories are reviewed.

18 See Part 2(a), Chapter 2.

19 See also M.E. Tigar & M.R. Levy, *Law and the Rise of Capitalism* (New York: Monthly Review Pr., 1977) at 196-201.

20 See further Ziff & Litman, *supra*, note 14, at 178-81. John Baker has rejected this rationale: J.H. Baker, *An Introduction to English Legal History*, 3rd ed. (London: Butterworths, 1990) at 324.

provides a simplified example of what is called a 'settlement' of property. A settlement arises when land is divided up among successive owners. The settlement scheme that invokes *Shelley's* rule also raises something that will be later described as a 'perpetuities' issue.[21]

In addition, the rule represents one of a host of traps for the unwary drafter, to be studiously avoided in the preparation of wills and other documents of transfer. It highlights the importance of appreciating the underlying rationales of property law. If it is true that the rule arose out of a struggle over feudal obligations, then it has long since become obsolete and should never have been received into Canada.[22] However, as a means of improving donative intention, *Shelley's* rule is not a complete anachronism, because a present gift to be shared among countless future generations of descendants is still a legal impossibility.[23] An empirical study has suggested that it is unlikely that such a meaning would be intended by a gift to 'heirs'.[24] And in Alberta, under statute,[25] a different construction of a gift to heirs is presumed. That being so, at best this ancient rule has a very limited ambit. Better yet, the law might be reformed to provide that the terms 'heirs' *must* mean immediate heirs, that is, those heirs who would take on the life tenant's intestacy. Sensibly, the Ontario Law Reform Commission concluded that it would be appropriate to replace the rule in *Shelley's Case* with a provision to that effect.[26]

3.   THE FEE TAIL: ITS LIFE AND TIMES

An estate in fee tail devolved only to lineal descendants. Its principal purpose was to perpetuate family dynasties. The origins of the fee tail as a full-fledged estate can be traced to the *Statute De Donis Conditionalibus* of 1285.[27] Prior to this, an attempt to create such a form of lineal descent was easily frustrated. For example, before 1285, a gift 'to A, and thereafter to the heirs of his body', though apparently intended to create a chain of title that would pass along a route of lineal descent, produced instead a conditional fee simple in A. Once an heir capable of inheriting was born the condition was regarded as having been met and the fee simple was held absolutely by A, who was then free to transfer it out of the family. The introduction of legislation in 1285 gave efficacy to the initial idea of a devolution in favour of a designated line of issue. The functional upshot

---

21 See Part 5, Chapter 7.

22 It has been held that the rule in *Shelley's Case* does not apply in Alberta: *Re Simpson* (1927) 23 Alta. L.R. 374, [1927] 3 W.W.R. 534, [1927] 4 D.L.R. 817 (C.A.) affirmed on other grounds [1928] S.C.R. 329, [1928] 3 D.L.R. 773; *Re Budd* (1958) 24 W.W.R. 383, 12 D.L.R. (2d) 783 (Alta.S.C.). *Cf. Re Ruse* (1923) 18 Sask. L.R. 62, [1924] 1 W.W.R. 119, [1924] 1 D.L.R. 437 (K.B.); *Re Rynard, supra,* note 14 and the authorities cited there.

23 See *LePage v. Communist Party of Canada* (1999) 209 N.B.R. (2d) 58, 535 A.P.R. 58 (Prob.Ct.) where a will was treated as providing a gift of the residue to all present and future members of the Communist Party of Canada. This was held to be contrary to the rule against perpetuities and therefore void.

24 Ziff & Litman, *supra,* note 14, at 194*ff.*

25 *Wills Act,* R.S.A. 1980, c. W-11, s. 27; *Interpretation Act,* R.S.A. 1980, c. I-7, sub. 24(3).

26 Ontario Law Reform Commission, *Report on Basic Principles of Land Law* (Toronto: A.G. (Ont.), 1996) at 71.

27 18 Edw. 1, c. 1.

of the statute was to raise the fee tail from being a qualified fee simple to the status of a distinct freehold estate. Thereafter, a conveyance containing the language 'to A and the heirs of her (or his) body' or some acceptable variation (of which there were several[28]) created what is sometimes termed an 'entailed' interest.

A fee tail estate would last as long as there were direct lineal descendants of the holder. The acceptable line included children or their issue, but excluded collaterals (uncles, nieces, *etc.*). Unlike the fee simple, the route of descent could be further refined, so that the interest might be made to pass to only male or female heirs (a tail male or tail female, respectively)[29] or, even more narrowly, to those lineal heirs of a named person: at common law, a gift 'to the daughters of Reuben by Kate begotten' produces a 'tail female special'.

While the estate tail was born out of the desire to preserve the family estate forever, the full history of the entail chronicles the ultimate success of policy forces favouring alienability over these dynastic aspirations. The tension between these values is significant. A tenant in tail, X, interested in realizing on the value of the property immediately, could dispose of the land to Y, but this gave the donee only an interest for life (which was not a very marketable commodity). Once X died, Y's interest ended and the property passed to X's lineal heir. Equally, the inherent limitations of the entail impeded an owner's ability to mortgage or lease the property. In its pristine form, the fee tail was thus able to operate effectively as a means of passing the family house and grounds on to future generations along a course of devolution established immutably by the original grantor.[30]

Two nefarious means of liberating land that had been locked into fee tail descent were eventually concocted by conveyancers, with the courts apparently acting as willing accomplices in this enterprise. By the late fifteenth century processes had been developed through which a fee tail could be 'barred', *i.e.*, enlarged into a fee simple estate.[31] There were a number of complicated steps that had to be taken, but the details are not worth recounting. In essence, the barring of a fee tail was accomplished by commencing litigation in which the relevant parties to the action collusively participated in alleging and admitting fictitious claims as to title. The court order that would be sought in these proceedings would result in the barring of the fee tail. One form of action, called a common recovery, was available to a fee tail owner in possession and resulted in the enlargement of the entail into a fee simple. When the fee tail holder was not in possession, and if that party could not obtain the consent of the person who was, the action taken was called a 'fine', and the estate created through barring was known as a 'base fee'. This was a transferable interest that would last only so long as the original

---

28 See generally A.H. Oosterhoff & W.B. Rayner, *Anger & Honsberger Law of Real Property*, 2nd ed. (Aurora, Ont.: Canada Law Book, 1985) ch. 6. See also *Doe d. McIntyre v. McIntyre* (1849) 7 U.C.Q.B. 156; *Sisson v. Ellis* (1860) 19 U.C.Q.B. 559.

29 See, *e.g.*, *Riddell v. McIntosh* (1885) 9 O.R. 606 (Ch.D.).

30 See further P. Butt, *Land Law*, 3rd ed. (Sydney: Law Book Co., 1996) at 128.

31 See *Taltarum's Case*, reproduced in A.K.R. Kiralfy, *A Source Book of English Law* (London: Sweet & Maxwell, 1957) at 86*ff* (described as *Hunt v. Smith (Talcarn's Case)*).

line of fee tail descent continued. In other words, the sale of a base fee from A to B gave B an estate that would last so long as the lineal descendants of A subsisted.

In the nineteenth century the chicanery of the fine and common recovery actions was obviated by the introduction of legislation that permitted barring by the execution of a special form of deed, which is sometimes referred to as a disentailing assurance. In any of these forms the barring process was highly effective: virtually all attempts to insulate a fee tail from being barred, in other words, to create an unbarrable entail, proved fruitless.[32] While the technique of barring through fines and common recoveries does not appear to have been practised in Canada, legislation permitting the granting of disentailing deeds was received[33] or later introduced.[34] The procedures conferred by the statutes were designed "to discourage estates tail and to get rid of such estates by a simple and easy process".[35]

The impetus for the practice of barring, i.e., the promotion of alienation, eventually led to the demise of the fee tail;[36] now only traces remain. Following abolition, an attempt to grant a fee tail is generally treated as having produced a fee simple. One mode of creation has been singled out for special treatment. After the enactment of the *Statute De Donis Conditionalibus*, a gift 'to A, but should (s)he die without issue, then to B' conferred a fee tail on A.[37] In Alberta, this language (presumptively) creates a conditional fee simple, the condition being the birth of a child.[38] In these instances the pre-1285 interpretation of the gift is again correct!

Another feature may also survive the statutory destruction of the estate tail: the desire of some to keep property within their family for generations to come. Perhaps it is difficult to conceive of dynastic visions in connection with a suburban home. Yet, there may exist for some a heartfelt desire, say, to maintain the farm and homestead within the family. For instance, in 1992 a court in New Brunswick was called upon to consider the will of one David McKenzie. He had devised his farm to two donees. Both gifts were made subject to the condition that the property was not to be sold for "as long as the grass grows and the water runs".[39] The

---

32 One method that will work is to protect the fee tail by statute. This was done in relation to Blenheim Palace, which is near Woodstock in Oxfordshire. Blenheim is the ancestral home of the Dukes of Marlborough. Under 5 Anne, c. 3, an estate in fee tail was created. The Act further provided that any attempt to bar the entail would be void. This fee tail still exists: for recent litigation involving both the property and the n'er-do-well tenant in tail in remainder (the Marquis of Blandford), see *Hambro v. Duke of Marlborough*, [1994] 3 All E.R. 332 (Ch.D.).

33 See *Reid v. Whiteford* (1883) 1 Man.L.R. 19 (Q.B.).

34 In *Wright v. Riach* (1924), 54 O.L.R. 404, [1924] 2 D.L.R. 273 (C.A.) at 276 D.L.R. it was said that there was no way of barring an entail in Ontario until the enactment of legislation permitting the granting of disentailing assurances in 1846.

35 *Lawlor v. Lawlor* (1882) 10 S.C.R. 194, at 206 (*per* Ritchie C.J.).

36 See, *e.g., Law of Property Act*, R.S.A. 1980, c. L-8, s. 9.

37 See, *e.g., Doe d. Anderson v. Fairfield* (1846) 3 U.C.Q.B. 140 (Full Ct.) where the devise read: "should it so happen that my daughter shall not have heirs, then . . . ". This was found to create a fee tail.

38 *Wills Act*, R.S.A. 1980, c. W-11, s. 28.

39 *McEachern v. New Brunswick Housing Corp.* (1991) 117 N.B.R. (2d) 174, 295 A.P.R. 174 (Q.B.) at 176.

ability of a prior owner to limit the present holder's rights to transfer property is quite circumscribed under the current law (the condition in the McKenzie will was struck down). The law on this point will be considered in greater detail in Chapter 7.[40]

4.   THE LIFE ESTATE

(a)   introduction

The life estate as understood in Anglo-Canadian law is at least as old as Norman feudalism. The first grants after the Conquest involved not pure rights over land, but personal obligations between lord and tenant, and it is by no means clear that these lasted beyond the life of either party.[41] The true nature of these rights is bound up with the development of the fee simple into an inheritable estate throughout the early decades of Norman rule. Within the feudal hierarchy, the lord initially guarded carefully the right to control the nomination of the immediate tenant.

The life estate still exists as an integral part of Canadian land law, though it is unlikely that it is widely used. There are probably few, if any, contemporary Canadian counterparts of the complex settlements adopted by the aristocracy in England. However, it is possible for even modest properties to be devised, say, by A 'to my widow for life, remainder to our children'.[42] This ostensibly simple limitation can pose difficult problems, primarily in the balancing of entitlements and obligations of present and future owners.

A life estate may be created to last for the life of the recipient(s) (known as a life estate *pur sa vie*) or some other person (*pur autre vie*). The person designated as the measuring life, the *cestui que vie* (which means '(s)he who lives') need not have any connection with the parties or the property and serves merely as a reference point, marking the duration of the estate. More than one life may be chosen, and unless the estate is intended to continue for joint lives, it will not end until the last *cestui que vie* has died. The transfer of a life estate *pur sa vie* transforms it into one *pur autre vie*, with the original life tenant remaining as the measuring life.[43]

A life estate may be created under a will or conveyance by carving this limited freehold interest out of the larger fee simple. Life estates may also arise by operation of law, that is, through a rule of law that can override the intentions of the property owner. The common law recognized two life estates of this type, known as dower and curtesy.[44] In western Canada, these have been replaced by comparable homestead life estates. A life estate may also serve as a remedial tool

---

40 See the discussion of restraints on alienation in Part 3(e), Chapter 7.

41 Brian Simpson has said that in this early period "all feudal holdings, all fiefs, were probably for the lives of lord and vassal and no more": A.W.B. Simpson, *A History of the Land Law*, 2nd ed. (Oxford: Clarendon Pr., 1986) at 70. See also S.E. Thorne, "English Feudalism and Estates in Land", [1959] C.L.J. 193.

42 See, *e.g.*, *Re Barrett's Estate* (1984) 46 Nfld. & P.E.I.R. 169, 135 A.P.R. 169 (Nfld.T.D.).

43 See, *e.g.*, *St-Coeur v. Chiasson* (1985) 64 N.B.R. (2d) 177, 165 A.P.R. 177 (C.A.).

44 See Part 5, *infra*.

that can be invoked, for example, to rectify unjust enrichment. This use will be explained further in Chapter 6.[45]

Here, then, is a schema of life estates:

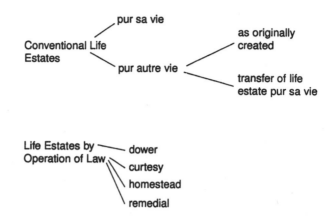

(b)   the language of creation

Unlike the fee simple, no special terminology is needed for the creation of a life estate at common law. Moreover, as we have seen, a failed attempt to confer a fee simple could produce a life estate instead.[46] This means that there is no strict code of construction for the life estate. Occasionally, a question of interpretation arises concerning whether a life estate has been given away, or whether some lesser right has been conferred, such as a mere permission (or licence) to use the land.[47] Gifts reserving a "privilege" to live on the land,[48] allowing "free use",[49] permitting the donee to "use" the property, with a gift over "[w]hen she no longer needs" the premises,[50] or the conferring of a right to occupy a dwelling house rent-free, have been found to confer a life estate.[51]

An issue of construction sometimes arises as to whether the donee was meant to receive a life estate or the fee simple. This problem can occur when an absolute gift (or one that looks absolute) is coupled with an inconsistent gift over of the same property. In its most aggravated form it might appear that the testator has

---

45 See Part 4(d), Chapter 6.

46 See the text accompanying notes 3 to 6, *supra*.

47 See, *e.g.*, *Re Walker's Application for Judicial Review*, [1999] N.I. 84 (Q.B.).

48 *Bartels v. Bartels* (1877) 42 U.C.Q.B. 22 (C.A.).

49 *Re Richer* (1919) 46 O.L.R. 367, 50 D.L.R. 614 (C.A.).

50 *Public Trustee v. Christiensen* (1999) 70 Alta.L.R. (3d) 78, 172 D.L.R. (4th) 367, [1999] 10 W.W.R. 417 (C.A.).

51 See also *Lapointe v. Cyr* (1950) 29 M.P.R. 54 (N.B.S.C.). *Cf. Re Stevenson Estate* (1990) 36 E.T.R. 289, 80 Nfld. & P.E.I.R. 277, 249 A.P.R. 277 (P.E.I.S.C.); *Powell v. Powell* (1988) 62 Alta.L.R. (2d) 379, 31 E.T.R. 105, 90 A.R. 291 (Q.B.); *Moore v. Royal Trust Co.*, [1956] S.C.R. 880, 5 D.L.R. (2d) 152; *Re Murley Estate* (1995) 130 Nfld. & P.E.I.R. 271 (Nfld.T.D.); *Re the Will of Mayer*, [1995] 2 Qd.R. 149 (S.C.).

tried to create a fee simple for life, such as where a gift reads '[to A] absolutely and forever during her lifetime'.[52] This, of course, is virtually indecipherable; the patent conflict must somehow be resolved. Three basic solutions are possible. One is to read the first gift as being absolute and to discard the subsequent stipulation as being repugnant. A second possibility is to cut down the absolute gift to a life estate, with the remainder going to the donee(s) of the second gift. A third option, lying notionally somewhere between the first two, is to treat the first gift as a life estate to which a 'power of appointment' has been appended. This power might allow the life tenant to overreach the life interest and to mortgage, sell or lease the property. Normally, when such powers are conferred they are tenable during the currency of the life estate, and whatever remains of the property can thereafter pass to the holders of the subsequent gift.

Re Walker[53] involved a repugnancy problem of this type. There, the will read as follows:

> I give . . . [to my wife] all of my real and personal property . . . and also should any portion of my estate still remain in the hands of my said wife at the time of her decease undisposed of by her the remainder shall be divided as follows . . .

Embarking on an inquiry as to the dominant intention, the Court concluded that the wife had been given an absolute gift, rendering the remainder after her death of no effect.[54] However, the search for that intention was a curt one and there is no indication given in the Walker judgment as to how this process was undertaken. The testator had two goals in mind – to confer a benefit on his widow, and to provide something for the other beneficiaries.[55] It would therefore seem to be more consonant with those desires to cut down the interest given to the widow than to exclude the other intended beneficiaries completely.

Given that either reducing the first gift to a life estate, or alternatively, ignoring the remainder, are both extreme measures, there is an allure to the third option under which the first taker is regarded as having received the hybrid interest of a life estate coupled with a power to encroach on the remainder. This possibility was regarded as unavailable in Walker because of the wording in the will (quoted above). The Court said that such a power could not be implied from the language used. Other cases suggest that greater flexibility is possible. For example, a power to encroach was found in Re Taylor, where the will gave to the testator's widow

---

52 See Re Robichaud's Will (1979) 25 N.B.R. (2d) 36, 51 A.P.R. 36 (Q.B.). This language was held to confer an absolute interest.

53 (1925) 56 O.L.R. 517 (C.A.). Cf. Re Schumacher, [1971] 4 W.W.R. 644, 20 D.L.R. (3d) 487 (Man.C.A.) affirmed (1973) 38 D.L.R. (3d) 320n (S.C.C.). For an analysis of the early authorities, see G.D. Kennedy, "Gift By Will to W: At Her Death 'What Remains' to the Children" (1950) 28 Can.B.Rev. 839.

54 See also Re MacInnis & Townshend (1973) 35 D.L.R. (3d) 459, 4 Nfld. & P.E.I.R. 211 (P.E.I.C.A.); Doe d. Humberstone v. Thomas (1834) 3 O.S. 516 (C.A.). For a host of antipodean authorities, see I.J. Hardingham et al., Wills and Intestacy in Australia and New Zealand, 2nd ed. (Sydney: Law Book Co., 1989) at 317-9.

55 This intention was pronounced in Re Loveless (1929) 36 O.W.N. 340 (H.C.). Despite this, the dominant intention was said to favour an absolute gift to the first taker.

all of his real and personal property to "have and use during her lifetime". The will also provided that "[a]ny estate, of which she may be possessed at the time of her death is to be divided equally between my daughters".[56] The widow was found to have received a life estate coupled with a power to encroach on the remainder for the purposes of her maintenance. This limit on the power to encroach, not set out explicitly in the will, was imported by the Court, presumably to respond to the claim that here the life estate + the power to encroach = a fee simple (in all but form). However, the power did not seem to cover the right to dispose of the property by will; therefore, even without the imposed constraint, the left side of the equation would not equal the right.[57] Putting aside the dubious restriction on the ambit of the power, one wonders whether this is what the testator had in mind in *Walker*, a desire that was perhaps frustrated by the rigid stance adopted by the Court in that case.

Reforms in England have attempted to reduce the uncertainty inherent in this type of gift. English law now provides that when an apparently absolute interest is given to a former spouse, followed by a gift over to any issue, it is presumed that the first gift is absolute.[58] This is only a rule of construction, so it will not avoid all future controversy. However, it would appear that the gift over to the issue cannot on its own count as a contrary intention, because otherwise the presumption would be rebutted in every case. The advantage of this drastic reading of the will (which is like that adopted in *Re Walker*) is not apparent if the donor's expectations are to count as the guiding and paramount concern. The reforms subordinate the intention to impart a benefit on the offspring. The most that can be said for the new English rule is that it works to simplify title by placing full ownership in one person. At the same time, it produces a result rather close to the effect of *Shelley's* rule![59]

(c) *rights, powers and obligations of the life tenant*

(i) *generally*

The ability to carve life estates from the larger fee simple creates two related pressure points to which the law must respond. One concerns the proper allocation of the rights and duties as between current life tenants and the succeeding owners. The second involves the impact of a life interest on alienability.

---

56 (1982) 12 E.T.R. 177, [1982] 6 W.W.R. 109, 19 Sask.R. 361 (Surr.Ct.) at 179 E.T.R. See also the various authorities on this issue referred to in the case, and also *Henderson v. Henderson* (1922) 52 O.L.R. 440 (H.C.); *Burgess v. Burrows* (1871) 21 U.C.C.P. 426 (Full Ct.). See further H.J.L. Irwin, "Annotation: Contending With Testamentary Ambiguity in Quantity of Interest Cases" (1978) 2 E.T.R. 108; *Bergmann-Porter v. Porter Estate* (1991) 44 E.T.R. 218, 110 N.S.R. (2d) 401, 299 A.P.R. 401 (T.D.); *Re Cowan Estate*, [1992] 6 W.W.R. 212, 103 Sask.R. 165 (Surr.Ct.).

57 Likewise, it cannot be said that a broader reading of the power would contravene the rule that one cannot interfere with the course of devolution: see further *Re Gee* (1973) 41 D.L.R. (3d) 317, [1974] 2 W.W.R. 176 (B.C.S.C.).

58 *Administration of Justice Act, 1982*, c. 53, s. 22.

59 However, to be fair, the English provision establishes a rule of construction, not one of law.

The balancing of rights of use and occupation between a life tenant and subsequent owners can be understood by introducing an analogous relationship – that which exists between income and capital beneficiaries. Assume that A dies leaving a large fund of money (the capital) on trust, with instructions that the interest derived from the investment of the trust funds is to be accumulated and paid annually to B (the surviving spouse) for life. Assume further that the will provides that the capital is to be divided among the surviving children on the death of the widow. The creaming off of the income for the widow should leave the capital undiminished. The trustee must walk a tightrope, attempting to optimize the income for the widow, while not jeopardizing the capital through improvident investments. This balancing act is performed in substantially the same way when settled land is involved. The copious rules that apply here can be understood if one treats the life tenant as an income beneficiary and the subsequent owners as being entitled, ultimately, to the capital (*i.e.*, the land in fee simple).[60]

(ii)   *waste*

The law of waste, which serves to limit the extent to which a life tenant may alter the *physical* complexion of real property, provides a graphic example of how the law tries to accommodate the rights of successive title holders. Waste doctrines serve an economic function. They seek to prevent those with limited interests from drawing positive externalities from the remainder. One might say that the law of waste is designed to prevent a variant of the tragedy of the commons from occurring.[61] Recall that in the tragedy parable a problem arises because there are a number of concurrent owners, each capable of over-exploiting the shared property. There is no assurance that each of these limited owners will "cherish the land".[62] The predicament here is identical except that the potential for conflict exists among a string of sequential interest holders. In particular, there is a danger that the life tenant will exploit the property in a way that reduces the value of the remainder. Something, therefore, needs to be done to control the level of exploitation undertaken during the currency of the life estate; enter the law of waste.

The principles of waste possess certain characteristics that are all too typical of English land law – they are elaborately embroidered and archaic. Much of the law was developed in the context of agrarian English society, where it is thought to have worked well to promote a land-use ethic that minimized degradation.[63] Sensibly, Canadian courts have resisted slavish adherence to "[a]ll the niceties of the ancient learning as to waste which obtain in England".[64] Still, the basic structures of English law have been applied in Canada. In theory, any conduct that permanently alters the nature of the freehold constitutes waste. However, this description is too vague. The liability of a life tenant is better understood by

---

60 See further *Trust Company of Australia Ltd. v. Braid*, [1998] 4 V.R. 97 (S.C.).
61 See Part 3(b)(ii), Chapter 1.
62 A. Ryan, *Property* (Minneapolis: U. of Minn.Pr., 1987) at 73.
63 J. Brasden & R. Fowler, "Land Degradation Issues and Institutional Restraints" in A. Chisholm & R. Dumsday, eds., *Land Degradation: Problems and Policies* (Cambridge: C.U.P., 1987) 129, at 131.
64 *Hixon v. Reaveley* (1904) 9 O.L.R. 6 (Ch.D.) at 6 (*per* Boyd C.).

reference to four distinct categories of waste: (i) *ameliorating* – acts that enhance the value of land; (ii) *permissive* – damage resulting from the failure to preserve or repair property; (iii) *voluntary* – conduct that diminishes the value of the land; and (iv) *equitable* – severe and malicious destruction.

The liability of a life tenant is not nearly as comprehensive as these stern definitions seem to suggest. Courts appear reluctant to prohibit or punish the commission of *ameliorating* waste,[65] since the end result of improving the property is to confer a financial benefit on those who own the remainder. However, there may be costs associated with this action that may in the end burden those holding the remainder: in particular, property taxes may rise as a result of the improvements. Plus, we know that there is often more to the enjoyment of property than that represented by its net worth. Therefore, ameliorating waste that significantly transforms the property may be actionable. Indeed, it has been suggested that this form of waste reflects values related to the personhood justification of private property. As Margaret Jane Radin has argued:

> [t]he doctrine of ameliorative waste probably now rests implicitly on the assumption that the remainderperson has personhood interests at stake that are irrelevant to the valuations of the marketplace.[66]

Responsibility for *permissive* waste is not automatically imposed on a life tenant. The instrument under which the estate is created must contain such a requirement and unless this is done the life tenant assumes no obligation to repair buildings on the property.[67] I suppose this posture flows from the reluctance of the law to impose, by implication, positive obligations of unpredictable dimensions on a tenant. However, the result of this reluctance is also problematic: a life tenant who is not bound to prevent permissive waste can, with impunity, allow the property to deteriorate, with the likely result that the worth of the capital holding (the freehold) declines.

The control of *voluntary* waste places the greatest fetter on the exploitation of land in the hands of a tenant for life. The rules governing voluntary waste are supposed to prevent the over-cultivation of timber estates, the destruction of buildings, the opening of new mines, and other conduct that will diminish the property in the long run. However, the common law recognizes a number of qualifications on this form of liability. As a general rule it is not wasteful to clear land for cultivation; such action is consonant with good husbandry. Nor is the felling of trees to make certain types of repairs actionable.[68]

---

65 See *Doherty v. Allman* (1878) 3 App.Cas. 709 (H.L.).

66 M.J. Radin, ''Property and Personhood'', 34 Stan.L.Rev. 957 (1982) at 1013, n. 202. Personhood theories of ownership are discussed in Chapter 1, Part 3(e).

67 See generally *Patterson v. Central Canada Loan & Savings Co.* (1898) 29 O.R. 134 (Div.Ct.).

68 A life tenant may cut timber to repair the premises (housebote), agricultural implements (ploughbote), and fences (haybote): see *Hiltz v. Langille* (1959) 42 M.P.R. 333, 18 D.L.R. (2d) 464 (N.S.C.A.). In Canada, the wood that is cut need not be used for these purposes; instead it can be sold to raise money for the purchase of more suitable materials: *Hixon v. Reaveley, supra,* note 64.

Not every life tenant is necessarily required to comply with the limitations on land use imposed through the law of waste. For one thing, a grantor may render a life tenant 'unimpeachable' (*i.e.*, exempt from responsibility) for waste. This waiver permits the life tenant to commit all forms of waste, except for that egregious type of destruction referred to as *equitable* waste. Modern legislation frequently provides that exemption from liability for this type of waste must be more explicitly conferred.[69] Additionally, present and future landowners can always bargain for a different result than that dictated by waste principles.

The concept of waste was called into service in the important Aboriginal land rights case of *Delgamuukw v. British Columbia*. There it was held that land under Aboriginal title cannot be used in a manner that is irreconcilable with the nature of the attachment to that land underscoring the claim. While acknowledging that the *sui generis* nature of Aboriginal title means that traditional land law concepts should not automatically be applied to such lands, the restrictions on exploitation were likened to the concept of equitable waste. Taking the term equitable waste to mean wanton or extravagant acts of destruction, Lamer C.J.C. said that "[t]his description of the limits imposed by the doctrine of equitable waste capture[s] the kind of limit I have in mind here".[70] If that is the standard, then Aboriginal landholders have a good deal of scope for development. However, the examples cited by the Chief Justice as potentially unacceptable uses – strip mining, paving a parking lot – more closely resemble forms of voluntary waste, at worst.[71] This is a more confining limitation on land use.

(iii)   *other management issues*

The doctrine of waste confronts just one issue affecting the successive freehold owners.[72] Maintaining property is often expensive: who must pay the costs of upkeep? The general rule is that a life tenant is liable for all current expenses, including property taxes in an amount up to the annual value of the land[73] and interest due on a mortgage debt.[74] Given that mortgages commonly call for blended payments of interest and principal,[75] a life tenant should be able to seek reimbursement from the owners of the remainder for the principal sums paid on

---

69 See, *e.g.*, *Law of Property Act*, R.S.A. 1980, c. L-8, s. 62.

70 *Delgamuukw v. British Columbia*, [1997] 3 S.C.R. 1010, [1998] 1 C.N.L.R. 14, 153 D.L.R. (4th) 193, at 1090-1 S.C.R.

71 Accord W.F. Flanagan, "Piercing the Veil of Real Property Law: *Delgamuukw v. British Columbia*" (1998) 24 Queen's L.J. 279, at 313*ff.*

72 Moreover, principles of waste apply in other circumstances, including these: as between landlord and tenant, joint tenants, tenants in common, mortgagor and mortgagee, a tenant in fee simple subject to defeasance and those entitled to the remainder, and vendor and purchaser. See further *New Westminster (City) v. Kennedy*, [1918] 1 W.W.R. 489 (B.C.Co.Ct.) where the situations in which the doctrine of equitable waste applies are listed. *Cf. Re Gilbert*, [1959] O.W.N. 294 (H.C.).

73 See the *obiter* comments in *Mayo v. Leitovski*, [1928] 1 W.W.R. 700 (Man.K.B.); *Re Denison* (1893) 24 O.R. 197 (Ch.D.). See also *Biscoe v. Van Bearle* (1858) 6 Gr. 438 (U.C.Ch.D.).

74 *Re Morrison Estate* (1921) 16 Sask.L.R. 7, [1922] 3 W.W.R. 493, 68 D.L.R. 787 (K.B.).

75 See Part 4(b), Chapter 11.

their behalf.[76] The owner of the life estate is in some ways in a fiduciary relationship with those entitled to the remainder, but this does not impose an obligation on the life tenant to insure the premises. Nor is there a duty to repair (unless permissive waste obligations are contained in the settlement). By the same token, the life tenant has no claim against those holding the remainder for the costs of improvements or repairs that have been undertaken unilaterally except, perhaps, for repairs done in the name of preserving the property from further deterioration (*i.e.*, as acts of salvage).[77]

The host of issues that can arise in the regulation of entitlements and duties can be dealt with explicitly when the life estate is created.[78] One method of management involves placing the legal title to the lands in trustees, who then hold the property on trust for the life tenant and those who own the remainder. The responsibility for making payments can be delegated to the trustees with instructions as to how to allocate the cost of expenses. Under a trust such as this the trustee might be directed to recoup expenses by charging the remainder, or by spreading the costs among the successive owners in a manner that is consistent with the income/capital analogy.

When the trust approach is adopted the life tenant's right to possession of the premises may be abridged. When the land is held on trust, there is authority that "the right to give possession to the life-tenant is discretionary with the Court".[79] This restriction on a life tenant's rights may be reasonable if the trustees are charged with duties for which possession is normally required. However, when the trust clearly bestows (or denies) a right of possession on a life tenant, then conferring a special and sweeping discretion on the court seems inappropriate. This discretion should be subordinate to the intention of the donor and should operate only when that intention is equivocal as to the right of possession, or when the basic law governing the variation of a trust is satisfied.[80] A logical starting point should be that an equitable life tenant, like all owners, is entitled to possession unless the trust document expressly or impliedly suggests otherwise. It is far from clear that this is the present law.[81]

(iv)   *settled estates legislation*

The life estate was a constituent element of the strict family settlement, which was at one time a prevalent estate planning device used by England's

---

76 See *Macklem v. Cumings* (1859) 7 Gr. 318 (U.C.Ch.D.).

77 *Re Buhr Estate* (1993) 90 Man.R. (2d) 118 (Q.B.).

78 See, *e.g.*, *Re Waters* (1978) 21 O.R. (2d) 124, 89 D.L.R. (3d) 742 (H.C.).

79 *Re Cunningham* (1917) 12 O.W.N. 268 (H.C.) at 269 (*per* Masten J.). See also H.G. Hanbury, *Godfroi on Trusts and Trustees*, 5th ed. (London: Stevens & Sons, 1927) at 428-9.

80 As to which, see D.W.M. Waters, *The Law of Trusts in Canada*, 2nd ed. (Toronto: Carswell, 1984) ch. 27.

81 See further *Whiteside v. Miller* (1868) 14 Gr. 393 (U.C.Ch.D.); *Hefferman v. Taylor* (1888) 15 O.R. 670 (Ch.D.); *Orford v. Orford* (1884) 6 O.R. 6 (Ch.D.). See also *Homfray v. Homfray* (1936) 51 B.C.R. 287 (S.C.). And a court may call for the posting of security or a promise of an indemnity, as a way of protecting those entitled to the remainder: P. Butt, *Land Law*, 3rd ed. (Sydney: Law Book Co., 1996) at 139-40.

landed class. Stripped to essentials, under a strict settlement, the family mansion and grounds might be given to A for life, with a remainder to A's issue in fee tail.[82] Typically, the settlement was gender-biased. Though the detailed terms often made provision for all members of the family, the information we have suggests that settlements were, in the main, "patrilineal, primogenitive, and patriarchal".[83] They helped to maintain a certain social order.

The inefficiency produced by the division of estates under complex settlements was quite pronounced; for this reason it incurred the wrath of political economists such as Bentham, Mill and Adam Smith.[84] Under a settlement the life tenant's ability to exploit the land was circumscribed by the law of waste. Absent a power to encroach on the remainder, the life tenant's power to sell, mortgage or lease was also limited: it extended only to the life interest itself.[85] The life tenant's ability to impose repair costs on the estate in remainder was, as we have just seen, rather limited.[86] These fetters could be overcome by conferring powers to sell, lease, mortgage, etc., but apparently this was infrequently done. That should not be surprising, given that the aim of the settlement was to preserve the lands. Settlements usually made it as clear as day that the lands were not supposed to circulate and wind up in the hands of those who valued them most. The strict settlement, standing in the way of free commercial trade in land, demonstrates that personhood values seem to have affected the ways in which members of England's propertied elite treated their holdings.

Throughout the period of industrial expansion in England in the nineteenth century a series of legislative reforms were introduced that were aimed at allowing property tied up in family settlements to be set free. The first wave of reform augmented slightly the powers of the life tenant to encumber the remainder. Most of these new powers required judicial sanction before they could be exercised.[87] The second wave, embodied principally in the English Settled Land Act, 1882,[88] resulted in significantly greater control being given to the life tenant to manage the entire estate. The 1882 legislation accorded the holder of a life estate wide powers to lease, mortgage and sell. The monies received had to be held under a

---

82 To prevent the fee tail in remainder from being barred, an accommodation had to be made with the heir holding the entail. The process of co-opting (i.e., bribing) the heir is explained in E. Spring, "The Settlement of Land in 19th Century England", 8 Am.J.Leg.Hist. 209 (1964). As to the social significance of the settlement, see M.R. Chesterman, "Family Settlements on Trust: Landowners and the Rise of the Bourgeoisie" in G.R. Rubin & D. Sugarman, eds., Law, Economy & Society: Essays in the History of English Law (Abingdon: Professional Books, 1984) 124. See also E. Spring, Law, Land and Family: Aristocratic Inheritance in England, 1300 to 1800 (Chapel Hill: U.N.C. Pr., 1993) ch. 5; A. Pottage, "Proprietary Strategies: The Legal Fabric of Aristocratic Settlements" (1998) 61 Mod.L.Rev. 162.

83 Spring, Law, Land & Family, supra, note 82, at 144.

84 Ibid. at 125.

85 See, e.g., Doe d. Fields v. M'Kay (1844) 4 N.B.R. 435 (S.C.).

86 See the text accompanying note 77, supra.

87 See, e.g., Settled Estates Act, 1877.

88 45 & 46 Vict., c. 38.

trust for sale for the benefit of the life tenant as well as for those entitled to the remainder.[89]

Some Canadian provinces enacted settled estates legislation along the lines of the first wave of English reforms.[90] These confer limited unilateral rights of disposal on life tenants. The statutes also provide, *inter alia*, for mortgages or sales, with court approval. Other provinces have acquired some of the English reforms through the operation of the laws governing the reception of English law into the colonies. In Alberta, the Court of Queen's Bench is clothed with the same powers in relation to leases and sales of settled estates that existed in England on July 15, 1870.[91] Given that date, the law in that province is principally contained in the English *Settled Estates Act, 1856*.[92] This cumbersome and prolix statute, which was part of the first wave of English reforms, provides for restricted rights of transfer by sale or lease. But no right to mortgage is conferred, on approval or otherwise. The only unilateral action permitted is the granting of leases of twenty-one years or less. This power can be precluded by the settlement and it does not apply to the "principal Mansion House"[93] and surrounding lands. In short, the powers conferred under the 1856 Act are so emaciated as to be virtually worthless in a modern setting.

In 1996, the Ontario Law Reform Commission (following Manitoba's lead[94]) suggested that the law governing settled estates be replaced by a different regime. They proposed that for successive interests in land a trust (to hold or retain the land) would be presumed to exist when one is not expressly established. As a general matter, the basic law of trusts would apply.[95]

5.   LIFE ESTATES ARISING BY OPERATION OF LAW

A life estate may be created not only by private conveyance, but also by operation of law, *i.e.*, through the invocation of a legal doctrine which, when applicable, automatically confers an estate on A in the lands of B. Early English law found the life estate to be a useful instrument of social policy and in this context two estates were recognized: dower and curtesy. A similar concept can be found in modern western Canadian homestead legislation.

---

89 English law has recently undergone reform: see the *Trusts of Land and Appointment of Trustees Act 1996*, c. 47, outlined in N. Hopkins, "The Trustees of Land and Appointment of Trustees Act" [1996] Conv. 410.

90 See, *e.g.*, *Settled Estates Act*, R.S.O. 1990, c. S.7, the first version of which was enacted in 1895.

91 *Judicature Act*, R.S.A. 1980, c. J-1, para. 6(2)(a).

92 19 & 20 Vict., c. 120. This Act was received into Saskatchewan: *Re Moffat Estate* (1955) 16 W.W.R. 314 (Sask.Q.B.).

93 S. 32.

94 *The Perpetuities and Accumulations Act*, R.S.M. 1987, c. P33, especially s. 4.

95 Ontario Law Reform Commission (Toronto: A.G. (Ont.), 1996) at 30*ff*, 157-8. However, it would be made clear that a beneficiary with a present vested interest in the land (typically a life tenant) would be entitled to possession.

(a) dower

Dower was designed to provide shelter for widows. The common law rules for the inheritance of land, the rules of primogeniture, did not contemplate the transmission of land to a surviving spouse on the death of the owner-spouse. Hence, another means was needed if land was to be used to provide fall-back support for a widow. This was to be the function of dower, which conferred on the widow a life interest in the freehold lands of her deceased husband. At common law this was an entitlement that took precedence over a testamentary transfer of dowerable lands.

The genesis of English (and *ergo* Canadian) dower law has been traced to Germanic and Anglo-Saxon law and custom, but the precise origins of dower are mired in uncertainty. The ancient practice of voluntarily providing the wife with a dowry on marriage[96] seems to have evolved into an entitlement to a portion of her husband's lands on his death. During the marriage the wife had a right to dower inchoate (or dower initiate) once the husband became seised of dowerable property. While this did not provide a direct power to deal with that land or to prevent its alienation, a wife's dower rights would run with the land unless she consented to the transfer. The wife's dower rights remained intact even if the purchaser had no notice of the dower claim. Understandably, then, the presence of a potential dower claim could have a chilling effect on transactions. On the death of the husband the inchoate dower right became a consummate one and could be enjoyed by the widow in possession. The quantum of the entitlement evolved over time, and centuries before the reception of English law into Canada, an allotment of one-third of the deceased-husband's lands had become the norm.[97]

Dower looks strange today. Its ambit was narrow, more so than one finds under more modern spousal support regimes. Dower did not apply to a variety of property interests, including leaseholds, joint tenancies, land held by a corporation, and reversionary interests or remainders. It did not apply to equitable interests until 1833. Furthermore, an entitlement to dower was unconnected to actual need. The one-third share was invariable, and the enjoyment of dower consummate was not abridged by the widow's remarriage. Unlike current matrimonial property law, dower entitlements were not premised on direct or indirect contributions to

---

96 See further C.M.A. McCauliff, "The Medieval Origin of the Doctrine of Estates in Land: Substantive Property Law, Family Considerations, and the Interests of Women", 66 Tul.L.Rev. 919 (1992).

97 The influence of English dower law in Canada was strong, and the links with the ancient past were sometimes quite evident. For example, the *Magna Carta* of 1215 enshrined the right of a widow to remain in her deceased husband's house for 40 days, the quarantine period, immediately after his death. During that time, the dower lands were to be assigned to her. A comparable right was contained in the Ontario *Dower Act* and remained good law until 1978, when the Act was abolished. The *Magna Carta* provides that "[a]fter the death of her husband, a widow may remain in her husband's house for forty days after his death, within which time her dower shall be assigned to her". Section 1 of the *Dower Act*, R.S.O. 1970, c. 135 (now repealed) stated that "[a] widow, on the death of her husband, may tarry in his chief house for forty days after his death, within which time her dower shall be assigned to her". See further G.L. Haskins, "The Development of Common Law Dower", 62 Harv.L.Rev. 42 (1948-9).

the acquisition of property.[98] Common law dower had an uneven fit with the modern constellation of rights and remedies governing property-sharing on death; most of these developed long after the emergence of dower. On intestacy, far from being excluded from the right to inherit land (as would occur under primogeniture), the widowed spouse is placed in a preferred position in relation to offspring and all other claimants. Family relief legislation permits a spouse to seek financial support where adequate provision out of the deceased's estate is lacking. In proceedings brought under these statutes there is a case-specific consideration of desert and need. Additionally, rights to possession of the matrimonial home during and after marriage are nowadays dealt with under marital property legislation.

Perhaps the most remarkable aspect of dower was the degree to which it could be avoided altogether by a recalcitrant husband. The assertion that "a widow shall have her dower"[99] was farcical. Through a form of conveyance known as a 'deed to uses' a husband could effectively enjoy the incidents of fee simple ownership and yet insulate the property from his wife's dower claims. Until the abolition of dower in Ontario, the use of such deeds was a standard feature of conveyancing and a mound of jurisprudence had developed concerning the practice.[100] More simply, in England after 1833 dower rights could be terminated by means of an *inter vivos* conveyance or a devise. Owing to these theoretical and practical deficiencies, common law dower is now a creature of the past.[101] In some provinces it has been completely overrun by the reforms mentioned above. In western Canada, as we will see, a dower-like interest has been created through homestead legislation.[102]

(b) curtesy

A widower's interest in the lands of his deceased wife was known as an estate by the Curtesy of England. Smoothing over the technical differences between dower and curtesy, the two estates look equivalent. However, their elements were not identical, nor were their respective functions. There is controversy surrounding the original purpose of curtesy. The most commonly accepted view is that it was designed to finesse or postpone the claims of feudal lords to certain incidents of tenure (primarily the right of wardship) that might otherwise arise on the devolution of land from a woman to an infant heir. As long as the father was alive, this "gracious rule"[103] (*i.e.*, curtesy) prevented the lands from passing to

---

98 See Part 7, Chapter 9.

99 This declaration is recited in R. St. J. McDonald, "Observations on the Land Law in the Common Law Provinces of Canada" in E. McWhinney, ed., *Canadian Jurisprudence: The Civil Law and Common Law in Canada* (Toronto: Carswell, 1958) 197, at 218.

100 One of the most peculiar and intriguing of the many decisions in this area is *Re Hazell* (1925) 57 O.L.R. 290, [1925] 3 D.L.R. 661 (C.A.).

101 See, *e.g.*, *Law of Property Act*, R.S.A. 1980, c. L-8, s. 3.

102 See Part 5(c), *infra*.

103 F. Pollock & F.W. Maitland, *The History of English Law*, 2nd ed. (Cambridge: C.U.P., 1923) vol. 2, at 417. See also T.F.T. Plucknett, *A Concise History of the Common Law*, 4th ed. (London: Butterworths, 1948) at 537. *Cf.* S. Staves, *Married Women's Separate Property in England, 1660-1833* (Cambridge: H.U.P., 1990) at 83.

the infant, an event that would have allowed the lord to reap profits from the land during that heir's minority.

Farrer's view is different: he saw curtesy as promoting family cohesion, by serving as a means of mediating the claims of widower and offspring.[104] On the mother's death, the child would eventually be able to assume control of her separate estate to the exclusion of the father. Curtesy prevented this. Farrer maintained further that although curtesy first arose in relation to land conferred on a wife through a marriage settlement, "a time when the interest of the whole prospective family is . . . considered",[105] it was later applied to the wife's other acquisitions.

The right of curtesy conferred upon the widower a life estate in all of the realty undisposed of at the death of the wife,[106] as long as heritable issue had been born – and heard to cry within the four walls – during the marriage. As with dower, there is little evidence that curtesy was of much good to widowers in England. It has been abolished in Canada[107] and the family property and support laws that are now in place here are formally gender-neutral.

(c)   homestead protections[108]

Common law dower was abolished in the prairie provinces in the 1880s and in British Columbia in 1925.[109] But amidst the perilous economic climate in western Canada in the early twentieth century a need arose for protection of the matrimonial home from seizure by creditors of the husband. The response came in the form of homestead legislation.

The Canadian statutes that were introduced drew heavily on developments occurring in the United States.[110] Typically, homestead laws (i) exempt the family home from seizure by creditors; (ii) enable the non-owning spouse to prevent dispositions of the home; and (iii) confer a life estate in the home on that spouse after the death of the owner. In Alberta, this latter right includes a life estate in personalty.[111] Generally speaking, these three elements remain part of the law in the four western provinces. While the Canadian statutes are clearly derivative of their American counterparts, a faint resemblance with common law dower can

---

104 F.E. Farrer, "Tenant by the Curtesy of England" (1927) 43 L.Q.R. 87, at 90-1.

105 *Ibid.*

106 See *McLellan v. Taylor* (1901) 40 N.S.R. 275 (S.C. *in banco*); *De Bury v. De Bury* (1903) 36 N.B.R. 57 (Eq.) affirmed (1903) 36 N.B.R. 90 (C.A.). By the twentieth century, legislation in many common law jurisdictions permitted a married women to dispose of her real property by will.

107 See, *e.g., Law of Property Act*, R.S.A. 1980, c. L-8, s. 4.

108 See generally W.N. Renke, "Homestead Legislation in the Four Western Provinces" in J. G. McLeod & A.A. Mamo, eds., *Matrimonial Property Law in Canada* (Toronto: Carswell, 1993) (looseleaf).

109 See further R.E. Hawkins, "Dower Abolition in Western Canada: How Law Reform Failed" (1997) 24 Man.L.J. 635. See also W.F. Bowker, "Our Earliest 'Homestead' or 'Dower' Act" (1986) 24 Alta.L.Rev. 522.

110 See generally A. Milner, "A Homestead Act for England?" (1959) 22 Mod.L.Rev. 458.

111 *Dower Act*, R.S.A. 1980, c. D-38, s. 23.

also be seen: common law dower trumped the claims of the husband's creditors; the refusal of a wife to bar common law dower often functioned to prevent dispositions; and, of course, the essence of dower consummate was the life estate.

The survival of homestead law in the west suggests that it has been more effective than its common law counterpart, but little is known about whether dower does protect the interests of the non-owning spouse. Indeed, although the introduction of homestead law in Alberta was thought to mark a major victory for the women's movement in that province, it was soon realized what a limited gain this had been. Cavanaugh has described this disillusionment:

> By 1917 feminists in Alberta had fought for and won dower rights guaranteeing the married woman a voice in the management and control of family property and a life interest in her deceased husband's estate. Yet, many women were left with a sense that the justice they had sought had, in the end, eluded them. To paraphrase Henrietta Muir Edwards, the wife had still not got what she wanted. While the Dower Act granted protection to the married woman in her home, it did not extend to her the full recognition of her contribution to the family farm that most women sought.[112]

Granted, the modern law confers a spectrum of rights on the non-owning spouse (whether the husband or wife). The sanctions that can be imposed in response to a wrongful disposition are sharp: transactions may be set aside;[113] in Alberta a right of action for damages may accrue[114] and a wrongful transfer is treated as a quasi-criminal offence.[115] Whether dower serves as a useful support mechanism may be questioned. With the introduction of modern intestacy, dependants' relief, and marital property laws, protections now exist for spouses that were not in place when common law dower first emerged. Given this, and the likelihood that many widows and widowers are, in fact, provided for by will, one wonders just how many dower life estates fall into possession. Even if this rarely happens, an Alberta Law Reform Institute report for discussion has suggested that dower be preserved in a modified form.[116] If nothing else, requiring that a non-owning spouse consent to a disposition of the family home is a valuable protection in its own right. It prevents the sale of the home that might eliminate one's ability to seek an order of exclusive possession under the *Matrimonial Property Act*.[117] Moreover, little is lost by providing a right of a widow or widower to remain in the home as a dower right, as a last resort.

---

112 C.A. Cavanaugh, *The Women's Movement in Alberta as Seen Through the Campaign for Dower Rights 1909-1929*, M.A. Thesis, Department of History, University of Alberta (1986) at 95 [copy on file at the University of Alberta]. See also M. McCallum, "Prairie Women and the Struggle for a Dower Law, 1905-1920" (1993) 18 Prairie Forum 19.

113 See, *e.g.*, *Meduk v. Soja*, [1958] S.C.R. 167, 12 D.L.R (2d) 289.

114 *Dower Act*, R.S.A. 1980, c. D-38, s. 11.

115 See, *e.g.*, *Dower Act*, R.S.A. 1980, c. D-38, sub. 2(3).

116 Alberta Law Reform Institute, *The Matrimonial Home* (Edmonton: A.L.R.I., 1995).

117 R.S.A. 1980, c. M-9, Part II. There is no general requirement of consent to dispositions of the home under the *M.P.A.*

6. TIMESHARING[118]

With the advent of timesharing over the last two decades, principally in relation to holiday resorts, a new challenge has been thrown to real estate practitioners. The purpose of entering into timeshare arrangements is usually to allow enjoyment of an interest in property for a limited period of time every year. This period may be fixed in advance for all time, or may be settled by reservations, lotteries, or through some other method. A typical timesharing arrangement might involve one condominium unit that is divided into 52 shares of one week each. Two weeks might be blocked off for repairs to the premises and the other 50 allotted to willing timesharers. In the context of resort properties the aim is often to reduce the costs and inconveniences of vacationing, while securing for the participant a proprietary interest in an appreciating asset. Absent special legislation, the conveyancing problem is this: what sort of timesharing bricolage can be manufactured with the materials supplied under the general law, including the fusty relics of the law of estates?

A number of arrangements have been tried.[119] A recurring right of occupation can be secured easily enough by using a series of discontinuous leases or licences.[120] Direct ownership of the timeshare property is also possible, with all holders obtaining an interest in the freehold as tenants in common. If this method is adopted, the individual times of enjoyment must still be fixed because in the absence of an agreement to the contrary co-owners are entitled at all times to possession of the whole property.[121]

Another means of establishing timesharing involves indirect ownership of the land. For example, title may be placed in a corporation, co-operative, club, or trust, with individuals receiving a share of that asset. The units of time that the 'owners' would receive would then be determined through an agreed system. One way of orchestrating this arrangement is for the developer to set up a timeshare corporation and then to grant this company a long-term lease. The fee simple is then sold to the participants, along with shares in the company. Although they are all then co-owners of the land, their co-ownership rights are subject to the prior lease to the company. Even if the freehold is sold this will not affect the continuation of the lease. That company (or other agency) then confers the time units on the holders in accordance with rules established by the shareholders.

An untested approach in Canada, and one that would *not* mesh with orthodox doctrine, is to create a series of recurring short-term freehold estates. To say that X owns Blackacre exclusively and permanently, but only for a set time each year,

---

118 See further D.T. Anderson, ''The Law Relating to Timeshared Property in the Common Law Provinces of Canada'' in Canadian Comparative Law Association, *Contemporary Law* (Cowansville, P.Q.:Yvon Blais, 1992) 220; T. Eastman, ''Time Share Ownership: A Primer'', 57 N.D.L.Rev. 151 (1981); M.L. Savage *et al.*, ''Time Share Regulation: The Wisconsin Model'', 77 Marq.L.Rev. 719 (1994).

119 See further Ontario Law Reform Commission, *Report on Timesharing* (Toronto: A.G. (Ont.), 1988) at ch. 2.

120 For the distinction between the two, see Part 2(c), Chapter 8.

121 See Part 2(a), Chapter 9.

would be novel. The common law has been reluctant to recognize 'fancy' new real property rights,[122] so it is quite risky to establish a scheme based solely on this approach. If accepted, some account would have to be made of issues of waste, taxes, and related management matters. Requiring all owners to contribute, say, to the cost of repairs, can be made part of the initial contract. As we will see, though, the transmissibility of such positive obligations into the hands of new purchasers of freehold interests cannot be accomplished easily.[123] Indeed, as a result of the difficulties associated with the 'fragmented fee' tack, the timesharing devices that were described above are those that tend to be adopted.

As we have seen, because timesharing projects exist in a legal world that is not designed for this new arrangement, the governing regimes are usually stitched together by using aspects of the laws of freehold and leasehold estates, general contract principles, and basics of company law. In place of this patchwork, the Ontario Law Reform Commission has proposed the introduction of a comprehensive *Timeshare Act*, designed to regulate the legal structure, marketing, management, registration and termination of timeshare projects.[124] It would apply to all projects with more than ten units that are intended to last for longer than five years. The Act contemplates the creation of special timeshare ownership concepts, together with mechanisms for allocating responsibilities among the owners of the fee. If enacted, the legislation would formally recognize interval ownership as a valid form of landholding.

7.   ESTATES IN ABORIGINAL LANDS

The doctrine of estates applies to land held under the general law; however, this is not the only system of land ownership in Canada. By virtue of the rights preserved under common law Aboriginal title, property rules can exist under customary native law. Additionally, unique rules for landholding exist in the more than 2,300 reserves presently under federal regulation. Entitlements to land on a reserve may be granted to individual Band members by the governing Band Council, with the approval of the responsible federal minister.[125] That right, held under a Certificate of Possession, is somewhat analogous to a fee simple interest. Such an entitlement conferred under the *Indian Act* has many of the trappings of ownership in fee: it confers exclusive rights of occupation and it may be devised.[126] This interest is capable of being transferred on the consent of the federal minister, although the potential recipients are restricted to the Band or Band members.[127] A provisional grant of two years (subject to renewal) may also be granted under a Certificate of Occupation.[128] All of these ownership rights are conditional on the holder remaining resident on the reserve. If this should no longer be the case,

---

122 See Part 4(a)(iii), Chapter 1.
123 See Part 9, Chapter 10.
124 *Supra*, note 119, at 82-3.
125 *Indian Act*, R.S.C. 1985, c. I-5, s. 20.
126 As to the rules governing transmission on death, see ss. 45-50 [as am.]. See further J. Woodward, *Native Law* (Toronto: Carswell, 1989) (looseleaf) ch. XVI, *passim*.
127 S. 24. See also sub. 58(3) [as am.].
128 Subs. 20(4) to (6).

a transfer to the Band or a member must be made, normally within six months. Failing this, the land reverts to the Band, which is required to provide compensation to the former holder.[129]

In Alberta, a new property-holding regime has been established for eight Métis communities.[130] The system adopts some of the *Indian Act* structures, but it does so in a way that provides a more explicit detailing of the incidents of ownership. Under the Métis legislation, rights in settlement lands can be created by a General Council.[131] A Land Policy has been enacted that contemplates three main types of interests: Métis title, provisional Métis title, and allotments.

An individual holding Métis title has the exclusive right to (i) use and occupy the land; (ii) make improvements on the land; (iii) transfer the title; (iv) grant lesser interests as set out in the Land Policy; and (v) determine who receives the title on the holder's death.[132] However, the land may not be given as security for a debt, and may not be held under a joint tenancy or a tenancy in common. As with rights under the *Indian Act*, to describe this form of ownership as a fee simple estate is inapposite. Title to the fee has been transferred by the Province of Alberta to a General Council by way of conditional grants under letters patent.[133]

A provisional title, which is granted for a fixed (but renewable) term, resembles a conditional grant under the *Indian Act*. It is intended to serve as a stepping stone for those wishing to acquire full Métis title. The grant must specify the conditions (such as the making of improvements) which, if met, will give the holder the right to acquire a Métis title in the land.[134] An allotment, the third type of interest, can be granted for a set time period for the purpose of allowing the holder to use the parcel to operate a farm, ranch or other business.[135]

The three forms of Métis title, together with the system of land registration under which they are recorded,[136] are unique. As with the federal system, there are restrictions on alienation, title may pass by descent in accordance with special

---

129 S. 25.
130 *Metis Settlements Act*, S.A. 1990, c. M-14.3 [as am.]. See also the *Metis Settlements Land Protection Act*, S.A. 1990, c. M-14.8; *Metis Settlements Accord Implementation Act*, S.A. 1990, c. M-14.5 [as am.]; and the *Constitution of Alberta Amendment Act, 1990*, S.A. 1990, c. C-22.2. For a full analysis of these developments, with a detailed consideration of the numerous land law issues that are raised, see C.E. Bell, *Alberta's Metis Settlements Legislation: An Overview of Ownership and Management of Settlement Lands* (Regina: Canadian Plains Research Center, 1994). See also C.E. Bell, *Contemporary Metis Justice: The Settlement Way* (Saskatoon: Native Law Centre, 1999) at 71*ff.*
131 By virtue of s. 99 of the *Metis Settlements Act*, an interest in settlement lands can arise only under the *Metis Settlements Act*, another statute, General Council Policy, or Settlement By-laws.
132 *Metis Settlements General Council Land Policy*, subcl. 2.4(1). Subclause (2) provides that the "holder of the Metis title also has any additional rights with respect to the parcel that are specifically provided for by General Council Policy or any other enactment".
133 A sample Crown patent is set out in Bell (1994), *supra*, note 130, at Appendix 2.
134 Clause 2.5.
135 Clause 2.6.
136 See Bell (1994), *supra*, note 130, at ch. 4, *passim*. The registration system that is in place on the settlement lands is based on the Alberta Law Reform Institute's *Model Land Recording and Registration Act*, which is discussed in Part 6(a), Chapter 12.

rules, and the lands are liable to seizure and expropriation. In short, these forms of ownership possess many of the attributes described by Honoré in his depiction of fulsome ownership.[137] Even if the bundle is not complete, the same can be said for most (if not all) proprietary entitlements tenable under the general law of property.

8.   PERSONALTY AND THE DOCTRINE OF ESTATES

The doctrine of estates is inapplicable to personalty; chattels can be owned outright. As a result, at common law an *inter vivos* gift of a chattel for life, or even for an hour,[138] is treated, in theory, as absolute. The imprint of the English ecclesiastical courts is evident here. These courts, which possessed some jurisdiction over the rules governing personalty, were influenced by Roman law, which had no concept of estates.

The common law rule is subject to several substantial qualifications. First, the granting of a temporary interest in a chattel – a bailment – is possible.[139] Borrow a book from the library for two weeks and you will hold a possessory estate-*like* interest. Second, equity will recognize time-limited gifts of personalty contained in a trust. For instance, stocks and bonds might be given to trustees to hold for the benefit of a succession of beneficiaries.[140] Third, it is accepted that the dividing up of the legal title of personalty under a will is valid.[141] If a chattel is bequeathed 'to A for life, then to B absolutely', this creates a type of future interest.[142] Three theories have been advanced to explain the nature of these consecutive rights.[143] Either (i) the title vests immediately in B, with a usufructuary right in A for life; (ii) A becomes the absolute owner, with something called an executory gift over to B; or (iii) A takes the property subject to a trust in favour of B.[144] In addition, sometimes estate interests in personalty are introduced through

---

137 See Part 2(a), Chapter 1.

138 *Anon* (1548) Brooke Abr. Devise, pl. 13, reproduced in J.H. Baker & S.F.C. Milsom, *Sources of English Legal History: Private Law to 1750* (London: Butterworths, 1986) at 186. See also *Re Troup* (1944) 52 Man.R. 384, [1945] 1 W.W.R. 364, [1945] 2 D.L.R. 450 (K.B.).

139 Bailments are examined in Part 8, Chapter 8.

140 See *Read v. Rayner* (1943) 16 M.P.R. 554, [1943] 2 D.L.R. 225 (P.E.I.S.C. *in banco*) affirmed [1943] 4 D.L.R. 803 (S.C.C.), where a gift of stocks and bonds was given by a father to his daughter, subject to his right to receive interest and dividends during his life. This seems explicable only if the daughter is to be regarded as a trustee; otherwise the common law rule seems to be violated. The point does not seem to have been raised. See also *Re Henry*, [1969] 2 O.R. 878, 7 D.L.R. (3d) 310 (H.C.).

141 See *Re Mackay* (1972) 20 F.L.R. 147 (S.A.Insolv.Ct.) at 160*ff. Cf. Re Troup*, *supra*, note 138.

142 See, *e.g.*, *Re Bangs* (1962) 39 W.W.R. 623, 38 D.L.R. (2d) 99 (Man.Q.B.).

143 D.T. Oliver, ''Interests for Life and Quasi-Remainders in Chattels Personal'' (1908) 24 L.Q.R. 431. However, an attempt to create a fee tail in personalty, even by will, has been held to create an absolute gift: *In re McDonald* (1903) 6 O.L.R. 478 (Div.Ct.). Executory interests are discussed in Part 4(b), Chapter 7.

144 Under this third reading, the trustee may be taken to be either the life tenant or the personal representative of the deceased: see further N. Crago, ''Bequests of Chattels in Succession'' (1999) 28 U.W.Aust.L.Rev. 198, at 204. The author calls for legislative reform under which the life tenant would be fixed with duties of trusteeship. See also R. Chambers, ''Conditional Gifts'' in N. Palmer & E. McKendrick, eds., *Interests in Goods*, 2nd ed. (London: L.L.P., 1998) ch. 18.

statute. In Alberta, for example, a widowed spouse may acquire a dower right in some of the personal property of the decedent.[145] Despite all of these qualifications on the general rule, estates cannot be created over consumable items; there can be no estate in a pizza![146]

Even though personal property can be owned absolutely, provision must still be made for the state of the title when the owner of personalty dies with no heirs (next of kin) to whom entitlements can pass. At common law such property becomes vested in the Crown, by prerogative, as *bona vacantia* (ownerless goods).[147] In a jurisdiction devoid of any form of subinfeudation and where, accordingly, all land is held of the Crown, there seems to be very little difference between the operation of *bona vacantia* and the escheat of land. Hence, under modern escheat legislation in Alberta, for example, no distinction is drawn between realty and personalty concerning the ultimate fate of property once held by a person who has died with no lawful next-of-kin.[148]

---

145 *Dower Act*, R.S.A. 1980, c. D-38, s. 23.

146 See further E.E. Nemmers, "Legal Relations of Owners of Present and Future Interests in Personalty – Consumables", 27 Marquette L.J. 82 (1942-3).

147 The complexities of this doctrine are reviewed in A. Bell, "Bona Vacantia" in N. Palmer & E. McKendrick, eds., *Interests in Goods*, 2nd ed. (London: L.L.P., 1998) ch. 8. See also N.D. Ing, *Bona Vacantia* (London: Butterworths, 1971).

148 See *Ultimate Heir Act*, R.S.A. 1980, c. U-1 [as am.].

6

THE ORIGINS AND NATURE OF EQUITABLE INTERESTS

Headline: "Wife left 'without even a spoon' and court agrees."

Edmonton Journal, October 3rd, 1973, at 1, reporting on the *Murdoch* decision[1]

1. INTRODUCTION

Earlier in the text it was noted that Canadian law distinguishes between 'legal' and 'equitable' ownership.[2] In this chapter we return to this fundamental dichotomy, developing further the concept called equity. The short-term goal of this presentation is to introduce those aspects of equity that will be treated later in the text. More generally, this chapter tries to provide an introduction to the equitable doctrines that are found in all reaches of private law in the common law jurisdictions of Canada.

In order to understand the nature of equity it is necessary to explore its origins. Much of this chapter will trace the growth of the concept. The discussion will chart, in a cursory way, the development of principles of equity in the English Court of Chancery, their incorporation into Canadian law, and the present position. In this analysis, the emergence of the 'trust' will be the central concern.

2. THE ORIGINS OF EQUITY

The term 'equity' has several connotations. In a broad sense, to do equity is to act fairly or justly. One also speaks of homeowners or investors holding or gaining equity in some property or business enterprise. These meanings are tied to the use of equity as a cognate set of rules, separate from the common law, which give rise to rights enforceable in a court of equity. This body of jurisprudence emerged first from the Crown's residual prerogative over the administration of justice, a power capable of being used as a corrective measure for defects or omissions in the common law. The story of this development is long and fascinating; it is told only briefly here.[3]

The need for remedial institutions for the courts of common law was manifested by complaints of injustice, levelled by unsuccessful litigants, and directed to the Crown as the fount of English justice. At this formative stage, in the

---

1 *Murdoch v. Murdoch*, [1975] 1 S.C.R. 423, [1974] 1 W.W.R. 361, 41 D.L.R. (3d) 367, discussed in Part 4(d), *infra*.

2 See Part 4(b), Chapter 2.

3 See further J.H. Baker, *An Introduction to English Legal History*, 3rd ed. (London: Butterworths, 1990) ch. 6, and the references cited there.

thirteenth century, a variety of approaches were used to respond to these grievances. Sometimes directions were given to the common law courts to do justice
in a given case. On occasion matters were referred to Parliament (if a general
change in the law was thought to be appropriate). Some petitions were delegated
either to the royal council, or to individual council members, including the Chancellor.

The office of the Chancellor served as the royal secretariat. It was responsible
for such matters as the impressing of official documents with the Great Seal of
England, and the issuance of writs. These writs were connected to the commencement of legal proceedings in the common law courts (the Courts of King's Bench,
Exchequer and Common Pleas). By the end of the thirteenth century, the capacity
of the Chancellor to devise new writs, when it was decided that new causes of
action should be recognized, had been severely restricted. This increased the
practice of presenting special petitions, as mentioned above. In time, the Chancery
emerged as the principal authority charged with the responsibility of assessing
these special pleas.

The early Chancery did not resemble a court. Its operation was divided into
two chambers. On the Latin side[4] (the records were in that language), the Chancery
served mainly as an administrative agency, though it could hold inquiries into
some property law matters. It could also entertain complaints *against* the Crown.
On the English side, bills of complaint delegated by the Crown were sometimes
heard. It was in the latter part of the fourteenth century that the Chancellor
increasingly undertook to hear petitions and issue decrees. By the fifteenth century
the Chancery was being regarded as a court of conscience that could cure the
harshness that sometimes resulted from the application of an unyielding common
law, with its penchant for rigid certainty and technicality.[5] Eventually, the brand
of justice dispensed by the Chancery came to be referred to as 'equity'.

Until the beginning of the sixteenth century, equity was not a body of fixed
substantive rules and precedents. Even as principles began to emerge under the
rubric of equity, their application remained a matter of discretion. In the middle
of the seventeenth century, John Selden remarked that the standard of justice
varied with each successive Chancellor:

> Equity is a roguish thing: for law we have a measure, know what to trust too; equity is according
> to ye conscience of him that is Chancellor, and as that is larger or narrower so is equity. 'Tis
> all one as if they should make the standard for the measure we call foot, a Chancellor's foot;
> what an uncertain measure would be this. One chancellor has a long foot, the other a short
> foot, a third an indifferent foot: 'tis the same thing in the Chancellor's Conscience.[6]

These famous words must have resonated in the ears of future Chancellors,
for in 1818 Lord Eldon confided that ''[n]othing would inflict on me greater pain,

---

4 See further A.D. Hargreaves, ''Equity and the Latin Side of Chancery'' (1952) 68 L.Q.R. 481.
5 A helpful example is found in equity's compassionate response to the common law of mortgages:
   see Parts 3 and 4, Chapter 11.
6 John Selden's Table Talk, as reproduced in M. Evans & R.I. Jack, eds., *Sources of English Legal
   and Constitutional History* (Sydney: Butterworths, 1984) at 223-4.

in quitting this place, than the recollection that I had done anything to justify the reproach that the equity of this Court varies like the Chancellor's foot".[7] In fact, in the period between these two statements equity was changing, its rules solidifying. The practice of appointing ecclesiastics as Chancellors (most of whom had training in ecclesiastical law but not secular law) gave way to the selection of lawyers. (The last non-legally trained Chancellors in England were the Bishop of Lincoln (who served from 1621 to 1625) and Lord Shaftsbury (1672-73)). In truth, even before Selden's rebuke, Chancellors had begun to rely on past decisions.[8] In 1727, a treatise on equitable maxims was published, and this aided the process of encoding basic principles. Among the maxims of equity set out in the treatise were these: "equity is equality", "he that hath committed inequity, shall not have equity", and "equity regards not the circumstance but the substance of the transaction".[9] These broad propositions of fairness (and a host of others) still guide courts of equity.

Equity has always been conceived of as a means of perfecting the common law. It was designed to improve and supplement, but not supplant, the law. The workings of these two discrete regimes were, in theory, harmonious. The thinking was that "[e]quity does not destroy the law, nor create it, but assist it".[10] However, it was inevitable that political and jurisdictional friction would ensue. When an order emanating from a common law court was regarded as unjust it could be stayed by a 'common injunction' issued in the Chancery. When, in the early seventeenth century, the effect of the common injunction was challenged, unsuccessfully, it was resolved that when a conflict between the common law and equity arose, it was equity that would prevail;[11] that remains so. Therefore, while the starting position was – and remains – that equity purports to follow the law, it is also true that it does not do so slavishly. Otherwise, its curative function would be rather limited.

From the seventeenth to the nineteenth century the overall complexion of equity changed vastly. It lost its original elasticity and became a more predictable system of rules. Equity was still somewhat pliable, but so was the common law, which has always developed through analogical extension in the face of new circumstances. However, these two juristic systems remained separate. That state of affairs could create difficulties, since rights and remedies available through one court might not be tenable in another. The common law courts applied only

---

7 *Gee v. Prichard* (1818) 2 Swan. 402, at 414, 36 E.R. 670, at 674. See also *Davis v. Duke of Marlborough* (1819) 2 Swan. 108, at 163, 36 E.R. 555, at 569 (*per* Lord Eldon): "It is not the duty of a Judge in equity to vary rules, or to say that rules are not to be considered as fully settled here as in a court of law."

8 See further W.H.D. Winder, "Precedent in Equity" (1941) 57 L.Q.R. 245, where it is suggested that past decisions were being consulted by the Chancery by the beginning of the seventeenth century.

9 R. Francis, *Maxims of Equity* (1727) reprinted in *Classics of English Legal History in the Modern Era* (New York: Garland Pr., 1978).

10 *Dudley v. Dudley* (1705) Prec. Ch. 241, at 244, 24 E.R. 118, at 119.

11 *Earl of Oxford's Case* (1615) 1 Rep. Ch. 1, 21 E.R. 485. The political conflict that underscored this tension is considered in J.P. Dawson, "Coke and Ellesmere Disinterred: The Attack on the Chancery in 1616", 36 Ill.L.Rev. 127 (1941).

common law doctrine (as altered by statute), and possessed the power to grant a limited set of remedies, the principal one being damages. Equity developed additional remedies, including the injunction and the order of specific performance.[12] Furthermore, the procedures adopted in these two systems differed. From its genesis as a system of inordinate informality, Chancery practice eventually became so convoluted that litigating a case under that system was no simple matter for the uninitiated.[13]

Minor reforms of the procedures used in the Court of Chancery were undertaken in the 1850s, but it was not until the 1870s that the administration of justice underwent large-scale restructuring in England. The primary development was the fusion of courts of law and equity. The effect of fusion is that a single court can apply both sets of rules. Importantly, the conventional view is that these administrative reforms did not directly alter or meld the substantive rules that each system had developed. This means that equitable interests in land remain distinct from those recognized by courts of law. For example, under common law principles, an equitable interest is of no consequence: the holder of equitable title to land or other property would be regarded as a trespasser in the eyes of the common law. We will return to these ideas shortly.[14]

By and large, the incorporation of the principles of equity into the common law jurisdictions of Canada was straightforward.[15] However, the process was not a completely smooth one in some provinces. For example, Upper Canada had no court of equity until 1837. And the abuses known to have plagued the English Chancery generated apprehension about reforms designed to introduce a court of equity into that colony; an attempt to establish a court in the 1820s failed.[16] In Nova Scotia, the Lieutenant-Governor served as the Chancellor from 1749 until 1825.[17] (From about the 1790s on, members of the Supreme Court of the Province

---

12 As to the power of a court of equity to award damages, see P.M. McDermott, "Jurisdiction of the Court of Chancery to Award Damages" (1992) 108 L.Q.R. 652. See now *Canson Enterprises Ltd. v. Boughton & Co.*, [1991] 3 S.C.R. 534 [1992] 1 W.W.R. 245, 85 D.L.R. (4th) 129.

13 The complexity of the Chancery's procedures prompted Dickens's famous reproach in the novel *Bleak House* (New York: W.W. Morton & Co., 1977 ed., 1853) at 5-6: "Fog everywhere . . . . And hard by Temple Bar in Lincoln's Inn, at the very heart of the fog, sits the Lord High Chancellor in his High Court of Chancery . . . This is the Court of Chancery; which has its decaying houses and its blighted lands in every shire; which has its lunatic in every madhouse, and its dead in every churchyard; which has its ruined suitor, with his slipshod heels and threadbare dress, borrowing and begging through the round of every man's acquaintance; which gives to monied might the means abundantly of wearying out the right; which so exhausts finances, patience, courage, hope; so overthrows the brain and breaks the heart; that there is not an honourable man among its practitioners who would not give – who does not often give this warning: 'Suffer any wrong that can be done you, rather than come here!' " A claim has been made that the Chancery was more benign in the fifteenth century: see M.E. Avery, "An Evaluation of the Court of Chancery under the Lancastrian Kings" (1970) 86 L.Q.R. 84.

14 See Part 3(a), *infra*.

15 See generally Part 2(b), Chapter 2.

16 See generally E. Brown, "Equitable Jurisdiction and the Court of Chancery in Upper Canada" (1983) 21 Osgoode Hall L.J. 275. As to how that colony coped without a court of equity, see J.D. Falconbridge, "Law and Equity in Upper Canada" (1914) 34 Can.L.T. 1130.

17 C.J. Townshend, "History of the Court of Chancery in Nova Scotia" (1900) 20 Can.L.T. 14, 37, 74, 105.

provided legal assistance.[18]) As in England, the Court of Chancery was a thoroughly unpopular institution. It was abolished in Nova Scotia in 1855, and its jurisdiction was transferred to the Supreme Court. This move was influenced by a more modest initiative in New Brunswick introduced a year earlier (which was itself based on American developments). The Nova Scotia legislation conferred equitable jurisdiction on the Supreme Court: this produced a procedural fusion of sorts. However, by 1864 the separate jural position of 'judge in equity' was created in the Nova Scotia Supreme Court, thereby reducing the extent to which the two systems had been merged.[19]

In Alberta, the general rule governing the reception of English law was supplemented by a provision that gave the Supreme Court of the Northwest Territories the same powers as those held by the English High Court of Chancery as of July 15, 1870.[20] This remains the case. Statute law also provides that "the rules of decision" are to be "the same as governed the Court of Chancery of England in like cases on July 15, 1870".[21] Despite the apparent tenor of this provision, established principles of equity have not been frozen in time; they have been allowed to develop.

3.   THE EMERGENCE OF THE 'USE' AND THE 'TRUST'

(a)   the development and functions of the 'use'

From a contemporary standpoint the emergence of the 'trust' stands as the chief contribution of equity to the law of property. It is sometimes said that the trust represents one of the supreme accomplishments of the English system of justice. However, some see the genesis of the trust concept in Roman, German and Islamic law.[22] Casting back to the evolution of English law and our immediate colonial experience is often sensible, but it is important to recognize that this delves down only one layer in the archaeological dig-site of the law.

The modern trust arose out of the 'use', a concept with feudal origins. The use was a device under which the legal title was granted to one person to hold for the benefit of another. Accordingly, under a grant to uses, land was transferred by A (who was called the feoffor to uses), to B (the feoffee), to be held for the benefit of C (the *cestui que use*). The goal of such a conveyance was to place legal title in B, who was intended to hold it for uses destined to serve C. As we will see below, the arrangement was deployed in circumstances in which it was thought expedient to separate the legal title from the person who was intended to

---

18 C. Greco, ''The Superior Court Judiciary of Nova Scotia, 1754-1900: A Collective Biography'' in P. Girard & J. Phillips, eds., *Essays in Canadian Legal History: Nova Scotia*, vol. III (Toronto: Osgoode Society & U. of T.Pr., 1990) 42, at 44. In 1825, this responsibility was given to the Master of the Rolls. Thereafter, the Lieutenant-Governor exercised an appellate function: *ibid.*

19 See P. Girard, ''Married Women's Property, Chancery Abolition, and Insolvency Law: Law Reform in Nova Scotia 1820-1867'', in Girard & Phillips, *supra*, note 18, at 106*ff*.

20 *Judicature Act*, R.S.A. 1980, c. J-1, subs. 5(1), (3).

21 Sub. 5(4).

22 See W.F. Fratcher, ''The Uses of Uses'', 34 Missouri L.Rev. 39 (1969) and the references cited there.

have the real benefit of the land, usually because of some disadvantage or disability associated with the holding of the legal title.

The practice of transferring land to uses pre-dated the Chancery's involve-
ment in the process, and it has been suggested that some uses were initially
enforced by the Church.[23] There is also some evidence that at one time the common
law recognized uses,[24] but that position did not endure for long. As far as the law
was concerned, the *cestui que use* had "no more to do with the land than the
greatest stranger in the world".[25] In essence, then, the person whom the use was
designed to benefit had no rights in a common law court – no entitlement at law
to any interest in the land. Again, in a grant 'to B to the use of C', legal title was
held by B, and C had no legally enforceable claim.

The Chancellor, by contrast, eventually recognized C's rights, and over time
the enforcement of uses became a central function of the Chancery. Its orders
were meant to fix on the conscience of the feoffee (B) to compel that person to
carry out the purposes for which the use had been created. C, having a right that
a court of equity would enforce, came to be thought of as holding an equitable
proprietary interest. The Chancellor would not deny that B held the legal title.
This entitlement was duly acknowledged, and the rights in equity were in fact
premised on the existence of that common law interest. However, equity regarded
the legal interest as purely managerial. B's title was coated with obligations that
were imposed in favour of C, and these were treated as paramount.

The use had many applications.[26] In the sixteenth century decision in *Chudleigh's Case* it was complained that "[t]here were two inventors of uses, fear and
fraud; fear, in the times of troubles and civil wars, to save . . . inheritances from
being forfeited; and fraud, to defeat due debts, lawful actions, wards, escheats,
mortmains, [etc.]."[27] There is some merit to this cynical appraisal, given the ways
in which the use was invoked. For example, the use provided a convenient means
through which a husband could avoid his wife's dower rights. You may recall
(from Chapter 5) that common law dower would attach only to *legal* estates
owned by the husband.[28] Hence, property given to B to the use of C (a husband),
who would hold in equity, was not affected by the wife's dower. The widower's
right to curtesy could also be side-stepped in this way.

However, not all uses were so obviously malevolent. For instance, the use
allowed property to be enjoyed by married women, free from the control of their
husbands. We saw in Chapter 2 that under the doctrine of marital unity the property
of a married woman fell under the control of her husband.[29] However, as with
dower, this rule applied only to interests recognized at common law. Therefore,

---

23 R.H. Hemholz, "The Early Enforcement of Uses", 79 Colum.L.Rev. 1503 (1979).
24 See J.L. Barton, "The Medieval Use" (1965) 81 L.Q.R. 562.
25 Anon. (1502) Keil. 42, pl. 7, quoted in Baker, *supra*, note 3, at 286.
26 See generally Fratcher, *supra*, note 22.
27 *Chudleigh's Case; Dillon v. Freine* (1595) 1 Co. Rep. 113b, at 121b, 76 E.R. 261, at 275.
28 Transfers through deeds to uses as a dower-avoidance device remained current in Ontario until
     dower was abolished in that Province in 1978: see, *e.g.*, *Armstrong v. Brown*, [1952] O.W.N.
     55 (C.A.); *Re Rowe*, [1957] O.R. 9, 10 D.L.R. (2d) 215 (H.C.).
29 See Part 3(a), Chapter 2.

one means of avoiding the impact of the doctrine was to place legal title in the hands of a feoffee to uses, who would hold the property for the 'separate use' of a married woman.

Uses could also be invoked to circumvent the restrictions on property holdings applicable to corporations and religious orders.[30] Additionally, the use could function as an early form of will. The common law did not provide for testamentary transfers; instead, the rules of primogeniture governed the devolution of land throughout most of England. However, a simple form of will could be constructed through a properly drafted deed to uses. In general, the granting of future interests through the deployment of equitable uses allowed for greater flexibility than permitted at common law. This feature is addressed in more depth in Chapter 7.[31]

Importantly, uses provided a way for the feudal obligations of tenants to be avoided. And, as we will soon see, this prompted legislative action (in 1535) designed to eliminate the use in England. Uses could be employed to circumvent feudal incidents, principally (but not only) wardship, relief and primer seisin. These were apparently lucrative sources of royal income.[32] Those incidents, which were in effect feudal taxes, fell due to the lord on the descent of land from an owner to his or her heir. Uses could be inserted lawfully into land transfers so that the property would pass on death in a way that did not attract this 'tax' liability. For example, if legal title were conferred on several feoffees, as joint tenants, holding to the use of a beneficial owner, the tax-triggering event could be postponed indefinitely. This is because on the death of a joint tenant, the interest of that tenant does not descend to an heir; instead it merges with the title of the surviving joint tenants.[33] If the scheme was competently constructed, new joint tenants would be appointed as others died, so that the legal title to the property would never pass by descent. Meanwhile, the beneficial (equitable) interest under the use could be enjoyed without regard to the impact of the feudal incidents.

(b)   the Statute of Uses

It has been said that by the fifteenth century a majority of the land in private hands in England was held to uses.[34] However, the capacity of the use mechanism to impede the operation of the incidents of feudal tenure provoked the introduction of reforms during the reign of Henry VIII. Obviously, it was not in everyone's interest that something be done about uses; the landed gentry, well-represented in Parliament, steadfastly opposed change to the *status quo*. After attempts at

---

30 See further A.H. Oosterhoff, ''The Law of Mortmain'' (1977) 27 U.T.L.J. 257.

31 See Part 4(b), Chapter 7.

32 See further A.R. Buck, ''The Politics of Land Law in Tudor England, 1529-40'' (1990) 11 J. Legal Hist. 200, at 201*ff*.

33 The concept of survivorship is explained more fully in Part 2(a), Chapter 9.

34 Fratcher, *supra*, note 22, at 41.

reaching a political solution reached an impasse,[35] and following a failed attempt to enact reforms in 1529, the *Statute of Uses, 1535*[36] was passed.[37]

The use, as we have seen, separated legal title from the beneficial ownership of property. In response to this, the legislation of 1535 reunited legal and equitable title by removing the legal title from the feoffee and placing it in the hands of the *cestui que use*. The operative section, as reproduced in the Statutes of Ontario,[38] is as follows:

> Where any person stands or is seized of and in lands, tenements, rents, services, reversions, remainders, or other hereditaments, to the use, confidence or trust, of any other person, or any body politic, by reason of any bargain, sale, feoffment, covenant, contract, agreement, will, or otherwise, by any means whatsoever it be, in every such case such person and body politic that shall have any such use, confidence or trust, in fee simple, fee tail, for term of life, or for years, or otherwise, or any use, confidence or trust, in remainder or reversion, shall from henceforth stand and be seized, deemed and adjudged in lawful seizin, estate and possession of and in the same lands, tenements, rents, services, reversions, remainders, and hereditaments, with their appurtenances, to all intents, constructions and purposes in the law, of and in such like estates as they had, or shall have, in use, trust or confidence, of or in the same. And the estate, right, title and possession, that was in such person, that was, or shall be hereafter seized, of any lands, tenements, or hereditaments, to the use, confidence or trust, of any such person or body politic, shall be henceforth deemed and adjudged to be in him that hath such use, confidence or trust, after such quality manner, form and condition, as he had before him in or to the use, confidence or trust, that was in him.

This is an imposing provision. A modern rendering of the salient passages might read as follows:

> Where one person is seised to the use, confidence or trust of another person (including a 'body politic' or 'corporation'), the legal interest of the person seised will be expropriated, and that interest will be given to that other person, but in all other respects that second person will hold the same entitlements as that person would have enjoyed under the use, confidence or trust as originally granted.

The Statute works this way: Prior to 1535, a grant 'to A and his/her heirs, to the use of B and his/her heirs' created a separation of the legal title (which would have been held by A as the feoffee) from the equitable title (which would have been enjoyed by B as the *cestui que use*). The Statute deprived A of the legal title. That estate was 'executed' by the Statute and given to the *cestui que use*, who then would possess both the legal and equitable interests in the land.

By this means, the use was collapsed; the tax loophole was sealed off. It is thought that the Statute did increase revenues, as intended, at least in the imme-

---

35 See further Buck, *supra*, note 32, at 203.

36 *An Act Concerning Uses and Wills, 1535*, 27 Hen. 8, c. 10. This Act is a diluted version of its 1529 predecessor.

37 See further E.W. Ives, "The Genesis of the Statute of Uses" (1967) 82 Eng.Hist.Rev. 673; D.H. Brown, "Historical Perspective on the Statute of Uses" (1979) 9 Man.L.J. 409. See also W.H. Holdsworth, "The Political Causes Which Shaped the Statute of Uses", 26 Harv.L.Rev. 108 (1926) where it is argued that the final result was the product of compromise and diplomacy.

38 *Statute of Uses*, R.S.O. 1897, c. 331, reprinted in R.S.O. 1980, Appendix A.

diate aftermath of its passage.[39] Supposedly, "the use was made to enter the Valley of Humiliation, goaded by the two pronged fork wielded by Henry VIII".[40] Given the pervasiveness of the use across England, the enactment of the *Statute of Uses* was a political event of some consequence. In the rebellion known as the Pilgrimage of Grace (in 1536 and 1537) a demand was made for the repeal of the Statute. The rebellion was crushed; the Statute remained in force.[41] The legal historian John Baker maintains that several lawyers paid for their efforts to evade the Statute by being banished to the Tower of London.[42] However, even in the face of this somewhat drastic sanction, methods were soon devised to escape the full impact of the Statute. In consequence, purely equitable interests could be created once again. How could this be accomplished? The answers to this question, first developed in the Tudor and Stuart periods, remain applicable today.

The Statute, despite its rather overbearing tone, does not affect all transfers under uses. Therefore, by constructing transfers in a way not pinpointed by the Statute, a purely equitable interest can be produced.[43] A convention has developed of describing these post-Statute uses as 'trusts'. Other changes in terminology have also been adopted. Whereas before the Statute the transferor was described as the feoffor to uses, the modern term is 'settlor'; a 'trustee' is a direct descendant of the feoffee to uses; and the *cestui que use* is the counterpart of today's *'cestui que trust'*, or beneficiary. But take caution: apart from these conventions, the terms 'use' and 'trust' are jural synonyms, and nothing should turn on which of these words happens to appear in a transfer document.[44]

There are two primary methods of overcoming the impact of the *Statute of Uses*: (i) avoidance; and (ii) exhaustion.

(c)   avoidance

One method of creating a trust after the Statute is to construct a limitation that does not fit within the four corners of the legislation. The words of the Statute quoted above establish a set of operational predicates. To paraphrase the key provision, the Statute applies where a person is seised to the use or trust of another person or corporation. With this in mind, one can think of at least two situations in which the operation of the main provision is avoided. First, the Statute does not apply when the feoffee/trustee holds a leasehold estate, since a leaseholder

---

39 See further J.L. Barton, "The Statute of Uses and the Trust of Freehold Lands" (1966) 82 L.Q.R. 215.

40 H.G. Hanbury, *Modern Equity*, 3rd ed. (London: Stevens & Sons, 1943) at 7.

41 Buck, *supra*, note 32, at 211. F.W. Maitland, *Equity* (Cambridge: C.U.P., 1916) at 35, describes the Statute as one of the "excuses, if not one of the causes" of the Pilgrimage of Grace, which was primarily a rebellion against the Reformation. The Statute is mentioned only in passing in M.H. Dodds & R. Dodds, *The Pilgrimage of Grace 1536-1537 and the Exeter Conspiracy 1538*, 1971 ed. (London: Frank Cass & Co., 1915) vol. 1, at 12.

42 J.H. Baker, "Introduction to the Reports of Sir John Spelman" (1977) 94 Seld.Soc. 1, at 203.

43 For a view that the Statute was only meant to have a limited scope, see D.E.C. Yale, "The Revival of Equitable Estates in the Seventeenth Century: An Explanation by Lord Nottingham", [1957] C.L.J. 72.

44 See *Bayliss v. Balfe* (1917) 38 O.L.R. 437, 35 D.L.R. 350 (H.C.) at 439 O.L.R.

cannot be 'seised' to the use of another. Seisin is the possession enjoyed by a *freeholder.* Therefore, a gift 'to B for 99 years to hold for the use of C' is not executed. Instead, a trust is created for the benefit of C.

Second, the Statute applies when a person holds to the use of a corporation (called a body politic in the section) but not *vice versa*: it does not apply when a corporation holds property to the use of someone else. Accordingly, a grant in which B. Ltd. holds to the use of C also creates a trust. Again, such a transfer does not fit within the formula created by the Statute. Nor would a transfer 'to A to the use of A' be executed. Under the Statute, a use is executed only when one is seised to the use of *another*. Still, this limitation produces the same result as if the Statute had been invoked: the words 'To A, to the use of A', if nothing more is added, gives the grantee both legal and equitable title by virtue of the language of the conveyance itself.[45]

There is another circumstance in which the Statute does not apply, even though it appears to be called for on a plain reading of the provision quoted above. It has been suggested that "most mediaeval uses were 'dry' in the sense that the feoffee had no obligation except to hold naked legal title",[46] leaving the *cestui que use* with the enjoyment of the land. The Statute does apply in those instances. However, not all uses are of this nature; some deeds to uses cast real responsibilities on the feoffee. In time it was accepted that the Statute should not be invoked if the feoffee/trustee was given active duties to perform, duties that would require that legal title should be retained.[47] The Statute, it seems, does not abjure uses altogether, but only those that are pure shams, *i.e.*, those in which the feoffee was holding as a mere shell to avoid the operation of some common law doctrine. In modern trust documents language is often used that would seem to (but does not) invite the application of the *Statute of Uses*, such as a transfer 'to my trustees, to hold land on trust for X, Y and Z'. The trust document might also outline various duties of maintenance that the trustees are to carry out. In jurisdictions where the Statute is in force, it is the principle that uses involving active duties are not executed that saves such trusts from being ruined by this legislation.

The Statute does not apply to personalty. The reforms of 1535 related to the incidents of land tenure. From the seventeenth century forward this limitation on the ambit of the Statute became increasingly significant. The nascent forms of capitalism that were emerging in Europe led to the creation of joint-stock companies, and a new brand of mercantilism. Agriculture was being replaced as the prime basis of economic organization, and land, the only property to which the Statute applied, was being overtaken as the dominant source of economic power. Money, stocks, and other instruments of commerce came to the fore, and trusts of these forms of capital became more common. As trusts of personalty ascended in importance, the practical relevance of the Statute diminished accordingly.

---

45 *Cf. Re Young* (1883) 9 P.R. 521 (Ont.Ch.D.).
46 J.C. Payne, "The English Theory of Conveyances Prior to the Land Registration Acts", 7 Ala.L.Rev. 227 (1954-5) at 250.
47 See, *e.g.*, *Romanes v. Smith* (1880) 8 P.R. 323 (Ont.Ch.D.) at 325. *Cf. Tunis v. Passmore* (1872) 32 U.C.Q.B. 419 (C.A.) at 421; *Bingham v. Wrigglesworth* (1882) 5 O.R. 611 (Ch.D.).

(d)   exhausting the operation of the Statute

The *Statute of Uses* has a limited potency. It was eventually decided that it was capable of executing only one fee simple of uses. This allowed conveyancers an opening to create instruments that triggered the Statute, but which also contemplated uses that the legislation was unable to execute. To explain, consider a transfer 'to A (in fee simple) to the use of B (in fee simple) to the use of C (in fee simple)'. A is seised to the use of B, and this falls within the purview of the Statute. As a result, A's interest is executed and conferred, by operation of law, on B. It is at this stage that the Statute has run its course; it is 'exhausted', for lack of a better term, for the full fee simple has been shifted from the feoffee and bestowed on the *cestui que use*. This also means that although B is seised to the use of C, the Statute will not execute this use. What is the effect of the second use? In *Tyrrel's Case* (1557)[48] it was said to be void. The second use would have been an inexplicable interest to a court of equity prior to the Statute, and it remained so, according to a line of authorities flowing from the *Tyrrel* decision.

However, by 1635 (and perhaps even earlier than this) the attitude of the courts had changed. This 'use upon a use', as it is now commonly called, today results in the creation of an enforceable equitable title held by C. The leading authority, *Sambach v. Daston*,[49] though not involving a limitation containing precisely this language, nevertheless paved the way for the recognition of the use-upon-a-use device. However, the date of this turnaround is in doubt, and there is some evidence of the enforcement of the second use some ten years before *Sambach*. It has also been suggested that recognition may have come as early as 1560.[50] No matter what view is adopted, it is likely that this willingness to enforce the second use was influenced by the fact that the Statute was no longer of practical fiscal value. That was certainly true by the time of *Sambach*. By the seventeenth century the importance of the feudal incidents had declined, and it will be recalled that the *Statute of Tenures* of 1660 marked an end to that aspect of the feudal economy. That Statute abolished most of the incidents of tenure, including those that had prompted the introduction of the *Statute of Uses* in the first place.[51]

As a result of these developments, the phrase 'to A, to the use of B to the use of C' creates a trust, with B as trustee, and C as the beneficiary. Other carefully drafted transfers can also exhaust the Statute, such as a transfer 'to A to the use of B in trust for C'. (Remember that the words 'use' and 'trust' are synonyms in this context.) Another functionally equivalent shorthand formulation is 'to B to the use of B, to the use of (or in trust for) C', which can be further truncated to 'unto and to the use of B to the use of C'. Even though the first use was not executed (as A is seised to his or her own use) it was eventually accepted that the

---

48 (1557) 2 Dyer 155a, 78 E.R. 336. See further N.G. Jones, "Tyrrel's Case (1557) and the Use Upon a Use" (1993) 14 Leg.Hist. 75.

49 (1635) Toth. 188, reproduced in J.H. Baker & S.F.C. Milsom, eds., *Sources of English Legal History: Private Law to 1750* (London: Butterworths, 1986) at 126. See further J.E. Strathdene, "*Sambach v. Dalston*: An Unnoticed Report" (1958) 74 L.Q.R. 550.

50 J.H. Baker, "The Use Upon a Use in Equity 1558-1625" (1977) 93 L.Q.R. 33.

51 See Part 2(a), Chapter 2.

second use was not touched by the Statute.[52] Of equivalent effect is a transfer 'to the use of B in trust for C'. But a further contraction, 'to B in trust for C', flirts with the Statute – indeed should invoke it[53]– because the Statute applies when a person is seised to the use, confidence, or *trust* of another. So, apart from this last example, any of these expressions can produce a separation of the legal and equitable title, thereby creating a trust.

It is not merely the existence of one use-interest after another that has the effect of exhausting the Statute and separating the equitable and legal titles; this is possible only after one full fee simple has been executed. Therefore, a gift 'to B in fee simple to the use of C for life, with the remainder to the use of D in fee simple', would leave C with a legal and equitable life estate, and D with a legal and equitable remainder in fee simple. The Statute would coat C's and D's equitable interests with a legal veneer.[54] At that point, but not before, the Statute is exhausted.

(e)   a reprise

The learning that developed in response to the *Statute of Uses* now appears to be little more than a perverse exercise in semantics. It seems inane that the phrase 'unto and to the use of B in trust for C' creates a trust, but that 'to B in trust for C' does not. Yet in theory that is so, and by merely adding a few words to a transfer the Statute is neutralized.[55] Perhaps this is why Maitland declared that the 1535 Act ''is not a mere Statute of Uselessness but a Statute of Abuses''.[56]

The failure to take account of the Statute, and to employ the deft circumventing strategy, can undermine an otherwise valid trust. *If* the *Statute of Uses* is part of received law in a given jurisdiction,[57] then the methods used to create a trust today should be based on the contrivances adopted in the decades after the

---

52 See *Doe d. Lloyd v. Passingham* (1827) 6 B. & C. 305, 108 E.R. 465.

53 See *Fair v. McCrow* (1871) 31 U.C.Q.B. 599 (C.A.) where land was devised ''in trust for the sole benefit of [A] during the term of her natural life''. See also *Bayliss v. Balfe, supra*, note 44; *Snyder v. Masters* (1850) 8 U.C.Q.B. 55.

54 See also *Bayliss v. Balfe, supra*, note 44.

55 ''The student is told almost in one breath that the only effect of the statute was to add three words to a conveyance, and that this is the foundation of the modern system of conveyancing'': F.W. Holdsworth, *A History of English Law* (Boston: Little, Brown, 1926) vol. 4, at 449.

56 H.A.L. Fisher, ed., *The Collected Papers of Frederic William Maitland* (Cambridge: C.U.P., 1911) vol. 1, at 191.

57 The *Statute of Uses* was held to have been received into Manitoba law in *Sinclair v. Mulligan* (1886) 3 Man.R. 481 (Eq.), which was affirmed on other grounds, *sub nom. Mulligan v. Hubbard* (1888) 5 Man.R. 225 (C.A.). The trial decision (at 490) contains this extraordinary passage (*per* Killam J.): ''The Statute of Uses must have been as applicable as it has been considered to be in other colonies; it must be considered to have been introduced into the Red River Settlement. By the charter to the Hudson's Bay Co. the lands granted were to be held in free and common socage. The conveyance by the chiefs of [the] Salteux and Crees to Lord Selkirk in the year 1817 exhibits an attempt at strict legal form and language, purporting to grant the lands to the King to the use of the Earl of Selkirk and of the settlers being established thereon.'' See also *Doe d. Hanington v. McFadden* (1836) 2 N.B.R. 260 (C.A.). The reception of English law into Canada is discussed in Part 2(b), Chapter 2.

Statute came into force. The *Statute of Uses* was abolished in England in 1925.[58] The chief architect of the 1925 reforms, Lord Birkenhead, said that the Statute "was the barbarous, if necessary, invention of a number of scholastic legal pedants, but that it had no contact with any kind of modern life".[59] Nevertheless, this relic may be part of the law in Canada.

Based on the analysis above, the following gifts, if contained in an *inter vivos* transfer, create a trust:

    To B for 99 years, in trust for C (for 99 years)
    To B. Ltd. in trust for C
    To B, to collect rent and profits and invest these to the use of C
    To B, the sum of $10,000, to hold in trust for the benefit of C
    To A to the use of B to the use of C
    To B to the use of B to the use of C
    Unto and to the use of B to the use of C
    Unto and to the use of B in trust for C
    To the use of B in trust for C

Assuming the *Statute of Uses* applies, the following transfers of land will *not* produce a separation of legal and equitable title:

    To B to the use of C
    To B to the use of C. Ltd.
    To B in trust for C
    To B in trust for C for life, then in trust for D in fee simple

(f) incidental effects of the Statute of Uses

The *Statute of Uses* was directed at the eradication of certain equitable interests but its ultimate impact has been more widespread. The operation of the Statute has affected the law of property transfers in three significant ways.

First, the *Statute of Uses* revolutionized conveyancing practices. Before 1535, legal title to a freehold estate in possession was conveyed through the ceremony of feoffment by livery of seisin. The Statute allowed that procedure to be replaced. The effect of the Statute, as we have seen, is to move legal title from the feoffor to the *cestui que use*. That being so, the Statute could be harnessed by conveyancers to transfer the legal title from A to B, eliminating the need for livery. Using a method called 'bargain and sale', A would agree to transfer the property to B at a stated price (eventually even a nominal sum was taken to suffice). The bargain and sale raised a use in equity, imposed on A in favour of B. The Statute would then operate, taking the legal title from A and placing it in B. This result, which would thereafter allow transfers of legal title absent a public ceremony of livery, was apparently anticipated by the framers of the Statute. In

---

58 *Law of Property Act, 1925*, 15 & 16 Geo. 5, c. 20, Sch. 7.
59 See P. Bordwell, "Repeal of the Statute of Uses", 39 Harv.L.Rev. 466 (1926) at 466, quoting 50 *Parliamentary Debates* (H.L.) 5S, at 1101.

response, in the same sitting of Parliament the *Statute of Enrolments*[60] was enacted. The Statute mandated the registration of bargain and sale transactions. However, the requirement of enrolment was, in the end, successfully avoided by convey-ancing conventions, and it soon fell into desuetude. Nevertheless, the deed of land as a mode of transfer and the current law of land registration can both be traced to these developments.

Second, the Statute was thought to have removed the power of landowners to make testamentary transfers. This was erroneous,[61] but pressures for the intro-duction of a power to devise property led to the enactment of the *Statute of Wills, 1540.*[62] Modern wills law stems from this legislation.[63]

Third, the Statute, in fusing legal and equitable title, created a hybrid form of property, known as a 'legal executory interest'. The basis upon which this occurred and the special nature of this type of interest will be discussed in Chapter 7.[64]

4.   THE ESSENCE OF MODERN EQUITY AND THE TRUST[65]

(a)   introduction

It is now possible to describe the nucleus around which today's equitable principles have formed. Equity continues to serve its initial function as a gloss on an imperfect common law. As such, it remains a tool for reform.[66] Equity and law remain fused, procedurally, though their substantive doctrines are distinct. This is not to say that principles of law and equity do not influence each other as they develop; they do,[67] perhaps more so in recent times than before. Accordingly,

---

60 *An Act Concerning Enrolments and Contracts of Lands and Tenements, 1535,* 27 Hen. 8, c. 16. Doubts as to whether this was the purpose of the Statute of Enrolments are expressed in J.M. Kaye, "A Note on the Statute of Enrolments" (1988) 104 L.Q.R. 617.

61 See R.E. Megarry, "The Statute of Uses and the Power to Devise", [1941] C.L.J. 354.

62 32 Hen. 8, c. 1.

63 For a review of the theories as to why the *Statute of Wills* followed so closely on the heels of the *Statute of Uses,* see generally Buck, *supra,* note 32, at 212*ff. Cf.* Barton, *supra,* note 39, at 222*ff.*

64 In particular, see Part 4(b), Chapter 7.

65 See generally D.W.M. Waters, *Law of Trusts in Canada,* 2nd ed. (Toronto: Carswell, 1984); A.H. Oosterhoff & E.E. Gillese, eds., *Text, Commentary and Cases on Trusts,* 5th ed. (Toronto: Carswell, 1998); E.E. Gillese, *The Law of Trusts* (Concord, Ont.: Irwin Law, 1997); J.E. Penner, *The Law of Trusts* (London: Butterworths, 1998); P.H. Pettit, *Equity and the Law of Trusts,* 7th ed. (London: Butterworths, 1993); J.E. Martin, *Hanbury & Martin: Modern Equity,* 15th ed. (London: Sweet & Maxwell, 1997); A.J. Oakley, *Parker and Mellows: The Modern Law of Trusts,* 7th ed. (London: Sweet & Maxwell, 1998); J.G. Riddall, *The Law of Trusts,* 5th ed. (London: Butterworths, 1996); T.G. Youdan, ed., *Equity, Fiduciaries and Trusts* (Toronto: Carswell, 1989).

66 *Canson Enterprises Ltd. v. Boughton & Co.,* [1991] 3 S.C.R. 534, [1992] 1 W.W.R. 245, 85 D.L.R. (4th) 129, at 585-6 S.C.R. (*per* La Forest J.). See also A.W. Scott, "The Trust as an Instrument of Law Reform", 21 Yale L.J. 45 (1922).

67 Several of these developments are discussed in J. Maxton, "Some Effects of the Intermingling of Common Law and Equity" (1993) 5 Canterbury L.Rev. 299.

there is today a confluence of these separate streams of justice in some areas.[68] This is a natural result of the fact that the same judges apply and refine both law and equity. Yet, it has been cautioned that "[t]here might be room for concern if one were indiscriminately attempting to meld the whole of the two systems"[69] and to treat them as fully integrated for all purposes. Differences remain, irreconcilable conflicts between law and equity can therefore still emerge, and these are resolved in favour of equity. Alberta law explicitly declares that "[i]n all matters in which there is any conflict or variance between the rules of equity and common law with reference to the same matter, the rules of equity prevail".[70] This is a codification of a long-standing principle.

Equity continues to focus on the conscience, creating, on one view, mere personal (or *in personam*) rights enforceable against an individual. In theory, therefore, these rights are not proprietary (or *in rem*). However, the effect of recognizing the rights of enforcement of the *cestui que trust* is normally described as creating an equitable interest in property that has been impressed with a trust.[71] The result of this characterization is that equitable rights are regarded as proprietary. Even so, in important respects an equitable interest is more fragile than a legal entitlement. A right in equity is dependent on the availability of equitable remedies, the granting or withholding of which is still a matter of judicial discretion. Additionally, equity will not impose an obligation against a *bona fide* purchaser for value of a legal interest who had no notice of an antecedent equitable claim.[72] Such a person acquires the legal title free from the obligations of equity.

(b) *modern usage of the trust*[73]

The ancient functions of the 'use' have been eclipsed over time, but the modern trust possesses its own vitality as a mechanism of private law estate planning and commercial practice. For example, a trust can be set up to allow property to be held for the benefit of minor children or other dependants. In

---

68 See *Canson Enterprises Ltd. v. Boughton & Co.*, *supra*, note 66. See also *United Scientific Holdings Ltd. v. Burnley Borough Council*, [1978] A.C. 904, [1977] 2 All E.R. 62 (H.L.). In *Canson* (at 591 S.C.R.) Stevenson J. commented that "the Judicature Acts were not a new Statute of Uses". In other words, these reform Acts did not conflate legal and equitable principles in the same way that the *Statute of Uses* united the legal and equitable estates in the *cestui que use*. See also A. Mason, "The Place of Equity and Equitable Doctrines in the Contemporary Common Law World: An Australian Perspective" in D.W.M. Waters, ed., *Equity, Fiduciaries and Trusts* (Toronto: Carswell, 1993) ch. 1.

69 *Canson Enterprises Ltd. v. Boughton & Co.*, *supra*, note 66, at 587 S.C.R. (*per* La Forest J.). See also *Chan v. Cresdon Pty. Ltd.* (1989) 168 C.L.R. 242, 64 A.L.J.R. 110 (Aust.H.C.). But see P. Sparkes, "*Walsh v. Lonsdale*: The Non-Fusion Fallacy" (1988) 8 O.J.L.S. 350.

70 *Judicature Act*, R.S.A. 1980, c. J-1, s. 16. See generally P.M. Perell, *The Fusion of Law and Equity* (Markham, Ont.: Butterworths, 1990).

71 The contrasting views on the characterization of the interest of the *cestui que trust* as *in rem* or *in personam* are presented in K. Gray, *Elements of Land Law*, 2nd ed. (London: Butterworths, 1993) at 40*ff*. See also D.W.M. Waters, "The Nature of the Trust Beneficiary's Interest" (1967) 45 Can.B.Rev. 219.

72 The *bona fide* purchaser for value is discussed in Part 2(b), Chapter 12.

73 See generally D. Waters, "The Use of the Trust in Canada Today" in D. Hayton, ed., *Modern International Developments in Trust Law* (Hague: Kluwer Law Int., 1998) 103.

general, protective trusts can be established to allow a person to enjoy the benefit of trust income while preventing that beneficiary from having full control over the property. It was seen (in Chapter 5) that when rights over real property are divided between present and future owners, the interposition of a trust can provide one means of regulating the management of this settled property.[74] Similarly, trusts can be deployed in a testamentary context to allow for the management of a decedent's estate. Property can be donated to charity via a trust. A trust is useful in this context because there are principles of equity (and statute law) that create special (generally advantageous) rules for charitable trusts.[75] Within the commercial realm, pension plans, mutual fund investments, debt security, indeed many types of financial ventures, can be undertaken by using a trust instrument in some way. The trust can also serve as a form of business organization.[76] The administration of trusts is itself a field of commercial endeavour. Trusts are sometimes created under statute as a means of effecting public policy.[77] The trust can be of value in tax planning, that is, it can be invoked to assist in the ordering of one's (personal or business) affairs in a way that minimizes tax liability.[78] Indeed, it has been offered that "[t]he trust is the estate planning vehicle *par excellence*".[79] This, plainly, is the strongest analogue to the early deployment of uses as a means of circumventing the payment of feudal dues.

This overview intimates that trusts are principally of value to wealthy organizations or individuals, and that for others they are of marginal utility.[80] In the main this reading is accurate. By the same token, it should be recognized that trusts can arise in wholly mundane circumstances, involving modest items. Even something as ostensibly worthless as season tickets to see the Calgary Flames play hockey can be the subject of a trust.[81] Moreover, charitable trusts facilitate the redistribution of wealth, and as such these are concerned with more than just elite practices. As we will soon see,[82] principles of equity in Canada have become increasingly directed toward the prevention of unjust enrichment. In this way the trust has affected the lives of many ordinary Canadians. It is also possible that

---

74 See Part 4(c)(iii), Chapter 5.

75 See further Waters, *supra*, note 65, at ch. 14, *passim*.

76 See further A.I. Ogus, "The Trust as Governance Structure" (1986) 36 U.T.L.J. 186; P. Finn, ed., *Equity and Commercial Relationships* (1986); R. Flannigan, "Business Applications of the Express Trust" (1998) 36 Alta.L.Rev. 630.

77 Such as under Alberta's residential tenancy law, which provides that a landlord is a trustee for any monies of the tenant that are held as a security deposit: *Residential Tenancies Act*, R.S.A. 1980, c. R-15.3, s. 37.1. But see *British Columbia v. Henfrey Samson Belair Ltd.*, [1989] 2 S.C.R. 24, [1989] 5 W.W.R. 577, 59 D.L.R. (4th) 726.

78 Detailed advice as to how this may be orchestrated can be found in G. Christopoulos & L.A. Kolinsky, *Taxation of Trusts and Beneficiaries* (Toronto: Richard De Boo, 1991) (looseleaf).

79 M. Cullity & C. Brown, *Taxation and Estate Planning*, 3rd ed. (Toronto: Carswell, 1992) at 527. A list of functions of the trust is found at 529-30.

80 See also the analysis in R. Cotterall, "Power, Property and the Law of Trusts: A Partial Agenda for Critical Legal Scholarship" (1987) 14 J.Law & Soc. 77.

81 *Thomas v. Whitwell* (1991) 45 E.T.R. 75 (Alta.Q.B.). See also *Byers v. Foley* (1993) 16 O.R. (3d) 641, 2 E.T.R. (2d) 55, 109 D.L.R. (4th) 761 (Gen.Div.). *Cf. Eng v. Evans* (1991) 83 Alta.L.R. (2d) 107 (Q.B.); *Fobasco Ltd. v. Cogan* (1990) 72 O.R. (2d) 254, 38 E.T.R. 193 (H.C.).

82 See Part 4(d), *infra*.

the trust can help to provide a response to environmental concerns. In the United States the 'public trust doctrine', which has traditionally been invoked as a means of ensuring public access to tidelands, shores, and navigable waters, has begun to serve more broadly as a basis for environmental control.[83] There may be lessons here for Canada.[84]

Trusts that are expressly created (such as those that we have discussed above[85]) are regulated by a vast battery of principles concerning such matters as the required formalities,[86] other issues as to the correct constitution of the trust, and the rights, responsibilities and powers of trustees.[87] These matters are beyond the purview of this text. However, there are two kinds of trust that are germane to topics that are covered elsewhere in the book – resulting and constructive trusts. These are introduced below.

(c)   resulting trusts[88]

A resulting trust may arise in several ways. First, it may occur when the beneficial entitlement under a trust has not been fully or properly disposed of by the settlor. Second, when property is gratuitously conferred by A to B, a resulting trust may be found in favour of A. It may also arise as a result of what is sometimes called 'common intention'.[89] These are general propositions that require further elaboration.

Turning to the first situation, if, in a grant of property on trust, some element of the beneficial interest is not transferred, it will 'result' back to the settlor. Consider a gift by A 'to the Baker Trust Co. in fee simple, in trust for C for life'. Reviewing what was said above, Baker Trust Co. is installed as the trustee; because it is a corporation, its interest would not be executed by the *Statute of*

---

83 See further S.B. Yates, "A Case for the Extension of the Public Trust Doctrine in Oregon", 27 Environ. L. 663 (1997); I. R. Cohen, "The Public Trust Doctrine: An Economic Perspective", 29 Cal.West L.Rev. 239 (1992); D.S. Sheehan, "Extending Public Trust Duties to Vermont's Agencies: A Logical Interpretation of the Common Law Public Trust Doctrine", 19 Vt.L.Rev. 509 (1995); J.M. Kehoe, "The Next Wave in Public Beach Access: Removal of States as Trustees of Public Trust Properties", 63 Fordham L.Rev. 1913 (1995).

84 See further B. von Tigerstrom, "The Public Trust Doctrine in Canada" (1998) 7 J.E.L.P. 379; J.C. Maguire, "Fashioning an Equitable Vision for Public Resource Protection and Development in Canada: The Public Trust Doctrine Revisited and Reconceptualized" (1998) 7 J.E.L.P. 1. See also D.W.M. Waters, "The Role of the Trust in Environmental Protection Law", in Waters, *supra*, note 68, ch. 17. Professor Waters considers other functions of the trust in this context, including the use of "environmental trust funds" to finance the reclamation of closed mines. But see *Green v. R.*, [1973] 2 O.R. 396, 34 D.L.R. (3d) 20 (H.C.).

85 See Part 3(e), *supra*. Sometimes this intention must be deduced from the circumstances. Here one might speak of an implied trust. However, take warning: there is no uniformity as to the meaning of the term implied trust.

86 See further T.G. Youdan, "Formalities for Trusts of Land, and the Doctrine in *Rouchefoucald v. Boustead* ", [1984] C.L.J. 306.

87 See, *e.g.*, *Trustee Act*, R.S.A. 1980, c. T-10 [as am.].

88 See generally R. Chambers, *Resulting Trusts* (Oxford: Clarendon Pr., 1997). For an Australian perspective, see J. Glover, "Re-Assessing the Uses of the Resulting Trust: Modern and Medieval Themes" (1999) 25 Monash U.L.Rev. 110.

89 *Cf.* C.E.F. Rickett, "The Classification of Trusts" (1999) 18 N.Z.U.L.Rev. 305, at 313*ff*.

Uses. Baker would hold the legal title on trust for C, the beneficiary, for life. Notice that the remainder of the beneficial fee simple estate after the grant of the equitable life estate to C is unaccounted for in the settlement. That portion of the equitable title, not having been given away, results back to the settlor (A). It likely does not belong to Baker, which holds only the legal estate, although it might have been given a beneficial interest had the settlor been inclined to do so. Similarly, assume that property is conveyed on trust, 'for my first child to turn 21 years of age'. Until the age-condition is met, the equitable title cannot pass to the intended beneficiary. In the meantime, the beneficial interest results back to the settlor.

A resulting trust can also arise if a deed of trust is somehow ineffective, such that it fails totally or partially. That might occur when, for example, the trust is found to contravene public policy, or if it was created through the perpetration of fraud or duress. Here, as in the case of an incomplete transfer of the beneficial interest, normally[90] the equitable title results back to the settlor.

The second type of resulting trust involves gratuitous transfers. As a general rule, when A buys property and places title to it in the name of B, a resulting trust is presumed to arise in favour of A. The same is true when A voluntarily transfers property that she or he presently owns to B. In both of these situations the legal title is in B, and B may even be registered as the owner. However, equity will treat that interest as subordinate to the resulting trust held by A; B is regarded as a bare trustee. Equity presumes bargains and not gifts and therefore leans against treating a transfer as a donation. But the presumption that arises in these circumstances serves merely a protective function and is not designed to impose a prohibition on gift-giving. The presumption of resulting trust can be rebutted by showing that a gift was truly intended.[91] If this is proved, then the legal and equitable titles are held by the donee (B in the example), and no trust arises.[92]

The presumption of resulting trust forms the general rule. However, in some circumstances the position is reversed, and a presumption of advancement (or gift) obtains. Whether this presumption applies depends on the nature of the relationship of the parties to the transaction. For example, a gift is presumed in a

---

90 There are some exceptions to this outcome. Under the rule in *Hancock v. Watson*, [1902] A.C. 14, [1900-03] All E.R.Rep. 87 (H.L.) when an absolute gift is bequeathed, to which are added trust conditions, if those conditions are invalid (for example, because of illegality), the donee holds the gift absolutely; no resulting trust arises: see, *e.g.*, *Re Goodhue Trusts* (1920) 47 O.L.R. 178 (H.C.). If the settlor knew of the illegality before the trust was created, a resulting trust may be denied: see Waters, *supra*, note 65, at 367, and 319*ff*. See also *Provincial Plasterers' Benefit Trust Fund (Trustees of) v. Provincial Plasterers' Benefit Trust Fund* (1990) 71 O.R. (2d) 558, 36 E.T.R. 157, 65 D.L.R. (4th) 723 (H.C.).

91 See, *e.g.*, *Fediuk v. Gluck* (1990) 26 R.F.L. (3d) 454 (Man.Q.B.).

92 A party may be precluded from relying on an illegal agreement to rebut the presumption: see, *e.g.*, *Reaney v. Reaney* (1990) 38 E.T.R. 252, 28 R.F.L. (3d) 52, 72 D.L.R. (4th) 532 (Ont.H.C.); *Sodhi v. Sodhi* (1998) 20 E.T.R. (2d) 242, 53 B.C.L.R. (3d) 280, [1998] 10 W.W.R. 673 (S.C.) affirmed (1998) 23 E.T.R. (2d) 235 (B.C.C.A.). See generally Waters, *supra*, note 65, at 319*ff*, where the contours of this principle are carefully defined. See also *Tribe v. Tribe*, [1995] 4 All E.R. 236 (C.A.); Oosterhoff & Gillese, *supra*, note 65, at 351*ff*.

transfer of property from father to child.[93] The transfer is described as an advancement because it is seen as fulfilling the expectation that the child will eventually receive some of the father's estate through inheritance. Owing to the presumption of advancement, the child holds both the legal and equitable interests. This reading of the transaction can be rebutted, and a resulting trust found in favour of the father, if it can be shown that a gift was not intended.[94] The case law in Canada is divided on the issue of whether a transfer from a mother to her child should also be presumptively treated as an advancement.[95] Given that nowadays it is reasonable to expect that mothers have the means to provide for their children, and that they would wish to do so, one would assume that gender parity now exists. It should.[96]

Traditionally an advancement was presumed when a husband purchased property in the name of his wife, but not *vice versa*. In other words, a gift by H to W triggered a rebuttable presumption of advancement in favour of W. In a gift from W to H, a resulting trust was presumed, also in favour of W. In the case of cohabiting spouses the presumption of advancement has not been applied: gifts between cohabitees are subject to the presumption of resulting trust.[97]

In some jurisdictions the rules governing transfers between spouses have been reformed. The general approach has been to render the rules gender-neutral and to limit or abolish the application of the presumption of advancement. For example, in proceedings under Alberta's *Matrimonial Property Act* for a division of property, the presumption of resulting trust generally applies to transfers made by one spouse to the other.[98] An exception exists for assets that are purchased by the spouses as joint owners: in that case the presumption is that both hold a share of the equitable title.[99] In other words, here a gift may be presumed.

On the judicial front it is also apparent that the presumption of advancement, as between spouses, is on the wane. In the Supreme Court of Canada decision in

---

93 This also applies when an individual stands in the place of a parent (*in loco parentis*): see, *e.g.*, *Evong Estate v. Lawton* (1990) 100 N.S.R. (2d) 133, 272 A.P.R. 133 (T.D.); *Young v. Young* (1958) 15 D.L.R. (2d) 138 (B.C.C.A.).

94 See, *e.g.*, *Marwin v. Bourque* (1990) 96 N.S.R. (2d) 12, 253 A.P.R. 12 (T.D.).

95 The presumption of advancement does not apply: *Lattimer v. Lattimer* (1978) 18 O.R. (2d) 375, 1 E.T.R. 274, 82 D.L.R. (3d) 587 (H.C.) relying on *Edwards v. Bradley*, [1957] S.C.R. 599, 9 D.L.R. (2d) 673. See *contra Re Wilson* (1999) 27 E.T.R. (2d) 97 (Ont.Gen.Div.); *Dagle v. Dagle* (1990) 38 E.T.R. 164, 70 D.L.R. (4th) 201, 81 Nfld. & P.E.I.R. 245, 255 A.P.R. 245 (P.E.I.C.A.) leave to appeal to S.C.C. refused (1991) 74 D.L.R. (4th) viii (S.C.C.); *Dreger v. Dreger (Litigation Guardian of)*, [1994] 10 W.W.R. 293 (Man.C.A.). See also *Taylor Estate v. Taylor* (1995) 9 E.T.R. (2d) 15 (B.C.S.C.); *Oulton Estate v. Oulton* (1996) 14 E.T.R. (2d) 214, 183 N.B.R. (2d) 186, 465 A.P.R. 186 (Q.B.).

96 Accord A. Dowling, "The Presumption of Advancement Between Mother and Child", [1996] Conv. 274, which reviews developments in Canada and other jurisdictions.

97 See further *Wilson v. Munro* (1983) 42 B.C.L.R. 317, 13 E.T.R. 174, 32 R.F.L. (2d) 235 (S.C.) where the traditional view is affirmed.

98 *Matrimonial Property Act*, R.S.A. 1980, c. M-9, sub. 36(1). This provision applies only to proceedings under the *Matrimonial Property Act*. In some provinces the reforms have general application: see, *e.g.*, *Family Law Act*, R.S.O. 1990, c. F.3, s. 14.

99 Sub. 36(2). Under para. 36(2)(b), money deposited in a joint account is treated as being jointly owned for the purposes of this exception.

Rathwell v. Rathwell, discussed below, it was said that the "old presumption of advancement has ceased to embody any credible inference of intention".[100] This is weighty language, coming as it does from the Supreme Court, and it may well point to the end of the doctrine. Some courts, mindful of this *dictum*, have treated the presumption as still extant, while at the same time noting that its significance has declined in recent years.[101] One might surmise, therefore, that it is now easier to rebut the presumption of gift than was the case in the past.

The 'common intention' resulting trust is a variant on the idea that a trust arises in favour of the party advancing the purchase price.[102] This kind of resulting trust has been found in cases in which it is shown that the party on title intended some other person (usually the spouse of the legal owner) to share beneficial ownership. What normally triggers the trust is an agreement, often only implicit, that the non-titled spouse should acquire some proprietary right, owing to that person's contributions to the acquisition, preservation or enhancement of the property. In the past, the recognition of the common intention resulting trust served as a way of rewarding the non-monetary contributions of one spouse, when title was held by the other. As we will see below, that function has been overtaken in the last 25 years or so by the emergence of two very robust equitable concepts: the doctrine of unjust enrichment and the remedial constructive trust. In Chapter 9, the role played by marital property laws in responding to these situations will also be explained.

(d)   constructive trusts

A constructive trust is one imposed by equity, irrespective of an intention to create a trust. Influenced by the orthodox English position, the constructive trust in Canada was at one time regarded as having a narrow compass. In this traditional or 'institutional' form, the constructive trust is situationally based, that is, it arises in a number of established specific instances. For example, an express trustee who wrongfully obtains profits from his or her position will hold those monies under a constructive trust.[103] A person who unlawfully deals with trust property in circumstances in which that person knew or ought to have known of the trust will be treated as a (constructive) trustee '*de son tort*'. Likewise, a constructive trust may be imposed to prevent a wrongdoer from profiting from a crime.[104]

---

100 *Rathwell v. Rathwell*, [1978] 2 S.C.R. 436, [1978] 2 W.W.R. 101, 83 D.L.R. (3d) 289, at 452 S.C.R. (*per* Dickson J., as he then was).

101 See *Aleksich v. Konradson* (1995) 5 B.C.L.R. (3d) 240, 12 R.F.L. (4th) 177, [1995] 6 W.W.R. 268 (C.A.).

102 The Canadian law concerning the common intention resulting trust is based on a reading of the decisions in *Gissing v. Gissing*, [1971] A.C. 886, [1970] 2 All E.R. 780 (H.L.) and *Pettitt v. Pettitt*, [1970] A.C. 777, [1969] 2 All E.R. 385 (H.L.). For a critique of this type of resulting trust, see Oosterhoff & Gillese, *supra*, note 65, at 322*ff.*

103 A trust may be imposed when the person profiting is not a trustee *per se*, but is acting as a 'fiduciary'. As to the meaning of that term, see *LAC Minerals Ltd. v. International Corona Resources Ltd.*, [1989] 2 S.C.R. 574, 35 E.T.R. 1, 61 D.L.R. (4th) 14, and *Hodgkinson v. Simms*, [1994] 3 S.C.R. 377, 5 E.T.R. (2d) 1, 117 D.L.R. (4th) 161.

104 See, *e.g.*, *Sangha Estate v. Sovereign Life Insurance Co.* (1991) 56 B.C.L.R. (2d) 395, 4 C.C.L.I. (2d) 239, [1991] 5 W.W.R. 652 (S.C.). See generally T.G. Youdan, "Acquisition of

These illustrations[105] suggest that a constructive trust arises in those instances in which equity wishes to respond to unconscionable conduct. While this is a common ingredient, it is not always a necessary one. A vendor in a standard house transaction normally assumes the position of a constructive trustee prior to the closing of the transaction. The purchaser acquires an equitable interest in the property provided that equity would be prepared to order specific performance of the contract of sale.[106] This places obligations on the vendor to maintain the property and not to deal with it in a manner that would be detrimental to the interests of the purchaser. However, the position of the vendor is not in all respects identical to that of other constructive trustees. Until the price is paid in full, an array of beneficial rights may still be enjoyed by the vendor, including rights to possession and to any rents or profits derived from the property.

The English jurisprudence demonstrates rote familiarity with the situations in which constructive trusts have previously been imposed; however, the absence of a unifying or explanatory theory has been a troublesome feature of the law. In consequence, even though the situations in which English law is prepared to impose a trust do not form a closed set, there has been resistance to the expansion of the concept beyond its established domain. One English response, cautiously developed and invoked, has been the recognition of a residual category of constructive trusts based on notions of unconscionability or 'good conscience'.[107] In Canada, the institutional constructive trust continues to apply, and it is now clear that the 'good conscience' trust is part of this package.[108] Moreover, the idea of good conscience may be the best overarching description of the institutional constructive trusts that now exist, or may later be recognized:

> Good conscience as a common concept unifying the various instances in which a constructive trust may be found has the disadvantage of being very general. But any concept capable of embracing the diverse circumstances in which a constructive trust may be imposed must, of necessity, be general. Particularity is found in the situations in which judges in the past have found constructive trusts. A judge faced with a claim for a constructive trust will have regard not merely to what might seem ''fair'' in a general sense, but to other situations where courts have found a constructive trust. The goal is but a reasoned, incremental development of the law on a case-by-case basis.[109]

Property By Killing'' (1973) 89 L.Q.R. 235. This principle is also applied in connection with the murder of one joint tenant by another: see Part 4(d), Chapter 9.

105 There are other circumstances in which equity has traditionally recognized a constructive trust: see Waters, *supra*, note 65, at 398*ff*. See also Oosterhoff & Gillese, *supra*, note 65, chs. 8, 9.

106 *Lysaght v. Edwards* (1876) 2 Ch. D. 499, at 506-10. See also *Martin Commercial Fueling Inc. v. Virtanen* (1997) 31 B.C.L.R. (3d) 69, [1997] 5 W.W.R. 330, 144 D.L.R. (4th) 290 (C.A.). But see S. Gardner, ''Equity, Estate Contracts and the Judicature Acts: *Walsh v. Lonsdale* Revisited'' (1987) 7 O.J.L.S. 60. On the suitability of specific performance in land deals, see the *dictum* of Sopinka J. in *Semelhago v. Paramadevan*, [1996] 2 S.C.R. 415, 3 R.P.R. (3d) 1, 136 D.L.R. (4th) 1, at 427-8 S.C.R.

107 See, *e.g.*, *Hussey v. Palmer*, [1972] 1 W.L.R. 1286, [1972] 3 All E.R. 744 (C.A.).

108 *Soulos v. Korkontzilas*, [1997] 2 S.C.R. 217, 146 D.L.R. (4th) 214, 17 E.T.R. (2d) 89. See also *Yorkshire Trust Co. v. Empire Acceptance Corp. (Receiver of)* (1986) 69 B.C.L.R. 357, 22 E.T.R. 96, 24 D.L.R. (4th) 140 (S.C.).

109 *Soulos v. Korkontzilas, supra*, note 108, at 236-7 S.C.R. (*per* McLachlin J., as she then was). As to the general grounds upon which a constructive trust based on wrongful conduct should

Modern Canadian law does not stop there; it has, in fact, moved rather far afield from the restrained English position. Since the 1970s, 'remedial' constructive trust has developed as a highly effective means of responding to unjust enrichment.[110] It is a flexible instrument, available in a variety of circumstances beyond purview of the 'institutional' constructive trust. So, the use of the constructive trust as a means of remedying unjust enrichment has provided a basis for rewarding those engaged in household labour. Specifically, the imposition of this form of trust furnishes a proprietary remedy as compensation for such work. However, its application has been much broader: it has also been applied in a commercial context. This type of remedial trust, influenced by American law, is a relatively recent innovation in Canada. A helpful way of understanding its present complexion is through a brief historical review, beginning with the infamous decision of the Supreme Court of Canada in *Murdoch v. Murdoch*.[111]

Murdoch involved a claim by a wife to an interest in her husband's ranch properties. In that case the wife had worked with her husband as a hired hand on various ranches from 1943 to 1947. During this period, both of their pay packets were given to the husband. In 1947 the husband and his father purchased a guest ranch. This was sold in 1951, and a second property was later purchased by the husband, with the title to that land being taken in his name alone. This property was paid for with the proceeds of sale from the first property, together with money drawn from the wife's bank account. The wife had obtained that money from her mother. Several other parcels were later acquired, and these properties were operated collectively as a ranch. Mrs. Murdoch worked tirelessly: for five months of the year, while her husband was away on business, she attended to the daily ranching chores (which included various forms of arduous physical labour). When the marriage broke down she claimed an interest in the ranch, based partly on the financial contributions made prior to the purchase of the lands, and partly on the indirect contributions that she had provided through her work. Her action failed.

A majority of the Supreme Court assessed the claims on the basis of whether or not a *resulting* trust arose. In the view of the majority, the necessary intention required to create a resulting trust could not be found on the facts. Remarkable as the wife's contributions appeared to be, Mr. Murdoch testified that these were

---

be awarded, see *ibid*. at 240-1 S.C.R. These criteria were not satisfied in *Terra Energy Ltd. v. Kilborn Engineering Alberta Ltd.* (1999) 43 C.L.R. (2d) 190, 170 D.L.R. (4th) 405, [1999] 6 W.W.R. 483 (Alta.C.A.) reconsideration refused (1999) 232 A.R. 297 (C.A.) leave to appeal to S.C.C. refused (January 27, 2000) Doc. 27341 (S.C.C.). See further K.B. Farquhar, "Unjust Enrichment and Constructive Trust: A Comment on *Korkontzilas v. Soulos*" (1996) 31 U.B.C.L.Rev. 341. *Cf.* C. Rickett & R. Grantham, "Towards a More Constructive Classification of Trusts", [1999] L.M.C.L.Q. 111, commenting on *Fortex Grp. Ltd. v. Macintosh*, [1998] 3 N.Z.L.R. 171 (C.A.).

110 See generally D.W.M. Waters, "The Constructive Trust in Evolution: Substantive and Remedial" (1990-91) 10 E. & T.J. 334.

111 [1975] 1 S.C.R. 423, [1974] 1 W.W.R. 361, 41 D.L.R. (3d) 367. The Canadian case law prior to *Peter v. Beblow, infra,* note 119, is surveyed in R.E. Scane, "Relationships 'Tantamount to Spousal', Unjust Enrichment and Constructive Trusts" (1991) 70 Can.B.Rev. 260. See also M.M. Litman, "The Emergence of Unjust Enrichment as a Cause of Action and the Remedy of Constructive Trust" (1988) 26 Alta.L.Rev. 407.

no more than would be expected of an ordinary ranch wife in the circumstances. This characterization seems to have been accepted by the trial judge and the majority of the Supreme Court. Her work could not therefore support a finding that there was a common intention that title was to be shared. Additionally, the Supreme Court apparently discounted the financial contributions made by the wife during the early years of the marriage when the spouses had both worked as hired hands. It was held that the first property was bought by the husband with his own assets. The money received from the wife's bank account was found to be a loan from the wife's mother. In dissent, Laskin J. (as he then was) was prepared to hold that a constructive trust should be imposed. His Lordship concluded that it was necessary to respond to the unjust enrichment enjoyed by the husband. Unlike the majority, Laskin J. was prepared to take into account the wife's contributions before the lands were purchased, as well as her participation in the ranching operations over the years.

The *Murdoch* case was more than a harsh judgment;[112] it became a *cause célèbre*, and was a catalyst in the process of family property reform that was already underway in Canada.[113] Through Laskin J.'s dissent, the seeds had also been sown for the growth of a new conceptualization of the constructive trust. Equitable doctrines underwent a rapid transition after *Murdoch*, starting with the Supreme Court judgment in *Rathwell v. Rathwell*,[114] which was decided only a few years later. There, a claim similar in nature to that advanced in *Murdoch* succeeded. While all members of the Court were able to find a resulting trust based on an implied common intention, a three-member minority went further. They endorsed the existence in Canada of a general doctrine of unjust enrichment, applicable when the facts display (i) an enrichment; (ii) a corresponding deprivation; and (iii) the absence of a juristic reason for the enrichment. One of the ways in which this unjust enrichment can be remedied, it was said, would be to treat the legal owner as holding part of the legal title on a constructive trust for the party suffering the deprivation.

In *Pettkus v. Becker*,[115] a case involving a *de facto* relationship that lasted almost 20 years, the minority position in *Rathwell* was adopted by a majority of the Supreme Court. From that point on the doctrine of unjust enrichment, with the remedy of constructive trust in aid, has been firmly entrenched in Canadian law. Only a few years after *Murdoch*, equitable principles had changed so dramatically that it is almost certain that Mrs. Murdoch would have received a share in the ranch (probably half of it) had her case been litigated in the wake of *Pettkus v. Becker*.

In *Sorochan v. Sorochan*[116] these doctrines were refined. The Sorochans lived together for 42 years, separating in 1982. During the period of co-

---

112 Among the stinging criticisms is P. Jacobson, "*Murdoch v. Murdoch*: Just About What the Ordinary Rancher's Wife Does" (1974) 20 McGill L.J. 308.

113 See Part 7, Chapter 9, where these reforms are briefly described.

114 *Supra*, note 100.

115 [1980] 2 S.C.R. 834, 8 E.T.R. 143, 117 D.L.R. (3d) 257.

116 [1986] 2 S.C.R. 38, 46 Alta.L.R. (2d) 97, 29 D.L.R. (4th) 1. See also *Rawluk v. Rawluk*, [1990] 1 S.C.R. 70, 36 E.T.R. 1, 65 D.L.R. (4th) 161.

habitation Mrs. Sorochan collaborated with her common law husband on a farm-ing venture. She also assumed virtually all of the caregiving responsibilities for their six children. Although they never married, the prospect of marriage was held out to Mrs. Sorochan on a number of occasions. All of the land was registered solely in Mr. Sorochan's name, and in 1971 he refused a request that part of the land be transferred to her. Following the separation, Mrs. Sorochan sought a remedy in equity in relation to the farm lands.

The prerequisites for the establishment of unjust enrichment were found to exist. The husband had been enriched: the benefit he received included the essen-tial farm services and domestic work performed by Mrs. Sorochan. The wife's contributions, which were significant, were made without compensation having been provided: this constituted the necessary corresponding deprivation. In *So-rochan* the farm property had been owned by the husband at the beginning of the common law relationship. Therefore, its initial acquisition could not be connected to Mrs. Sorochan's labours. The Supreme Court held that this was not determi-native – a contribution relating to the preservation, maintenance or improvement of property can suffice. Finally, it was held that there was no juristic reason to deny relief; Mrs. Sorochan was under no obligation to perform the services. Moreover, she had prejudiced her position on the reasonable expectation of receiving something in return. Mr. Sorochan accepted these benefits in circum-stances in which he should have appreciated her expectation.

A finding of unjust enrichment having been made, the next step was to determine the best method of providing restitution. A finding of unjust enrichment does not invariably lead to the imposition of a constructive trust. This is only one of the remedies available. Another option open to a court is to award monetary compensation.[117] And the granting of an interest in land need not amount to the fee simple estate; in some circumstances a more limited interest (*e.g.,* a life estate) may be the most appropriate response.[118] In *Sorochan* the Supreme Court granted a proprietary remedy and imposed a constructive trust of a one-third interest in the disputed property. The factors that seem to have been most important in this decision were these: (i) the presence of a clear link between her contributions and the land; (ii) Mrs. Sorochan's reasonable expectation of obtaining a proprietary interest; and (iii) the length of the relationship.

An issue often present in these cases relates to whether or not the provision of domestic services, of the sort normally undertaken by spouses during cohabi-tation, could serve as the basis for an unjust enrichment suit. In these earlier cases there had always been some additional, often monumental, contribution to the material well-being of the parties. In *Peter v. Beblow*[119] the Supreme Court of

---

117 See, *e.g., Everson v. Rich* (1988) 31 E.T.R. 26, 16 R.F.L. (3d) 337, 53 D.L.R. (4th) 470 (Sask.C.A.); *Lakusta v. Jones* (1997) 34 R.F.L. (4th) 431, 56 Alta.L.R. (3d) 214, [1998] 5 W.W.R. 453 (Q.B.).

118 See, *e.g., Bannister v. Bannister*, [1948] 2 All E.R. 133 (C.A.). See also *Ungurian v. Lesnoff*, [1990] Ch. 206; *Le Compte v. Public Trustee*, [1983] 2 N.S.W.L.R. 109 (Eq.Div.).

119 [1993] 1 S.C.R. 980, 77 B.C.L.R. (2d) 1, [1993] 3 W.W.R. 337. There are two judgments: that of McLachlin J. (as she then was), with La Forest, Sopinka, Iacobucci JJ., concurring; and that

Canada sustained a claim of unjust enrichment based on conventional domestic labour.

In this case the parties had cohabited for 12 years, during which Catherine Peter had undertaken most of the domestic work. William Beblow, in whose name the family home was registered, had maintained and improved the property in the ways that owners customarily do. Over the course of the relationship the mortgage on the home was paid off; Beblow also bought a houseboat and van during that period. Ms. Peter purchased a parcel of land with money earned during the currency of the relationship. When the parties separated the beneficial title to the Beblow house was at issue. In the result, the Court found that Mr. Beblow had been unjustly enriched by Ms. Peter's contributions and that a proprietary remedy was appropriate. Due to the extent of the contributions to the overall financial welfare of the family, the entire equity in the home was awarded to Ms. Peter. Ultimately, the Supreme Court of Canada upheld this order.

The elements of unjust enrichment were made out: the housekeeping constituted a benefit to Beblow; there was no compensation to Peter (the deprivation); plus, there was no obligation to provide the services, and no other plausible reason to deny compensation. Her work in the home was not regarded as having been provided as a gift.[120] The suggestion that ordinary household services cannot support a claim of unjust enrichment was repudiated, given the basic principles of that doctrine, and the obvious value of such contributions. (Prior to this relationship, Beblow had hired a housekeeper to perform some of the work that was later undertaken by Peter.) The idea that domestic services cannot found a claim was flatly rejected as "a pernicious one that systematically devalues the contributions which women tend to make to the family economy".[121] It was added that such a notion had in the past "contributed to the phenomenon of the feminization of poverty".[122]

The Supreme Court held as well that for a constructive trust to be ordered, whether in family law cases or otherwise,[123] a court should find that (i) a monetary compensation is inadequate; and (ii) that a link exists between the services rendered and the property in dispute.[124] (These are general rules: because equity is inherently flexible, they are not rigid requirements.) The nature of the requisite causal connection remains vague. A minor or indirect contribution should not be sufficient to prompt the constructive trust remedy. In *Beblow* the contributions

of Cory J., with Gonthier and L'Heureux-Dubé JJ. concurring. The decision in favour of the appellant (Catherine Peter) was unanimous.

120 See further A. Drassinower, "Unrequested Benefits in the Law of Unjust Enrichment" (1998) 48 U.T.L.J. 459; *Campbell v. Campbell* (1999) 173 D.L.R. (4th) 270 (Ont.C.A.).

121 *Supra*, note 119, at 993 S.C.R. (*per* McLachlin J.).

122 *Ibid.* English law has not embraced the doctrine of unjust enrichment, or the idea of a remedial constructive trust. The English approach is exemplified by *Lloyd's Bank plc. v. Rosset*, [1991] 1 A.C. 107, [1990] 1 All E.R. 1111 (H.L.) noted in (1991) 54 Mod.L.R. 126. See also *Hammond v. Mitchell*, [1991] 1 W.L.R. 1127, [1992] 2 All E.R. 109 (Fam.Div.) noted in (1993) 56 Mod.L.Rev. 224.

123 The majority placed commercial and family cases on the same footing. *Cf.* the minority judgment of Cory J.

124 *Supra*, note 119, at 997 S.C.R. (majority judgment).

had been substantial and they were found to be sufficiently connected to the family home, presumably because Ms. Peter's contributions allowed Beblow to pay off the mortgage and improve the property. A money payment was held to be inadequate given the nature of her work in the home and the chance that a damages award might not be paid. The measure of her assistance, based on the manner in which it enhanced the holdings of the parties,[125] was treated as roughly equivalent to the value of the family home. For this reason, the home was awarded to Ms. Peter. This outcome does seem extreme – Beblow, the sole legal owner of the house, lost out completely. In granting the award the Supreme Court suggested that the proper course was to consider the manner in which the contributions of Ms. Peter enhanced the value of all of the family assets. Having done so, one of these assets, the home, was segregated out and made the subject of the trust. Still, this left Beblow with very little (mainly a van, a houseboat, and his veteran's allowance).[126]

Another consideration in disputes of this nature is the extent to which the benefits received by the claimant during cohabitation should be taken into account. The non-owning party in many of these cases has lived rent-free, while the owner of the property may have paid all of the current expenses associated with the upkeep of the home. It is obviously important that this side of the balance sheet not be overlooked. After all, if it is unrealistic to suppose that the cohabitee in a case like *Beblow* is intending to make a gift of services, then the same must be true of the tangible benefits provided by the other party.[127] In the *Beblow* case the trial judge divided the financial contributions of Peter by 50%, presumably to take account of the benefits that she had received from Beblow.[128]

It was argued in *Peter v. Beblow* that because matrimonial property legislation excludes non-married couples from the right to seek a division of family assets under these statutory schemes, the courts should not use the equitable doctrine of unjust enrichment to provide such a right. In response it was said that ''[i]t is precisely where an injustice arises without a legal remedy that equity finds a role''.[129] That reply leads the discussion back to the starting point of this chapter. The story of the growth of the remedial constructive trust in Canada serves as a

---

125 This is described in the judgment as the 'value survived' approach. By contrast, under a 'value received' approach, the value of the services rendered is computed. This was said to be appropriate when a monetary payment is ordered. However, it would be appropriate only if the purpose of the order is to provide payment for those services. When the payment is intended to estimate the value of property, the amount by which that property is augmented (the 'value survived') should form the basis of the award. The value survived approach was applied in *Regnier v. O'Reilly* (1997) 31 R.F.L. (4th) 122, 39 B.C.L.R. (3d) 178 (S.C.).

126 See also *Crick v. Ludwig* (1994) 4 E.T.R. (2d) 213, 95 B.C.L.R. (2d) 72, [1994] 9 W.W.R. 754 (C.A.) leave to appeal to S.C.C. refused (1995) 6 E.T.R. (2d) 159n (S.C.C.).

127 See J.G. McLeod, Annot: *Herman v. Smith* (1984) 42 R.F.L. (2d) 154, also reported at 34 Alta.L.R. (2d) 90, 18 E.T.R. 169, 56 A.R. 74 (Q.B.). McLeod's position is criticized in Litman, *supra*, note 111, at 438-9. See further M.M. Litman, ''Recent Developments in the Law of Unjust Enrichment: Survival of Actions, Accounting and Beyond'' (1988-89) 9 E. & T.J. 287. See also K. Farquhar, ''Causal Connection and Constructive Trusts'' (1986-88) 8 E. & T.Q. 161, at 188.

128 *Supra*, note 119, at 1000 S.C.R. (majority judgment).

129 *Ibid*. at 994 S.C.R. (*per* McLachlin J.).

contemporary manifestation of the very essence of equity as a curative gloss on the common law. At the same time, the reluctance of English law to follow a similar course of development is premised on another part of the story of equity. The broadly framed nature of unjust enrichment principles reminds some of ''earlier times when equity was said to vary like the Chancellor's foot''.[130] These opposing attitudes reflect the tension that often emerges between the need for certainty and flexibility in property law, and in the law generally.

---

130 P.H. Pettit, *Equity and the Law of Trusts*, 7th ed. (London: Butterworths, 1993) at 62. Sometimes these concerns are referred to as fears of 'palm tree justice'. See also the doubts about the doctrine of unjust enrichment in the judgment of Martland J. in *Rathwell v. Rathwell*, *supra*, note 100, at 473 S.C.R. Likewise in *Springette v. Defoe*, [1992] 2 F.L.R. 388 (C.A.) at 393, Dillon L.J. commented that English courts do not yet ''sit, as under a palm tree, to exercise a general discretion to do what the man [sic] in the street, on a general overview of the case, might regard as fair''.

7

CONDITIONAL TRANSFERS
AND FUTURE INTERESTS

Clutching the parchment
with shaking hands.
a sigh.

Louis J. Sirico, Jr.,
The Duke of Norfolk's Case[1]

1. INTRODUCTION

Throughout this text we have been exploring the ways in which property can be used as a basis of power. Property, with its right of exclusion, mediates relationships among people, conferring control on the designated owner. This chapter introduces several methods by which this type of empowerment is exercised.

Property rights can be used by present owners to impose restrictions on future ones. In the world of legal liberalism, the freedom of owners to use or dispose of property as they wish is extensive. Among other things, they may attach strings to property transfers. This chapter deals primarily with (i) the ways in which conditional gifts can be created; and (ii) the limitations on the freedom of transfer that are imposed under the law. A number of policy goals will be addressed throughout the discussion, including those tied to market efficiency. However, the issues that are canvassed here go far beyond economic concerns. The wielding of private power through the use of property can engage a broad range of social issues.

In essence, we will see how the law balances proprietary freedoms against other values. Of course, this type of balancing act permeates everything that has been or will be dealt with in this text. Again, speaking in general terms, all principles of property law are the product of an unending tug of war between competing interests. The interplay here is quite plain to see and the stresses of conflict are more apparent than in other areas of the law. Therefore they are of especial importance in this chapter.

As a prelude to the examination of public policy, some of the mechanisms of private control will be explained. To begin this analysis we return to a foundational concept: the doctrine of estates. It was seen (in Chapter 5) that the temporal division of property leads to the creation of present and future interests. The examples that were considered earlier involved pure-form freehold estates, namely, the fee simple absolute and the life estate. In this chapter a fuller array

---

1 "Future Interest Haiku", 67 N.C.L.Rev. 171 (1988) at 174. The *Duke of Norfolk's Case* laid the foundation for the modern rule against perpetuities, to be studied in Part 5 of this chapter.

of proprietary interests will be described. These include the following: remainders, reversions, vested and contingent interests, determinable and defeasible estates, possibilities of reverter, and rights of re-entry. The meaning of these terms will be described in the first section of the chapter; they form the building blocks for the concepts that follow.

2.   BASIC CONCEPTS

(a)   remainders and reversions

Remainders and reversions are associated with the doctrine of estates in land. Consider a conveyance by a fee simple owner, G, which reads 'to A for life'. The interest granted to A is a mere 'particle' of the fee simple; hence, the life estate is occasionally referred to as a *particular estate*. The grantor retains a *reversion* – the property returns or reverts to G on the expiration of A's life interest. Consider next a transfer by G that reads 'to A for life, then to B in fee simple'. The interest conveyed to B is a *remainder*; instead of reverting to the grantor on the death of A, the property moves to B, to be enjoyed in possession when the prior particular life estate given to A has ended. While one speaks of remainders and reversions as future interests, they are more accurately described as present rights to future enjoyment.

(b)   defeasible and determinable interests

An interest is *defeasible* if it may be brought to a premature end on the occurrence of a specified event. Imagine a devise 'to the School Board in fee simple, on the condition that if the property shall no longer be needed for school purposes, my estate may re-enter'.[2] Here the School Board receives a defeasible interest, or more precisely in this instance, *a fee simple subject to a condition subsequent*. The decedent's estate retains a *right of re-entry* (or more simply, a right of entry), which may be exercised if the stated event comes to pass. In other words, the School Board holds a present estate in fee simple and if the condition is adhered to that interest will continue on.[3] If the condition is broken the right of re-entry may be relied upon by the estate to reclaim the land. Conceptually, this re-entry cuts short the fee simple estate. It is like a dark *cloud* that hovers over the fee.

A *determinable* interest closely resembles its defeasible counterpart.[4] In a devise 'to the School Board *until* the land is no longer required for school pur-

---

2 See *Fitzmaurice v. Monck (Township) School Trustees*, [1949] O.W.N. 786 (H.C.). *Cf. Moser v. Barss*, [1947] 4 D.L.R. 313 (N.S.S.C.); *Spruce Grove v. Yellowhead Regional Library Bd.* (1985) 37 Alta.L.R. (2d) 70, 59 A.R. 304 (Q.B.).

3 As it turns out, the right of re-entry would be void because it is contrary to the rule against perpetuities at common law: see Part 5, *infra*. Under Alberta law, this condition would now have a limited lifespan, which would be 40 years: *Perpetuities Act*, R.S.A. 1980, c. P-4, s. 19.

4 Determinable limitations are sometimes referred to (confusingly) as conditional limitations: see, *e.g.*, *In re Melville* (1886) 11 O.R. 626 (Ch.D.) at 631. They are sometimes taken to refer to conditions subsequent: see B. Murdoch, *Epitome of the Laws of Nova Scotia* (Halifax: J. Howe, 1832-3) vol. 2, at 139-40. The term conditional limitation is not used in this text.

poses', a *determinable fee simple* is produced. Again, the Board receives a present possessory right. Should the determining event occur, the fee will end and the property will pass to the grantor (or that person's estate). The interest that is retained is called a *possibility of reverter*. The estate in the School Board will end automatically on the happening of the prescribed event and no formal entry or demand for possession is required by the person holding the possibility of reverter. The determining event is like a *fence post* that demarcates the durational extent of the entitlement.

Defeasible and determinable interests bear a very, very strong resemblance to each other. But make no mistake – beyond the superficial similarities lie vital juridical differences, particularly when questions of invalidity arise.[5] The phrases employed in the examples above foreshadow the disquieting fact that distinguishing between these interests is often difficult, and usually turns on linguistic nuances.

Whether a condition subsequent or a determinable limitation has been created is a matter of construction, and so depends, in principle, on the intention of the grantor. However, certain phrases have come to be associated with these interests, and given that there may be no reliable evidence of intention, these stock phrases are often used to help construe a grant or devise. Terms such as 'while', 'during', 'so long as', and 'until' are taken to connote a determinable interest. These are words of duration; they have a temporal sound. Remember, the determinable interest is treated as marking the chronometric limit of the grant, as a refinement of the normal durations fixed by the doctrine of estates. Conversely, language such as 'on condition that', 'but if', 'provided that', 'if it happens that', is normally taken to refer to a condition subsequent. A stipulation that appears in another part of a gift suggests the same result, because it is not integral to the definition of the estate, but rather describes an event that may supervene to terminate prematurely an otherwise absolute interest.[6]

Although these are the chief indicators, it is not always an easy matter to apply the standard phrases. Drafters do not always use this type of wording,[7] and a disposition may contain mixed signals. A gift 'to A so long as she continues to reside in Canada', found in a clause that appears after the main gift, provides support for either construction.[8] So does a clause that reads 'but only so long as the railway shall occupy or use the lands'.[9] Additionally, though courts are supposed to disregard the consequences of their rulings when resolving questions of construction, one wonders if this is always done; some courts seem to have warped

---

5 See Part 3(b), *infra.*

6 See generally the discussion in *Tilbury West Public School Bd. v. Hastie*, [1966] 2 O.R. 20, 55 D.L.R. (2d) 407 (H.C.) order varied [1966] 2 O.R. 511, 57 D.L.R. (2d) 519 (H.C.). See also P. Devonshire, "Possibilities of Reverter and Rights of Re-entry for Condition Broken: The Modern Context for Determinable and Conditional Interests in Land" (1990) 13 Dal.L.J. 650.

7 See, *e.g.*, *Re Essex County Roman Catholic Separate School Board* (1977) 17 O.R. (2d) 307, 2 R.P.R. 223, 80 D.L.R. (3d) 405 (H.C.).

8 *Sifton v. Sifton*, [1938] A.C. 656, [1938] 3 D.L.R. 633, [1938] 3 All E.R. 435 (P.C.). In this case it was held that a condition subsequent was created.

9 *Re McKellar*, [1972] 3 O.R. 16, 27 D.L.R. (3d) 289 (H.C.) affirmed [1973] 3 O.R. 178n (C.A.).

the categories in a struggle to reach a result that avoids the destruction of some interest.[10] Presumably, this is done on the view that the strictures imposed by certain property 'rules of law'[11] can sometimes work in an over-broad way, destroying gifts that do not seem in fact to offend public policy. That attitude is sometimes prevalent in cases involving potential violations of the rule against perpetuities.[12]

The legal characterization of a right of re-entry was considered in *St. Mary's Indian Band v. Cranbrook (City)*.[13] There, a Native Band surrendered reserve land to the Crown for use as an airport. The document of surrender contained the 'condition' that "should at any time the said lands cease to be used for public purposes they will revert to the St. Mary's Indian Band free of charge". In 1992, the Band tried to impose a property tax on the current occupiers of the lands. In a dispute over the validity of the levy, the British Columbia Court of Appeal decided that the Band had no interest in the lands and therefore retained no powers of taxation in relation to that property. The Court concluded that the surrender was subject to a condition subsequent and that the Band held the right of re-entry. But here is the crux of the matter: it was also decided that the right of re-entry was not an interest in land.[14] I doubt whether that holding is correct. Rights of re-entry and possibilities of reverter are unique rights, that much is certain. They apparently are not reversions or remainders in the strict sense.[15] But they do possess some of the hallmarks of interests in land: for example, they seem capable of binding third parties who acquire an interest in the property. While a right of entry may take the form of a personal covenant, valid only as a matter of contract and therefore subject to the rules governing privity of contract, it seems to me that it can also be made to run with the land.

In 1997, the Supreme Court of Canada affirmed the decision of the Court of Appeal but on other grounds. Although, in the process of doing so the issue of the correct characterization of a right of re-entry was essentially side-stepped, the Supreme Court's analysis nevertheless aids our understanding of the appropriate treatment of conditional grants of Aboriginal lands. Placing emphasis on the *sui generis* nature of Aboriginal land rights, the Court declined to indulge in an examination of the minutiae of the language in the surrender document in order to decide whether the qualification fell within the general real property categories of conditional or determinable rights. Instead, looking at the transaction as a whole, including the legislative and factual contexts in which it occurred, it was

---

10 Such a case may well be *Sifton v. Sifton, supra*, note 8. See also A. Brudner, *The Unity of the Common Law* (Berkeley: U. of Calif.Pr., 1995) at 28*ff.*

11 Recall the definition of this term in Part 2(a), Chapter 5.

12 See Part 5, *infra.*

13 (1995) 126 D.L.R. (4th) 539, 10 B.C.L.R. (3d) 249 (C.A.).

14 The British Columbia Court of Appeal relied on *In re Taxation of University of Manitoba Lands*, [1940] 1 W.W.R. 145, [1940] 1 D.L.R. 575 (Man.C.A.) and A.H. Oosterhoff & W.B. Rayner, *Anger & Honsberger Law of Real Property*, 2nd ed. (Aurora, Ont.: Canada Law Book, 1985) vol. 1, at 125.

15 R.E. Megarry & H.W.R. Wade, *The Law of Real Property*, 5th ed. (London: Stevens & Sons, 1984) at 237.

held that an absolute surrender was intended. Again, the words and phrases used to interpret conditional grants were not regarded as helpful.[16]

(c) vested interests, contingent interests and conditions precedent

Property interests are either *vested* or *contingent*. An interest is vested when no condition or limitation (including the ascertainment of the identity of the recipient) stands in the way of enjoyment. The natural termination of the prior particular estate is not treated as such a condition. So, in a devise 'to A for life, remainder to B', the interests of both donees are vested. The life estate is *vested in possession*. B's interest is also vested since the right to possession is not delayed by any condition other than the natural termination of the prior particular estate (of A). This remainder is *vested in interest* (but not in possession).

An interest is *contingent* if vesting is delayed pending the occurrence of some *condition precedent*, the happening of which is not inevitable. A condition precedent is like a *bridge* that must be crossed before the property can be enjoyed. This is true of a remainder that reads 'to the first person to find a cure for cancer'. Similarly, a gift 'to A for life, remainder to B but only if and when B marries' imposes a condition precedent on B's remainder.

The contrast between vested and contingent interests can be shown by returning to the fee simple subject to a condition subsequent and the companion concept, the right of re-entry. That type of fee is vested, but it may be lost (or divested) if the condition is breached. The right of re-entry is subject to a condition precedent, namely, the violation of the condition; therefore it is contingent. Only a fiction precludes the same analysis in relation to a determinable interest followed by a possibility of reverter. The determinable fee is vested. The possibility of reverter would logically appear to be contingent, just as the right of re-entry, but a different view has prevailed in Canada. The determining event is regarded as marking a natural limitation of the estate granted and not as imposing a super-added condition. This means the possibility of reverter is treated as being vested at common law.[17]

Ascertaining whether a gift is vested or contingent is a matter of construction.[18] In resolving disputes of this nature it has been said that "[t]he courts have followed a rule of construction favouring vesting or 'early vesting', particularly where the property is land, and this is a principle of law that has universal applications".[19] This view finds expression in at least two ways. First, courts are loath to imply contingencies and, when possible, adopt an interpretation that

---

16 *St. Mary's Indian Band v. Cranbrook (City)*, [1997] 2 S.C.R. 657, 35 B.C.L.R. (3d) 218, [1997] 8 W.W.R. 332. For subsequent proceedings, see *Cranbrook (City) v. British Columbia (Registrar of Land Titles)*, [1999] B.C.J. No. 230 (S.C., Chambers).

17 See further Devonshire, *supra*, note 6. However, see the reforms introduced in connection with the rule against perpetuities, mentioned in Part 5, *infra*.

18 See *Re Porter*, [1975] N.I. 157 (S.C.) for an analysis of how one might discern whether a condition should be found to be precedent or subsequent.

19 *Canada Permanent Trust Co. v. Lasby* (1984), [1985] 1 W.W.R. 489, 37 Sask.R. 193 (Q.B.) at 492 W.W.R. (*per* McIntyre J.).

leaves an interest indefeasibly vested.[20] Second, there is a preference in favour of vesting gifts at the earliest occasion possible. This attitude has spawned several rules of construction. For example, when it is unclear whether a gift creates (i) a condition precedent; (ii) a condition subsequent; or (iii) a determinable limitation, the latter two options are preferred because these readings lead to an immediate vesting of the interest. The condition or limitation is then treated as a basis for termination.[21] At best, only a rebuttable presumption in favour of early vesting arises, which can be overcome by language that shows that a contingent interest was intended. It is, of course, also possible that a given condition is intended to serve as both a condition of acquisition (a condition precedent) *and* one of retention (a condition subsequent or a determinable limitation).[22] A devise that reads 'to A for life, remainder to B so long as B is married' might produce that result.

By and large, Canadian courts have faithfully adhered to the ethos of promoting early vesting even though there has been little judicial scrutiny of the reasons that underlie it. In 1613, Coke C.J. put the matter this way: "the law always delights in vesting of estates, and contingencies are odious in the law, and are the causes of troubles, and vesting and settling of estates, the cause of repose and certainty".[23] More specifically, construing an interest as vested insulates the gift from those rules that may vitiate contingent interests, including the rule against perpetuities (which applies only to contingencies).[24] Furthermore, early vesting can allow for the early distribution of a deceased's estate into the hands of the ultimate beneficiaries. On a more general plane, a preference for vesting promotes the free alienation of property, at least when the interpretation given to the gift removes ostensible contingencies, and therefore means that the property is unfettered.[25] A property to which strings are attached may not be easy to sell.

The rule in *Phipps v. Ackers*[26] is premised on the preference for early vesting and illustrates this notion.[27] As initially cast, the rule provided that in a devise (or grant) to A, 'if' or 'when' A attains a given age, with a gift over in the event that he or she were to die before reaching that age, the age threshold is to be regarded

---

20   See, *e.g.*, *Re Ross* (1984) 6 D.L.R. (4th) 193 (B.C.S.C.) quoting *Duffield v. Duffield* (1829) 3 Bli.N.S. 260, at 331, 4 E.R. 1334, at 1358. See also *Browne v. Moody*, [1936] A.C. 635, [1936] 2 All E.R. 1695 (P.C.); *Re Lysiak* (1975) 7 O.R. (2d) 317, 55 D.L.R. (3d) 161 (H.C.); *Re Goian Estate* (1995) 139 Sask.R. 29, [1996] 2 W.W.R. 614 (Q.B.).

21   See, *e.g.*, *Sifton v. Sifton, supra*, note 8; *Goguen v. Godwin* (1978) 82 D.L.R. (3d) 547 (N.S. T.D.). See also *Woykin v. Nemanishen* (1990) 88 Sask.R. 105 (Q.B.).

22   See *Jordan v. Dunn* (1887) 13 O.R. 267 (Q.B.) affirmed (1888) 15 O.A.R. 744 (C.A.). This type of construction was raised, but not applied, in *Re Tepper's Will Trusts*, [1987] Ch. 358, [1987] 1 All E.R. 970, where its application would have made sense.

23   *Roberts v. Roberts* (1613), 2 Bulst. 123, at 131, 80 E.R. 1002 (K.B.) at 1009.

24   The rule is explained in Part 5, *infra*.

25   See further E.H. Rabin, "The Law Favors the Vesting of Estates. Why?", 65 Colum.L.Rev. 467 (1965).

26   (1842) 9 Cl. & Fin. 583, 8 E.R. 539 (H.L.). See also *Edwards v. Hammond* (1684) 3 Lev. 132, 84 E.R. 614; *In re Johnston Estate*, 53 Man.R. 143, [1945] 2 W.W.R. 324, [1945] 3 D.L.R. 213 (K.B.). *Cf. Balkaran v. Davidson*, [1980] 4 W.W.R. 1 (Man.Q.B.).

27   For other manifestations of the policy, see T.G. Feeney, *The Canadian Law of Wills*, 3rd ed. (Toronto: Butterworths, 1987) vol. 2, at ch. 8 *passim*.

as a condition subsequent and not precedent. As a result, A would take an immediate vested estate, subject to being divested if he or she dies before reaching the specified age. The rule has been applied to gifts of pure realty or personalty (and to mixed gifts),[28] and to conditions other than those relating to age.[29] However, it is only a rule of construction, and an unusual one at that, since it can twist clear language for the sake of promoting early vesting. The somewhat facile reasoning behind *Phipps v. Ackers* is that the gift over implies that the first taker is to enjoy the property first; it is to be 'given over' only if the prescribed event does not occur.[30]

Some very fine distinctions have been drawn in the application of the rule in *Phipps v. Ackers*. For instance, it has been suggested that a devise (i) 'to the children of A when they turn 21, but if no child reaches that age, then to B' attracts the operation of the rule. Yet a limitation (ii) 'to all of the children of A who shall attain 21, but if no child attains 21, then to B', arguably does not. In the second case the age requirement is considered so integral to the definition of the class that it must be treated as a requirement for the acquisition of the property; that is not so in the first example. Limitation (i) is described as a gift to a class on a contingency, while (ii) is a gift to a contingent class.[31]

(d) precatory words and in terrorem conditions

Terms are said to be purely precatory if they fall short of establishing conditions, limitations or any kind of binding obligation whatsoever. They are, in essence, toothless tigers, expressing no more than a wish, hope or desire that a donee act or refrain from acting in a specified manner, without providing for legal consequences should the donee fail to abide by the terms. So, for example, to 'request' that a beneficiary maintain accounts for the gifted property, coupled with a stated 'understanding' that the property shall pass on that person's death to others, has been treated as precatory; this language denoted neither a condition nor a gift over.[32] By contrast, it is plausible to see these directions as creating a 'precatory trust'. This "misleading nickname"[33] means, simply, a trust, albeit one couched in polite language. As can be appreciated, the difference between words that are precatory (and of no effect) and those that establish a precatory trust (binding in equity) is a question of construction, and one which can be quite difficult to resolve at the margins.

---

28 *In re Heath*, [1936] Ch. 259, [1935] All E.R.Rep. 677. See also *In re Kilpatrick's Policies Trusts*, [1966] Ch. 730, [1966] 2 All E.R. 149 (C.A.).

29 See, *e.g.*, *Kotsar v. Shattock*, [1981] V.R. 13 (S.C. Full Ct.). See also *Collins v. The Equity Trustees Executors and Agency Ltd.*, [1997] 2 V.R. 166 (S.C.).

30 *Cf. Re Monroe Estate* (1995) 135 Sask.R. 155, 9 E.T.R. (2d) 174, [1995] 9 W.W.R. 372 (Q.B.), where the *absence* of a gift over supported the conclusion that a vested gift was intended. Remarkably, the Court found that a gift to the decedent's daughter, "if and only if" she reached the age of 30, created a vested entitlement.

31 J.H.C. Morris & W.B. Leach, *The Rule Against Perpetuities*, 2nd ed. (London: Stevens & Sons, 1962) at 45. Class gifts are encountered again, briefly, in Parts 4(a)(ii) and 5(e), *infra*.

32 *Re Vance*, [1945] 2 D.L.R. 593, [1945] O.W.N. 323 (H.C.). See also *Perry v. Perry* (1918) 29 Man.R. 23, 40 D.L.R. 628, [1918] 2 W.W.R. 485 (C.A.).

33 *In re Williams*, [1897] 2 Ch. 12 (C.A.) at 27 (*per* Rigby L.J.).

In addition, some testamentary conditions attached to bequests of personalty (or a blended gift of realty and personalty) may be treated as *in terrorem*, that is, as an idle threat, not intended to lead to a loss of an interest. This interpretation has been applied when the conditions impose a restraint on marriage, or where they seek to prevent a beneficiary from disputing a will, if there is no apparent gift over of the property contained in the will that could be triggered by a breach of the condition.[34]

(e)   transferability

Interests that are vested in possession are fully alienable, as are reversions and vested remainders. The position for contingent remainders was at one time somewhat less clear. In a strict sense, until the condition precedent is met, and the bridge crossed, no interest exists, and so there should be no transferable entity. However, currently it seems to be accepted that these interests can pass by will. The ability to convey a contingent interest by means of an *inter vivos* transfer was expressly provided for in the English *Real Property Act, 1845*.[35] At common law, the right of re-entry after a condition subsequent could not be created to benefit a stranger when contained in a simple *inter vivos* grant. Whether this is now possible is a more difficult matter, but there is no current policy reason that might stand in the way of the validity of such a transfer.[36] Likewise, the possibility of reverter, as a vested future interest, *ought* to be fully transferable by deed or will.

3.   STATE LIMITATIONS ON PRIVATE POWER

(a)   introduction

The ability of property owners to attach stipulations to gifts of property provides a basis for control, which I have sometimes referred to above as 'private power'. This power can be wielded in a variety of ways including: in *inter vivos* transfers, testamentary dispositions, leasehold covenants, restrictive covenants running with freehold property,[37] or via a trust.[38] And, of course, conditions governing use might also be established under a simple contract.[39] The discussion

---

34 See *Re Kent* (1982) 38 B.C.L.R. 216, [1982] 6 W.W.R. 165, 139 D.L.R. (3d) 318 (S.C.).

35 8 & 9 Vict., c. 106, s. 6.

36 See also *Conveyancing and Law of Property Act*, R.S.O. 1990, c. C.34, s. 10. But see *Clark v. Vancouver (City)* (1901) 10 B.C.R. 31 (Full Ct.) affirmed (1904) 35 S.C.R. 121, where it was held that a possibility of a reverter, retained after the creation of a defeasible fee simple interest, could not be assigned. (Under the terminology used in this text, the right at issue would be called a 'right of re-entry'.)

37 See Chapter 10.

38 See, *e.g., Roman Catholic Episcopal Corp. of Halifax v. Denson* (1998) 168 N.S.R. (2d) 356, 505 A.P.R. 356 (S.C.) affirmed (1998) 173 N.S.R. (2d) 199, 527 A.P.R. 199 (C.A.). See generally Chapter 6.

39 It is also possible for a testator to create a charge on property, or a personal obligation, short of a trust, binding on a recipient in equity, in favour of a third party, where the transferee takes a gift that is made subject to an obligation set out in the will. See T.C. Thomas, ''Conditions in Favour of Third Parties'', [1952] C.L.J. 240, at 251*ff*, where the early decisions are reviewed. See also C.J. Davis, ''The Principle of Benefit and Burden'', [1998] C.L.J. 522, at 528*ff.*

that follows examines the policy of the law as it relates to stipulations attached by means of conditions precedent, conditions subsequent and determinable limitations when used in wills and deeds. You should appreciate, however, that public policy does not apply just in these situations.

The limits of the law's tolerance for conditional transfers ushers the tension between private and public interests onto centre stage. Ownership rights are always subject to the qualification that a private act will not be treated as valid if it offends a countervailing state policy. Remaining on this general level, two discrete categories of public policy may be identified. In the first I would place those policies related directly to the use of property. Prominent among these is the promotion of alienability; another is the need for certainty in property dealings. As we know, property law is heavily affected by efficiency considerations such as these. As a result, private action that could prove to be inefficient might call for some sort of state reaction. The second category of public policy contains a larger spectrum of social policy considerations, including matters that may only incidentally have a property dimension. This second group emerges from the recognition of the lure of property and the potential for this to be used in a harmful fashion. Here proprietary freedom must be balanced against any number of other values that the law might wish to promote.

As we saw in Chapter 1, aspects of both 'freedom' and 'efficiency' can serve to found the basic idea of private property. Yet the interests imbricated in these two concepts can clash when specific rules of allocation are framed. Indeed, even the basic notion of freedom of testation can chafe against principles of efficiency. The argument here is that conferring a broad discretion on testators will motivate would-be donees to engage in what economists call 'rent seeking'. In its most general sense, this term refers to conduct induced by the prospect of an expected windfall.[40] Rent seeking, to the extent that it goes unrewarded, *may* be wasteful. (It might not be if the donee manages to gain the sought-after legacy, or if some other beneficial result is produced.) In this context, rent seeking encompasses anything done to curry favour with a property owner. The goal of this activity is to capture a rent, that is, to gain a profit beyond that which normal market conditions might yield. This type of action can be eliminated in this context by constricting donative freedom, because this will render the rent-seeking conduct of hopeful donees a rather pointless exercise:

> Rent seeking will tend to be eliminated where the donor's *discretion* over the selection of the beneficiary is absent, even if the donor is allowed to carry out transfers. So long as there exist well-defined and widely known enforceable rules or laws that determine the identity of the potential recipients, independent of the choice of the donor, there is no profit to be gained from engaging in rent seeking.[41]

---

40 As to the nature of rent-seeking, see further R.D. Tollison, ''Rent Seeking: A Survey'', 35 Kyklos 575 (1982); C.K. Rowley *et al.*, eds., *The Political Economy of Rent-Seeking* (Boston: Kluwer, 1988).

41 J.M. Buchanan, ''Rent Seeking, Noncompensated Transfers, and Laws of Succession'', 26 J.L. & Econ. 71 (1983) at 78.

But to reduce so severely the freedom of transfer would erode the liberty interests of property owners. A balance therefore must be struck. As donors *do* have a great deal of scope in determining the fate of their property, this might well mean that the present law is inefficient. An interesting feature of this analysis is that the identified inefficiency relates to conduct that transpires *before* a transfer occurs. As we will see in the discussion of the rule against perpetuities, limits on ownership rights are sometimes imposed because of the inefficiencies that can plague property *after* it has been passed from one generation of holders to the next.[42]

(b)   the effects of invalidity

In this part of the book, a number of rules that can invalidate all or part of a property transfer will be described. Before doing so, the effects of a finding of invalidity will be explained.

For conditions subsequent and determinable interests (whether of realty or personalty), the results of a finding of invalidity are clear: an invalid condition subsequent is eliminated and the gift is rendered absolute; the dark cloud over the property is removed. In contrast, if a determinable limitation is void the entire gift fails. Theoretically, this is so because the quantum of the estate is rendered uncertain by the removal of the event (the fence post) that was inserted to mark its temporal limit.

So great a legal difference, based as it is on the slight linguistic differences between these two types of interest,[43] has been described as "little short of disgraceful to our jurisprudence".[44] Certainly, it smacks of the worst sort of legalistic pettifoggery. In consequence, in 1996 the Ontario Law Reform Commission recommended that the distinction between the two be abolished, so that, as a general rule, language that would result in the creation of a determinable interest at common law should be construed as creating a condition subsequent instead.[45] I see the basic logic of this proposal. As we will see shortly, some conditions which violate the rules of public policy when framed as a condition subsequent will pass muster if drafted as a determinable interest. If public policy is offended under one version, it is hard to accept that the formulation of the stipulation should be so critical. I accept that a donor should not be able to side-step a public policy dictate just by framing a gift in a certain way.

However, when it comes to the *effects* of invalidity I do not think that the same considerations apply. There seems nothing wrong with a donor saying this: 'I wish to make a gift with strings attached. I recognize that what I propose may run contrary to law. In that event – which I cannot control – I have a second plan:

---

42 See Part 5(a), *infra*.

43 See Part 2(b), *supra*.

44 *Re King's Trusts* (1892) 29 L.R.Ir. 401, at 410. See also *Heath v. Lewis* (1853) 3 De G.M. & G. 954, at 956, 45 E.R. 374, at 375.

45 Ontario Law Reform Commission, *Report on Basic Principles of Land Law* (Toronto: A.G. (Ont.), 1996) at 64. They did not include certain determinable interests contained within a protective trust within this recommendation: *ibid.*

the property will then pass to . . .'. I see no reason why a grantor should not be able to implement the alternative gift (assuming that it is otherwise lawful).[46] In other words, the difference in the treatment of defeasible and determinable interests can be deftly and legitimately exploited in the drafting of transfers. By selecting the right form, one can control the fate of the gift should a condition prove to be unenforceable. A donor who is worried that invalidity might sabotage the whole gift should use a condition subsequent: if the condition is struck out, the property will remain in the hands of the donee. On the other hand, if the attitude of the donor is that the stipulation is closely tied to the very reasons for giving the gift, then the transfer should be drafted as a determinable limitation. If this construct is used, then a void stipulation would nullify the entire transaction. In this instance the donee takes either a qualified (and valid) gift, or nothing at all. A hidden feature of the Ontario proposals is that this type of planning may not be prevented. As matters now stand, the two formulations create default rules, that is, by merely creating a determinable interest one triggers the rule that dictates what will happen in the event the gift is invalid. If the proposals become law, then it will be necessary for this result to be stated explicitly. And again, there is no reason to prohibit this type of estate planning.

When a condition precedent is attached to realty, invalidity destroys the gift. The law is less simply stated in the case of a contingent gift of personalty. Some courts[47] have adopted a rule that is derived from civilian legal systems. The following formulation of this 'civil rule' is drawn from the venerable English text, *Jarman on Wills*:

> [W]here the condition precedent is originally impossible, or is illegal as involving *malum prohibitum*, the bequest is absolute, just as if the condition had been subsequent. But where the performance of the condition is the sole motive of the bequest, or its impossibility was unknown to the testator, or the condition which was possible in its creation has since become impossible by the act of God, or where it is illegal as involving *malum in se*, in these cases the civil [law] agrees with the common law in holding both gift and condition void.[48]

---

46 Such a stipulation was upheld in *Girard Trust Co. v. Schmitz*, 20 A.2d. 21 (N.J.Ch., 1941). See further W.J. Klockau, "The Effect of Illegal Conditions Annexed to Dispositions of Property", 40 Ill.L.Rev. 464 (1946).

47 See, *e.g.*, *Re Fairfoull* (1973) 41 D.L.R. (3d) 152 (B.C S.C.) affirmed on reconsideration, [1974] 6 W.W.R. 471, 18 R.F.L. 165 (S.C.); *Re McBride* (1980) 27 O.R. (2d) 513, 6 E.T.R. 181, 107 D.L.R. (3d) 233 (H.C.). See also *Re A.T. St. George*, [1964] N.S.W.R. 587, 80 W.N. (N.S.W.) 1423 (S.C.); *Re Hamilton* (1901) 1 O.L.R. 10 (Ch.D.). But see *Re Gross*, [1937] O.W.N. 88 (C.A.).

48 R. Jennings & J.C. Harper, *Jarman on Wills*, 8th ed. (London: Sweet & Maxwell, 1951) vol. 2, at 1457-8. Compare the description of the law in J.B. Clark & J.G.R. Martyn, *Theobald on Wills*, 15th ed. (London: Sweet & Maxwell, 1993) at 649-50: "[A]s regards personalty, a gift made upon a condition precedent involving a physical impossibility, such as to drink up the ocean, takes effect notwithstanding the condition. On the other hand, if the condition precedent, though not in fact impossible at the date of the will, or becoming impossible by subsequent events, involves no physical impossibility, the gift will not take effect. As regards personalty, a condition precedent, which becomes impossible by the act of the testator, is discharged. . . . If the fulfilment of a condition precedent is rendered impossible by operation of law before the date of the will, a gift of personalty which depended upon the condition becomes absolute. It is said that, as regards personalty, a condition precedent which is *contra bonos mores*, i.e. malum prohibitum as opposed to malum in se . . . may be rejected . . .".

Reading this statement is heavy sledding. Restated, the rules seem to provide that the gift *survives* when a condition precedent (i) is originally impossible (and, presumably, the donor is aware of this); (ii) becomes impossible owing to some act of the donor; or (iii) is illegal because it is *malum prohibitum*. However, when (i) the performance of the condition is the sole motive for the bequest; (ii) its impossibility was unknown to the donor; (iii) the condition was possible in its creation but has since become impossible by an act of God; or (iv) it is illegal because it is *malum in se*, then both the gift and condition are void (as in the case of realty).

There is a lot to be confused about here. The distinction between conditions that are *malum in se* (inherently wrong or immoral) and those *malum prohibitum* (in conflict with other facets of law or public policy) is often far from obvious.[49] Moreover, using the motivation of the donor as a factor affecting the results of invalidity seems problematic. Are motives ever straightforward? How are these to be proven? Despite all of this, the civil law rule appears to be based on what the donor might have wanted had the question been considered, and that is compatible with the basal function of these invalidating rules. On this ground the civil rule may be preferable to the rule that is applied to realty.[50] In any event, there is little justification for different approaches for realty and personalty, whichever one should govern.

(c)   public policy

(i)   generally

Conditions that contravene public policy will not be enforced. In a sense, all law is a manifestation of public policy, but the term is used here to denote a more narrow sphere, that is, those rules that seek to eradicate offensive elements of private transactions.

Public policy as a basis for invalidity has been described as an 'unruly horse', *i.e.*, it is an unsafe foundation on which to rest a judgment.[51] Though there are many areas of indeterminacy in the law of property, perhaps none is more prone to vagueness than that which allows courts to strike down transfers (or conditions attached to transfers) under the mantle of public policy. For those who assert that legal doctrine cannot sensibly constrain judges from introducing – under the guise of *ex cathedra* objectivity – their own subjective beliefs and political ideologies, no better example can be cited than this basis of judicial intervention.[52] The

---

49 See further A.H. Oosterhoff, Note (1980) 5 E. & T.Q. 97.

50 But see Oosterhoff, *ibid.*, for a critique of the rule and the Canadian cases that have applied it.

51 This equine metaphor has proved popular: "public policy . . . is a very unruly horse, and when once you get astride it you never know where it will carry you": *Richardson v. Mellish* (1824) 2 Bing. 229, at 252, 130 E.R. 294, at 303 (*per* Burrough J.); "With a good man in the saddle, the unruly horse [of public policy] can be kept in control. It can jump over obstacles. It can leap fences put up by fictions and come down on the side of justice": *Enderby Town Football Club Ltd. v. Football Association Ltd.* (1970), [1971] Ch. 591, [1971] 1 All E.R. 215 (C.A.) at 606-7 Ch. (*per* Lord Denning M.R. (who regarded himself as quite a good legal equestrian)).

52 See also K.J. Vandevelde, "The New Property of the Nineteenth Century: The Development of the Modern Concept of Property", 29 Buff.L.Rev. 325 (1980) at 366-7.

potential of this doctrine to transform judges into tin gods is well recognized in the authorities. While the appropriate standard for contraventions of public policy must remain open-ended, it has been warned that public policy should be invoked only when the harm is "substantially incontestable", and that the application of the doctrine should not depend upon the "idiosyncratic inferences of a few judicial minds".[53] Accordingly, the courts are reluctant to develop new heads of public policy, although at the same time it is clear that existing categories are not closed or inflexible. Moreover, public policy is not static – "[t]he wind of change blows on it".[54] Accordingly, even established grounds may be reconsidered as time passes and mores shift.

Some conditions are rendered invalid because they affect state interests in a very direct way, such as by encouraging a recipient to violate the criminal law. In a contemporary setting, many prohibitions relate to conditions that touch on family life in some way. For example, conditions that seek to undermine parental rights and obligations may be found void, especially those directed at separating parent from child.[55] In the past, general restraints on marriage have been held to contravene public policy. Some subtle qualifications emerge from the case law concerning the treatment of marriage-related conditions. A gift to X on the condition that she or he remain unmarried can be construed as creating an invalid financial inducement to remain single. Yet, it might also be read, more innocently, as a way of providing support to someone who is living alone. As a canon of construction (only), the use of a condition subsequent is taken to denote the former (invalid) intention;[56] a determinable limitation suggests the latter.[57] Moreover, prohibitions against remarriage have been tolerated.[58] Partial restraints, limiting the age at which the recipient of a gift may marry,[59] or excluding a given person as a potential spouse,[60] have also been upheld. More troubling is the judicial attitude found in relation to restrictions based on religion: these have generally withstood challenge. For instance, a condition that Y must not marry outside of the Jewish faith has been upheld.[61]

---

53 *Fender v. St. John-Mildmay* (1937), [1938] A.C. 1, [1938] 3 All E.R. 402 (H.L.) at 12 A.C. (*per* Lord Atkin). See also *Re Millar* (1937), [1938] S.C.R. 1, [1938] 1 D.L.R. 65.

54 *Nagle v. Feilden*, [1966] 2 Q.B. 633, [1966] 1 All E.R. 689 (C.A.) at 696 All E.R. (*per* Danckwerts L.J.). See also *Evanturel v. Evanturel* (1874) L.R. 6 P.C. 1, at 29.

55 See, *e.g.*, *Re Thorne* (1922) 22 O.W.N. 28 (H.C.). *Cf.* the analysis concerning gifts designed to influence parental decisions concerning religious adherence in *Blathwayt v. Baron Cawley*, [1976] A.C. 397, [1975] 3 All E.R. 625 (H.L.). See further K. Mackie, "Testamentary Conditions" (1998) 20 U.Q.L.J. 38, at 44-5.

56 See, *e.g.*, *Re Cutter* (1916) 37 O.L.R. 42, 31 D.L.R. 382 (H.C.). *Cf. In re Hewett*, [1918] 1 Ch. 458; *Jones v. Jones* (1876) 1 Q.B.D. 279.

57 See, *e.g.*, *In re Hewett*, *supra*, note 56.

58 See, *e.g.*, *Re Goodwin* (1969) 3 D.L.R. (3d) 281 (S.C.); *In re Muirhead Estate*, 12 Sask.L.R. 123, [1919] 2 W.W.R. 454 (K.B.); *Doe d. Livingston v. Corrie* (1847) 5 N.B.R. 450 (S.C.); *cf. In re Tucker* (1910) 16 W.L.R. 172 (Sask.Q.B.).

59 *Stackpole v. Beaumont* (1796) 3 Ves. 89, 30 E.R. 909.

60 *Jarvis v. Duke* (1681) 1 Vern. 19, 23 E.R. 274: "[s]he being only prohibited to marry with one man by name, and nothing in the whole fair garden of Eden would serve her turn but this forbidden fruit".

61 *Re Tepper's Will Trusts*, [1987] Ch. 358, [1987] 1 All E.R. 970, referring to *Blathwayt v. Baron*

Conditions affecting married couples have also been subjected to careful scrutiny. Gifts promoting separation have been found to be invalid,[62] but not those that terminate on the reconciliation of a couple already apart, or that encourage continued cohabitation.[63] A gift that provides that the donee's share will increase on death or divorce may also be upheld on the basis that it is designed to provide additional financial support, which might well be needed once the marriage ends.[64]

(ii)   sources of public policy

The task of locating the current state of public policy in disputes of first impression can resemble a treasure hunt. The quest is for an adequate sense of what the law should tolerate. In this process, the courts have tended to look beyond potential analogies in the case law, to such other sources as human rights legislation, international laws[65] and conventions, and even political speeches. The *Canadian Charter of Rights and Freedoms* can also serve as a barometer of public policy. In a strict sense, the *Charter* does not apply to private transactions.[66] Yet it can influence the evolutionary development of public policy; in this indirect way the *Charter* can affect the law governing private dealings.[67]

Precisely how the *Charter* can be used in practice to help define public policy is a matter of debate. The *Charter* promotes equality and prohibits state discrimination on a number of grounds, including race and gender. But just because the government is constrained from infringing these basic rights does not mean that donors will be held to the same standard. Unlike the government, private property owners are not required to keep an even hand among constituents. A direct, unqualified gift to the sons, but not the daughters, of a testator, or a gift to one religious order to the exclusion of all others, is almost certainly beyond legal reproach. By contrast, a legislative scheme that conferred comparable advantages would raise the spectre of unconstitutionality. Moreover, through section 1 of the

---

Cawley, supra, note 55. *Cf. Re Hurshman* (1956) 6 D.L.R. (2d) 615 (B.C.S.C.). Compare also the decision in *Fox v. Fox Estate* (1996) 28 O.R. (3d) 496, 10 E.T.R. (2d) 229, 88 O.A.C. 201 (C.A.) leave to appeal to S.C.C. refused (1996) 207 N.R. 80 (note) (S.C.C.), especially the judgment of Galligan J.A.

62 See, *e.g.*, *Cartwright v. Cartwright* (1853) 3 De G.M. & G. 982, 43 E.R. 385.

63 *In re Hope-Johnstone*, [1904] 1 Ch. 470.

64 See, *e.g.*, *MacDonald v. Brown Estate* (1995) 6 E.T.R. (2d) 160, 139 N.S.R. (2d) 252, 397 A.P.R. 252 (S.C.).

65 "The common law does not necessarily conform with international law, but international law is a legitimate and important influence on the development of the common law, especially when international law declares the existence of universal human rights. A common law doctrine founded on unjust discrimination in the enjoyment of civil and political rights demands reconsideration": *Mabo v. Queensland (No. 2)*, [1992] 5 C.N.L.R. 1, 175 C.L.R. 1, 107 A.L.R. 1 (Aust.H.C.) at 36 C.N.L.R. (*per* Brennan J.).

66 *Canadian Charter of Rights and Freedoms*, Pt. I of the *Constitution Act*, 1982 [en. by *Canada Act, 1982* (U.K.), c. 11, s. 1]. See *R.W.D.S.U., Local 580 v. Dolphin Delivery Ltd.*, [1986] 2 S.C.R. 573, 9 B.C.L.R. (2d) 273, 33 D.L.R. (4th) 174. For an effective critique of this case, see A.C. Hutchinson & A. Petter, "Private Rights/Public Wrongs: The Liberal Lie of the Charter" (1988) 38 U.T.L.J. 278.

67 See *Dolphin Delivery, supra*, note 66, at 603 S.C.R. (*per* McIntyre J.). See also *Hill v. Church of Scientology of Toronto*, [1995] 2 S.C.R. 1130, 126 D.L.R. (4th) 129, 184 N.R. 1.

Charter derogations from the protections in the entrenched guarantees may be upheld if the state action can be shown to be demonstrably justifiable in a free and democratic society. Section 1 cannot, without difficulty, be applied to test private donative actions. So, while the *Charter* can be useful in identifying core values, its utility in shaping and refining the actual contours of public policy is a complicated matter.

(iii)   *a case in point: the Leonard trust*[68]

The *Leonard Foundation*[69] case demonstrates how public policy pits rights of private ownership against other social values, and how the law patrols the line between permissible and impermissible uses of property. The case involved a trust established by Col. Reuben Wells Leonard (1860–1930). An engineer by training, Leonard became a multi-millionaire as the owner of a silver-rich mine in Cobalt. His fortune having been made, he was, in his day, one of Canada's most generous philanthropists. It was said that he regarded his money as a public trust.

In 1916, Leonard established a Foundation to provide scholarships. It was revised in 1920 and took its final form in 1923. The trust deed contains a lengthy preamble that was designed to explain the underlying principles of the Foundation. It begins with a statement of Leonard's belief that "the White Race is, as a whole, best qualified by nature to be entrusted with the development of civilization and the general progress of the world along the best lines". The document also recites that the progress of the world depends in the future, as it has in the past, on the maintenance of the Christian religion, and that the advancement of civilization throughout the world rests upon the independence, stability and prosperity of the British Empire. The Empire, he asserted, must remain under the control of British nationals who are not beholden to foreign powers, whether temporal or spiritual. Based on these premises, student awards were created under the trust available only to persons who were White Protestants of British nationality or parentage. Both males and females were eligible, although no more than one-quarter of the funds awarded annually could be given to female recipients.

Leonard was a Canadian nationalist who supported something known as imperial federation, and who believed, among other things, that Canada was destined to assume a leading role in the British Empire. One can see this ideology (and others such as a belief in social Darwinism) in the language of the recitals. As the Empire shaded into Commonwealth, and the world view implied by the trust began to evanesce, Leonard's scheme nevertheless continued undeterred. Odd-sounding, even disturbing as the language of the trust may now appear, the

---

68 See further B. Ziff, *Unforeseen Legacies: Reuben Wells Leonard and the Leonard Foundation Trust* (forthcoming) [copy on file at the University of Alberta].

69 *Canada Trust Co. v. Ontario (Human Rights Commission)* (1990) 74 O.R. (2d) 481, 38 E.T.R. 1, 69 D.L.R. (4th) 321 (C.A.). See J. Phillips, "Anti-Discrimination, Freedom of Property Disposition, and the Public Policy of Charitable Educational Trusts: A Comment on *Re Canada Trust Co. and Ontario Human Rights Commission*" (1990) 9(3) Philanthropist 3. See also *Hermitage Methodist Homes of Virginia, Inc. v. Dominion Trust Co.*, 387 S.E.2d 740 (Va.S.C., 1990).

Leonard Foundation operated under these terms for over 60 years. Throughout this period hundreds of scholarships were awarded, the recipients being selected by a board of governance that has included university presidents, high-placed Anglican clerics, a justice of the Supreme Court of Canada (Henry Davis), and a member of Parliament (Reginald Stackhouse). Membership on the selection committee was subject to the same exclusionary rules.

In 1956 the first note of public criticism of the trust was sounded (in the Ontario Legislature), but it was not until the 1980s that public concern mounted. Led by the Ontario Human Rights Commission, pressure began to build (including from within the Foundation) to seek a way to alter the terms of the trust. At the same time, some supported the trust's validity in its original form. Consider this editorial from the *Toronto Sun*:

> If a black philanthropist wishes to leave scholarships for blacks only, or a donor wishes to give money for women or hunchbacks or Latvians – that is their prerogative. In fact, that is what makes us especially mad. We have a very strong suspicion that if this was an endowment helping blacks, women or the handicapped, there wouldn't be a murmur from our Human Rights Commissioners. It is because WASPs are a great pariah of our society that this has come up. Well, apart from the obvious fact that there are such things as needy poor WASPs of British nationality, we will not desist from pointing out that even if every WASP lived in Rosedale, a free society should permit a man to leave his money as he sees fit and more importantly, a university to accept it – if they see fit.[70]

In 1986, when the Ontario Human Rights Commission launched a formal complaint, alleging that the Foundation was acting in violation of the Province's human rights code, the trustees countered by applying to the court for advice and direction as to the validity of the eligibility criteria. At first instance the trust was upheld.[71] Accepting the deplorable nature of racism, the Court nevertheless plumped in favour of proprietary freedom as the dominant value.[72]

The Ontario Court of Appeal reached a different result: it ordered that the discriminatory elements of the document be excised, but it allowed the rest of the trust to stand. Robins J.A. (with whom Osler J. concurred) took the view that this charitable trust, which was capable of existing in perpetuity to provide scholarships to the *public*, for attendance at *publicly* funded institutions, ought to be regarded, functionally, as *public*, or at least quasi-*public*. A trust of this type, based on notions of racism and religious superiority, patently contravened contemporary public policy.

---

70 "Human Wrongs", *Toronto Sun*, November 1, 1982. See also C. Hoy, "A discriminating opinion", *Toronto Sun*, November 23, 1982; C. Hoy, "WASPs also have rights", *Toronto Sun*, December, 1982; C. Hoy, "Pretentious rights code", *Toronto Sun*, December 12, 1982; C. Hoy, "Rights turn into wrongs", *Toronto Sun*, November 9, 1982. See also *Hansard, Legislative Assembly of Ontario*, 2nd. Sess., 32 Parl., November 22, 1982, at 5327; "Human Rights are Not For WASPs" *Orillia Packet*, December 6, 1982.

71 *Canada Trust Co. v. Ontario (Human Rights Commission)* (1987) 61 O.R. (2d) 75, 27 E.T.R. 193, 42 D.L.R. (4th) 263 (H.C.) [reversed *supra*, note 69], criticized in J.C. Shepherd, "When the Common Law Fails" (1988-9) 9 E. & T.J. 117.

72 See also *Blathwayt v. Baron Cawley, supra*, note 55.

Although the Court was advised that there were numerous scholarships in Canada that discriminated on a host of grounds, the majority was not prepared to establish a framework for future guidance. They regarded the Leonard trust as idiosyncratic. Tarnopolsky J.A., in a separate judgment, endeavoured to provide some direction. In his view, the validity of any similar scholarship should be assessed under a standard of scrutiny analogous to that used in human rights law to review discriminatory conduct. In essence, he suggested that discriminatory scholarships could be saved if directed towards acceptable policy ends. Under such a standard, scholarships to promote the education of women or Aboriginals would likely be acceptable. Given the importance of bilingualism and multiculturalism, scholarship restrictions based on language would probably also be valid. In general, a specific evaluation of the context, purpose and effect of the restrictions would have to be undertaken in each case. However, Tarnopolsky J.A. expressly excluded family trusts from the ambit of his ruling. Indeed, in both judgments the public policy analysis is directed only at trusts with a public dimension. Leonard's own attitude about his wealth – it was to be treated as a public trust – seems now at once ironic and prescient.

The *Leonard* ruling, important as it is, is still somewhat ambiguous as regards the scope of public policy. It is unclear to what extent the majority holding turns on the language of the recitals. It is there, and there alone, that the trust speaks explicitly of racial and religious superiority. As mentioned above, the majority, though aware that there were many restrictive scholarships in Canada, seemed to have said that, while they were not going to draw a bright line rule, the Leonard scheme was clearly on the wrong side of any line that might be drawn. The difficulty of discerning the rule to be derived from the *Leonard* litigation is evident in the 1996 case of *Re Ramsden Estate*.[73] There, a scholarship at the University of Prince Edward Island tenable only by Protestants was upheld. *Leonard* was distinguished on the ground that it "was based on blatant religious supremacy and racism"[74] that was absent from the Ramsden bequest.

(d)   uncertainty

Conditions attached to property transfers that are too imprecise may be found to be void. Uncertainty may arise in a number of ways. Earlier in the chapter we saw that it is sometimes unclear whether a condition should be treated as being imposed before (precedent) or after (subsequent) vesting. This type of vagueness does not render that condition invalid; instead, a court will attempt to make the correct designation by applying rules such as the preference for early vesting. Likewise, a gift is not invalid just because several people might legitimately claim to be the named donee. When faced with this dilemma, courts will struggle to find out who was meant to receive the property. The same approach will be taken in instances of evidential uncertainty, such as when it is unclear whether or not

---

73 (1996) 139 D.L.R. (4th) 746, 14 E.T.R. (2d) 239, 145 Nfld. & P.E.I.R. 156 (P.E.I.T.D.).
74 *Ibid.* at 751 D.L.R. (*per* MacDonald C.J.T.D.).

some relevant event has occurred.[75] The problems addressed here involve the standard of clarity to be applied in giving meaning to conditions of acquisition (*i.e.*, conditions precedent) or retention (conditions subsequent and determinable limitations). This is a problem of conceptual uncertainty.

The English language is rife with ambiguity: few statements are so clear that their meaning is totally incontrovertible. Indeed there are those who argue that words alone can never enjoy universal understanding, and that in construing language readers necessarily rely on their own experiences and personal epistemologies. This is not to say that understanding is so much a part of individual experience that meaningful communication is impossible. The argument is not that interpretation is purely subjective, that anything goes, or that one construction of a document must be as valid as any other. Rather, the claim here is that if we recognize that language is always bound up with the context in which it is found, it follows that a given text – in this case the 'text' being a document of transfer of some kind – is likely to yield conflicting interpretations in the minds of different readers.

Lawyers may construe words very differently from the way others do. Additionally, we might find that some common ground exists among property lawyers about the meaning of words contained in a deed or will. Within this specialized 'interpretive community' a greater degree of consensus about language might be found than would result within the general population.[76] Notice that a consensus among lawyers arises because the *readers* tend to agree about what the language is saying. Such an analysis effectively confers on the reader a power over the ultimate meaning that a document is taken to possess. Put another way, while we might think that the writer of a text gives meaning to it, that the author is fully in charge of what the words stand for, that job is really shared with the reader.[77]

What I am driving at is that language is inherently flexible and that its ultimate meaning is bound up with its setting. How does the law cope with all of this?

The importance of context is recognized in some rules of interpretation, especially those that apply to wills. Courts appreciate that the interpretations arrived at in prior wills cases are of limited value when trying to determine what some other testator might have intended. Instead, "[e]ach judge must endeavour to place [himself or herself] in the position of the testator at the time the will was made".[78] Although such an approach ignores the suggestion that the reader is also playing a part in the process of giving meaning to words, one can understand why that posture is adopted in this instance. The attempt to privilege the view of

---

75 See further *In re Tuck's Settlement Trusts*, [1978] Ch. 49, [1978] 1 All E.R. 1047 (C.A.); *Re Coxen*, [1948] Ch. 747, [1948] 2 All E.R. 492.

76 See generally S. Fish, *Is There a Text in This Class?: The Authority of Interpretive Communities* (Cambridge: H.U.P., 1980). See also J.P. Kaplan, "Syntax in the Interpretation of Legal Language: The *Vested* Versus *Contingent* Distinction in Property Law", 68(1) American Speech 58 (1993).

77 See further M. Davies, *Asking the Law Question* (Sydney: Law Book Co., 1994) at 245*ff*, where the author draws on works by Roland Barthes and others.

78 *Re Burke*, [1960] O.R. 26, 20 D.L.R. (2d) 396 (H.C.) at 30 O.R. (*per* Laidlaw J.).

the author/testator seems appropriate because the task at hand is to ascertain that person's preferences. However, whether that privileging is actually possible is an open question.

When it comes to the assessment of whether the language of a disposition is sufficiently clear to pass the test of conceptual certainty (our main focus here), the judicial approach is quite different. We do not ask whether the language used was clear from the testator's vantage point. Instead, the courts attempt to apply objective tests. Given what was said about the significance of context, the plurality of meanings that can arise as a result, and the role that interpretive communities can play, I wonder whether any general objective test of certainty can be formulated. As we will see in the discussion below, not all conditions will be invalid on the ground of uncertainty; only a practical level of clarity is demanded. In other words, the task is to assess the language used on a so-called common sense basis; it has been opined that a zealous urge to detect ambiguities should be repressed.[79] And complex questions about semiotics, language, and the 'meaning of meaning' do not seem to make their way into the jurisprudence.

The tests for uncertainty are aimed, theoretically, at enabling the recipients of property to understand the scope of any conditions affecting their entitlements. For conditions subsequent (and probably determinable limitations), the donee must be able to see clearly and distinctly from the outset those actions that will lead to a loss of the interest.[80] So, in the leading Canadian case of *Sifton v. Sifton*,[81] a condition requiring the donee to continue to reside in Canada was held to fall below this minimum standard, because there were no adequate guidelines as to what sorts of temporary absences or sojourns would contravene the condition.

A lower threshold of certainty is demanded for a condition precedent. All that need be shown is that the condition is capable of being given some plausible meaning. Moreover, a comprehensive mapping out of the full extent of the condition is not needed and the donee may enjoy the gift so long as it can be shown that he or she falls within a reasonable meaning of the term used. Therefore, to draw on a standard example, a gift to A 'if he is tall' will not fail for uncertainty. Although views may differ as to just what this means, we can give it some meaning; it is not gibberish. As long as A (who we will say is 6' 6") can show that he fits within a reasonable definition of that term, the gift can pass, even if this determination might not have been as easy had the gift been given to me (I am approximately 5' 10").

Owing to the difference between these two tests, conditions subsequent are more vulnerable to invalidity than conditions precedent. As a result, a requirement that X remain within the Jewish faith may fail as a condition of retention, though

---

79 See also *Church Property Trustees v. Ebbeck* (1960) 104 C.L.R. 394 (Aust.H.C.) at 406; *Blathwayt v. Baron Cawley*, *supra*, note 55, at 424-5 A.C.

80 *Clavering v. Ellison* (1859) 7 H.L. Cas. 707, 11 E.R. 282.

81 [1938] A.C. 656, [1938] 2 W.W.R. 465, [1938] 3 D.L.R. 577 (P.C.). See also *Re Cotton* (1982) 13 E.T.R. 19 (B.C.S.C.). *Cf. Kotsar v. Shattock*, *supra*, note 29; *Beadle v. Gaudette* (1985) 21 E.T.R. 117 (B.C.S.C.).

it might be valid as a condition of acquisition.[82] This difference has been criticized,[83] and it appears to create a paradox, as the following example illustrates. Consider a gift of Blackacre to A for life, which provides also that the property shall pass to B should B "need to return to live here".[84] Let us accept that this raises an issue of uncertainty. The devise creates a life estate subject to a condition subsequent, looked at from A's perspective. From B's standpoint what is given is a fee simple subject to a condition precedent. This single stipulation can be described either way, and both characterizations are correct; the description we give (precedent or subsequent) is merely a matter of the vantage point from which the gift is viewed. Moreover, the antinomy revealed by this example is widespread: one person's condition subsequent is, it seems, always someone else's condition precedent. That being so, which test of certainty should apply?

Presumably both tests are applicable, but since the test for a condition subsequent is the hardest to meet, it would determine validity in all cases. It could be argued that the condition precedent test is the appropriate one here, because the stated event relates to B's conduct (not A's). When the event relates to something that A must do (or not do), then the condition subsequent test would seem to be the appropriate one to apply. However, a problem would still remain for conditions relating to some third party or an external event.

In a world in which words are imprecise, and where uncertainty can lead to invalidity, lawyers should play a preventive role by using crisp language. A further hedge against litigation might be to create a mechanism within the granting document that is designed to resolve uncertainties if they should ever arise. This was attempted in *Re Tuck*,[85] where the will called for defeasance if a donee married outside of the Jewish faith. The will also provided that a reference could be made to the Chief Rabbi of England to resolve disputes as to whether a marriage would violate (or had violated) the stipulation. One member of the Court of Appeal (Lord Denning M.R.) endorsed this clause as a valid preventive measure; the other members of the Court did not comment on the point. This method has been criticized on the basis that if the language was too uncertain for the parties, then a non-judicial arbiter cannot likely do better,[86] particularly where (unlike *Tuck*) that person has no special expertise.[87] However, the provision in *Tuck* was tantamount to saying that defeasance would occur when – in the *opinion* of the Chief Rabbi – the marriage would be to a person outside of the Jewish faith. That opinion is ascertainable.[88] Although this opinion cannot be known from the outset, as the test for a condition subsequent appears to require, as long as the donee can

---

82 For an extensive review of the early authorities, see P. Butt, "Testamentary Conditions in Restraint of Religion" (1977) 8 Syd.L.Rev. 400. See also *Re Tepper's Will Trusts*, [1987] Ch. 358, [1987] 1 All E.R. 970.

83 See *Re Tuck, supra*, note 75, at 60 (*per* Lord Denning M.R.).

84 *Bernard Estate v. Bernard* (1986) 29 D.L.R. (4th) 133, 72 N.B.R. (2d) 267, 183 A.P.R. 267 (Q.B.).

85 *Supra*, note 75.

86 See *Re Coxen, supra*, note 75; *In re Jones*, [1953] Ch. 125, [1953] 1 All E.R. 357. See also R. Scane, Note (1978) 4 E. & T.Q. 169.

87 See *Re Lichtenstein*, [1986] 2 N.Z.L.R. 392 (H.C.).

88 *Cf. Re Lysiak* (1975) 7 O.R. (2d) 317, 55 D.L.R. (3d) 161 (H.C.).

be in a position to appreciate the consequences of potentially ruinous action before it occurs, that should suffice to meet the needs of fairness.

(e) restraints on alienation

(i) the rationale of the rules

The law promotes alienability and therefore conditional transfers that impose unacceptable restraints on the transfer of property are invalid.[89] To take the clearest example, a devise that reads 'to A on the condition that the property never be sold, leased or mortgaged' will run afoul of the rules limiting restraints that are described in this section.

The rules governing restraints on alienation are sometimes described in terms of the doctrine of repugnancy: restraints are invalid if they are inconsistent with an inherent attribute of ownership, *i.e.*, the right to transfer property freely. This characterization of the problem has been decried as circular because it requires one to assume that free alienability is an ever-present core element of ownership.[90] More important, reliance on repugnancy alone is unpersuasive unless one also looks to the policy underpinnings on which it is premised. What are these?

In general terms, the rules seem to have something to do with the idea of freedom: people should be able to do with their property whatever they wish to do. This sounds convincing, except that it begs the question of whose freedom we are talking about. An owner might argue that her autonomy is limited if she cannot impose restrictions on the fate of her property. That is a rational complaint, because the rules governing restraints sacrifice the interests of present owners out of a preference for future ones. In terms of proprietary freedom, there is a trade-off here.

Rather than seeing freedom at the heart of the rules, economic efficiency seems the better explanation. The factors that support the promotion of free alienability reflect the twinned beliefs that allowing property to circulate as a commodity of exchange furthers economic efficiency and that the market provides the best mechanism, on the whole, for allocating resources. This general refrain takes us back to the economic case for private property. We have seen that transferability is regarded as one of the key components of a property system that is based on wealth maximization principles.[91] Still, the idea that alienability should not be stifled is not an insight derived from the modern law and economics movement. Long ago Blackstone maintained that "experience hath shewn, that property best answers the purposes of civil life, especially in commercial countries, when its transfer and circulation are totally free and unrestrained".[92]

---

89 See generally C. Sweet, "Restraints on Alienation" (1917) 33 L.Q.R. 236 and 342.
90 See G.L. Williams, "The Doctrine of Repugnancy – I: Conditions in Gifts" (1943) 59 L.Q.R. 343, at 346 and *passim*.
91 See the discussion in Part 3(b)(i), Chapter 1.
92 W. Blackstone, *Commentaries on the Laws of England* (Chicago: U. of Chi.Pr.ed. 1979, 1765-9) vol. 2, at 288.

The economics-based reasoning in support of the law regulating restraints on alienation takes many forms. It is sometimes argued that restrictions on transfer, if left in place, allow the 'dead hand' control of prior owners, not ever-changing market conditions, to dictate land use. Fetters on transferability mean that an investor cannot change investments in response to shifts in financial opportunities.[93] Limits on transfer will tend to lower the profitability of investments; if land cannot be traded, the desire to invest in and improve the property may be dampened.[94] In most jurisdictions this will adversely affect the property tax base and so can result in a reduction in public revenues. Restraints that prevent land from being mortgaged will of course reduce the availability of property as loan-security; this, in turn, can impede other forms of development.[95] Finally, some say, invoking the language of social Darwinism, that restrictions on transfer permit the " 'survival' of the least fit".[96] In other words, the removal of restraints on alienation allows inept wealth maximizers to be weeded out of the market. The premise is that a fool and his or her money will soon be parted once (s)he is no longer insulated from the consequences of foolish transactions.

The promotion of free alienability is not pursued relentlessly in the law. Restrictions on the right of transfer will occasionally accord with public policy.[97] This is apparent when we consider the controls that exist over transfers of minors' property; in the restrictions imposed on transfers of the matrimonial home without spousal consent; in the laws preventing the sale of prescription drugs by patients;[98] and in the controls placed on foreign ownership.[99] The offensive act of auctioning sacred objects, such as preserved Maori heads (*moko mokai*), might also be precluded out of ordinary human decency and respect.[100] In Upper Canada it was an offence to purchase lands reserved for Aboriginal peoples.[101] As we have seen,

---

93 O.E.G. Johnson, "Economic Analysis, The Legal Framework and Land Tenure Systems", 15 J.Law & Econ. 259 (1972) at 267.

94 *Stephens v. Gulf Oil of Canada Ltd.* (1976) 11 O.R. (2d) 129, 25 C.P.R. (2d) 64, 65 D.L.R. (3d) 193 (C.A.) at 220 D.L.R., leave to appeal to S.C.C. refused (1976) 11 O.R. (2d) 129n (S.C.C.). It was also suggested in *Stephens* (*ibid.*) that the taking of property out of commercial circulation has "a tendency to result in a concentration of wealth". It is not obvious to me why this result will necessarily occur.

95 It has been argued that restraints on alienation work an "obvious hardship" on creditors, who are precluded from resorting to the restrained property to satisfy unpaid claims: see, *e.g.*, M.I. Schnelby, "Restraints Upon the Alienation of Legal Interests – I", 44 Yale L.J. 961 (1935) at 964. See also H. Bernhard, "The Minority Doctrine Concerning Direct Restraints on Alienation", 57 Mich.L.Rev. 1173 (1957) at 1180. But surely creditors must take responsibility for ensuring that debtors have sufficient collateral or exigible assets.

96 Bernhard, *supra*, note 95, at 1180.

97 See also S. Sterk, "Restraints on Alienation of Human Capital", 79 Va.L.Rev. 383 (1993).

98 See, *e.g.*, *Pharmacy Act*, S.N.B. 1983, c. 100, s. 37.

99 See, *e.g.*, *Lands Protection Act*, R.S.P.E.I. 1988, c. L-5. See further *Reference Re Lands Protection Act (P.E.I.)* (1987) 64 Nfld. & P.E.I.R. 249, 197 A.P.R. 249, 40 D.L.R. (4th) 1 (*sub nom. Reference re Prince Edward Island Lands Protection Act*) (P.E.I.C.A.).

100 See R.G. Hammond, *Personal Property: Commentary and Materials*, Rev. ed. (Auckland: O.U.P., 1992) at 72*ff.*

101 A conviction for this offence was upheld in *The Queen v. Hagar* (1858) 7 U.C.C.P. 380, applying 13 & 14 Vict., c. 74.

Aboriginal title is inalienable except to the Crown.[102] In Alberta, not too long ago, the law imposed harsh restrictions on dealings with Hutterite communities.[103]

(ii)   the testing of restraints

The law governing restraints on alienation in private transactions is designed to limit the scope of allowable restraints. However, this does not mean that all privately imposed restrictions on transfer are void; some will be tolerated. The principles considered below have arisen in an attempt to provide guidance as to the acceptable range.

Three types of restraints are possible: forfeiture, promissory and disabling.[104] A *forfeiture restraint* is one for which a right of re-entry or possibility of reverter may be invoked in the event of a breach. A *promissory restraint* is one that is purely contractual. As will be seen, in Canada it is unclear whether the rules considered in this section apply to this type of restriction.[105] A *disabling restraint*, a term that I have not found in use in the Canadian case law, simply removes from the owner a power of disposal. Unlike a forfeiture restraint, an attempted transfer that is in violation of a disabling restraint does not divest the holder of the property. It merely deprives that owner of some aspect of the power of transfer normally found in the bundle of proprietary rights. A disabling restraint may be difficult to discern in a given case from a forfeiture restraint because courts sometimes imply a right of termination into a grant or devise when that right has not been expressly conferred.

When the validity of a restraint is at issue, the extent of the restriction must be assessed. In general, powers of disposal may be abridged in three ways: by restricting the *mode* of alienation (*e.g.*, the property may not be sold or mortgaged); by prohibiting alienation to some *class* of recipients; or by precluding dealings for a specified *time*.[106] In the Canadian cases no explicit attention appears to be given to the reasons for the inclusion of restraints affecting private transactions as a basis for upholding restrictions.[107] Instead, the three elements of mode, class and time seem to be of paramount importance. In ascertaining whether the combined effect of the mode, class and time restrictions is unacceptable, the

---

102 See Part 3(b), Chapter 2.

103 "No person shall sell or agree to sell any land to any Hutterite, or to any trustee or other person on behalf of any Hutterite": *An Act to Prohibit the Sale of Lands to any Hutterites for the Duration of the War*, S.A. 1944, c. 15, s. 3. After the war, this was replaced by the slightly less disgraceful *Communal Property Act*, S.A. 1947, c. 16, as amended by S.A. 1955, c. 42 (and consolidated in R.S.A. 1955, c. 52). The constitutional validity of the Act was upheld in *Walter v. Alberta (Attorney General)*, [1969] S.C.R. 383, 66 W.W.R. 513, 3 D.L.R. (3d) 1. The legislation was repealed by S.A. 1972, c. 103, s. 1. See further W. Janzen, *Limits on Liberty: The Experience of Mennonite, Hutterite and Doukhobor Communities in Canada* (Toronto: U. of T.Pr., 1990) at 67*ff*.

104 These terms are borrowed from the *Restatement of the Law of Property 2d* (St. Paul: A.L.I., 1983) vol. 1, at ch 3, *passim*.

105 See the text accompanying notes 117 to 119, *infra*.

106 *Re Macleay* (1875) L.R. 20 Eq. 186.

107 See the analysis in V. Di Lorenzo, "Restraints on Alienation in a Condominium Context: An Evaluation and Theory for Decision Making", 24 Real Prop., Prob. & Trust J. 403 (1989).

test is sometimes said to be "whether the condition takes away the whole power of alienation substantially".[108] Obviously, this is a highly flexible standard; it provides little guidance as to how the amalgam of factors should be assessed. There is authority that when a condition imposes too great a restriction on the mode and class, it cannot be redeemed by virtue of the fact that there is a limitation on the duration of the embargo.[109] Whether this reasoning would prevail in the case of a very short time restriction remains untested, but to do so seems anomalous. Why should an absolute restraint (as to class and mode), lasting a matter of weeks or days, be void?

Assessing whether a condition unacceptably restrains alienation is a matter of substance, not form.[110] Therefore it should be immaterial whether the restraint is direct, relating explicitly to the three criteria, or whether the indirect effect of the imposition of some stipulation is to impede the owner's ability to transfer the property. The potential for indirect restraints to be invalidated is exemplified by the case of *Re Rosher*.[111] There, a son received a devise of Blackacre subject to the proviso that he (or his heirs) could not sell the land without first offering it to his mother for £3,000. At the time the devise took effect the property was worth about £15,000. A loving son might make such an offer, but the Court must have thought that a rational wealth maximizer would not: it was held that the proviso was an invalid restraint on alienation.[112] What is more, it is not necessary for the restraint to be tied explicitly to a transfer at all, if a stipulation could have a chilling effect on alienation. Accordingly, in *Fuji Builders Ltd. v. Tresoor* a detailed restrictive covenant that contained a clause providing that any construction on the affected land had to be carried out by a designated builder was declared to be

---

108 *Re Macleay, supra*, note 106, at 189 (*per* Jessel M.R.). Limited restrictions were upheld in *Re Dalton* (1921) 20 O.W.N. 344 (H.C.); *Cook v. Nova Scotia* (1982) 53 N.S.R. (2d) 87, 109 A.P.R. 87 (T.D.); *Martin v. Dageneau* (1906) 11 O.L.R. 349 (H.C.) (see also the review of the early authorities cited there). Compare the results in *Re Carr* (1914) 20 B.C.R. 82, 28 W.L.R. 776, 20 D.L.R. 74 (S.C.); *Re Quinn* (1975) 13 N.B.R. (2d) 181 (Q.B.); *Re Collier* (1966) 52 M.P.R. 211, 60 D.L.R. (2d) 70 (Nfld.T.D.); *Doherty v. Doherty*, 10 M.P.R. 286, [1936] 2 D.L.R. 180 (N.S.S.C. *in banco*); *Faucher v. Tucker* (1993) 109 D.L.R. (4th) 699, 92 Man.R. (2d) 41, [1994] 2 W.W.R. 1 (C.A.).

109 *Blackburn v. McCallum* (1902) 33 S.C.R. 65; *Buchanan v. Barnes* (1913) 25 O.W.R. 421, 5 O.W.N. 524 (H.C.); *Re Buckley* (1910) 15 O.W.N. 329, 1 O.W.N. 427 (H.C.). *Cf. Dominion of Canada General Insurance Co. v. Wickford Development Corp.* (1988) 50 R.P.R. 50, 69 Sask.R. 78 (Q.B.) at 80 Sask.R., criticized in *Hongkong Bank of Canada v. Wheeler Holdings Ltd.* (1990) 77 Alta.L.R. (2d) 149, 14 R.P.R. (2d) 1, 111 A.R. 42 (*sub nom. Canada Mortgage & Housing Corp. v. Hongkong Bank of Canada*) 75 D.L.R. (4th) 307 (C.A.) additional reasons at (1991) 78 Alta.L.R. (2d) 236, 112 A.R. 85, 75 D.L.R. (4th) 561 (C.A.) reversed in part [1993] 1 S.C.R. 167, 100 D.L.R. (4th) 40, 148 N.R. 1.

110 *Re Macleay, supra*, note 106, at 189.

111 (1884) 26 Ch.D. 801. See also *Re Dowsett* (1926) 31 O.W.N. 353 (H.C.); *Re Metcalf* (1925) 27 O.W.N. 438 (H.C.); *In re Cockerill*, [1929] 2 Ch. 131; *Re Katzman* (1983) 17 E.T.R. 70 (Ont.H.C.). A right of sale conditioned on the consent of the grantor was held to be void in *Pardee v. Humberstone Summer Resort Co. of Ontario Ltd.*, [1933] O.R. 580, [1933] 3 D.L.R. 277 (H.C.). Compare the mode of analysis used in *Allen v. Allen*, [1994] 6 W.W.R. 323, 2 E.T.R. (2d) 276, 121 Sask.R. 121 (Q.B.).

112 See also *Trinity College School v. Lyons* (1995) 47 R.P.R. (2d) 95 (Ont.Gen.Div.).

void because it created a substantial restraint on alienation.[113] Again, the covenant did not forbid the sale of the property; probably nothing could have been further from the minds of the developers when the covenant was drafted. Nonetheless it was decided that the stipulation could adversely affect the marketability of the land.

Without challenging the economic rationale of alienability (indeed accepting it), one may question whether there is any need to impose special rules here to regulate the market. Consider *Re Rosher* anew.[114] Even if the son were not willing to offer the house to his mother, he might still be open to the idea of buying the right of first refusal from her. In theory, any deal that leaves him with more than a £3,000 profit would make him better off than if he were to sell the house to his mother. She has no present right to own or sell the property, so its present value to her is less easy to determine. However, she cannot count on the son offering it to her at the prescribed price: the whole basis of the current rule is that he would not do such an improvident thing. If she is willing to forego the right of first refusal for anything less than £12,000 a deal might be struck (assuming for the moment that the restriction is valid).

Even if a deal cannot be made, I am not convinced that the law should intervene to strike down the right of first refusal. After all, the son has been given an asset that is not actually worth £15,000 *to him*. He should accept the fact that his interest, which is subject to his mother's right of pre-emption, has a limited market value. Once that bitter pill is swallowed, that is, once he realizes the real value of the gift he has received, he might be more willing to deal with the property. The same is true of the covenant in *Fuji Builders*. Assume that the presence of the covenant would reduce the sale value of the property. My response is that this impediment can be removed, for a price. The current owner can bargain with the party holding the benefit of the covenant and it is plausible the two will agree to its removal. Failing that, the owner must accept that the property is not worth as much as a house that is not lumbered with this type of restrictive covenant.

If this analysis is correct, then I ask again: why do we need rules about restraints on alienation? These rules are necessary only if the market cannot iron out problems such as those occurring in *Rosher* and *Fuji Builders*. In most cases it is theoretically possible for parties who are affected by a restraint to reach a mutually advantageous agreement to remove the restriction. For example, a restraint in the form of a condition subsequent can be bought off by purchasing the right of re-entry. However, bargaining is not always feasible in practice. In the laboratory of economic theory, bargains may be arrived at to achieve an optimum result. Real life is often quite different. Those who control the benefit of the restraint may be unavailable, or obstreperous, or part of a large class. In the latter case, there is a chance that some members of the class would hold out and not settle, thereby undermining the bargaining process. Moreover, when the restraint is disabling, that is, when it simply removes the power of disposal from the bundle

---

113 *Fuji Builders Ltd. v. Tresoor*, [1984] 5 W.W.R. 80, 28 Man.R. (2d) 115, 33 R.P.R. 78 (Q.B.).
114 *Supra*, note 111. My analysis here applies also to *Trinity College School v. Lyons, supra*, note 112, which cites *Rosher* with approval.

of rights of a fee simple owner, there is no one with whom to bargain. When the market cannot easily overcome these impediments to exchange on its own, some form of legal intervention is necessary. This, then, explains why we appear to need rules prohibiting restraints on alienation. The rules are necessary because it may be difficult, as a general matter, to overcome the barriers to bargaining that restrictions erect.

If rules about restraints are explicable on this basis, it may be suggested that the present law is actually under-inclusive. The principles concerning restraints on alienation have been held to apply to conditions that attach directly to an interest in property, as is the case when the restriction is disabling or one of forfeiture. The rules should also apply to interests such as options to purchase, restrictive covenants,[115] and mortgages.[116] In these cases, the restraints attach to, and derogate from, the real estate. Conversely, it is by no means clear that the rules apply when the restraint is purely contractual, because the contract would not 'run with the land'.[117] If the policy of the law is to promote the circulation of property, and if this is offended by a conditional grant, the harmful effects of stagnation can also occur when the restriction is imposed through a contract. This view accords with the position that the law is concerned with substance not form. The argument being made here also assumes that the rules against restraint are not merely concerned with repugnancy, that is, with whether an essential feature of a property right is missing, but rather with a more pervasive policy issue (*i.e.,* economic efficiency).

In *C.M.H.C. v. Hongkong Bank of Canada*[118] the Supreme Court of Canada addressed, in passing, the applicability of the rules governing restraints and their applicability to contracts. But the Court's treatment of the issue is a bit puzzling. Sopinka J. said this:

> To the extent that the policy against restraints on alienation applies to contractual provisions that are not annexed to the land so as to run with the land, it does not render such provisions unenforceable for all purposes. Contractual provisions are simply ineffective to prevent the

---

115 See, *e.g., Fuji Builders v. Tresoor, supra,* note 113; *Re Drummond Wren,* [1945] O.R. 778, [1945] 4 D.L.R. 674 (H.C.).

116 See B. Ziff, "Restraints on Alienation in Mortgages" (1989) 67 Alta.L.R. (2d) 346. See also E.J. Murdock, "The Due-On-Sale Controversy: Beneficial Effects of the Garn – St. Germain Depository Institution Act of 1982", 1984 Duke L.J. 121.

117 *British Columbia Forest Products Ltd. v. Gay* (1978) 7 B.C.L.R. 190, 89 D.L.R. (3d) 80 (C.A.). Compare the somewhat confusing analysis in *Laurin v. Iron Ore Co.* (1977) 82 D.L.R. (3d) 634, 19 Nfld. & P.E.I.R. 111, 50 A.P.R. 111 (Nfld.T.D.). Compare also the *obiter* comments in *Stephens v. Gulf Oil Canada Ltd., supra,* note 94. It has been held that when a question of construction arises as to whether a purely contractual covenant or a condition has been created, the courts should incline in favour of the former because "[c]onditions subsequent are not favoured in law": *Pearson v. Adams* (1912) 27 O.L.R. 87, 7 D.L.R. 139 (Div.Ct.) at 144 D.L.R. (*per* Riddell J.) reversed (1913) 28 O.L.R. 154, 12 D.L.R. 227 (C.A.) which was reversed (1914) 50 S.C.R. 204. See also *McIntosh v. Samo* (1875) 24 U.C.C.P. 625 (C.A.). In Australia, contractual restraints are covered by these rules: see *Hall v. Busst* (1960) 104 C.L.R. 206, [1961] A.L.R. 508 (Aust.H.C.) reviewed in W.N. Harrison, "Hall v. Busst" (1961) 35 A.L.J. 3.

118 *Supra,* note 109.

owner of land from conveying a good title to a purchaser but other *in personam* remedies remain available.[119]

This view seems to be both tautologous and naive. Of course, a term which does not run with the land cannot prevent a purchaser from acquiring title free from that condition. However, the prospect that a vendor who sells contrary to the terms of a contractual restraint might be mulcted in damages (being an *in personam* remedy that remains available) can be enough to induce a party not to sell a property, thus keeping it out of circulation.

4. THE LEGAL REMAINDER RULES

(a) the four rules and inter vivos transfers

(i) *words of warning*

In this section four ancient rules that regulate the validity of legal remainders will be reviewed. In brief, these rules restrict the manner in which future legal interests can be created. The common law held an antipathy toward future interests in general, and contingent remainders in particular. This attitude probably arose because interests of this kind clouded title, generated uncertainty, and inhibited transfers. For similar reasons, the law sought to reduce the number of 'fancy' interests that could be created. In Chapter 1 we observed that new rights over real property are not readily accepted by the courts (a concept that has been labeled the *numerus clausus* principle).[120]

In addition, we will see that two of the four rules to be reviewed below were designed to promote the smooth passage of 'seisin' from one owner of land to the next. The term seisin has shown up several times already.[121] In short, it is a feudal concept that refers to the possession enjoyed by a freeholder. It was from the person seised that feudal incidents could be claimed, and only such a person could launch a real action to recover possession of land. In sum, the identity of the person seised was significant[122] and so was carefully regulated. Today it is still correct to say that a life tenant or fee simple owner who is vested in possession is seised of the land.

There was a time, which I think has long since passed, when detailed tutelage about the legal remainder rules was essential for Canadian property lawyers. Over

---

119 *Ibid.* at 206-7 S.C.R.

120 See Part 4(a)(iii), Chapter 1.

121 See, *e.g.*, Part 2(a), Chapter 2, and Part 5(a), Chapter 4.

122 Seisin has remained important in the context of Canadian constitutional law, in a limited way. To qualify as a Senator one must be seised of land of a value of $4,000 or more: *Constitution Act, 1867* (U.K.) 30 & 31 Vict., c. 3 [formerly the *British North America Act*], s. 23. This provision affected the eligibility of Michael Forestall, who was appointed to the Senate in 1990 as part of the Conservative government's strategy to stack the Senate so as to ensure passage of the goods and services tax legislation. Mr. Forestall held only a remainder interest in a certain property in Nova Scotia, and so was not *seised* of land; he was not entitled to possession. The niceties of feudal land law involving seisin were debated in the Senate: *Senate Debates*, October 26, 1990, 2nd Sess., 34th Parl., vol. 133, at 3264*ff.*

the centuries a good deal of learning has been deposited in the law reports and texts about the finer points of legal future interests. The English writer Charles Fearne was one of several scholars who wrote about this convoluted area of law, and his work might still come in handy. However, in the discussion that follows most of this detail is omitted. My advice is to consult Fearne's eighteenth-century classic *Essay on the Learning of Contingent Remainders and Executory Devises* (or some later edition of that work) if a knotty issue arises in practice.[123] The goal is to outline the main elements of the four rules, which then allows for an understanding of the nature of certain special entitlements (in particular 'legal executory interests'). This treatment also sets the stage for the analysis of the rule against perpetuities, which is found in the final part of the chapter.

(ii)   *the rules*

The first rule (this ordering is arbitrary) demonstrates the rigid common law attitude toward the movement of seisin. The rule provides that *an estate of freehold is void if it is designed to take effect in the future, unless it is supported by a prior particular estate.* This means that a deed given to A on Day #1, which is stated to take effect on Day #2, is void.[124] There is a gap in seisin here (albeit for only one day) which the common law has resolutely refused to tolerate, overlook or remedy. Instead of invalidating the transaction, the common law might have considered the grantor to have remained seised for that extra day, the property then springing forward to the grantee at the appointed hour. Part of the reason for this strictness may have been to ensure that there was no dissonance between the symbolic act of conveyance, which represented the transfer of ownership and seisin, and the date in the document. The rule emerged at a time when there was no comprehensive registry system that could be used to check the state of ownership. Importantly, the rule is not violated when the future interest is preceded by the granting of a prior particular estate, as in the case of a grant 'to A for life, remainder to B and her heirs'. The gift to B is supported by the prior particular estate in A; hence there is no gap in seisin. Once A dies, seisin passes automatically to B.

The second rule provides that a legal contingent remainder is void unless it vests at or before the termination of the prior particular estate. This rule is concerned with the 'timely vesting' of contingent remainders. Thus, a gift 'to A for life, remainder to B if B remarries *after* A's death' is void *ab initio* (from the outset), because the marriage requirement, as stated, will produce an inevitable

---

123 There are also several helpful modern reviews of the arcane area: see R.E. Megarry & H.W.R. Wade, *The Law of Real Property*, 5th ed. (London: Stevens & Sons, 1984) at Appendix IV; M.A. Neave *et al.*, eds., *Sackville & Neave Property Law: Cases and Materials*, 6th ed. (Sydney: Butterworths, 1999) at 190*ff*; J. Makdisi, *Estates in Land and Future Interests* (Boston: Little, Brown, 1991); R.J. Hopperton, "Teaching Present and Future Interests: A Methodology for Students That Unifies Estates in Land Concepts, Structures, and Principles", 26 U.Tol.L.Rev. 621 (1995).

124 *Barwick's Case* (1597) 5 Co.Rep. 93b, 77 E.R. 199. This rule was acknowledged, but avoided on the facts, in *Nolan v. Fox* (1865) 15 U.C.C.P. 565. See also *Re Smith and Dale* (1919) 46 O.L.R. 403, 55 D.L.R. 274 (H.C.) which is criticized in E.D. Armour, "Grant of Freehold Estates *In Futuro*" (1920) 55 D.L.R. 276.

gap in seisin. B has been given a contingent interest that cannot vest until the condition precedent (the marriage) has occurred. An interest that remains contingent is too inchoate to allow its holder to enjoy seisin. In contrast, a gift 'to A for life, remainder to B if she marries *before* A's death' is unquestionably a valid remainder, because there is no possibility of a gap in seisin. True, B may not marry at all, but this means only that she has failed to meet the condition precedent, not that the condition or the remainder is contrary to law. By the way, in this limitation, the grantor has not parted with the full estate: no provision is explicitly made for the chance that B will not marry. Here, the grantor is said to have retained a reversion in order to take account of the possibility that A might die without B having married.

So far I have given two examples to illustrate this rule: in the first a gap is inevitable; in the second it is impossible. There is a third type of factual permutation under this second rule, and it is one that will require analysis later on.[125] Consider a grant 'to A for life, remainder to B if B marries'. The time for the marriage is not indicated (as it was in the two earlier examples). Therefore, it is unclear whether a timely vesting of that contingent remainder will occur; that is, we do not know whether the remainder will vest at or before the end of the life estate, as required by Rule 2. Should B marry on time, the remainder will be valid, because the baton of seisin can be passed, without interruption, to B. Again, whether this will happen is unknown at the outset – we must 'wait and see'. This second rule has the effect of limiting the period during which a contingency can linger; that is why we say that the rule promotes timely vesting. It will be seen below that a rule of broader application (the rule against perpetuities[126]) also arose to prevent the remote vesting of contingent interests.

The second legal remainder rule can reduce the number of recipients claiming under a 'class gift'. A limitation 'to A for life, with a remainder to all of B's children who reach 21' creates a class gift. Here, the recipients are determined by reference to whether they fit within the defined class: the children of B who manage to reach 21. It is of course possible that only some of the children will have reached 21 at the time of A's death. The interests of those children who comply with Rule 2 will be valid, and the children reaching 21 afterwards will be shut out. This is the effect of the rule in *Festing v. Allen*,[127] which, as we have just seen, provides for a premature closing of the class in these circumstances. Its effect is to save the gift for those members of the class who vest on time, while excluding the latecomers.

The third and fourth rules are not directly concerned with the uninterrupted flow of seisin, but rather with the law's reluctance to recognize new forms of land interests (the *numerus clausus* policy).[128] The *third rule* declares that *a remainder is void if it is to take effect by cutting short a prior particular estate*. Such a

---

125 See Part 4(b), *infra*.
126 See Part 5, *infra*.
127 (1843) 12 M. & W. 279, 152 E.R. 1204. The rule is applicable only to legal remainders, including those so considered under the rule in *Purefoy v. Rogers*: see Part 4(b), *infra*.
128 See Part 4(a)(iii), Chapter 1.

transfer has been described as being "foreign to the simplicity of the conveyances before uses and devises were introduced".[129] To explain, consider a gift 'to A for life, provided he does not remarry, but if he does, then to B'. This wording gives a valid life estate to A, which is subject to a condition subsequent. However, the right given to B could cut short A's life estate and would therefore be invalid under Rule 3. According to this rule, at common law only the grantor (or that person's estate) can enjoy the benefit of this right of re-entry. Careful drafting can avoid this restriction, while leaving the substance of the gift virtually unchanged. Consider a grant 'to A for life or *until* A remarries, and then to B'. This creates a determinable life estate, which does not violate the third rule: owing to the fiction described earlier[130] the determining event marks the natural end of the estate and does not cut short the life estate or prematurely terminate it.

Under *the fourth rule, a remainder after a fee is void.*[131] For example, in a gift 'to A in fee simple, remainder to B in fee simple', the remainder to B is a nullity. Of course, this is no more than an application of the Statute *Quia Emptores*, which abolished the process of subinfeudation.[132] Once the grantor has parted with the full fee simple by conferring it on A, there remains no additional interest that can be given to B.

The fourth rule, however, also applies to possibilities of reverter and rights of re-entry following the grant of a fee simple. Hence, a gift 'to A in fee simple, but should liquor be sold on the premises, then to B in fee simple' is invalid. Here, re-casting the gift in the form of a determinable fee simple will not avoid the operation of Rule 4: a gift 'to A in fee simple, until liquor is sold on the premises, and then to B in fee simple' still creates a remainder after a fee, and is therefore void. Any attempt to mount a fee after (or upon) a fee is invalid and the second interest will be ignored. The main gift will stand and the rights arising on the happening of the prescribed event are retained by the grantor. If it is now the case that possibilities of reverter and rights of re-entry are fully alienable, the fourth rule catches only remainders after fees contained in the same instrument (or perhaps the same transaction). In other words, it seems possible to create a fee simple subject to a right of re-entry in the grantor and later on pass that right of re-entry to someone else. That being so, this rule seems utterly anachronistic.

(b) equitable and legal executory interests

One of the advantages of creating equitable interests in land (before and after the *Statute of Uses, 1535*[133]) is that they are not subject to the *legal* remainder rules. The Chancellor was uninterested in the niceties of seisin and was not *as* concerned with the dangers associated with the creation of unconventional interests. As a result, none of the grants above would have been invalid had purely

---

129 *In re Melville* (1886) 11 O.R. 626 (Ch.D.) at 632, quoting *Smith's Real and Personal Property*, 8th ed., s. 170.
130 See Part 2(b), *supra*.
131 See, *e.g.*, *Re Chauvin* (1920) 18 O.W.N. 178 (H.C.).
132 Subinfeudation is explained in Part 2(a), Chapter 2.
133 *An Act Concerning Uses and Wills, 1535*, 27 Hen. 8, c. 10. See Part 3(b), Chapter 6.

equitable interests been involved. A gift of an equitable interest 'to A for life, remainder to B if B marries after A's death' would produce the following entitlements: A would receive an equitable life estate; B gets an equitable contingent remainder. In the inevitable interval of time after A's death but before B's marriage it would be presumed (as a matter of construction) that the equitable title would return to the settlor. That interest is a resulting trust, a term introduced in Chapter 6.[134] On B's marriage the settlor would be divested and the right to possession would move forward to B, as a *springing* trust. If no marriage ever takes place, title will remain with the settlor. Similarly, any gap occasioned by a gift *in futuro* would be remedied by the imposition of a resulting trust in favour of the settlor. Therefore, a notional hiatus in possession, so detrimental to the validity of legal future interests under the first two legal remainder rules, poses no threat to equitable rights.

Similarly, Rules 3 and 4 are irrelevant if purely equitable interests in land are involved. A gift of an equitable interest 'to A and his heirs, but should she remarry then to B', which may result in the cutting short of A's interest in favour of B, gives B a *shifting* equitable interest. As we saw above, a comparable gift of the legal estate would be invalid because it contravenes the fourth rule. Therefore, by creating a valid trust the strictures imposed by the law of common law future interests are rendered irrelevant. In jurisdictions such as Manitoba, where transfers of successive interests in land are impressed with a statutory trust, the legal remainder rules are totally devoid of significance.[135]

If the legal remainder rules apply to legal interests proper, but not at all to purely equitable interests, what then is the position for *legal executory interests,* the hybrid created by virtue of the operation of the *Statute of Uses*? We saw earlier that the *Statute of Uses* could coat a purely equitable interest with the veneer of legal title. When the Statute applied, a gift 'to A to the use of B' would place the legal and equitable titles in the hands of B; A retained nothing. Recall also that the Statute provides that the *cestui que use* (to whom the Statute transferred the legal title of the feoffee) is supposed to hold the same estate that he or she formerly had in the use.[136] With one glaring and troublesome exception, this has been taken to mean that legal executory interests are not subject to the legal remainder rules.

The exception relates to the 'wait and see' permutation under the second rule. We saw above that when a transfer is made, say, 'to A for life, remainder to B if B marries', one must wait and see if the rule of timely vesting (Rule 2) is violated. All other transfers that trigger the legal remainder rules involve violations that are apparent from the moment of the grant; this is the one occasion in which one must wait in order to find out if invalidity ensues. In this example, if B does not marry before A dies, the remainder is invalid. In the notorious case of

---

134 See Part 4(c), Chapter 6.
135 *Perpetuities and Accumulations Act*, R.S.M. 1987, c. P33, sub. 4(1). *Cf.* the discussion accompanying notes 142 to 150, *infra*.
136 See Part 3(b), Chapter 6.

Purefoy v. Rogers[137] it was decided that the legal remainder rules would apply to legal executory interests in this wait-and-see situation. In the words of the Court,

> where a contingency is limited to depend on an estate of freehold which is capable of supporting a remainder, it shall never be construed to be an executory devise, but as a contingent remainder only.[138]

To reiterate, the impact of Rule 2 is felt only if an executory interest is capable of complying with the legal remainder rules. If a remainder can comply with those rules it must comply. As a mantra it might be recited this way: if it can it must! The remainder ('to B if she marries') might vest on time. Therefore, by virtue of *Purefoy*, if that remainder does not vest on time it becomes void. Why the rule emerged is a matter of conjecture, but it may have been a reaction against the freedoms otherwise enjoyed by legal executory interests after the introduction of the *Statute of Uses* in 1535. Whatever the rationale, its effect can be prevented by careful drafting. Inserting an inevitable gap in seisin avoids the operation of *Purefoy*, such as if property is given 'to A for life, remainder one day later to B if B is 21'. This executory interest cannot comply with the legal remainder rules, so, curiously, it need not.

(c)   testamentary gifts

Whether the legal remainder rules apply to devises of land is not clear. It was never settled in England whether the *Statute of Uses* applied to interests created under the *Statute of Wills, 1540*.[139] The *Statute of Uses* does refer to interests created by will, and there is Canadian authority in which the Statute was applied to a testamentary disposition.[140] In any event, the *Statute of Uses* was invoked as an analogous rule of construction, and in this way uses in wills were executed as in the case of *inter vivos* conveyances. Whether it still makes sense to apply such a rule is debatable, given that it is likely that the use of words such as 'in trust' would probably be intended to create a valid trust, which the application of the *Statute of Uses* would frustrate.

Additionally, it has been decided that legal interests in devises should be treated as legal executory interests, even if uses are not recited in the will itself. This attitude arose out of a generous reading of the first wills legislation, which allowed interests to be transferred at the "free will and pleasure" of the donor.[141] This is an important idea, because it can, on its own, negate the application of the *Statute of Uses*. Here is how it works: An executory devise (i) 'to A, but if B marries then to B' is treated as creating a valid shifting devise and is the functional equivalent of a grant (ii) 'to X in fee simple, to the use of A, but if B marries,

---

137 (1671) 2 Wms. Saund. 380, 85 E.R. 1181. See B.D. Stapleton, ''*Purefoy v. Rogers* and the Rule Against Perpetuities'' (1980) 29 U.N.B.L.J. 263.

138 *Supra*, note 137, at 1192 E.R. (*per* Lord Hale).

139 32 Hen. 8, c. 1.

140 *Fair v. McCrow* (1871) 31 U.C.Q.B. 599. See also *Hall v. Urquhart* (1928) 35 O.W.N. 201 (H.C.).

141 See further Megarry & Wade, *supra*, note 123, at 1180.

then to the use of B'. Again, in a will, legal interests may shift or spring, just like legal executory interests. Therefore, apart from the possible effect of the rule in *Purefoy v. Rogers*, the legal remainder rules have no application to devises.

The position concerning land given away by will is complicated further. It has been suggested that devises should *never* be subject to the legal remainder rules and that the rule in *Purefoy v. Rogers* has no application to testamentary gifts. This view emerges out of the English decision in *Re Robson*.[142] There, property was devised "unto and to the use of my said daughter Helen during her life and from and after her decease to the use of such of her children in fee simple as shall attain the age of twenty-one years".[143] On the death of the daughter, some children had reached the prescribed age while others had not. Therefore, the question was whether the underage children would be cut out by applying the common law class closing rule in *Festing v. Allen*.[144] The Court said no.

Under the *Land Transfer Act, 1897*,[145] which applied to this will, the property of a deceased person was temporarily treated as being held on trust, with legal title being given to the deceased's personal representatives. Once an 'assent' was granted under the Act, the estate could be distributed. Until that assent, the interests conferred by the will were purely equitable and as such would be immune from the operation of the legal remainder rules. *Re Robson* held that even after the assent had occurred, any devises of the legal interests retained the initial protection from destruction enjoyed by equitable interests. If compliance with the timely vesting legal remainder rule (Rule 2) was not required, then the children who were still under 21 years of age could vest at some future time, that is, even after the death of the life tenant (Helen). If this holding is good law, a conclusion that has been resisted by some,[146] its effect is to render the legal remainder rules inapplicable to wills. In short, this would mean that *Purefoy* would never apply to testamentary gifts. At least that would be the case in those jurisdictions that have a law that is comparable to the *Land Transfer Act, 1897*, the statute relied upon in *Robson*.[147]

---

142 [1916] 1 Ch. 116.

143 *Ibid.* at 116-7. It may appear that this language creates a contingent equitable interest in the children, because their gift appears to be a use upon a use, given the recital of 'unto and to the use of Helen'. The Court's interpretation must have been as follows: 'to Helen for life to the use of Helen for life. Thereafter, the estate is to hold to the use of those children who turn 21'. That reading suggests that the children's interest was legal (subject, of course, to the ultimate holding of the Court on point).

144 *Supra*, note 127.

145 60 & 61 Vict., c. 65.

146 See the caustic attack of G.C. Cheshire in "The Case of *Re Robson; Douglass v. Douglass*" (1920) 6 Conv. (O.S.) 44. (Consider also *Commr. of Stamp Duties (Qld.) v. Livingston*, [1965] A.C. 694 (P.C.) and the discussion in D.W.M. Waters, *Law of Trusts in Canada* (Toronto: Carswell, 1984) at 34-5, n. 11.) But similar reasoning was adopted in *Re Beavis* (1906) 7 S.R. (N.S.W.) 66, 23 W.N. 245 (S.C.) before *Robson*, and in *Barrett v. Barrett* (1918) 18 S.R. (N.S.W.) 637, 35 W.N. 180 (S.C.) afterwards.

147 See, *e.g.*, *Devolution of Real Property Act*, R.S.A. 1980, c. D-34, ss. 2, 3. But see s. 7. See also *Estates Administration Act*, R.S.O. 1990, c. E.22, sub. 2(1).

An opportunity to reconsider the case law, and, for that matter, to assess whether there was a continuing need for the legal remainder rules, arose in the 1984 Ontario case of *Re Crow*.[148] Sadly, that chance was squandered, for the Court did not evaluate fundamental doctrines in resolving the dispute placed before it. In *Crow*, property was given to A and B for life, with remainders to their children, and with alternative remainders to their nieces and nephews in the event that A and B had no children of their own. On the death of A, there was no one then alive who was able to claim the remainder, though potential recipients were subsequently born. This raised the question of whether the rule in *Purefoy v. Rogers* was applicable. If it was, Rule 2 applied and the remainder was void. The gifts under that remainder had not vested in time, because there was no one who could hold seisin on the death of the life tenant. In *Re Crow* the Court applied the timely vesting rule and *Purefoy*, striking off the remainder.

There were other options available to the trial judge. It is arguable that the interests created in the will were equitable in the first place.[149] Even if this is not the proper way to read the will, another possibility was for the Court to apply the reasoning found in *Robson*. That was not done, and apparently *Robson* was not cited to the Court.[150] Alternatively, the suitability of retaining *Purefoy* as part of the modern law of property could have been assessed. Canadian courts must certainly have the power (perhaps even the duty) to remove archaic judge-made law. Granted, it is one thing to brush aside the operation of the *Statute of Uses* itself, especially in Ontario, where the Act is incorporated into provincial law by statute.[151] However, nothing prevented a court, in 1984, from refusing to follow a decision that was not binding upon it and which appears to possess no contemporary *raison d'être*. Even if there remains a reason to demand the timely vesting of contingent remainders, the policing of such interests is the function of the rule against perpetuities, to which the discussion now turns.

5. THE RULE AGAINST PERPETUITIES[152]

(a) introduction

The common law's concern about contingent remainders explains the rule governing timely vesting (Rule 2, above), which strives to limit the period during

---

148 (1984) 48 O.R. (2d) 36, 17 E.T.R. 1, 12 D.L.R. (4th) 415 (H.C.). For a detailed examination of this case and a review of the relevant policies, see T.G. Youdan, "Future Interests and the Rule in *Purefoy v. Rogers*: The Unnecessary Application of Archaic and Capricious Rules" (1984) 17 E.T.R. 3.

149 The interests may have been equitable owing to the duties cast upon the executors: see Youdan, *supra*, note 148, at 7*ff.* The significance of such a finding is discussed in Part 3(c), Chapter 6.

150 See *Re Crow, supra*, note 148, at 416-7 D.L.R. (Editorial Note).

151 *An Act Concerning Uses*, R.S.O. 1897, c. 331.

152 See further J.C. Gray, *The Rule Against Perpetuities*, 4th ed., R. Gray, ed. (Boston: Little, Brown, 1942); H.C. Morris & W.B. Leach, *The Rule Against Perpetuities*, 2nd ed. (London: Stevens & Sons, 1962). For a primer on how to work through standard perpetuity problems (and for references to other primers), see J.W. Weaver, "Fear and Loathing in Perpetuities", 48 Wash. & Lee L.Rev. 1393 (1991). See also M. Reutlinger, "When Words Fail Me: Diagramming the Rule Against Perpetuities", 59 Missouri L.Rev. 157 (1994); L.A. Mc-

which contingencies can linger. That rule applies only to legal (and select legal executory) interests. In time, rules of wider application developed to limit the lifespan of both legal and equitable interests. These doctrines eventually coalesced under the rubric of 'the rule against perpetuities'.[153] Its modern function is to promote alienability; contingent interests are targeted as potential fetters. Accordingly, the rule establishes a period of time during which contingencies will be permitted to remain unvested. Put another way, the rule against perpetuities tries to strike a balance between the rights of a prior owner to control the destiny of her or his property, and the autonomy of present owners to act without being controlled by the dead hand of the past.[154] In essence, then, the rule against perpetuities is connected to the goal of promoting economic efficiency, and it attempts to broker the liberty interests of present and future owners.

The basic common law rule is as follows: *an interest is valid if it must vest, if it is going to vest at all, within the perpetuity period. That period is calculated by taking the lives in being at the date the instrument takes effect, plus 21 years.*

This statement possesses a lyrical simplicity that is highly deceptive. The rule presents, as is sometimes said, a trap for the unwary. Consider a will in which the residue of an estate is given "to the Communist Party of Canada". This inoffensive-looking little clause was found to contravene the rule against perpetuities.[155] The Party is an unincorporated association; as such it is incapable of holding title. In consequence, the gift was construed as one to present and future members, and this reading[156] led inescapably to the conclusion that some of those interests would vest outside of the perpetuity period, thereby rendering the whole gift void. Indeed, so difficult can a perpetuities issue be to detect that in the California case of *Lucas v. Hamm*[157] it was held that the failure of an attorney to appreciate the impact of the rule in the drafting of a specific testamentary instrument did not place that lawyer's conduct below the standard of the ordinary

---

Crimmon, "Understanding the Rule Against Perpetuities: Adopting a Five Step Approach to a Perpetuities Problem" (1997) 5 Aust.Prop.L.J. 130.

153 The modern rule is normally traced to the *Duke of Norfolk's Case* (1681) 2 Swans. 454, 22 E.R. 930. However, the rule was not cast in its modern form until the early nineteenth century: see *Cadell v. Palmer* (1833) 1 Cl. & F. 372, 6 E.R. 956. The reference to the 'modern' rule against perpetuities distinguishes it from the 'old rule against perpetuities' (which is also known as the rule in *Whitby v. Mitchell* (1890) 44 Ch.D. 85 (C.A.)). The old rule prohibits a gift to the offspring of an unborn person.

154 See further D.E. Allan, "The Rule Against Perpetuities Restated" (1963) 6 U.W.Aust.L.Rev. 27. A classic statement of the rationale of the rule can be found in L. Simes, *Public Policy and the Dead Hand* (Ann Arbour: U. of Mich. Law School, 1955). See also J.E. Stake, "Darwin, Donations and the Illusion of Dead Hand Control", 64 Tul.L.Rev. 705 (1990).

155 *LePage v. Communist Party of Canada* (1999) 209 N.B.R. (2d) 58, 535 A.P.R. 58 (Prob.Ct.). In Alberta, it is possible that this clause could have been saved by s. 20 of the *Perpetuities Act*, R.S.A. 1980, c. P-4.

156 Other, non-invalidating, constructions are possible: see A.H. Oosterhoff & E.E. Gillese, eds., *Text, Commentary and Cases on Trusts*, 5th ed (Toronto: Carswell, 1998) at 972*ff*. See also D.W.M. Waters, *Law of Trusts in Canada*, 2nd ed. (Toronto: Carswell, 1984) at 505*ff*.

157 364 P.2d 685 (Cal.S.C., 1961) lampooned in (1965) 81 L.Q.R. 478, at 481. See also D.M. Becker, "If You Think You No Longer Need to Know Anything About the Rule Against Perpetuities, Then Read This!", 74 Wash.U.L.Rev. 713 (1996).

practitioner. As a result, the attorney, who accidentally drafted a clause that violated the rule, avoided civil liability for professional negligence.

What follows is a look at the common law rule through an examination of its ingredients.

(b)   'an interest'

The rule against perpetuities applies to almost all contingent interests in property, real or personal, legal or equitable. Outside of the common law rule's grasp in Canada is the possibility of reverter, which is regarded as a vested interest.[158] Other property interests have been excepted, including the following: a right of re-entry arising from the breach of a condition under a lease, a gift over from one charity to another, and an option to renew a lease.[159] It has also been maintained that the rule does not apply to invalidate contractual obligations as between the parties. If so, it is plausible that the grant of an option over land, even if void for remoteness, is still enforceable against the parties to the contract.[160] On the other hand, there is Canadian authority stating that if an interest (such as an option) offends the rule, there remains no personal covenant or contractual term that can be enforced in its place.[161]

(c)   'must vest'

The rule against perpetuities is not concerned with interests that last indefinitely;[162] the fee simple is capable of enduring forever, and is not objectionable on that ground. The rule is solely concerned with contingent property rights. They must vest, either in possession or interest, within the perpetuity period.

Vesting in this context has a more elaborate meaning than that introduced above.[163] In addition to referring to interests that are not subject to a condition

---

158 *Tilbury West Public School Bd. v. Hastie*, [1966] 2 O.R. 20, 55 D.L.R. (2d) 407 (H.C.) order varied [1966] 2 O.R. 511, 57 D.L.R. (2d) 519 (H.C.); *Caroline (Village) v. Roper* (1987) 82 A.R. 72, 37 D.L.R. (4th) 761 (Q.B.); *Women's Christian Association of London v. McCormick Estate* (1989) 34 E.T.R. 216 (Ont. H.C.). See *contra Hopper v. Liverpool Corp.* (1944) 88 Sol.J. 213, noted in (1946) 62 L.Q.R. 222. As to reform of this facet of the rule, see note 183, *infra.*

159 However, the rule does apply to a right of renewal of a *profit à prendre: Canadian Export Gas & Oil v. Flegal* (1977), [1978] 1 W.W.R. 185, 9 A.R. 105, 80 D.L.R. (3d) 679 (S.C.); *PanCanadian Petroleum Ltd. v. Husky Oil Operations Ltd.* (1994) 26 Alta.L.R. (3d) 203, [1995] 4 W.W.R. 40 (Q.B.) and to an option to purchase the freehold: *Newsome v. Sullivan* (1987) 52 Alta.L.R. (2d) 304, 78 A.R. 297, 38 D.L.R. (4th) 1 (C.A.) leave to appeal to S.C.C. refused (1988) 87 N.R. 74n (S.C.C.).

160 See, *e.g., Hill Housing Ltd. v. Lynch* (1985) 64 N.B.R. (2d) 229, 165 A.P.R. 229 (Q.B.) affirmed (March 20, 1986) Doc. No. 147/85/CA, Stratton C.J.N.B., Ryan and Hoyt JJ.A. (C.A.). See also *Radbourne v. Radbourne* (1977) 2 E.T.R. 85 (Sask.Q.B); Megarry & Wade, *supra*, note 123, at 287*ff*; P. Butt, *Land Law*, 3rd ed. (Sydney: Law Book Co., 1996) at 203-5.

161 See *PanCanadian Petroleum Ltd. v. Husky Oil, supra*, note 159, at 57-8, and the authorities cited there.

162 *Aldercrest Developments Ltd. v. Hunter*, [1970] 2 O.R. 562, 11 D.L.R. (3d) 439 (C.A.).

163 See Part 2(c), *supra*.

precedent,[164] it also includes a requirement that the exact size of the interest of the donee(s) be known. This means that the size of all portions enjoyed under a class gift must be determined within the period. If this does not occur, then even those members of the class who had vested on time will be deprived of their share. The common law rule against perpetuities took an all-or-nothing attitude: one bad apple could spoil the entire barrel.[165] The common law rule is also impatient: one does not normally 'wait and see' whether or not vesting will occur.[166] Instead, to comply with the rule it must be known from the outset that a remote vesting of the interest granted is impossible. If, looking at the matter from the date the disposition took effect, it is possible, however unlikely, that the interest may vest outside the perpetuity period, the gift is void. An examination of the limitation in *Lucas v. Hamm*[167] illustrates this demanding posture. There, the property was to vest five years after probate had been obtained. In uncontested cases the issuance of probate can typically take a few months, and even in a contested case, a dispute would likely be resolved within a few years. However, these are not ironclad certainties, and it was within the realm of possibility that the condition might not have been met until the perpetuity period had elapsed, which in *Hamm* was 21 years.[168] Even if it had been shown that probate was actually obtained before expiration of the period, the gift would still be void. The vantage point from which to determine whether a possibility of remote vesting exists is the time the disposition becomes operative. For an *inter vivos* transfer, the completion of the transaction is the crucial moment; for a will, it is the death of the decedent that starts the clock.

(d) 'if at all'

This qualification reveals an important element of the common law rule: it is completely and utterly indifferent as to whether a contingent interest actually does vest. Rather, the rule seeks to know merely whether or not a timely vesting will occur. The rule poses the following question: when will we know, one way

---

164 See generally R.E. Megarry & H.W.R. Wade, *The Law of Real Property*, 5th ed. (London: Stevens & Sons, 1984) at 242-3.

165 But see the discussion of the class closing rules in *Andrews v. Partington*, in the text accompanying notes 173 to 175, *infra*.

166 In certain situations, mainly involving alternative contingencies, the rule will wait and see whether the gift is void: see further Morris & Leach, *supra*, note 152, at 152-4, 159-63.

167 *Supra*, note 157. See also *Re Wood*, [1894] 3 Ch. 381 (C.A.).

168 In *Van Hees v. Higgins*, 64 B.C.L.R. (2d) 150, [1992] 3 W.W.R. 530, 86 D.L.R. (4th) 193 (S.C.) affirmed (1993) 81 B.C.L.R. 109, 102 D.L.R. (4th) 449, [1993] 7 W.W.R. 332 (C.A.), a clause similar to that used in *Hamm* was considered. There, an option to purchase was supposed to last for one year after the notification of the death of the survivor of A and B. Conceivably, that notice might not occur until 21 years after the death. The Court offered that "in this day and age, possibilities considered should not be fanciful or contrived" and that "[i]f they verge on the absurd they should be ignored": *ibid.* at 199 D.L.R. (*per* Hood J.). However, instead of simply ignoring the rule, the clause was taken to mean that the option was to last only for a reasonable time, that is, well before the perpetuity period would expire. This construction therefore finessed the application of the perpetuities rule. The Court of Appeal held that the trial judge "arrived at the right conclusion for the reasons which he gave": 81 B.C.L.R. (2d) at 117 (*per* Cummings J.A.).

or the other, whether this contingent interest will vest? If we know that this question will be resolved within the period, either way, that will satisfy the rule. A gift 'to my first grandchild to marry within 21 years of my death' is valid, even if no marriage occurs, and even if no grandchild is ever born. In this situation it is certain that any vesting that does occur must take place before the perpetuity period expires. This is because the condition precedent has been carefully set to remain open only for the duration of the allowable period of time. In other words, if a marriage were to take place outside of the period, it would be irrelevant to the gift. Perpetuity rule or no perpetuity rule, that married child would not receive the gift because that marriage does not fall within the scope of the stated condition precedent.

(e)   'within the perpetuity period'

The perpetuity period is calculated according to a formula that consists of the duration of all 'lives in being' plus a period of 21 years. The selection of this time frame seems to have been influenced by limitations in family settlements, because the period calculated under the rule permits a postponement of vesting until the grandchildren of the settlor reach the age of majority (which was at one time 21 years of age). Note, however, that the time limit applies in all circumstances, not just to those involving inter-generational transfers.

The lives-in-being variable imbues the rule with complexity. Determining the catalogue of lives in being can be difficult. As a starting point, I take the view that any human being alive at the date of the gift is a life in being; even a child that is then *en ventre sa mère* qualifies.[169] However, this definition is only partially helpful in calculating the period. Once a few examples are considered, it will become apparent that only individuals who are directly or indirectly connected with the gift are potentially 'helpful' lives in being. By this qualifier I mean that these people are helpful in resolving perpetuity problems. Included within this category would normally be the donor, potential recipients, and those entitled to prior interests. Others might have a sufficient nexus to be considered as useful in calculating the perpetuity period. For instance, a devise 'to my grandchildren who turn 21' implicates the children of the donor, since their offspring are the potential takers.

A helpful life in being can be described in another way: someone who is alive at the time of the gift and who can be used to demonstrate that vesting cannot possibly occur outside of the period. A devise 'to my grandchildren who marry during the life of X' does not violate the rule, the reference to X being crucial in this determination. Any vesting under this devise must occur during X's life. Therefore, she is a life in being who can be used to demonstrate that the gift must vest, if at all, during the perpetuity period. Consider a more subtle example – an *inter vivos* grant 'to the children of A who turn 21'. Assume that A is still alive. Here, we know that if any children are going to turn 21, they must do so no more than 21 years after the life of their parent (A). Put another way, this gift must vest,

---

169   See also C. Sappideen, "Life After Death – Sperm Banks, Wills and Perpetuities" (1979) 53 A.L.J. 311.

if it is going to vest at all, during the life of A (a life in being) plus 21 years. Remember though, the identification of what I call helpful lives in being serves merely as an aid in the solving of perpetuities problems. It does not negate the starting premise that any person alive at the time that a gift takes effect counts as a life in being.

A doctrine with such destructive capacities as the rule against perpetuities demands grudging respect. Ignore it at your peril. However, having said that, it is not a difficult matter to create interests that acknowledge the rule's cruel bent. A gift 'to my first grandchild to marry within 21 years of the death of X,Y, and Z' is valid; it permits a vesting to occur right up until the end of the perpetuity period. Importantly, the three named lives in being that I have used here do not have to be associated in any other way with the donor or donee. In a similar way, a large class of lives in being can be chosen to serve as measuring lives for the computation of the perpetuity period. For instance, a 'royal lives' clause, one that postponed vesting until 20 years after the death of the last lineal descendant of Queen Victoria, was upheld in the 1929 case of *Re Villar*.[170] When the will took effect (in 1922) there were some 120 lineal descendants, all of whom served as what I have called 'helpful' lives in being.[171] The use of royal lives clauses can be employed to ensure compliance with the common law rule. However, this technique has its limitations. The use of too large a class might be invalid on the grounds of administrative uncertainty. For example, a gift in which vesting is postponed until all persons then living are deceased would likely be found to be void.[172]

In the case of class gifts, we saw that the possibility that one member might vest outside of the period ruined the entire gift. This result can be avoided by providing that only those members of the class who meet the stated conditions within the period will be entitled to receive a share, and that latecomers are to be excluded. This would be the effect of a devise (i) 'to all my grandchildren who marry within 21 years of my death', or one that read (ii) 'to all my grandchildren, alive at my death, who marry'. In the first case it is clear that the period is confined to 21 years from the date that the devise takes effect. In the second example the only grandchildren who may take are themselves lives in being.

---

170 [1929] 1 Ch. 243 (C.A.). See also *Clay v. Karlson* (1998) 19 W.A.R. 287 (S.C.) which reviews the leading authorities.

171 It is possible that Prince Louis Ferdinand 'of Prussia', a great-great grandson of Queen Victoria, who was born in 1907, was the last life in being to pass away. He died in 1994. If so, the 21-year period has now begun to run: see T. Aldridge, ''A Prince Passes'' (1994) 138 Sol.J. 1062.

172 See *In re Moore*, [1901] 1 Ch. 936, [1900-3] All E.R.Rep. 140. The issue of administrative uncertainty is not resolved merely by determining whether or not the numbers are too large. For example, a gift that allowed for vesting 'at any time until, but not after, the last person now living has died' is probably *not* invalid on the grounds of administrative uncertainty. A potential recipient who had met the stated contingency would merely have to produce a life in being to show that the contingency had been met during the time period called for under the gift. What is required is the continued existence of a life in being who can be used to show that the vesting had happened before the period had run out. To underline the point, in this example it would never be necessary to show that all of the lives in being had died, just that one was still living.

A comparable interpretation of a gift can also result through the application of rules of construction designed to close classes prematurely.[173] A leading example is the rule in *Andrews v. Partington*,[174] under which a class will close as soon as one member is entitled to receive a share. Hence, a devise 'to all my grandchildren who marry', without more, violates the rule against perpetuities (if there are children of the testator still living). A marriage might occur after all the lives in being have died and 21 years have passed. All of the grandchildren alive when the gift takes effect are lives in being; however, another grandchild might be born afterwards (who is therefore not a life in being). That person might marry at some distant time in the future, that is, more than 21 years after the last of the lives in being had died. Therefore, at common law the whole gift is void; no grandchild can take. Now consider the impact of *Andrews v. Partington*. If one of the grandchildren had met the requirement when the will took effect (*i.e.*, by the time the donor had died) the outcome would change. The class of potential takers is then frozen (by virtue of *Andrews*). That class would include not only the one married grandchild, but all those alive when the testator died. Each such person is a life in being whose interest must vest, if at all, within their own lifetime. (Afterborn grandchildren are shut out by virtue of the operation of this class closing rule.) This rule of construction (for that is all it is[175]) creates a limitation that is the functional equivalent of example (ii) set out above.

(f) further examples

Consider an *inter vivos* transfer from 1965 that reads 'to my first grandchild to turn 21'. Does this contravene the common law rule against perpetuities? Assume that at the time of the grant the grantor had one child, a daughter aged 20. In that instance, there would be two potentially helpful lives in being: the grantor and that daughter. Imagine what might happen next: The grantor may have a child after the grant is made (say in 1966) who would not be a life in being. The two existing lives in being might then die (in 1967); the 21-year period would then begin to run and would expire in 1988. It is possible that at some point, say 1984, the second child might have a child, and if that (grand)child turned 21, this event would occur outside of the perpetuity period (in 2005). This is one possible scenario that could result in remote vesting and that is enough to destroy the gift, no matter how far-fetched this might be, or how differently the events actually turn out.

However, the same gift contained in a devise would be valid. In that case, there would be only one helpful life in being, the daughter. The testator, of course, cannot then have further children. Any child of the daughter would have to turn 21 within 21 years after the daughter's death; the devise is therefore good.[176] The

---

173 This was the effect of the rule in *Festing v. Allen*, *supra*, note 127.

174 (1791) 3 Bro.C.C. 401, 29 E.R. 610, [1775-1802] All E.R.Rep. 209. For a detailed account of the interaction between *Andrews v. Partington* and the rule against perpetuities, see J.H.C. Morris, ''The Rule Against Perpetuities and the Rule in *Andrews v. Partington*'' (1954) 70 L.Q.R. 61.

175 *In re Chapman's Settlement Trusts*, [1977] 1 W.L.R. 1163, [1978] 1 All E.R. 1122 (C.A.).

176 *Cf. Meyers v. Hamilton Provident & Loan Co.* (1890) 19 O.R. 358 (C.P.D.).

daughter serves as a life in being who can be used to demonstrate that it is impossible for the gift to vest beyond the perpetuity period. The same result would occur if the devise was 'to all of my children to reach 30' or 'to all the grandchildren of A to reach 21' provided that in the second case A had predeceased the donor;[177] if it is otherwise then the second gift fails.

Imagine now a devise, effective in 1962, that reads 'to A for life, remainder to A's widow for life, remainder in fee simple to their eldest surviving child'. Assume that A was not married when the devise was drafted or when it took effect. The remainder to the widow is contingent, since it is obvious that the donor is not referring to a specific person (sometimes referred to as a *persona designata*) but rather to an individual, presently unascertained, who may someday be the widow of A. Whether such a person will emerge to take the second life estate when A dies is unknown, but because A is a life in being the contingent gift to the widow is valid. In other words, whether there will be a widow to take the remainder will be known as soon as A (a life in being) dies.

It is the remainder in fee to the eldest child that is vulnerable to a perpetuities challenge; indeed it is void on that ground. That interest will vest, if at all, on the death of the widow; only then will it be known who, if anyone, is the surviving eldest child. But the widow may not turn out to be a life in being, for there is no guarantee that this person will have been alive at the date the limitation took effect (1962). That being so, consider this possible turn of events: in 1983, A marries B (who was born in 1963); a child, C, is born in 1984; A dies in 1985; B dies in 2007; C is still alive and is the eldest surviving child. Since the perpetuity period is based on A's life plus 21 years, the period ended in 2006 and the vesting was therefore too remote. Because this was possible from the outset, the remainder is void *ab initio*.

Finally, consider a devise that creates an otherwise valid trust for 'A's first grandchild to turn 21'. A is a woman aged 65, who has two children, B and C. Logic and medical science suggest that this would be a valid gift. A can have no more children, so any grandchildren (*i.e.*, the children of B and C) who turn 21 must do so within 21 years of the death of B and C; they are both lives in being. However, the common law rule against perpetuities does not care about the biological realities of this situation. It is enough that there is a theoretical possibility of another child being born, and that other child would not be a life in being. (This thinking was not based on the possibility that A might have adopted a child in the future, since the common law rule pre-dates legal adoptions.) That afterborn child might produce a grandchild, who might be the first grandchild to turn 21. That might occur outside of the period, which is enough to infringe the rule.

(g) reform measures

Reform of the rule against perpetuities has occurred in a number of Canadian provinces and elsewhere. Calls for change have come in response to what was seen to be the over-zealous and unrelenting nature of the common law rule. As

---

177 *Re Lawson* (1981) 33 N.B.R. (2d) 462, 80 A.P.R. 462 (Q.B.).

we have just seen, it can vitiate even those gifts that are unlikely to vest at some unacceptable point in the future. Professor Barton Leach, writing in the early 1950s, characterized the rule as giving rise to a 'slaughter of the innocents'.[178] There is some doubt as to just how many unnecessary fatalities have been caused, given that a perpetuities violation might not necessarily lead to litigation, let alone a reported judgment. Nevertheless, the examples considered above illustrate that the rule, however well-intentioned, attacks transfers that seem pretty harmless.

Several different types of reform have been tried. Under one approach the basic rule is maintained, but some problems are rectified. This tack has been taken in Alberta,[179] where the key revision has been the implementation of a 'wait and see' rule. Generally speaking, one calculates the perpetuity period in accordance with the common law rule and if the gift satisfies that standard, the inquiry ends there and the gift is treated as valid. If the gift would violate the common law rule then a perpetuity period is calculated using a statutory definition of lives in being. Then one waits to see if a timely vesting results. Moreover, realistic presumptions apply as to the capacity to have children.[180] If a violation occurs, or is inevitable, other remedial devices may then be deployed. These include a reduction of the stated age of vesting[181] and class-splitting (that is, eliminating the late vesters and preserving the gift for those members of the class who vest on time).[182] If all this fails, there is a general power to rewrite the gift to give effect to the general intention of the donor within the limits imposed by the rule against perpetuities.[183]

The Alberta model retains some of the complexity of the old rule, including the life in being formula. A more streamlined approach is to select instead a set period, usually 80 or 90 years, to serve as a proxy for the common law calculation.[184] Another mode of reform, suggested for Saskatchewan in the early 1960s,

---

178 W.B. Leach, "Perpetuities: Staying the Slaughter of the Innocents" (1952) 68 L.Q.R. 35.

179 *Perpetuities Act*, R.S.A. 1980, c. P-4, s. 5. For a critique of wait-and-see style reforms, see I.M. Bloom, "Perpetuities Refinement: There is an Alternative", 62 Wash.L.Rev. 23 (1987).

180 S. 9. A male is presumed to be able to have a child (!) at 14, but not before; for females the window is between 12 and 55. Evidence of complete incapacity may be presented. When a determination as to capacity is made but turns out to be erroneous, that determination will stand, but the court may make an order for the benefit of a child born afterwards: subs. 9(2), (3). The power to make such an order applies also to adopted or legitimated children: sub. 9(4).

181 S. 6. This age reduction rule allows the stated age to be reduced to 21, but no lower.

182 S. 7.

183 S. 8. S. 11 sets out the batting order for the application of these provisions. The order is as follows: (i) capacity to have children; (ii) wait and see; (iii) age reduction; (iv) class splitting; and (v) general *cy-près* (as s. 8 is called). S. 19 of the Alberta Act renders possibilities of reverter following a fee simple subject to the statutory rule. Under the Act, this type of possibility of reverter is rendered void on the expiration of a 40-year perpetuity period. The same rule applies to a right of re-entry.

184 The American Uniform Statutory Rule Against Perpetuities uses a 90-year period: see generally L.W. Waggoner, "The Uniform Statutory Rule Against Perpetuities: Oregon Joins Up", 26 Willamette L.J. 259 (1990); A. M. Hess, "Freeing Property from the RAP Trap: Tennessee Adopts the Uniform Statutory Rule Against Perpetuities", 62 Tenn.L.Rev. 267 (1995). See also P.G. Haskell, "A Proposal for a Simple and Socially Effective Rule Against Perpetuities", 66 N.C.L.Rev. 545 (1988); A.J. Hirsch & W.K.S. King, "A Qualitative Theory of the Dead

is to confer a general judicial power of modification for dispositions that run afoul of the rule.[185]

The wave of reform that yielded these models accepted that some type of rule against perpetuities was warranted. In 1983 the Province of Manitoba abandoned this position and abolished the rule altogether;[186] there have been recommendations in Saskatchewan and in England to do likewise.[187] In Manitoba, the policy of limiting dead hand control was not seen as spent, but the potential for unfairness, the rule's complex nature, and its limited relevancy, supported the point of view that it causes more harm than good. As a countervail, the judicial power to vary trusts was extended, and this now serves as an *ad hoc* means of controlling problems previously dealt with by the perpetuities rule, at least when trusts are involved. With the rule now dead in Manitoba, one wonders whether the general rules governing restraints on alienation – of which perpetuities law may be seen as a part[188] – may also increasingly be called into play in Manitoba in response to gifts that create enduring contingent rights.

Iland'', 68 Indiana L.J. 1 (1992). Some commercial interests are subject to an 80-year period in Alberta: see s. 18.

185 O.E. Lang, "A Perpetuities Act for Saskatchewan" (1962) 40 Can.B.Rev. 294.

186 *The Perpetuities and Accumulations Act*, R.S.M. 1987, c. P33. See further Manitoba Law Reform Commission, *Report on the Rules Against Accumulations and Perpetuities* (Winnipeg: M.L.R.C., 1982). See further R.L. Deech, "The Rule Against Perpetuities Abolished!" (1984) 4 O.J.L.S. 454; J.M. Glenn, "Perpetuities to *Purefoy*: Reform by Abolition in Manitoba" (1984) 62 Can.B.Rev. 618; A.J. McClean, "The Rule Against Perpetuities, *Saunders v. Vautier*, and Legal Future Interests Abolished" (1983) 13 Man.L.J. 245.

187 Law Reform Commission of Saskatchewan, *Proposals Relating to the Rule Against Perpetuities and Accumulations* (Saskatoon: L.R.C.S., 1987); Law Commission, *The Law of Trusts – The Rules Against Perpetuities and Excessive Accumulations* (London: H.M.S.O., 1993). Reform of the current English law is preferred in C. Emery, "Do We Need a Rule Against Perpetuities?" (1994) 57 Mod.L.Rev. 602, and P. Sparkes, "How to Simplify Perpetuities", [1995] Conv. 212. Down-sizing of the rule in some American states is briefly noted in J. Dukeminier & J. Krier, eds., *Property*, 4th ed. (New York: Aspen Law, 1998) at 316.

188 See *Cambridge Co. v. East Slope Investment Corp.*, 700 P.2d 537 (Colo.S.C., 1985).

8

LEASES, LICENCES AND BAILMENTS

I went next door
To see my friend.
Landlord won't fix the building
And the roaches let me in.

Going on a rent strike,
Got to end these blues.
Well, if the landlord don't fix the building,
Gonna have to try and move.

Jimmy Collier[1]

1. INTRODUCTION

The principal topic of this chapter is the leasehold estate. Over the last three decades significant changes in the law of residential tenancies have taken place across Canada, with the result that today there are really two 'laws' of landlord and tenant, one covering commercial property and the other residential. Although many incidental aspects of the law have been altered in the process, there remains a common structure and this will be presented here. Features of residential tenancy law reform will also be addressed.

The law of landlord and tenant is a composite of contract and property principles, for a lease can be both a contract and the basis of an estate in land. Moreover, the patterns of change in the law can be understood as oscillations between the magnetic poles of contract and property. As initially conceived, the lease was regarded as a contract, which was laid over the feudal system of freeholds. In these ignoble beginnings it served as a means of providing security for debts, the lender going into possession of the land as a tenant.[2] Increased protection for the tenant developed with the growth of a class of agrarian lease-holders, tilling the soil over which they held fragile tenancy rights.[3] Security of tenure was provided by treating the lease as a proprietary entitlement, which bound third parties and conferred exclusive possession of the demised lands on the tenant.[4] In the latter part of the twentieth century a pull back toward contract principles occurred, not so far as to deny the reification of the lease, but enough to provide a more viable set of remedies and rights for the modern era.[5] These swings will be apparent as the discussion proceeds.

---

1 "Rent Strike Blues" (1966) performed on *We Won't Move: Songs of the Tenants' Movement* (Folkways, FS5287, 1983).

2 See the brief discussion in Part 2, Chapter 11.

3 J.H. Baker, "Introduction to the Reports of Sir John Spelman" (1977) 94 Seld.Soc. 1, at 180-7.

4 W.M. McGovern, "The Historical Conception of a Lease for Years", 23 U.C.L.A.L.Rev. 501 (1976).

5 See generally D.R. Stollery, "The Lease as a Contract" (1981) 19 Alta.L.Rev. 234.

Leaseholds are used in Canada in a variety of contexts. The law studied in this chapter governs the large retail outlet in a shopping mall, the law firm in a commercial skyscraper, and also the corner grocer, or the wholesale distributor renting a warehouse in an industrial park. About 35% of Canadians live in rental accommodations.[6] Here, the law of landlord and tenant applies to luxury apartments, and to those who choose, for lifestyle reasons, to rent. It will also affect, of course, those who cannot afford to buy a house.

A review of the demographics of renters reveals some interesting patterns. On the whole, the percentage of a renter's income devoted to shelter costs has risen through the 1980s and early 1990s, though there is evidence that this is starting to stabilize.[7] Most likely to be living in rental accommodations are households that are non-elderly one-person (66% rent), multi-family (61%), and single-parent with children under the age of 18 (66.3%).[8] About half of the single parents who are renting have an affordability problem:[9]

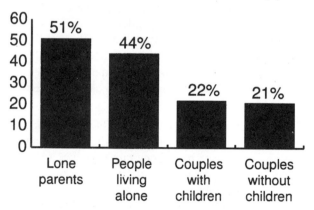

% of renter households with an affordability problem

The design of landlord and tenant law is noticeably affected by its socio-economic context. In this realm, apartment owners are generally pitted against an economically weaker renting population, composed mainly of low income earners, the young, and the elderly, all of whom tend to devote large portions of their income toward paying the rent; many live in units that form part of a decaying infrastructure. The economic power of tenants increases along with the vacancy

---

6 Statistics Canada, *Households by Dwelling Characteristics*, as reproduced in <www.statcan.ca>.

7 Statistics Canada, Household Facilities by Income and Other Characteristics (Cat.13-218, 1996) at 18-9.

8 *Ibid.* at 19.

9 O. Lo & P. Gauthier, "Housing Affordability Problems Among Renters", Canadian Social Trends (Spring, 1995) 14, at 17.

rate, and is diminished as units become scarce. Legal regimes sometimes attempt to alter the balance of power by conferring statutory protections on leaseholders. Whether these measures are adequate or necessary is something that might be considered when the reform of residential tenancy law is reviewed below.[10]

Leases are often contrasted with licences, and the nature and importance of this distinction will be considered below. The issues here involve the dividing line between personal and proprietary rights and the proper place of the licence within this dichotomy. The chapter concludes with an analysis of bailments, or leases of chattels, as these might (imprecisely) be called. Some comparisons will be drawn between the basic law of landlord and tenant and this personal property counterpart.

2.   THE NATURE OF A LEASE[11]

A lease is a demise of land under which exclusive occupation is conferred by a landlord on a tenant. A leasehold estate, as with all estates, delimits the duration of the tenant's holdings. While the lease continues in force the landlord retains a reversionary interest; the landlord's right to actual possession is suspended during the term of the tenancy. This is not a true reversion of the freehold, for even while the lease is in existence the landlord remains 'seised' of the land.[12] However, the relationship is tenurial: the tenant holds of the landlord.[13]

(a)   five types of leases

A lease may exist for a *fixed term*. Although this is sometimes referred to as a 'term of years', it may last for any interval, however irregular or lengthy. The term must be certain as to both its date of commencement[14] and termination. For instance, a lease that is stated to last for the "duration of [the] war" [15] fails to

---

10 In Part 6, *infra*.

11 See generally C. Bentley *et al.*, *Williams & Rhodes Canadian Law of Landlord and Tenant*, 6th ed. (Toronto: Carswell, 1988) (looseleaf).

12 Seisin, it will be recalled, is the possession of a freeholder: see Part 2(a), Chapter 2.

13 S. 3 of the *Commercial Tenancies Act*, R.S.O. 1990, c. L.7 [as am.], provides that the relationship between a landlord and tenant does not depend on tenure, and a reversion is not necessary before the incidents of that relationship are applicable. The origins and function of this enigmatic provision are explained in R.J. Balfour, ed., *Landlord and Tenant Law* (Toronto: Emond Montgomery, 1991) at 43*ff*.

14 *Reinhart v. Bast* (1966) 57 W.W.R. 757, 59 D.L.R. (2d) 746 (Sask.Q.B.); *Omsac Developments Ltd. v. Colebourne* (1976) 28 O.R. (2d) 455, 110 D.L.R. (3d) 766 (H.C.); *Hillmond Investments Ltd. v. Peel (Regional Municipality)* (1992) 23 R.P.R. (2d) 161 (Ont.Gen.Div.). *Cf. Canada Square Corp. v. VS Services Ltd.* (1981) 34 O.R. (2d) 250, 15 B.L.R. 89, 130 D.L.R. (3d) 205 (C.A.). See also the review of the authorities in that case. The starting date of the lease must at least be ascertainable.

15 *Trerise v. Evanocke* (1944) 60 B.C.R. 301, [1944] 3 W.W.R. 319, [1944] 3 D.L.R. 220 (S.C.); *Lace v. Chantler*, [1944] K.B. 368, [1944] 1 All E.R. 305 (C.A.). See also *Casson v. Handisyde* (1974) 3 O.R. (2d) 471 (Co.Ct); *Prudential Assurance Co. v. London Residuary Body*, [1992] 2 A.C. 386, [1992] 3 All E.R. 504 (H.L.) discussed in P. Sparkes, "Certainty of Leasehold Terms" (1993) 109 L.Q.R. 93.

meet this standard.[16] Likewise, a lease that is stated to end "on the 31st day of December in the year of the Lessor's death" does not achieve the required level of certainty.[17] In contrast, a lease with a stated fixed terminal date, but which may be ended prematurely on the happening of a specified event, is valid. It is the maximum length that must be certain. A lease 'for life' is not governed by this requirement, because, at common law,[18] this creates a freehold interest (a life estate). As a matter of convention, when property is conferred for life without a rent being exacted, this is referred to as a life estate. Where rent is payable the interest is frequently described as a lease for life.[19]

A *periodic tenancy* is one that is to be enjoyed for some recurring unit of time (*e.g.*, month by month) that, in the normal course, continues until terminated by notice. Unless otherwise agreed to, or altered by statute,[20] the notice required is equivalent to the length of the tenancy period, although in the case of a yearly tenancy, a six-month notice is the rule at common law. A periodic tenancy may arise from inference, such as when the tenant under a fixed term lease remains in possession and pays a rent that is accepted by the landlord.[21]

A *tenancy at will* has no set period or term and continues only so long as both landlord and tenant wish. Either may bring the tenancy to an end by notice, even if this right is stated to be at the sole prerogative of the lessor.[22] The creation of such a tenancy may be implied. For instance, when a tenant remains on the premises after the expiration of a previous tenancy with the landlord's consent the law may imply that a tenancy at will has arisen. If so, the terms of the original lease apply in so far as these are compatible with the new arrangement.[23] Under appropriate circumstances the payment and acceptance of rent will convert a tenancy at will into a periodic tenancy, if this can be fairly implied from the circumstances.[24] Even if no rent obligation is expressed, a tenant at will may be liable to a claim based on use and occupation. Just as a tenancy at will can arise by implication, so may it be ended in this way. In other words, the notice to

---

16 The same would be true of a lease that is stated to last until the lessee of a service station has purchased a specified amount of gasoline from the landlord: *Shell Canada Ltd. v. Shafie* (1989) 93 N.S.R. (2d) 115, 242 A.P.R. 115 (T.D.).

17 *Black v. Blair Athol Farms Ltd.* (1996) 110 Man.R. (2d) 84, [1996] 5 W.W.R. 516, 118 W.A.C. 84 (C.A.).

18 *Cf. Life Lease Act*, S.M. 1998, c. 42, proclaimed in force as of December 1, 1999. See also J. MacLennan & I. Ellingham, "Issues of Life Tenure Housing in Ontario" (1999) 27 R.P.R. (3d) 269. Can a lease for 90 years 'unless the tenant shall die beforehand' qualify as a leasehold grant?

19 See *Greco v. Swinburne Ltd.*, [1991] 1 V.R. 304 (S.C.) and the authorities cited there. See also *Jones v. Jones* (1868) L.R. 4 C.P. 422, at 424 (*per* Bovill C.J.): "Most persons who hold property on a lease for life consider it a leasehold, and it is only the strict law which calls it [a] freehold".

20 See, *e.g.*, *Residential Tenancies Act*, R.S.A. 1980, c. R-15.3, ss. 4-7.

21 *Young v. Bank of Nova Scotia* (1915) 34 O.L.R. 176, 23 D.L.R. 854 (C.A.).

22 *Winslow v. Nugent* (1903) 36 N.B.R. 356 (C.A.) at 358.

23 *Newfoundland (Attorney General) v. Newfoundland Quick Freeze Ltd.* (1980) 14 R.P.R. 5, 30 Nfld. & P.E.I.R. 139, 84 A.P.R. 139 (Nfld.T.D.).

24 See, *e.g.*, *Rocca Group Ltd. v. Margaris* (1978) 21 N.B.R. (2d) 562, 37 A.P.R. 562 (C.A.).

terminate need not be express and the conduct of either party may demonstrate that the tenancy is being treated as if it is over.[25]

A *tenancy at sufferance* arises when a tenant remains on the premises without permission after the termination of one of the other types of tenancies. Unlike all other forms, a tenancy at sufferance is non-consensual and in fact does not produce a tenurial relationship; its classification as a tenancy is therefore questionable. Moreover, even though there is no obligation to pay rent, the overholding tenant will be liable to the landlord for use and occupation of the premises.

Generally speaking, a *perpetual lease*, with no fixed term or stated period, no right of termination on notice, and which can accordingly last forever, is not tenable at common law. An attempt to confer such an interest is treated as creating either a yearly periodic tenancy or an outright sale of the freehold to which a rentcharge might be attached instead of a leasehold rent.[26] (As we will soon see, such an arrangement cannot amount to a licence if exclusive possession is granted.) Still, perpetual leases are found in the law. In some Australian states the Crown has granted land in the form of perpetual leases instead of fee simple estates and this has produced a wide array of tenures in those jurisdictions.[27] The same power to create special forms of tenure exists in Canada.[28] Moreover, a lease for a term of years may validly provide for a perpetual right of renewal.[29]

(b) essential and formal elements

An unimpeachable lease should contain a demise of exclusive possession, plus the identification of the parties, the property, the term, the date of commencement, and the rent (if any[30]) to be paid.[31] The common law does not establish any strict formal requirement for the creation of a lease. And because a leaseholder cannot be seised of land, the rule prohibiting grants *in futuro*[32] does not apply. A lease can therefore be granted to take effect at some designated later date. However, at common law, the tenant holds only an *interesse termini*, an interest in the term, until possession is taken. This remains true in those Canadian jurisdictions in which the *interesse termini* has not been abolished.[33] Functionally, a tenant holding a mere *interesse termini* may not maintain an action for use and occu-

---

25 See, *e.g.*, *Doe d. Lyon v. Slavin* (1846) 5 N.B.R. 258 (C.A.); *Henderson v. Harper* (1845) 1 U.C.Q.B. 481 (Full Ct.); *Brewing v. Berryman* (1873) 15 N.B.R. 115 (C.A.).

26 *Wotherspoon v. Canadian Pacific Ltd.*, [1987] 1 S.C.R. 952, 45 R.P.R. 138, 39 D.L.R. (4th) 169.

27 See A. Bradbrook *et al.*, *Australian Real Property Law*, 2nd ed. (Sydney: Law Book Co., 1997) ch. 6.

28 *Wotherspoon v. Canadian Pacific Ltd.*, *supra*, note 26.

29 See *Clinch v. Pernette* (1895) 24 S.C.R. 385, at 393.

30 Rent is not an essential element of a lease: *Ashburn Anstalt v. W.J. Arnold & Co.*, [1989] Ch. 1, [1988] 2 All E.R. 147 (C.A.). See also *British American Oil Co. v. DePass*, [1960] O.R. 71, 21 D.L.R. (2d) 110 (C.A.) leave to appeal to S.C.C. refused [1960] O.R. 82n.

31 See *607113 Alberta Ltd. v. Saskatoon Business College Ltd.* (1996) 8 R.P.R. (3d) 186, [1997] 1 W.W.R. 583, 149 Sask.R. 174 (Q.B.). See also *Ossory Canada Inc. v. Wendy's Restaurants of Canada Inc.* (1997) 36 O.R. (3d) 483, 16 R.P.R. (3d) 204 (C.A.).

32 See Part 4(a)(ii), Chapter 7.

33 See, *e.g.*, *Law of Property Act*, R.S.A. 1980, c. L-8, s. 59.3 [as am.].

pation, trespass,[34] or for breach of the covenant of quiet enjoyment. Nonetheless, the tenant's interest in the property is binding on third parties.[35]

Formal requirements were introduced in the *Statute of Frauds, 1677*,[36] which provides that leases must be in writing and signed by the lessor (or an agent). Failing this, the Statute provides that a tenancy at will is created if the tenant takes possession with the landlord's consent. The requirement of some form of writing does not apply to leases of less than three years, if the rent to be paid is at least two-thirds of the annual value of the premises.[37] Some of these requirements were altered by the English *Real Property Act, 1845*,[38] which provides that a lease required to be in writing is void unless made by deed. Likewise, in Alberta the *Land Titles Act* states that when land is demised for a term of more than three years (or for life) the owner must execute a lease in the prescribed form and the document must identify the land sufficiently.[39]

As with other measures taken under the *Statute of Frauds*, the Statute itself (and the 1845 Act, *etc.*) can produce unfairness, because the absence of formal compliance can undermine a perfectly fair and otherwise unimpeachable contract. In response, several principles have emerged to mitigate the impact of non-compliance. If a tenant enters into possession under a void lease and pays rent (and if it is accepted by the landlord), a periodic or yearly tenancy is presumed by the common law; the term of that lease will depend upon the basis on which the rent is paid. Covenants in the void lease that are consistent with the presumed lease will be implied as part of the arrangement.

Equity may also intervene. Under the principle in *Walsh v. Lonsdale*[40] an agreement for a lease is treated as an equitable demise: this is an application of the maxim 'equity regards as done that which ought to be done'.[41] (Even a verbal agreement may be enforced in equity as an agreement for a lease if there are sufficient acts of part performance that can serve to prove the existence of the

---

34 But see *St. Leger v. Manahan* (1836) 5 U.C.Q.B. (o.s.) 89 (Full. Ct.).

35 *Cleveland v. Boice* (1862) 21 U.C.Q.B. 609.

36 29 Cha. 2, c. 3, s. 1.

37 Compare the wording of the Ontario Statute, which provides that the exception is only satisfied if the rent "amounts to at least two-thirds of the full improved value of the thing demised": *Statute of Frauds*, R.S.O. 1990, c. S.19, s. 3. This has been taken to mean rental not sale value: *Hoj Industries Ltd. v. Dundas Shepard Square Ltd.* (1978) 23 O.R. (2d) 295, 95 D.L.R. (3d) 354 (Co.Ct.). The Court held that even though a lease fell within the exception, it was still necessary to comply with s. 4 of the Ontario *Statute of Frauds*, which requires the existence of a note or memorandum in writing signed by the party to be charged. It has been held that a lease for less than three years with an option to renew for a duration that would take the total term beyond three years is not caught by the writing requirement: *Roman Catholic Episcopal Corp. de St. Albert v. R.J. Sheppard & Co.* (1913) 6 Alta.L.R. 128, 3 W.W.R. 814, 9 D.L.R. 619 (S.C.). See *contra Pain v. Dixon* (1923) 52 O.L.R. 347, [1923] 3 D.L.R. 1167 (H.C.).

38 8 & 9 Vict., c. 106, s. 3.

39 *Land Titles Act*, R.S.A. 1980, c. L-5, subs. 98(1), (2).

40 (1882) 21 Ch.D. 9 (C.A.).

41 Whether a given document is a lease or merely an agreement for a lease may depend on whether the accord purports to effect a present demise, or whether it contemplates that some further document (*i.e.*, the lease) be drawn up: see *Kyle v. Stocks* (1871) 31 U.C.Q.B. 47 (Full Ct.).

agreement.[42]) By virtue of the *Walsh v. Lonsdale* doctrine it is sometimes said that an agreement for a lease is as good as a lease, but that is not strictly accurate. When the doctrine applies it gives rise to an equitable, not a legal, leasehold interest.[43] When the terms of an agreement for a lease that is enforceable in equity are at variance with the lease presumed at common law (as mentioned in the paragraph above), the rights and obligations recognized by equity will prevail; this accords with general principles that were described earlier.[44]

(c)   leases v. licences

A lease is a grant of exclusive possession: this is the key feature that distinguishes a lease from a licence.[45] The juridical differences between these two entitlements can be significant. A lease creates an interest in land; the grant of a licence, without more, does not. A licence is merely a permission to do that which would otherwise amount to a trespass.[46] Therefore, a licensee does not have standing to sue in trespass; a licence is not binding on a purchaser of the land over which the licence is granted; the right to revoke a licence may (and often will) differ from the principles governing the termination of tenancies; and a licensee of residential premises may not (there is provincial variation here) enjoy the panoply of statutory protections afforded to residential tenants.

The disparity between the protections given to a tenant and those available to a licensee has been particularly acute in England. A mass of jurisprudence from that jurisdiction on the lease–licence distinction has grown in response to attempts by landlords to avoid statutory protections (designed for tenants) through the creation of residential licences. Some of these avoidance manoeuvres have, in turn, been countered by judicial attempts to confine their ambit. Of course, this interplay represents a larger dynamic: property rules are sometimes finessed by artful dodgers wishing to avoid the full impact of the law. This phenomenon was

---

42 See further *Starlite Variety Stores Ltd. v. Cloverlawn Investments Ltd.* (1978) 22 O.R. (2d) 104, 5 B.L.R. 215, 92 D.L.R. (3d) 270 (H.C.) affirmed (1979) 26 O.R. (2d) 394n (C.A.).

43 Accord *Chan v. Cresdon Pty. Ltd.* (1989) 168 C.L.R. 242, 89 A.L.R. 522 (Aust.H.C.). The contrary view is that since the fusion of the courts of law and equity an agreement for a lease creates a legal interest. In my opinion this is based on a misunderstanding of the effect of the *Judicature Acts*, which produced a procedural fusion of law and equity while leaving these two cognate bodies of doctrine separate. See further *Chan v. Cresdon Pty. Ltd.*, *ibid.* But see P. Sparkes, "*Walsh v. Lonsdale*: The Non-Fusion Fallacy" (1988) 8 O.J.L.S. 350. See also S. Gardner, "Equity, Estate Contracts and the Judicature Acts: *Walsh v. Lonsdale* Revisited" (1987) 7 O.J.L.S. 60; and Part 4(a), Chapter 6.

44 See Part 4(a), Chapter 6.

45 See, *e.g.*, *Metro-Matic Services Ltd. v. Hulman* (1973) 4 O.R. (2d) 462, 48 D.L.R. (3d) 326 (C.A.). A question may also arise as to whether a lease or a *profit à prendre* has been created: see, *e.g.*, *Nywening v. Melton Holdings Ltd.* (1998) 16 R.P.R. (3d) 302, 58 Alta.L.R. (3d) 333, [1998] 7 W.W.R. 317 (Q.B.) (lease found); *OH Ranch Ltd. v. Patton* (1996) 5 R.P.R. (3d) 29, 43 Alta.L.R. (3d) 445, 138 D.L.R. (4th) 381 (C.A.) (same). Profits are discussed in Part 3, Chapter 10.

46 See further Part 7, *infra*.

first illustrated in the learning relating to the *Statute of Uses,*[47] and it is readily apparent in this context as well.[48]

In the leading English decision of *Street v. Mountford*[49] exclusive possession was found to lie at the heart of the lease–licence distinction. If exclusive possession has been conferred then, generally, the interest granted is a tenancy. Past Canadian decisions seem to have waffled between this approach and one that centres on the more general issue of whether a personal or a proprietary right was intended. However, it seems that, as in England, the fundamental criterion is whether exclusive possession has been conferred on the transferee.[50]

The English courts have said that whether exclusive possession has been granted is resolved not only by looking at the terms of the lease but also at other attendant circumstances. It is not enough simply to label the arrangement a licence or a lease. The question is one of substance and not form,[51] though this is not to say that the language contained in the document is irrelevant.[52] Moreover, the inquiry in England extends beyond the four corners of the signed documents. For this reason, the inclusion of the incantation that 'the tenant shall not have exclusive possession' does not necessarily create a licence. If such a term is a sham, not meant to reflect the reality of the situation, and if the tenant in fact enjoys exclusive rights and was really meant to, then a tenancy will be found. Even if the landlord reserves the right to place additional lodgers in the premises, or to stay there personally at whim from time to time, this will not invariably mean that exclusive possession has been withheld. A factor in this determination is whether one can realistically expect that these powers will be exercised. If the leased premises are too small to be used in this way it is likely that the rights that have been reserved will be treated as a (failed) smokescreen.[53]

The judgments in *Street v. Mountford* recognize that while there is no tenancy without exclusive possession, one may still enjoy exclusive possession without

---

47 See Parts 3(b) to (e), Chapter 6.

48 See further D. McBarnett, ''Law, Policy, and Legal Avoidance: Can Law Effectively Implement Egalitarian Policies?'' (1988) 15 Law & Soc.Rev. 113; S.S. Juss, *Judicial Discretion and the Right to Property* (London: Pinter, 1998) ch. 4.

49 [1985] A.C. 809, [1985] 2 All E.R. 289 (H.L.). The most recent ruling from the House of Lords on this issue is *Bruton v. London & Quadrant Housing Trust*, [1999] 3 W.L.R. 150 (H.L.) where *Street v. Mountford* was applied.

50 See, *e.g.*, *Wal-Mac Amusements Ltd. v. Jimmy's Dining & Sports Lounge (Receivership)* (1997) 200 A.R. 31, 146 W.A.C. 31, [1997] 7 W.W.R. 358 (C.A.); *Naegele v. Oke* (1916) 37 O.L.R. 61, 31 D.L.R. 501 (C.A.) at 504 D.L.R.; *Metro-Matic Services v. Hulman, supra*, note 45. See also *Pacific Wash-a-Matic Ltd. v. R.O. Booth Holdings Ltd.*, [1979] 6 W.W.R. 458, 105 D.L.R. (3d) 323 (B.C.C.A.); *Phillips v. Glenwood Lumber Co.* (1904) 8 Nfld. R. vii (appendix) (P.C.). *Cf. Read Marketing Inc. v. British Columbia (Minister of Transportation and Highways)* (1995) 56 L.C.R. 55 (B.C.Exprop.Comm.Bd.), where the element of exclusive possession does not appear to be treated as the paramount concern.

51 *Street v. Mountford, supra*, note 49; *Reliance Petroleum Ltd. v. Rosenblood*, [1953] O.W.N. 115 (Co.Ct.).

52 See *Metro-Matic Services Ltd. v. Hulman, supra*, note 45.

53 See generally *A.G. Securities v. Vaughan; Antoniades v. Villiers*, [1990] 1 A.C. 417, [1988] 3 All E.R. 1058 (H.L.); *Westminster City Council v. Clarke*, [1992] A.C. 288, [1992] 1 All E.R. 695 (H.L.).

being a tenant. Exclusivity can be enjoyed by the owner in fee simple (or a life tenant), a trespasser, a mortgagee in possession, or a service occupier (such as a building superintendent). These people are not tenants; nor are individuals who are in occupation under circumstances that are not intended to give rise to legal obligations, including those occupying under some family arrangement or by virtue of an act of charity.[54] Additionally, a resident may be considered a lodger, and not a tenant, if the owner provides services for the living unit that require, for their performance, regular access to the premises. This last qualification is no more than a reiteration of the requirement of exclusive possession as the *sine qua non* of a lease.

The intensity of the struggle between occupiers and owners in England may not be as apparent in the reported Canadian jurisprudence, but the implications of the distinction can be just as substantial. The chasm between the rights of tenants and licensees is still great in some provinces. As a result, rooming house lodgers, part of a lamentably large underclass in some large Canadian cities, gain no solace or protection from laws designed only for 'tenants' and not licensees.

Some provinces have amended their residential tenancy legislation to include lodgers. Until 1992, Alberta law defined residential premises as ''a self-contained dwelling unit used for residential purposes''.[55] Not only was the typical lodger excluded by this definition, but even when exclusive possession was granted to a designated space, the arrangement fell outside the purview of the Act if the lodger did not live in a self-contained unit. The law now defines residential premises as ''any place occupied by an individual as a residence'', and a tenant as a ''person who is permitted to occupy residential premises under a residential tenancy agreement''.[56] This wording appears to include lodgers, a view that is fortified by the explicit exclusion of hotel guests from the application of the Act.[57] But such a reading assumes that the stated requirement of occupation does not import a test of *exclusive* possession. Far clearer is the current Ontario definition, which provides that ''residential unit'' includes ''a boarding house, rooming house or lodging house and a unit in a care home''.[58]

3.   ASSIGNMENTS AND SUBLEASES

(a)   the effect at law and in equity

Under the common law a tenant's interest is freely alienable and may be assigned or sublet as long as there is no term in the lease to the contrary. An

54 See, *e.g.*, *Rutherford v. Cross* (1931) 39 O.W.N. 495 (C.A.). See also *Gray v. Taylor*, [1998] 1 W.L.R. 1093, [1998] 4 All E.R. 17 (C.A.). But see *Family Housing Association v. Jones*, [1990] 1 All E.R. 397 (C.A.) noted in J. Warburton, ''Leases, Licences and 'an Object of Charity' '', [1990] Conv. 397.

55 *Landlord and Tenant Act*, R.S.A. 1980, c. L-6, para. 1(e). See also *Maxwell v. Brown* (1982) 35 O.R. (2d) 770 (Co.Ct.).

56 *Residential Tenancies Act*, R.S.A. 1980, c. R-15.3, paras. 1(e), (l) [as am.]

57 Para. 2(2)(d) [as am.].

58 *Tenant Protection Act, 1997*, S.O. 1997, c. 24, sub. 1(1) (definition of ''residential unit''). See also the definition of ''rental unit''. Encompassed also by these two definitions is a mobile home and a land lease home.

assignment occurs when the tenant's full interest in the lease is conveyed. A transfer of a shorter period, even if only one day less than the full term, creates a sublease. Of course, it does not matter what the parties have called the transaction; it is the extent of the rights granted that determines the correct characterization.[59]

An assignee acquires the estate initially held by the original (or head) tenant. That tenant remains liable to the (head) landlord on the basis of privity of contract,[60] unless the original parties to the lease agree to some other arrangement.[61] Privity of contract does not exist between the landlord and the assignee. However, there is a direct tenurial relationship between the two – a *privity of estate* exists between them – and this affects greatly the rights and obligations that obtain between the original landlord and the new tenant by assignment.[62] Not all of the terms contained in the head lease will apply: under the rule in *Spencer's Case*[63] only the 'real covenants' in the original lease will run with the transfer of that lease into the hands of the assignee. Liability for the assignee will end if that person later transfers his or her interest under the lease fully.[64] Comparable rules apply when the landlord assigns the reversionary interest in the property.[65] If that occurs the new landlord does not share privity of contract with the original tenant, but they are in privity of estate with one another.

Real covenants are rather hard to define precisely. Covenants that 'touch and concern' the land, and that affect the landlord *qua* landlord, or the tenant *qua* tenant, fall within the meaning of the concept. However, this terse description doesn't say much. In essence, the underlying notion is that covenants of a personal nature entered into between the original landlord and tenant do not apply to the new relationship. Real covenants relate to the subject-matter of the lease; they are terms that affect the nature, quality or value of the land, or the use to which it may be put.[66] Further, real covenants are those that would lose most of their usefulness if they were no longer connected to the land. If the value of a contractual

---

59 See further *Pin's Buildland Investment Ltd. v. Von Dehn* (1991) 54 B.C.L.R. (2d) 222, 16 R.P.R. (2d) 59, 77 D.L.R. (4th) 566 (C.A.).

60 *Haines v. Garson* (1942) 16 M.P.R. 476, [1943] 2 D.L.R. 525 (N.B.K.B.) at 529 D.L.R.; *McCrohan v. Edwards*, [1927] 1 W.W.R. 9, [1927] 1 D.L.R. 490 (Alta.S.C.); *Athan Holdings Ltd. v. Merchant Holdings* (1982) 40 A.R. 199 (Chambers); *Norwich Union Life Insurance Ltd. v. Low Profile Fashions Ltd.*, [1992] 1 E.G.L.R. 86 (C.A.).

61 *Hum v. Mosher* (1977) 33 N.S.R. (2d) 135, 57 A.P.R. 135 (Co.Ct.) at 143.

62 The principles considered here are in addition to those affecting the contractual assignment of benefits, and the rules governing the running of covenants, as discussed in Chapter 10.

63 (1583) 5 Co. Rep. 16a, 77 E.R. 72, [1558-1774] All E.R.Rep. 68.

64 *Dambrill v. Dunscome* (1818) Nfld.S.C., reproduced in R.A. Tucker, ed., *Select Cases of Newfoundland* (Toronto: Carswell, 1979) 91.

65 This principle was introduced in the *Grantees of Reversions Act, 1540*, 32 Hen. 8, c. 34, which pre-dates *Spencer's Case*. In Alberta, a person who acquires the landlord's or the tenant's interest has all the rights and is subject to all of the obligations based on the real covenants relating to the tenancy, during the time that the interest is held: *Law of Property Act*, R.S.A. 1980, c. L-8, s. 59.21 [as am.]. Hence, the two early sources have been replaced and the positions of the landlord and tenant have been made identical.

66 See *P & A Swift Investments v. Combined English Stores Group Plc.*, [1989] A.C. 632, [1988] 2 All E.R. 885 (H.L.) at 642 A.C. See also *Merger Restaurants v. D.M.E. Foods Ltd.* (1990) 12 R.P.R. (2d) 261, [1990] 5 W.W.R. 489, 71 D.L.R. (4th) 356 (Man.C.A.) leave to appeal to S.C.C. refused (1991) 79 D.L.R. (4th) vii (note) (S.C.C.).

term would evaporate if it were severed from the property, that promise is likely to be viewed as a real covenant.[67]

Some covenants are destined to run with the land, including obligations to repair,[68] or pay rent,[69] or restrictions on the right to assign and sublet.[70] Conversely, an undertaking by the landlord to purchase chattels belonging to the tenant at the end of the lease is personal to the contracting parties and so will not usually run.[71] However, there is a peripheral area of vagueness here. A promise by a retail-lessee to buy products from the supplier-landlord runs with the land,[72] but a covenant by the landlord not to establish a competing business within a specified radius of the leased property may not.[73] An option to renew the leasehold will pass,[74] but not a mere privilege to renew a lease,[75] nor a right to purchase the (freehold) reversion.[76]

There is a paucity of Canadian case law on the application of the touching and concerning requirement, a fact that may be explained by the practice of landlords to require that a new lease be entered into with assignees of the original tenant.[77] When that is done, a new landlord and tenant relationship is struck between the landlord and the original tenant's assignee, creating both privity of contract and estate. Even if this approach is commonly followed when one tenant is replaced by another, this is less likely to occur when it is the reversion that is transferred by the landlord to a new owner of the freehold.[78] Unless the incoming landlord enters into fresh leases with all existing tenants, the ensuing relationships will be based on the rules governing privity of estate and the running of covenants.

So thorny is the distinction between real and 'other' covenants that it has been proposed that it be scrapped. This is the position taken by the Manitoba Law Reform Commission, which has recommended that all covenants contained in a lease, even those involving personal services, should pass on an assignment.[79]

---

67 *P & A Swift Investments v. Combined English Stores Group Plc.*, supra, note 66. See also *Coronation St. Industrial Properties Ltd. v. Ingall Industries Plc.*, [1989] 1 W.L.R. 304, [1989] 1 All E.R. 979 (H.L.).

68 *Perry v. Bank of Upper Canada* (1866) 16 U.C.C.P. 404 (Full Ct.).

69 *Parker v. Webb* (1693) 3 Salk. 5, 91 E.R. 656.

70 *Goldstein v. Sanders*, [1915] 1 Ch. 549; *In re Robert Stephenson & Co.*, [1915] 1 Ch. 802.

71 *Gorton v. Gregory* (1862) 3 B. & S. 90, 122 E.R. 35 (Ex.Ch.).

72 *Clegg v. Hands* (1890) 44 Ch.D. 503. See also *Rudd v. Manahan* (1913) 5 Alta.L.R. 19, 4 W.W.R. 350, 11 D.L.R. 37 (C.A.).

73 *Thomas v. Haywood* (1869) L.R. 4 Ex. 311. *Cf. Coast-to-Coast Industrial Developments Ltd. v. Gorhim Holdings Ltd.* (1960) 22 D.L.R. (2d) 695 (Ont.H.C.).

74 *Rogers v. National Drug & Chemical Co.* (1911) 24 O.L.R. 486 (C.A.).

75 *Alexander v. Herman* (1912) 21 O.W.R. 461, 2 D.L.R. 239 (H.C.).

76 *Woodall v. Clifton*, [1905] 2 Ch. 257, [1904-07] All E.R.Rep. 268 (C.A.).

77 N. Bankes & N. Rafferty, "A Tenant's Remedies for a Landlord's Breach: The Impact of *Lehndorff Canadian Pension Properties Ltd. v. Davis Management Ltd.*" (1990) 24 U.B.C.L.Rev. 155, at 166, n. 38.

78 See further the catalogues of covenants that do and do not run with the land in C. Bentley *et al.*, *Williams & Rhodes Canadian Law of Landlord and Tenant*, 6th ed. (Toronto: Carswell, 1988) (looseleaf) vol. 2, at 15-78ff.

79 Manitoba Law Reform Commission, *Covenants in Commercial Tenancies* (Winnipeg: M.L.R.C., 1995) at 35-9.

This would render the effect of an assignment more certain, and would probably accord with the expectations of the parties to the assignment. Under the Manitoba proposals only covenants contained in the lease would pass and not collateral contracts. This might raise questions as to whether a given personal covenant falls within 'the lease' (whatever that may mean), which may raise new problems in the drawing of a bright line between the promises that pass to an assignee and those that do not.

Different principles apply if the assignee of the tenant acquires purely equitable rights.[80] Equitable interests may be involved either because the assigned interest was initially equitable or by virtue of the fact that the assignment is enforceable only in equity (perhaps owing to some formal defect). The concept of privity of estate is foreign to equity; but without it, *Spencer's Case* does not apply. That being so, the basic position in equity is this: an assignment of the tenant's interest that is valid only in equity transfers the benefits of the term to the assignee (which can be enforced against the original landlord), but none of the burdens.[81]

This state of affairs seems to put the landlord in an awful position; in actuality it is not that serious. A breach of the original lease giving rise to a right of forfeiture may entitle the landlord to terminate the initial tenancy. The original lease still exists, of course, and the landlord does not lose the right to recover the land just because an equitable assignment has occurred. With this termination, the assignee is also without an estate. To avoid that result, one can see that an assignee might well wish to comply with the terms of the head lease in order to ensure that the tenancy remains on foot. In addition, the assignee may be bound by restrictive covenants. As we will see in Chapter 10, these covenants can be enforceable even absent both privity of contract or estate.[82] It is also conceivable that a new lease or periodic tenancy will be implied simply by the payment of rent by the new tenant (in equity) to the original landlord. There is support for this viewpoint;[83] it seems logical.[84]

A sublease involves fewer complications. Here it is clear that the original landlord and subtenant have no direct relationship under either privity of contract or estate. The sublessor (the original tenant) retains a leasehold interest, having carved out only a portion of it through the granting of the sublease. The direct tenurial and contractual relationship between the head landlord and tenant remains intact. However, the sublease is dependent on the continued existence of the main lease and, as we saw in relation to an equitable assignee of the tenant, if the main

---

80 See generally R.J. Smith, ''The Running of Covenants in Equitable Leases and Equitable Assignments of Legal Leases'', [1978] C.L.J. 98.

81 See *contra Boyer v. Warbey*, [1953] 1 Q.B. 234, [1953] 1 All E.R. 269 (C.A.). See also *Rogers v. National Drug & Chemical Co.*, *supra*, note 74.

82 Restrictive covenants are considered in Chapter 10.

83 See further K. Gray, *Elements of Land Law*, 2nd ed. (London: Butterworths, 1993) at 871-3. *Cf.* R.E. Megarry & H.W.R. Wade, *The Law of Real Property*, 5th ed. (London: Stevens & Sons, 1984) at 665-6.

84 In Alberta, this problem *may* have been eliminated by s. 59.21 [as am.] of the *Law of Property Act*, R.S.A. 1980, c. L-8.

lease is terminated, the common law rule is that the sublease also ceases to exist. Consequently, it is usually in the subtenant's interest to avoid conduct that contravenes the head lease.[85]

(b) limits on a tenant's right to alienate

Leases frequently restrict the tenant's powers of alienation. These may take the form of (i) an absolute prohibition; (ii) a right to transfer conditioned on the consent of the landlord;[86] or (iii) a right of transfer conditioned on the consent of the landlord that is qualified in some manner. Typically, the third type of clause provides that the landlord's consent shall not be unreasonably withheld.[87] Specific grounds for refusal may also be expressly set out in the lease.[88] In some jurisdictions, the qualification that the landlord's refusal must be based on reasonable grounds is implied under statute, either as a rule of construction or law.[89]

A landlord's right of refusal creates a potential clog on alienability. We have seen how the right of alienation is regarded as an important stick in the bundle of property rights and how transferability is treated as essential to the operation of an economically efficient property regime.[90] So, while landlords are entitled to restrict a tenant's right to sell or lease, such terms are construed strictly. Accordingly, it has been held that a prohibition on assigning and subletting does not prevent the granting of a mere licence,[91] or a sharing of the property.[92] Given these rulings, tenants may wish to transfer rights under a licence arrangement.

---

85 In some provinces the sublessee can be protected against a forfeiture of the head lease: see, *e.g.*, *Commercial Tenancies Act*, R.S.O. 1990, c. L.7, s. 21.

86 This, in substance, is the same as the first form, since the landlord can always unilaterally waive the absolute prohibition.

87 There is American case law suggesting that a reasonableness requirement should be implied when the consent of the landlord is required under a commercial lease: see, *e.g.*, *Kendall v. Ernest Pestana, Inc.*, 709 P.2d 837 (Cal.S.C., 1985). This is not yet the majority rule. See generally A.M. Johnson, "Correctly Interpreting Long-Term Leases Pursuant to Modern Contract Law: Toward a Theory of Relational Leases", 74 Va.L.Rev. 751 (1988). One Canadian commentator has argued that the right to withhold consent must be exercised in good faith: see S.K. O'Byrne, "Good Faith Contractual Performance: Recent Developments" (1995) 74 Can.B.Rev. 70.

88 See, *e.g.*, *Sundance Investment Corp. v. Richfield Properties Ltd.* (1983) 24 Alta.L.R. (2d) 1, 27 R.P.R. 93, [1983] 2 W.W.R. 493 (C.A.) discussed in M.M. Litman & B.H. Ziff, Annotation, 24 Alta.L.R. (2d) 2.

89 For example, such a clause is implied as a rule of law in the *Residential Tenancies Act*, R.S.A. 1980, c. R-15.3, sub. 16.1(2) [as am.]. A rule of construction can be found in the *Commercial Tenancies Act*, R.S.O. 1990, c. L.7, s. 23.

90 See Part 3(b)(i), Chapter 1.

91 *Carmichael v. Dolmage*, [1947] 1 W.W.R. 193, [1947] 1 D.L.R. 559 (B.C.C.A.) leave to appeal to S.C.C. refused [1947] 1 W.W.R. 286, [1947] 1 D.L.R. 781 (B.C.C.A.); *Brockville (Town) v. Dobbie* (1929) 64 O.L.R. 75, [1929] 3 D.L.R. 583 (C.A.); *Just v. Stewart* (1913) 23 Man.R. 517, 4 W.W.R. 780, 12 D.L.R. 65 (K.B.); *389079 B.C. Ltd. v. Coast Hotels* (1998) 63 B.C.L.R. (3d) 359, 19 R.P.R. (3d) 131 (S.C.).

92 *Stapleton Enterprises of Manitoba Ltd. v. Bramer Machine Shop Ltd.*, [1978] 1 W.W.R. 297, 81 D.L.R. (3d) 717 (Man.Q.B.); *Jan Vargas Industries Inc. v. 737552 Ontario Ltd.* (1990) 15 R.P.R. (2d) 265 (Ont.Gen.Div.) quoting with approval *Outdoor Neon Displays Ltd. v. Toronto*, [1959] O.R. 26, 16 D.L.R. (2d) 624 (C.A.) affirmed [1960] S.C.R. 307, 22 D.L.R. (2d) 241.

There is a touch of irony here: to avoid being caught by the covenant restraining alienation, tenants can employ the same forms of legal legerdemain sometimes used by landlords to avoid the creation of a true landlord and tenant relationship.[93] To plug this loophole, that is, to prevent a transfer by the granting of a licence, a landlord must impose an additional restriction.[94]

A prohibition against transfer is not violated if the assignment or sublease is made conditional on the approval of the landlord.[95] Additionally, in those instances in which the landlord has a right to object only when based on reasonable grounds, a transfer without consent will be valid if it can be shown that the landlord has no reasonable basis to refuse. Moreover, damages have been recovered where the landlord's refusal was found to be unreasonable, even if this power of veto was couched in the lease as a qualification of the tenant's powers of alienation, and not as a separate covenant given by the landlord. In other words, a wrongful refusal has been treated by *some* courts as an actionable violation of an independent promise by the lessor.[96]

There is no doubt that a landlord has a legitimate interest to protect in regulating transfers. So, when a landlord is permitted to object to a transfer on reasonable grounds, it has been accepted that consent may be withheld when there is a valid concern about the personality of the proposed new tenant, or the use to which the premises will be put if transferred. While these were once regarded as the exclusive bases upon which a landlord might reasonably object, the modern approach is more open-ended.[97] In *International Drilling Fluids Ltd. v. Louisville Investments (Uxbridge) Ltd.*[98] the English Court of Appeal, while recognizing that each case is fact-specific, nevertheless provided some guiding principles.

First, the Court of Appeal said that the function of the qualified veto is to protect the landlord from the chance that the premises might be occupied in an undesirable way, or by an undesirable tenant.[99] This is the conventional viewpoint. Second, a refusal must relate to the relationship of landlord and tenant and to the subject-matter of the lease. Third, the onus of proving unreasonableness lies on the tenant. Fourth, it is not necessary for the landlord to demonstrate that the conclusions drawn were justified, so long as they might have been arrived at by

---

93 See Part 2(c), *supra*.

94 However, a lease prohibiting a parting with possession is not breached by sharing the premises: *Stapleton Enterprises of Manitoba Ltd. v. Bramer Machine Shop Ltd.*, *supra*, note 92.

95 *LaJeffries v. Roberts*, [1946] O.R. 10, [1946] 1 D.L.R. 602 (C.A.).

96 See *Cudmore v. Petro Canada Inc.* (1986) 2 B.C.L.R. (2d) 113, [1986] 4 W.W.R. 38 (S.C.). See also *Lehndorff Canadian Pension Properties Ltd. v. Davis Management Ltd.* (1989) 37 B.C.L.R. (2d) 306, [1989] 5 W.W.R. 481, 59 D.L.R. (4th) 1 (C.A.). But see Williams & Rhodes, *supra*, note 78, at 15-64, and the authorities cited there.

97 See *Shields v. Dickler*, [1948] O.W.N. 145, [1948] 1 D.L.R. 809 (C.A.); *Lehndorff Canadian Pension Properties Ltd. v. Davis Management Ltd.*, *supra*, note 96; *Ayre's Ltd. v. Atlantic Shopping Centres Ltd.* (1989) 62 D.L.R. (4th) 12, 79 Nfld. & P.E.I.R. 347, 246 A.P.R. 347 (Nfld.C.A.).

98 [1986] Ch. 513, [1986] 1 All E.R. 321 (C.A.).

99 See *Canada Safeway Ltd. v. Triangle Acceptance Ltd.* (1980) 14 R.P.R. 90, [1980] 5 W.W.R. 259, 19 Man.R. (2d) 292 (C.A.) affirming 11 R.P.R. 279, [1980] 3 W.W.R. 352, 5 Man.R. (2d) 22 (Co.Ct.).

a reasonable person in the circumstances; therefore, a reasonable mistake will not vitiate the legitimacy of the refusal. Fifth, a refusal may be upheld even if the proposed use is permitted under the lease. Sixth, generally the landlord is entitled to consider his or her own interests exclusively, and not those of the tenant. However, when the benefit to the tenant far outweighs the potential detriment to the landlord, it is possible that a refusal to allow the tenant to assign or sublet would be found to be unreasonable. In Canada, it has been held that the landlord may take into account the position of other tenants (at least when this may work to the detriment of the landlord),[100] and may also have regard to 'commercial realities'.[101] When the landlord merely wants a surrender of the term so as to capture the benefits of a rising market, this basis for refusing has been treated as unreasonable.[102] It is apparently not within the sole prerogative of the landlord to make a profit on the sale of leasehold space.[103]

4.   OBLIGATIONS OF LANDLORDS AND TENANTS

(a)   sources of obligations

By and large, the permissible rights and obligations of landlords and tenants are as plenary as contractual autonomy permits. The logical starting point in seeking to understand the terms governing the relationship is, therefore, the lease itself. However, the documents alone, or the verbal understanding if there is no writing, do not always tell the full story. Terms may be inserted by implication under the common law, in equity, or by statute.

At common law the implication of rights and obligations can arise in two ways. If the parties simply agree to import the 'usual covenants' into their lease, this will lead to the incorporation of a standard set of terms, though the composition of this set varies depending on the current conventions followed in the jurisdiction, and the nature of the property to be leased.[104] An agreement for a lease, which can create an equitable term, will likewise be treated as adopting the usual clauses if nothing is set out. Despite the protean nature of the usual covenants, they typically include the following: a covenant by the landlord for quiet enjoyment; and covenants by the tenant to pay the rent (with a provision for forfeiture on default), keep and deliver up the premises in repair, pay taxes not required by law to be paid by the landlord, and allow the landlord to enter and

---

100 *Coopers & Lybrand Ltd. v. William Schwartz Construction Co.* (1980) 36 C.B.R. (N.S.) 265, 31 A.R. 466 (*sub nom. Community Drug Marts P & S Inc. v. William Schwartz Construction Co.*) (Q.B.).

101 See *Federal Business Development Bank v. Starr* (1986) 55 O.R. (2d) 65, 41 R.P.R. 151, 28 D.L.R. (4th) 582 (H.C.) affirmed (1988) 65 O.R. (2d) 793 (C.A.).

102 See, *e.g., Cowitz v. Siegel,* [1954] O.W.N. 833, [1955] 1 D.L.R. 678 (C.A.); *Dominion Stores Ltd. v. Bramalea Ltd.* (1985) 38 R.P.R. 12 (Ont.Dist.Ct.).

103 See further the review of authorities in H.M. Haber, "Assignment and Subletting" in H.M. Haber, ed., *Tenant's Rights and Remedies in a Commercial Lease: A Practical Guide* (Aurora, Ont.: Canada Law Book, 1997) 31, at 38-40.

104 See generally L. Crabb, " 'Usual Covenants' in Leases: A Misnomer", [1992] Conv. 18.

view the state of repair of the property.[105] An implied term will yield to an express one covering the same subject-matter. More generally, the parties may waive the application of terms implied by the common law.

Incorporation under statute can occur in three ways. First, certain clauses may be inserted as rules of law, so that the parties cannot contract out of their application. That approach is common in relation to terms implied in residential leases that are designed for the benefit of tenants.[106] Second, a statute may imply clauses through rules of construction that yield to a contrary intention (as with the terms implied at common law). Third, terms may be incorporated by reference, under 'short forms of leases' legislation. Such statutes allow for highly abbreviated clauses to be inserted in a lease, and these are infused with an expanded meaning by virtue of the statute. To illustrate, a clause entered into pursuant to the short forms of leases provisions in Alberta might simply state that the tenant "will not, without leave in writing, assign or sublet". That term will have this meaning:

> The covenantor, his executors, administrators or transferees, will not, during the said term, transfer, assign or sublet the land and premises hereby leased, or any part thereof, or otherwise by any act or deed procure the said land and premises, or any part thereof, to be transferred or sublet without the consent in writing of the lessor or his transferees first had and obtained.[107]

Given the ambit of contractual freedom generally accorded parties to a lease, especially in the context of commercial tenancies, and recalling also the variety of lease provisions that may be implied, it is impossible to tabulate fully all of the rights and obligations that might apply to a landlord and tenant under a specific lease. Only two common matters are outlined here: the covenants relating to (a) quiet enjoyment (and related matters), and (b) repair.

(b)   quiet enjoyment (and non-derogation)

The tenant's right to quiet enjoyment is normally (perhaps invariably) conferred in a tenancy. The right will be implied through the usual clauses and is often explicitly included. The express covenant may take a variety of forms and need not replicate the covenant implied under law. Therefore, general statements about the meaning of the covenant must be read with these factors in mind.

In essence, quiet enjoyment involves a right to take possession, and to be protected against interference with the tenant's use and enjoyment of the premises by the landlord or others claiming under the landlord. This includes protection against direct physical interference.[108] Indirect action can also produce a breach, such as when the landlord allows carbon monoxide fumes to seep into an apart-

---

105 C. Bentley *et al.*, *Williams & Rhodes Canadian Law of Landlord and Tenant*, 6th ed. (Toronto: Carswell, 1988) (looseleaf) vol. 1, at 3-48.
106 See the text accompanying note 176, *infra*.
107 *Land Titles Act*, R.S.A. 1980, c. L-5, Schedule A, cl. 1. See also s. 102 [as am.].
108 See, *e.g.*, *Acropolis Restaurants Ltd. v. Corval Motels Ltd.* (1980) 5 Sask.R. 55 (Q.B.).

ment, rendering it unlivable.[109] Persistent conduct by the landlord designed to force the tenant out is now regarded as a patent contravention of the covenant (and may even support a claim for punitive damages).[110] A recent Ontario case adopted this general definition:

> [A] breach of the covenant should arise from any acts which result in the tenant's reasonable peace, comfort, or privacy being interfered with, whether due to liquids, gases, vapours, solids, odours, vibration, noise, abusive language, threats, fire, the total or partial withholding of heat, electricity, water, gas, or other essential services, or the removal of windows, doors, walls or other parts of the rented premises.[111]

There are a number of matters that are wrongly thought to fall within the domain of the implied covenant for quiet enjoyment. The covenant is not directed against noise *per se*, although excessive noise may produce a significant interference with the tenant's use of the premises.[112] The covenant does not protect against the *wrongful* acts of other tenants.[113] However, if the contemplated use for which Apt. A is let is one that interferes with the use and enjoyment of Apt. B, a landlord can be held liable for a breach of the covenant for quiet enjoyment given to the tenant of Apt. B, based on the otherwise lawful acts undertaken under the lease of Apt. A.[114]

In addition, it is sometimes said that the covenant serves as a warranty of title,[115] but whether this is so depends on how widely the covenant is framed. If it applies only to acts of the landlord or any persons taking *under* the landlord, then there is no protection against an eviction by someone with a *superior* right (a title paramount). The covenants that are implied merely from the letting of premises, or under the usual covenants, appear limited in this way.[116]

---

109 *Federic v. Perpetual Investments Ltd.*, [1969] 1 O.R. 186, 2 D.L.R. (3d) 50 (H.C.). *Cf. B.G. Preeco 3 Ltd. v. Universal Explorations Ltd.*, 54 Alta.L.R. (2d) 65, [1987] 6 W.W.R. 127, 42 D.L.R. (4th) 673 (Q.B.).

110 As it did in *Parkes v. Howard Johnson Restaurants Ltd.* (1970) 74 W.W.R. 255 (B.C.S.C.) where the landlord broke a padlock, removed doors, interrupted elevator service, and shut off the electrical supply and heating. Similar tactics led to a breach of the covenant in *Franco v. Lechman* (1962) 36 D.L.R. (2d) 357 (Alta.C.A.). Damages based on loss of profit and the need to relocate were ordered, but exemplary damages were not. The right to recover damages for injured feelings and mental distress was denied in *Branchett v. Beaney*, [1992] 3 All E.R. 910 (C.A.).

111 *Caldwell v. Valiant Property Management* (1997) 33 O.R. (3d) 187, 145 D.L.R. (4th) 559, 9 R.P.R. (3d) 227 (Gen.Div.) at 567 D.L.R. (*per* D.S. Ferguson J.) adopting part of the proposal found in Ontario Law Reform Commission, *Report on Landlord and Tenant Law* (Toronto: A.G. (Ont.), 1976) at 96-7.

112 See *e.g.*, *Caldwell v. Valiant Property Management*, *supra*, note 111. *Cf. Southwark London Borough Council v. Mills*, [1999] 2 W.L.R. 409 (C.A.).

113 See *Curtis Investments Ltd. v. Anderson* (1981) 24 Man.R. (2d) 220 (Co.Ct.).

114 See *Baxter v. Camden London Borough Council*, unreported, 20 June 1997 (Eng.C.A.). See also the text accompanying, and the references mentioned in, note 119, *infra*.

115 See *Stranks v. St. John* (1867) L.R. 2 C.P. 376.

116 See further M.J. Russell, "Landlord's Covenant for Quiet Enjoyment", [1976] Conv. 427; M.J. Russell, "Leasehold Covenants for Title", [1978] Conv. 418. It has been said that the covenant will provide protection against eviction by title paramount if the word 'demise' is used in the lease, but this view has been questioned: see R.E. Megarry & H.W.R. Wade, *The*

Allied to the right to quiet enjoyment, but distinct from it, is the principle that a landlord must not derogate from the lease.[117] By virtue of this doctrine, the lessor must not use the property retained in a way that renders the demised premises substantially less fit for the purposes for which they were let. This obligation covers physical interference with the rental property, but it may extend further. For example, in *Harmer v. Jumbil (Nigeria) Tin Areas, Ltd.*[118] a leased warehouse was to be used for storing explosives. The lessor, aware of this intended use, was prevented from building on neighbouring land at a proximity that was prohibited by regulations governing the storage of explosive materials. Going beyond this, in a 1997 English decision, a derogation was found when the business operations of one tenant in a mall, a pawnbroker, significantly interfered with the retail trade of another tenant. In that instance, the landlord was held liable for not availing itself of its powers (under the leases) to prevent the substantial interference that resulted. Its failure to act constituted the derogation.[119]

(c)   repair

Obligations of repair form a central feature of most modern commercial and residential leases. The common law reads into a lease a requirement that the tenant must act in a tenant-like manner. This stipulation means that certain action must be taken to preserve the property (say, by trying to prevent damage by frost[120] or infestation by insects[121]). Lord Denning's account captures the essence of this obligation:

> [W]hat does 'to use the premises in a tenantlike manner' mean? It can, I think, best be shown by some illustrations. The tenant must take proper care of the place. He must, if he is going away for the winter, turn off the water and empty the boiler. He must clean the chimneys, when necessary, and also the windows. He must mend the electric light when it fuses. He must unstop the sink when it is blocked by his waste. In short, he must do the little jobs about the place which a reasonable tenant would do. In addition, he must, of course, not damage the house, wilfully or negligently; and he must see that his family and guests do not damage it: and if they do, he must repair it. But apart from such things, if the house falls into disrepair through

---

Law of Real Property, 5th ed. (London: Stevens & Sons, 1984) at 695. *Cf. Williams & Rhodes*, *supra*, note 105, at 9-14, and *Forrest v. Greaves* (1923) 17 Sask. L.R. 460, [1923] 3 W.W.R. 658, [1923] 3 D.L.R. 816 (K.B.).

117 See generally D.W. Elliott, "Non-Derogation from Grant" (1964) 80 L.Q.R. 244.

118 [1921] 1 Ch. 200, [1920] All E.R.Rep. 113 (C.A.). See also *Ostry v. Warehouse on Beatty Cabaret Ltd.* (1992) 21 R.P.R. (2d) 1 (B.C.S.C.) for an interesting variation on this theme.

119 *Chartered Trust plc v. Davies*, [1997] 2 E.G.L.R. 83 (C.A.). Andrew Bruce has suggested that "*Chartered Trust* will breathe new life into the implied term not to derogate from grant": A. Bruce, "Nuisance and the Common Landlord" (1997) 141 Sol.J. 922, at 923. See also *Nynehead Developments Ltd. v. R.H. Fibreboard Containers Ltd.*, [1999] 1 E.G.L.R. 7 (Ch.D.). For comparable developments in Australia, see P. Butt, "Covenant for Quiet Enjoyment" (1998) 72 A.L.J. 495. *Cf. Romulus Trading Co. Ltd. v. Comet Properties Ltd.*, [1996] 2 E.G.L.R. 70 (Q.B.); *Caplan v. Acadian Machinery Ltd.* (1976) 13 O.R. (2d) 48, 70 D.L.R. (3d) 383 (Div.Ct.). See also *Clark's-Gamble of Canada Ltd. v. Grant Park Plaza Ltd.*, [1967] S.C.R. 614, 61 W.W.R. 472, 64 D.L.R. (2d) 570, quoting (at 625 S.C.R.) the leading authority of *Browne v. Flower*, [1911] 1 Ch. 219, [1908-10] All E.R.Rep. 545, at 227 Ch.

120 *Ryan & Co. v. Weilgoesz* (1913) 4 W.W.R. 982 (Man.Co.Ct.).

121 *Martin v. Larsen* (1943) 59 B.C.R. 398, [1944] 1 D.L.R. 303 (Co.Ct.).

fair wear and tear or lapse of time, or for any reason not caused by him, then the tenant is not liable to repair it.[122]

A landlord and tenant are in a relationship that resembles that which exists between a life tenant and a remainderperson. There, as we have seen, the law of waste applies to regulate the rights and obligations relating to the physical upkeep and deterioration of the property. Principles of waste apply here too. Liability for wasteful conduct may be found when wilful (and arguably even negligent) conduct on the part of a tenant leads to damage; this is a form of voluntary waste.[123] Liability for permissive waste may also attach: the nature and extent of this duty varies according to the type of tenancy involved (*i.e.*, depending on whether it is periodic, or for a fixed term, *etc.*). A tenant who damages the property in the course of removing tenant's fixtures will also be liable for waste.

5. TERMINATION AND REMEDIES

At common law, a lease for a fixed term expires naturally on the expiration of the stated term. If the tenant remains in possession, the acceptance of rent may be taken to mean that a renewal has been agreed to, though the circumstances may dictate that only a periodic term or a tenancy at will has been created. A periodic tenancy may be ended by a timely notice, the extent of which depends on the period of the lease.

A lease may end through the unification of the tenant's term and the landlord's reversion in the tenant or in a third party (known as merger), or as a result of a denial by the tenant of the lessor's title (disclaimer).[124] It is now accepted that the contractual doctrine of frustration applies to leases; when applicable, the tenancy is terminated.[125]

A breach by a tenant may lead to forfeiture of the tenancy. However, not every breach will necessarily produce this result: under traditional analysis, it depends on how the tenant's obligation is set out. In brief, the right of forfeiture applies when the tenant has breached an obligation that has been framed in the lease as a condition and not as a covenant.[126] A condition is imported by the use of such language as 'on condition that' in the lease. Likewise, the lease may provide explicitly that a breach triggers a right of re-entry.

---

122 *Warren v. Keen*, [1954] 1 Q.B. 15, [1953] 2 All E.R. 1118 (C.A.) at 20 Q.B.

123 *Tudor Developments Ltd. v. Van Es* (1975) 53 D.L.R. (3d) 716 (Alta.T.D.). See also *Nichols v. R.A. Gill Ltd.* (1974) 5 O.R. (2d) 741, 51 D.L.R. (3d) 493 (H.C.).

124 See, *e.g.*, *Doe d. Nugent v. Hessell* (1846) 2 U.C.Q.B. 194. It is sometimes said that this is a form of forfeiture that can arise without the need to insert a proviso for re-entry: see Megarry & Wade, *supra*, note 116, at 670.

125 See *National Carriers Ltd. v. Panalpina (Northern) Ltd.*, [1981] A.C. 675, [1981] 1 All E.R. 161 (H.L.) noted in J.T. Robertson, "Frustrated Leases: No to Never – But Rarely if Ever" (1982) 60 Can.B.Rev. 619. See also *Residential Tenancies Act*, R.S.A. 1980, c. R-15.3, s. 32; *Tenant Protection Act, 1997*, S.O. 1997, c. 24, s. 10. But see *Binder v. Key Property Management Corp.* (1992) 26 R.P.R. (2d) 80 (Ont.Gen.Div.).

126 Except in the case of forfeiture arising from the denial of the landlord's title: see note 124, *supra*.

Of course, the landlord may choose not to exercise the right of forfeiture and instead may sue on the breach. An additional and powerful remedy available to the landlord at common law is the right to levy distress for the non-payment of rent. The law of distress allows the landlord to impound the goods of the tenant until payment is received. In 1689, a power of sale was added by statute.[127] Distress, that "relic of feudalism",[128] is still used in Canada, mainly in commercial settings.[129]

Although forfeiture provides the landlord with a drastic remedy, its impact is tempered in several ways. First, it has been offered that "[c]ourts do not look with favour upon forfeitures and will take advantage of even trifling reasons to avoid upholding them".[130] This means, among other things, that forfeiture terms will be strictly construed.[131] Additionally, a landlord must carefully comply with all prerequisites for re-entry under a forfeiture clause.

Second, even if the lease states that breaches render the tenancy void, the landlord is not compelled to enter, and may waive those breaches that have triggered the right of forfeiture. A waiver need not be express and may be found if the landlord implicitly affirms the continued existence of the lease. The classic demonstration of this condonation is the acceptance of rent, accruing due after, and with knowledge of, the breach.[132]

Third, even if there has not been a waiver, a court may grant relief from forfeiture to a supplicating tenant. Speaking generally, equity is willing to provide relief against forfeiture as long as compensation to the landlord is possible (in damages or costs, *etc.*),[133] without adversely affecting innocent third parties. Equity is ready to respond (by granting relief) in cases in which the tenant's breach relates to the failure to pay rent on time, but it may also do so in other instances. In some jurisdictions the right to seek relief for breaches other than the non-payment of rent has been broadened by statute.[134] The reasoning behind the granting of relief against forfeiture is that the right of entry by the landlord is treated as security for the performance of the obligations of the lease, a security that is unnecessary once the tenant has made good on the default. (This is an

---

127 *Distress for Rent Act, 1689*, 2 Will. & Mar., c. 5.

128 Law Commission, *Landlord and Tenant: Interim Report on Distress for Rent* (London: H.M.S.O., 1966) at para. 5.

129 See further *Williams & Rhodes, supra*, note 105, at ch. 8, *passim*; Manitoba Law Reform Commission, *Distress for Rent in Commercial Tenancies* (Winnipeg: M.L.R.C., 1993).

130 *Big Valley Collieries Ltd. v. MacKinnon* (1915) 9 W.W.R. 4, 23 D.L.R. 62 (Alta.S.C.) at 63 D.L.R. (*per* Hyndman J.).

131 See, *e.g., Fetherston v. Bice*, [1917] 1 W.W.R. 224, 31 D.L.R. 554 (Alta.S.C.).

132 *Straus Land Corp. v. International Hotel Windsor Ltd.* (1919) 45 O.L.R. 145, 48 D.L.R. 519 (C.A.). Compare the result in *Nuytten v. Stein*, 12 W.W.R. (N.S.) 465, [1954] 2 D.L.R. 785 (B.C.S.C.). See also *Law of Property Act*, R.S.A. 1980, c. L-8, s. 59.4 [as am.].

133 *Edwards v. Fairview Lodge*, 28 B.C.R. 557, [1920] 3 W.W.R. 867 (S.C.).

134 See, *e.g., Law of Property Act*, R.S.A. 1980, c. L-8, s. 67; *Judicature Act*, R.S.A. 1980, c. J-1, s. 10. See generally *Snider v. Harper*, 18 Alta.L.R. 82, [1922] 2 W.W.R. 417, 66 D.L.R. 149 (C.A.).

attitude of sympathetic indulgence that we will encounter again, when the equitable rules designed to stave off mortgage foreclosures are examined.[135])

Conventionally, a lease does not confer on the tenant a right comparable to
the landlord's remedy of forfeiture. Furthermore, traditionally covenants in leases
have been viewed as independent of each other. Therefore, generally, the breach
of one term does not enable the innocent party to withhold the performance of
obligations in response.[136] At common law nothing short of an eviction would
suspend the obligation to pay rent.[137] There was a time when the word 'eviction'
carried the narrow connotation of an expulsion by someone with a better right to
the property than the landlord (title paramount), or a removal brought about under
some process of law. Now it means "every class of expulsion or amotion of a
grave and permanent character done by the landlord with the intention of depriving
the tenant of the enjoyment of the demised premises".[138] This more encompassing
approach includes acts of constructive eviction, that is, conduct by the landlord
that evidences an intention to deprive the tenant of the enjoyment of the property,
and which has forced the tenant to leave.[139] This was found, for example, when a
lessee left the premises after the lessor had refused to comply with a covenant to
repair damage caused by fire.[140]

A lease may be terminated through an express surrender of the term, such
as where the tenant reconveys the demised premises. A surrender may also arise
by operation of law. This second form occurs, for instance, when acts of repudiation committed by the tenant are accepted by the landlord as proof of an intention
to forego the remainder of the lease.[141] Commonly, the surrendering action is the
abandonment of the property; the corresponding acceptance occurs when the
landlord resumes possession.[142]

When an abandonment occurs the landlord may pursue one of four options.
The first is to ignore the abandonment, refuse to bring about a surrender, and
patiently stand by, suing for the rent as it falls due. Second, the landlord may
choose to accept the surrender and terminate the tenant's interest in the property,
all the while retaining the right to sue for past breaches. Third, the landlord may
advise the tenant that the premises are going to be re-let, with the landlord acting
as agent for the tenant, and retaining the right to sue for any shortfall in the rent
received. This action is not treated as an act inconsistent with the continued

---

135 See Part 4(d), Chapter 11.
136 *Primeridian Farms Ltd. v. Guyot* (1986) 42 Man.R. (2d) 206 (Q.B.); *Winfield Developments
     Ltd. v. J.E.R. Associates Inc.* (1985) 36 Man.R. (2d) 301 (Q.B.). See generally S.J. Stoljar,
     "Dependent and Independent Covenants" (1957) 2 Syd.L.Rev. 217.
137 *Cross v. Piggott*, 32 Man.R. 362, [1922] 2 W.W.R. 662, 69 D.L.R. 107 (K.B.).
138 *Upton v. Greenlees* (1855) 17 C.B. 30, at 64-5, 139 E.R. 976, at 991 (*per* Jervis C.J.) quoted
     in *Corse v. Moon* (1889) 22 N.S.R. 191 (C.A.) at 198.
139 *Maunsell v. The Queen*, [1925] Ex.C.R. 133.
140 *Seven Seas Restaurant v. Central & Eastern Trust Co.* (1978) 24 N.B.R. (2d) 491, 48 A.P.R.
     491 (Q.B.).
141 Other forms of surrender by operation of law are discussed in *Williams & Rhodes, supra,* note
     105, at 12-12*ff.*
142 See, *e.g., Queen Square Development Ltd. v. Financial Collection Agencies Ltd.* (1989) 94
     N.S.R. (2d) 229, 247 A.P.R. 229 (T.D.).

existence of the lease, and it explains why the posting of a 'for rent' sign may not necessarily lead to the conclusion that the landlord has treated the lease as being over.[143] Likewise, merely handing over the keys is regarded as equivocal, because this may be done to allow the landlord to inspect the premises.[144] A fourth option, often more valuable to the landlord than the first three, was added in the ground-breaking Supreme Court of Canada decision in *Highway Properties Ltd. v. Kelly, Douglas & Co.*[145] That case held that the landlord may (i) accept the surrender, and (ii) serve notice on the tenant that an action may be brought to recover for prospective losses caused by the tenant's repudiation of the unexpired portion of the term.

In *Highway Properties* the landlord-plaintiff owned a small shopping centre. The tenant-defendant agreed to lease a large space for a supermarket under terms that required the tenant to carry on business continuously once possession was taken up. However, the store was not a success, and within two years the property was abandoned. That departure seriously undermined the viability and profitability of the entire venture: the defendant was the major (or 'anchor') tenant in the shopping centre. The landlord subsequently advised the tenant that it intended to retake the premises and to hold the tenant liable for the damages resulting from its wrongful repudiation of the lease.

The basis of damages in contract is that the innocent party should be placed in the same position that he or she would have been in had the contract been duly performed. The traditional rule in relation to the surrender of leaseholds was different: the acceptance ended the tenant's estate, and with this the obligation to pay rent vanished, as did the right to sue for ancillary future losses. The rule was premised on the notion that a lease was first and foremost an interest in land. In *Highway Properties* the Supreme Court of Canada concluded that it was no longer sensible to preclude the landlord from enjoying the range of remedies available on the breaching of a commercial contract.[146] To this extent, the 'propertyness' of the lease was diminished by the Supreme Court.

This recasting of the lease has had a major impact in cases of surrender and abandonment, augmenting the landlords' armoury in a very valuable way.[147] Whether the law of landlord's remedies is now on par with those available for the breach of contract generally is not altogether certain. It is likely that the contract law duty to mitigate damages has been incorporated as part of this branch of landlord and tenant law.[148] That is so at least when the fourth option (the one

---

143 See *Green v. Tress* (1927) 60 O.L.R. 151, [1927] 2 D.L.R. 180 (C.A.).

144 See, *e.g.*, *Hum v. Mosher* (1977) 33 N.S.R. (2d) 135, 57 A.P.R. 135 (Co.Ct.). *Cf. Machula v. Tramer*, [1972] 1 W.W.R. 550 (Sask.Dist.Ct.).

145 [1971] S.C.R. 562, [1972] 2 W.W.R. 28, 17 D.L.R. (3d) 710. See further G. Sustrik, "Highway Properties – Look Both Ways Before Crossing" (1986) 24 Alta.L.Rev. 477.

146 *Supra*, note 145, at 576 S.C.R.

147 For an interesting application, see *Applewood Lane West Ltd. v. Scott*, [1987] 3 W.W.R. 665, 35 D.L.R. (4th) 287, 48 Man.R. (2d) 77 (C.A.).

148 See, *e.g.*, *West Edmonton Mall Ltd. v. McDonald's Restaurants of Canada Ltd.* (1995) 50 R.P.R. (2d) 1, 35 Alta.L.R. (3d) 305, [1996] 3 W.W.R. 191 (C.A.). See also *Adanac Realty Ltd. v. Humpty's Egg Place Ltd.* (1991) 78 Alta.L.R. (2d) 383, 15 R.P.R. (2d) 77, 113 A.R. 215 (Q.B.).

added in *Highway Properties*) is chosen. When the landlord prefers to keep the lease in effect it has been maintained that the duty to mitigate is not engaged,[149] although some have questioned that position.[150] And, unlike the general law, the courts require that notice be given by the landlord in order to trigger the right to sue for prospective losses. That notice need not be contemporaneous with the termination of the lease and it is possible that the *timely* filing of documents in a law suit (the pleadings) can satisfy the notice requirement.[151]

How much further should a contract-based analysis of the lease go? Does the holding mean that a fundamental breach of a covenant now allows the landlord to treat the lease as having ended, even if the tenant has not abandoned the premises? If so, a lease may be terminated by a fundamental breach of a covenant, just as it can when the breach of a condition triggers a right of forfeiture. This position has prevailed in both Australia[152] and New Zealand[153] where parallel developments in the contractualization of remedies for breaches of a lease have occurred. English law seems to be inclining in this direction as well.[154]

The real conceptual hurdle in the analogical progress of *Highway Properties* concerns the availability of contractual remedies to *tenants*. The Supreme Court moved the law of leases closer to that governing contracts. It should follow that a fundamental breach by a landlord gives the tenant the right to treat the lease as at an end, even if the landlord's conduct falls short of actual or constructive eviction. A few Canadian courts have recognized this possibility. For example, in *Lehndorff Canadian Pension Properties Ltd. v. Davis Management Ltd.*[155] it

149 See *Almad Investments Ltd. v. Mister Leonard Holdings Ltd.*, [1996] O.J. No. 4074 (C.A.); *607190 Ontario Inc. v. First Consolidated Holdings Corp.* (1992) 26 R.P.R. (2d) 298 (Ont.Div.Ct.). But see *Toronto Housing Co. Ltd. v. Postal Promotions Ltd.* (1982) 39 O.R. (2d) 627, 140 D.L.R. (3d) 117, 26 R.P.R. 184 (C.A.) affirming (1981) 34 O.R. (2d) 218, 128 D.L.R. (3d) 51, 22 R.P.R. 89 (H.C.).
150 See further A. Sternberg, "The Commercial Landlord's Duty to Mitigate Upon a Tenant's Abandonment of the Premises" (1985) 5 Advocates' Q. 385, where the case for a duty to mitigate is advanced. *Cf.* C.S. Goldfarb, "Abandonment of Premises by Tenant: The Damages Issue" in Haber, *supra*, note 103, 167.
151 See further *Langley Crossing Shopping Centre Inc. v. North-West Produce Ltd.* (1998) 20 R.P.R. (3d) 112 (B.C.S.C.) [reversed on the facts (2000) 73 B.C.L.R. (3d) 55, 30 R.P.R. (3d) 180 (C.A.)] where the leading cases are reviewed.
152 *Progressive Mailing House Pty. Ltd. v. Tabili Pty. Ltd.* (1985) 157 C.L.R. 17, 57 A.L.R. 609 (Aust.H.C.); *Laurinda v. Capalaba Park Shopping Centre Pty. Ltd.* (1989) 63 A.J.L.R. 372 (H.C.). See further A.J. Bradbrook *et al.*, *Australian Real Property Law*, 2nd ed. (Sydney: Law Book Co., 1997) at para. 12.72*ff*, and the additional references cited there. For a review of American developments, see R.H. Kelley, "Any Reports of the Death of the Property Law Paradigm for Leases Have Been Greatly Exaggerated", 41 Wayne L.Rev. 1563 (1995).
153 *Morris v. Robert Jones Investments Ltd.*, [1994] 2 N.Z.L.R. 275 (C.A.).
154 See the discussion in *Nynehead Developments Ltd. v. R.H. Fibreboard Containers Ltd.*, *supra*, note 119, at 12. See also *Chartered Trust plc v. Davies*, *supra*, note 119. For an English perspective on these developments, see M. Pawlowski, "Acceptance of Repudiatory Breach in Leases", [1995] Conv. 379.
155 [1989] 5 W.W.R. 481, 5 R.P.R. (2d) 1, 59 D.L.R. (4th) 1 (B.C.C.A.). The recognition of the tenant's contractual right to terminate as a supplement to the remedies offered under a strict property law analysis was welcomed in N. Bankes & N. Rafferty, "A Tenant's Remedies for a Landlord's Breach: The Impact of Lehndorff Canadian Pension Properties Ltd. v. Davis

was held that a landlord's unreasonable refusal to allow a transfer by a tenant was a breach of such severity that the tenant was entitled to bring the lease to an end. Having decided to move, the right to assign or sublet constituted the only remaining item of value for the tenant, making the harm produced by the landlord's breach seem especially severe. In another case the landlord's interference with the tenant's access to its delivery area was found to be a breach of such significance as to entitle the tenant to terminate the lease.[156] Drawing support from such cases, in 1996 the Manitoba Law Reform Commission recommended the implementation of a statutory rule that recognizes a right of both landlords and tenants to terminate a commercial lease on the ground that the other party has committed a fundamental breach.[157]

6.   REFORM OF RESIDENTIAL TENANCY LAW[158]

Just as the rules pertaining to leases as security interests became rather inappropriate once tenancies for agricultural purposes became increasingly common, the recognition that the general law of landlord and tenant was ill-suited to urban residential tenancies has prompted substantial reform in the last three decades. These changes were a long time coming. It has been suggested that the impetus for change in the United States came from the civil rights movement, which exposed the gravity of the housing problems of the poor.[159] This does not serve all that well as a basis for explaining the parallel Canadian developments, many of which actually pre-dated the so-called American revolution in landlord and tenant law. I see these developments as one facet of the general wave of consumer protectionism that emerged after the Second World War. Whatever the spark, the old law was a "tinderbox waiting to be ignited".[160]

These developments are premised on the recognition that, to the landlord, the residential unit is an investment, a going concern. To the tenant, it is a home, and,

> [a] home is . . . a reflection of our personality, a signature of our identity . . . Emotionally, the investment in a home – *rented or owned* – is often far greater than the monetary expenditure it represents. Financial investments may become sunk costs, but the emotional commitments to a home remain fresh in the mind and grow with the accumulation of memories. It should become apparent, therefore, that actions that are perceived as threats to the continued security

---

Management Ltd." (1990) 24 U.B.C.L.Rev. 155. However, the authors question the finding in *Lehndorff* that the landlord's breach was sufficient to allow the tenant to terminate the lease.

156 See, *e.g.*, *Homer v. Toronto-Dominion Bank* (1990) 83 Sask.R. 300 (C.A.); *Prince Business Inc. v. Vancouver Trade Mart Inc.* (1994) 99 B.C.L.R. (2d) 226, 43 R.P.R. (2d) 228, [1995] 2 W.W.R. 617 (C.A.); *Bastarache (Antoine L.) Ltd. v. Bouctouche Chrysler Dodge Ltd.* (1996) 184 N.B.R. (2d) 108, 469 A.P.R. 108 (C.A.).

157 Manitoba Law Reform Commission, *Fundamental Breach and Frustration in Commercial Tenancies* (Winnipeg: M.L.R.C., 1996) at 14-5.

158 For an overview of developments in Australia, see A.J. Bradbrook, "Residential Tenancies Law – The Second Stage of Reforms" (1998) 20 Syd.L.Rev. 402.

159 E.H. Rabin, "The Revolution in Residential Landlord-Tenant Law: Causes and Consequences", 69 Cornell L.Rev. 517 (1984).

160 *Ibid.* at 547, n. 160.

of possession of one's home could evoke a strong response not only from the persons directly involved, but also from other members of the community who empathise with them.[161]

The modernization of the feudal-based law of leaseholds recognizes that Canada's housing stock is privately owned, and that the law needs to be sensitive to problems affecting economic efficiency. However, these concerns must be balanced against the privacy, personhood and economic interests of tenants.

Reform in Canada has involved ten major areas of change (although not every provincial initiative deals with each area). These are:

1. greater security of tenure for tenants and *lodgers*;[162]

2. increased termination notice periods;

3. the fixing of standard obligations of both landlords and tenants in a way that endeavours to allocate responsibilities and rights in a rational and fair manner;

4. an increase in tenants' remedies;

5. the curtailment of landlords' self-help remedies;[163]

6. the establishment of dispute resolution procedures that are designed to be informal, effective, expeditious and inexpensive;[164]

7. the establishment of prohibitions on the bargaining away of statutory rights;

8. the elimination of various anachronisms affecting the general law of landlord and tenant;

9. the creation of landlord and tenant advisory boards; and

10. rent control mechanisms.[165]

Alongside these developments, human rights protections have been introduced to respond to discriminatory rental practices. In general, all of these changes build on the pre-existing framework of the law of landlord and tenant.

---

161 W.T. Stanbury, *The Normative Bases of Rent Regulation* (Toronto: Commission of Inquiry into Residential Tenancies, Research Study No. 15, 1985) at 3-10 (emphasis added).

162 See generally D.H. Bell, "Providing Security of Tenure for Residential Tenants: Good Faith as a Limitation on the Landlord's Right to Terminate", 19 Ga.L.Rev. 483 (1985).

163 For example, the right to levy distress has been abolished in Ontario for residential tenancies: *Tenant Protection Act, 1997*, S.O. 1997, c. 24, s. 31.

164 See, *e.g.*, *Tenant Protection Act, 1997*, S.O. 1997, c. 24, Part VII, establishing the Ontario Rental Housing Tribunal. The constitutionality of the procedures planned for Nova Scotia was upheld in *Reference Re Amendments to the Residential Tenancies Act (N.S.)*, [1996] 1 S.C.R. 186, 131 D.L.R. (4th) 609, discussed in P.S. Rapsey, "Case Comment: *Reference re Residential Tenancies Act, 1992, Nova Scotia*: Throwing Residential Tenants to the Political Wind" (1997) 12 J.Law & Soc.Pol. 233.

165 See, *e.g.*, *Tenant Protection Act, 1997*, S.O. 1997, c. 24, Part VI, which transforms the Ontario rent control from a unit-specific to a tenant-specific regime. In short, the landlord may negotiate a new rent with each new tenant. Thereafter increases are subject to regulation.

Alberta's attempts at reform exemplify that Province's conservative political culture. In the 1970s modest reforms were undertaken: notice periods for tenants were increased, but there was little in the legislative regime to provide security of tenure. A landlord could, generally speaking, terminate a periodic tenancy without cause simply by giving the required notice to vacate.

Reforms in 1992 have changed that.[166] Presently, a periodic tenancy cannot be terminated by simply giving notice, unless the landlord can rely on certain prescribed reasons (such as that the property is required because major renovations are going to be undertaken, or the premises are being converted into condominium units).[167]

The Alberta *Residential Tenancies Act* of 1992 inserts basic terms into all residential tenancy agreements. Under the Act every residential tenancy agreement contains the following landlord's covenants:

(a) that the premises will be available for occupation by the tenant at the beginning of the tenancy;

(b) that neither the landlord nor a person having a claim to the premises under the landlord will in any significant manner disturb the tenant's possession or peaceful enjoyment of the premises;

(c) that the premises will be habitable by the tenant at the beginning of the tenancy.[168]

A tenant impliedly covenants that:

(a) the rent will be paid when due;

(b) the tenant will not in any significant manner interfere with the rights of either the landlord or other tenants in the premises, the common areas or the property of which they form a part;

(c) the tenant will not perform illegal acts or carry on an illegal trade, business or occupation in the premises, the common areas or the property of which they form a part;

(d) the tenant will not endanger persons or property in the premises, the common areas or the property of which they form a part;

(e) the tenant will not do or permit significant damage to the premises, the common areas or the property of which they form a part;

(f) the tenant will maintain the premises and any property rented with it in a reasonably clean condition;

(g) the tenant will vacate the premises at the expiration or termination of the tenancy.[169]

In my opinion these provisions still give little to the tenant that the common law would not have provided by implication. Additionally, the covenant for quiet enjoyment is subject to the landlord's right to enter the premises if there are reasonable grounds to believe (i) that emergency repairs are needed; or (ii) that the tenant has abandoned the premises. The landlord may also enter at a reasonable

---

166 *Residential Tenancies Act*, R.S.A. 1980, c. R-15.3.
167 Sub. 4.1(1) [as am.]; *Residential Tenancies Ministerial Regulation*, Alta. Reg. 229/92.
168 S. 14.
169 S. 16.

time, after serving a written notice, to inspect the state of repairs, to make repairs, or to show the property to prospective purchasers, mortgagees, or tenants.[170]

The responsibility for repair is not defined with the type of specificity that is required to reduce squabbles that sometimes arise over who is responsible for what. Anyone who has ever been a tenant knows that this is a common source of conflict. The tenant is responsible for cleanliness (see para. (f)), but nothing is said directly about the landlord's ongoing responsibilities. By contrast, the Ontario Act is far more explicit, establishing rules of eminent common sense:

> 24(1) A landlord is responsible for providing and maintaining a residential complex, including the rental units in it, in a good state of repair and fit for habitation and for complying with health, safety, housing and maintenance standards.
>
> (2) Subsection (1) applies even if the tenant was aware of a state of non-repair or a contravention of a standard before entering into the tenancy agreement.
>
> . . .
>
> 29. The tenant is responsible for ordinary cleanliness of the rental unit, except to the extent that the tenancy agreement requires the landlord to clean it.
>
> 30. The tenant is responsible for the repair of damage to the rental unit or the residential complex caused by the wilful or negligent conduct of the tenant, other occupants of the rental unit or persons who are permitted in the residential complex by the tenant.[171]

Various other elements of residential tenancy reform are present in the Alberta statute. For example, the landlord's self-help remedies have been severely curbed[172] and those of the tenant have been expanded. A breach by the landlord of the lease gives the tenant the right to seek (a) damages; (b) an abatement of rent; (c) compensation for the performance of the landlord's obligations; and (d) termination of the tenancy (if the breach is significant).[173] Furthermore, the Act provides for summary proceedings before the Provincial Court,[174] and for the establishment of a Landlord and Tenant Advisory Board, which is given a mandate to provide advice, receive and investigate complaints, mediate disputes, and provide educational services.[175]

The rights conferred for the benefit of tenants in Alberta cannot be waived or surrendered under the lease. When a residential tenancy agreement is in writing it must state that "if there is a conflict between [the] agreement and the Act, the Act prevails".[176] This restriction on contracting out, designed for the benefit of tenants, assumes that the bargaining power between landlord and tenant is likely to be unequally held. But the Ontario case of *Pinheiro v. Bowes*[177] demonstrates how these protections can sometimes backfire. There, the lease provided for a 30-day notice period to terminate the tenancy; the law calls for a 60-day period.

---

170 S. 17.
171 *Tenant Protection Act, 1997*, S.O. 1997, c. 24, ss. 24, 29, 30.
172 See Part 3, "Remedies of Landlords and Tenants", and especially ss. 20 to 23.1 [as am.].
173 S. 29.
174 See Part 5 of the Act.
175 S. 49.
176 S. 2.1 [as am.].
177 (1994) 109 D.L.R. (4th) 315, 37 R.P.R. (2d) 199 (Ont.Gen.Div.).

When the tenant gave the 30-day notice, the landlord maintained that this shorter period was contrary to law. The Court agreed, holding that public policy did not prevent a landlord from relying on the protections contained in the *Landlord and Tenant Act*, even though these were intended for the benefit of tenants.

Pinheiro may be an exceptional case in some senses, but it does typify the ways in which measures designed to empower tenants can be arrogated or subverted by landlords. This is especially noticeable when rent controls are imposed. Over the years, some Canadian jurisdictions have ambitiously attempted to impose controls on a landlord's right to exact rent, in an effort to provide a sufficient supply of affordable housing. Rent control prevents landlords from implementing radical rent increases in the expectation that renters will suffer a rent hike rather than assume the financial and personal burdens of finding a new home (aptly called a 'hold-up' problem[178]). Another goal is to enhance security of tenure: under a rent control system, tenants are protected against 'economic eviction', that is, the imposition of an astronomic rent hike designed to induce a tenant to quit the premises.[179]

One approach to rent regulation is to allow automatic annual increases to be levied by landlords to keep pace with inflation. This is supplemented with procedures under which landlords may seek a larger raise in rent. For instance, the law might allow an increase that is above the norm if the rent for a given apartment has been historically low, or if significant improvements have been made to the premises.[180]

Economists have questioned the efficacy of rent control mechanisms. The success of these devices, as measured by a demonstrable improvement in the lives of tenants, is uncertain. Sometimes the schemes falter because of the ways that property owners adapt. One potential effect is that landlords will try to reduce maintenance on properties in order to optimize profits. In addition, rent controls can reduce the earning power of a property below its opportunity costs, so that landowners seek better investments elsewhere. Some landlords may pursue ways of removing tenants (such as through harassment or vexatious litigation) in order to allow the premises to be used more profitably. Plus, controls can result in a capital flight from the rental housing market, the conversion of apartment buildings into freehold units operating under condominium legislation (to the extent that conversions are not prohibited by law) and a reduction in the number of new units coming onto the market. When these events occur, rental housing stocks will eventually shrink and age.[181] A reduced supply in the face of a steady or increasing demand may also lead to the emergence of various black market

---

178 See further E. Iacobucci, ''Rent Control: A Proposal for Reform'' (1995) 27 Ottawa L.Rev. 311, at 326*ff*.

179 *Ibid.* at 326.

180 *Cf. ibid.* at 330*ff*.

181 C. Rydell *et al.*, *The Impact of Rent Control on the Los Angeles Housing Market* (Santa Monica: Rand, 1981) at 82.

practices, including the exacting of 'key money' from prospective tenants at the behest of either landlords or outgoing tenants.[182]

In the end, the problem to be remedied – a dearth of affordable rental housing – may be exacerbated. Moreover, the benefits that controls do produce may be spread unevenly. Tenants that are happily ensconced in controlled premises will be in a superior position when compared to latecomers to the rental market. Additionally, those who gain an advantage from the suppressed rents may not be those who are most deserving: "rent review is a blunt instrument: for every needy household assisted, two households without affordability problems are also assisted".[183]

However, it is not inevitable that rent controls will fail. Even if they suppress profits, it does not follow that earnings for landlords will dip below acceptable levels; the best use of the property might still be as leasehold accommodations. New rental housing is sometimes exempted from controls; therefore, the replenishing of this type of housing stock is not inhibited. Removing rent controls does not mean that the invisible hand of the market will now determine allocations in an unfettered way – there are copious subsidies and tax breaks that affect housing market practices; rent control is just one of these. And while there may be disadvantages in favouring present renters over latecomers, it may also be true that the security of tenure acquired by current renters enhances their personhood interests. That result has some virtue.[184]

The cat-and-mouse game of rent regulation provides a useful demonstration of the idea that the law can be seen, not as a way of prohibiting behaviour, but rather as a means of affecting the cost of conduct.[185] The law is little more than an enormous pricing mechanism in the eyes of some economic thinkers.[186] If we reduce the profitability of certain economic opportunities, this public policy initiative merely gets factored-in when investment decisions are made. Unless rent controls can make the financial costs of non-compliance heavy enough, the wealth-maximizing landlords among us will find other ways to put their money to work.

All in all, attempts by the state to transform the rental market through rent control regulations expose the highly political nature of the law of landlord and tenant, which, like labour law, is associated with issues of class stratification. This interrelationship is sometimes made explicit: rent controls were described in the Reagan Commission on Housing as an implicit, inequitable and inefficient

182 Key money refers to a one-time finder's fee that is collected as a condition of granting a lease to a prospective tenant.

183 J.R. Miron & J.B. Cullingwood, *Rent Control: Impacts on Income Distribution and Security of Tenure* (Toronto: Centre for Urban and Community Studies, 1983) at 51.

184 See J.W. Singer, ed., *Property Law: Rules, Policies and Practices*, 2nd ed. (New York: Aspen Law, 1997) at 804-7, and the references cited there.

185 See further Part 3(b)(i), Chapter 1.

186 C. Veljanovski, *The Economics of Law* (London: Institute of Economic Affairs, 1990) at 15.

tax on landlords for the benefit of tenants.[187] Rent control is a form of income subsidy. Another perspective is that the machinery of a liberal democratic state is not normally capable of bringing property owners to heel, in order to improve the living conditions for others, at least as long as the weapon of the capital strike is available to landlords and other business people.[188]

7.   THE PROPRIETARY STATUS OF LICENCES

A licence is a permission to do that which would otherwise constitute a trespass. Such a privilege may be expressly conferred, such as through a contract to enter a theatre to see a show, or it may be implied, such as when a shop is open for business to the public at large. Even a householder is generally taken to invite strangers to call at the front door, for lawful purposes at least.

Licences may take several forms. A bare licence, one unsupported by a contract, is fully revocable. Such is the nature of private property that the implied general invitation may be withdrawn at any time.[189] In the past, even a contractual licence was treated as being revocable at will,[190] the licensor being liable only in damages for revoking in breach of the contract.[191] Today, when a licence expressly or impliedly precludes or limits revocation, the licensor may be prevented, by injunction if necessary, from revoking contrary to the contract.[192] So, for example, a baseball fan lawfully attending a Toronto Blue Jays game at Skydome holds (in substance) an irrevocable licence for the duration of the game, provided that the fan complies with all of the requirements of the licence, express or implied.[193] While irrevocability confers upon some licences a measure of permanence it does not on its own elevate the licence into an interest in land. In other words, an irrevocable licence would not bind a purchaser of the land over which the licence is exercised. At any rate that is the conventional position.[194]

There are, however, accepted instances in which a licence will bind subsequent purchasers. A licence may blossom into an interest in land, in equity, under the principles of estoppel and unjust enrichment. A licence by estoppel may be imposed, for example, when the owner of land requests or allows another to spend money under an expectation, created by the owner of a parcel, that the other party

---

187 *Report of the President's Commission on Housing* (Washington, D.C.: P.C.H., 1982) at 91. *Cf.* Note, "Reassessing Rent Control: Its Economic Impact in a Gentrifying Housing Market", 101 Harv.L.Rev. 1835 (1988).

188 A public sector response is advocated in R.G. Lee, "Rent Control – The Economic Impact of Social Legislation" (1992) 12 O.J.L.S. 543.

189 Following a revocation of permission, police officers (and presumably all licensees) have a reasonable time to leave: *R. v. Thomas* (1991) 67 C.C.C. (3d) 81, 91 Nfld. & P.E.I.R. 341, 286 A.P.R. 341 (Nfld.C.A.) affirmed [1993] 1 S.C.R. 835, 78 C.C.C. (3d) 575.

190 *Wood v. Leadbitter* (1845) 13 M & W. 838, 153 E.R. 351.

191 *Thompson v. Park*, [1944] K.B. 408, [1944] 2 All E.R. 477 (C.A.).

192 *Winter Garden Theatre (London) Ltd. v. Millennium Productions Ltd.*, [1948] A.C. 173, [1947] 2 All E.R. 331 (H.L.).

193 *Davidson v. Toronto Blue Jays Baseball Ltd.* (1999) 170 D.L.R. (4th) 559 (Ont.Gen.Div.).

194 See the discussion of the *Errington* case in the text accompanying notes 200 to 208, *infra*.

will be able to remain there.[195] Recognizing the existence of an irrevocable licence is one way that a court can respond to unjust enrichment, though other remedies, such as the awarding of damages, or the granting of a freehold, might be more appropriate in a given case.[196]

In *Stiles v. Tod Mountain Development Ltd.*[197] the remedy granted was an irrevocable licence. There, A purchased from B Ltd. a lot in a proposed recreational subdivision. The company encouraged A to develop the property and eventually a cottage was built. B Ltd. later sold its interest to C Ltd., which acknowledged the rights of A (and others in the same position). However, the plan of subdivision was subsequently rejected by the provincial authorities, and this threw the entire development into disarray. It was held that A did not have a freehold interest, because the subdivision, and the interests dependent on it, could not be registered. The failure to obtain subdivision approval meant that there was no patch of ground that A could legally claim as his. Despite this, it was found that A's right to enter the land before registration was a contractual licence. This licence was protected by the doctrine of proprietary estoppel and was binding on C Ltd., which had notice of A's rights. The estoppel arose from the acts of detrimental reliance undertaken by A, including the building of the cabin.

A constructive trust may be imposed to protect a licence over land that has been transferred to a third party. This principle does not apply merely because the purchaser is aware of the presence of the licence when the land is bought; notice is not enough. Even purchasing property that is described in the transfer documents as being 'subject to' a licence may not be sufficient to support the imposition of a constructive trust on the interest acquired by the purchaser.[198] However, this remedy is appropriate when the purchaser's conduct is unconscionable. That might be so when a party acquires title to Blackacre, knowing of a licence, expressly taking title subject to it, *and* enjoying a benefit, such as a reduction in the price of the land, as a consequence of agreeing that the licence will continue.[199]

Some would go further than this. There is English authority that a contractual licence, pure and simple, can enjoy the status of an equitable interest in land. This controversial position developed out of the judgment of Lord Denning L.J. (as he then was) in *Errington v. Errington*, in which it was said that in the eyes of equity "[n]either the licensor nor anyone who claims through [that person] can disregard the contract except a purchaser for value without notice".[200] In that case, a father purchased a house in his own name. He allowed his son and daughter-in-law to live there and promised that the property would be transferred to them if they

---

195 See, *e.g.*, *Inwards v. Baker*, [1965] 2 Q.B. 29, [1965] 1 All E.R. 446 (C.A.); *Jarvis v. Toronto (City)* (1895) 25 S.C.R. 237; *Collier v. Salisbury (Village)* (1999) 208 N.B.R. (2d) 60, 531 A.P.R. 60, 169 D.L.R. (4th) 560 (C.A.).

196 For more on the doctrine of unjust enrichment, see Part 4(d), Chapter 6.

197 (1992) 64 B.C.L.R. (2d) 366, 22 R.P.R. (2d) 143, 88 D.L.R. (4th) 735 (S.C.).

198 *Ashburn Anstalt v. Arnold*, [1989] Ch. 1, [1988] 2 All E.R. 147 (C.A.) petition to the House of Lords dismissed; noted in [1988] C.L.J. 353 and [1988] Conv. 201.

199 See, *e.g.*, *Binions v. Evans*, [1972] Ch. 359, [1972] 2 All E.R. 70 (C.A.).

200 [1952] 1 K.B. 290, [1952] 1 All E.R. 149 (C.A.) at 299 K.B.

remained in occupation and made the remaining mortgage payments; this they did. But the house was later left by will to the mother (widow). She, in turn, sought possession against the daughter-in-law, who was then in sole occupation. A majority of the Court of Appeal held that the rights created by the earlier arrangement would ripen into an equitable interest once the payments on the mortgage were all made. In the meantime, the daughter (and the son) held what amounted to a licence coupled with an equity, which was binding on the widow.

Lord Denning's bold position has been applied in subsequent decisions,[201] but it has always lived under clouds of disapproval and doubt.[202] When the authorities were reviewed in the 1988 English Court of Appeal decision in *Ashburn Anstalt v. Arnold*[203] the Denning analysis was caustically rejected as being "neither practically necessary nor theoretically convincing".[204] It was not necessary, the Court suggested, because the result in *Errington* could have been supported on other grounds: (i) there was an estate contract, creating an equitable interest binding on the widow; (ii) there had been an estoppel by representation; and (iii) a constructive trust might have been warranted.[205]

The theoretical deficiencies of the Denning licence 'coupled with an equity' alluded to by the Court in *Arnold* are less obvious. Certainly it blurs the line between contractual and proprietary interests over land. And it suggests some odd possibilities. The notion that everyone who attends a Spirit of the West concert at the Winspear Centre acquires an interest in land for the duration of the show seems fabulous, of course.[206] On the other hand, if parties wish to create a binding right stopping short of a grant of exclusive possession (this being a matter of intention), there may be occasions when this is entirely suitable. The rejection in *Arnold* of the idea that a contractual licence can create an interest in land in England was *obiter dictum* because the interest in question was found to be a lease and not a licence. However, the House of Lords seems to have an accordant viewpoint, for it has stated (also in *obiter*) that "[a] licence in connection with land while entitling the licensee to use the land for the purposes authorized by

---

201 *D.H.N. Food Distributors Ltd. v. Tower Hamlets London Borough Council*, [1976] 1 W.L.R. 852, [1976] 3 All E.R. 462 (C.A.); *In re Sharpe (a bankrupt)*, [1980] 1 W.L.R. 219, [1980] 1 All E.R. 198 (Ch.D.).

202 They gathered soon after the decision was rendered: see H.W.R. Wade, "Licences and Third Parties" (1952) 68 L.Q.R. 337; A.D. Hargreaves, "Licensed Possessors" (1953) 69 L.Q.R. 466. But the result was welcomed in G.C. Cheshire, "A New Equitable Interest in Land" (1953) 16 Mod.L.Rev. 1.

203 *Ashburn Anstalt v. Arnold, supra*, note 198.

204 *Ibid.* at 22 Ch. (*per* Fox L.J.). *Ashburn Anstalt* was endorsed in *I.D.C. Group Ltd. v. Clark*, [1992] 2 E.G.L.R. 184 (Ch.D.).

205 See further A. Lyall, *Land Law in Ireland* (Dublin: Oak Tree Pr., 1994) at 494.

206 See *Cowell v. Rosehill Racecourse Co.* (1937) 56 C.L.R. 605, 43 Argus L.R. 273, 11 A.L.J. 32 (Aust.H.C.) at 616 C.L.R. (*per* Latham C.J.): "[f]ifty thousand people who pay to see a football match do not obtain fifty thousand interests in the football ground".

the licence does not create an estate in the land''.[207] The modern Canadian position has not yet been tested.[208]

A licence 'coupled with an interest' can also bind third parties in some circumstances. For example, a licence normally attaches to the grant of a *profit à prendre*. As will be seen later,[209] a *profit* is a real property interest entitling the holder to enter onto the land of another to exploit some natural resource. The licence, as an integral part of the grant, will bind subsequent owners of the servient lands over which the profit is enjoyed. The key is that the binding nature of the licence on third parties is dependent on the status of the interest to which it is 'coupled'. If that interest cannot bind third parties, neither will the licence. Therefore, this parasitic type of licence does not really amount to a distinct proprietary interest.[210]

8. BAILMENT[211]

A bailment is a temporary transfer of personalty under which the goods of a bailor are handed over to a bailee. As such it resembles, to a degree, a lease of land.[212] And just as the law affecting land leases is an amalgam of principles of property and contract, so too is the law of bailment, with the added dimension that the impact of tort law is also apparent.[213] The law of bailment draws from each of these areas, but it emerges as a branch of the law that is distinct from all three.[214]

(a) the nature of a bailment[215]

A bailment may be contractual or gratuitous. According to one school of thought, the bailment relationship is inherently consensual. Even if so, there are

---

207 *Street v. Mountford*, [1985] A.C. 809, [1985] 2 All E.R. 289 (H.L.) at 814 A.C. (*per* Lord Templeman). See further G. Battersby, "Contractual and Estoppel Licences as Interests in Land", [1991] Conv. 36.
208 But see *Freeborn v. Goodman*, [1969] S.C.R. 923, 6 D.L.R. (3d) 384, discussed in Part 8(c), Chapter 9.
209 See Part 3, Chapter 10.
210 Accord G.W. Hinde *et al.*, *Introduction to Land Law*, 2nd ed. (Wellington: Butterworths, 1986) at 382-3.
211 See generally N.E. Palmer, *Bailment*, 2nd ed. (London: Sweet & Maxwell, 1991).
212 A tenant of land has a property interest (a chattel real), but whether a bailee has rights of a similar quality is, at best, contentious. A lease runs with the sale of Blackacre, but the bailment does not *per se* bind a purchaser of the chattel. See further W. Swadling, "The Proprietary Effect of a Hire of Goods" in N. Palmer & E. McKendrick, eds., *Interests in Goods*, 2nd ed. (London: L.L.P., 1998) ch. 20. The resolution of this latter point turns in part on the extent to which covenants can run with chattels, an issue I examine in Part 12, Chapter 10.
213 Even this has an analogue in leases of land, given that the restrictions on use imposed by the law of waste are tort-based.
214 "An action against a bailee can often be put, not as an action in contract, nor in tort, but as an action on its own, sui generis, arising out of the possession had by the bailee of the goods": *Building & Civil Engineering Holidays Scheme Management Ltd. v. Post Office*, [1966] 1 Q.B. 247, [1965] 1 All E.R. 163 (C.A.) at 261 Q.B. (*per* Lord Denning M.R.). See also *American Express Co. v. British Airways Board*, [1983] 1 W.L.R. 701, [1983] 1 All E.R. 557 (Q.B.) at 560 All E.R.
215 See further A. Bell, "The Place of Bailment in the Modern Law of Obligations" in N. Palmer

instances when this element is attenuated. For example, a finder is sometimes described as a quasi-bailee on the basis that the true owner would probably agree to the finder taking possession on his or her behalf. Similarly, when goods are foisted on a party who then assumes control, this creates what is inelegantly called an 'involuntary bailment'.[216] Taking possession of goods under the mistaken impression that they belong to you may mean that you become an 'unconscious bailee', as unflattering as that may sound.[217]

Another view is that a bailment does not, of necessity, contain a consensual element, and that all that must be shown is that the bailee has voluntarily assumed control over the chattel.[218] This would explain the bailee status of a finder, but may also mean that a thief is a bailee of the victim. Another way to describe the basic idea is to say that the bailee must be in possession *with authority*, whether that emanates from an agreed transfer or a right implied by law.[219] Still, this may not account for the situation that arises when a landlord lawfully and unilaterally distrains the goods of a tenant for non-payment of rent: here it has been doubted that the landlord is a bailee, even though possession is obtained under lawful authority (*i.e.*, the law of distress).[220]

Under a garden-variety bailment, the bailed goods must eventually be re-delivered in their original or altered form. To send a ring for repair is a bailment, even if a new setting is cast and the old one discarded. However, it is not always essential that the goods be returned to the bailor. For example, the bailee's obligation may be to deliver goods to a third party. And a bailment exists when an item is left with a bailee for sale on consignment, to be returned only if it is not sold.[221]

When the arrangement gives the transferee the option to return the very goods bailed or to substitute others, this transaction should probably be characterized as a sale or barter and not a bailment.[222] This seems to be true also when fungibles are delivered and intermixed with those belonging to other people.[223] Here, the return of a *pro rata* (proportionate) share of the goods is not a return of the specific goods. The bailor cannot realistically expect to get the very same items back from the commingled mass. However, the line between sales and

---

& E. McKendrick, eds., *Interests in Goods*, 2nd ed. (London: L.L.P., 1998) ch. 19. See also A. Tay, "The Essence of a Bailment: Contract, Agreement or Possession?" (1965-7) 5 Syd.L.Rev. 236.

216 See further *Cosentino v. Dominion Express Co.* (1906) 16 Man.R. 563, 4 W.L.R. 498 (C.A.).

217 See further *A.V.X. v. E.G.M. Solders Ltd.*, *The Times*, July 7, 1982 (Q.B.). On discovery of the mistake, the holder becomes an involuntary bailee.

218 See *The "Pioneer Container"*, [1994] 2 A.C. 324, [1994] Lloyd's Rep. 593, [1994] 2 All E.R. 250 (P.C.). This case is discussed further in Part 8(f). See also Palmer, *supra*, note 211, at 37*ff.*

219 A.P. Bell, *Modern Law of Personal Property in England and Ireland* (London: Butterworths, 1989) at 90.

220 See *Martyn v. Omega Investments Ltd.* (1980) 30 Nfld. & P.E.I.R. 13, 84 A.P.R. 13 (Nfld.Dist.Ct.). See *contra* Palmer, *supra*, note 211, at 35.

221 See, *e.g.*, *Langley v. Kahnert* (1904) 9 O.L.R. 164 (C.A.) affirmed (1905) 36 S.C.R. 397.

222 *Crawford v. Kingston*, [1952] O.R. 714, [1952] 4 D.L.R. 37 (C.A.). See also *Oliver v. Newhouse* (1883) 8 O.A.R. 122 (C.A.).

223 *Lawlor v. Nicol* (1898) 12 Man.R. 224 (C.A.).

bailments of fungible goods is perhaps a little less clearly demarcated than one might initially think. A bailment relationship can arise, some argue, even when goods are handed over on the understanding that the bailee will be allowed to commingle.[224] In effect, the bailor is saying the following: 'I am giving you possession of my property, which you may dispose of and replace with other property. In either case you must hold the property in your possession as my bailee'. If this does produce a bailment, perhaps the governing rule should be stated this way: a bailment exists even in the case of commingled goods if those goods are transferred under circumstances in which the bailor controls their ultimate fate. That occurs in those situations in which the bailor agrees to let the bailee mix, sell and later replace the bailed objects.

Bailments are typically either for a fixed term (as in the case of a long-term lease of machinery), or at will (as in the case of a gratuitous loan). When there is a fixed term, one supported by consideration, the bailor's right to possession is postponed until the term has ended, provided that the bailee has not committed a serious breach that would allow the bailor to retake possession. Of course, when the bailment is at will, the bailor has a right to immediate possession and, in theory, may demand the article back at any time.

The lease–licence dichotomy, of great importance in the realm of landlord and tenant law, also marks an important threshold in the application of bailment principles. The placing of a chattel with X may amount to a bailment (X being a bailee), or a licence (X, having given permission to the presence of the chattel, being a licensor). The correct legal characterization can be vital, because a bailee has a duty of care over goods that is higher than that applicable to a licensor. This difference will be explained more fully below.[225]

Issues of categorization have arisen in a variety of settings,[226] including on numerous parking lots across Canada.[227] In determining the question of classification in such a context the courts have considered a number of factors, such as whether there is a handing over of keys; whether an attendant supervises the lot; the terms, if any, contained on the parking stubs;[228] the degree of supervision imposed over the vehicle;[229] the value of the goods; whether fees are charged;[230] the nature of past dealings; the layout of the premises; and the proximity of the

224 These ideas are explored in L.D. Smith, "Bailment with Authority to Mix – And Substitute" (1995) 111 L.Q.R. 10, assessing the decision in *Mercer v. Craven Grain Storage Ltd.*, Unreported, March 17, 1994 (H.L.). See further L. Smith, *The Law of Tracing* (Oxford: Clarendon Pr., 1997) at 91*ff.*

225 See Part 8(b), *infra*.

226 See, *e.g.*, *Seaspan International Ltd. v. The "Kostis Prois"*, [1974] S.C.R. 920, 33 D.L.R. (3d) 1; *Robertson v. Stang* (1997) 38 C.C.L.T. (2d) 62 (B.C.S.C.).

227 See also *Allison Concrete Ltd. v. Canadian Pacific Ltd.* (1973) 40 D.L.R. (3d) 237 (B.C.S.C.) where a payloader was hired by the defendant. Even though the plaintiff provided an operator, it was held that the defendant had control over the operations and was therefore a bailee.

228 *Bata v. City Parking Canada Ltd.* (1973) 2 O.R. (2d) 446, 43 D.L.R. (3d) 190 (C.A.).

229 See *Walton Stores Ltd. v. Sydney County Council*, [1968] 2 N.S.W.R. 109, 70 S.R. (N.S.W.) 244, 88 W.N. (Pt. 2) 153 (C.A.).

230 See, *e.g.*, *Maritime Coastal Containers Ltd. v. Shelburne Marine Ltd.* (1982) 52 N.S.R. (2d) 51, 106 A.P.R. 51 (T.D.).

owner to the vehicle.[231] The control of the keys is perhaps the 'key' factor, but this has not determined the outcome in all of the parking cases.[232] In addition, it has been suggested that if the owner of a chattel has "the exclusive right to the use of a particular identified portion of [the] premises for storage and safekeeping, this agreement will frequently provide conclusive evidence against the creation of a bailment".[233] Here a lease of the premises might be found to exist.

These clues are important, though one should not lose sight of the central question that must be resolved: has there been a transfer of possession? Some of these listed factors may be quite equivocal as guides in resolving that issue. Thus, the absence of a system of supervision may mean either that no bailment was intended, or that it was being poorly performed.[234] The fact that cars are not *generally* under the control of an attendant does not prevent a bailment from being found in any given case if control was in fact assumed.

Generally, when a bailment exists there will be a constructive bailment of other items that one would expect to be in the principal chattel. So, for instance, a bailment of a car carries with it all items one might normally find inside. Conversely, goods that one would not normally expect to accompany the bailed chattel are not covered by the bailment obligations unless the bailee has some notice of their presence.[235]

(b)   obligations of the bailee

As alluded to above, the distinction between a lease and a licence affects the nature and extent of the responsibilities that arise in relation to chattels. A licensor who allows a chattel to be left on his or her premises assumes no obligations over it other than those imposed by the general law. Such a person would be liable for stealing or converting the goods, for trespass or detinue, or when his or her positive acts of negligence cause damage. At the same time, there is no need for the licensor to be vigilant against such things as the prospect of theft or damage.

A bailee, on the other hand, must be more conscientious,[236] and is governed by the general law (for example, the bailee may not convert the property) as well as principles that relate specifically to the bailment relationship. First, if a contract requires the chattels to be dealt with in a specified fashion, a deviation from that course gives rise to strict liability.[237] The wrongful delivery of the goods is

---

231 See, *e.g.*, *McLennan v. Charlottetown Flying Services* (1979) 24 Nfld. & P.E.I.R. 72, 65 A.P.R. 72 (P.E.I.S.C.); *Albert v. Breau* (1977) 19 N.B.R. (2d) 476, 30 A.P.R. 476 (Q.B.).

232 See, *e.g.*, *Palmer v. Toronto Medical Arts Building Ltd.*, [1960] O.R. 60, 21 D.L.R. (2d) 181 (C.A.).

233 Palmer, *supra*, note 211, at 409.

234 See *Spagnolo v. Margesson's Sports Ltd.* (1981) 127 D.L.R. (3d) 339 (Ont.Co.Ct.) reversed on other grounds (1983) 41 O.R. (2d) 65, 145 D.L.R. (3d) 381 (C.A.).

235 *Minichiello v. Devonshire Hotel (1967) Ltd.*, [1976] 3 W.W.R. 502, 66 D.L.R. (3d) 619 (B.C.S.C.) affirmed [1978] 4 W.W.R. 539, 87 D.L.R. (3d) 439 (C.A.).

236 While a bailment is occasionally described as a delivery of a chattel 'in trust', it does not *per se* give rise to the equitable obligations of a trustee.

237 See *Lilley v. Doubleday* (1881) 7 Q.B.D. 510, [1881-85] All E.R.Rep. 406. See also *Blumenthal v. Tidewater Automotive Industries Ltd.* (1978) 29 N.S.R. (2d) 291, 45 A.P.R. 291 (C.A.).

normally treated as a deviation (or a tortious conversion) and liability will be imposed even if the misdelivery was prompted by a reasonable mistake.[238] Along the same lines, the refusal to redeliver as directed by the bailor will normally render the bailee liable; so will a denial of the bailor's title.[239] Second, a contract of bailment may set out the general level of care required in the care and possession of the bailed item(s). Unless this is done the law will imply levels of responsibility in accordance with the principles explained below.

The implied duties of a bailee have evolved over time, having passed through three phases. During the first, the bailee was strictly liable for just about any conduct that resulted in damage or loss.[240] Bailment was viewed through the juridical optic of contract law, under which parties are normally bound to perform their obligations to the letter. This meant that showing that all care was taken in trying to perform one's obligations was not good enough: if a bailee took possession and promised to return the goods in a certain state, this undertaking was strictly enforced.

In the second phase, beginning in the early eighteenth century, the implied obligations were defined by reference to calibrated levels of diligence. In the leading case of *Coggs v. Bernard*[241] this position became entrenched. Borrowing from Roman law, after the *Coggs* case the forms of bailment were placed under six headings: (i) *depositum* (safekeeping without charge); (ii) *commodatum* (a loan for use by the bailee); (iii) *locatio et conductio* (a hiring of chattels); (iv) *vadium* (a pawn or pledge); (v) *operis faciendi* (possession for performing paid services); and (vi) *mandatum* (a transfer for a specific purpose of the bailor). Although there are six types of bailment described here, in essence, these boil down to three levels of liability:

1.   Bailments for the benefit of the bailor. Here the bailee assumes a low duty of care and is liable for gross negligence.[242] Put another way, only slight diligence is required.

2.   Bailments for the sole benefit of the bailee. In this situation, the bailee is liable for slight negligence and therefore owes a duty of great diligence.[243]

---

238   "In cases of conversion by misdelivery notions of care are . . . irrelevant . . . Expressed simply, a bailee is liable for loss or damage resulting from his dealing with the goods bailed in a manner not authorised by the bailor": *Jackson v. Cochrane*, [1989] 2 Qd.R. 23 (Full Ct.) at 26 (*per* McPherson J.).

239   This obligation is subject to the bailee's ability to raise a defence of *jus tertii*: see further S. Fisher, *Commercial and Personal Property Law* (Sydney: Butterworths, 1997) at 205*ff.* The *jus tertii* defence is introduced in Part 4(c), Chapter 4.

240   *Southcote's Case* (1601) 4 Co.Rep. 83b, 76 E.R. 1061 (K.B.).

241   (1703) 2 Ld. Raym. 909, 92 E.R. 107.

242   See, *e.g.*, *Remme v. Wall* (1978) 29 N.S.R. (2d) 39, 45 A.P.R. 39 (T.D.). See also *Campbell v. Pickard* (1961) 36 W.W.R. 222, 30 D.L.R. (2d) 152 (Man.C.A.). *Cf. Brewer v. Calori* (1921) 29 B.C.R. 457 (C.A.).

243   See, *e.g.*, *Riverdale Garage Ltd. v. Barnett Bros.*, 65 O.L.R. 616, [1930] 4 D.L.R. 429 (C.A.).

3.   Bailments of mutual benefit. In these instances a duty of ordinary diligence applies.

The pigeonholes contemplated by this scheme were constructed before the modern law of negligence developed,[244] and it has been suggested that the 'postmodern' approach (the third phase) is to apply a general standard of negligence across the board. All of the circumstances of the bailment, including a consideration of whom the arrangement was intended to benefit, are taken into account under this mode of analysis.[245] However, courts still pay lip-service to the three levels of liability,[246] and so it is perhaps too early to say that the postmodern era has fully arrived in Canada.

The benefit needed to invoke the standard of ordinary diligence may be quite minor;[247] it does not have to be money, and need not amount to a separate charge for the bailment. For instance, the cost of a bus ticket may include a charge for baggage. The price paid for dry cleaning can be taken to cover storage. Even in the case of a restaurant offering 'free' parking to customers, a bailment of mutual benefit *may* (this is a contentious point) be found to exist. The advantage to the customer is obvious enough. The restaurant is treated as benefiting from the increased patronage that the offer of parking is designed to produce.[248] And by taking possession, the parking spaces can be used more efficiently. Moreover, the costs of this service to the restaurant are not zero, and are likely recouped through the menu. The old saying that there is no such thing as a free lunch can be extended to include 'free parking' as well.

The fixing of the level of care required cannot be understood merely by invoking the schema of duties described above. When one gets down to cases it is clear that the specific circumstances will always play a part in determining how a bailee will be expected to act. Some chattels require a particular type of care, owing to their nature or value. Storage of a Porsche[249] requires different action than that needed for the care of horses,[250] or human remains.[251] Moreover, a bailee

---

244 Starting of course with *Donoghue v. Stevenson*, [1932] A.C. 562, [1932] All E.R.Rep. 1 (H.L.). But the trend can be discerned from far earlier authorities dealing with bailments for the benefit of the bailor: see *Giblin v. McMullen* (1868) 2 L.R. 2 P.C 317.

245 See, *e.g., Houghland v. R.R. Low (Luxury Coaches) Ltd.*, [1962] 1 Q.B. 694, [1962] 2 All E.R. 159 (C.A.); *MacNaughton v. Farrell* (1982) 54 N.S.R. (2d) 361, 112 A.P.R. 361 (T.D.) at 369. See also the Canadian cases cited in Palmer, *supra*, note 211, at 547-8, n. 29. See also *Lifestyles Kitchens & Bath v. Danbury Sales Inc.*, [1999] O.J. No. 3097 (S.C.J.) at para. 34.

246 See, *e.g., Kinsella v. Club '7' Ltd.* (1993) 115 Nfld. & P.E.I.R. 150, 360 A.P.R. 150 (Nfld.T.D.).

247 See, *e.g., Carpenter v. Cargill Grain Co.*, 19 Alta.L.R. (2d) 354, [1982] 4 W.W.R. 292, 36 A.R. 598 (Q.B.).

248 See *Murphy v. Hart* (1919) 53 N.S.R. 79, 46 D.L.R. 36 (C.A.) concerning a 'free' coat check. But see *Martin v. Town N' Country Delicatessen Ltd.* (1963) 45 W.W.R. 413, 42 D.L.R. (2d) 449 (Man.C.A.).

249 *Zubrecki v. M.C.L. Motor Cars Ltd.* (June 12, 1990) Cooper Co. Ct. J. (B.C.Co.Ct.) summarized at 21 A.C.W.S. (3d) 975.

250 *Romo Seafood Ltd. v. James* (1990) 112 N.B.R. (2d) 305, 281 A.P.R. 305 (Q.B.).

251 *Mason v. Westside Cemeteries Ltd.* (1996) 135 D.L.R. (4th) 361, 29 C.C.L.T. (2d) 125 (Ont.Gen.Div.)

who claims to have a particular skill and knowledge will be expected to act accordingly and will be held to the avouched standard.

The surrounding circumstances, including the presence of special perils or risks, are also relevant factors in defining what one can expect from a bailee. For example, a bailee is not generally required to insure goods kept in storage and this is consistent with the fundamental idea that a bailee is not expected to guarantee the safety of bailed chattels in all events.[252] Nevertheless, the circumstances at play may well demand that a bailee obtain insurance. So, in the Ontario case of *Punch v. Savoy*[253] expensive jewellery was being shipped via a carrier that the bailee had not used before. Obtaining insurance for the value of the goods was a term of the contract for transport, but the bailee had under-insured the jewellery. This was found to be an actionable failure by the bailee. The Ontario Court of Appeal held that obtaining adequate insurance was "a minimal step that a prudent owner would take for goods of this type".[254]

Finders and involuntary bailees are Good Samaritans in the eyes of the law, and this affects the bailment duties that are imposed on them.[255] Their duties are quite minimal: those of a gratuitous bailee. Moreover, the liability for wrongful redelivery seems to be less stringent than in the case of other bailees: they are not strictly liable for the failure to return goods to the rightful owner. Instead, a negligence standard applies.[256]

A bailee may be held liable for acts of an employee committed in the course of employment by virtue of the general principles of vicarious liability.[257] Furthermore, a bailee cannot fob off responsibility by delegating the goods to an employee: that employee's negligence[258] or intentional dishonesty will render the employer bailee liable.[259] Some have gone so far as to suggest that a bailee can

---

252 See *Mason v. Morrow's Moving & Storage Ltd.* (1978) 5 C.C.L.T. 59, [1978] 4 W.W.R. 534, 87 D.L.R. (3d) 234 (B.C.C.A.). See also *Longley v. Mitchell Fur Co.* (1983) 45 N.B.R. (2d) 78, 118 A.P.R. 78 (C.A.) especially at 81, where Stratton J.A. adopts the reasoning in M.M. Litman, Annotation: *Morden v. Adamson* (1976) 2 C.C.L.T. 45. See also M.M. Litman, "Bailee's Liability for Failure to Warn Bailor of Lack of Insurance: Source of the Duty of Care" (1978) 16 Alta.L.Rev. 20.

253 *Punch v. Savoy's Jewellers Ltd.* (1986) 54 O.R. (2d) 383, 35 C.C.L.T. 217, 26 D.L.R. (4th) 546 (C.A.) discussed in N. Bankes & N. Rafferty, "The Liability of Bailee and Sub-Bailees: A Comment on *Punch v. Savoy's Jewellers Ltd.*" (1988) 14 Can.Bus.L.J. 97.

254 *Supra*, note 253, at 227 C.C.L.T. (*per* Cory J.A., as he then was).

255 This is true even though they enjoy possessory rights enforceable against others. Therefore, their actions are not regarded as purely altruistic in law.

256 See, *e.g.*, *Elvin & Powell, Ltd. v. Plummer Roddis, Ltd.* (1933) 50 T.L.R. 158 (K.B.). *Cf. Hiort v. Bott* (1874) L.R. 9 Ex. 86. In *Hiort* the defendant was held to be strictly liable, but the Court appears to have concluded that the defendant had *not* become an involuntary bailee. That being so, it was merely meddling with someone else's property.

257 See generally J.G. Fleming, *The Law of Torts*, 9th ed. (Sydney: Law Book Co., 1998) ch. 19.

258 See, *e.g.*, *Manitoba Public Insurance Corp. v. Midway Chrysler Plymouth Ltd.*, [1978] 1 W.W.R. 722, 82 D.L.R. (3d) 206 (Man.C.A.).

259 *Morris v. C.W. Martin & Sons*, [1966] 1 Q.B. 716, [1965] 2 All E.R. 725 (C.A.). See also *Port Swettenhan Authority v. T.W. Wu & Co. (M.) Sdn. Bhd.*, [1979] A.C. 580, [1978] 3 All E.R. 337 (P.C.). There is a suggestion in *Morris v. Martin, ibid.* at 725 and 737 Q.B., that a gratuitous bailee will not be liable for a theft by an employee entrusted with the goods, or any theft arising from that employee's negligence. Is this a sensible limitation?

be vicariously liable when the delegation is made to an independent contractor, *i.e.*, someone who is not an employee.[260] Even when the goods are not entrusted to a dishonest employee, the bailee may be liable if it can be shown that the bailee was negligent in some way.[261] That might be true (i) if the bailee had hired an untrustworthy employee under circumstances in which that could have been prevented; or (ii) if the bailee has carelessly created an opportunity for theft.

(c)   the onus of proof in bailment claims

Whether one conceives of a bailee's liability as being based on gradations of negligence, or on separate categories, the law of bailment still differs from general tort law with regard to an important element – the burden of proof. In civil actions the general rule is that the plaintiff bears a burden of persuasion and must therefore prove all elements of liability on the balance of probabilities. In bailment claims a presumption of negligence can arise, which the bailee must then rebut in order to avoid liability. The presumption contains three components: (i) *the triggering facts* – facts that must be proven by the bailor; (ii) *the short-cut to proof* – the facts that are then presumed against the bailee; and (iii) *the escape route* – the matters that the bailee must prove in order to overcome the shift in onus.

The presumption that is available in bailment suits is not easily invoked. The plaintiff-bailor must show that the acts complained of occurred during the course of the bailment, not before or afterwards. So, if items have gone missing the presumption will not apply unless it is shown that the loss occurred while the goods were in the possession of the bailee.[262] When the complaint is that the goods have been damaged, the condition of the goods when bailed and returned must be proved.[263] The rationale of the reverse onus is that the bailee is in a position to know what has transpired.[264] In *National Trust Co. v. Wong Aviation*[265] a bailed airplane and its bailee-pilot were lost in unknown circumstances. The bailee was, of course, not available to account for what had transpired. Therefore, it was held that the presumption of negligence could not be applied in these circumstances.

If, despite these hurdles, the triggering facts are all in place, negligence is presumed against the bailee, the degree of negligence being dictated by the type

---

260 See the *dictum* in *British Road Services, Ltd. v. Arthur V. Crutchley & Co.*, [1968] 1 All E.R. 811, at 820.

261 See *Morris v. C.W. Martin & Sons Ltd.*, *supra*, note 259. *Cf. Bamert v. Parks*, [1965] 2 O.R. 266, 50 D.L.R. (2d) 313 (Co.Ct.).

262 See, *e.g.*, *Calgary Transport Services Ltd. v. Pyramid Management Ltd.*, [1976] 6 W.W.R. 631, 1 A.R. 320, 71 D.L.R. (3d) 234 (C.A.); *Lifestyles Kitchen & Bath v. Danbury Sales Inc.*, *supra*, note 245.

263 See *Charrest v. Manitoba Cold Storage Co.* (1908) 17 Man.R. 539 (C.A.) affirmed (1909) 42 S.C.R. 253.

264 *The "Ruapehu"* (1925) 21 Ll.L.Rep. 310 (C.A.) at 315.

265 [1969] S.C.R. 481, 3 D.L.R. (3d) 55, discussed in N.E. Palmer, *Bailment*, 2nd ed. (London: Sweet & Maxwell, 1991) at 1264*ff. Cf. Amo Containers Ltd. v. Mobil Oil Canada, Ltd.* (1989) 62 D.L.R. (4th) 104, 75 Nfld. & P.E.I.R. 208, 234 A.P.R. 208 (Nfld.C.A.).

of bailment arrangement.[266] In order to pass through the escape route the bailee must disprove negligence (whether slight, gross, or ordinary, to use the modern tags) on the balance of probabilities. The defendant does not have to explain fully what happened; rather, what needs to be shown is that the system in place for the care and safekeeping of the bailed goods was up to the standard required by bailment law.[267]

(d)   the bailor's duties

The bailor assumes responsibility in relation to the state of a bailed chattel. While the delineation of the duty of a bailee is drawn on terms inspired by tort law, the bailor's obligations resemble the contractual liability of a seller of goods. Hence, a bailor for reward has a duty to ensure that the chattels are reasonably fit and suitable for the purposes of the hire. So, if a shopping cart has a defective wheel (not that this ever happens), leading to the collapse of the cart and injury to the bailee, a breach of the bailor's duty can be made out.[268] Canadian cases commonly speak of an obligation to take *reasonable* care that the goods supplied are safe and suitable. The bailor must protect against all defects that *skill and care* can discern and remedy.[269] On that reading, the standard of liability is essentially one of negligence. As a result, if a defect is latent (not patent), such that a careful detection would not have uncovered it, the bailor will not be liable. Liability under sales of goods legislation imposes a higher duty, under which the absence of negligence on the part of the seller is irrelevant.

In the case of a gratuitous bailment for the benefit of the bailee, it has been held that the bailor will be liable for failing (wilfully or through gross negligence) to warn the borrower of known defects that might make the item unfit for its purpose.[270] Logically, it should be the case that a gratuitous bailment for the benefit of the bailor (such as when A stores B's goods as a favour to B) should give rise to a more exacting duty on the part of the bailor: the bailor must make sure that the goods are not somehow harmful to the gratuitous bailee. This question has not yet been decided. It may be that liability here may follow the lead seen in relation to the bailee's duty of care – general principles of negligence may inform the standard of liability.[271] As alluded to in the preceding paragraph, such an

---

266 See Part 8(b), *supra*.
267 See *United Refrigerator Parts Co. v. Consolidated Fastfrate Ltd.*, [1974] 5 W.W.R. 166, 46 D.L.R. (3d) 290 (Man.C.A.).
268 *Cottee v. Franklins Self-Serve Pty. Ltd.*, [1997] 1 Qd.R. 469 (C.A.).
269 See, *e.g.*, *Crawford v. Ferris*, [1953] O.W.N. 713 (H.C.) drawing on the judgment of Lindley J. in *Hyman v. Nye & Sons* (1861) 6 Q.B.D. 685, at 687-8. See also *Matheson v. Watt* (1956) 19 W.W.R. 424, 5 D.L.R. (2d) 437 (B.C.C.A.); *Coleshaw v. Lipsett* (1973) 33 D.L.R. (3d) 382 (Sask.Q.B.); *Boorman v. Morris*, [1944] 3 D.L.R. 382, [1944] 2 W.W.R. 12 (Alta.S.C.). See *contra Neilson v. Atlantic Rentals* (1974) 8 N.B.R. (2d) 594 (C.A.). Absolute liability is the standard in Australia: *Derbyshire Building Co. Pty. Ltd. v. Becker* (1962) 107 C.L.R. 633 (Aust.H.C.); *Cottee v. Franklins Self-Serve Pty. Ltd.*, *supra*, note 268.
270 *Coughlin v. Gillison*, [1899] 1 Q.B. 145, [1895-99] All E.R.Rep. 730 (C.A.) discussed and criticized by Palmer, *supra*, note 265, at 632*ff. Cf. MacTague v. Inland Lines Ltd.* (1915) 8 O.W.N. 183 (H.C).
271 Palmer, *supra*, note 265, at 583-4.

approach is already somewhat apparent in the Canadian cases concerning bailments for reward.

(e)   avoiding liability

The basic rules of liability merely provide a starting point in the analysis. The contract of bailment may augment or diminish the responsibilities and rights of either party. The bailee may assume an absolute obligation to return the chattel,[272] or may seek to limit liability through an exemption or exculpatory clause.[273] We have all seen signs in cloak rooms and parking lots that declare something like: 'Not responsible for lost goods', or 'Park at Own Risk'. There is no general statutory or common law impediment to sheltering behind such protections. Nevertheless, the courts have reacted to these shields with circumspection;[274] this attitude is manifested through the ways in which judges have been able to ignore or constrict clauses that seek to reduce or eliminate the standard duty of care.

An exculpatory clause will apply only if it is accepted by the bailor (or bailee as the case may be). In written contracts, agreed to by the parties before the bailment begins, this aspect may be clear-cut; but not every bailment is created that way. Consider again the parking lot situation. Signs are sometimes placed on the lot to put the bailor on notice that no responsibility will be assumed for the cars that are left there. These warnings will not apply unless the bailor had either actual or constructive notice of the clause at the time when the bailment agreement was struck.[275] The location of the sign will be a factor in determining whether constructive notice was given, and a repeat customer is more likely to be fixed with notice than one who is not.

There are other avoidance techniques. A bailee may be estopped from relying on the clause by conduct suggesting that it will not be enforced according to its tenor.[276] In one case, the "unforgivably small print"[277] of the contract of bailment required a bailor to give notice of any damage to the goods in writing within 36 hours of the termination of the bailment. An inspection of the damage by an employee of the bailee in the presence of a representative of the bailor within 24

---

272 *Grant v. Armour* (1893) 25 O.R. 7 (H.C.).

273 See, *e.g., Miida Electronics Inc. v. Misui O.S.K. Lines Ltd.*, [1986] 1 S.C.R. 752, 34 B.L.R. 251, 28 D.L.R. (4th) 641.

274 Accord A. Samuels, "Car Park and Garage Mishaps" (1977) 121 Sol.J. 364.

275 See *Spooner v. Starkman*, [1937] O.R. 542, [1937] 2 D.L.R. 582 (C.A.). See also *Pickin v. Hesk*, [1954] O.R. 713, [1954] 4 D.L.R. 90 (C.A.); *Williams & Wilson Ltd. v. OK Parking Stations Ltd.*, [1971] 2 O.R. 151, 17 D.L.R. (3d) 243 (Co.Ct.); *Appleton v. Ritchie Taxi*, [1942] O.R. 446, [1942] 3 D.L.R. 546 (C.A.); *Way Sagless Spring Co. v. Bevradio Theatres, Ltd.*, [1942] O.W.N. 236, [1942] 3 D.L.R. 448 (C.A.); *Thornton v. Shoe Lane Parking*, [1971] 2 Q.B. 163, [1971] 1 All E.R. 686 (C.A.). Indeed, the small print on a signed form will not always be found to be part of the contract: see Fridman, *infra*, note 279, at 610*ff.*

276 See, *e.g., Schnelle v. City Parking Canada Ltd.*, [1972] 2 W.W.R. 550 (Alta.Dist.Ct.).

277 *Fraser Valley Milk Producers Cooperative Assn. v. Kaslo Cold Storage Ltd. Partnership* (1994) 92 B.C.L.R. (2d) 304 (C.A.) at 305 (*per* McEachern C.J.B.C.).

hours was held to suffice as notice, even though no written statement was delivered within the required time period.[278]

Generally, a contract will be construed against the party proffering it (under the *contra proferentem* rule[279]) and this can be pertinent when an exculpatory clause is ambiguous. In this context, the rule is applied to produce narrow readings of seemingly wide exemptions, so that a court may find that an exculpatory clause does not, as a matter of construction, cover the act(s) complained of by the bailor.[280] Accordingly, a clause will not normally be considered to apply once the bailee is acting outside of the four corners of the bailment. For example, a bailee who undertakes to store goods in warehouse A might not be able to invoke an exemption clause if the items were stored in warehouse B.[281]

In the past it has been questioned whether a party to a contract can, as a matter of law, exact a clause excluding that party from liability for breaches of a fundamental term of the contract. In the context of bailment, one would ask whether, by such a term, a bailee can be absolved from contractual liability for a failure to undertake the very core of the bailment obligations. The general issue of whether one can contract out of liability for fundamental breach has now been resolved in Canada: it is possible to bargain for such an exemption.[282] However, as a matter of construction, the courts will not readily construe an exculpatory clause as having such a sweeping effect. Additionally, it is possible that the arrangement will be treated as invalid because it is unconscionable under general contract law principles. In England it has been suggested that in cases involving a breach by 'deviation', that is, a serious departure from the agreed bailment, exclusion clauses are void.[283] Given that acts of deviation in bailment are merely a form of the more generic fundamental breach, one struggles to find a persuasive

---

278 See also *Davidson v. Three Spruces Realty Ltd.*, [1977] 6 W.W.R. 460, 79 D.L.R. (3d) 481 (B.C.S.C.).

279 See further G.H.L. Fridman, *The Law of Contract in Canada*, 4th ed. (Toronto: Carswell, 1999) at 495*ff.*

280 In *Leva v. Lam*, [1972] 2 O.R. 353, 25 D.L.R. (3d) 513 (C.A.) the clause read "Cars Parked at Owner's Risk". An attendant damaged the plaintiff's car while placing it in a spot. An action against the bailee-lot succeeded. The clause was held to exclude only liability for the car once parked. See also *Brown v. Toronto Auto Parks Ltd.*, [1955] O.W.N. 456, [1955] 2 D.L.R. 525 (C.A.); *Gray v. Canwest Parking Ltd.* (1965) 52 W.W.R. 56 (B.C. Co. Ct.); *Noble v. Brooks Chevrolet Ltd.* (1978) 5 Alta.L.R. (2d) 117, 11 A.R. 41 (Dist. Ct.). See also *Meditek Laboratory Services Ltd. v. Purolator Courier Ltd.* (1995) 102 Man.R. (2d) 85, [1995] 6 W.W.R. 738, 125 D.L.R. (4th) 738 (C.A.) leave to appeal to S.C.C. refused (1996) 131 D.L.R. (4th) vii (S.C.C.). *Cf. Samuel Smith & Sons Ltd. v. Silverman*, [1961] O.R. 648, 29 D.L.R. (2d) 98 (C.A.). A *bailor's* attempt to limit liability was narrowly construed in *Arrow Transfer Co. Ltd. v. Fleetwood Logging Co. Ltd.* (1961) 30 D.L.R. (2d) 631 (B.C.C.A.).

281 But see *Gibaud v. Great Eastern Ry. Co.*, [1921] 2 K.B. 426, [1921] All E.R.Rep. 35 (C.A.).

282 See generally *Hunter Engineering Co. v. Syncrude Canada Ltd.*, [1989] 1 S.C.R. 426, [1989] 3 W.W.R. 385, 57 D.L.R. (4th) 321. In a bailment setting, see *Punch v. Savoy's Jewellers Ltd.*, *infra*, note 291. *Cf. A.C.A. Co-operative Association Ltd. v. Associated Freezers of Canada Inc.* (1990) 97 N.S.R. (2d) 91, 258 A.P.R. 91 (T.D.) reversed (1992) 93 D.L.R. (4th) 559, 113 N.S.R. (2d) 1, 309 A.P.R. 1 (C.A.). Some of the uncertainty surrounding the *Hunter* judgments is discussed in Fridman, *supra*, note 279, at 635*ff.*

283 See A.P. Bell, *Modern Law of Personal Property in England and Ireland* (London: Butterworths, 1989) at 116*ff.*

reason for a different rule here, and it seems doubtful that Canadian courts need to resort to this type of reasoning to avoid an exemption, given the other means at their disposal.

(f)   assignment and sub-bailment

A bailee may sub-bail or assign, provided that the terms of the initial bailment expressly or impliedly permit this to be done. Even if not, the assignment or sub-bailment may later be ratified by the bailor.[284]

The analogy between sub-bailments and subleases of land should be obvious here, but the law has developed differently in relation to these two kinds of transactions. In the case of a sublease of land we saw that the common law does not confer on a landlord a direct cause of action against a subtenant.[285] At one time a comparable rule restricted the bailor's right of recourse against a sub-bailee, so long as the main bailment was still in existence. However, there were always exceptions. A tort action is available against third parties whenever a permanent injury to the bailor's reversionary interest has been inflicted. This cause of action is available even when the right of the bailor to possession is postponed.[286] Once a bailment has been terminated (which could arise by virtue of the bailee's wrongful act), the bailor can pursue a remedy against the person then in possession.

Modern authorities confer on the bailor a direct right of action against a sub-bailee when (i) the bailor has an immediate right to terminate the principal bailment;[287] and (ii) the sub-bailee accepts the goods knowing that the goods belong to someone other than the sub-bailor.[288] Notice here that a right to sue may exist even if there is no direct contractual relationship between the bailor and the sub-bailee.[289] At one time it seemed clear that when the bailor sues the sub-bailee, the primary basis of liability rests on the terms of the sub-bailment. This *should* mean that if the sub-bailment contains an effective exculpatory clause, then recovery by the bailor can be precluded.[290] However, in *Punch v. Savoy's Jewellers Ltd.*[291] this result was avoided. In the *Punch* case a valuable ring was given by A to a bailee (B) in Sault Ste. Marie for repair. The ring was then sub-bailed to C

---

284   See, *e.g.*, *Chapman v. Robinson* (1969) 71 W.W.R. 515 (Alta.Dist.Ct.).

285   See Part 3(a), *supra*.

286   *Mears v. London & South West. Ry. Co.* (1862) 11 C.B. (N.S.) 850, 142 E.R. 1029. See also A. Tettenborn, "Reversionary Damage to Chattels", [1994] C.L.J. 326. This action is roughly equivalent to the right of a remainderperson of land to sue for waste: see Part 4(c)(ii), Chapter 5.

287   See, *e.g.*, *Scott Maritimes Pulp Ltd. v. B.F. Goodrich Canada Ltd.* (1977) 72 D.L.R. (3d) 680, 19 N.S.R. (2d) 181 (C.A.).

288   See *The "Pioneer Container"*, [1994] 2 A.C. 324, [1994] Lloyd's Rep. 593, [1994] 2 All E.R. 250 (P.C.) at 262 All E.R. See further A. Phang, "Sub-Bailments and Consent" (1995) 58 Mod.L.Rev. 422. *Cf.* N. Bankes & N. Rafferty, "Privity of Bailment – Liability of Sub-Bailee to Owner of Goods: *The Pioneer Container*" (1997) 28 Can.Bus.L.J. 245, at 252*ff.*

289   *Pioneer Container, supra*, note 288.

290   See *Singer Co. (U.K.) Ltd. v. Tees & Hartlepool Port Authority*, [1988] 2 Lloyd's Rep. 164 (Q.B.).

291   (1986) 54 O.R. (2d) 383, 35 C.C.L.T. 217, 26 D.L.R. (4th) 546 (C.A.).

in Toronto where the work was performed. Following that, the ring was sub-bailed to D who was supposed to return it to the Soo. The item vanished somewhere along the way. The bailor, A, sued D (and B and C) but was met with the defence that an exculpatory clause in the sub-bailment to D limited its liability.

There had been no express authorization given from A to B to sub-bail, but the Court must have found that there was either an implied power to do so, or that there had been a subsequent ratification by the bailor (perhaps shown by A's law suit against the sub-bailee for breach of bailment). It was also held that the exculpatory clause could protect D only if the bailor had expressly or impliedly consented to such a clause.[292] The principle is that the bailor will be bound by the sub-bailment only if (s)he has expressly or impliedly consented to (or ratified) that sub-bailment. As the bailor in the case had not consented to that very exculpatory clause, it was held that the clause did not apply.

While the outcome of *Punch v. Savoy's Jewellers* seems to accord with the judicial tendency to side-step exculpatory clauses, I think that the treatment of the clause in this instance is questionable. If the decision is correct the law would seem to be that the bailor may select and adopt the beneficial parts of a sub-bailment and discard the rest. There is another possible mode of analysis, however, that could still result in liability in a case such as *Punch*. If the sub-bailment was made on terms outside of the warrant initially given by the bailor, it is an unlawful sub-bailment and the putative sub-bailee (D here) is no more than a wrongful possessor.[293] Furthermore, the bailee should be strictly liable for the transfer to D, which had been undertaken in breach of the head bailment. Alternatively, if the arrangement is ratified, the bailor, by this condonation, must surely take the sub-bailment as it is, like it or not. Ratification is no more than an *ex post facto* consent and it is hard to understand therefore why any different principle should apply when the consent is given before the sub-bailment instead of afterwards. In either case, one would assume that the bailor takes the sub-bailment with all its imperfections, or not at all.[294]

The *Punch* ruling does not stand alone, and in fact it can now be placed in the esteemed company of the Privy Council decision in *The Pioneer Container*.[295] In that case the Board was faced with the same type of issue that arose in *Punch* (albeit that a different contractual clause was involved). The Privy Council saw the problem as one going to the very nature of the bailment construct (which is so). It was reasoned that if a bailment arises only if the bailor consents to the transfer of possession to the bailee (or, as I would add, if the possession is assumed under *authority* that binds the bailor),[296] then the bailor has to accept the terms of the sub-bailment "warts and all".[297] However, if this consent is not a prerequisite to the establishment of a bailment, and all that is needed is that the bailee volun-

---

292 See *Morris v. C.W. Martin & Sons Ltd.*, *supra*, note 259.

293 See *Chapman v. Robinson*, *supra*, note 284.

294 Accord *Johnson Matthey & Co. v. Constantine Terminals Ltd.*, [1976] 2 Lloyd's Rep. 215 (Q.B.).

295 *Supra*, note 288.

296 See Part 8(a), *supra*.

297 *Supra*, note 288, at 341 A.C. (*per* Lord Goff).

tarily take the goods of another into custody, then a different conclusion follows. It means, among other things, that even a sub-bailment on terms that were not authorized is still a bailment; also, the head bailor may sue the sub-bailee for a breach. The basis of liability in that suit can be affected only by terms to which the bailor has agreed. Therefore, one can look to the sub-bailment to see if any terms found there might apply to *alter* the already-existing bailor/sub-bailee relationship. This second approach, which is thoroughly consistent with *Punch*, was held to be the correct one.[298]

(g)   bringing suit

Depending on the nature of the wrongful act, a breach by the bailee may give the bailor a right to pursue remedies in tort, contract or 'in bailment'. A bailee who appropriates goods may be liable for conversion. A wrongful withholding may also be actionable under the tort of detinue.[299] When a bailee acquires possession with the consent of the bailor, an overholding by the bailee is not actionable *per se* in tort. A demonstration of the wrongfulness of the bailee's retention must be shown, and this is typically accomplished by the plaintiff-bailor proving that a demand for the return of the chattel was ignored or refused, or that to have demanded a return of the item would have been futile. As a temporary measure, when recovery of the chattel is sought (as is normally the case in a detinue action), interim possession may be claimed by bringing a replevin action. The bailor may also resort to self-help (recaption). However, when goods lawfully come into the possession of a non-owner (again, such as under a bailment), the right of recaption is severely limited: if the bailor uses force, an action for trespass to the person or land of the bailee may result.[300]

It was once the law that a bailee's repudiation, if accepted by the bailor, brought the bailment to an end with the bailor obtaining no right to sue for prospective losses. This rule was influenced by the law of landlord and tenant that obtained prior to *Highway Properties Ltd. v. Kelly, Douglas & Co.*[301] It was reasoned that the bailor should be in no better position than the lessor of land. Owing to *Highway Properties*, the law governing land leases has been reversed on this point. Until recently, the bailor was left in the ironic position of having rights that were based on a land law analogue that no longer existed. This anom-

---

298 The holding in *The Pioneer Container* was endorsed in A. Tettenborn, ''Contract, Bailment and Third Parties – Again'', [1994] C.L.J. 440, at 442. *Cf.* Bankes & Rafferty, *supra*, note 288. *The Pioneer Container* was applied in *Sonicare International Ltd. v. East Anglia Freight Terminals Ltd.*, [1997] 2 Lloyd's Rep. 48 (Co.Ct.) and *Spectra International Plc. v. Hayesoak Ltd.*, [1997] 1 Lloyd's Rep. 153 (Co.Ct.). On the facts of *The Pioneer Container*, the bailor was found to have consented to the clause in issue (which conferred on Taiwanese courts exclusive jurisdiction to settle disputes). *The Pioneer Container* has not yet been considered by a Canadian court.

299 The torts of conversion and detinue are explained in J.G. Fleming, *The Law of Torts*, 9th ed. (Sydney: Law Book Co., 1998) ch. 4.

300 For an overview of the law regulating the right of self-help, see Ontario Law Reform Commission, *Study Paper on the Wrongful Interference With Goods* (Toronto: A.G. (Ont.), 1989) ch. 8.

301 [1971] S.C.R. 562, [1972] 2 W.W.R. 28, 17 D.L.R. (3d) 710.

alous situation has since been rectified, and the right of a lessor of chattels to seek damages for prospective loss has been authoritatively recognized.[302]

Like a tenant of land, a bailee acquires a possessory interest that can support a remedy whenever that possession is disturbed. This right is not dependent on injury to the bailor's interest; rather, it is a manifestation of the law's protection of prior possession and an application of the axiom that, as against subsequent actors, possession is title.[303] It is possible therefore that a tortious act by A in relation to the chattels of B, which are in the possession of a bailee (C), gives both B and C a cause of action. However, once the defendant (A) has paid the damages claim of the bailee (C) in full this constitutes a complete answer to a subsequent claim by the bailor (B). The converse is also true: if the bailor's claim is satisfied, the bailee cannot later recover from the wrongdoer.[304]

---

302 *Keneric Tractor Sales Ltd. v. Langille*, [1987] 2 S.C.R. 440, 43 D.L.R. (4th) 171, 82 N.S.R. (2d) 361.

303 See *The "Jag Shakti"*, [1986] A.C. 337, [1986] 1 All E.R. 480, [1986] 1 Lloyd's Rep. 1 (P.C.) applying *The "Winkfield"*, [1902] P. 42, [1900-3] All E.R.Rep. 346 (C.A.); *Swire v. Leach* (1865) 18 C.B.N.S. 479, 144 E.R. 531, [1861-73] All E.R.Rep. 768. See also *Irvine v. Hagerman* (1863) 22 U.C.Q.B. 545 (C.A.); *Sanford v. Bowles* (1873) 9 N.S.R. 304 (S.C.); *Knickle v. Silver Garage Ltd.* (1971) 4 N.S.R. (2d) 681 (T.D.); *Trailways Transport Ltd. v. Thomas* [1996] 2 N.Z.L.R. 443 (H.C.).

304 See *O'Sullivan v. Williams*, [1992] 3 All E.R. 385 (C.A.).

9

SHARED OWNERSHIP

The law doth punish man or woman
That steals the goose from off the common,
But lets the greater felon loose
That steals the common from the goose.

Anon.

1. INTRODUCTION

This chapter is concerned with the principles that govern the concurrent ownership of property. The first half of the discussion deals with the traditional forms of co-ownership found in Canadian law. The common law recognized four types: (i) joint tenancy; (ii) tenancy in common; (iii) tenancy by entireties; and (iv) co-parcenary. The first two, which are introduced immediately below, retain contemporary significance; the latter two are (at the very least) functionally extinct in Canada. The co-ownership of chattels will also be considered, principally in relation to the basic rules governing joint bank accounts.

This, however, is too narrow a focus for a proper treatment of the idea of shared property. This topic was introduced in the opening chapter through the brief discussion of common and public property.[1] It has also been pursued in other chapters: the law of leaseholds concerns the respective rights of landlords and tenants. The doctrine of estates deals with balancing the rights of present and future owners. In particular, the rules governing the life tenant[2] are vaguely similar to the law's regulation of co-ownership. Even the trustee-beneficiary relationship can be understood as involving concurrent rights of ownership. The law of servitudes and mortgages will provide further illustrations in the chapters that follow.

There are other areas in which shared entitlements play a prominent role. For example, under Canadian matrimonial property law a stylized form of co-ownership has been created. Shareholding in corporations also involves collective rights that can be characterized as a kind of co-ownership. And, as we will see, the corporate model provides the basis for co-operative housing and condominium regulatory schemes. Finally, there are notions of 'communal' rights that have a social and historical presence in Canadian law and culture. These various conceptions of sharing will be surveyed in the second half of the chapter.

---

1 See Part 2(b), Chapter 1.
2 See Part 4(c), Chapter 5.

2.   CONVENTIONAL FORMS OF CONCURRENT OWNERSHIP

(a)   joint tenancy and tenancy in common

The joint tenancy and the tenancy in common constitute the main forms of co-ownership in Canadian law. These interests have different attributes, and of the two, the joint tenancy involves a more elaborate set of rules. Adopting Blackstone's well-recognized analysis, to create a joint tenancy four unities must exist.[3] These describe the need for virtually perfect equality as between (or among) all of the joint tenants. So, the holdings of each joint tenant must be equal in nature, extent and duration (unity of interest); they must arise from the same act or instrument (unity of title); the interests of the joint tenants must arise at the same time (unity of time); and their rights must relate to the same piece of property (unity of possession); that is, "each of them have the entire possession, as well as every *parcel* as of the *whole*".[4]

The unity of time requirement has been modified by several exceptions that apply when the interests are created through a will or a deed to uses. For example, in a devise 'to A for life, remainder to the children of A as joint tenants', a joint tenancy may be created for those children who vest, even if they do so at different times, that is, as each is born.[5] There is no clear reason as to why this type of exception is permitted, but then the whole purpose of the unities is obscure and no light is shed by Blackstone's treatment of the subject. There is a certain conceptual purity in requiring a high degree of symmetry among joint tenants. The legal fiction underlying a joint tenancy is that there is only one tenant and that there are no distinct shares held by anyone. It is ownership *per my et per tout*: each holds for all.[6] Canadian courts have treated the four unities as if they were carved in (Black)stone.[7] Given the lack of modern function for these requirements, the Ontario Law Reform Commission has recommended that a joint tenancy should arise so long as (i) unity of possession exists; and (ii) there is an intention (presumed by statute or otherwise) to create a right of survivorship.[8]

While the four unities lie at the heart of the joint tenancy as it is now constituted, undoubtedly its most important characteristic is the right of survi-

---

3 W. Blackstone, *Commentaries on the Laws of England* (Chicago: U. of Chi. ed. 1979, 1765-9) vol. 2, at 180-2.

4 *Ibid.* at 182 (emphasis in the original).

5 See *Kenworthy v. Ward* (1853) 11 Hare 196, 68 E.R. 1245. See further R.E. Megarry & H.W.R. Wade, *The Law of Real Property*, 5th ed. (London: Stevens & Sons, 1984) at 421-2, for the ancient authorities cited to support this exception. Unities of time and title exceptions also exist for trustees under s. 17 of the *Trustee Act*, R.S.A. 1980, c. T-10.

6 In a joint tenancy *'totum tenet et nihil tenet'*: he (or she) holds the whole and yet holds nothing.

7 See, *e.g.*, *Re Speck* (1983) 51 B.C.L.R. 143 (S.C.) at 144, where the idea of a joint tenancy without unity of interest was described as a "monster unknown to the law". The monstrous attributes were not explained.

8 Ontario Law Reform Commission, *Report on Basic Principles of Land Law* (Toronto: A.G. (Ont.), 1996) at 107, 159. Recommendations have been advanced in British Columbia that the requirement of unity of interest be abolished: Law Reform Commission of British Columbia, *Report on Co-Ownership of Land* (Vancouver: L.R.C.B.C., 1988) at 33, 60.

vorship, the *jus accrescendi*.[9] In essence, joint tenants are engaged in a tontine pact. Once a joint tenant dies, his or her interest is extinguished, increasing the holdings of the survivors. On the death of the penultimate co-owner, the remaining tenant will hold the full interest. However, the chance of receiving the sole title by surviving one's co-tenants is a precarious one. As will be seen,[10] a joint tenancy may be converted into a tenancy in common even, in some instances, through the unilateral action of a tenant.[11]

The survivorship device has proven to be versatile. In the feudal context, the joint tenancy led to a simplified title, because the various interests would eventually coalesce into one, through survivorship. It could also serve the constituency of tenants. By placing legal title in the hands of several trustees as joint tenants, the transmission of that title on death was postponed indefinitely, since on the death of one trustee the legal estate did not devolve but was subsumed in the surviving trustees. This avoided tenurial liability arising from the descent of the legal estate – an event that could trigger feudal death duties.[12] Apart from this, it is generally sensible for trust assets to be held by the trustees as joint tenants, because on the death of one trustee, the property will continue to be held by the others, rather than pass to the decedent trustee's heirs, to whom this inherited managerial interest might be little more than an unwanted burden.

The Law Reform Commission of British Columbia thought it "safe to say that today the joint tenancy continues to be of use almost exclusively in the context of family holdings",[13] where it can be used as an estate planning mechanism. Survivorship occurs by operation of law and serves as an alternative to a transfer by will, thereby eliminating the need to seek probate to obtain a change in the registration of title. Property held in joint tenancy may also provide insulation from creditors. While a debtor/joint tenant's interest may be seized by a creditor, the right to do so is lost once that tenant dies, at which time the debtor's interest in the property vanishes.

Only the unity of possession must exist for a tenancy in common to arise, though of course all four unities may be present. Because there need not be a

---

9 Despite the appearance created by its name, the *jus accrescendi* was apparently unknown to Roman law: *Curmody v. Delehunt*, [1984] 1 N.S.W.L.R. 667 (C.A.) at 675, affirmed (1986) 161 C.L.R. 464, 68 A.L.R. 253 (Aust.H.C.).

10 See Part 4, *infra*.

11 In Saskatchewan the consent of all joint tenants is required to sever a legal joint tenancy (unless the joint tenants are trustees, executors or administrators): *Land Titles Act*, R.S.S. 1978, c. L-5, s. 240 [as am.]. See, *e.g.*, *Canada v. Peters* (1982) 21 Sask.R. 106, [1983] 1 W.W.R. 471, 141 D.L.R. (3d) 508 (Q.B.). But see *Royal Bank of Canada v. Oliver (Trustee of)* (1991) 10 C.B.R. (3d) 235, [1992] 1 W.W.R. 320, 85 D.L.R. (4th) 122 (*sub nom. Royal Bank v. Babiy*) (C.A.) leave to appeal to S.C.C. refused (1992) 10 C.B.R. (3d) 235n (S.C.C.). *Cf. Land Titles Act*, R.S.A. 1980, c. L-5, s. 68.1 [as am.]. For an examination of problems of severance of Torrens title land in Australia, see further J. Tooher, "Windfall by Wager or Will? Unilateral Severance of a Joint Tenancy" (1998) 24 Monash U.L.Rev. 399.

12 This tax avoidance technique is discussed in Part 3(a), Chapter 6.

13 *Report on Co-Ownership of Land, supra*, note 8, at 30. See also N.W. Hines, "Real Property Joint Tenancies: Law, Fact, and Fancy", 51 Iowa L.Rev. 582 (1966) which refers to an empirical study that found that the joint tenancy in Iowa was mainly used by married couples.

unity of interest, the parties may each hold a different quantum of the title (say, one-third to A and two-thirds to B). Under that arrangement there is still unity of possession and both parties are equally entitled to possession of the whole; their respective shares remain undivided during the currency of the relationship. Given that the pure-form tenancy in common does not involve a right of survivorship, an interest held in common devolves on the death of a tenant, by will or through the law of intestacy, in accordance with general principles.

The tenancy in common has many functions. While a joint tenancy may be ideal for family estate planning, or when trustees are holding title, the right of survivorship is usually seen as inappropriate in a commercial setting or in other arm's length dealings. So, for example, it is conventional for partnership assets to be held in common.[14] Likewise, for condominium property, where freehold interests in suites are involved, the common areas (such as the stairs, halls and foyers) are typically held by the condominium unit owners as tenants in common.[15]

(b)   co-parcenary and tenancy by (the) entireties

The forms of co-ownership known as co-parcenary and tenancy by entireties reveal the abject sexism of the common law. Co-parcenary arose where property devolved on intestacy pursuant to the rules of primogeniture. In the absence of a male heir, land would pass to all of the female children, who would rank equally as co-parceners. Collectively they were counted as one heir, equal to the oldest male. The introduction of modern intestacy principles has rendered this type of concurrent ownership obsolete.[16]

At common law a transfer of land to a husband and wife, without more, created a specialized joint tenancy, known as a tenancy by entireties. A fifth unity was present, the marital unity.[17] Property held in this way could not be alienated unless both spouses agreed and the entirety could not be severed other than through the termination of the marriage (which would transform the title into a joint tenancy). Until then, the husband was solely entitled to any income derived from the property. Several provinces have expressly abolished the tenancy by entireties,[18] and in others it has probably been destroyed as a by-product of the elimination of the doctrine of marital unity.[19] While the continued importance of the

---

14 But see notes 24 and 118, *infra*.

15 See further Part 8(b), *infra*.

16 Co-parcenary may still apply when a fee tail devolves on two or more daughters. Given that it is likely that no land in Canada is actually held in fee tail, co-parcenary is likely also non-existent: see J.M. Glenn, "Tenancy by the Entireties: A Matrimonial Regime Ignored" (1980) 58 Can.B.Rev. 711, at 718, n. 28.

17 See the discussion of the doctrine of marital unity in Part 3(a), Chapter 2.

18 See, *e.g.*, *Law of Property Act*, R.S.A. 1980, c. L-8, s. 5. See further Glenn, *supra*, note 16, at 721.

19 Glenn, *supra*, note 16, at 721-2. In *Campbell v. Sovereign Securities & Holding Co.*, [1958] O.W.N. 415, 16 D.L.R. (2d) 606 (C.A.) affirming [1958] O.W.N. 441, 13 D.L.R. (2d) 195 (H.C.), it was held that a tenancy by entireties could be created in Ontario, even in the face of the *Married Women's Property Act* then in force in that province. See also W.D. Goodman, "The Use of Tenancies by the Entireties in Estate and Tax Planning" (1996) 15 E. & T.J. 373.

estate by entireties has been promoted,[20] I find that difficult to accept. True, this form of holding did once serve to protect property from attachment by the creditors of one spouse, and it prevented alienation unless both husband and wife consented. However, similar protective measures can be (and have been) implemented without the need to resort to this rigid and archaic institution.[21]

3.   METHODS OF CREATION

Assuming the four unities are present, determining whether or not a joint tenancy or a tenancy in common has been created rests on the intention of the grantor. If the document is silent on this point, a rule of construction is required. The early common law demonstrated an ardent preference for the joint tenancy, presumably because of its effect on feudal rights, the convenience it provided for trustees, and the usefulness of survivorship in simplifying the state of title. As a result, a rule of construction emerged under which property conveyed simply 'to A and B' created a joint tenancy, absent a contrary intention.

Equity did not share this posture. Instead, it was thought that survivorship was regarded as "odious";[22] it made "no provision for posterity";[23] and it might wind up being applied in situations in which the owners were completely unaware of its effects. Although equity did reluctantly follow the law most of the time in presuming that a joint tenancy had been created, it refused to do so in a few circumstances. Equity presumes a tenancy in common (i) for partnership assets;[24] (ii) in cases where money is advanced and secured under a mortgage and (iii) when money to purchase property is provided in unequal shares. In addition, it has been held that if possession of a co-owned property is shared by individuals pursuing separate commercial enterprises, equity will presume a tenancy in common.[25]

Cf. *Demaiter v. Link*, [1973] 3 O.R. 140, 12 R.F.L. 314, 36 D.L.R. (3d) 164 (H.C.). See also B. Laskin, Note (1959) 37 Can.B.Rev. 370.

20 See Goodman, *supra*, note 19. See also the reform ideas advocated in J. Harper Porter, "Real Property – Tenancy by the Entirety in North Carolina: An Idea Whose Time Has Gone?", 58 N.C.L.Rev. 997 (1979-80); and Glenn, *supra*, note 16.

21 See the discussion of matrimonial property law in Part 7, *infra*. Newfoundland law comes close to employing something that looks like the tenancy by entireties. Section 8 of the *Family Law Act*, R.S.N. 1990, c. F-2, provides that each spouse has an equal interest in the home "[n]otwithstanding the manner in which the matrimonial home is held". This provision is deemed to create a joint tenancy: sub. 8(2). See further *Walsh v. Canadian General Insurance Co.* (1989) 60 D.L.R. (4th) 358, 77 Nfld. & P.E.I.R. 118, 240 A.P.R. 118 (Nfld.C.A.).

22 *R. v. Williams* (1735) Bunb. 342, at 343, 145 E.R. 694. See also *Gould v. Kemp* (1834) 2 My. & K. 304, at 309, 39 E.R. 959, at 961; *York v. Stone* (1709) 1 Salk. 158, 91 E.R. 146 (Ch.).

23 *Kent's Commentaries on American Law*, 12th ed., O.W. Holmes, ed. (Boston: Little, Brown, 1873) vol. 4, at 361. Of course, this critique overlooks that the ultimate survivor obtains a transferable interest and that a joint tenancy can be transformed into a tenancy in common.

24 But take note of the controversy and surrounding the case of *Harris v. Wood* (1915) 7 O.W.N. 611 (H.C.) discussed in *Report on Basic Principles of Land Law, supra*, note 8, at 77-8.

25 See further *Malayan Credit Ltd. v. Jack Chia-MPH Ltd.*, [1986] A.C. 549, [1986] 1 All E.R. 711 (P.C.). The parties in that case had divided the premises into unequal portions and paid expenses on a similar basis. The Privy Council held that a tenancy in common existed, treating

Over time the law's position shifted. Although the presumption in favour of the joint tenancy continued, courts began to adopt the view that the slightest indication that property was meant to be held in common could suffice to rebut it.[26] Accordingly, the common law presumption might be negated by the use of the following language: 'equally amongst them', 'equally',[27] 'in equal moieties', 'share and share alike', 'respectively', 'between', 'amongst', to 'each'.[28] Strange as it might seem, even the word 'jointly', in just the right context, might be taken to signify a tenancy in common.[29] Such terms and phrases are referred to as *words of severance*. At first glance some of the terms appear to be equivocal. Certainly a gift to two persons 'equally' could be taken to imply a joint tenancy. However, the thinking here is that these words of severance imply a division of the property into shares, and this is antithetical to the imagery of a joint tenancy, within which no distinct shares are held by any one person.

This judicial reaction was based on the same concerns that arose in equity: some joint owners might be unaware of the survivorship rule. The most colossal example of this type of transactional misconception to be found anywhere might be that which occurred in colonial Nova Scotia. At one time, letters patent over large tracts in that colony were issued to groups of settlers *en masse*. Little attention was paid to legal conventions, and so the grants did not describe the nature of the communal rights held: hence the presumption of joint tenancy applied. That being so, once the original settlers died, in theory, their shares would not descend down to their families, but rather would pass by survivorship – in effect, across the field – to their neighbours! However, "it had never been contemplated by the government or the grantees, that survivorship was to arise under these grants".[30] Eventually the problem was rectified through legislation that transformed all existing joint tenancies into tenancies in common.[31]

More generally, statutory modifications in some jurisdictions have established a presumption in favour of the tenancy in common, reversing the common law rule. For instance, Alberta law provides that:

> When, by letters patent, notification, transfer, conveyance, assurance, will or other assignment, land or an interest in land is granted, transferred, conveyed, assigned or bequeathed to 2 or

---

the unequal physical division and payments as analogous to a purchase in unequal portions. Perhaps there is a stronger analogy with the rule relating to partnership assets. See also the text accompanying note 137, *infra*.

26 R. Jennings & J.C. Harper, *Jarman on Wills*, 8th ed.(London: Sweet & Maxwell, 1951) vol. 3, at 1793-4. See also *McEwan v. Ewers*, [1946] 3 D.L.R. 494, [1946] O.W.N. 573 (H.C.); *Fisher v. Anderson* (1880) 4 S.C.R. 406.

27 See, *e.g.*, *Re Chafe Estate* (1995) 9 E.T.R. (2d) 196, 134 Nfld. & P.E.I.R. 345, 417 A.P.R. 345 (Nfld.T.D.); *Re Leaver*, [1997] 1 Qd.R. 55 (S.C.).

28 See *Jarman on Wills*, *supra*, note 26, at 1794. See also *Re Woodward* (1975) 64 D.L.R. (3d) 364 (B.C.S.C.).

29 *Re White* (1987) 59 O.R. (2d) 488, 38 D.L.R. (4th) 631 (H.C.). *Cf. Rafuse v. Borne* (1996) 16 E.T.R. (2d) 80, 157 N.S.R. (2d) 118, 462 A.P.R. 118 (S.C.) where a number of authorities are reviewed.

30 B. Murdoch, *Epitome of the Laws of Nova Scotia* (Halifax: Joseph Howe, 1832-3) vol. 2, at 148.

31 S.N.S. 1791, c. 10, which supplemented S.N.S. 1758, c. 2.

more persons, other than as executors or trustees, in fee simple or for any less estate, legal or equitable, those persons take as tenants in common and not as joint tenants unless an intention sufficiently appears on the face of the letters patent, transfer or conveyance, will or other assurance that they should take as joint tenants.[32]

By virtue of this section a purposeful act is now required to create a joint tenancy and thereby invoke survivorship. However, the statute does not replace the common law totally. It remains applicable in the case of transfers to executors and trustees, which is sensible given that the practical advantages of employing joint tenancies remain in those contexts. Furthermore, words of severance retain importance when language that appears to denote a joint tenancy is jumbled with accepted words of severance, so that the question as to what was really intended must be answered. In such instances, when all else fails, there is a default rule that in a deed the first direction is to be regarded as controlling, while in a will, the last will normally govern.[33] Additionally, the Alberta statute, like those in other provinces, does not change the rule of construction governing *personal* property. Therefore, the common law presumption still applies to personalty. That being so, the traditional learning on words of severance remains relevant in determining whether that presumption has been rebutted.

Owing to these statutory reforms, the creation of a joint tenancy of land now generally requires the existence of the four unities coupled with a sufficiently stated intention. Assuming that the unity of possession is present, a tenancy in common can be created in a variety of ways: (i) by express creation; (ii) pursuant to a statutory presumption; (iii) as a result of a failed attempt to create a joint tenancy (such as where there is no unity of interest); or (iv) by operation of law.[34] Moreover, a validly created joint tenancy may later be transformed into a tenancy in common through *acts* of severance, as we will see below.[35]

It is possible for parties to hold *legal* title to a parcel of land in one form of co-ownership, while holding in another form in *equity*. For example, a transfer of land 'unto and to the use of A and B in trust for A and B' [36] would make the parties joint tenants in law, but tenants in common in equity. Different titles at law and equity might also be produced through the imposition of a resulting or constructive trust.[37] Consider a situation in which A and B purchase property, each person advancing the same amount of money. Assume further that title is placed in the name of A alone. Absent a contrary intention, a resulting trust will be implied, giving both parties a share in the equitable interest equivalent to the ratio of their respective contributions (here, 50:50). In other words, A, the regis-

---

32 *Law of Property Act*, R.S.A. 1980, c. L-8, s. 8. Compare *Family Law Act*, R.S.N. 1990, c. F-2, s. 8, which is discussed in passing in note 21, *supra*.

33 *Joyce v. Barker Brothers (Builders) Ltd.* (1980) 40 C. & P.R. 512 (Ch.D.).

34 See, *e.g.*, *Conveyancing and Law of Property Act*, R.S.O. 1990, c. C.34, s. 14: "Where two or more persons acquire land by length of possession, they shall be considered to hold as tenants in common and not as joint tenants". The law of adverse possession, to which this provision relates, is outlined in Part 3, Chapter 4.

35 See Part 4, *infra*.

36 Recall the discussion of the meaning of this cryptic language in Part 3(d), Chapter 6.

37 See Parts 4(c) and (d), Chapter 6.

tered owner, would be treated as holding the legal title on trust for A and B, who would hold the equitable title as tenants in common. Additionally, acts of severance may transform a joint tenancy into a tenancy in common in equity while leaving the legal title unaltered. This is possible because some acts of severance may be regarded as effective in equity, but not in the eyes of the common law.

In all of these instances the dissonance that occurs between the rights at law and those in equity poses no logistical or conceptual problem because, generally, the state of the beneficial (*i.e.*, equitable) title is paramount. Assume, for example, that A and B are joint tenants in law, and tenants in common in equity. If B dies first, A assumes full legal title by survivorship. B's equitable interest, being held in common, passes to B's estate, leaving A to hold legal title as trustee for the beneficial owners, namely B's estate and A.

4.   SEVERANCE OF JOINT TENANCIES[38]

(a)   the policy mix

As mentioned above, the right of survivorship is not immutable. The destruction of that right is referred to as a 'severance'. Before the presumption in favour of joint tenancy was reversed by statute, we noticed that there was a perceived danger that parties sometimes held as joint tenants without realizing that the right of survivorship would control ownership entitlements on death. As we have just seen, one response to this is to treat words of severance as revealing an intention to create a tenancy in common.[39] Another tactic is to find that subsequent events have transformed – severed – the joint tenancy. However, in those jurisdictions in which the creation of a joint tenancy now requires cognizant and deliberate action, that is, an express intention to create a joint tenancy, finding severance as a way to avoid the dramatic results of survivorship may be excessive, even unfair.[40]

When questions of severance emerge, "[n]owadays everyone starts with the judgment in *Williams v. Hensman*".[41] This oft-cited case declares that a joint tenancy can be severed in three ways: (i) by one person acting on his or her own share; (ii) by mutual agreement; or (iii) by "any course of dealing sufficient to intimate that the interests of all were mutually treated as constituting a tenancy in common".[42] These methods will be considered in turn.

(b)   severance through unilateral action

The first 'rule' builds on the straightforward idea that any act that destroys an essential unity must bring the joint tenancy to an end. Therefore, where A and

---

38 See generally A.J. McClean, "Severance of Joint Tenancies" (1979) 57 Can.B.Rev. 1.

39 See the text accompanying notes 26 to 29, *supra*.

40 McClean, *supra*, note 38, at 25, quoted with approval in *Morgan v. Davis* (1984) 17 E.T.R. 271, 58 N.B.R. (2d) 235, 151 A.P.R. 235 (Q.B.).

41 *Burgess v. Rawnsley*, [1975] Ch. 429, [1975] 3 All E.R. 142 (C.A.) at 438 Ch. (*per* Lord Denning M.R.). See further P. Luther, "*Williams v Hensman* and the Uses of History" (1995) 15 Leg.Stud. 219.

42 *Williams v. Hensman* (1861) 1 John & H. 546, at 557, 70 E.R. 862, at 867 (*per* Page Wood V.C.).

B hold as joint tenants, and A conveys to C, the new co-ownership relationship between B and C must be a tenancy in common because the unities of title and time are now absent.[43] Likewise, where A, B and C hold jointly, and C conveys to D, the title then reads as follows: A and B continue to hold as joint tenants *inter se*, but D holds a one-third interest as a solitary tenant in common. This means, in effect, that the interests of A and B will pass on survivorship. The one-third portion owned by D will devolve to D's heirs. Similarly, the contorted action of a conveyance to oneself also produces a severance,[44] because the new title resulting from this process is obtained at a different time and under a different document than that of the other joint owners.[45]

A partial alienation by one joint tenant, such as the granting of a life estate, *should* also produce a severance, because this leaves the grantor with only a reversion, thus destroying the unity of interest.[46] Likewise, a transfer of an equitable interest results in a severance of the equitable title.[47] However, an attempted severance by will is ineffective. The idea behind the *jus accrescendi* is that it determines the course of title after the death of an owner. The right of survivorship trumps that owner's will (*jus accrescendi praefertur ultimae voluntati*).[48] Of course, it also prevails over the normal rules for the devolution of property on an intestacy. Additionally, the granting of an easement or a rentcharge will not sever.[49] These transactions do not destroy a unity, they merely encumber a tenant's interest with some additional right.

---

43 Consent among all of the joint tenants is required to perfect a severance of legal title in Saskatchewan: see *Land Titles Act*, R.S.S. 1978, c. L-5, s. 240. *Cf. Land Titles Act*, R.S.A. 1980, c. L-5, s. 68.1. See further, note 11, *supra*.

44 See, *e.g.*, *Knowton v. Bartlett* (1984) 16 D.L.R. (4th) 209, 60 N.B.R. (2d) 271, 157 A.P.R. 271 (Q.B.); *Walker v. Dubord* (1992) 67 B.C.L.R. (2d) 302, 45 E.T.R. 209, 92 D.L.R. (4th) 257 (C.A.). At common law, a conveyance directly to oneself was a legal impossibility. This impediment could be avoided by a conveyance to uses (*e.g.*, A grants 'to X to the use of A'). A number of jurisdictions now permit direct conveyances to oneself: see, *e.g.*, *Law of Property Act*, R.S.A. 1980, c. L-8, para. 12(1)(d), *Conveyancing and Law of Property Act*, R.S.O. 1990, c. C.34, s. 41. See also *Murdoch v. Barry* (1975) 10 O.R. (2d) 626, 64 D.L.R. (3d) 222 (H.C.); *Re Summon* (1979) 22 O.R. (2d) 721, 94 D.L.R. (3d) 594 (C.A.). In *Murdoch v. Barry*, it was intimated that even an ineffective attempt to convey to oneself might nevertheless estop that co-owner from claiming by survivorship. *Cf. Freed v. Taffel*, [1984] 2 N.S.W.L.R. 322 (S.C.).

45 Furthermore, a transfer of a family home to oneself does not offend statutory restrictions on dispositions of the home, because these are designed to preserve rights of possession (which are unaffected by such a transfer), not the *jus accrescendi*: see *Re Horne and Evans* (1987) 60 O.R. (2d) 1, 26 E.T.R. 233, 39 D.L.R. (4th) 416 (C.A.).

46 But see *Sorenson v. Sorenson*, [1977] 2 W.W.R. 438, 3 A.R. 8, 90 D.L.R. (3d) 26 (C.A.). Leave to appeal to the S.C.C. was granted ((1977) 6 A.R. 540) but the dispute was apparently settled. Accordingly, a notice of discontinuance was filed: [1979] 1 S.C.R. xiii.

47 See, *e.g.*, *Re Mee* (1971) 23 D.L.R. (3d) 491, [1972] 2 W.W.R. 424 (B.C.C.A.); *In the Marriage of Badcock* (1979) 5 Fam.L.R. 672. See also *Stonehouse v. British Columbia (Attorney General)*, [1962] S.C.R. 103, 37 W.W.R. 62, 31 D.L.R. (2d) 118. Compare *Re Foort & Chapman*, [1973] 4 W.W.R. 461, 37 D.L.R. (3d) 730 (B.C.S.C.) criticized (and rightly so) in McClean, *supra*, note 38, at 14.

48 Suggestions that this rule should be abolished are critiqued in L. Tee, "Severance Revisited", [1995] Conv. 105.

49 *Re Chernetski Estate* (1985) 66 A.R. 79 (C.A.).

Whether or not the granting of a mortgage by one joint tenant will produce a severance depends on the applicable law of mortgages. In those jurisdictions in which a mortgage involves the transfer of title to the lender, a severance results when one joint tenant mortgages his or her interest.[50] This is because the granting of the mortgage involves a transfer of title to the lender. The interest of the mortgagor-tenant is necessarily affected. The mortgagee acquires a property right that differs in time, title and interest from those of the other owner(s). Conversely, in some provinces a mortgage is characterized by the relevant law as creating a 'charge' on the owner's title; so no severance results.[51] As in the case of an easement, the unities remain intact, even if the interest of one of the owners has been coated with an encumbrance (the charge).

An assignment or sublease of a leasehold joint tenancy leads to a severance of that interest. However, the proper outcome when a lease is granted by a freeholder is a more contentious matter. Some say this does not produce the destruction of a unity. Certainly, the unity of possession is not altered, since otherwise there would be no tenancy in common either. It has been maintained, however, that the surrendering of the immediate right of possession alters the interest of the lessor, who then has only a postponed right to possession.[52] An alternative view is that the freehold interest is merely encumbered with an additional interest, as in the case of an easement, and the freeholder is still seised of the land, albeit through the instrumentality of the tenant. Another approach is to say that the lease suspends the right of survivorship until the expiration of the term, at which point it operates. A further alternative is to treat the interference with the right of survivorship as a basis for finding that a severance has occurred. If so, then only when the lease endures beyond the life of the lessor will a severance result.[53] In reply, it might be suggested that a lease invariably ends on the death of the lessor and therefore can never interfere with survivorship.[54]

In addition to the methods of severance mentioned above, proceeding all the way to judgment in an action for a partition or sale of the joint property will result in a severance.[55] More controversial is the idea that a clear unilateral *statement*

---

50 *York v. Stone, supra,* note 22.

51 *Lyons v. Lyons,* [1967] V.R. 169 (S.C.). See also *Sorenson v. Sorenson, supra,* note 46; *Re Brooklands Lumber & Hardware Ltd.* (1956) 64 Man.R. 1, 18 W.W.R. 328, 3 D.L.R. (2d) 762 (Q.B.).

52 See McClean, *supra,* note 38, at 9.

53 This reasoning was applied to support the conclusion that a lease for life by one joint tenant to the other did not produce a severance, because such a lease could never affect the right of survivorship of either co-owner: *Sorensen v. Sorenson, supra,* note 46. Note, however, that this supposed lease should be treated as a *freehold* life estate. See also *Groves v. Christiansen,* [1978] 4 W.W.R. 64, 86 D.L.R. (3d) 296 (B.C.S.C.).

54 The conventional view is that a lease by a joint owner can survive the death of that owner: see McClean, *supra,* note 38, at 8, and the ancient authorities cited in support of that view. See also R.H. Buttery, "Leases By Joint Tenants" (1944) 17 A.L.J. 292.

55 *Gillette v. Cotton,* [1979] 4 W.W.R. 515, 99 D.L.R. (3d) 693 (Alta.T.D.). *Cf. Munroe v. Carlson* (1975) 21 R.F.L. 301, [1976] 1 W.W.R. 248, 59 D.L.R. (3d) 763 (B.C.S.C.); *Grant v. Grant,* [1952] O.W.N. 641 (Master); *In re Wilks,* [1891] 3 Ch. 59; *Rodrique v. Dufton* (1976) 13 O.R. (2d) 613, 30 R.F.L. 216, 72 D.L.R. (3d) 16 (H.C.).

should be enough to sever. To date, no Canadian court has gone that far.[56] I think that a statement alone should not be enough. Allegations about who said what to whom, which might be raised only after the death of one co-owner, can add an element of uncertainty. Given that a unilateral transfer is possible it is a simple matter for a joint owner to show an intention to sever by concrete action. This 'ceremony' serves both notice and reflective functions (in a way that is analogous to the delivery requirement found in the law of gifts.[57]) At the very least, the law should mandate that the declaration be in writing and served on the other co-owner(s).[58]

(c) by agreement or a course of dealing

A severance under the last two rules operates only in equity. For centuries it has been axiomatic that 'equity regards as done that which ought to be done'. This may explain why effect is given to an agreement to sever by joint tenants. However, if the agreement is not enforceable – and apparently it does not have to be an enforceable contract to produce a severance[59] – then what is it that equity insists ought to be done? Perhaps the best way to regard matters is to say that equity will intervene to estop the parties, because of their conduct, from attempting to assert a right of survivorship.

The final two rules in *Williams v. Hensman* are distinct. However, it does seem sensible to combine them, because an agreement must surely also qualify as a course of conduct by which the joint tenants effectively declare that they hold their interests in common.[60] Here, a severance may result even if the owners are unaware of the attributes of the joint tenancy. This exemplifies the use of severance as a means of avoiding the imposition of the survivorship rule on co-owners who might not have had the slightest idea that it applies to their property. Due to the fact that this is likely to be less problematic today (given that most joint tenancies must be expressly created), it may be that the cases decided under the last two rules of severance should be reassessed, and that the aggressive, severance-minded attitude of the courts should now be tempered.

A sale or lease by all of the joint owners does not itself result in a severance, because this arrangement is compatible with the continuation of joint ownership in relation to the proceeds of sale.[61] It follows that an agreement to sell the property

---

56 See further *Sorenson v. Sorenson*, *supra*, note 46; *O'Connor Estate v. Lindsay* (1987) 51 Man.R. (2d) 65 (Q.B.). *Walker v. Dubord*, *supra*, note 44, contains a useful discussion of this issue and the relevant case law.

57 See Part 5(a), Chapter 4.

58 This is the gist of the proposal advanced by the Law Reform Commission of Ontario, *supra*, note 8, at 118-9, 162-3.

59 See K. Gray, *Elements of Land Law*, 2nd ed. (London: Butterworths, 1993) at 498. Opinion is divided as to whether an agreement to sever must comply with the writing requirements of the *Statute of Frauds*: see Gray, *ibid*. See also *Ginn v. Armstrong* (1969) 3 D.L.R. (3d) 285 (B.C.S.C.) where it is doubted that the *Statute of Frauds* applies here.

60 See also McClean, *supra*, note 38, at 16.

61 See *Flannigan v. Wotherspoon* (1952) 7 W.W.R. (N.S.) 660, [1953] 1 D.L.R. 768 (B.C.S.C.) where the authorities are reviewed. *Cf. Re McKee* (1975) 7 O.R. (2d) 614, 56 D.L.R. (3d) 190

at some future time will not transform the nature of the co-ownership until (at least) the sale occurs. On the other hand, if there is an agreement to sell *and divide* the proceeds of sale afterwards this might result in a reading of the accord in a way that shows that an immediate severance was contemplated.[62] If that is the case, then arguably the severance cannot be altered *ex post facto* by an abandonment of the plan to sell (such that the joint tenancy is restored).

The third method, a 'course of dealing', has supported a finding of a severance when the dealings fall short of a firm or explicit agreement. For example, although a will cannot effect a severance, a course-of-dealing severance may be found to have occurred when co-owners execute mutual or joint wills. These testamentary arrangements are typically used when spouses wish to establish a common course of succession for their pooled property. For instance, a couple might decide that all of their respective property is to go to the survivor for life, with a remainder to their children. This agreement might be reflected in two mutual wills, or in a joint will that they both sign.[63] If the spouses own some property as joint tenants, their new arrangement *might* be viewed as showing an intention to replace the right of survivorship with the pattern of distribution contained in the will(s). That is a matter of interpretation, however. As a will does not normally affect a joint tenancy it is quite conceivable that jointly owned property was never meant to be included within the agreed testamentary arrangement. In other words, co-owners might draw mutual wills to cover just the property that would normally be governed by a will. Of course, the jointly owned property may be expressly mentioned, and this suggests, in the strongest of ways, a course of dealing producing a severance. Moreover, an implication that the joint property was meant to be included in the will may be warranted when, for example, that property comprises the parties' only substantial asset.[64]

Canadian courts have held that *failed* negotiations over joint assets can lead to the finding that the owners regarded the joint tenancy as having been severed. Often this issue arises in the wake of negotiations between spouses in the midst of marriage breakdown.[65] The back and forth bargaining is treated as the course of dealing that supports the conclusion that a severance has occurred. While it has been maintained that a simple offer and counter-offer cannot destroy a joint

---

(C.A.); *Sampaio Estate v. Sampaio* (1992) 22 R.P.R. (2d) 314, 90 D.L.R. (4th) 122 (Ont.Gen.Div.).

62 See, *e.g.*, *Schofield v. Graham* (1969) 69 W.W.R. 332, 6 D.L.R. (3d) 88 (Alta. S.C.). See also *Philippson v. van Gruting* (1993) 85 B.C.L.R. (2d) 46, [1994] 2 W.W.R. 73 (S.C.).

63 See generally T.G. Feeney, *The Canadian Law of Wills*, 3rd ed. (Toronto: Butterworths, 1987) vol. 1, at 22*ff.* See, *e.g.*, *Szabo v. Boros* (1967) 60 W.W.R. 754, 64 D.L.R. (3d) 48 (B.C.C.A.); *Bryan v. Heath*, [1980] 3 W.W.R. 666, 108 D.L.R. (3d) 245 (B.C.S.C.); *Re Gillespie*, [1969] 1 O.R. 585, 3 D.L.R. (3d) 317 (C.A.). *Cf. Palmer Estate v. Cunningham* (1985) 22 E.T.R. 8 (B.C.S.C.).

64 See *Szabo v. Boros, supra*, note 63.

65 See, *e.g.*, *Re Walters* (1978) 17 O.R. (2d) 592n, 84 D.L.R. (3d) 416n (C.A.) affirming (1977) 16 O.R. (2d) 702, 1 R.P.R. 150, 79 D.L.R. (3d) 122 (H.C.); *Ginn v. Armstrong, supra*, note 59; *Robichaud v. Watson* (1983) 42 O.R. (2d) 38, 14 E.T.R. 135, 147 D.L.R. (3d) 626 (H.C.). *Cf. Nielson-Jones v. Fedden*, [1975] Ch. 222, [1974] 3 All E.R. 38; *Tompkins Estate v. Tompkins* (1992) 86 D.L.R. (4th) 759 (B.C.S.C.) affirmed (1993) 76 B.C.L.R. (2d) 323, 99 D.L.R. (4th) 193 (C.A.).

tenancy,[66] it is unclear just how much haggling must occur to produce a severance. The reason why this can lead to a severance at all must be that the negotiation of *shares* and separate interests represents an attitude that shows that the notional unity of ownership under a joint tenancy has been abandoned.

There is something curious and perhaps unfair about finding a severance based on a failure to agree. Parties negotiating in the shadow of litigation typically bargain on a 'without prejudice' basis. In other words, offers made in this setting cannot generally be taken as admissions of responsibility to be thrown back in the face of the offeror should the dispute proceed to court. The unfairness (and irony) here is that failed negotiations, if found to produce a severance, may actually prejudice one of the parties, who otherwise would have taken by survivorship.[67] Perhaps the policy driving these cases is that it is unwise to allow survivorship rights to continue when the parties have separated. I would guess that most estranged spouses would no longer want survivorship to govern the fate of their property. Perhaps this should mean that separation works to suspend, and divorce should terminate, the right of survivorship; to date this is not the law.[68]

The 1999 case of *Agro Estate v. C.I.B.C. Trust Corp. (Guardian of)*[69] may be understood as a further example of a nuanced application of the course-of-conduct form of severance. There, four siblings held farm property as joint tenants. Following the death of two of them, the survivors began a business venture as partners. It was found that they held the land as tenants in common. Even if originally the four owners intended to hold as joint tenants, this intention was said to have changed once the two-person partnership was formed. The Court applied the principle that partners are presumed, absent a contrary intention, to hold as tenants in common. However, that presumption is germane at the time of the initial transfer.[70] There was no follow-up conveyance here. This is why I believe that the outcome is intelligible (if at all) only if we treat the formation of the partnership as a course of conduct severing, in equity, the original joint tenancy. Note, however, that this line of reasoning was not expressly set out in *Agro Estate*.

(d)   severance by other means

The three modes listed in *Williams v. Hensman* do not account for all of the recognized acts of severance. For example, a severance will also occur on bankruptcy,[71] by judicial sale, and probably by seizing the property via lawful execu-

---

66 *Burgess v. Rawnsley, supra*, note 41, at 447.
67 See also *Tompkins Estate v. Tompkins, supra*, note 65.
68 See *Morgan v. Davis, supra*, note 40.
69 (1999) 26 E.T.R. (2d) 314 (Ont.Gen.Div.).
70 See the text accompanying note 24, *supra*.
71 See, *e.g.*, *Royal Bank v. Oliver (Trustee of)* (1991) 24 R.P.R. (2d) 107, [1992] 1 W.W.R. 320, 85 D.L.R. (4th) 122 (Sask. C.A.) leave to appeal to S.C.C. refused (1992) 88 D.L.R. (4th) vi (note) (S.C.C.).

tion procedures (but not merely on the filing of a writ of execution[72]). In Ontario, if a spouse dies owning property as a joint tenant in a matrimonial home together with a third party (*i.e.*, not with the other spouse), that joint tenancy will be deemed to have been severed immediately before the death of the owning-spouse.[73] (This provision allows for a spouse's share in the home to be available for division under the Province's matrimonial property law.) Finally, while the murder of one joint tenant by another may in one sense be called unilateral action, it is best regarded as producing a severance (in equity) by operation of law,[74] based on the principle that one should not be permitted to profit from an illegal act.

5.   RESOLVING CONCURRENT OWNERSHIP DISPUTES[75]

(a)   termination

Disputes may ultimately lead to the winding up of the co-ownership relationship. Termination can occur through the release of one owner's interest to the other, or by a transfer by all of the co-owners to a third party. Alternatively, a co-owner may invoke the judicial power to order a physical division of the land (partition), or a sale.

The common law provides no remedies of partition and sale to joint tenants or tenants in common; they are left to their own devices to resolve irreconcilable differences. The power to order a partition was conferred by statute in the mid-sixteenth century.[76] The English partition statutes required the courts to grant a division "however inconvenient or undesirable partition may be".[77] The power of sale, added in the nineteenth century, allowed a court to order a sale in lieu of

---

72 See, *e.g.*, *Power v. Grace*, [1932] O.R. 357, [1932] 2 D.L.R. 793 (C.A.). See also *Canadian Imperial Bank of Commerce v. Muntain*, [1985] 4 W.W.R. 90 (B.C.S.C.). In Alberta, see now *Civil Enforcement Act*, R.S.A. 1980, c. 10.5, s. 76.

73 *Family Law Act*, R.S.O. 1990, c. F.3, sub. 26(1) which was applied in *Fulton v. Fulton* (1994) 17 O.R. (3d) 641, 2 E.T.R. (2d) 113, 113 D.L.R. (4th) 266 (C.A.).

74 See *Schobelt v. Barber*, [1967] 1 O.R. 349, 60 D.L.R. (2d) 519 (H.C.) where it was held that the legal title merged in the accused by reason of survivorship, but that one half of the title in equity was held on a constructive trust for the estate of the victim. See also *Novak v. Gatien* (1975) 25 R.F.L. 397 (Man.Q.B.); *Merkley v. Proctor* (1989) 33 E.T.R. 175, 59 Man.R. (2d) 199 (Q.B.). As to the position where three joint tenants are involved, see *Rasmanis v. Jurewitsch*, [1968] 2 N.S.W.R. 166 (S.C.). A constructive trust has been impressed following a conviction for manslaughter in *Re Stone*, [1989] 1 Qd.R. 351 (S.C.). *Cf. Manitoba (Public Trustee) v. LeClerc* (1981) 123 D.L.R. (3d) 650, 8 Man.R. (2d) 267 (Q.B.).

75 See generally L. Berger, "An Analysis of the Economic Relations Between Cotenants", 21 Ariz.L.Rev. 1015 (1979). See also Ontario Law Reform Commission, *Report on Basic Principles of Land Law* (Toronto: A.G. (Ont.), 1996) ch. 6, where the present law of Ontario is reviewed. Recommendations for reform are offered, which are, in essence, a slight modification of the present law of Alberta.

76 *Partition Act, 1539*, 31 Hen. 8, c. 1; *Partition Act, 1540*, 32 Hen. 8, c. 32.

77 *Patel v. Premabhai*, [1954] A.C. 35 (P.C.) at 42 (*per* Lord Porter).

partition.[78] But a court did not have the power to refuse an order altogether. The assumption was that a co-owner had a right to end the relationship.

In those common law provinces that do not rely on the received English law, it is assumed that the courts have a discretion, to some degree, to refuse to grant an order.[79] Under current Alberta law a court must grant some form of partition and sale order, except in defined circumstances.[80] For example, when a matrimonial home is involved, partition and sale proceedings may be stayed pending an application under the *Matrimonial Property Act*, or while an order under that Act remains in force.[81] Conversely, the court may make an order terminating co-ownership, despite an agreement between co-owners to the contrary, if the continuance of the relationship would cause undue hardship to one of the parties.[82] Once it is decided that an order should be made, the options available are to direct (i) a physical division; (ii) a sale, followed by a distribution of the proceeds; or (iii) a sale among the co-owners.[83] A court may refuse to approve a sale if the highest offer on the property is unacceptably low.[84]

In some jurisdictions the governing legislation has been treated as conferring a broader judicial discretion to deny an application. So, even though it is recognized that a co-owner has a *prima facie* right to partition or sale,[85] some courts have assumed that they may refuse an order in the interests of fairness and justice.[86] It is mainly in relation to disputes over the matrimonial home that the jurisprudence has developed. Some cases say that an order can be refused if the relative hardship of granting an order would be greater than in refusing one.[87] Other courts have spoken of economic oppression,[88] vexatiousness, or malice[89] as relevant criteria.[90] The obvious concern in the family homes cases is that an order might

---

78 *Partition Act, 1868*, 31 & 32 Vict., c. 40.

79 Accord J.M. Glenn, Note (1976) 54 Can.B.Rev. 149, at 150.

80 *Law of Property Act*, R.S.A. 1980, c. L-8, sub. 15(2). See also *Westlock Foods Ltd. v. Bonel Properties Ltd.* (1981) 33 A.R. 1 (Q.B.).

81 S. 22.

82 S. 28.

83 Sub. 15(2). None of these options has any presumptive priority. Under Ontario law, a sale can be ordered only if partition is not feasible: *Dibattista v. Menecola* (1990) 75 O.R. (2d) 443, 14 R.P.R. (2d) 157, 74 D.L.R. (4th) 569 (C.A.); *Cook v. Johnston*, [1970] 2 O.R. 1 (H.C.).

84 S. 16.

85 *Davis v. Davis*, [1954] O.R. 23, [1954] 1 D.L.R. 827 (C.A.); *Rayworth v. Prefontaine* (1997) 45 B.C.L.R. (3d) 251 (S.C.); *Canadian Imperial Bank of Commerce v. Mulholland Construction Inc.* (1998) 37 O.R. (3d) 759, 16 R.P.R. (3d) 85 (Gen.Div.).

86 *Harmeling v. Harmeling*, 6 R.P.R. 129, [1978] 5 W.W.R. 688, 90 D.L.R. (3d) 208 (B.C.C.A.) at 212 D.L.R. (*per* Seaton J.A.). In *Hrynkiw v. Hrynkiw* (1979) 9 R.F.L. (2d) 374 (Ont.H.C.) an order was refused because one co-owner had granted a contractual licence to the other.

87 See *Fernandes v. Fernandes* (1975) 24 R.F.L. 289, [1976] 3 W.W.R. 510, 65 D.L.R. (3d) 684 (B.C.S.C.) and the authorities reviewed there. See also *Re Yale and MacMaster* (1974) 3 O.R. (2d) 547, 18 R.F.L. 27, 46 D.L.R. (3d) 167 (H.C.). But see the review of authorities in *Silva v. Silva* (1990) 1 O.R. (3d) 436, 30 R.F.L. (3d) 117, 75 D.L.R. (4th) 415 (C.A.).

88 See, *e.g.*, *Korolew v. Korolew* (1972) 7 R.F.L. 162 (B.C.S.C.).

89 *Reitsma v. Reitsma* (1974) 17 R.F.L. 292, [1975] 3 W.W.R. 281 (B.C.S.C.).

90 Under Ontario law, "where substantial rights in relation to jointly owned property are likely to be jeopardized by an order for partition and sale, an application under the *Partition Act* should

be too disruptive to children or a spouse, and the cases which expand the discretion to refuse an order beyond situations of malice or vexatiousness are typically those involving families.[91]

(b)   financial issues

Disagreements among co-owners over financial matters and other entitlements are commonplace. For starters, there may be a dispute about the very existence of a co-ownership relationship. Merely because A is on title does not prevent a claim by B to an equitable interest based, say, on the principles governing resulting and constructive trusts.[92] Moreover, left unregulated, co-ownership can provide a setting for the emergence of a classic tragedy of the commons problem.[93] According to the parable, each co-owner is supposedly motivated to exploit the property fully, even if this leaves the other owners less well off. How are financial disputes resolved? How, if at all, is the tragedy averted?

It is typically recited that in settling the financial issues that emerge on the termination of co-ownership, the court has a discretion to make all allowances that are just and fair under the circumstances.[94] Despite the generality of this starting position, a number of basic principles guide the courts. In Alberta, an attempt has been made to codify (with a few minor adjustments) the common law rules that govern 'accounting' on a partition or sale. The court must consider whether:

> (a) one co-owner has excluded another co-owner from the land;
> (b) an occupying co-owner was a tenant, bailiff or agent of another co-owner;
> (c) a co-owner has received from third parties more than [a] just share of the rents from the land or profits from the reasonable removal of its natural resources;
> (d) a co-owner has committed waste by an unreasonable use of the land;
> (e) a co-owner has made improvements or capital payments that have increased the realizable value of the land;
> (f) a co-owner should be compensated for non-capital expenses in respect of the land;
> (g) an occupying co-owner claiming non-capital expenses in respect of land should be required to pay a fair occupation rent.[95]

While the list seems to cover most of the problems that can arise, it is not exhaustive.[96] For example, it is not entirely clear whether the list contemplates

---

be deferred until the matter is decided under the [*Family Law Act*]'': *Silva v. Silva, supra*, note 87, at 424 D.L.R. (*per* Finlayson J.A.).

91 Provincial partition legislation is not available on Aboriginal reserves: *Simpson v. Ziprick* (1995) 10 B.C.L.R. (3d) 41, 126 D.L.R. (4th) 754 (S.C.).

92 See Parts 4(c) and (d), Chapter 6.

93 See Part 3(b)(ii), Chapter 1.

94 *Mastron v. Cotton*, [1926] 1 D.L.R. 767, 58 O.L.R. 251 (C.A.); *Davis v. Davis, supra*, note 85. As to the rules governing financial disputes prior to the launching of partition and sale actions, see Ontario Law Reform Commission, *supra*, note 75, at 80*ff*.

95 *Law of Property Act*, R.S.A. 1980, c. L-8, s. 17. See also para. 17(2)(h), which requires the court to consider the effect of an order on dower rights.

96 Sub. 17(2).

claims based on non-monetary contributions.[97] To understand fully the meaning of the Alberta list some elaboration is needed.

All else being equal, each party is liable for capital expenditures (such as the repayment of the principal due under a mortgage) and current expenses (such as taxes, utilities, insurance and mortgage interest) in accordance with her or his ownership share. Therefore, the payment by one tenant of the full amount owing gives rise to a claim for reimbursement, unless it can be shown that paying off the obligation of another co-owner was intended as a gift. A liability to account may also arise when one owner acts as an agent or tenant of the other, or, of course, when they have agreed to some payment arrangement that deviates from the standard rules.

Owing to the fact that all co-tenants are inherently entitled to possession of each and every part of the property, no matter the size of their individual shares, one co-owner cannot exclude or 'oust' another (say, by changing the locks). If one party is locked out, the owner remaining behind may be charged with an occupation rent.[98] In addition, when the conduct of one co-owner is so egregious that the other is forced to leave the premises, this may amount to a constructive ouster; an occupation rent may be claimed in this situation as well.[99] There seems to be a good deal of variation in how courts in Canada have determined the quantum of the rent. At times, the amount is based on an estimation of the market value of the property, or the cost of the current expenses, or of alternative accommodations.[100]

An occupation rent is not normally payable simply because one owner has enjoyed exclusive possession.[101] However, when, on a partition or sale, the party in possession makes a claim for reimbursement based on the payment of current expenses, a counterclaim for occupation rent may be entertained.[102] I do not find

---

97 See further *Aleksich v. Konradson* (1995) 5 B.C.L.R. (3d) 240, 12 R.F.L. (4th) 177, [1995] 6 W.W.R. 268 (C.A.).

98 The ousting of a co-owner may also give rise to a claim in trespass: *Petrie v. Taylor* (1847) 3 U.C.Q.B. 457; *Stedman v. Smith* (1857) 8 El. & Bl. 1, 120 E.R. 1; *Jacobs v. Seward* (1872) L.R. 5 H.L. 464. See also *Bull v. Bull*, [1955] 1 Q.B. 234, [1955] 1 All E.R. 253 (C.A.) at 237 Q.B.; *Ferguson v. Miller*, [1978] 1 N.Z.L.R. 819 (S.C.). *Cf. Elliot v. Smith* (1858) 3 N.S.R. 338 (S.C.).

99 See, *e.g.*, *Baker v. Baker*, 24 R.F.L. 145, [1976] 3 W.W.R. 492 (B.C.S.C.).

100 See generally G. Blancy, "Commentary: Occupation Rent" in *Payne's Divorce and Family Law Digest* (Don Mills: De Boo, 1982) (looseleaf) at 82-651.

101 See, *e.g.*, *Kaplan v. Kaplan* (1974) 15 R.F.L. 239 (B.C.S.C.). See, however, *Chhokar v. Chhokar* (1984) 5 F.L.R. 313 (Fam.D.) reversed on other grounds (1984) 14 Fam. Law 269 (C.A.). In that case it was said basic principles of fairness should govern when determining whether an occupation rent should be ordered. See also *Opie v. Zegil* (1997) 100 O.A.C. 197, 28 R.F.L. (4th) 405 (C.A.) leave to appeal to S.C.C. refused (1997) 225 N.R. 398 (note) (S.C.C.) where an occupation rent was ordered because one spouse had been excluded from the family home pursuant to a court order of exclusive occupation granted in favour of the other spouse.

102 See *Osachuk v. Osachuk*, [1971] 2 W.W.R. 481, 18 D.L.R. (3d) 413 (Man.C.A.) and the cases cited there. See also *Bernard v. Bernard* (1987) 12 B.C.L.R. (2d) 75 (S.C.) which also canvasses the authorities. In *Balzar v. Balzar* (1990) 67 Man.R. (2d) 196 (Q.B.) a claim for occupation rent was denied for the period during which the occupant had provided support for the child of the marriage.

this approach entirely satisfactory, at least as an abstract proposition of fair play. Assuming that the absent owner could reasonably return to the property (I accept that this is not always true), I am not convinced that the party remaining in occupation must cover all of the expenses and not expect *full* compensation for the portion paid on the other person's account. If the price for seeking reimbursement is the payment of an occupation rent, the result will often be that the party leaving will be able to shirk some or all of the existing obligations to share expenses (because the occupation rent will produce a full or partial set-off). And in this case, the occupying co-owner will be paying a rent for something (occupation) that they are entitled to as of right. Only when it is unrealistic to expect the parties to resume cohabitation – again, this may be the most common situation – does it make sense to allow the departing party this indulgence.

Under the *Statute of Anne* of 1705[103] a co-owner who appropriates more than his or her just share of any rents or profits issuing out of the land must account to the other(s).[104] (The gist of the Statute is contained in paragraph (c) of the Alberta provision quoted above). The Statute is relevant if profits are actually reaped: the failure to capture a rent for the property does not trigger its operation.[105] Nor is there a right of sharing for profits derived from a business venture carried out on the land. Only rents and profits obtained directly from the land itself are caught. So, in *Henderson v. Eason*[106] it was held that there was no liability to account for profits earned by farming the land. After all, the tenant-farmer could not have demanded that a loss be shared with the absent co-owner had the crop failed. A less convincing conclusion was reached in *Spelman v. Spelman*,[107] in relation to a rooming house operation. There, the rent paid by the roomers was not just for their living quarters, but also for the services provided by the proprietor. The services affected the gross income, but surely some of the rent, and hence some portion of the profit, related to the provision of space in the house. Nonetheless, the Court refused to order an accounting to determine the extent of the profit that related solely to the provision of space.

A co-owner, even one holding in fee simple, may be liable for waste.[108] In Alberta, waste occurs when there is an "unreasonable use of the land".[109] In my view, this means that the principles governing voluntary (and therefore also 'equitable') waste define, *roughly*, the bases of liability.[110] Although a co-owner can probably exploit the land to a somewhat greater extent than a life tenant, one must remember that deriving a profit from the realty, for instance, through mining,

---

103 4 & 5 Anne, c. 3, s. 27.

104 See, *e.g.*, *Curtis v. Coleman* (1875) 22 Gr. 561 (Ont.Ch.D.).

105 *Osachuk v. Osachuk, supra*, note 102. *Cf. Crooks v. Crooks* (1977) 30 R.F.L. 351, [1977] 3 W.W.R. 22 (B.C.S.C.).

106 (1851) 17 Q.B. 701, 117 E.R. 1451.

107 (1944) 59 B.C.R. 551, [1944] 1 W.W.R. 691, [1944] 2 D.L.R. 74 (C.A.). See also *Reid v. Reid*, [1978] 4 W.W.R. 460, 87 D.L.R. (3d) 370 (Sask.Q.B.).

108 See *Linton v. Wilson* (1841) 3 N.B.R. 223 (S.C.); *Hersey v. Murphy* (1920) 48 N.B.R. 65 (Ch.D.). *Cf. Griffies v. Griffies* (1863) 8 L.T. 758 (Ch.D.). See also *Dougall v. Foster* (1853) 4 Gr. 319 (U.C.Ch.D.).

109 *Law of Property Act*, R.S.A. 1980, c. L-8, para. 17(2)(d).

110 Waste was introduced in Part 4(c)(ii), Chapter 5.

can trigger a claim for recovery under the *Statute of Anne*. An action in nuisance may also be tenable, though there is a division of opinion as to whether this type of claim can be launched by one co-owner against another.[111]

The costs of repairs undertaken to maintain the property in its present state are regarded as being similar to current expenses. Therefore, when reimbursement for reasonable repairs is sought, the claimant may be required to pay an occupation rent. The position concerning improvements is more controversial. I use the term improvements in this setting to describe renovations or additions that enhance the value of the capital holding. They are analogous to payments of the principal amount owing under a mortgage, except, of course, that there may be no prior agreement that the improvements are to be undertaken. If, despite this difference, the comparison is apt, improvement costs should be recoverable without at the same time opening up the improving co-owner to a charge for occupation rent. That is the law in Alberta under statute,[112] but there is case law suggesting that a rent may be sought.[113]

As a rule, compensation for improvements cannot be claimed on its own.[114] However, if the property is to be sold or partitioned, the non-improving party cannot enjoy the full value of the property without shouldering a share of the cost of the improvements.[115] In such a case, the improver should be able to recoup no more than the actual outlay even if the property's value has increased by a larger amount. At the same time, the increased purchase price should work as a cap on the improver's claim, even if more has been expended.[116]

6. SHARED OWNERSHIP OF PERSONALTY

(a) generally[117]

Much of the jurisprudence concerning the co-ownership of land applies equally to personalty, though some significant differences do exist. While the prerequisites for the creation of joint tenancies and tenancies in common are the same, the rules of construction may differ. Notice that the Alberta provision (quoted above) presumes a tenancy in common only in transfers of land.[118] There-

---

111 See *Ferguson v. Miller, supra*, note 98, which suggests (in *obiter*) that such an action may be brought. The authorities to the contrary are also cited.

112 This is an implication drawn from the coverage of paras. 17(2)(e) to (g) quoted above.

113 See the review of authorities in E.E. Gillese, ed., *Property Law: Text, Cases and Materials*, 2nd ed. (Toronto: Emond Montgomery, 1990) at 18:30.

114 *Ruptash v. Zawick*, [1956] S.C.R. 347, 2 D.L.R. (2d) 145.

115 See also *Re Kneebone and Matheson* (1981) 124 D.L.R. (3d) 538, 31 Nfld. & P.E.I.R. 372, 87 A.P.R. 372 (P.E.I.S.C.); *Ruptash v. Zawick, supra*, note 114.

116 See *Boulter v. Boulter* (1898) 19 L.R. (N.S.W.) Eq. 135, at 137, quoted with approval in *Squire v. Rogers* (1979) 39 F.L.R. 106, 27 A.L.R. 330, at 125-6 F.L.R. See further R. Stein, "Co-owner's Profits Revisited: Now You Have Them, Now You Don't – *Squire v. Rogers*" (1989) 63 A.L.J. 631.

117 See generally J. Hill & E. Bowes-Smith, "Joint Ownership of Chattels" in N. Palmer & E. McKendrick, eds., *Interests in Goods*, 2nd ed. (London: L.L.P., 1998) ch. 10.

118 See the text accompanying note 32, *supra*. Under Alberta law, partnership assets are presumed to be held *inter se* as personal property: *Partnership Act*, R.S.A. 1980, c. P-2 , s. 24. This

fore, the common law presumption applies to chattels: a joint tenancy is presumed, unless overcome by the insertion of words of severance.[119] In most jurisdictions, there is no power to order a partition or sale of personalty. In the case of intractable disputes the parties must somehow find their own solution.[120] There is, however, authority that permits the unilateral appropriation of property held in a common bulk of equal quality, provided that the share to be taken can be ascertained.[121]

By virtue of long-standing authority, one co-owner of chattels cannot be rendered liable to the other in the tort of conversion unless there has been a destruction of the goods or some equivalent act,[122] such as excluding a co-owner from possession, or destroying the right to possession. In essence, this means that a sale to a third party is not normally actionable. In the typical case, all that the purchaser can acquire through the sale is the vendor's share, which that person has the power to convey. The title of the other co-owner is not affected; therefore, the reasoning goes, no wrong has been done. Canadian cases have generally followed this rule.[123] It has been abolished by statute in England,[124] and rejected in New Zealand.[125] In Canada, two law reform commissions have recommended that the law be changed to allow an action to be brought following a purported sale to a third party of the whole property.[126] This would be a step in the right direction, because it would recognize that such a sale will often deprive the non-consenting co-owner of the practical benefits of ownership.

---

means that the presumption of a tenancy in common for land, found in s. 8 of the *Law of Property Act*, R.S.A. 1980, c. L-8, will not normally apply. The result is curious: partnership assets (realty and personalty) are presumed to be held jointly at law, but under a tenancy in common in equity (in accordance with the principle described in the text accompanying note 24, *supra*).

119   In the case of joint bank accounts, equity may have recognized a further exception to the presumption of a joint tenancy: see the text accompanying note 135, *infra*.

120   A recommendation has been that a remedy be provided: see Law Reform Commission of British Columbia, *Report on Wrongful Interference With Goods* (Vancouver: L.R.C.B.C., 1992) at 64.

121   See *Re Gillie* (1996) 150 A.L.R. 110 (F.C.).

122   *Morgan v. Marquis* (1854) 9 Ex. 145, at 148, 156 E.R. 62, at 63; *Mayhew v. Herrick* (1849) 7 C.B. 229, 137 E.R. 92. See further *Re Gillie, supra,* note 121, drawing on *Kitano v. The Commonwealth of Australia* (1974) 129 C.L.R. 151 (Aust.H.C.) at 172, application for special leave to appeal to Privy Council dismissed as incompetent (1975) 132 C.L.R. 231 (P.C.); and also D.P. Derham, "Conversion by Wrongful Disposal as Between Co-Owners" (1952) 68 L.Q.R. 507.

123   See *Strathy v. Crooks* (1844) 2 U.C.Q.B. 51; *McNabb v. Howland* (1861) 11 U.C.C.P. 434; *Wiggins v. White* (1836) 2 N.B.R. 179 (S.C.). But see *Rathwell v. Rathwell* (1866) 26 U.C.Q.B. 179. Compare the analysis of Macdonald C.J.A. in *Henderson v. Rouvala*, 31 B.C.R. 515, [1923] 1 W.W.R. 467 (C.A.).

124   *Torts (Interference With Goods) Act, 1977,* c. 32, s. 10.

125   *Coleman v. Harvey,* [1989] 1 N.Z.L.R. 723 (C.A.) especially at 731.

126   Law Reform Commission of British Columbia, *supra,* note 120, at 62*ff*, and 78; Ontario Law Reform Commission, *Study Paper on Wrongful Interference With Goods* (Toronto: A.G. (Ont.), 1989) at 26, 167.

(b)   joint bank accounts

When money is pooled by spouses or others in joint bank accounts difficult issues of concurrent ownership can emerge. These relate to (i) rights to the capital and interest; (ii) the applicability of survivorship; and (iii) rights to property acquired by using money drawn from the account.

The first of these issues (who holds what rights to the money in a joint account?) depends, sensibly enough, on who is the beneficial owner. When both parties contribute to a joint account it is presumed that the beneficial interest is to be shared. The interest each possesses is a "fluctuating and defeasible asset",[127] that is, their respective rights are dependent on the balance in the bank account as it rises and falls over time.

When just one party makes deposits there may be either a resulting trust in favour of that person, or an advancement, giving each a share. This determination (gift or no gift) turns on the same fulcrum that is applicable to the presumptions of resulting trust and advancement.[128] The presumption of resulting trust, when applicable, can be rebutted by showing that a gift was intended.[129] A presumed advancement may be rebutted, for example, by showing that the arrangement was one of convenience, designed to allow the non-contributor to have easy access to the funds.[130] As we saw in Chapter 6, the modern role of these presumptions has been questioned by the courts and modified by statute in some provinces.[131] In Alberta, for instance, money held jointly is presumptively treated as being jointly owned in equity.[132]

On the opening of a joint account, rights over the deposited money are typically set out in an agreement with the bank. The primary purpose of that document is to allow the bank to carry out transactions without fear of liability; it is its authority to act. These forms do not directly govern the rights of the account holders *inter se*, although they may provide an indication as to their relative rights. From the bank's point of view, both account holders are normally afforded separate and unrestricted access, absent an agreement to the contrary, and both are entitled to a share of any interest that accrues.

Even if one speaks of a 'joint' bank account, this does not necessarily mean that a right of survivorship exists;[133] that is a question of construction. Again, the

---

127 *Re Figgis; Roberts v. MacLaren*, [1969] 1 Ch. 123, [1968] 1 All E.R. 999 (Ch.D.) at 1014 All E.R. (*per* Megarry J., as he then was).

128 See Part 4(c), Chapter 6.

129 See, *e.g.*, *Halfpenny v. Holien* (1997) 37 B.C.L.R. (3d) 186, 19 E.T.R. (2d) 84 (S.C.).

130 See, *e.g.*, *Dobson v. Dobson* (1981) 26 R.F.L. (2d) 49, 16 Sask.R. 64 (Q.B.); *Greskow v. Greskow* (1990) 73 O.R. (2d) 388 (H.C.). See further A.P. McGlynn & K.T. Grozinger, "Joint Ownership of Property in the Context of Inter-Generational Transfers of Estates: Convenience and Conflict" (1996) 16 E. & T.J. 105.

131 See Part 4(c), Chapter 6.

132 *Matrimonial Property Act*, R.S.A. 1980, c. M-9, s. 36.

133 "Because rights exist between the account holders for the period of the joint lives, and also for the period of survivorship, the two periods must be seen separately. For instance, there will be a *prima facie* resulting trust as to the right of survivorship even when two persons pay equally into a joint account": D.W.M. Waters, *The Law of Trusts in Canada*, 2nd ed. (Toronto:

forms signed on the opening of the account may provide some clue as to what was intended, but these documents are not controlling.[134] Moreover, in the Ontario case of *Frosch v. Dadd* it appears to have been held that the account will be presumed to be held in common, even in the case of equal contributions, because otherwise a ''joint tenancy could be created by inadvertence, a proposition which [is] wholly untenable''.[135] In jurisdictions in which the statutory reversal of the presumption in favour of a joint tenancy does not embrace personalty (such as Alberta),[136] the holding in *Frosch* seems to provide a further instance in which equity prefers not to follow the common law.[137]

Determining the ownership of property purchased with money held in a joint account can also be problematic. In *Jones v. Maynard*[138] money was pooled by a married couple in a joint account from which the husband drew in order to acquire, among other things, certain corporate shares. It was held that there was an equal entitlement to draw money from the account and that the purchases were owned by both spouses even though purchased by the husband. It was suggested that had the wife purchased the investments, beneficial title would have remained in her; the use of the husband's money would have been treated as an advancement. It was also held that the shares were owned equally; the Court was not prepared to indulge in a minute dissection of every deposit and withdrawal made by the spouses throughout the history of the account.

A different result was reached in *Re Bishop*,[139] where property bought with money deposited in a joint bank account was found to belong to the spouse in whose name that property had been taken; both husband and wife had made purchases. In *Bishop* the facts suggested that the account was not restricted in its purpose, and there were ''positive indications''[140] that separate purchases could be made. Additionally, there was no suggestion that individual acquisitions were to be held on trust for both parties, or that the cash in the joint account should be

---

Carswell, 1984) at 333. Rather than speaking of a resulting trust as to survivorship, is it not better to describe equitable title as being held in common, so that there is simply no right of survivorship? See *ibid.* at 334, describing the reasoning in *Frosch v. Dadd*, [1960] O.R. 435, 24 D.L.R. (2d) 610 (C.A.).

134 *Niles v. Lake*, [1947] S.C.R. 291, [1947] 2 D.L.R. 248; *Whitford v. Whitford*, [1942] S.C.R. 166, [1942] 1 D.L.R. 721; *Re Mailman*, [1941] S.C.R. 368, [1941] 3 D.L.R. 449; *Edwards v. Bradley*, [1957] S.C.R. 599, 9 D.L.R. (2d) 673; *Purchase v. Pike Estate* (1991) 42 E.T.R. 75, 90 Nfld. & P.E.I.R. 79, 280 A.P.R. 79 (Nfld.T.D.); *Re McKenna Estate* (1994) 5 E.T.R. (2d) 160, 134 N.S.R. (2d) 218, 383 A.P.R. 218 (Prob.Ct.).

135 *Supra*, note 133, at 616 D.L.R. (*per* Schroeder J.A.).

136 See the text accompanying note 32, *supra*.

137 However, in *Frosch* it was also said that the account holders were ''partners or stood in a like relationship'': *supra*, note 133, at 617 D.L.R. Equity has traditionally presumed a tenancy in common for partnership assets: see the text accompanying note 24, *supra*. Cf. *Whittle v. Fewer* (1984) 49 Nfld. & P.E.I.R. 165, 145 A.P.R. 165 (Nfld.T.D.).

138 [1951] Ch. 572, [1951] 1 All E.R. 802. See also *Warm v. Warm* (1969) 70 W.W.R. 207, 8 D.L.R. (3d) 466 (B.C.S.C.).

139 *Re Bishop*, [1965] Ch. 450, [1965] 1 All E.R. 249. See also *De Ross v. De Ross* (1980) 19 R.F.L. (2d) 359 (Ont. H.C.).

140 *Supra*, note 139, at 464 Ch. (*per* Stamp J.).

treated as shared savings.[141] It was on this basis that *Jones v. Maynard* was distinguished. That case was regarded as turning on an understanding that the account was a pool for joint savings, which in turn coloured the subsequent investments as joint assets.

Is this an accurate reading of the decision in *Jones v. Maynard*? In *Jones* it was said that purchases in the wife's name would have been presumed to belong to her alone. This remark suggests that there was no actual agreement in the case, at least none that the Court in *Jones* found to be relevant.[142] The *ratio* in *Jones* appears to be based on the application of the presumption of resulting trust.[143] More generally, the ability of a joint owner of an account to use funds to make individual investments, as held in *Bishop*, has been doubted in Canada. In *Rathwell v. Rathwell*, Dickson J. (as he then was) expressed "difficulty in understanding the basis upon which it can be said that the joint owner who reaches the bank first can divert jointly owned funds to the purchase of investments upon which the other joint owner will have no claim".[144]

7. CONCURRENT OWNERSHIP THROUGH MARITAL PROPERTY LAW

An understanding of the basic principles governing the co-ownership of property within the family setting is enhanced by examining the special rules relating to matrimonial property. Statutory reforms that were introduced in the common law jurisdictions in Canada during the 1970s have created systems that recognize, in effect, an additional type of co-ownership; one that is applicable to the holdings of married couples.

The common law treated marriage as, among other things, an economic partnership. But it was not a partnership of equals, for the husband was given the upper hand in the control of property. This was one feature of the doctrine of marital unity, under which the legal personality of a wife was merged into that of her husband.[145] Facets of the doctrine were eventually abolished with the introduction of married women's property legislation.[146] These changes produced the "non-system"[147] of separate property: with a few exceptions, the rules governing property rights between spouses were those applicable to all property owners, under the general law. Although this created a grand illusion of spousal equality,

---

141 *Ibid.*
142 The attempt to explain this away in *Re Bishop* is unconvincing. Stamp J. stated: "That question had not been argued before [the trial judge in *Jones v. Maynard*] and, again, in my judgment, he was not attempting to lay down any general principles of law, but was merely stating his conclusion on the facts of that particular case": *ibid.* at 463 Ch.
143 See further A. Samuels, "The Joint Matrimonial Banking Account and Its Proceeds" (1965) 28 Mod.L.Rev. 480, where the reasoning in *Re Bishop* is questioned.
144 *Rathwell v. Rathwell*, [1978] 2 S.C.R. 436, [1978] 2 W.W.R. 101, 83 D.L.R. (3d) 289, at 459 S.C.R.
145 See Part 3(a), Chapter 2.
146 See *ibid.*
147 R. Bartke, "Ontario Bill 6, or How Not to Reform Marital Property Rights" (1977) 9 Ottawa L.Rev. 321, at 324.

bitter experience demonstrated that such an approach would tend to operate to the detriment of women. Not all forms of contribution within a household are adequately recognized under a separate property approach.

It has already been explained that work lacking a cash-nexus, such as child care and domestic services of various sorts, has traditionally been undervalued; some would say these tasks are rendered economically invisible.[148] The potential for the rules of separate property to produce inequitable results was dramatized by the case of *Murdoch v. Murdoch*,[149] which we considered earlier.[150] The perceived unfairness that resulted in *Murdoch* was mitigated by judicial revision of the law of trusts. The case also influenced a far more ambitious process of reform through which contemporary Canadian matrimonial property law in the common law provinces and territories was forged.

Different approaches have been taken. A possible model for reform, but one that has not been adopted in the common law provinces, is known as 'community property'.[151] Here, all property accumulated through onerous title, that is, through the efforts of the spouses (and not by gift) falls into the regime. Generally, this means that both spouses acquire an interest in the property regardless of who may have paid for it. Either party has the power to alienate most personalty, but consent is required for transfers of realty. At the termination of the marriage, whether through death or divorce, each is entitled to half of the community holdings, subject only to a judicial power to override this norm to prevent extreme unfairness.

The matrimonial property statutes now found in common law Canada establish systems of deferred equal sharing; in effect, these are diluted community property regimes. These systems are described as deferred because the rules of separate property continue to apply until some event denoting marriage breakdown (such as separation or divorce) occurs. In a number of provinces the death of a spouse can bring the rules into operation.[152] Once a triggering event has occurred, a right to apply for a judicial division of property accrues. Generally, there is a presumption of equal sharing of certain property. In some provinces, the presumption applies primarily to property accumulated during the marriage. In others, items used as 'family assets' by the spouses or their children are caught by the presumption. Some schemes adopt an amalgam of the accumulations and family use criteria. The presumption of equal sharing can be rebutted in appropriate circumstances, such as when it can be shown that there has been an improvident disposal of property, or when there has been a severe dereliction of

---

148 See also the cursory discussion in Part 3(f), Chapter 1.

149 (1973), [1975] 1 S.C.R. 423, [1974] 1 W.W.R. 361, 41 D.L.R. (3d) 367.

150 See Part 4(d), Chapter 6.

151 A compelling case for the adoption of community property is found in K.J. Gray, *Reallocation of Property on Divorce* (Abingdon: Professional Books, 1977).

152 In Alberta, death is not presently a triggering event, though in some cases an action, otherwise available, may be maintained on the death of a spouse: ss. 11, 16. Recently, a report for discussion has recommended that the death of a spouse should serve as a triggering event: Alberta Law Reform Institute, *Division of Matrimonial Property on Death* (Edmonton: A.L.R.I., 1998).

familial duties. If so, an unequal division can be ordered; in some jurisdictions it is even possible to seek a division of property that is not available for sharing under the presumption of equality. Marital property statutes also typically regulate rights to transfer or occupy the matrimonial home. Finally, wide latitude is granted to the spouses to enter into a contract in order to create entitlements that deviate from the standard distributional rules.

Alberta's *Matrimonial Property Act*[153] illustrates an accumulations approach (which is the most common form). The value of all property acquired during marriage is subject to the norm of equal distribution on marriage breakdown. The value of property acquired before marriage is exempt, as is money acquired by gift or inheritance, or as damages or insurance proceeds paid in relation to injuries to one spouse.[154] Any increase in the value of these items can be shared however. Even though no statutory presumption of equality applies here, if these items are in fact used for the mutual benefit of the spouses, increases in their value will usually be divided equally.[155]

The norm of equality will not be applied if it would appear unjust to do so, having regard to 13 discretion-structuring factors.[156] Under the last of these, the court may consider "any fact or circumstance that is relevant".[157] However, it has been maintained that judges should be loath to deviate from the standard of equal distribution.[158] An important rationale supporting a 'hard' presumption of equality is that departing from that norm would diminish the predictability of outcomes, increase transaction costs, and therefore reduce the frequency of out-of-court settlements. Once the entitlements are ascertained, the court may order a sale, grant a declaration of title, or order a money payment.[159] The parties are free, before, during or after marriage, to contract out of the rules governing division on breakdown.[160] Finally, an order of exclusive possession of the home and contents can be granted, even if a division of assets is not being sought.[161]

One can see from this overview that a semblance of co-ownership is visible primarily at the end of the marriage. At that time the template of marital property law is placed over the standard rules of separate property. How, then, do marital property laws interrelate with the general law governing concurrent ownership? The continued importance of separate property prior to the accrual of the right to

---

153 R.S.A. 1980, c. M-9.

154 S. 7.

155 *Mazurenko v. Mazurenko* (1981) 15 Alta.L.R. (2d) 357, 23 R.F.L. (2d) 113, 124 D.L.R. (3d) 406 (C.A.) leave to appeal to S.C.C. refused (1981) 39 N.R. 539 (S.C.C.).

156 S. 8.

157 Para. 8(m).

158 *Mazurenko v. Mazurenko, supra*, note 155. See also *Fair v. Jones* (1999) 44 R.F.L. (4th) 399 (N.W.T.S.C.) at 413*ff*, which reviews the law concerning the very high theshold for deviation in Ontario and the Northwest Territories.

159 Sub. 9(2).

160 Ss. 37-8.

161 Part 2. Changes to this Part have been recommended in a report for discussion: see Alberta Law Reform Institute, *The Matrimonial Home* (Edmonton: A.L.R.I., 1995) which is referred to extensively in *Verburg v. Verburg* (1995) 30 Alta.L.R. (3d) 290, 172 A.R. 380, [1995] 9 W.W.R. 522 (Q.B.).

deferred sharing provides the key to understanding how these two areas of the law interact. Before matrimonial property can be divided, there must be a reckoning of the separate holdings of each spouse. Without this determination one cannot determine who owns exempt property. This, in turn, will affect the size of shares and the orders that would have to be made to produce a fair reallocation. For the purposes of determining the separate property of each spouse, it is logical that the rights of the joint tenants or tenants in common (if applicable on the facts) first be determined. This may include claims by one spouse against the other for occupation rent, or for the payment of current or capital expenses. Only then can a court know how the matrimonial property order should be used to rearrange the entitlements of the spouses.

The dilemma that courts once faced in applications for partition or sale of the family home should no longer be of concern in most (if not all) provinces, at least for spouses (however defined). Under the prior law, an order for partition or sale could lead to a judicially enforced ouster from the home; and to prevent that untoward result some judges looked to factors relating to hardship and prejudice when deciding whether or not to grant an order dissolving the co-ownership relationship. Marital property rules allow for a wider variety of possible orders and outcomes. For instance, in Alberta possession may be granted to one spouse independently of orders as to title, transfer or compensation. In sum, the advent of marital property regimes has meant that the straightjacket of the traditional law of partition and sale has been loosened in this context.

8.   THE NATURE OF CONDOMINIUMS AND CO-OPERATIVES[162]

(a)   the limits of the common law

A condominium exists when two or more property owners band together under an arrangement in which there are individually owned units, coupled with the shared ownership of other lands, all of which is subject to a scheme of management. Condominiums have been common in Canada since the 1960s, largely in the context of high-rise residential buildings, row housing, vacation properties, and retirement estates. In Canada, condominiums account for about 4% of all households.[163] Condominiums also have commercial uses, mainly in aid of small service-industry firms wishing to share facilities. In this modern setting it is easy to overlook the fact that the condominium has a venerable history in some civil law jurisdictions (such as France, Germany and Switzerland). It has also been employed in Scotland and in England, where a simple type of condominium ownership has been practised through the sale of flats.[164] The word

---

162 See generally A.H. Oosterhoff & W.B. Rayner, *Anger & Honsberger Law of Real Property*, 2nd ed. (Aurora, Ont.: Canada Law Book, 1985) vol. 2, Part X.

163 Lo, ''Condominium Living'', Canadian Social Trends 27 (Summer, 1996).

164 See further J. Leyser, ''The Ownership of Flats – A Comparative Study'' (1958) 7 I.C.L.Q. 31.

'condominium' means co-ownership in Latin, but Roman law did not recognize the condominium forms that are found today.[165]

The condominium projects that now exist in Canada are governed by statutory codes,[166] but condominium-like arrangements could be crafted through the use of common law principles. There is nothing remarkable about the idea of a group of nearby property owners joining forces to acquire common areas, with contractual terms affecting their mutual rights and obligations. However, the common law is not always as flexible as property owners might like. Two main problems tend to emerge in the creation of a common law condominium: one has to do with the nature of airspace rights; the other with the establishment of a workable network of reciprocal duties.

The ability to own a home in the sky, separate from ownership of the surface, has never been free from doubt. However, there are comforting statements in the learning about the acceptability of the idea of a 'flying fee' (as it is sometimes called). In the Canadian case of *Iredale v. Loudon* (decided in 1908) it was said that, "[i]t is too late to dispute the proposition that an upper room not resting directly upon the soil but supported entirely by the surrounding parts of a building might at common law be the subject of a feoffment and livery as a corporeal hereditament, that is to say, as land".[167]

However, even if a separate title to airspace is possible, logistical difficulties can arise. One problem concerns the unresolved question of what rights, if any, would survive the destruction of the premises.[168] The initial grant should deal with the implications of this event: buildings do not last forever. One method of anticipating the problem is to confer on all unit holders a share in the surface area when the building is destroyed. However, the nature of this future right is itself problematic: if what is created is a contingent interest, it would be subject to the rule against perpetuities.[169] In addition, land recording laws may not allow for the registration of title to airspace. Even if registration is possible, there may be troublesome (though not insurmountable) issues relating to the proper description of the boundaries. The imprecise nature of airspace title may have an impact on the willingness of a lender to advance money secured against the project. In addition, the horizontal or vertical severance of a plot of land, as part of a condominium venture, will normally require the approval of local planning authorities.

---

165 "Roman law, reasonable and flexible in most ways, was unremittingly hostile to the concept of horizontal property": R. G. Natelson, *Law of Property Owners Associations* (Boston: Little, Brown, 1989) at 23. See also R.G. Natelson, "Comments on the Historiography of the Condominium", 12 Okla. City U.L.Rev. 17 (1987).

166 The first purpose-built condominium legislation in common law Canada was enacted in British Columbia in 1966: see *Strata Titles Act*, S.B.C. 1966, c. 46. It was based on the New South Wales reforms of 1961.

167 (1908) 40 S.C.R. 313, at 333 (per Duff J.). The case is discussed in Note, "Castles in the Air" (1908) 44 Can.L.J. 593.

168 See J.E. Cribbet, "Condominium – Home Ownership for the Megalopolis", 61 Mich.L.Rev. 1207 (1963).

169 The rule is explained in Part 5, Chapter 7.

The second major problem relates to the creation of a satisfactory mesh of rights and obligations. Condominium owners are likely to wish to impose various restrictions and positive duties on each other, relating both to the privately held units and the common areas. It is also necessary to anticipate problems that might emerge in relation to tax levies. As a general rule, all joint tenants are fully liable for taxes that fall due. Therefore, the common law condo participant runs the risk (in theory at least) of having to shoulder the entire tax burden. These matters can be dealt with by contract, but to be fully effective against all owners, present and future, the contractual solution is limited. New owners will not be bound by past agreements; ideally, each newcomer would have to enter into a contract that would be enforceable by all. Private restrictions on land use, if properly framed, can be registered on title so as to run with the land, automatically binding each successive owner, but neither the common law nor equity allow *positive* obligations to run with freehold title in this way.[170] Even if these responsibilities could be made to run, the needs of the condominium may change over time. At common law, any amendments to the scheme would have to be accepted by everyone, and the chances of someone holding out against an increase in fees or rates probably rises exponentially as the number of relevant stakeholders mounts.

In addition, the conventional law of co-ownership lacks a suitable mechanism for resolving disputes among owners. In the absence of an agreement the only solutions available to resolve conflicts are the drastic measures of partition and sale. Finally, agreements aside, one co-owner may sell his or her share in the common areas separately from an individual unit, or seek an order for a partition or sale of the whole common property.

(b)   styles of condominium regulation

Modern condominium statutes attempt to overcome the limitations of the common law. In general, the Canadian legislation provides for the creation, registration, regulation and termination of condominiums. Special consumer protection mechanisms, applicable in connection with the sale of condominium units, are also commonly dealt with as part of the regime. In essence, the statutory condominium is analogous to a municipality. The legislation creates a micro-sovereignty that can enact and enforce a type of local law, provided, of course, that the rules are promulgated in conformity with both the general law and the enabling condominium statute. A person buying into a condominium project is then subject to the rules and becomes a part of the community of governance.

These are the basic features of the Canadian condominium statutes. However, the provinces rode off in all directions in pursuit of a suitable legislative framework. As to the broad issues of creation and governance, two basic approaches are used. These alternatives can be seen through an outline of the Ontario and Alberta systems.

---

170 See further the discussion of restrictive and positive covenants in Chapter 10.

In Ontario, the declaration is of central importance; this document, together with the Act, comprise the 'constitution' to which any by-laws enacted by the governing body must conform. The declaration *must* include the following:

1. a statement of intention that the lands are to be governed by the Act;
2. the consent of registered mortgagees;
3. a statement of the proportions of the property that are the common areas, described in percentage terms;
4. a statement of the proportionate contributions of the units to the common expenses;
5. addresses for the condominium corporation;
6. a statement of the common areas that are to be available to some but not all owners of the units;
7. certain conditions that may be imposed by provincial planning authorities; and
8. other material required by regulation.[171]

The declaration *may* contain provisions concerning:

1. a specification of the common expenses;
2. conditions or restrictions pertaining to the occupation or use of the units and the common elements;
3. conditions or restrictions concerning gifts, leases and sales of the units or the common interests;
4. the duties of the corporation; and
5. the allocation of the obligations to maintain the units and the common elements or repair them from damage.[172]

The declaration is entrenched; it is not easily amended. For some amendments, 80% approval of the unit owners is required; for others 90% must consent.[173] A corporation is created for each registered condominium, but it does not assume ownership of the units, and it need not have any direct property interest in the premises. This corporation is the principal organ for the administration of the project and is responsible for its day-to-day operation. A condominium must elect a board of directors, on a one vote per unit basis. The directors are empowered to pass by-laws, which become effective once they are ratified by a majority of the unit holders and registered.

In Alberta, the main documents are the by-laws and a condominium plan describing the property. There is no declaration, so the constitutional structure is formed through the combined effect of the Act and the by-laws. The *Condominium Property Act* contains a set of standard by-laws, which include provisions con-

---

171 *Condominium Act*, S.O. 1998, c. 19, sub. 7(2). At the time of publication, this version of the list had not yet been proclaimed in force.
172 Sub. 7(4).
173 The elaborate rules are contained in s. 108. A limited right to seek an amendment by court order is contemplated by s. 110.

cerning the following: the duties of the owners; the creation of the corporation; the constitution of the board and the officers of the corporation; meetings; notice and voting; and general restrictions as to the use of the property.[174] The standard by-laws serve merely as default rules; they may be altered through the democratic processes of the corporation.

Rules and regulations are determined by the membership, which acts through the instrumentality of a corporate structure. The members may choose to delegate certain responsibilities to a management board. Some basic structural or organizing rules are set out in the Act. For example, certain items of general business, including the setting of the amounts to be levied for common expenses, require majority approval of the unit holders.[175] A special resolution is required for changes to the by-laws, which must be passed by a 75% majority.[176] In the case of a transfer or lease of the common property, a decision to take the benefit of a restrictive covenant or, more importantly, a decision to terminate the condominium, unanimous consent must be obtained, though there is legislation pending that will treat these matters as being subject to 75% approval.[177]

Participation in condominium projects necessarily involves a surrender of some degree of proprietary independence. An owner is at the mercy of the rules enacted through the internal decision-making process. This is only logical. The imposition of obligations of repair for party walls and ceilings is fully understandable when, as in the usual case, the fee simple units are all within a single building. Likewise, uses that directly and adversely affect the physical enjoyment of neighbouring properties need to be regulated. These are problems that occur in all communities, and one of the attractions of the condominium lifestyle is that there can be a measure of control over the petty annoyances that often occur in urban habitats. However, the loss of autonomy can go further still. Consider the standard by-laws in Alberta,[178] which provide that an owner must not:

1. use the unit for an illegal purpose;
2. keep an animal in the unit or on the common property after a date specified in a notice to remove it;
3. use a residential unit for other than residential purposes; or
4. hang or place anything on the property of the corporation or the common property or within or on a unit ''that is, in the opinion of the board, aesthetically unpleasing when viewed from outside the units''.[179]

---

174 *Condominium Property Act*, R.S.A. 1980, c. C-22, s. 27, Appendices 1, 2 [as am.].

175 Voting is based on the ''unit factor'' for each unit, which appears to be the portion of that unit, as a share of the full complement of units: see paras. 1(1)(w), 6(1)(g), and sub. 21(1).

176 S. 26.

177 Ss. 40, 42, 51. See the *Condominium Property Amendment Act*, S.A. 1996, c. 12, s. 59. But see also s. 61. As at the time of publication of this text, the amending act had not yet been proclaimed in force.

178 Appendix 1, s. 37.

179 Appendix 1, paras. 37(2)(c), (e), (f) and (i).

One right that cannot be abridged in Alberta is the freedom to alienate: the by-laws cannot prohibit or restrict transfers, leases, mortgages or other dealings with the unit.[180] Apart from this, there are very few limitations on the potential content of the by-laws, and it is likely, based on clause 3 above, that broad restrictions on the *mode* of occupation are permissible.

The meaning of the right to control non-residential uses, as found in clause 3, was considered in the *Condominium Plan No. 8810455 v. Spectral Capital Corp.*,[181] where an injunction was granted against the owner of one unit, Spectral, which had begun selling timeshare interests in its suite. Under the by-laws, a notification had to be served whenever there was a change of ownership. Also, the by-laws prohibited commercial activity, or any conduct that might be a nuisance to other tenants and that could increase insurance premiums. The complaint against Spectral was that it was using the unit for commercial purposes. In response, the defendant argued that it would be incongruous to allow the granting of leases of units to new residents, but not to permit timesharing arrangements. However, the Court concluded that the "driving force"[182] behind the defendant's action was the pursuit of profit. This goal was at odds with the underlying purpose of this condominium development, which was to allow the unit holders "to escape to the 'peace and solitude' of the mountains".[183]

The Ontario provisions governing the permissible ambit of the declaration allow for controls on use, but appear to go further, by permitting clauses that restrict gifts, leases and sales.[184] However, it has been recognized that because the right of alienation is a fundamental incident of ownership, provisions in the declaration purporting to restrict the power to transfer should be strictly construed.[185] Moreover, attempts to limit ownership or occupation, say, on the grounds of race or nationality, may be contrary to the laws that prohibit private acts of discrimination.[186]

---

180 Subs. 26(4).

181 (1990) 14 R.P.R. (2d) 305, 112 A.R. 213 (Q.B.).

182 *Ibid.* at 218 A.R. (*per* Moore C.J.Q.B.).

183 *Ibid.*

184 *Condominium Act*, S.O. 1998, c. 19, sub. 7(4).

185 *Metropolitan Toronto Condominium Corp. No. 699 v. 1177 Yonge St. Inc.* (1998) 39 O.R. (3d) 473, 18 R.P.R. (3d) 9, 109 O.A.C. 192 (C.A.) at 194 O.A.C., which relies on *Re Peel Condominium Corp. No. 11 and Caroe* (1974) 4 O.R. (2d) 543, 48 D.L.R. (3d) 503 (H.C.).

186 As to the legality of 'adults only' restrictions, see *Dudnik v. York Condominium Corp. No. 216* (1990) 12 R.P.R. (2d) 1, 12 C.H.R.R. D/325 (Ont.Bd. of Inquiry) reversed in part (1991) 3 O.R. (3d) 360, 79 D.L.R. (4th) 161, 16 R.P.R. (2d) 177 (Div.Ct.) (restrictions invalid). See contra *Marshall v. Strata Plan No. NW 2584* (1996) 3 R.P.R. (3d) 144, 27 B.C.L.R. (3d) 70 (S.C.) and *York Condominium Corp. No. 216 v. Borsodi* (1983) 42 O.R. (2d) 99, 148 D.L.R. (3d) 290 (Co.Ct.) noted in G. Richardson (1984) 62 Can.B.Rev. 656. See also *Condominium Plan No. 931 0520 v. Smith* (1999) 24 R.P.R. (3d) 76 (Alta.Q.B.). See generally V. Di Lorenzo, "Restraints on Alienation in a Condominium Context", 24 Real Prop., Prob. & Trust J. 403 (1989). Restrictions concerning pets have generally been upheld: see J. Mascarin, "The Enforceability of No Pet Clauses in Condominium Documents" (1992) 24 R.P.R. (2d) 24. But see *Waterloo North Condominium Corp. No. 198 v. Donner* (1997) 36 O.R. (3d) 243, 15 R.P.R. (3d) 134 (Gen.Div.) and, especially, *Niagara North Condominium Corp. No. 46 v. Chassie* (1999) 173 D.L.R. (4th) 524, 23 R.P.R. (3d) 25 (Ont.Gen.Div.).

(c)   co-operatives[187]

Housing co-operatives appear to have first emerged in Canada during the Depression. The idea enjoyed a revival in the 1960s, and today it represents a noticeable, if not prevalent, form of property arrangement. In 1971, there were only 2,000 units (representing 0.03% of all housing units in Canada). In 1981, there were 23,000 (0.3%). And by 1989 there were just under 61,000 housing units run under the auspices of about 1,500 not-for-profit organizations; this accounted for 0.6% of all housing units in the country. The demographic breakdown of those living in co-ops is interesting. A study reporting in 1990 found that single parents were over-represented. Incomes were lower than the national average, but levels of education were higher.[188]

As with condominiums, a co-operative is typically designed to create a community comprised of shared amenities and individual entitlements. In addition, members co-operate in the administration of the project. There are a variety of ways in which this can be accomplished. Under one method, the freehold is held in common and leases are granted in favour of the members. Under another, the entire property is owned by a corporation. Participants purchase shares in the corporation, which in return leases residential units to its shareholders. In either case, there is usually an assumption of a portion of the mortgage obligation and a levy for operating expenses. When financing is required, the property may be covered by a blanket mortgage or mortgages. Remember, if the title to property is placed in a company, only it can provide the land-security for the mortgage. One potential problem is that the failure of some members to contribute to the mortgage affects everyone, even those who have paid their full share. For this reason, co-operative agreements often provide for a claim against a member's corporate interest in the event of a failure to contribute as agreed.

The case of *Freeborn v. Goodman*[189] involved an attempt to establish a business co-operative by employing the meagre supply of legal tools available at common law. At issue were the proprietary rights, if any, of a party to a cooperative venture. In *Freeborn*, a development company sold exclusive rights of occupancy to several suites. Participants in the plan were required to purchase shares in the company. The right of occupancy that they acquired as part of the package was subject to the provisos that the occupant must retain the company shares, and must abide by all of the other terms and conditions of the agreement, including any rules and regulations established by the corporation. A failure to comply with these terms gave the company a right to terminate the interest. After a number of these occupancy agreements had been signed, the developer defaulted on mortgages secured against the land. A question arose as to whether the rights of occupancy were interests in land, thereby binding on, and with priority over,

---

187 See B. Woodrow, "Co-operative Housing: A Proposal for Reform" (1983) 41 U.T.Fac.L.Rev. 34; S. Bailey, "Legal Aspects of Continuing Housing Co-operatives" (1978) 4 Queen's L.J. 230; *Anger & Honsberger, supra*, note 162, at 1806*ff.*

188 M.A. Burke, "Co-operative Housing: A Third Tenure Form", Social Trends (Spring 1990) 11.

189 [1969] S.C.R. 923, 6 D.L.R. (3d) 384.

a subsequent mortgage security. The owners of these occupancy rights had not been in breach of their contracts.

The interests that had been granted contained many of the trappings of a lease, including a right to quiet enjoyment. However, unlike a lease there was no specified term; nor was the duration capable of being ascertained. Therefore, the occupancy interests, whatever else they might be, were not leases. Yet, a majority of the Supreme Court of Canada said that "at the very least the interest was a demise secured by a covenant for quiet possession which a Court of equity would undoubtedly enforce".[190] It was conceded that there were no authorities "which characterize the exact interest acquired by the purchasers in terms of any of the categories heretofore accepted by the Courts"[191] in Canada. However, these unique interests have been recognized in American law in connection with co-operative apartments;[192] that now appears to be the case in Canada in light of the *Freeborn* ruling: the co-op 'tenants' were found to have an interest in land. Whether *Freeborn*-style arrangements are commonly used is another matter. Of course, there seems little need to do so now that it is possible to set up a condo-minium under legislation designed for that purpose. Whatever else may be said, the decision in *Freeborn v. Goodman* represents a rare instance of a Canadian court sanctioning a new interest in land.[193]

9. OTHER VISIONS OF COMMUNAL PROPERTY

The tenancy in common and the joint tenancy are the prime forms of co-operative ownership in Canadian law. But they are not the only conceptions of sharing that one can imagine. In the introductory chapter the basic notion of common property was considered. There are few commodities today that might correctly be said to be held in common, to be shared and enjoyed by everyone. The air (to the extent that it has not been placed in containers) or the world's oceans (outside of national boundaries and economic zones) are part of the heritage of all. These are not entitlements that one acquires by private grant or through succession on the death of a prior holder. Quite the reverse: they belong to us (if at all) automatically, at birth.

---

190 *Ibid.* at 933 S.C.R. (*per* Ritchie J.) applying the *dictum* of Strong J. in *Trust & Loan Co. of Canada v. Lawrason* (1881) 10 S.C.R. 679, at 703-4. Martland J. dissented in *Freeborn*.

191 *Supra,* note 189, at 934 S.C.R.

192 "Apparently there has arisen in the field of real property a type of interest, peculiar to the co-operative apartment concept, which does not fit precisely in any of the ancient legal pigeonholes and which is not fully or adequately defined by existing legal terminology": Reeve, *The Influence of the Metropolis on the Concepts, Rules and Institutions Relating to Real Property* (1954) at 198, as noted in P.J. Rohan, "Cooperative Housing: An Appraisal of Residential Controls and Enforcement Procedures", 18 Stan.L.Rev. 1322 (1965-66) at 1329, n. 43, quoted by Ritchie J. in *Freeborn v. Goodman, supra,* note 189, at 934 S.C.R.

193 See Part 4(a)(iii), Chapter 1. For another unusual treatment of co-owned property, in this instance among members of a small hunt club who shared property as tenants in common, see *MacDonald v. Bezzo* (1998) 38 B.L.R. (2d) 1, 108 O.A.C. 232 (C.A.).

Communal systems are found all over the world.[194] In Canada, some groups have established shared arrangements within the strictures of the common law. In Hutterite colonies, for instance, all property is vested in the congregation. If a member is excommunicated from the Church and expelled from the colony, there is no right to remain or to claim a portion of the assets.[195] Moreover, there was a time, not that long ago, when vast expanses of land on the Canadian Prairies were regarded as being used and enjoyed, effectively, as commons.[196]

In Chapter 2, we saw that common law Aboriginal title is regarded as communal.[197] Apart from this common law designation, the idea of communal title is found among the various conceptions of property held by Canada's First Nations. Consider Sákéj Henderson's description of Míkmaq conceptions of sharing:

> The relationship between Míkmaq and the land embodies the essence of [an] intimate social order. As humans, they have and retain an obligation to protect the order and a right to share its uses, but only the future unborn children in the invisible sacred realm of the next seven generations had any ultimate ownership of the land. In the custom of the Míkmaq, the Santé Mawíomi was and is the trustee of the sacred order and territory for future generations. . . .

> The sacred order itself is never individualized. The tenure is held for future generations. A family or an "individual" might enjoy wide administrative authority over a resource or space (a *legacy*), but they have no right to withhold the use of the resources or the products of their use to another insider. The system of kinship relations unites everyone in a web of complementary rights and responsibilities. . . . The continued strength of any claim in the indigenous tenure is a function of sound management and generosity. These legacies are "strong" enough to create incentives to conserve, but "weak" enough to create incentives to share.[198]

Leroy Little Bear, speaking in general terms, has described an Aboriginal vision of property that is quite different from that found in the common law:

> [I]f one attempts to trace the Indians' source of title, one will quickly find the original source is the Creator. The Creator, in granting land, did not give the land to human beings only but gave it to all living beings. This includes plants, sometimes rocks, and all animals. In other words, deer have the same type of estate or interest as any human being. This concept of sharing with fellow animals and plants is one that is quite alien to Western society's concept of land . . . Indian property concepts are [holistic]. Ownership does not rest in any one indi-

---

194 See K. Frimpong, "The Administration of Tribal Lands in Botswana", [1986] J. African L. 51. See also M. Trebilcock, "Communal Property Rights: The Papua New Guinea Experience" (1984) 34 U.T.L.J. 377; R.C. Ellickson, "Property in Land", 102 Yale L.J. 1315 (1993) and the references cited there.

195 See *Hofer v. Hofer*, [1970] S.C.R. 958, 73 W.W.R. 644, 13 D.L.R. (3d) 1. See also *Lakeside Colony of Hutterian Brethren v. Hofer*, [1992] 3 S.C.R. 165, [1993] 1 W.W.R. 113, 97 D.L.R. (4th) 17.

196 The story of the transformation of the commons to private property on the Canadian Prairies is told in I.M. Spry, "The Tragedy of the Loss of the Commons in Western Canada" in A.L. Getty & A.S. Lussier, eds., *As Long as the Sun Shines and the Water Flows* (Vancouver: U.B.C. Pr., 1983) 203.

197 See Part 3(b), Chapter 2.

198 S. Henderson, "Mikmaw Tenure in Atlantic Canada" (1995) 18 Dal.L.J. 196, at 232, 235. See further J.(S.)Y. Henderson *et al.*, *Aboriginal Tenure in the Constitution of Canada* (Toronto: Carswell, 2000).

vidual, but belongs to the tribe as a whole, as an entity. The land belongs not only to people presently living, but it belongs to past generations. Past and future generations are as much a part of the tribal entity as the living generations.[199]

Little Bear has also suggested that these rights resemble a joint tenancy, because "the members of a tribe have an undivided interest in land; everybody, as a whole, owns the whole".[200] However, this comparison is apt only at a very high level of abstraction. Unlike a joint tenancy the rights Leroy Little Bear describes belong to members of Aboriginal communities because they are part of that community, not by virtue of a grant; and their rights cannot be alienated. This is also true of both common law Aboriginal rights, as well as those property rights conferred under the *Indian Act*,[201] which are reposed in the Band unless and until they are allocated to individual members.[202]

There is, however, another analogue that the common law can offer. English law recognizes an eclectic assortment of customary rights that are proprietary in nature; as such they can bind subsequent owners of the affected lands. To qualify, the right must be ancient, meaning that it must have existed since time immemorial (1189 or earlier).[203] It must also be reasonable, certain as to its nature and locality, and it must have been used continuously.[204] If these elements are found, customary rights can be conferred on a fluctuating group, as long as its membership is ascertainable. Accordingly, in *Hall v. Nottingham* it was found that members of a parish had the right to enter on private land for the purpose of erecting and dancing around a maypole, and to otherwise use the land for lawful and innocent recreation throughout the year.[205] The claim was found to be reasonable despite the fact that the customary uses effectively deprived the landowner of the ability to use the land when those activities were taking place. And it was said to be sufficiently certain even though the types of recreation were not spelled out. One member of the Court, Kelly C.B., explicitly described the problem as one involving a clash of private and collective rights:

199 L. Little Bear, "A Concept of Native Title" , [1976] C.A.S.N.A.P. Bulletin 258, at 262. A general review of Aboriginal property systems, from an economist's viewpoint, is found in M.J. Bailey, "Approximate Optimality of Aboriginal Property Rights", 32 J. Law & Econ. 183 (1992).

200 *Supra*, note 199, at 262.

201 R.S.C. 1985, c. I-5 [as am.].

202 See further *Joe v. Findlay, Jr.*, 26 B.C.L.R. 376, [1981] 3 W.W.R. 60, 122 D.L.R. (3d) 377 (C.A.).

203 This was fixed by statute at 1189, the year of the ascension of Richard I to the throne of England: *Statute of Westminster, 1275*, 3 Edw. 1, c. 39. See further *Bryant v. Foot* (1867) L.R. 2 Q.B. 161, affirmed (1868) L.R. 3 Q.B. 493 (Ex.Ch.).

204 See *Adair v. National Trust for Places of Historic Interest or Natural Beauty*, [1998] N.I. 33 (Ch.D.) at 44-5, where the claim to a customary right to dig lugworms from the foreshore failed.

205 (1875) 33 L.T. 697 (Ex.D.). See also *Brocklebank v. Thompson*, [1903] 2 Ch. 344; *Wyld v. Silver*, [1963] Ch. 243, [1962] 3 All E.R. 309 (C.A.). The analogy between Aboriginal title and customary rights under English law was noticed by Lord Denning M.R. in *R. v. Secretary of State for Foreign and Commonwealth Affairs; ex parte Indian Association of Alberta*, [1982] 1 Q.B. 892, [1982] 2 All E.R. 118 (C.A.) at 910 Q.B.

> We are dealing . . . with a matter affecting an individual owner of a small piece of land on the one hand, and the rights and privileges of all the inhabitants of an entire parish on the other; and it is so much for the moral and physical benefit and advantage of those inhabitants that they should have rational and healthful recreation, and that they should have a piece of ground on which they may be able to indulge in the exercise of lawful sports, games and pastimes, that I think the benefit and advantage accruing to them from the right claimed outweigh the injury and disadvantage arising therefrom to the owner of the land.[206]

The right that was protected is an example of a rare form of communal interest recognized under law. Such rights acknowledge the past and preserve a tradition for present and future generations. Of course, this encompasses less than that described in the Little Bear account. There is no accommodation for the claims of non-humans;[207] nor, patently, are the English customary rights premised on a spiritual connection with the land.

---

206 *Supra,* note 205, at 699.
207 But see the statement of Douglas J. in *Sierra Club v. Morton,* 405 U.S. 727 (1972) at 752, quoted in Part 4(b), Chapter 1.

10

SERVITUDES OVER PROPERTY

The decision of Mr. Justice Keiller MacKay, in declaring void a
clause in a deed which stipulated that a certain parcel of land was
"not to be sold to Jews or persons of objectionable nationality",
was on the noblest level of jurisprudence. . . . It will no longer
be possible to prevent any person of any race or creed from living
where he wishes to live. This is the essence of freedom.

> Editorial, "Blow to Prejudice", *Globe & Mail*,
> November 2, 1945, 6, endorsing the decision in *Re
> Drummond Wren*

The Court of Appeal has sustained [a] judgment . . . upholding
the validity of a restrictive covenant applying to properties in a
Lake Huron summer resort colony . . . [that] binds owners of
these properties not to sell, lease or transfer to persons of Semitic
or Negro blood. . . . In this case, it cannot be seriously claimed
that basic rights to shelter are being denied by the covenant. But
to assert that any group of people should be forbidden to associate
themselves in a perfectly lawful manner would create problems
of a far-reaching character with all sorts of dangerous
implications. . . . There is much to correct in our treatment of
minorities in Canada, but force is not the way to do it.

> Editorial, "Tolerance and Law", *Globe & Mail*, June
> 11, 1949, 6, endorsing the Ontario Court of Appeal
> decision in *Re Noble & Wolf*

1. INTRODUCTION

This chapter explores the law governing 'servitudes', a term borrowed from
Roman law to refer to rights of use over property that belongs to another. Servitudes are like metaphysical fixtures, for they can be attached to, and pass with, a
transfer of realty. Owing to this quality, they resemble the real covenants that run
with the assignment of a leasehold interest under the rule in *Spencer's Case*.[1] As
with the study of real covenants in leases, the analysis here returns to the line that
separates contract and property. Other themes are also revisited: the distinction
between law and equity; the *numerus clausus* policy as it applies to land;[2] and the
nature of the power that can be wielded through ownership. The use of private
planning devices as mechanisms for environmental protection will also be discussed. The running of covenants with personalty will be broached, but the rights
studied here apply mainly in relation to land, and so this chapter is almost exclusively about the law of real property.

---

1 (1583) 5 Co.Rep. 16a, 77 E.R. 72, [1558-1774] All E.R.Rep. 68. See Part 3(a), Chapter 8.
2 See Part 4(a)(iii), Chapter 1.

Two servitudes will be considered in detail: easements and covenants. The essentials of their creation and transfer will be addressed. The rules are complex, and there is a lexicon in this area that needs to be mastered. As an aid to understanding the discussion to follow, examine this photograph of a residential duplex in Edmonton:

Assume that both sides of this duplex were originally owned by A. In 1999, the unit on the left, Blackacre, was sold to B. On the sale, B was given a right of access over the parcel retained by A, Whiteacre. At the same time, B promised not to change the colour of the exterior without A's consent, and to keep the roof in repair. A gave similar undertakings to B. This chapter is concerned with the means by which such promises can be made to 'run' with both properties, so as to be binding on any new owners of Blackacre and Whiteacre. It should be helpful to reflect back on this simple scenario as the discussion unfolds.

2.   THE ELEMENTS OF AN EASEMENT[3]

Easements fall within the category of interests known as incorporeal hereditaments. Also included under this head is the interest known as a *profit à prendre*,[4] along with an assortment of other property holdings of less current

---

3 See generally A.J. McClean, "The Nature of an Easement" (1966) 5 U.W.O.L.Rev. 32; J. Gaunt & P. Morgan, *Gale on Easements*, 16th ed. (London: Sweet & Maxwell, 1997); C. Sara, *Boundaries and Easements*, 2nd ed. (London: Sweet & Maxwell, 1996).

4 Profits are discussed in the text accompanying notes 43 to 46, *infra*.

significance.[5] Covenants running with property, a relative newcomer to land law, should perhaps now be included as well.[6]

The origins of the easement have been traced to the copyhold tenures of the English manor.[7] Today they constitute an integral part of the Canadian law of real property. A tenant's use of the common hallways of an apartment building, a pipeline right-of-way, a right to walk or drive along a lane, to use a park as a garden,[8] to stroll along a beach,[9] to use a ditch for water run-off,[10] to engage in acts of nuisance,[11] even the right to use a neighbour's kitchen[12] or toilet,[13] can be enjoyed as an easement. However, the range of easements is not endlessly elastic. On the contrary, four doctrinal limits circumscribe the allowable forms.[14]

First, there must be a dominant tenement (which enjoys the benefit of the easement) and a servient tenement (which is burdened). At common law, easements cannot exist in gross, but must be connected (appurtenant) to a dominant tenement.[15] Ordinarily that tenement is a freehold or leasehold estate, but apparently it can also be another incorporeal hereditament.[16]

---

5 Included here is a rentcharge, which is an annuity charge on property. Unlike the requirements for rent under a lease at common law, a rentcharge need not be attached to a reversionary interest. As to other incorporeal hereditaments, none of which appears to have taken hold in Canada, see R.E. Megarry & H.W.R. Wade, *The Law of Real Property*, 5th ed. (London: Stevens & Sons, 1984) at 814-7. Rentcharges are discussed in detail at 818*ff.*

6 The law of restrictive covenants is not mentioned in E.D. Armour, *A Treatise of the Law of Real Property* (Toronto: Canada Law Book, 1901) the leading real property text of its day in Canada.

7 "The common lands of the manor required an adjustment of the conflicting claims of many persons trying simultaneously to derive benefit from the same land. This process set in motion much of what is now known as the law of easements": *Powell on Real Property*, Rev.ed. (New York: Matthew Bender & Co., 1990) vol. 1, at para. 25.

8 *In re Ellenborough Park*, [1956] Ch. 131, [1955] 3 All E.R. 667 (C.A.).

9 *Dukart v. Surrey (District)*, [1978] 2 S.C.R. 1039, [1978] 4 W.W.R. 1, 86 D.L.R. (3d) 609.

10 *Ryslephaniuk v. Prosken* (1951) 59 Man.R. 142, 3 W.W.R. (N.S.) 76 (K.B.).

11 See, *e.g.*, *British Columbia Forest Products Ltd. v. Nordal* (1954) 11 W.W.R. (N.S.) 403 (B.C.S.C.).

12 *Heywood v. Mallalieu* (1883) 25 Ch.D. 357.

13 *Miller v. Emcer Products Ltd.*, [1956] 1 Ch. 304, [1956] 1 All E.R. 237 (C.A.). For more examples, see *Gale on Easements*, *supra*, note 3, at 38*ff.*

14 The leading case on this subject is *In re Ellenborough Park*, *supra*, note 8, where this four-part analysis, developed by G.C. Cheshire, was employed.

15 See *Miller v. Tipling* (1918) 43 O.L.R. 88, 43 D.L.R. 469 (C.A.); *Union Bank of Canada v. Foulds* (1924) 26 O.W.N. 179 (Chambers); *Voice v. Bell* (1993) 68 P. & C.R. 441 (C.A.). For a critique of this requirement, see M.F. Sturley, "Easements in Gross" (1980) 96 L.Q.R. 557 and G. Morgan, "Easements in Gross Revisited" (1999) 28 Anglo-Am.L.Rev. 220. In *Hubbs v. Black* (1918) 44 O.L.R. 545, 46 D.L.R. 583 (C.A.), one member of the Court of Appeal, Riddell J., held that the right to bury a corpse in another's freehold was an exception to the general rule that an easement cannot exist in gross. See also *Griffin v. Klassen Estate*, Unreported (November 29, 1991) Brockenshire J. (Ont.Gen.Div.) discussed in the text accompanying notes 67 to 69, *infra*. In Alberta, various utility rights of way may be created without being attached to a dominant tenement: *Land Titles Act*, R.S.A. 1980, c. L-5, s. 72 [as am].

16 See *Vannini v. Public Utilities Commission of Sault Ste. Marie*, [1973] 2 O.R. 11, 32 D.L.R. (3d) 661 (H.C.). See also *Re Salvin's Indenture*, [1938] 2 All E.R. 498 (Ch.D.) (noted in (1938) 54 L.Q.R. 487) where the dominant tenement was comprised of both corporeal and incorporeal hereditaments.

The reason why a dominant property is required may relate to ancient (and long-since abandoned) rules concerning the remedies available to an easement holder.[17] Absent this constraint, there remains a policy argument that pertains to the very idea of servitudes as land-based rights: their function is to improve the utility of land. Since easements can inhibit the productive use of servient lands, the burdening of one property is permitted only as long as some reciprocal benefit is conferred on another. Requiring a dominant property also limits the number of parcels that can enjoy an easement, and hence reducing (but not preventing altogether) the danger that a servient tenement might become overburdened with easements. Following the lead of the United States and New Zealand, where easements in gross may be created, in 1996 the Ontario Law Reform Commission recommended that this approach be adopted.[18]

Second, the easement must accommodate the dominant land. Some real benefit must accrue to the dominant tenement, making it a better and more convenient property. This underscores the policy of tolerating burdens on one parcel only if another is thereby improved. In the nineteenth century case of *Hill v. Tupper*[19] it was decided that an exclusive right to place boats on a lake did not accommodate the dominant tenement, because this monopoly was unconnected with the normal use and enjoyment of the land.[20] The case is an important one in the development of the law of easements, but the general principle it establishes is not obvious. If this ruling means that an easement does not meet the second requirement if it serves only to enhance business activity, then it seems both illogical and inconsistent with other authority.[21] In *Hill*, the dominant land was used in connection with the boating operations, and the monopoly obviously made that enterprise more viable, so the ruling might be too restrictive, even wrong.[22] Another approach to this issue, one that would support the holding in the case, is to regard easements as serving to supply an attribute of ownership normally or frequently associated with land. Viewed in this way, the law of easements is designed to allow such deficiencies to be remedied. Because the bundle of rights over land does not include monopolies of the type found in *Hill v. Tupper*, the Court in that case was correct in denying the easement claim.

---

17 See Ontario Law Reform Commission, *Report on Basic Principles of Land Law* (Toronto: A.G. (Ont.), 1996) at 141.

18 *Supra*, note 17, at 145, 164. In the United States it has been necessary to develop principles designed to deal with the possibility of overburdening an easement held in gross. See A.D. Hegi, "The Easement in Gross Revisited: Transferability and Severability Since 1945", 39 Vanderbilt L.Rev. 109 (1986). As to New Zealand, see *Property Law Act 1952*, s. 122. See also *Faloon v. District Land Registrar*, [1997] 3 N.Z.L.R. 498 (H.C.).

19 (1863) 2 H. & C. 121, 159 E.R. 51, [1861-73] All E.R.Rep. 696.

20 See also *In re Ellenborough Park*, *supra*, note 8, at 175 Ch. (*per* Lord Evershed M.R.): "It is clear that what the plaintiff [in *Hill*] was trying to do was to set up, under the guise of an easement, a monopoly which had no normal connexion with the ordinary use of his land, but which was merely an independent business enterprise. So far from the right claimed subserving or accommodating the land, the land was but a convenient incident to the exercise of the right."

21 See, *e.g.*, *Moody v. Steggles* (1879) 12 Ch.D. 261.

22 See further R.N Gooderson, "Easement – *Jus Spatiandi*", [1956] C.L.J. 24, at 25.

The 'accommodation' requirement also means that there must be a reasonable proximity between the dominant and servient tracts. We know that the properties do not have to be contiguous to comply with this rule. But just how close the two must be is something that cannot be defined precisely: the permissible extent of physical separation cannot simply be measured in metres. In determining whether an easement is able to accommodate the dominant land, the type of right involved should be an important factor.

Third, the dominant and servient tenements cannot both be in the hands of the same person. To have an easement over one's own land is nonsensical given that ownership of the servient land carries with it a far more extensive set of rights of use and exploitation than an easement could possibly confer. However, an easement might be given, say, in favour of a tenant over lands retained by the landlord. In this instance, freehold title to the dominant and servient tenements remains under the ownership of the landlord, but possession is divided. As a result, such an easement is not contrary to the third rule. Additionally, some jurisdictions have departed from the common law by permitting the registration of easements over lands owned and occupied by one person. This enables a land developer to establish easements in a subdivision prior to the sale of individual lots, eliminating the need to grant separate easements on the sale of each parcel.[23]

Fourth, the easement must be capable of forming the subject-matter of a grant. The need for a grant stems from the treatment of easements as *incorporeal rights*: because a transfer of possession is not possible, a grant is required in order to pass ownership. However, more is involved in the fourth element than just this. If one opens up this rule one exposes several additional limitations: there must be a capable grantor and grantee; rights under an easement must not be too vague; the easement cannot be a mere right of recreation without benefit or utility; and (apart from fencing easements[24]) it cannot require the servient owner to spend money.[25] Furthermore, to count as an easement, the grant cannot confer a right to possession or control of the servient lands to an extent that is inconsistent with the possessory rights of the servient owner: "[t]here is no easement known to the law which gives exclusive or unrestricted use of a piece of land. A grant of the exclusive or unrestricted use of land beyond all question passes the ownership of that land."[26]

The requirement that easements be non-possessory raises both theoretical and practical concerns. The rationale of this limitation is that easements that bestow possessory rights may sterilize the servient lands. However, non-possessory easements can create the same problem. For example, it is well accepted that once an easement has been granted, the servient lands cannot be altered so as to

---

23 See, *e.g.*, *Land Titles Act*, R.S.A. 1980, c. L-5, s. 71.

24 For this reason it is sometimes referred to as a "spurious easement": *Lawrence v. Jenkins* (1873) L.R. 8 Q.B. 274, [1861-73] All E.R.Rep. 847, at 279 L.R. 8 Q.B. (*per* Archibold J.).

25 See *Nordin v. Faridi* (1996) 17 B.C.L.R. (3d) 366, [1996] 5 W.W.R. 242 (C.A.).

26 *Weeks v. Rogalski*, [1956] O.R. 109, 1 D.L.R. (2d) 709 (C.A.) at 117 O.R. (*per* Roach J.A., quoting from *Gale on Easements*, 12th ed. (1950) at 25). See also *Aircraft Maintenance Enterprises Inc. v. Aerospace Realties (1986) Ltd.* (1992) 94 Nfld. & P.E.I.R. 271, 298 A.P.R. 271 (Nfld.T.D.).

interfere with the enjoyment of the easement. Moreover, all easements involve some degree of possession-taking, however ephemeral this may be in some instances.[27] And it is not clear as to what counts as the servient lands for these purposes: the entire tract owned by the servient owner, or only the place where the easement is actually being enjoyed.[28] Given all of this uncertainty, it is not surprising to find that this principle has been applied unevenly.[29] One route out of the maze would be to reduce the inquiry to an assessment of whether or not the easement creates a 'substantial interference' with the servient property, and not to focus narrowly on possession alone.[30]

The fourth rule also includes the idea that a claim made for a novel type of easement, even one that meets all of the other requirements, might not succeed. While it is true that the "category of servitudes and easements must alter and expand with the changes that take place in the circumstances of [humankind]",[31] nevertheless there is a general hesitancy to add new forms to the catalogue of valid easements.[32] Additionally, it has been maintained that new types of positive easements are more readily recognized than negative ones.[33] Positive easements permit the holder to engage in some activity on the servient tenement (*e.g.*, using a right-of-way). Negative easements restrict activities on the servient land. Included here, for instance, is a right to receive light into a window on the dominant land, which, as a necessary consequence, prohibits the servient owner from blocking that window.[34] By way of contrast, it is generally said that the right to a prospect or view cannot be protected as a negative easement.[35] The stricter scrutiny for negative easements must be due to the assumption that, on balance, they are more prone to impede the productive use of servient property. As we will see below, these fears surface in relation to easements arising by prescription.[36]

---

27 B. Ziff & M.M. Litman, "Easements and Possession: An Elusive Limitation", [1989] Conv. 296, at 297.

28 See further *Gale on Easements*, *supra*, note 3, at 32.

29 See also K. Gray, *Elements of Land Law*, 2nd ed. (London: Butterworths, 1993) at 1076*ff.*

30 See, *e.g.*, *Shelf Holdings Ltd. v. Husky Oil Operations Ltd.* (1989) 65 Alta.L.R. (2d) 300, [1989] 3 W.W.R. 692, 56 D.L.R. (4th) 193 (C.A.) leave to appeal to S.C.C. refused (1989) 57 D.L.R. (4th) viii (note) (S.C.C.). See *Grant v. MacDonald* (1992) 68 B.C.L.R. (2d) 332, [1992] 5 W.W.R. 577, 24 R.P.R. (2d) 234 (C.A.) which can be explained, if at all, on this basis. For further proceedings relevant to this point, see *MacDonald v. Grant* (1993) 85 B.C.L.R. (2d) 180, 35 R.P.R. (2d) 50 (S.C.). See also *London & Blenheim Estates Ltd. v. Ladbroke Retail Parks Ltd.*, [1992] 1 W.L.R. 1278 (Ch.D.) affirmed on other grounds [1994] 1 W.L.R. 31 (C.A.).

31 *Dyce v. Lady Hay* (1852) 1 Macq. 305, 149 R.R. 11 (H.L.) at 16 R.R. (*per* Lord St. Leonards L.C.). See also A.F. Conrad, "Easement Novelties", 30 Cal.L.Rev. 125 (1942).

32 See generally Part 4(a)(iii), Chapter 1.

33 "[T]he law has been very chary of creating any new negative easements": *Phipps v. Pears*, [1965] 1 Q.B. 76, [1964] 2 All E.R. 35 (C.A.) at 83 Q.B. (*per* Lord Denning M.R.).

34 See, *e.g.*, *Ough v. King*, [1967] 1 W.L.R. 1547, [1967] 3 All E.R. 859 (C.A.). See generally M.A. Bowden, "Protecting Solar Access in Canada: The Common Law Approach" (1984-5) 9 Dal.L.J. 261. More generally, see I. Dawson & A. Dunn, "Negative Easements – A Crumb of Analysis (1998) 18 Leg.Stud. 510.

35 See *Aldred's Case* (1610) 9 Co.Rep. 57b, at 58b, 77 E.R. 816 (H.L.), which denied a right to a prospect. See further P. Polder, "Views in Perspective", [1984] Conv. 429. But see *Brumell v. Wharin* (1866) 16 Gr. 283 (U.C.Ch.D.).

36 Part 4(e), *infra*.

3. INTERESTS ANALOGOUS TO EASEMENTS

There are a number of interests or rights that resemble easements in one way or another. Think of a simple agreement between landowners to allow B's car to be parked on A's driveway. This arrangement could take the form of a lease of a parking space, an easement,[37] a licence,[38] or perhaps even a bailment.

There are other rights that overlap with easements, in purpose or design. Some property rights closely resemble negative easements. Here are some examples. In Chapter 3 it was shown that ownership of land carries with it natural or inherent rights of lateral and vertical support.[39] A comparable easement of support can be obtained for buildings on land (arguably a negative easement), and this gives the easement holder the right to repair neighbouring buildings when the support they provide is in jeopardy of being lost or reduced.[40] Under the doctrine of non-derogation from grant, discussed in relation to leases, we saw that a tenant may have a right to limit activity taking place on nearby lands owned by the landlord.[41] As will become apparent later on in this chapter, negative easements are similar to restrictive covenants. Because of this similarity, rights which have not been accepted into the legion of negative easements, such as a right to protection from weather,[42] may be made to run – via covenants – with the servient and dominant lands.

The incorporeal hereditament known as a *profit à prendre* is somewhat akin to a positive easement. A profit entitles the holder to enter onto the land of another to take some part of the produce, such as timber, crops, turf, soil, grass, or animals.[43] It may entitle the holder to extract oil and natural gas: this is the type of grant sometimes used in modern drilling operations.[44] A profit can be either held with others (in common), or exclusively (in severalty). Title to the objects covered by the grant of a *profit à prendre* is acquired through capture, not before: it is a right to win or extract (thus the term '*prendre*').[45]

Unlike an easement, a profit may exist in gross; or it may be tied (or 'appurtenant') to a dominant tenement. In the case of a profit in gross, the extent of the permitted exploitation is assumed to be unlimited; the resource may be ex-

---

37 See *London & Blenheim Estates Ltd. v. Ladbroke Retail Parks Ltd.*, supra, note 30. See also S. Bridge, "Rights to Park: Re-Drawing a Single Yellow Line", [1994] C.L.J. 229, *Handel v. St. Stephens*, [1994] 1 E.G.L.R. 159 (Q.B.) discussed in H.W. Wilkinson, "The Right to Park" (1994) 144 N.L.J. 579.

38 See, *e.g.*, *Imperial Oil Ltd. v. Young* (1998) 167 Nfld. & P.E.I.R. 280, 513 A.P.R. 280, 21 R.P.R. (3d) 65 (Nfld.C.A.). As to the distinction between easements and licences, see *Gypsum Carrier Inc. v. The Queen*, [1978] 1 F.C. 147, 78 D.L.R. (3d) 175 (T.D.).

39 See Part 4(b), Chapter 3.

40 Some riparian rights also resemble negative (and positive) easements. See Part 3(c), Chapter 3.

41 See Part 4(b), Chapter 8.

42 Such a right was rejected as an easement in *Phipps v. Pears*, supra, note 33.

43 It is not, therefore, confined to fugacious substances: *Amoco Canada Resources Ltd. v. Potash Corp. of Saskatchewan*, [1992] 2 W.W.R. 313, 86 D.L.R. (4th) 700, 93 Sask.R. 300 (C.A.).

44 See, *e.g.*, *Berkheiser v. Berkheiser*, [1957] S.C.R. 387, 7 D.L.R. (2d) 721; *Canadian Export Gas & Oil Ltd. v. Flegal*, [1978] 1 W.W.R. 185, 9 A.R. 105, 80 D.L.R. (3d) 679 (T.D.).

45 See generally *British Columbia v. Tener*, [1985] 1 S.C.R. 533, [1985] 3 W.W.R. 673, 17 D.L.R. (4th) 1; H.H. Hahner, "An Analysis of Profits à Prendre", 25 Ore.L.Rev. 217 (1946).

hausted. The scope of a profit appurtenant is restricted to the needs of the dominant lands. Even so, it has been recently held that a right to graze animals, though created as a right appurtenant to nearby land, may be transformed into a profit in gross, so long as the pre-existing right of pasture was limited to a defined number of animals. If so, the interests of the servient owner are not prejudiced by severing the profit from the dominant tenement.[46]

In Chapter 9 we saw that English common law recognizes ancient customary rights.[47] These create a "local common law"[48] and may run with land even though the necessary features of an easement are absent. In order to be recognized, the customary use must be certain, reasonable, continuous, and it must have existed since time immemorial (1189 or earlier).[49] This last requirement rules out the possibility of claims succeeding in Canada, at least those made by non-indigenous settlers.[50]

Aboriginal rights, some of which are analogous to *profits à prendre*,[51] can also be recognized under the common law, or by way of treaty.[52] A right to hunt or fish may be established when it is shown that the practice, custom or tradition was a central and significant part of the claimant Aboriginal group's culture at the time of European contact. To find such a right, therefore, the courts do not have to resort to the English law governing customary rights based on usage from time immemorial. And although such a claim does not amount to Aboriginal *title*, it is normally connected to the land in some way. As with a profit, the right relates to some ascertainable territory; it is 'site-specific'.[53]

Some public usufructuary rights resemble incorporeal hereditaments. We all enjoy general rights to use public roadways[54] and watercourses. Our rights over these public lands are subject, of course, to various restrictions (such as those

---

46 *Bettison v. Langton*, [1999] 3 W.L.R. 39, [1999] 2 All E.R. 367 (C.A.).

47 See Part 9, Chapter 9.

48 *Hammerton v. Honey* (1876) 24 W.R. 603 (Ch.D.) at 603 (*per* Jessel M.R.).

49 This was fixed by statute at 1189, the year of the ascension of Richard I to the throne of England: *Statute of Westminster, 1275*, 3 Edw. 1, c. 39. See further *Bryant v. Foot* (1867) L.R. 2 Q.B. 161, affirmed (1868) L.R. 3 Q.B. 493 (Ex.Ch.).

50 See *Grand Hotel Co. v. Cross* (1879) 44 U.C.Q.B. 153. See also *Gibbs v. Grand Bend (Village)* (1989) 71 O.R. (2d) 70, 7 R.P.R. (2d) 13, 64 D.L.R. (4th) 28 (H.C.) additional reasons at (1990) 72 O.R. (2d) 697, 68 D.L.R. (4th) 474 (H.C.) at 64 D.L.R. (4th) 67, reversed (1995) 26 O.R. (3d) 644, 49 R.P.R. (2d) 157, 129 D.L.R. (4th) 449 (C.A.). At trial, Chilcott J. suggested that "perhaps the law of custom in Ontario could be looked at afresh" with regard to the requirement of usage since time immemorial. See also S.W. Bender, "Castles in the Sand: Balancing Public Custom and Private Ownership Interests in Oregon's Beaches", 77 Ore.L.Rev. 913 (1998).

51 See *Bolton v. Forest Pest Management Institute*, [1985] 6 W.W.R. 562, [1986] 2 C.N.L.R. 26, 21 D.L.R. (4th) 242 (C.A.) where a trap line registered under provincial law was treated as a *profit à prendre*.

52 See, *e.g.*, *R. v. Marshall* (1999) 178 N.S.R. (2d) 201, 177 D.L.R. (4th) 513, [1999] 4 C.N.L.R. 161 (S.C.C.) reconsideration refused (1999) 179 N.S.R. (2d) 1, 179 D.L.R. (4th) 193, [1999] 4 C.N.L.R. 301 (S.C.C.)

53 See *R. v. Van der Peet*, [1996] 2 S.C.R. 507, [1996] 4 C.N.L.R. 177, 137 D.L.R. (4th) 289. See also *R. v. Sparrow*, [1990] 1 S.C.R. 1075, [1990] 3 C.N.L.R. 160, 70 D.L.R. (4th) 385. See further Part 3(b), Chapter 2.

54 But see *R. v. Trabulsey* (1995) 22 O.R. (3d) 314, 97 C.C.C. (3d) 147 (C.A.) leave to appeal to S.C.C. refused (1996) 27 O.R. (3d) xv (S.C.C.)

imposed by traffic rules).[55] In England, it has been recently affirmed that the public may use public roads for reasonable activities (conducted in reasonable ways), including peaceful assemblies arranged as part of a protest.[56] Of course, in Canada government regulation of the use of public property is itself subject to review under the *Canadian Charter of Rights and Freedoms*.[57] The state's control over its property is, therefore, affected by a special set of constraints (*i.e.*, the *Charter*). As I will explain immediately below, a by-product of the introduction of these protections has been the creation of certain easement-like rights.

Several important cases involving freedom of expression have prompted a consideration of the extent to which these *Charter* rights may be exercised on public property. In the leading decision of *Committee for the Commonwealth of Canada v. Canada*[58] the right to distribute leaflets at federally controlled airports was recognized. More precisely, the Supreme Court of Canada held (i) that attempts to prohibit the distribution of leaflets violated the right to freedom of speech; and (ii) that the regulations that had been used by the federal authorities were constitutionally unacceptable. American law blazed this trail some years ago, and it is clear that the American experience affected the way that the Supreme Court of Canada saw the issues. As it turns out, one year or so after the Canadian decision, the United States Supreme Court struck down a ban on the sale of literature in force at J.F.K. International Airport in New York City.[59] Although the patterns of constitutional reasoning in the two polities differ from each other, the bottom lines appear to be roughly parallel.

The opinions rendered in the *Commonwealth* case reflect the idea that public property is encrusted with certain unique obligations that require that this property be administered for the benefit of the nation. The members of the Court also recognized that airports are now common thoroughfares, very much like public streets and squares. Airports have become, in effect, public forums. In allowing

---

55 Private roads may become public roads or highways under the doctrine of dedication. The governing principles are reviewed in *Edmonton (City) v. Alberta (Registrar, North Alberta Land Registration District)* (1994) 26 Alta.L.R. (3d) 100, [1995] 3 W.W.R. 543 (Q.B.) and the judgment of Brooke J.A. in *Gibbs v. Grand Bend (Village)*, *supra*, note 50. In general, there must be an intention to dedicate on the part of the owner, the property must be made available for public use, and this dedication must be accepted by the public. These elements may be implied from surrounding circumstances. The doctrine of dedication has been held to be inapplicable to Aboriginal lands: *Skerryvore Ratepayers' Assn. v. Shawanaga Indian Band* (1993) 16 O.R. (3d) 390, 36 R.P.R. (2d) 23, 109 D.L.R. (4th) 449 (C.A.) leave to appeal to S.C.C. refused (1994) 17 O.R. (3d) xvii (S.C.C.).

56 *D.P.P. v. Jones*, [1999] 2 All E.R. 257, 237 N.R. 18 (H.L.).

57 Pt. I of the *Constitution Act, 1982* [en. by the *Canada Act, 1982* (U.K.), c. 11, s. 1].

58 [1991] 1 S.C.R. 139, 77 D.L.R. (4th) 385, 120 N.R. 241 reconsideration refused (May 8, 1991) Doc. 20334 (S.C.C.). For an analysis of the judgments in this case, see J. Ross, "*Committee for the Commonwealth of Canada v. Canada*: Expression on Public Property" (1991) 2 Constit.Forum 109.

59 See *International Society for Krishna Consciousness, Inc. v. Lee*, 112 S.Ct. 2701 (1992). See further B.W. Berg, "Diminishing the Freedom to Speak on Public Property: *International Society for Krishna Consciousness, Inc. v. Lee*", 29 Creighton L.Rev. 1265 (1993). See also *Benefit v. City of Cambridge*, 679 N.E.2d 184 (Mass. S.J.C., 1997) which held that peaceful begging in a public place constitutes communicative activity protected by the First Amendment.

for the exercise of free speech in these settings, citizens who do not themselves have the resources to exercise that right in a meaningful way are empowered to some measure. Madame Justice L'Heureux-Dubé recognized the interrelationship between wealth and freedom, a connection that was featured in the opening chapter.[60] She observed that "[o]nly those with enough wealth to own land, or mass media facilities (whose ownership is largely concentrated), [are] able to engage in free expression".[61] The case is a modest response to this property-based imbalance.

Of course, not all publicly owned land can be treated as a public forum in the same way as an airport. Additionally, private conduct, even the exercising of a constitutional freedom, cannot be allowed to interfere unduly with whatever use is being made of the public property. Free speech in an airport facility can be restricted to the extent necessary to operate the terminal properly. As in all cases in which the *Charter* is invoked, a balance must be struck. Nonetheless, the Supreme Court has opened the way for challenges against attempts to regulate speech and assembly on other accessible public property sites, such as parks and streets. Indeed, the *Charter* has been applied to strike down excessive restrictions on the right to post signs on public utility poles.[62] But the removal of a 'peace camp' on Parliament Hill by governmental authorities has been upheld. Even though establishing the camp fell within the right of freedom of *expression*, the method used to control the use of the lawn in front of the Parliament Buildings was found to be a reasonable limitation on the enjoyment of that right.[63]

These *Charter* cases concern public lands, but an off-shoot of this jurisprudence may someday take root in the domain of private property. A landowner has a general right to exclude members of the public,[64] but even as against other citizens this power may not be as comprehensive as is sometimes thought. Certainly, it was not absolute at common law: for example, innkeepers could not unreasonably refuse services to members of the public.[65] Likewise, it may be that quasi-public forums, such as modern shopping malls, to which the public is generally invited, cannot be closed – at the pure whim of the owners – to those

---

60 See Part 3(d), Chapter 1.

61 *Supra*, note 58, at 198 S.C.R.

62 *Peterborough (City) v. Ramsden*, [1993] 2 S.C.R. 1084, 106 D.L.R. (4th) 233, 16 M.P.L.R. (2d) 1. *Cf. Beaumier v. Brampton (City)* (1998) 46 M.P.L.R. (2d) 32 (Ont.Gen.Div.) affirmed (1999) 7 M.P.L.R. (3d) 219 (C.A.), discussed in B.I. Colangelo, "Keep Off the Grass: By-law Prohibits Federal Election Signs on Public Property – Case Comment: *Beaumier v. Brampton (City)*" (1998) 46 M.P.L.R. (2d) 37.

63 *Weisfeld v. Canada (Minister of Public Works)* (1994) 116 D.L.R. (4th) 232, 171 N.R. 28 (Fed.C.A.).

64 *Harrison v. Carswell*, [1976] 2 S.C.R. 200, [1975] 6 W.W.R. 673, 62 D.L.R. (3d) 68.

65 See *Carriss v. Buxton*, [1958] S.C.R. 441, 13 D.L.R. (2d) 689, at 446 S.C.R.; *Whiting v. Mills* (1850) 7 U.C.Q.B. 450. See also M.M. Litman, "Freedom of Speech and Private Property: The Case of the Mall Owner" in D. Schneiderman, ed., *Freedom of Expression and the Charter* (Calgary: Carswell, 1991) 361, at 366*ff*. The argument that a similar rule should apply to shopping malls fell flat on its face in *C.I.N. Properties Ltd. v. Rawlins, The Times*, Feb. 9, 1995 (C.A.) noted in M. Haley, "Shopping Centres: Private Rights, Public Rights?", [1995] Conv. 332.

who wish to take advantage of these latter-day public squares as sites of protest.[66] To call these easements of free speech and assembly is perhaps far-fetched, but this label at least allows one to see how these rights compare to conventional easements.

A final analogous (and somewhat anomalous) interest should be mentioned. In *Griffin v. Klassen Estate*[67] a question arose as to whether the owners of (deceased) animals buried in a pet cemetery had a property right enforceable against the successors to the lands on which the graveyard was situated. It was held that "[s]uch rights, like, or as easements, are enforceable against the successors".[68] This innominate entitlement, applicable to human and animal burials,

> vests in the grantee and his legal representative, family and friends, a right in perpetuity to his burial in the grave, to have the grave remain forever undisturbed, to erect such monument, tombstone, headstone curbing, enclosures, flowers and plants as are 'seemly and customary' by and about the grave in perpetuity, and to forever maintain the same, and to visit the grave. For purposes of visitation and maintenance, [an] 'implied easement of necessity' attaches, to and from the grave if separated from a public way by private lands.[69]

4.   CREATION AND TRANSFER OF EASEMENTS

All easements 'lie in grant'; as *incorporeal* hereditaments they cannot, by definition, be conveyed by a transfer of *possession*. Moreover, an element of consent underlies all easements. At common law, they cannot arise by unilateral appropriation. However, a review of the full array of accepted methods for bringing easements into existence reveals that the idea of a consensual grant can, at times, be rather fictional. This will become quite apparent in relation to the creation of legal rights through long-term usage (under the law of prescription), but it is also evident in connection with easements arising through implied grants, reservations, estoppel and statute. First, the most straightforward method of creation will be described: the express grant.

(a)   express grant

Easements may be acquired through an express grant made by the owner of the servient lands. When no words of limitation are recited, the duration of the easement is determined with regard to the surrounding circumstances. In the absence of words of limitation, one would think that it should be presumed that an easement will continue for as long as the dominant interest to which it is attached subsists (*e.g.*, a fee simple, or a term of years), though it may be created to last for a shorter period.[70] It is not necessary that the dominant tenement be

---

66 See further K. Gray, "Equitable Property", [1994] C.L.P. 157, at 172-81; R. Moon, "Access to Public and Private Property Under Freedom of Expression" (1988) 20 Ottawa L.Rev. 339.

67 Unreported (November 29, 1991) Brockenshire J. (Ont.Gen.Div.).

68 *Ibid.* at 9.

69 *Ibid.* See further A. Dowling, "Exclusive Rights of Burial and the Law of Real Property" (1998) 18 Leg.Stud. 438.

70 See *Craig v. Craig* (1878) 2 O.A.R. 583 (C.A.); *Bratt v. Malden*, 60 O.L.R. 102, [1927] 1 D.L.R. 1116 (C.A.). See also *Smith v. Curry*, 29 Man.R. 97, [1918] 2 W.W.R. 848, 42 D.L.R. 225 (C.A.).

described expressly in the granting document, if it can be identified through extrinsic evidence.[71] As an interest in land, an easement must comply with any formal requirements that are mandated for a valid transfer of land. However, an agreement for an easement may produce an equitable easement under the doctrine of *Walsh v. Lonsdale*.[72] Even a verbal agreement can be enforced in equity if sufficient acts of part performance can be proven.[73]

(b)   implied grant

An easement may be implied as a necessary incident of a property transaction. For example, an easement of strict necessity of access will arise in favour of land that is landlocked at the time of the transfer, provided that there is some land retained by the grantor over which this access can be exercised.[74] A tenant on the twentieth floor of an apartment building acquires such an easement over the common areas including the elevators and stairs, even if these rights of passage are not spelled out in the lease. Returning to the example at the beginning of the chapter,[75] let us assume that on the sale of Blackacre to B, the only means of access to a public road is by crossing the land retained by A, the vendor. An easement of necessity over that land (Whiteacre) will normally sprout up.

The right of access arising from necessity is based on the implied intentions of the parties and therefore is not invoked by operation of law.[76] In other words, the implication of an easement of necessity is based on a rule of construction and so yields to a contrary intention. The rule emanates from the principle that a grantor cannot derogate from the grant. Indeed, this idea may be said to lie at the base of all implied easements. Given this rationale, and the manifest utility of easements of necessity, one would think that very explicit language should be required before this implied right is not found to be part of a given transaction (assuming, of course, that an easement of necessity is called for on the facts).

Within the category of implied grants is a sub-group that is sometimes referred to as 'intended easements'. These interests arise by implication to give effect to the common intention of the parties, having regard to the purposes for

---

71 *Laurie v. Winch*, [1953] 1 S.C.R. 49, [1952] 4 D.L.R. 449. See also *Montador v. Cerenzia* (1991) 60 B.C.L.R. (2d) 135, [1992] 1 W.W.R. 439, 19 R.P.R. (2d) 301 (C.A.).

72 (1882) 21 Ch.D. 9 (C.A.). See also *Leon Asper Amusements Ltd. v. Northmain Carwash & Enterprises Ltd.* (1966) 56 D.L.R. (2d) 173 (Man.Q.B.).

73 See *Campbell, Wilson & Horne Ltd. v. Great West Saddlery Co.*, 16 Alta.L.R. 465, [1921] 2 W.W.R. 63, 59 D.L.R. 322 (C.A.) at 327-8 D.L.R.

74 See *B.O.J. Properties Ltd. v. Allen's Mobile Home Park Ltd.* (1979) 11 R.P.R. 260, 108 D.L.R. (3d) 305, 36 N.S.R. (2d) 362 (C.A.); *MacKinnon v. MacDonald* (1988) 1 R.P.R. (2d) 185, 88 N.S.R. (2d) 255, 225 A.P.R. 255 (T.D.). An easement based on strict necessity will not arise if there is a legal means of access over navigable water: *Fitchett v. Mellow* (1897) 29 O.R. 6 (H.C.); *Drammeh v. Manjang* (1990) 116 N.R. 153 (P.C.). See *contra Hirtle v. Ernst* (1991) 21 R.P.R. (2d) 95, 110 N.S.R. (2d) 216, 299 A.P.R. 216 (T.D.).

75 See Part 1, *supra*.

76 *Nickerson v. Barraclough*, [1981] Ch. 426, [1981] 2 All E.R. 369 (C.A.). See further P.J. Jackson, "Easements of Necessity", [1981] C.L.P. 133; L. Crabb, "Necessity: the Mother of Intention", [1981] Conv. 442; A.J. Bradbrook, "Access to Landlocked Land: A Comparative Study of Legal Solutions" (1983) 10 Syd.L.Rev. 39.

which the land has been granted.[77] Intended easements are very similar to what I have called easements of necessity, and sometimes the two are treated as equivalent. This similarity can be seen by considering the leading case of *Wong v. Beaumont*.[78] There, an intended easement for proper ventilation of a basement was found, because *inter alia* without it the premises, which were rented solely for use as a restaurant, would not have complied with the applicable public health codes nor the lease itself. It would not have been possible for the tenant to have used the property legally and in compliance with the lease without the enjoyment of the easement of ventilation being claimed. Looked at in another way, given the purpose and terms of the demise, it would have amounted to a derogation from the grant not to recognize the easement over part of the property that had been retained by the landlord. The English Court of Appeal spoke of an easement of necessity arising on these facts.

Easements may be implied under the rule in *Wheeldon v. Burrows*.[79] Assume again that A owns and occupies the duplex containing Blackacre and Whiteacre and that she has often used Whiteacre as a convenient means of going to Blackacre. Given that there is unity of title and possession, Whiteacre does not constitute a servient tenement and the right-of-way is not an easement, strictly speaking. Instead, the law calls this ostensible right-of-way a 'quasi-easement'. When the quasi-dominant land is transferred the rule in *Wheeldon v. Burrows* may come into play, and if so, the quasi-easement will blossom into a real easement in the hands of the new owner of the quasi-dominant tenement (Blackacre). The same result would occur if both lots were sold (or devised) simultaneously to different parties.

The *Wheeldon* rule is a pronounced application of the principle of non derogation. It serves as a form of consumer protection, allowing a purchaser to acquire amenities (*i.e.*, easements) that the purchased land appears to enjoy. As such, it is a minor deviation from the principle of *caveat emptor* (let the buyer beware). For *Wheeldon* to be attracted, the quasi-easement must be in use at the date of the transfer. Furthermore, it must be reasonably necessary for the enjoyment of the property *and/or* be continuous and apparent. There is uncertainty as to whether or not these last two components are alternatives, though the weight of scholarly opinion suggests that both criteria must be satisfied.[80] The 'continu-

---

77 See *Pwllbach Colliery Co. v. Woodman*, [1915] A.C. 634, [1914-5] All E.R.Rep. 124 (H.L.).

78 *Wong v. Beaumont Property Trust Ltd.*, [1965] 1 Q.B. 173, [1964] 2 All E.R. 119 (C.A.) noted in (1964) 80 L.Q.R. 322. See also *Cringle v. Strapko* (1994) 41 R.P.R. (2d) 74 (Ont.Gen.Div.).

79 (1879) 12 Ch.D. 31, [1874-80] All E.R.Rep. 669 (C.A.). Concerning the origins of the doctrine, see A.W.B. Simpson, "The Rule in *Wheeldon v. Burrows* and the Code Civile" (1967) 83 L.Q.R. 240.

80 See K. Gray, *Elements of Land Law*, 2nd ed. (London: Butterworths, 1993) at 1099, where it is suggested that the majority view is that both elements must be found to exist. In *Israel v. Leith* (1890) 20 O.R. 361 (C.A.) at 367 (*per* Street J.), an accordant view was expressed: "It is clearly established that where the owner of two adjoining lots conveys one of them he impliedly grants to the grantee all those continuous and apparent easements which are necessary to the reasonable use of the property granted, and which are at the time of the grant used by the owner of the entirety for the benefit of the part granted". See *Sovmots Investments Ltd. v. Secretary of State for the Environment*, [1979] A.C. 144, [1977] 2 All E.R. 385 (H.L.) at 168 and 175 A.C., where

ous' and 'apparent' elements, whatever their roles in the creation of an easement under *Wheeldon*, have developed special meanings. Initially, a 'continuous' easement was defined as one that is enjoyed passively (such as a drain pipe). This limited category has been extended to include interests that have a continuing physical presence, such as a well-worn path or road.[81] A quasi-easement is 'apparent' when it is discoverable by a person reasonably conversant with such matters.[82]

Legislation may provide that a transfer of land will incorporate by implication a host of ancillary rights, in much the same way that the law provides that all fixtures normally pass on a sale.[83] In addition, in some jurisdictions an easement may be created by implication through the conveyancing process. For instance, Ontario law provides as follows:

> *Every conveyance of land, unless an exception is specially made therein, includes* all houses, outhouses, edifices, barns, stables, yards, gardens, orchards, commons, trees, woods, underwoods, mounds, fences, hedges, ditches, *ways*, waters, watercourses, lights, liberties, *privileges*, easements, profits, commodities, emoluments, hereditaments and appurtenances whatsoever to such land belonging or in anywise appertaining, or with such land demised, held, *used, occupied or enjoyed* or taken or known as part or parcel thereof, and, if the conveyance purports to convey an estate in fee simple, also the reversion and reversions, remainder and remainders, yearly and other rents, issues and profits of the same land and of every part and parcel thereof, and all estate, right, title, interest, inheritance, use, trust, property, profit, possession, claim and demand whatsoever of the grantor into, out of or upon the same land, and every part and parcel thereof, with their and every of their appurtenances.[84]

This section serves to make all pre-existing easements pass on the sale of the dominant tenement. Moreover, it can also have the effect of creating new easements. This has been held to occur by virtue of the phrase "ways . . . used, occupied or enjoyed" in the section quoted above.[85] Even if a right of way was not a true easement before the conveyance, it may crystallize into one on the transfer. Assume that a tenant of A, renting Blackacre, enjoys a personal right of access over Whiteacre, which is occupied by the landlord. A sale of the leased premises (Blackacre) to the tenant in these circumstances can lead to the transformation of the personal privilege into an easement.[86] The reasoning is that the personal right amounted to a 'way' that was 'used, occupied or enjoyed' during

---

passages are quoted from *Wheeldon* that suggest that the criteria are alternatives. Recent English decisions have not resolved the issue: see *Wheeler v. J.J. Saunders Ltd.*, [1995] 2 All E.R. 697 (Ch.D.) especially at 707, where the criteria are treated as alternatives. However, in *Millman v. Ellis* (1995) 71 P. & C.R. 158 (C.A.) both elements were regarded as being essential. The latter case is discussed in J. West, "*Wheeldon v. Burrows* Revisited", [1995] Conv. 346.

81 See also *Wilcox v. Richardson* (1997) 43 N.S.W.L.R. 4 (C.A.) at 16.

82 *Pye v. Carter* (1857) 1 H. & N. 916, at 922, 156 E.R. 1472, at 1475.

83 See, *e.g.*, *Law of Property Act*, R.S.A. 1980, c. L-8, s. 7.

84 *Conveyancing and Law of Property Act*, R.S.O. 1990, c. C.34, sub. 15(1) (emphasis added).

85 The phrase "taken or known to be part or parcel thereof" might also be of significance here.

86 See *International Tea Stores Co. v. Hobbs*, [1903] 2 Ch. 165, [1900-3] All E.R.Rep. 303. See further C. Harpum, "Easements and Centre Point: Old Problems in a Novel Setting", [1977] Conv. 415; L. Tee, "Metamorphoses and Section 62 of the Law of Property Act 1925", [1998] Conv. 115.

the lease, even though it was not a property right at that time. It may be, as English case law provides, that the section will not produce an easement unless there is a diversity of ownership and occupation prior to the conveyance.[87]

Unless one interprets the section in this restrictive fashion, it in effect covers the same terrain as the rule in *Wheeldon v. Burrows*. Indeed, it is even broader: unlike *Wheeldon* there is no explicit requirement that the easement be continuous or apparent, or reasonably necessary for the use and enjoyment of the dominant property. Occasionally, this provision can result in the creation of an easement quite out of the blue. With this in mind, the Ontario Law Reform Commission has recommended that the law should declare that the section quoted above does not work to create new easements, profits or similar rights.[88]

(c)   reservations

A reservation refers to an interest retained by a grantor on a transfer of land to some other person.[89] For example, in the context of estates a grantor may transfer Blackacre while at the same time carving out and reserving a life estate in the lands. Likewise, on the sale or lease of property an owner may wish to reserve an easement over the land that has been transferred, for the benefit of an adjacent or nearby tract that has been retained.

Easements may be impliedly reserved in cases of strict necessity, just as in the case of grants.[90] Intended easements may also arise by implied reservation,[91] though it has been suggested that this implication will less readily be drawn in the case of a reservation,[92] because to do so here grates against the notion that the vendor should not be permitted to derogate from the grant by impliedly imposing

---

87 *Sovmots Investments Ltd. v. Secretary of State for the Environment, supra*, note 80. See further P. Jackson, "Easements and General Words", [1966] Conv. 340. *Cf. Hardy v. Herr*, [1965] 2 O.R. 801, 52 D.L.R. (2d) 193 (C.A.) where the property, held initially in common, was divided and sold to those persons previously sharing as co-owners. Section 15 was applied.

88 Ontario Law Reform Commission, *Report on Basic Principles of Land Law* (Toronto: A.G. (Ont.), 1996) at 146-7 and 164.

89 The term 'reservation' is a misnomer when used here. A reservation pertains to matters connected with tenure. Technically, what occurs here is not a reservation but a re-grant. This should be accomplished by the grantee signing either the original transfer or a separate grant. In either case a question then arises as to whether that disposition should be strictly construed against the party re-granting the easement: see further R.E. Megarry & H.W.R. Wade, *The Law of Real Property*, 5th ed. (London: Stevens & Sons, 1984) at 858. Even absent this re-granting, it has been held that although the grantee does not execute the conveyance, the 'reservation' will be effective in equity: see *Adamson v. Bell Telephone Co. of Canada* (1920) 48 O.L.R. 24, 55 D.L.R. 157 (C.A.); *Patterson v. Bagnall*, [1948] 1 D.L.R. 702 (P.E.I.S.C.); *Canada Cement Co. v. Fitzgerald* (1916) 53 S.C.R. 263, 29 D.L.R. 703; *May v. Belleville*, [1905] 2 Ch. 605. If that were not so, it is hard to understand how *implied* reservations can ever be effective. In some jurisdictions, the need for a re-grant has been eliminated: see, *e.g, Conveyancing and Law of Property Act*, R.S.O. 1990, c. C.34, s. 44.

90 See, *e.g., Comet Investments Ltd. v. Newfoundland* (1990) 88 Nfld. & P.E.I.R. 271, 274 A.P.R. 271 (Nfld.T.D.).

91 See, *e.g., Barton v. Raine* (1980) 29 O.R. (2d) 685, 15 R.P.R. 287, 114 D.L.R. (3d) 702 (C.A.) leave to appeal to S.C.C. refused (1980) 114 D.L.R. (3d) 702n (S.C.C.); *Chaffe v. Kingsley* (1997) 77 P. & C.R. 281 (Ch.D.).

92 See *In re Webb's Lease*, [1951] Ch. 808, [1951] 2 All E.R. 131 (C.A.).

an easement on the parcel that has been sold. Building on this idea, it is well established that the rule in *Wheeldon v. Burrows* does not apply to reservations.[93] There is no need to confer rights on the reserving owner that ostensibly attach to the land retained, because the owner should be aware of the legal rights affecting that parcel. Likewise, the rules governing the automatic transmission of easements on a conveyance of dominant lands[94] are not germane to reservations.

(d)   estoppel

Easements can be created through the application of the doctrine of proprietary estoppel.[95] Two cases should help explain the basic concept. In *Adams v. Lougham*[96] a representation was made to a prospective purchaser that a lane was going to be set aside for the use of the land being offered for sale. It was on the faith of this statement that the purchaser agreed to buy the property. Accordingly, the grantor, and those claiming through him, were estopped from preventing the grantee from using the lane as a right-of-way, even though the development plans for the lane were subsequently changed.[97] Similarly, in *Zelmer v. Victor Projects Ltd.*[98] an underground reservoir was built by Z (and several others) on a nearby lot owned by V, on the expectation, prompted by V, that an easement would be granted (gratuitously) to provide access to the water works. V, unhappy with the location of the reservoir on his lands, refused to grant the easement. Invoking the doctrine of proprietary estoppel, the British Columbia Court of Appeal upheld the claim for an easement over V's land.[99]

(e)   prescription[100]

The common law recognizes that rights to an easement may emerge out of continuous use, under the rules for prescription.

Prescription is premised on "a judicially-endorsed piece of pious perjury".[101] The fabrication is that an easement was granted at some time in the past, as

---

93 *Attrill v. Platt* (1884) 10 S.C.R. 425.

94 See the text accompanying notes 83 to 88, *supra*.

95 See generally M. Pawlowski, *The Doctrine of Proprietary Estoppel* (London: Sweet & Maxwell, 1996).

96 (1876) 39 U.C.Q.B. 247 (Full Ct.). See also *Hendry v. English* (1871) 18 Gr. 119 (Ont.C.A.); *Carew v. Rockwood* (1993) 112 Nfld. & P.E.I.R. 299 (Nfld.S.C.). *Cf. Atlas Acceptance Corp. v. Lakeview Development of Canada Ltd.*, [1991] 6 W.W.R. 366, 74 Man.R. (2d) 276 (Q.B.) affirmed [1992] 4 W.W.R. 481, 92 D.L.R. (4th) 301, 78 Man.R. (2d) 161 (C.A.).

97 Additionally, when land that is described in a conveyance as abutting a street, lane or way that is also owned by the grantor, it has been held that the grantee may use the adjacent property as an easement: see, *e.g.*, *Pugh v. Peters* (1876) 11 N.S.R. 139 (S.C.); *McLennan v. Hutchins* (1917) 50 N.S.R. 358 (C.A.); *Butt v. Barrett* (1930) 12 Nfld.R. 441 (S.C.). *Cf. Phillips v. Ross* (1926) 58 N.S.R. 326, [1926] 1 D.L.R. 605 (C.A.). Although this is described as an interest arising through estoppel, it is perhaps best understood as an intended easement.

98 (1997) 34 B.C.L.R. (3d) 125, 9 R.P.R. (3d) 313, 147 D.L.R. (4th) 216 (C.A.).

99 See also *Ellis v. Eddy Holding Ltd.* (1996) 7 R.P.R. (3d) 70 (B.C.S.C., Chambers); *Hill v. Nova Scotia (Attorney General)*, [1997] 1 S.C.R. 69, 142 D.L.R. (4th) 230, 462 A.P.R. 81, additional reasons at (1997) 155 D.L.R. (4th) 767, 61 L.C.R. 241 (S.C.C.).

100 See further Ontario Law Reform Commission, *Report on Limitation of Actions* (Toronto: A.G. (Ont.), 1969) at 143*ff*.

101 G. Teh & B. Dwyer, *Introduction to Property Law* (Sydney: Butterworths, 1988) at 200.

evidenced by long, uninterrupted use. The doctrine protects reliance on, and enjoyment of, long-held and unchallenged rights.[102] But courts tend to proceed cautiously when prescriptive rights are being claimed. After all, the finding of a prescriptive right imposes a burden on some servient land without compensation being payable to the servient owner. It can sometimes punish (and thereby discourage) neighbourly co-operation. When the doctrine is applied to protect an easement it can serve to reward the aggressive property owner who has been using neighbouring land under a falsely claimed right to do so.[103]

Although prescription resembles adverse possession,[104] the two concepts are distinct. Prescription, as that term is used in this context, applies to non-possessory rights, and so can be supported by acts amounting to far less than the degree of control that is required to make out a squatter's claim.[105] Prescription involves the acquisition of a right that encumbers some other landowner's interest, and may limit further use of the servient tenement, whereas in most jurisdictions adverse possession serves to extinguish the right of action of the true owner and effectively leads to the usurpation of that owner by the squatter. Therefore, the potential for prescriptive rights to stultify the course of activity on the servient lands has no equivalent result in cases of adverse possession, where one owner is replaced with another.

Negative easements that are recognized under the law of prescription can develop in an incipient and passive way. In other words, completely inert behaviour can found a claim. For example, the right to receive light through a defined aperture (normally a window) can count as an easement. Accordingly, a prescriptive entitlement can arise simply because there has been unobstructed enjoyment of solar access to a window for the required prescription period (generally 20 years). Furthermore, acts of a positive nature, such as the perpetration of actionable nuisance through pollution activities, can also gain legal protection under the doctrine of prescription.[106] Concern that the operation of the prescriptions rules can impede development on servient lands has prompted the abolition of the doctrine for certain types of easements. For example, in Ontario, no one may now acquire a prescriptive right to air or light for the benefit of a house, workshop or other building.[107] In locales governed by land titles registration, the ability to obtain rights through prescription is typically abolished altogether. Hence, for those parts of Ontario under the *Land Titles Act* of that Province, it is not possible

---

102 See further S. Anderson, "Easements and Prescription – Changing Perspectives" (1975) 38 Mod.L.Rev. 640.

103 See *Henderson v. Volk* (1982) 35 O.R. (2d) 379, 132 D.L.R. (3d) 690 (C.A.) at 384 O.R.

104 See Part 3, Chapter 4.

105 See *Reynolds v. Laffin* (1909) 7 E.L.R. 100 (N.S.S.C.) where a prescriptive easement was granted as appurtenant to a property that had been acquired by adverse possession at the same time.

106 See, *e.g.*, *Gambo (Town) v. Dwyer* (1990) 49 M.P.L.R. 257, 82 Nfld. & P.E.I.R. 232, 257 A.P.R. 232 (Nfld.T.D.).

107 *Limitations Act*, R.S.O. 1990, c. L.15, s. 33. See also s. 35.

to acquire any rights via the rules for prescription.[108] Here the need for certainty of title is treated as paramount.

The common law devised two methods of acquisition through prescription; a third has been added by statute. The first mode is based on a claim of use extending back to time immemorial (1189). After 20 years a presumption arises that the grant was ancient, but this is rebuttable on proof that the usage does not extend back to 1189. Therefore, as with those rights asserted on the basis of custom, that requirement leaves this method of prescription unavailable to non-indigenous claimants in Canada.[109]

Under the doctrine of 'lost modern grant', the second mode of acquisition, a prescriptive right can emerge out of continuous use for a specified period; normally 20 years will do.[110] Here the pretence is that a grant was made but has gone missing. The doctrine will operate even if there is proof that no such grant ever existed,[111] unless it can be shown that there was no grantor who had the capacity to confer an easement during the period when the transfer must have taken place.[112] This limitation might come into play, for example, if the owner of the servient land was a corporation with no power under its articles of incorporation to confer such a right.[113]

The premise of a fictional grant explains the main prerequisites for prescription. The easement must have been enjoyed without (i) violence (*nec vi*); (ii) secrecy (*nec clam*); and (iii) permission (*nec precario*).[114] These three elements must be in place throughout the duration of the relevant period. To be a valid easement the right that is being claimed through prescription must also, of course, comply with the four rules outlined earlier in this chapter.[115]

Usage without violence (*nec vi*) means not only that there has been no physical obstruction of the easement, but also that the use did not proceed in the face of protests from the servient owner that might be seen as challenging the claimed right. At the same time, the use cannot have occurred with the permission of that owner during the period of time relied on to support the prescriptive claim; otherwise this might suggest that the alleged easement was being enjoyed by

---

108 *Land Titles Act*, R.S.O, 1990, c. L.5. s. 51. See also *Law of Property Act*, R.S.A. 1980, c. L-8 sub. 60(3) [as am].

109 *Jones v. Jones* (1843) 4 N.B.R. 265 (C.A.). See also *Abell v. Woodbridge (Village)* (1917) 39 O.L.R. 382, 37 D.L.R. 352 (H.C.) at 388 O.L.R., reversed (1919) 45 O.L.R. 79, 46 D.L.R. 513 (C.A.) which was reversed (*sub nom. Abell v. York (County)*) (1920) 61 S.C.R. 345, 57 D.L.R. 81. At the trial level in *Abell* judicial notice was taken of the fact that America was 'discovered' in 1492.

110 See *Henderson v. Volk*, *supra*, note 103. *Cf.* Ontario Law Reform Commission, *supra*, note 100, at 145, where it is suggested that a longer or shorter period may be applied and that each case must turn on its own facts.

111 *Jones v. Jones*, *supra*, note 109. *Cf. Crowe v. Cabot* (1899) 40 N.S.R. 177 (S.C.).

112 See *Avery v. Fortune* (1908) 11 O.W.R. 784 (C.A.). Remember, an easement cannot exist unless there is a capable grantor and grantee: see Part 2, *supra*.

113 See, *e.g.*, *Canadian Southern Railway v. Lewis* (1884) 20 Can.L.J. 241 (Ont.Co.Ct.).

114 As in adverse possession, tacking by successive owners of the dominant land is possible: *Ker v. Little* (1898) 25 O.A.R. 387. *Cf. Tupper v. Campbell* (1876) 11 N.S.R. 68 (C.A.).

115 See Part 2, *supra*.

virtue of that permission.[116] Likewise, if the putative dominant owner actually acknowledges that the use was not as of right, this will undermine a claim to a prescriptive interest.[117] Somewhere between these very close poles – between a use that is not objected to, but not permitted – one finds the servient owner who acquiesces in, or does not complain about or impede, the exercising of easement-like rights.[118] When that occurs, a claim to an easement through prescription can succeed.

Predictably, the acts required to demonstrate the ownership of an easement will depend on the type of right claimed. At the very least, they must be continuous,[119] and must serve to put the owner of the servient lands on notice. If the use is covert there is no basis for inferring that the servient owner has accepted the dominant owner's rights. This explains the requirement that the use must be *nec clam*: without secrecy. Additionally, as a general matter the easement must be claimed by a fee simple owner against a fee simple owner.[120]

Even these basics are intricate. In an effort to simplify and improve the law, the English *Prescription Act, 1832*[121] was introduced. However, this reform, which has been adopted in some provinces, is not a model of clarity, and whether it has improved the law of prescription is a debatable point. Under the Ontario version of these measures, a claim for prescription can be based on unobstructed 20-year use immediately before the commencement of an action relating to the prescriptive claim. An interruption of the running of the period will not be found merely because an obstruction was placed over the way, unless the claimant has submitted to it for one year. As with the doctrine of lost modern grant, it is not necessary to show that the exercise of the right dates back to time immemorial, though other defences against the acquisition of a prescriptive right remain open, such as the acknowledgment by the claimant that the use was by permission. A claimant relying on a 40-year period of use cannot be defeated by proof that a *verbal* permission was given by the servient owner.[122]

(f)   statute

Special rights may be conferred by statute, and this includes easements in favour of, or against, public or private entities. For example, under Alberta's

---

116 See *Smith v. MacGillivray* (1908) 5 E.L.R. 561 (N.S.S.C.). See also *Adrian v. McVannel* (1992) 11 O.R. (3d) 137, 28 R.P.R. (2d) 109 (Gen.Div.).

117 See *Garfinkel v. Kleinberg*, [1955] O.R. 388, [1955] 2 D.L.R. 844 (C.A.) at 848 D.L.R.

118 See, *e.g.*, *Mills v. Silver*, [1991] Ch. 271, [1991] 1 All E.R. 449 (C.A.).

119 A use may be intermittent yet still be continuous within the meaning of the law of prescription: see *Axler v. Chisholm* (1977) 16 O.R. (2d) 665, 79 D.L.R. (3d) 97 (H.C.).

120 *McKinnon v. Clark* (1908) 5 E.L.R. 102 (P.E.I.C.A.); *Walker v. Hennigar*, [1935] 1 D.L.R. 285 (N.S.T.D.). Unity of possession suspends the running of the period: *Stothart v. Hilliard* (1890) 19 O.R. 542 (Ch.D.). See also *Ferguson v. Innes* (1895) 24 S.C.R. 703, which adopts the reasons of Maclennan J.A. in (1894) 21 O.A.R. 323; *Margison v. Lanzarotta Investments Ltd.* (1985) 37 R.P.R. 1 (Ont.Dist.Ct.). See also *Simmons v. Dobson* (1991) 62 P. & C.R. 485 (C.A.) discussed in P. Sparkes, "Establishing Easements Against Leaseholds", [1992] Conv. 167. See also Note, [1992] C.L.J. 220, at 223, where this limitation is doubted in connection with the doctrine of lost modern grant.

121 2 & 3 Will. 4, c. 71.

122 *Limitations Act*, R.S.O. 1990, c. L.15, ss. 30-41.

condominium legislation an easement of subjacent and lateral support is implied in favour of every unit capable of enjoying these rights. The statute also creates easements over the common areas, and rights-of-way for water, sewage, drainage, gas, electricity, garbage, artificially heated and cooled air, telephone, and radio and television services.[123]

5.   SCOPE, LOCATION AND TERMINATION

(a)   scope and location

The ambit of an easement is a matter of contractual intention. Prudence suggests that the scope of the rights being granted should be described with as much precision as the nature of the easement allows. However, when this trite counsel of perfection is not followed, the determination of the proper scope becomes a matter of inference; disagreement and litigation will sometimes follow. A prime consideration in construing the breadth of an easement is the purpose for which the grant was initially made. Physical circumstances may be relevant to constrict the otherwise broad rights of use that an unrestricted grant suggests. The relevant factors include the physical nature of the servient lands,[124] and the extent to which an expansion of the easement would throttle activity on that tenement.[125] Circumstances relating to the dominant land may also be germane.[126]

One question of construction that frequently recurs concerns the effect of changed circumstances on the rights of the easement holder: can the initial grant be read to contemplate the possibility of a change in the nature of the use of the easement, or are the rights frozen at the time of the grant? Naturally, the grantee is not entitled to increase the burden on the servient lands beyond the rights initially conveyed, but it may have been contemplated (or taken as implied) that the easement's use would change over time. If so, an apparent increase in the burden can be a valid use of the initial right. For example, in *Laurie v. Winch*[127] farmland (the dominant tenement) was subdivided into residential lots. The easement, which was granted as a perpetual right-of-way over a slender lot near the farm, was split into a large number of easements, one of these being attached to

---

123 *Condominium Property Act*, R.S.A. 1980, c. C-22, s. 18 [as am]. See also s. 19.

124 See, *e.g.*, *Todrick v. Western National Omnibus Co.*, [1934] Ch. 190, varied [1934] Ch. 561, [1934] All E.R.Rep. 25 (C.A.). But see the cautionary remarks about the application of this principle in *Robinson v. Bailey*, [1948] 2 All E.R. 791 (C.A.) at 795.

125 This was one of several factors that was relevant in *Malden Farms Ltd. v. Nicholson*, [1954] O.R. 740, [1955] 1 D.L.R. 339 (H.C.) affirmed [1956] O.R. 415, 3 D.L.R. (2d) 236 (C.A.) in giving a restricted meaning to the rights enjoyed under a grant of a 'right of way'. Another consideration was the existence of a prior grant of a 'free uninterrupted right of way'. This broad language suggested that a narrower reading should be given to the grant in dispute. See also *Granfield v. Cowichan Valley (Regional District)* (1996) 16 B.C.L.R. (3d) 382, 1 R.P.R. (3d) 211 (C.A.). *Cf. British Columbia (Minister of Environment, Lands & Parks) v. Thomes* (1998) 61 B.C.L.R. (3d) 198, 161 D.L.R. (4th) 74, 18 R.P.R. (3d) 23 (C.A.).

126 See, *e.g.*, *S.S. & M. Ceramics Pty. Ltd. v. Kin*, [1996] 2 Qd.R. 540 (C.A.).

127 [1953] 1 S.C.R. 49, [1952] 4 D.L.R. 449. *Cf. Corbitt v. Wilson* (1891) 24 N.S.R. 25 (S.C. *in banco*).

each new lot. The Supreme Court of Canada treated this diffusion as valid.[128] There was nothing to suggest that it was contemplated that the lands would always be used for agricultural purposes, or that changes in the use of the dominant lands would affect the continued existence of the easement. (Indeed, at the time of the grant, nearby land had been converted into a residential subdivision.) The original easement of access remained available to the owners of the dominant lands, even though now there were a number of owners using the land as residential property, not as farmland. That holding is consistent with the rule of construction that provides that an easement is presumed to attach to every part of the dominant lands.[129]

In the case of implied easements, extrinsic evidence is often vital in determining the scope of the right.[130] The basis for the implication is, of course, *the central consideration*. The right granted should not be one iota greater than is necessary to give effect to the implied intention. When the easement is one of strict necessity, it is the grantor who selects the access route, and this assignment will govern unless it is shown to be unreasonable, or it is changed afterwards by agreement.[131] The scope of easements obtained through prescription is based on the nature of the conduct supporting that claim.[132]

Under the rule in *Harris v. Flower*, if an easement is granted for the benefit of Lot 1, the grantee, if she or he owns or acquires Lot 2, cannot use the easement, in substance, as a means of crossing over Lot 1 to get to Lot 2.[133] The crux of the matter is whether the use being made of the easement is colourable: is the easement really a servitude for the intended dominant tenement, or is it actually enhancing some other property? So, in *Pearsall v. Power Supermarkets Ltd.*[134] an easement obtained for the benefit of a grocery store was suspended when the store area was expanded. An injunction was ordered because the benefit to the new portion (which was seen as colourable under this rule) could not be separated from the exercising of the legitimate access rights held in relation to the original store.[135]

---

128 See also *Freeman v. Camden* (1917) 41 O.L.R. 179 (H.C.); *Yeomans v. Bourgeois* (1993) 128 N.S.R. (2d) 225, 359 A.P.R. 225 (S.C.).

129 *Gallagher v. Rainbow* (1994) 121 A.L.R. 129 (H.C.).

130 See, *e.g.*, *May v. Belson* (1905) 10 O.L.R. 686 (C.A.).

131 See *Noye v. Ocean Park Ltd.* (1991) 20 R.P.R. (2d) 73, 97 Nfld. & P.E.I.R. 55, 308 A.P.R. 55 (P.E.I.S.C.). See also *Wells v. Wells* (1994) 116 D.L.R. (4th) 524, 39 R.P.R. (2d) 269, 132 N.S.R. (2d) 388 (S.C.). But see *Greenwich Healthcare National Health Service Trust v. London and Quadrant Housing Trust*, [1998] 3 All E.R. 437 (Ch.D.). See also Note, "The Right of Owners of Servient Estates to Relocate Easements Unilaterally", 109 Harv.L.Rev. 1693 (1996).

132 See *Publicover v. Publicover* (1991) 101 N.S.R. (2d) 75, 275 A.P.R. 75 (T.D.).

133 (1904) 74 L.J. Ch. 127 (C.A.) at 132 (*per* Romer L.J.). See also *Purdom v. Robinson* (1899) 30 S.C.R. 64.

134 (1957) 8 D.L.R. (2d) 270 (Ont.H.C.). See also *Gamble v. Birch Island Estates Ltd.*, [1970] 3 O.R. 641, 13 D.L.R. (3d) 657 (H.C.); *Jobson v. Record*, [1998] 1 E.G.L.R. 113 (C.A.); *MacKenzie v. Matthews* (1998) 21 R.P.R. (3d) 307 (Ont.Gen.Div.) varied (1999) 46 O.R. (3d) 21, 28 R.P.R. (3d) 1, 180 D.L.R. (4th) 674 (C.A.). Compare the result in *National Trust for Places of Historical Interest v. White*, [1987] 1 W.L.R. 907 (Ch.D.).

135 See further P.L.J. Huff, "Overburdening the Right of Way: Where the Right of Way Ends" (1991) 4 Nat.Real Prop.L.Rev. 49.

(b)   termination

An easement may come to an end in a number of ways. It will die of natural causes when the time limit set for its duration runs its course. As a general rule, it will also end through a unity of ownership and occupation of both tenements.[136] An easement may be expressly released by agreement, or it may be released by implication, that is, through abandonment. As in the case of an abandonment of chattels, there must be an intention to abandon and a sufficient manifestation of relinquishment before the right is lost.[137] This intention may be inferred from a change in the nature of the dominant tenement that renders the easement useless, or by virtue of a similar change in the servient lands to which the easement holder does not seem to object. Whether these circumstances show a subjective intention to abandon is a question of fact, and the onus of proof on a party alleging that a property right has been relinquished is a heavy one. Owners are not normally taken to have cavalierly thrown away an entitlement.[138] And, just as an easement can arise by estoppel, so can it be lost in that way. Accordingly, while the surrounding circumstances may not prove abandonment, the actions of the dominant owner may support an estoppel, if it would be inequitable for that person to insist that the easement is still in existence.[139]

6.   COVENANTS RUNNING WITH PROPERTY[140]

(a)   introduction

As with easements, covenants over land can be used to create rights enforceable by one landowner against another, even in the absence of both privity of contract and estate between the parties.[141] Although they begin their life as contractual entities, covenants can be converted into real property rights. The rules governing this transformation will be considered below.

---

136 *Attrill v. Platt* (1884) 10 S.C.R. 425; *McDonald v. McDougall* (1897) 30 N.S.R. 298 (S.C. *in banco*).

137 See further *Liscombe v. Maughan*, 62 O.L.R. 328, [1928] 3 D.L.R. 397 (C.A.).

138 Accord C.J. Davis, "Abandonment of an Easement", [1995] Conv. 291, where it is argued that abandonment should be found only when it would be unconscionable to allow the easement to endure. Unconscionability might arise, for example, if the owner of the servient lands has relied on an apparent abandonment.

139 In British Columbia an order can be sought cancelling an easement (or a profit, as well as other interests) under sub. 35(2) of the *Property Law Act*, R.S.B.C. 1996, c. 377. An application was denied in *Kasch v. Goyan* (1992) 21 R.P.R. (2d) 199, 87 D.L.R. (4th) 123 (B.C.S.C.) affirmed (1993) 81 B.C.L.R. (2d) 268, 32 R.P.R. (2d) 297, 103 D.L.R. (4th) 51 (C.A.). See also Part 11, *infra*. Whether an easement of necessity ends once the necessity ceases is a question that is troubled by divided authority. The easement ends: *McCulloch v. McCulloch* (1910) 2 O.W.N. 331, 17 O.W.R. 639 (H.C.). See *contra B.O.J. Properties Ltd. v. Allen's Mobile Home Park Ltd.* (1979) 11 R.P.R. 260, 108 D.L.R. (3d) 305, 64 A.P.R. 362 (N.S.C.A.); *Gardner v. Horne* (1848) 3 N.S.R. 278 (S.C.). See also the discussion of this issue in *Wells v. Wells, supra*, note 131, at 528. Presumably, one may also be statute-barred from enforcing an easement when the disruption contnues beyond the relevant limitation period.

140 See generally G.L. Newson, *Preston & Newsom's Restrictive Covenants Affecting Freehold Land*, 8th ed. (London: Sweet & Maxwell, 1991).

141 Recall the definition of privity of estate found in Part 3(a), Chapter 8.

Covenants resemble public land use controls and, as with condominium regimes, they can be used to create a "local law".[142] Their use as planning devices pre-dates public land-use regulation inits current form and, in 1984, the English Law Commission considered whether the job performed by government instruments had eliminated the need for a law of private covenants. However, the extent to which covenants were still in use suggested that they remained important.[143] Along the same lines, a study conducted in Kitchener-Waterloo and Cambridge, Ontario revealed an increase in the use of covenants over the period from 1951 to 1991. Here are the results for Kitchener:[144]

Trends in the Registration of Development Plans With Restrictive Covenants in Kitchener, 1951-1991

Years	All Development Plans	Plans With Restrictive Covenants Limiting Affordable Housing and Non-Single Family Uses	Plans With Restrictive Covenants Limiting Non-Single Family Uses Only	Total of Plans With Such Restrictive Covenants
1985-91	70	43 (61.4%)*	3 (4.2%)*	46 (65.7%)*
1980-84	30	9 (30.0%)	2 (6.6%)	11 (36.7%)
1975-79	47	11 (23.4%)	3 (6.4%)	14 (29.8%)
1970-74	36	8 (22.2%)	0	8 (22.2%)
1965-69	52	14 (26.9%)	1 (1.9%)	15 (28.8%)
1960-64	74	5 (6.8%)	0	5 (6.8%)
1955-59	104	3 (2.9%)	1 (1.0%)	4 (3.8%)
1951-54	58	3 (5.2%)	0	3 (5.2%)

* Percentage of all development plans.

(b)   covenants in context

Covenants over land can cater to a variety of interests. They can be used to regulate commercial practices among tenants in a shopping centre. Malls tend to be heavily regulated spaces, and part of the structure of control is imposed through

---

142 *Scharf v. Mac's Milk Ltd.*, [1965] 2 O.R. 640, 51 D.L.R. (2d) 565 (C.A.) at 573 D.L.R. (*per* Schroeder J.A.).

143 Law Commission, *Transfer of Land: The Law of Positive and Restrictive Covenants* (London: H.M.S.O., 1984) at 7.

144 P. Filion, *The Impact of Restrictive Covenants on Affordable Housing and Non-Single-Family Uses of Homes: A Waterloo Region Case Study* (Ottawa: C.M.H.C., 1993) at 26. Of the 62 development plans filed in Waterloo for the period 1985-91, 44 (71%) contained restrictive covenants. There were fewer in Cambridge (26% of the 78 plans filed), but the trend there was an increase in the use of restrictive covenants in recent years.

covenants that limit the kinds of business operations that can be undertaken.[145] Another common function is the regulation of the nature or quality of construction in residential developments.[146] In this context, restrictive covenants can help to create an economic ghetto, where the wealthy can live apart from those who cannot afford the houses that a covenant might require. Restrictive covenants can, in theory, be used to repel those living in alternative lifestyles, to prevent the building of an AIDS hospice,[147] a youth shelter, or a home for quiescent schizophrenics.[148] In short, these conveyancing devices can be useful instruments in the hands of a 'nimby'.[149]

The point of using covenants in these ways can be understood by returning to the idea of externalities, which was introduced in Chapter 1.[150] That term refers to the spillover effects of ownership. A positive externality can result, for example, when the presence of an amenity (such as nice shopping) in a neighbourhood enhances the value of nearby properties. Proximity to some undesirable public work (for instance, a sewage treatment plant) can have the opposite effect. A covenant that insulates properties from low-cost or high-density housing is designed to prevent negative externalities, and promote positive ones. However, because such covenants can wind up constraining landowners to a greater degree than do zoning by-laws (which is one of the reasons that covenants are employed), they can affect municipal planning significantly.[151] The Waterloo study found that the increased presence of private covenants was subverting the implementation of planning policies aimed at the development of affordable housing in certain parts of the Region.[152]

On a more general level, it has been argued that restrictive covenants can adversely affect personhood values. In particular, the complaint is that the owner of a property that is burdened by a valid restrictive covenant loses some facet of the power of self-determination. These covenants,

> frustrate[] the notion of property as protecting personal identity, and [the] home as a favored context for individual flourishing. The central importance of the home to an individual's sense of self, and to the shaping of that individual's unique history and future by the expression of

---

145 See, *e.g.*, *Canada Safeway Ltd. v. Thompson (City)*, [1996] 10 W.W.R. 252, 5 R.P.R. (3d) 1, 112 Man.R. (2d) 94 (Q.B.) affirmed [1997] 7 W.W.R. 565, 11 R.P.R. (3d) 65, 118 Man.R. (2d) 34 (C.A.).

146 See further A. Oshinski, "Restrictive Covenants and Architectural Review: Some Suggested Standards", 27 John Marshall L.Rev. 939 (1994).

147 But see *Hill v. Community of Damien of Molokai*, 911 P.2d. 861 (N.M.S.C., 1996) where it was held *inter alia* that the covenant in issue did not preclude the use of the subject land as a group home for people with AIDS.

148 See *National Schizophrenia Fellowship v. Ribble*, [1994] 1 E.G.L.R. 181 (Ch.D.). But as in *Hill, supra*, note 147, the covenant in *Ribble* was ineffective.

149 An acronym that stands for 'not in my backyard'. See further G. Korngold, "Single Family Use Covenants: For Achieving a Balance Between Traditional Family Life and Individual Autonomy", 22 U.C.Davis L.Rev. 951 (1989); D. Hubbard, "Group Homes and Restrictive Covenants", 57 U.M.K.C.L.Rev. 135 (1988).

150 See Part 3(b), Chapter 1.

151 Filion, *supra*, note 144, at 17.

152 *Ibid.* at 46.

his or her distinctive personality, requires that – presumptively – each resident should control the details of his or her own residential uses.[153]

At one time in Canada, freehold covenants were deployed in an attempt to restrict ownership or occupation of land to certain classes or races. In time, the legality of these devices came into question, the test case being *Re Drummond Wren*.[154] This dispute, decided in 1945, concerned a residential lot in Toronto that was subject to a stipulation that the property could never be sold to "Jews or persons of objectionable nationality". Wren applied to court for a declaration that the covenant was invalid. Mr. Justice MacKay granted the order, holding, in part, that the covenant was void for uncertainty, and that it constituted a restraint on alienation. It was also held that the impugned clause was void as being contrary to the doctrine of public policy:[155]

> In my opinion, nothing could be more calculated to create or deepen divisions between existing religious and ethnic groups in this province, or in this country, than the sanction of a method of land transfer which would permit the segregation and confinement of particular groups to particular business or residential areas . . . It appears to me to be a moral duty, at least, to lend aid to all forces of cohesion, and similarly to repel all fissiparous tendencies which would imperil national unity. . . That the restrictive covenant in this case is directed in the first place against Jews lends poignancy to the matter when one considers that anti-semitism has been a weapon in the hands of our recently-defeated enemies, and the scourge of the world.[156]

---

153 J.L. Winokur, "The Mixed Blessings of Promissory Servitudes: Toward Optimizing Economic Utility, Individual Liberty, and Personal Identity", 1989 Wisc.L.Rev. 1, at 74. However, the creation of a neighbourhood identity through covenants can promote flourishing for those who seek out such communities. *Cf.* L. Berger, "A Policy Analysis of Promises Respecting the Use of Land", 55 Minn.L.Rev. 167 (1970).

154 [1945] O.R. 778 (S.C.). Discriminatory covenants had been before Ontario courts before, but the issue of whether these were invalid owing to the doctrine of public policy had never been extensively examined. In *Essex Real Estate Co. Ltd. v. Holmes* (1930) 37 O.W.N. 392 (H.C.) affirmed (1930) 38 O.W.N. 69 (C.A.) the covenant read as follows: " . . . the lands shall not be sold to or occupied by persons not of the Caucasian race nor to Europeans except such as are of the English-speaking countries and the French and the people of French descent". It was held that the applicant, a Syrian, being of the Caucasian race, was not precluded by this provision from purchasing the land. Public policy was not raised. In *Re Bryers and Morris* (1931) 40 O.W.N. 572 (H.C.) the question of invalidity (as an undue restraint on alienation) was side-stepped on procedural grounds. In *Re McDougall and Waddell*, [1945] 2 D.L.R. 244, [1945] O.W.N. 272 (H.C.) it was held that a racially restrictive covenant did not contravene the *Racial Discrimination Act*, S.O. 1944, c. 51. The broader public policy argument was not addressed. Invalidity based on public policy may explain a little-known 1911 British Columbia ruling. There, an application was brought to determine whether a covenant that prevented transfers to persons of Japanese or Chinese origin was valid. Hunter C.J. held that the covenant was inoperative and hence could not be registered. No further reasons for judgment were given. See further H.S. Robinson, "Limited Restraints on Alienation" (1950) 8 Advocate 250, at 251, where the short judgment is set out.

155 It was also argued that the registration of the deed contravened the *Racial Discrimination Act*. That Act had a narrow scope, prohibiting only the publication or display of representations expressing racial or religious discrimination. Although Mr. Justice MacKay said that this argument had merit, it was not made a basis for his decision.

156 *Supra*, note 154, at 782-3.

The *Globe & Mail* welcomed the decision, describing it as being "on the noblest level of jurisprudence", and suggesting that it would significantly advance the cause of social equality.[157] But this was not to be the last word on the subject. In *Re Noble and Wolf*,[158] which arose several years later, the validity of a land covenant was again in issue. The case involved a deed containing a prohibition against the sale of cottage lots near Lake Huron to any person of the "Jewish, Hebrew, Semitic, Negro or coloured race or blood". It also provided that the intention was to limit ownership in the lands to persons of the "white or Caucasian race".

At the first hearing, Mr. Justice Schroeder upheld the clause. The claim that the restrictions on transfer represented a danger to the public interest (the core of the reasoning in *Wren*) was described as fanciful. There was nothing in this case, nor had there been in *Wren*, that would justify an expansion of the doctrine of public policy to prohibit such a term. A five-member panel of the Ontario Court of Appeal agreed. Chief Justice Robertson said that to transform the efforts of these property owners from a modest attempt to create a congenial summer colony into a practice that offends public policy required "a stronger imagination than I possess".[159] Furthermore, the law was incapable of producing or imposing racial integration:

> Doubtless, mutual goodwill and esteem among the people of the numerous races that inhabit Canada is greatly to be desired, and the same goodwill and esteem should extend abroad, but what is so desirable is not a mere show of goodwill or a pretended esteem . . . To be worth anything, either at home or abroad, there is required the goodwill and esteem of a free people who genuinely feel, and sincerely act upon, the sentiments they express. A wise appreciation of the impotence of laws in the development of such genuine sentiments, rather than mere formal observances, no doubt restrains our legislators from enacting, and should restrain our courts from propounding, rules of law to enforce what can only be of natural growth, if it is to be of any value to anyone.[160]

The Court may have been unanimous, but the public reaction was mixed. The Association for Civil Liberties denounced the decision,[161] as did a *Toronto*

---

157 "Blow to Prejudice", *Globe & Mail*, November 2, 1945, 6. See also G.R. Schmitt, "Re Wren" (1946) 15 Fortnightly L.J. 264; "Anti-Semitic Land-Sale Clause Declared Illegal", *Globe & Mail*, November 1, 1945, 1. It was estimated that the decision could affect lands valued at $1 million in the City of Hamilton: "Says $1,000,000 Affected in Hamilton Property", *Toronto Star*, November 1, 1945, 1. The *Drummond Wren* case was followed by Mr. Justice Barlow in an unreported Ontario decision in 1946: D.A.L. Smout, "An Inquiry into the Law of Racial and Religious Restraints on Alienation" (1952) 30 Can.B.Rev. 863, at 869. See also this unusual article criticizing the result: "Re Wren [1945] O.R. 778 – Contributed" (1946) 15 Fortnightly L.J. 264.

158 [1948] O.R. 579, [1948] 4 D.L.R. 123 (H.C.) affirmed [1949] O.R. 503, [1949] 4 D.L.R. 375 (C.A.) reversed on other grounds [1951] S.C.R. 64 (*sub nom. Noble v. Alley*), [1951] 1 D.L.R. 321. The story behind this case is discussed in detail in J.W. St. G. Walker, *"Race", Rights and the Law in the Supreme Court of Canada* (Toronto: Osgoode Society & W.L.U. Pr., 1997) ch. 4.

159 *Re Noble and Wolf, supra*, note 158, at 522-3.

160 *Ibid.* at 523. Four judgments were issued.

161 "Protest Ruling in Racial Case", *Globe & Mail*, June 11, 1949, 4.

Star editorial.[162] Rabbi Abraham Feinberg of the Holy Blossom Temple in Toronto asserted that "[t]he language of the covenant, upheld by the court of appeal, differs only in degree from the dangerous nonsense and blood-worship of naziism".[163] A public opinion poll conducted following the Court of Appeal ruling indicated that 68% of the respondents claimed that they would not sign an agreement that contained a restriction against the sale or lease of property based on race or colour; 19% were prepared to agree to such a term; 13% were undecided.[164] The *Globe & Mail*, which had applauded the outcome in *Drummond Wren* four years earlier, endorsed the Court of Appeal decision in *Re Noble and Wolf*, echoing (and quoting) the reasoning of Chief Justice Robertson. It was said that, unlike *Drummond Wren*, this was not a case involving the provision of basic shelter. Moreover, "to assert that any group of people should be forbidden to associate themselves in a perfectly lawful manner, would create problems of a far-reaching nature with all sorts of dangerous implications. . . . There is much to correct in our treatment of minorities in Canada, but force is not the way to do it".[165]

An appeal was taken to the Supreme Court of Canada, but the ultimate result of the litigation was an anti-climax. Before the case reached the Supreme Court, the Ontario Legislature amended the law to prevent the creation of discriminatory covenants.[166] This did not render the Court's ruling moot, since the Act was designed to have only prospective effect. However, the Court resolved the dispute without regard to the public policy argument. Four (of seven) members of the panel held that the covenant was void for uncertainty; five justices thought that restrictions on the type of occupant (as opposed to, say, the type of *use* intended for the lands) could not be binding on a subsequent purchaser.[167]

This brief excursus might lead one to think that covenants are chiefly designed to do dirty work. That is not the case. On the side of the angels, we can see that covenants can serve different ends. They have been used for heritage preservation, both of green space and architecturally or historically significant buildings.[168] In fact, the nineteenth century genesis of the concept was connected to the pursuit of conservationist goals. With these objectives in mind, a number of jurisdictions have introduced legislation creating covenant-like devices, com-

---

162 See, *e.g.*, "The Law Should be Changed", *Toronto Star*, June 13, 1949, 6.

163 "Should Change Law Rabbi Feinberg Says as Covenant Upheld", *Toronto Star*, June 10, 1949, 3.

164 See also Walker, *supra*, note 158, at 218 and the accompanying note.

165 "Tolerance and Law", *Globe & Mail*, June 11, 1949, 6.

166 See now *Conveyancing and Law of Property Act*, R.S.O. 1990, c. C.34, s. 22. See also *Law of Property Act*, R.S.M. 1987, c. L90, sub. 7(1), which contains a long list of prohibited discriminatory practices, including discrimination on the basis of source of income or political belief. Subsection 7(2) allows restrictions intended to maintain land primarily for the use of elderly persons. See also *Land Title Act*, R.S.B.C. 1996, c. 250, s. 222.

167 In dissent, Locke J. expressed approval of the judgment of Robertson C.J.O.: [1951] S.C.R. at 80.

168 See R. Ward, "Heritage Conservation in British Columbia" (1988) 22 U.B.C.L.Rev. 61, at 103*ff.*

monly referred to as conservation easements. I will review some of these developments later in the chapter.[169]

(c)   outline of the analysis

The primary focus here will be on the basic rules for creating and transferring covenants as interests in land. As a prelude to this, several terms must be introduced. Strictly speaking, a covenant is a promise under seal. Of late, the need for a seal has been discarded in land transactions in some parts of Canada,[170] and therefore the continued reference to the law of 'covenants' is somewhat inappropriate. For our purposes, a covenant may be regarded as a valid contractual undertaking made by a covenantor (who assumes the burden of the promise) in favour of a covenantee (who obtains the benefit). Borrowing from the terminology of easements, we can call the land burdened by a covenant the servient tenement; the land to be benefited will be referred to as the dominant tenement.

The rules of transmission are multi-faceted because the principles operating at law are quite distinct from those applied in equity. These differences are vital. An individual seeking a legal remedy (damages) must hold an entitlement to the benefit of the covenant at law, and any action brought in pursuit of that remedy may be maintained only against an individual who, in the eyes of the law, is regarded as being subject to the burden. Likewise, equitable relief is available against someone whom equity sees as bound by the burden, and a remedy (if appropriate) will issue in favour of a holder of the benefit in equity. As the discussion develops it will become apparent that the equitable rules are of greatest utility. Not only is the equitable remedy of an injunction frequently the most useful enforcement device, but also it is in the Chancery that the notion of covenants running with land has flourished.

7.   THE RUNNING OF BENEFITS AND BURDENS AT LAW

(a)   benefits at law

The methods used for transferring the benefit of a covenant can be understood by reference to some basic principles of contract and property law. Consider the scenario introduced at the outset of this chapter: A holds a promise from his neighbour (B), that B will not change the colour of the exterior of B's house without first obtaining A's consent.[171] B has also promised to keep the roof in proper repair. Assume that at some later date A sells her property to C. Can C enforce the promises contained in the contract between A and B? Phrased more formally, using the vocabulary of this area of the law, one might ask: can the assignee of land owned by the covenantee enforce the benefit against the original covenantor?

---

169   These are discussed again in Part 10, *infra*.
170   See, *e.g.*, *Land Registration Reform Act*, R.S.O. 1990, c. L.4, s. 13; *Property Law Act*, R.S.B.C. 1996, c. 377, s. 16.
171   See Part 1, *supra*.

One way in which the right to sue might be passed from A to C is through the rules for the assignment of contractual benefits, rules that apply whether or not those benefits happen to concern land. In Chapter 2 we saw that the right to enforce a contract can be a chose in action, which is a property right that can usually be alienated.[172] The common law courts stubbornly refused to allow the benefit of any chose in action to be assigned by means of a contract. In 1873, a statutory right of assignment was introduced in England, a reform that has been implemented in Canada.[173] Today, a contractual assignment of the benefit of a covenant is valid at law provided (i) the initial promise is not personal to the covenantee; (ii) the ability to assign has not been bargained away; and (iii) the statutory requirements regulating the transfer of the chose in action have been met. This assignment will be effective only against the original covenantor; it is purely a contractual matter.

Before statute permitted contractual assignments at law, the transmission of a benefit was possible as an incident of a transfer of land. This method remains available. At common law, the benefit passes when (i) the transferee obtains the same legal estate as the transferor;[174] (ii) it was intended that the covenant would pass automatically; and (iii) the covenant relates to the land transferred: it must 'touch and concern' that land. If these conditions are met there is no need for an express contractual assignment, and the new owner of the dominant land acquires a right to enforce the covenant.[175] This is so even if the benefit is obtained without notice. To a purchaser of dominant property, the covenant can be "a hidden treasure which may be discovered in the hour of need".[176]

The requirement that the promise 'touch and concern' the dominant land arises throughout the law of covenants. It works to limit the variety of promises that can pass from owner to owner. The authorities state that to touch and concern the land, the covenant must either (a) relate to the mode of occupation; or (b) directly, and not in some collateral manner, affect the value of the land.[177] Restrictions on land use will normally pass the test. Moreover, controls imposed on the quality of structures that can be placed on the servient land have also been accepted as touching and concerning neighbouring dominant lands. However, as we saw above, an attempt to prevent sale to, or occupation by, an excluded class

---

172 See Part 4(a), Chapter 2.

173 See, *e.g.*, *Judicature Act*, R.S.A. 1980, c. J-1, s. 21.

174 This requirement has been abolished in England by virtue of the *Law of Property Act, 1925*, 15 & 16 Geo. 5, c. 20, s. 78: see *Smith v. River Douglas Catchment Board*, [1949] 2 K.B. 500, [1949] 2 All E.R. 179 (C.A.). A comparable provision is found in Ontario: *Conveyancing and Law of Property Act*, R.S.O. 1990, c. C.34, s. 24. A question has been raised as to whether the Ontario provision produces the same result as that which obtains in England: Ontario Law Reform Commission, *Report on Covenants Affecting Freehold Land* (Toronto: A.G. (Ont.), 1989) at 16.

175 See, *e.g.*, *Smith v. River Douglas Catchment Board*, supra, note 174.

176 *Lawrence v. South County Freeholds Ltd.*, [1939] Ch. 656, [1939] 2 All E.R. 503, at 680 Ch. (*per* Simmonds J.).

177 *Galbraith v. Madawaska Club Ltd.*, [1961] S.C.R. 639, 29 D.L.R. (2d) 153, adopting *Rogers v. Hosegood*, [1900] 2 Ch. 388, [1900-3] All E.R.Rep. 915 (C.A.). See also *Mayor of Congelton v. Pattison* (1808) 10 East 130, 103 E.R. 725 (K.B.).

has been held to fall outside of the concept in Canada.[178] These exclusions, it has been argued, have nothing to do with the mode of occupation, and although such restrictions might well affect land values, their tendency to do so is collateral and not direct.[179] As in the case of easements, an element of proximity (but not necessarily contiguity) must be shown in order for a covenant to touch and concern a dominant tenement.

(b)   burdens at law

The burden of a covenant will not run at law. Freehold covenants binding on the new owner of servient lands have never been tolerated, presumably owing to the *numerus clausus* policy.[180] This obviously limits the usefulness of legal remedies and the value of holding the benefit at law. Once the original covenantor parts with the servient land, the contractual right against that person may be of no practical value. Even when the original covenantor remains liable under the contract, it may be pointless to sue that person. The reluctance of the law to enforce covenants is one factor that sparked the introduction of condominium reforms. As we have seen (in Chapter 9), condominium statutes provide a means through which owners and their successors can be required, under law, to fulfil various obligations.

There are other means of skirting or overcoming the law's position. For example, burdens may be imposed by way of a condition subsequent or determinable limitation. Hence, one might provide that Blackacre is granted subject to the condition that the land should be preserved as a green space. But this approach has obvious drawbacks: the result of non-compliance is drastic (loss of the land) and so it is not something that a purchaser is likely to accept readily. Furthermore, the lifespan of a condition subsequent or determinable limitation may be affected by the rule against perpetuities.[181]

Additionally, a 'chain of covenants' may be used as an indirect means of obtaining enforcement at law. Assume in the duplex hypothetical that the covenantor, B, as part of the initial bargain, agreed to remain liable even after the land is sold to someone else, and that B also promised to extract the same covenants from the next owner of the burdened land. This should spark a chain reaction. If B sells to C, B would then bargain for the insertion of these covenants and seek an indemnity from C should any breach occur. Each departing owner of the servient land (C, D, E, F, *etc.*) will have a strong incentive to seek a new covenant to gain protection against personal liability for future breaches. In this circuitous

---

178   *Re Noble and Wolf, supra*, note 158; *Galbraith v. Madawaska Club, supra*, note 177. *Cf. Hemingway Securities Ltd. v. Dunraven Ltd.* (1994) 71 P. & C.R. 30 (Ch.D.); *North Vancouver (District) v. Lunde* (1998) 60 B.C.L.R. (3d) 201, 162 D.L.R. (4th) 402 (C.A.) (age restriction upheld).

179   See further J.E. Stake, "Toward an Economic Understanding of Touch and Concern", 1988 Duke L.J. 925.

180   *Keppell v. Bailey* (1834) 2 My. & K. 517, 39 E.R. 1042, [1824-34] All E.R.Rep. 10. See also Part 4(a)(iii), Chapter 1.

181   See Part 5, Chapter 7. For example, under Alberta law a condition subsequent or a determinable limitation attached to a fee simple created after July 1, 1973 can last for no more than 40 years: *Perpetuities Act*, R.S.A. 1980, c. P-4, s. 19.

fashion liability can be extended to the current owner of the land. However, this is a cumbersome method and it will break down if any party in the chain cannot be sued. If F, the current owner of the servient tenement, breaches the covenant in some way, A, the holder of the benefit, will sue B, with whom the first contract was made. B, in turn, will sue C, and so on. The longer the chain becomes the more likely it is that it will be broken. In the example here, unless E can be joined as a party to the action, the actual culprit (F) cannot be sued. (Only E has a contract-based action against F.)[182]

In spite of the basic rule (that burdens do not run at law), application of the so-called 'pure principle of benefit and burden' may give rise to the enforcement of a legal obligation. Under this doctrine, the acceptance of a benefit may entail the assumption of a related burden. The basis of the concept is rudimentary: sometimes the law will insist that an owner must take the bad with the good. So, in the case of *Halsall v. Brizell*[183] the acquisition and use of easements over Whiteacre, acquired with the purchase of Blackacre, carried with it the pre-existing obligation to contribute to the cost of their maintenance. As long as the dominant owner used these rights, the corresponding obligations were enforceable by the servient owner, even in the absence of privity of contract and estate between the two parties to the dispute.

The principle of benefit and burden was applied in the case of *Tito v. Waddell* (sometimes referred to as the *Ocean Island* case).[184] There, a claim was brought by a group of Banaban Islanders, whose predecessors in title had granted various mining rights to a British company decades earlier. The documents signed at the time of this arrangement included a promise by the company to plant trees following the completion of the excavation and mining operations. Those operations effectively gutted the island, and when the present holders of the mining rights refused to honour the planting obligations an action was commenced. In a complex and lengthy judgment, one finds a bold and embracing articulation of the pure principle of benefit and burden. It was found that the current holders of the benefit could not renounce the burden of planting. Although the right to mine and the duty to restore were created as independent terms, these were later married through the operation of the pure principle.

---

182 A method sometimes used in England is to attach affirmative conditions to the grant of a rentcharge: see generally S. Bright, "Estate Rentcharges and the Enforcement of Positive Covenants", [1988] Conv. 99. See also *Report on Covenants Affecting Freehold Land, supra*, note 174, at 24. A further exception, based on the effect of the assumption of mortgage obligations (as provided for under statute), is alluded to in *Webster v. Garnet Lane Developments Ltd.* (1992) 10 O.R. (3d) 576 (C.A.) leave to appeal to S.C.C. refused (1993) 13 O.R. (3d) xvi (S.C.C.).

183 [1957] Ch. 169, [1957] 1 All E.R. 371, noted in (1957) 73 L.Q.R. 154 and [1957] C.L.J. 35.

184 *Tito v. Waddell (No. 2)*, [1977] Ch. 106, [1977] 3 All E.R. 129, noted in [1977] Conv. 432. See also G.H. Treitel, *The Law of Contract*, 8th ed. (London: Sweet & Maxwell, 1995) at 618-20; R.E. Megarry & H.W.R Wade, *The Law of Real Property*, 5th ed. (London: Stevens & Sons, 1984) at 769-70; B. Ziff, "Positive Covenants Running With Land: A Castaway on Ocean Island?" (1989) 27 Alta.L.Rev. 354.

In the aftermath of *Tito v. Waddell* it was said that even though "[b]asic principles are now in conflict", the "prospects of justice are better".[185] The judgment itself conceded that there were many uncertainties to be clarified. A number come to mind: Is a dominant tenement required for the principle to apply? Does the rule apply to personalty? Does the rule not overwhelm the law of easements,[186] not to mention the principles governing the running of real covenants in legal and equitable leases?[187] One can see that the *Ocean Island* case might have enormous implications for the rules being considered here (that is, the rules pertaining to the running of burdens at law). For example, if A buys Blackacre, to which some burden is attached, should we say that the assumption of the benefit (the fee simple in Blackacre) cannot be taken by A unless she or he submits to a burden that was in place when the land was purchased?

From the time that *Tito v. Waddell* was handed down it was quite uncertain how it would be received. In 1990, in the first decision to scrutinize it extensively, *Tito* was rejected as a means of enforcing a positive building obligation.[188] A few years later, in *Rhone v. Stephens*,[189] the House of Lords also responded with disapproval to the apparent breadth of the *Tito* holding, staunchly resisting the suggestion that a party deriving a benefit from a conveyance normally had to accept a burden that was also associated with that land. For the doctrine to apply, the Law Lords insisted that the condition (or burden) has to be relevant to the right (the benefit) being exercised. They thought that this requirement was present in *Halsall v. Brizell*: use of the easements was properly tethered to the cost of maintenance. In addition, it was observed that in *Halsall* it was theoretically possible for a party to choose between taking the benefit or not, and therefore, assuming the burden or not. That was not an option in *Rhone*, where the benefit (support of a building) could not realistically be waived in order to avoid the burden (repair of a roof).[190]

---

185 Megarry & Wade, *supra*, note 184, at 770.

186 The argument would be that one cannot accept the benefit – the transfer of the servient land – without also accepting the burden of whatever easement-like rights happened to be imposed on that land.

187 See Part 3(a), Chapter 8.

188 *G.I.O. (N.S.W.) v. K.A. Reed Services Pty. Ltd.*, [1988] V.R. 829 (Full Ct.). For an endorsement of *Tito* and a response to *Reed Services*, see E.P. Aughterson, "In Defence of the Benefit and Burden Principle" (1991) 65 A.L.J. 319.

189 [1994] 2 A.C. 310, [1994] 2 All E.R. 65 (H.L.) critiqued in N.P. Gravells, "Enforcement of Positive Covenants Affecting Land" (1994) 110 L.Q.R. 346. *Rhone* is also discussed in Part 9, *infra*.

190 Doubts as to the applicability of *Tito* to Canadian law were expressed in *Weissbach v. Western World Communications Corp.*, [1994] B.C.J. No. 906 (S.C.). A general review of the various manifestations of the benefit and burden concept in private law is to be found in C.J. Davis, "The Principle of Benefit and Burden," [1998] C.L.J. 522.

8. THE RUNNING OF BURDENS AND BENEFITS IN EQUITY

(a) burdens in equity

Courts of equity have enforced restrictive covenants against later owners of burdened land since the landmark decision in *Tulk v. Moxhay*,[191] if not before.[192] In the *Tulk* case a covenant was entered into to maintain a parcel of land in central London as a public park. A purchaser of that property, who knew of the covenant, was held to be bound by its terms. While the Court said that the result did not turn on whether the covenant runs with the land, it added that "if an equity is attached to the property by the owner, no one purchasing with notice of that equity can stand in a different situation from the party from whom he purchased".[193] On this footing, the framework of the law of restrictive covenants running with freehold property has been built.

Tulk v. Moxhay appears to be out of step with its period. The decision permits the imposition of land restrictions of unlimited duration. Rendered in 1848, three years before the Great Exhibition in Brighton celebrated the fruits of industrial expansion, the ruling seems to reflect a reaction against the monumental changes that industrialization was producing throughout England. In 1832, a special commission had recommended to the British Parliament that reforms be introduced to allow covenants to pass with freehold land. These were promoted by the commissioners as serving a conservationist function, and it was reported that covenants were then being used to preserve parks and squares, and in circumstances "where an uninterrupted view of the sea, or of open country, is to be secured to the owners of adjoining houses".[194] The validity of these devices remained speculative, so a statute legitimizing these practices was recommended.[195] Parliament did not act, but the proposals tabled by the real property commissioners are similar to the approach adopted shortly afterwards in *Tulk v. Moxhay*.

The decision in *Tulk* did not lay down a series of prerequisites for the running of burdens. It seemed influenced primarily by the fact that the purchaser of the square bought that property knowing of the covenant.[196] Today, notice is a necessary but not a sufficient condition if a burden is to run with servient lands in equity. Additional conditions have been engrafted by later authorities; in modern Canadian law there are four principal requirements.

---

191 (1848) 2 Ph. 774, 41 E.R. 1143, [1843-60] All E.R.Rep. 9.
192 See *Whatman v. Gibson* (1838) 9 Sim. 196, 59 E.R. 333; *Mann v. Stephens* (1846) 15 Sim. 377, 60 E.R. 665.
193 *Supra*, note 191, at 778 Ph., 1144 E.R. (*per* Cottenham L.C.).
194 *Third Report of the Real Property Commissioners*, Parliamentary Papers (London: s.n., 1831-2) at 372.
195 See further S.I. George, "*Tulk v. Moxhay* Restored to its Historical Setting" (1990) 12 Liverpool L.Rev. 173.
196 The original purchaser stood to gain from the covenant, because, "[o]f course, the price would be affected by the covenant": *Tulk v. Moxhay*, *supra*, note 191, at 778 Ph., 1144 E.R. (*per* Cottenham L.C.).

First, the covenant must have been made for the protection of land held by the covenantee at the time the covenant was entered into, and that land (and the burdened land[197]) must be easily ascertainable from the document. These requirements have been interpreted in Canada to mean that for a burden to run it must enhance a dominant tenement:[198] the covenant must touch and concern that land.[199] Here the analogy with the accommodation rule in the law of easements is obviously quite strong.[200] And, as with easements, the dominant land need not be a freehold estate. Presumably, any valid interest in the dominant tenement will do.[201]

The stipulation that the dominant land be "easily ascertainable" from the original deed was endorsed by the Supreme Court of Canada in *Galbraith v. Madawaska Club*,[202] where the contest was between the original covenantee and the purchaser of the burdened land from the covenantor. If a covenant is stated to attach to some lands and is not meant to be merely personal, why should it be necessary to describe the *dominant* lands in the document in order for the burden to run with the *servient* lands? One answer is that this ensures that the new owner of the servient land knows who has title to sue, that is, who holds the benefit in equity. In *Galbraith* the action was brought by the original covenantee, who was still in possession, so patently that plaintiff had standing. However, that is not necessarily enough to meet the needs of certainty for the owner of the servient lands. There may, in theory, have been other lands to which the benefit was also attached. The ability to ascertain the perimeters of the benefited land is required so that the owner of the burdened land can know not only if a given plaintiff can sue, but also the full class of potential plaintiffs. Without this knowledge, a new owner of the burdened lands would not know with whom to strike a bargain to remove the restriction.

Second, it must have been intended that the burden was to run with the covenantor's land. If a given covenant was never meant to pass with a transfer of the servient land, it would be beyond the objectives of equity to make it do so. Furthermore, it has been suggested that in Canada there is a presumption against the running of restrictive covenants.[203]

---

197 See *Lorne Park Estates Assn. v. Ontario Regional Assessment Commissioner, Region No. 15* (1979) 23 O.R. (2d) 628, 97 D.L.R. (3d) 181 (H.C.) at 184 D.L.R.

198 *R. v. York (Township)* (*Ex Parte 125 Varsity Road Ltd.*), [1960] O.R. 238, 23 D.L.R. (2d) 465 (C.A.). See also *Page v. Campbell* (1921) 61 S.C.R. 633, [1921] 2 W.W.R. 552, 59 D.L.R. 215; *Mitcham (City) v. Clothier* (1994) 62 S.A.S.R. 394 (S.C.).

199 *Galbraith v. Madawaska Club, supra*, note 177. See also *Canadian Construction Co. v. Beaver (Alberta) Lumber Ltd.*, [1955] S.C.R. 682, [1955] 3 D.L.R. 502; *Re Noble and Wolf, supra*, note 158.

200 See Part 2, *supra.*

201 A leasehold qualifies: *Pacific International Equities Corp. v. Royal Trust Co.* (1994) 42 R.P.R. (2d) 66 (Ont.Gen.Div.).

202 *Supra*, note 177, at 653 S.C.R. (*per* Judson J.), building on *Beaver Lumber, supra*, note 199. See also *Guaranty Trust Co. of Canada v. Campbelltown Shopping Centre Ltd.* (1986) 44 Alta.L.R. (2d) 270, 72 A.R. 55 (C.A.). See contra *Marten v. Flight Refuelling Ltd.*, [1962] Ch. 115, [1961] 2 All E.R. 696.

203 *Lamvid Inc. v. 427654 Ontario Ltd.* (1985) 50 O.R. (2d) 782, 40 R.P.R. 50 (H.C.) at 784 O.R.

Third, the covenant must be negative in substance.[204] Only negative – restrictive – covenants will run. Equity's insistence that the covenant be negative 'in substance' merely underscores the idea that it is not the form of the words but the true nature of the duties that are imposed that is central. An obligation may be couched in positive terms but still be negative in its operation. That was true of part of the covenant in *Tulk v. Moxhay*,[205] where the document spoke, *inter alia*, of properly maintaining the park in its current form. Sometimes it is said that the test of negativity is whether the owner of the servient land is required to put her hand into her pocket. A more general approach is to say that a covenant is negative if compliance is possible by the covenantor (or an assignee) doing absolutely nothing. As a result, a covenant requiring that any construction on the lands must be undertaken by X Co. is negative, because this is satisfied if no building takes place.[206] Likewise, a promise not to change the colour of the exterior of a house without first obtaining consent is negative.[207]

Fourth, all general limitations imposed on the availability of equitable remedies apply. Included as the key element under this component is the enshrined rule that a *bona fide* purchaser for value (of a legal interest) without notice who acquires the burdened land will not be bound to comply with a restrictive covenant.[208] This is the starting point of the law as framed in *Tulk v. Moxhay* and it remains a critical feature. The required level of notice may be refined or altered in a given jurisdiction under the law governing the registration of land.[209]

(b) benefits in equity

There are three means by which the benefit of a covenant may be transmitted in equity: through (i) annexation; (ii) assignment; or (iii) a scheme of development. Under all three modes it is necessary that the covenant touch and concern the benefited land.

(i) annexation

Annexation refers to the automatic affixing of the benefit to the dominant land, so that it passes, like a fixture, on the sale of that property. An intention to annex may be expressly contained in the covenant. Stating that the covenantee acts in the capacity as owner of a described dominant land should suffice as explicit annexing language. Of course, one might state more directly that the covenant is annexed to the (fully described) dominant lands. The extent to which a benefit can run can also be limited in the document, such as when the promise

---

204 *Parkinson v. Reid*, [1966] S.C.R. 162, 56 D.L.R. (2d) 315; *Bowes Co. v. Rankin*, 55 O.L.R. 601, [1924] 4 D.L.R. 406 (C.A.); *Pacific International Equities Corp. v. Royal Trust Co.* (1994) 42 R.P.R. (2d) 66 (Ont.Gen.Div.).

205 *Supra*, note 191. Parts of the covenant seem positive. However, these promises were not in dispute in the case.

206 See *Cities Service Oil Co. v. Pauley*, [1931] O.R. 685 (H.C.).

207 See the example in Part 1, *supra*. See also *Ceda Dry Cleaners v. Doonan*, [1998] 1 N.Z.L.R. 224 (H.C.).

208 The *bona fide* purchaser for value is discussed in Part 2(b), Chapter 12.

209 See generally Chapter 12.

is stated to apply only in favour of the registered freeholder. If so, the benefit will not pass to a party acquiring a leasehold interest in the dominant lands.[210]

There is authority in England that annexation can be implied from the circumstances, that is, even absent words of annexation.[211] A more controversial suggestion has been made that there exists in English law a statutory presumption of annexation, applicable when a covenant relates to land of the covenantee.[212] Canadian law may be different. We saw above that in *Galbraith* the Supreme Court decided that the burden of a covenant does not run unless the dominant land is easily ascertainable from the documentation.[213] Drawing on that holding, it has been said that the language of the *Galbraith* case "clearly excludes any notion of annexation to dominant land by implication".[214] This is an extension of *Galbraith*, since that case did not involve the transmission of a benefit, but it is a logical (and minimal) extrapolation of that ruling. As suggested above,[215] an owner of the burdened land needs to know who holds the benefit.

(ii)   *assignment*

Equity has long permitted a benefit under a contract to be assigned, as an equitable chose in action, and this is effective to allow the grantee of that chose to maintain an action against the original covenantor under general principles of contract law. Therefore, in the absence of transmission by annexation, the benefit of a covenant may be expressly assigned.

However, when the dispute is between the assignees of both the covenantee and covenantor, contract principles are obviously no longer relevant. Under English law an express assignment passes the benefit so as to enable an action against an assignee of the covenantor when (i) the covenant touches and concerns the dominant land, and was taken for its benefit; (ii) the assignment occurs contemporaneously with the transfer of the dominant land; and (iii) that land is ascertainable, at least by extrinsic evidence.[216] Whether this mode of transfer is avail-

---

210 *Forestview Nominees Pty. Ltd. v. Perpetual Trustees WA Ltd.* (1998) 193 C.L.R. 154 (Aust. H.C.).

211 See, *e.g.*, *Marten v. Flight Refuelling Ltd.*, *supra*, note 202.

212 *Federated Homes Ltd. v. Mill Lodge Properties Ltd.*, [1980] 1 W.L.R. 594, [1980] 1 All E.R. 371 (C.A.). See further G.H. Newsom, "Universal Annexation?" (1981) 97 L.Q.R. 32; D. Hayton, "Revolution in Restrictive Covenants Law?" (1980) 43 Mod.L.Rev. 445. *Cf. Roake v. Chadha*, [1984] 1 W.L.R. 40, [1983] 3 All E.R. 503 (Ch.D.).

213 See the text accompanying note 177, *supra*.

214 *Sekretov v. Toronto (City)*, [1973] 2 O.R. 161, 33 D.L.R. (3d) 257 (C.A.) at 262 D.L.R. (*per* Schroeder J.A.). But see *Conveyancing and Law of Property Act*, R.S.O. 1990, c. C.34, s. 24, discussed briefly in *Report on Freehold Covenants Affecting Land*, *supra*, note 174, at 36. The Report also suggests that automatic transmission may occur under s. 15 of the *Conveyancing and Law of Property Act: ibid.* at 36-7. That provision is quoted in Part 4(b), *supra*. *Cf. Roake v. Chadha*, *supra*, note 212.

215 See the text accompanying note 202, *supra*.

216 See *Re Union of London & Smith's Bank Ltd.'s Conveyance*, [1933] Ch. 611, [1933] All E.R.Rep. 355. It has been suggested that an assignment creates a delayed annexation, eliminating the need for future assignments: see P.V. Baker, "The Benefit of Restrictive Covenants" (1968) 84 L.Q.R. 22, at 29. But this is far from having been accepted in England: see R.E.

able in Canada hinges on the same analysis that is applicable to implied annexation. This is because the need for an express assignment arises only when an express annexation has not occurred owing to the absence of some essential component of annexation. These same deficiencies will prevent the burden from running: that is the impact of *Galbraith*. If so, once the burdened land has found its way into the hands of a new owner, an express assignment of the benefit would be ineffective against that person.

(iii)   *schemes of development (or building schemes, or, more generally, common plans)*

Restrictive covenants are perhaps most often used today within the context of residential suburban developments. Covenants are one means of ensuring, for example, that the homes in the neighbourhood are all "made of ticky-tacky and . . . all look just the same".[217] When this type of goal is pursued, developers may wish to impose a blanket covenant to cover all of the lots in the planned neighbourhood. There are several ways that this can be accomplished. In some provinces it is possible to register a restrictive covenant against one's own land. Each parcel may be impressed with a burden, and receive the benefit of all other covenants, even before the individual lots are sold off.[218] A second method is to impose restrictions, individually, as each lot is transferred. However, this method is unwieldy, requiring that a careful pattern be followed involving the granting of reciprocal covenants on each initial sale.

Special rules for schemes of development permit a simpler procedure to be adopted. If the proposed covenants touch and concern the land, the traditional position is that a scheme will be created on the sale of the first lot if: (i) title to the affected parcels is derived from a common vendor; (ii) prior to the sale of the parcels, the vendor established restrictions consistent only with a scheme of development; (iii) the promises were intended to be for the benefit of all of the lots sold;[219] (iv) the parties purchased from a common vendor on the understanding that the restrictions were imposed for the benefit of the other lots included in the scheme;[220] and (v) the land covered is adequately described.[221]

The formulation of these requirements has been relaxed in England. There, building schemes will be enforced if it can be shown that a regime of reciprocal rights and obligations was intended.[222] That approach has so far enjoyed a mixed

---

Megarry & H.W.R. Wade, *The Law of Real Property*, 5th ed. (London: Stevens & Sons, 1984) at 789.

217 M. Reynolds, "Little Boxes" (Schroder Music Co. (A.S.C.A.P.)).

218 See, *e.g.*, *Land Titles Act*, R.S.A. 1980, c. L-5, s. 71.

219 See also *Re Lankin*, [1951] O.W.N. 821 (H.C.).

220 *Elliston v. Reacher*, [1908] 2 Ch. 374, affirmed [1908] 2 Ch. 665, [1908-10] All E.R.Rep. 612 (C.A.) quoted with approval in *Re Wheeler*, 59 O.L.R. 223, [1926] 4 D.L.R. 392 (C.A.) at 398 D.L.R.

221 See, *e.g.*, *McGregor v. Boyd Builders Ltd.*, [1966] 1 O.R. 424, 54 D.L.R. (2d) 112 (H.C.); *Munro v. Jaehrlich* (1994) 1 B.C.L.R. (3d) 388, 43 R.P.R. (2d) 220, [1995] 4 W.W.R. 85 (S.C.).

222 See, *e.g.*, *In re Dolphin's Conveyance*, [1970] Ch. 654, [1970] 2 All E.R. 664, noted in (1970) 86 L.Q.R. 445.

reception in Canada.[223] However, the foundational idea that the scheme of development creates a special community of interest, which is the very essence of the device, is well-accepted. As a result, it has been held that a right to accept or reject building plans, conferred on a developer under a scheme of development, must be exercised by that developer with regard to the interests of members of the scheme who might be affected. In other words, the discretion that is conferred under the covenant is not unbridled, even if no qualifications on how it is to be exercised are contained in the building scheme.[224]

9.   POSITIVE COVENANTS

The burden of a positive covenant will not run at law (because burdens do not run at law at all). Nor can such a burden run in equity: as we have seen, only negative or restrictive covenants fall within the rules now in place. Therefore, in the context of freehold land the orthodox position is that a positive covenant can be enforced only against the original covenantor. (The enforcing party may be either the original covenantee or an assignee of the benefit, at law or in equity.) As we have seen, there are some qualifications on these basic propositions: for instance, a chain of covenants might be formed; or the doctrine of benefit and burden might apply.[225]

In *Rhone v. Stephens*[226] the House of Lords affirmed the rule that positive covenants do not run in English law. The Lords were concerned about the danger of adopting a rule that would result in the enforcement of a personal obligation against someone who had not covenanted to undertake that obligation. That concern does not apply (they said) to restrictive covenants: "To enforce negative covenants is only to treat the land as subject to a restriction".[227] Restrictive covenants deprive an owner of a right that could otherwise be exercised. However, equity cannot compel the performance of a positive covenant agreed to by the prior owner without blatantly contradicting the common law rules concerning privity of contract. In brief, "[e]nforcement of a positive covenant lies in contract . . . Enforcement of a negative covenant lies in property; a negative covenant deprives the owner of a right over property".[228]

This is a surprising (and somewhat opaque) basis for the prohibition. The reluctance to impose positive obligations on others does not prevent positive

---

223 *Lakhani v. Weinstein* (1980) 31 O.R. (2d) 65, 16 R.P.R. 305, 118 D.L.R. (3d) 61 (H.C.) *Berry v. Indian Park Assn.* (1999) 44 O.R. (3d) 301, 174 D.L.R. (4th) 511, 23 R.P.R. (3d) 169 (C.A.). See also *Lim v. Titov* (1997) 56 Alta.L.R. (3d) 174, 14 R.P.R. (3d) 205, [1998] 5 W.W.R. 495 (Q.B.). *Cf. Spike v. Rocca Group Ltd.* (1979) 107 D.L.R. (3d) 62, 23 Nfld. & P.E.I.R. 493, 61 A.P.R. 493 (P.E.I.S.C.).

224 *Hemani v. British Pacific Properties Ltd.* (1992) 70 B.C.L.R. (2d) 91, 24 R.P.R. (2d) 248 (S.C.) affirmed (1993) 86 B.C.L.R. (2d) 378, 38 B.C.A.C. 304 (C.A.). See generally S.K. O'Byrne, "Good Faith in Contractual Performance: Recent Developments" (1995) 74 Can.B.Rev. 70.

225 See Part 7(b), *supra*.

226 [1994] 2 A.C. 310, [1994] 2 All E.R. 65 (H.L.).

227 *Ibid.* at 321 A.C. (*per* Lord Templeman).

228 *Ibid.* at 318 A.C.

burdens from running with leaseholds.[229] In addition, a person who buys land subject to a mortgage has got to realize that the failure to make the payments can produce dire results; in effect, the positive obligation is assumed, like it or not. In that instance, the purchaser of land subject to a positive covenant assumes those obligations with eyes open. As long as there is such notice, and assuming the covenant does not violate some rule of public policy, the owner who takes land subject to a burden can hardly complain.[230]

Several other reasons have been given as to why the refusal to allow positive covenants to run is sound, though the judicial analysis one finds on this point is rather sparing.[231] Part of the explanation must relate to the reluctance of some courts to break new ground. Hence, one finds the phobic reaction in *Haywood v. Brunswick Permanent Benefit Building Society* that to enforce positive covenants would be "making an equity, which we cannot do".[232] This concern relates directly to the judicial reluctance to create fancy new interests, a hesitancy that had earlier delayed the emergence of the running of restrictive covenants in equity.[233]

It is sometimes argued that positive covenants constitute indirect restraints on alienation.[234] If anything, this explanation serves to highlight the over-breadth and arbitrariness of the limitation. Restrictive covenants may also constitute restraints on alienation, and that issue, when it arises, is dealt with on a case-specific basis.[235] Moreover, the touch and concern requirement should prevent

---

229 See also *Juin v. Nepean (City)* (1992) 9 O.R. (3d) 11, 25 R.P.R. (2d) 1, 93 D.L.R. (4th) 641 (C.A.) leave to appeal to S.C.C. refused (February 11, 1993) Doc. 23250 (S.C.C.) and the authorities reviewed in the Court of Appeal.

230 This point forms the central thesis in R.A. Epstein, "Notice and Freedom of Contract in the Law of Servitudes", 55 S.Cal.L.Rev. 1353 (1982). See also Note, "Enforcement of Affirmative Covenants Running With Land", 47 Yale L.J. 821 (1938) at 826. *Cf.* S.E. Sterk, "Freedom From Freedom of Contract: The Enduring Value of Servitude Restrictions", 70 Iowa L.Rev. 615 (1985); S.E. Sterk, "Foresight and the Law of Servitudes", 73 Cornell L.Rev. 956 (1988).

231 See O.L. Browder, "Running Covenants and Public Policy", 77 Mich.L.Rev. 12 (1978) at 18-9. See also W.H. Lloyd, "Enforcement of Affirmative Agreements Respecting the Use of Land", 14 Va.L.Rev. 419 (1928) at 428-9.

232 (1881) 8 Q.B.D. 403 (C.A.) at 408 (*per* Brett L.J.). See also *London & South Western Railway v. Gomm* (1882) 20 Ch.D. 562 (C.A.) at 587 (*per* Lindley L.J.) and the judgment of Sir James Hannen, *ibid.* at 586-7.

233 It has been suggested that *Haywood* may "best be explained if one remembers the contemporary setting. The principle laid down in *Tulk v. Moxhay* was still at a formative stage, there was little upon which to assert that the burden of a positive covenant could run with freehold land in equity and the court may have refrained from endorsing the latter principle because of an inability to comprehend the consequences which would flow from so doing. The case may be legitimately considered as an example of the natural conservatism of the judiciary": C.D. Bell, "*Tulk v. Moxhay* Revisited", [1981] Conv. 55, at 59-60.

234 Browder, admittedly puzzled by the origins of the restriction on positive covenants, has suggested that this may lie at its root: "do English judges", he asks rhetorically, "assume that the greater the burden the greater the restraint on alienation, and that somewhere a line must be drawn?": *supra*, note 231, at 19.

235 See also F.H. Mann *et al.*, "Affirmative Duties Running With Land", 35 N.Y.U.L.Rev. 1344 (1960) at 1361.

some unreasonable burdens from encumbering servient lands.[236] There is also the more general response that market forces will take account of, and respond to, the effect of positive covenants on alienation: if a covenant renders a property less desirable, its price will fall until it again becomes attractive to purchasers.[237]

There is a superficial difference between positive and negative covenants that appears to support dissimilar treatment in the law. In the case of negative covenants, a prospective purchaser appears to be able to know from the outset the full extent of the obligation being assumed. If the restriction is agreed to, this will, by definition, involve no direct expenses. However, a landowner who covenants to maintain a wall or who undertakes to carry out construction at some future date is assuming an obligation of uncertain financial dimensions. No one can forecast future labour and material costs and this places a cloud over the property that may deter the risk-averse investor. This argument, although attractive, is premised on a view of costs that is rather narrow, focusing as it does on actual outlays, and not on opportunity costs.[238] In fact, the forgone investment opportunities incurred by being unable to convert property (owing to the presence of a restrictive covenant) can be significant, and the inability to respond to emerging opportunities is something with which the law governing restraints on alienation is supposed to deal.[239]

The limitation on the running of positive covenants has been explained as a problem of a lack of adequate remedies.[240] I am not sure why a mandatory injunction (which is an equitable remedy) would not be available if, as a matter of policy, the enforcement of positive covenants is the right thing to do. One dilemma relating to enforcement concerns the fair apportionment of liability among the original covenantor and future owners of the burdened land. This issue affects subsequent purchasers of the fee simple, as well as those who acquire more limited interests in the burdened property, such as a lessee, sub-lessee or a life tenant. In the case of a restrictive covenant, future owners of limited interests would be bound by the covenant. However, no particular problems arise, because they can all be forced to comply without any one of them incurring disproportionate expenses. Not all positive burdens will necessarily work that way.

It has been argued that the potentially infinite duration of positive covenants militates against their acceptance.[241] It is true that such an obligation may endure

---

236 See S.F. French, "Towards a Modern Law of Servitudes: Reweaving the Ancient Strands", 55 S.Cal.L.Rev. 1261 (1982) at 1308. See also S.F. French, "Servitudes Reform and the New Restatement of Property: Creation Doctrines and Structural Simplification", 73 Cornell L.Rev. 928 (1988).

237 See also S. Gardner, "The Proprietary Effect of Contractual Obligations under *Tulk v. Moxhay* and *De Mattos v. Gibson*" (1982) 98 L.Q.R. 279, at 295-6. See further Part 3(e)(ii), Chapter 7.

238 The undervaluing of opportunity costs is discussed in G.J. Stigler, "The Theory of Price", reproduced in A.I. Ogus & C.G. Veljanovski, eds., *Readings in the Economics of Law and Regulation* (Oxford: Clarendon Pr., 1984) 24.

239 See generally Part 3(e), Chapter 7.

240 A detailed explanation of equity's limitations in this regard are presented in Gardner, *supra*, note 237, at 296.

241 See Lloyd, *supra*, note 231, at 431. See also B. Rudden, "Economic Theory v. Property Law:

indefinitely (if framed that way), perhaps surviving long after its original objective has vanished. As a general matter, the rule against perpetuities has no application in limiting the duration of the benefit or burden of a covenant. Additionally, the removal of outmoded covenants through negotiations may be hampered by problems of holdouts in cases where a large number of property owners need to be involved in the negotiations. Nevertheless, these problems apply both to positive and negative covenants. As we will see shortly, there are statutory and equitable principles that allow for the early termination of covenants affecting realty.[242]

10.   COVENANTS AND CONSERVATION

Earlier in the chapter I mentioned that the doctrine of *Tulk v. Moxhay* can serve the needs of environmentalists.[243] Allusion was also made to the introduction of legislation aimed at facilitating private environmental control. Under these statutes, new interests in land, 'conservation easements', are contemplated.[244]

In Alberta, conservation easements may be created for the preservation or restoration of any land or building, and for the protection of the natural environment. In 1996 the *Environmental Protection and Enhancement Act*[245] was amended to allow for a landowner to grant a conservation easement for the protection, conservation and enhancement of the environment. The easement may also provide for recreational, open space, educational, and environmentally based scientific uses. Such an easement may be created to be enforceable not only by the grantee, but also by designated organizations. Included within this latter category are the government or a government agency, a local authority, and (essentially) environmental charitable organizations. A conservation easement is an interest in land, and once registered under the Province's land titles system it will run with the land. Importantly, the easement is enforceable even if it imposes positive obligations, and even though there is no dominant tenement to be benefited. Above all else, it is those two elements that distinguish these new rights from generic common law and equitable covenants.

The *Numerus Clausus* Problem" in J.M. Eekelaar & J. Bell, eds., *Oxford Essays in Jurisprudence*, 3rd series (Oxford: Clarendon Pr., 1987) 239, at 259-60.

242   See Part 11, *infra*.

243   See Part 6(b), *supra*.

244   There is a wealth of literature on this topic: see, *e.g.*, M.W. Baldwin, "Conservation Easements: A Viable Tool for Land Preservation", 32 Land & Water L.Rev. 89 (1997); A. Dana & M. Ramsay, "Conservation Easements and the Common Law", 8 Stan.Env.L.J. 2 (1989). See also S. Silverstone, "Open Space Preservation Through Conservation Easements" (1974) 12 Osgoode Hall L.J. 105; S. Lieberman, "New Game in Town: Conservation Easements and Estate Planning" (1995) 14 E. & T.J. 306; M.J. Mossman & W.F. Flanagan, eds., *Property Law: Cases and Commentary* (Toronto: Emond Montgomery, 1998) at 625*ff*, and the references cited there. For an English vantage point, see R. Castle & I. Hodge, "Covenants for the Countryside", [1994] Conv. 122.

245   *Environmental Protection and Enhancement Act*, R.S.A. 1980, c. E-13.3, ss. 22-22.3 [as am.]. See further A. Kwasniak, *Conservation Easement Guide for Alberta* (Edmonton: Environmental Law Centre, 1997). The modern prototype statute is the American *Uniform Conservation Easement Act*. See also *Historical Resources Act*, R.S.A. 1980, c. H-8, s. 25 [as am.].

A conservation easement does not lapse merely because of non-enforcement, or because the land is being used in a manner that conflicts with the easement, or if there has been a change in the use of surrounding lands. It may, however, be modified or terminated by agreement or by an order of the appropriate Minister, if that person is of the view that the public interest warrants such action. As will be seen in Part 11 (directly below), this differs from the treatment accorded to obsolete covenants generally. However, the basic rules governing the modification and termination of covenants under Alberta statute law do apply to conservation easements as well.

11.   MODIFICATION AND TERMINATION OF COVENANTS

A covenant may be framed to last for a stated or ascertainable period, or indefinitely.[246] Either way, it may be terminated prematurely by agreement, or through the unification of ownership and occupation in one person, except where legislation provides otherwise,[247] and, perhaps, when the property falls within a common plan.[248]

In addition, equitable remedies may be refused when a covenant has ceased to fulfil a useful function. Occasionally, the substratum of the covenant will drop out, for instance when the complexion of the surrounding neighbourhood has changed so dramatically that the covenant can no longer realistically serve as a land-use control mechanism.[249] Perhaps this is merely a way of looking at the touching and concerning requirement from another angle: when local conditions have changed there may no longer be a real and continuing benefit being enjoyed by the dominant lands.[250] If the continued utility of the burden depends on equitable remedies (that is, when the original servient owner has parted with the property), the loss of those remedies can effectively ring the death knell of the covenant. The operation of other equitable principles may preclude enforcement of the covenant, such as when the dominant owner is guilty of delay or acquiescence in the face of continuing breaches.[251]

---

246 See, *e.g.*, *R. v. Westminster City Council* (1989) 59 P. & C.R. 51 (Q.B.) which involved the park at Leicester Square, on land once owned by John Augustus Tulk. The covenant at issue there was given at least as early as 1874. Moreover, the Court noted: "There were, I may observe, many members of the Tulk family associated with the Square, one being the plaintiff in the ancient and famous case of *Tulk v. Moxhay*, a case concerning covenants in similar terms to those now in question, although raising wholly different legal issues": *ibid.* at 54 (*per* Simon Brown J.).

247 *Land Titles Act*, R.S.A. 1980, c. L-5, sub. 71(2).

248 See *Texaco Antilles Ltd. v. Kernochan*, [1973] A.C. 609, [1973] 2 All E.R. 118 (P.C.).

249 See, *e.g.*, *Cowan v. Ferguson* (1919) 45 O.L.R. 161, 48 D.L.R. 616 (C.A.); *cf. VanKoughnet v. Denison* (1885) 11 O.A.R. 699 (C.A.); *Chudley v. Buss*, [1979] 1 W.W.R. 447 (Man.Q.B.), affirmed [1980] 1 W.W.R. 478 (C.A.) leave to appeal to S.C.C. refused [1980] 4 W.W.R. 481 (C.A.).

250 See generally G.O. Robinson, "Explaining Contingent Rights: the Puzzle of 'Obsolete' Covenants", 91 Colum.L.Rev. 546 (1991).

251 See, *e.g.*, *Turney v. Lubin* (1979) 14 B.C.L.R. 329, 10 R.P.R. 89, [1980] 1 W.W.R. 35 (S.C.); *Lafortune v. Puccini* (1991) 2 O.R. (3d) 689, 16 R.P.R. (2d) 16 (Gen.Div.).

In many jurisdictions, legislation permits a party to apply to remove or alter a covenant. For example, in British Columbia an application may be brought to modify or discharge a covenant (as well as an easement, a profit, and other interests in land) when:

(a) because of changes in the character of the land, the neighbourhood or other circumstances the court considers material, the registered charge or interest is obsolete;[252]

(b) the reasonable use of the land will be impeded, without practical benefit to others, if the registered charge or interest is not modified or cancelled;

(c) the persons who are or have been entitled to the benefit of the registered charge or interest have expressly or impliedly agreed to it being modified or cancelled;

(d) modification or cancellation will not injure the person entitled to the benefit of the registered charge or interest; or

(e) the registered interest is invalid, unenforceable or has expired, and its registration should be cancelled.[253]

In Alberta, an order may be obtained if it can be shown that a modification or discharge would be beneficial to the persons principally interested in its enforcement. An order may also be granted if (i) the covenant conflicts with zoning laws or other regulatory instruments; *and* (ii) the modification or discharge would be in the public interest.[254] It is odd if the section is saying that a true conflict with public planning is necessary, but not sufficient, for a court order, and that it must *also* be determined that the order is in the public interest. This language seems to imply that not all conflicts with public planning instruments will be remedied.

12. COVENANTS OVER PERSONALTY

Not long after *Tulk v. Moxhay* was decided, the notion of enforcing covenants over personal property was addressed. However, this intriguing extension has never materialized to any great extent. The jurisprudential trail, modest though it may be, starts with the 1858 case of *De Mattos v. Gibson*.[255] There, the following proposition was offered: a donee or a purchaser of property who acquires it with knowledge of a previous contract designed to regulate its use "shall not, to the material damage of the third person, in opposition to the contract and inconsistently with it, use and employ the property in a manner not allowable to the giver or seller".[256] This sweeping language could quite possibly affect a wide assortment of obligations affecting personal property.

---

252 See *Alexander v. Luke* (1991) 16 R.P.R. (2d) 23 (B.C.S.C.) affirmed (March 18, 1994) Doc. CA013763, CA014239 (B.C.C.A.) (application denied).

253 *Property Law Act*, R.S.B.C. 1996, c. 377, sub. 35(2). See further *Fleischman v. British Pacific Properties Ltd.* (1997) 16 R.P.R. (3d) 103 (B.C.S.C.) where an application under this provision was dismissed. The principles governing modification and discharge in Ontario are reviewed in: Ontario Law Reform Commission, *infra*, note 267, at 51*ff*.

254 *Land Titles Act*, R.S.A. 1980, c. L-5, sub. 52(3). See further *Seifeddine v. Governor & Co. of Adventurers of England Trading into Hudson's Bay* (1980) 11 Alta.L.R. (2d) 229, 11 R.P.R. 224, 108 D.L.R. (3d) 671 (C.A.); *Tanti v. Gruden* (1999) 74 Alta.L.R. (3d) 110, 23 R.P.R. (3d) 186, [1999] 11 W.W.R. 294 (C.A.) additional reasons at (1999) 75 Alta.L.R. (3d) 97, [2000] 3 W.W.R. 46 (C.A.).

255 (1858) 4 De. G.& J. 276, 45 E.R. 108.

256 *Ibid.* at 282, 45 E.R. at 110 (*per* Knight Bruce L.J.).

The *dictum* from *De Mattos* was applied in the Privy Council decision of *Lord Strathcona Steamship Co. v. Dominion Coal Co.*, an appeal case originating in Nova Scotia.[257] The defendant had purchased a steamship with notice that it had been committed to sail under a charterparty arranged by the previous owner and the plaintiff. On the basis that "honesty forbids"[258] a rejection of this prior commitment, an action to compel the purchaser to uphold the pre-existing charterparty succeeded, even though there was no privity of contract between that purchaser and the plaintiff. The parameters of the rule after the *Strathcona* decision are not very clear and that case has not generally enjoyed a warm reception. It has been disapproved of as an unwarranted derogation of principles of contractual privity,[259] and confined in its application to the performance of charterparty obligations.[260] Nonetheless, the idea of a rule for chattels that is analogous to the doctrine introduced in *Tulk* has received some (but not much) guarded academic endorsement.[261]

Quite similar results can be achieved without resorting to the rule in *De Mattos*. The tort of interference with contractual relations prevents a person from inducing or procuring a breach of contract, when there is actual knowledge of that contract.[262] Additionally, it has been seen that if a purchaser agrees to assume existing contractual obligations over land, such as a licence, a constructive trust may be imposed to enforce that promise.[263] This remedy seems, in principle, as applicable to goods as it is to land.[264]

---

257 [1926] A.C. 108, [1925] All E.R.Rep. 87, [1926] 1 D.L.R. 873 (P.C.).

258 *Ibid.* at 120 A.C. (*per* Lord Shaw).

259 *Port Line Ltd. v. Ben Line Steamers Ltd.*, [1958] 2 Q.B. 146, [1958] 1 All E.R. 787. See also *Greenhalgh v. Mallard*, [1943] 2 All E.R. 234 (C.A.) at 239; *General Securities Ltd. v. Brett's Ltd.* (1956) 19 W.W.R. 385, 5 D.L.R. (2d) 46 (B.C.S.C.).

260 *Clore v. Theatrical Properties Ltd.*, [1936] 3 All E.R. 483 (C.A.) at 491 (*per* Lord Wright M.R.). *Cf. 1915 Holdings Ltd. v. Chateau Granville Inc.* (1992) 27 R.P.R. (2d) 77 (B.C.S.C.) at 89; *Southern Cross Pumps & Irrigation Pty. Ltd. v. Nicholls* (1996) 39 N.S.W.L.R. 501 (Eq.Div.).

261 A. Tettenborn, "Covenants, Privity of Contract, and the Purchaser of Personal Property", [1982] C.L.J. 58; H. McInnes, Note (1930) 8 Can.B.Rev. 304; Z. Chafee, "Equitable Servitudes on Chattels", 41 Harv.L.Rev. 945 (1928) (suggesting as much as a guarded endorsement may be a stretch here). It is easy to find writers who are averse to the whole idea: see, *e.g.*, G.H.L. Fridman, *The Law of Contract in Canada*, 4th ed. (Toronto: Carswell, 1999) at 213*ff*; M.H. Ogilvie, "Privity of Contract and the Third Party Purchaser" (1987-8) 13 Can.Bus.L.J. 402; J. Beatson, *Anson's Law of Contract*, 27th ed. (Oxford: O.U.P., 1998) at 438; W. Swadling, "The Proprietary Effect of a Hire of Goods" in N. Palmer & E. McKendrick, eds., *Interests in Goods*, 2nd ed. (London: L.L.P., 1998) ch. 20.

262 See also *Swiss Bank Corp. v. Lloyds Bank Ltd.*, [1979] Ch. 548, [1979] 2 All E.R. 853 (C.A.) affirmed on other grounds [1982] A.C. 584, [1981] 2 All E.R. 449 (H.L.) where it was said (at 575 Ch.) that *De Mattos v. Gibson* is the equitable counterpart of the tort of knowingly interfering with contractual rights.

263 See Part 7, Chapter 8. This doctrine was available on the facts of the *Strathcona* case, but the Privy Council seems to have relied on the rule in *De Mattos*, which does not require that there be an agreement to assume the existing contract: see further *Port Line Ltd. v. Ben Line Steamers Ltd.*, *supra*, note 259, at 165-6.

264 See also T. Arno, "Use Restrictions and the Retention of Property Interests in Chattels Through Intellectual Property Rights", 31 S.D.L.Rev. 279 (1994).

13. REFORM IDEAS

The law of freehold covenants, which is replete with "rigid categories, silly distinctions and unreconciled conflicts over basic values",[265] has been the subject of law reform efforts in various common law jurisdictions,[266] including Ontario.[267] Drawing on earlier English proposals, Ontario has recommended that a new property concept be introduced, in law and equity, to be known as a "land obligation". There would be five varieties: (i) restrictive; (ii) positive; (iii) reciprocal payment; (iv) positive user; and (v) access.[268] As with conservation easements, the new land obligation would be allowed to exist in gross. Permitting benefits in gross would enable covenants to be enforced by building scheme managers, or residential associations, even if these parties had no proprietary interest within the building scheme area. In response to the concern that covenants in gross might confer no appreciable or true benefit on those entitled to seek enforcement, it has been recommended that this possibility be dealt with by means of a judicial power of discharge and variation. This more flexible approach would replace the touch and concern requirement as the prime method of controlling the types of permissible covenant obligations.

---

265 See S.F. French, "Towards a Modern Law of Servitudes: Reweaving the Ancient Strands", 55 S.Cal.L.Rev. 1261 (1982) at 1261, n.1, for these and other scornful comments. For some time, the American Law Institute has been revising the *Restatement (3d) of Property (Servitudes)*. Under the latest version, the touch and concern concept would be abandoned; obsolete or otherwise unacceptable covenants would be subject to rules for modification and discharge. See further S.F. French, "The Touch and Concern Doctrine and the Restatement (Third) of Servitudes: A Tribute to Lawrence E. Berger", 77 Neb.L.Rev. 653 (1998) and A.D. Turlock, "Touch and Concern is Dead, Long Live the Doctrine", 77 Neb.L.Rev. 804 (1998).

266 See, *e.g.*, Law Commission, *Transfer of Land: Appurtenant Rights* (London: H.M.S.O., 1971); Law Commission of Victoria, *Easements and Covenants* (Melbourne: L.C.V., 1989); New Zealand Property Law & Equity Reform Committee, *Report on Positive Covenants Affecting Land* (Wellington: Dept. of Justice, 1985).

267 Ontario Law Reform Commission, *Report on Covenants Affecting Freehold Land* (Toronto: A.G. (Ont.), 1989).

268 *Ibid.* at 111-2. Positive obligations would involve the provision of services for the dominant lands, or the carrying on of works on the dominant or servient lands. Positive user obligations are those that require the servient lands to be used in a particular way.

11

MORTGAGES AND OTHER SECURITY INTERESTS

I was a farmer on the rocks of Bruce County.
I was plowing when the letter came.
Some bullshit banker, down in Toronto,
Money or the farm: to him 'twas all the same.

Doug McArthur, "Break the Law"

1. INTRODUCTION

The aim of this chapter is to outline the basic principles that govern security interests. The primary focus will be the mortgage of land.

The mortgage serves as an important adjunct to a loan. Under a loan, the borrower is typically required to repay the amount borrowed (the principal) together with interest, in accordance with a payment schedule (or on demand). The contractual obligation, standing by itself, creates only a personal right of action against the borrower. This right can turn out to be valueless if that borrower absconds or is insolvent: it has been estimated that on bankruptcy an unsecured creditor can generally expect to receive about a 5% return on any debt owed,[1] Even if a judgment is obtained and the creditor is able to pursue enforcement, by garnisheeing wages, or through the seizure of goods, the money extracted may not be enough to satisfy the deficiency. Consequently, a lender may seek additional protection. This is the primary function of the mortgage: it is an interest in property conferred by the borrower (the mortgagor) on the lender (the mortgagee) for the purpose of providing a fall-back if the repayment obligations are not met. In sum, the mortgage highlights the value of proprietary (as opposed to personal) remedies.

Mortgage law has moved rather far afield from the general principles that apply to contracts, money lending and banking. In particular, we will see throughout this chapter that freedom of contract has been deeply eroded in the mortgage context. Courts of equity have figured prominently in these developments, and in most jurisdictions equitable principles have been supplemented by statute.

The interaction between commercial activity and equity involves more than just the idea that mortgages should be regulated by special rules. The intervention of equity undoubtedly has an impact on the cost of loans. The higher the level of protection given by the courts to the borrower in arrears, the greater the expense of enforcement. In general, an increase in the risk of non-payment will typically

---

1 J.S. Ziegel *et al.*, eds., *Commercial and Consumer Transactions: Cases, Text and Materials*, 3rd ed. (Toronto: Emond Montgomery, 1995) vol. 3, at 5.

drive the lender to demand a higher rate of return. Therefore, additional risks assumed by lenders are ultimately borne by all consumers through higher interest rates or the reduced availability of financing. Poor risks (speaking figuratively and literally) typically pay more for the money they borrow. This is a predictable result, and one long appreciated by the courts. In the seventeenth century Lord Nottingham conceded that the availability of equitable relief for the cash-strapped borrower had the "ill consequence" of rendering it more difficult to obtain a mortgage loan.[2]

The mortgage is a social and economic institution as important as any covered in this text.[3] We live in a world dominated by credit, and within the credit system the mortgage plays a leading role. The lending of money secured by mortgages is highly lucrative to the financial institutions that are in a position to advance money. It is a multi-billion dollar industry, with banks being the major participants. Banks provide more than half of the over $400 billion loaned for home purchases under a mortgage in Canada.[4] In absolute terms, the rise in the total mortgage debt for residential property is remarkable:[5]

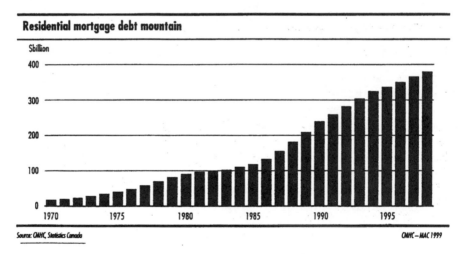

Residential mortgage debt mountain

$billion

Source: CMHC, Statistics Canada   CMHC—MAC 1999

Mortgage financing provides a vehicle for home ownership, a highly prized social aspiration for many Canadians. The mortgage system allows people to enter into the housing market long before they could have raised the purchase money on their own. For those regarded as creditworthy, the mortgage allows personhood

---

2 Quoted in J.H. Baker, *An Introduction to English Legal History*, 3rd ed. (London: Butterworths, 1990) at 356, n. 92. For a contrary view, see M.H. Schill, "An Economic Analysis of Mortgagor Protection Laws", 77 Va.L.Rev. 489 (1991). See also J. Hudson, "The Case Against Secured Lending," 15 Int.Rev.L. & Econ. 47 (1995). For other factors affecting the development of mortgage practices over time, see A.M. Burkhart, "Lenders and Land", 64 Missouri L.Rev. 249 (1999).

3 See further K. Gray, *Elements of Land Law*, 2nd ed. (London: Butterworths, 1993) at 932*ff*.

4 C.M.H.C., *Mortgage Market Trends* (Third Quarter, 1999) at 4.

5 C.M.H.C., *Mortgage Market Trends* (First Quarter, 1999) at 2.

and liberty interests to be realized.[6] Almost 65% of all Canadians live in a dwelling that is owned by a member of the household. Of these homes, just under half are encumbered by at least one mortgage.[7] The number of properties that at some time have been mortgaged is undoubtedly much higher.

This chapter, then, is concerned largely with banks and homeowners, and with the principles of law and equity that mediate their respective interests when the mortgage payments are not made and enforcement action is initiated. The analysis will develop as follows. In the first part, the development of the mortgage will be described, from its feudal forms to the present. Of importance in this overview will be the remedies available in the event of default, and the safeguards developed to protect the borrower during the course of enforcement. The laws in each province differ greatly on these points today. Accordingly, general principles will be stressed. At the end of the chapter a brief outline of personal property security devices will be presented.

2.   ORIGINS OF THE MORTGAGE

The modern mortgage has an ancient ancestry. However, even though there is a strong functional resemblance and a shared terminology, the early forms differ from the modern variants. The evolution of the mortgage resulted from the combined effects of changing social needs and the ingenuity of land conveyancers, who adapted accepted property concepts to develop the means needed to secure loans against land.

The Domesday Book, a census of property holdings in England as of 1086, records the presence of a simple security interest that we would now call a 'pledge'. Security under a pledge (or gage) is obtained by the lender (gagee) acquiring possession of some object; the earliest mortgages under English law are thought to have been pledges of land.[8] Several varieties existed. When the arrangement called for the creditor to apply income from the land to repay the principal debt this was termed a *vivum vadium*: the land had an enduring use to the debtor, given that it was helping to retire the debt. When the income issuing out of the land went to the gagee but did not affect the amount of the principal owing this was known as a *mortuum vadium*, or in French, a *mort gage*.[9] This latter arrangement was stigmatized as usurious and therefore sinful by the Church, because the lender obtained the income from the property, as interest. Nonetheless, this arrangement was not seen as unlawful in the eyes of the secular courts.

---

6 See Parts 3(d) and (e), Chapter 1.

7 Statistics Canada, *Households by Dwelling Characteristics*, as reproduced at <www.statcan.ca>.

8 Possession was not assumed under what was termed a 'Jewish mortgage'. See further T.F.T. Plucknett, *A Concise History of the Common Law*, 5th ed. (London: Butterworths, 1956) at 605-6.

9 Littleton proposed a different origin for the nomenclature. He maintained that the failure to pay the debt left the land dead ('mort') to the debtor; full satisfaction meant that the land was dead as a continuing security to the creditor: E. Coke, *The First Part of the Institutes of the Laws of England or, a Commentary Upon Littleton [Coke upon Littleton]* at s. 332.

In the mid-thirteenth century a practice emerged of leasing the land to the lender who, on default, was given the power to transform the lease into a freehold, thus eliminating the debtor's interest in the property. Not until the fifteenth century did the modern form of mortgage begin to develop out of this earlier approach. By that time it was common to grant the fee simple to the mortgagee, subject to a condition subsequent[10] that gave the mortgagor a right of re-entry on full payment. As a corollary, the failure to meet that condition meant that the mort-gagee could hold the land free from the condition. By the seventeenth century the right of re-entry had been refined to include a proviso for reconveyance by the lender once the loan was paid off. Until then, the lender was still entitled to possession. Along the way, the convention developed of allowing the mortgagor back into possession during the currency of the debt, usually under a lease, with the lender retaining a residual right to assume possession in the event of a breach.

A variation on this last approach, which as it turns out is comparable to that devised under Roman law,[11] is still used in some jurisdictions. In others, such as Alberta, a further modification has been introduced. Here, a mortgage that is registered in the land registration system is regarded as a *charge* on the land and not as a conveyance of title.[12] It does not involve a shifting of a freehold estate from borrower to lender, but rather the adding of a further layer of rights that encrust or encumber the borrower's title. This is not merely a formal difference, but neither is it one of major functional significance, given that the statutory rights that attach to this form of charge create a measure of parity with the common law mortgage. Ontario law now treats the mortgage and the charge as jural equals. Statute law in that Province provides that parties to a charge over land are entitled to all of the legal and equitable rights and remedies in the same way as if the borrower had "transferred the land by way of a mortgage, subject to a proviso for redemption".[13]

3.   THE CONTRIBUTIONS OF LAW AND EQUITY

(a)   generally

The development of mortgage law epitomizes the portrayal of equity as a set of principles devoted to mitigating the harshness of a rigid, ossifying and sometimes cold-hearted common law. This interplay defines the role of equity and is most evident in the protections afforded to a mortgagor: "[i]t seems that a borrower was such a favourite with courts of equity".[14] And this equitable pro-pensity to protect the borrower from oppression at the hands of the lender remains a feature of modern mortgage principles. It is an understandable posture if one

---

10 See Part 2(b), Chapter 7.

11 See B. Nicholas, *An Introduction to Roman Law*, 3rd ed. (Oxford: Clarendon Pr., 1987) at 151.

12 S. 106 of the *Land Titles Act*, R.S.A. 1980, c. L-5, states as follows: "A mortgage or encumbrance under this Act has effect as security but does not operate as a transfer of the land thereby charged."

13 *Land Registration Reform Act*, R.S.O. 1990, c. L.4, sub. 6(3).

14 *Salt v. Marquess of Northampton*, [1892] A.C. 1 (H.L.) at 19 (*per* Lord Bramwell).

assumes that there typically is a power relationship between lender and borrower, favouring the former.

Under a pure-form common law mortgage the legal title to the property is conveyed to the mortgagee as security. Commonly, the subject-matter is a freehold estate, but a leasehold can also be mortgaged, as can other interests, such as an easement,[15] or a mortgage itself (that is, the mortgagee's rights). The borrower has a contractual right to redeem (*i.e.*, recover) the mortgaged interest. At common law the due date for repayment was sacrosanct, and a failure to make the required payments on the 'law day' meant that the right to redeem was lost forever. This drastic result would occur even if the amount owing was equivalent to a mere fraction of the value of the land, or the payment was just one day late.

Quite predictably, the Chancery decided that this was unfair. Its response, initially invoked only in exceptional cases of inequity, but eventually as a matter of course, was to provide relief from forfeiture and to allow the borrower to make the overdue payment(s). We now say that the mortgagor holds an equitable right to redeem after the time for payment has passed. The mortgagor holds what is called an 'equity of redemption', which is an interest in land (enforceable in equity).[16] In common parlance, one speaks of the net value of a property after deducting the mortgage loan as the 'equity' and this is consistent with the nature of the debtor's juridical interest.[17]

The concerns of equity were that mortgage arrangements might "ruin the distressed and unwary, and give unconscionable advantage to greedy and designing persons",[18] and that mortgagees might "wrest the estate fraudulently out of the hands of the mortgagor".[19] Speaking in the eighteenth century, Lord Henley L.C. said: "necessitous men are not, truly speaking, free men, but, to answer a present exigency, will submit to any terms that the crafty may impose upon them".[20] Such sentiments were uttered long before the development of the huge market for residential mortgages or the advent of the rural landowner in the Canadian hinterland. In fact, it is significant that the protections in favour of the landowning borrower arose at a time when England was a "patrician polity"[21]

---

15 See also *Russell v. Mifflin (S.W.) Ltd.* (1991) 89 Nfld. & P.E.I.R 168, 278 A.P.R. 168 (Nfld.T.D.) where the mortgagor had an undefined right to build on the land of his father. This was found to be an interest in land capable of supporting a mortgage.

16 *Casborne v. Scarfe* (1738) 1 Atk. 603, 26 E.R. 377; *DeBeck v. Canada Permanent Loan & Savings Co.* (1907) 12 B.C.R. 409 (C.A.).

17 See further *Petranik v. Dale*, [1977] 2 S.C.R. 959, 69 D.L.R. (3d) 411. In the case of a charge, the language is misleading, since the mortgagor retains the legal estate, which is encumbered by the security. Still, the right held by the mortgagor (the borrower) is commonly described as an equity of redemption.

18 *Spurgeon v. Collier* (1758) 1 Eden 55, at 59, 28 E.R. 605, at 606, adopted in *Fallon v. Keenan* (1866) 12 Gr. 388 (U.C.Ch.D.) at 394.

19 *Mellor v. Lees* (1742) 2 Atk. 494, at 495, 26 E.R. 698, at 699, quoted in *Wilson v. Ward*, [1930] S.C.R. 212, [1930] 2 D.L.R. 433, at 221 S.C.R.

20 *Vernon v. Bethel* (1762) 2 Eden 110, at 113, 28 E.R. 838, at 839.

21 D. Sugarman & R. Warrington, "Land Law, Citizenship, and the Invention of 'Englishness': The Strange World of the Equity of Redemption" in J. Brewer & S. Staves, eds., *Early Modern Conceptions of Property* (London: Routledge, 1995) 111, at 121.

(even more so than today) in which the central place of land, and the landed, was refracted throughout the law of property:

> In addition to being an important instrument for preserving and consolidating landed wealth, the equity of redemption was also a set of political and cultural codes. It was a repository of stories signifying the central importance of the landed aristocracy and gentry to English society. It assumed a certain ordering of preferences and rights: of what was proper and what was illicit; and who and what should be recognized, protected, or excluded.[22]

The principles that were formed in aid of that elite class were later infused into Canadian law. And the felt need for empowerment in the mortgage market-place continues, whether it be for the benefit of the Prairie farmer in a troubled economy, or the lowly homeowner trying to cling to a modest house, bought at an astronomical price, and owned mainly by the bank.

(b)   'disguised' and other equitable mortgages

Equity will always look beyond the form or ostensible purport of a legal transaction in search of its underlying substance; its true meaning. In the case of mortgage transactions this is reflected, obliquely, by the maxim 'once a mortgage, always a mortgage'.[23] What this means is that a mortgage should be treated as a form of security only; therefore, the equity of redemption – the residual ownership rights that remain after the mortgage is granted – will fall under the protective wing of the Chancery.

The maxim also encodes the notion that equity will examine the nature of a transaction to see if it is, in fact, a mortgage parading around as some other form of arrangement. For example, consider a situation in which B agrees to sell Blackacre to L for $100,000.00. As a part of this deal, B is given the right to buy the property back three years later for $125,000.00. It is also agreed that this right to repurchase lapses after the three years has expired. Perhaps this is no more than it appears to be – a sale with a time-limited option given back to B, the vendor. On the other hand, a mortgage may be found to exist even though it is camouflaged to resemble some other dealing, as may be the case here.[24] It may be that this transaction should be regarded as a mortgage, with interest being set at $25,000.00, and with a three-year redemption period. The vague test that determines the real characterization is whether the dealing is set up merely to provide security for a loan. The documents themselves may hint at this intention[25] and parol evidence may be tendered on the issue.[26] At the end of the day, there

---

22 *Ibid.* at 126.

23 " '[O]nce a mortgage always a mortgage' is as fair an equitable doctrine today as it ever was": *Korpan v. Supynuk*, [1939] 1 W.W.R. 45 (Sask.K.B.) at 47 (*per* Taylor J.).

24 See the illustration of this principle in *Fleming v. Watts*, [1944] S.C.R. 360, [1944] 4 D.L.R. 353. *Cf. Kreick v. Wansbrough*, [1973] S.C.R. 588, [1973] 4 W.W.R. 350, 35 D.L.R. (3d) 275; *Athabasca Realty Co. v. Lee* (1976) 67 D.L.R. (3d) 272 (Alta.T.D.); *Herron v. Mayland*, [1928] S.C.R. 225, [1928] 2 D.L.R. 858.

25 See *Fleming v. Watts, supra*, note 24.

26 *Athabasca Realty Co. v. Lee, supra*, note 24. See also *Arnal v. Arnal* (1969) 6 D.L.R. (3d) 245 (Sask.C.A.).

must be "powerful collateral"[27] evidence to displace the apparent meaning of the documents when taken at face value. The point of pursuing the issue of characterization is plain enough: it determines whether or not the rights of the parties fall to be governed by the special rules of mortgage law.

Equitable mortgages can arise in other ways. Recall the maxim 'equity regards as done that which ought to be done'.[28] This proposition explains why an agreement for a lease is as good as a lease, and underscores the principle that an agreement for the sale of land can confer an equitable estate in the purchaser before the closing of the transaction.[29] The maxim applies here too: an agreement to advance money under a legal mortgage creates an equitable mortgage.[30] Similarly, a defective legal mortgage *may* be enforceable in equity if it reflects an agreement to grant a mortgage,[31] and a verbal agreement can create a charge if there are sufficient acts of part performance to prove that a mortgage contract exists. One traditional method of creating an equitable mortgage, which relies on an extrapolation of these principles, is for the mortgagor, in return for a loan, to deliver the documents of title to the lender (or an agent) to hold as security.[32] In such a situation no mortgage deed is prepared (although there is usually some form of written record); instead the borrower hands over the existing documents of title to perfect the security.

A mortgage of an equitable interest is, necessarily, an equitable mortgage. Therefore, any second or subsequent mortgages must be equitable, because after the granting of the first mortgage all that the mortgagor retains in the land is the equity of redemption. However, in those jurisdictions (such as Alberta) in which the mortgage has been redesigned as a statutory charge this is not so. The legal freeholder who grants a legal charge over the property nevertheless retains legal

---

27 *Herron v. Mayland, supra*, note 24, at 862 D.L.R. (*per* Duff J.). See also *Pierce v. Empey*, [1939] S.C.R. 247, [1939] 4 D.L.R. 672.

28 See, *e.g.*, Part 2(b), Chapter 8.

29 See, *e.g.*, *Bellabona v. Amaral* (1994) 94 Man.R. (2d) 52, [1994] 7 W.W.R. 560 (Q.B.).

30 See, *e.g.*, *Re Collens* (1982) 22 Alta.L.R. (2d) 258, 40 A.R. 336, 140 D.L.R. (3d) 755 (Q.B.); *Canadian Imperial Bank of Commerce v. Zimmerman* (1984) 27 B.L.R. 38, 33 R.P.R. 29 (B.C.S.C.); *Bellabona v. Amaral, supra*, note 29.

31 See, *e.g.*, *Chedore v. Bank of Montreal* (1986) 34 D.L.R. (4th) 177, 76 N.B.R. (2d) 99, 192 A.P.R. 99 (C.A.); *Luscombe v. Luscombe* (1990) 80 Nfld. & P.E.I.R. 325 (Nfld.T.D.).

32 This rule can be traced at least as far back as *Russel v. Russel* (1783) 1 Bro.C.C. 269, 28 E.R. 1121. See also *Royal Canadian Bank v. Cummer* (1869) 15 Gr. 627 (Ont.Ch.D.); *Masuret v. Mitchell* (1879) 26 Gr. 435 (Ont.Ch.D.). "The doctrine has been often regretted – e.g., by Lord Eldon – but it is too firmly established to be altered except by legislation": *Zimmerman v. Sprat* (1912) 26 O.L.R. 448, 5 D.L.R. 452 (H.C.) at 453 D.L.R. (*per* Riddell J.). This type of mortgage may arise even though the actual certificate of title is lodged in the land titles office, so that all that can be handed to the lender is the duplicate certificate: see *Bank of Nova Scotia v. David (Trustee of)* (1988) 60 Alta.L.R. (2d) 223, 50 R.P.R. 236, 89 A.R. 136 (Q.B.); *Royal Bank v. Mesa Estates Ltd.* (1985) 70 B.C.L.R. 7, [1986] 2 W.W.R. 641, 23 D.L.R. (4th) 753 (C.A.); *North West Trust Co. v. West* (1989) 70 Alta.L.R. (2d) 326, [1990] 2 W.W.R. 133, 62 D.L.R. (4th) 749 (C.A.) leave to appeal to S.C.C. refused (1990) 65 D.L.R. (4th) viii (S.C.C.). For a comment on the *North West* and *Mesa* cases, see P. Devonshire, "Equitable Mortgages and Lodgement of Title Agreements" (1990) 17 Can.Bus.L.J. 309. See also *Land Titles Act*, R.S.O. 1990, c. L.5, s. 114. The continued availability of this mode of creation has been doubted in England: see *United Bank of Kuwait Plc. v. Sahib*, [1995] 2 W.L.R. 94 (Q.B.).

title. The same should hold true after the granting of a subsequent legal charge (a 'second mortgage') and so on. The mortgagor retains the legal title throughout.

(c)   clogs and fetters on the equity of redemption

The maxim 'once a mortgage, always a mortgage' is a compendious expression of equity's tendencies to protect the mortgagor. To this can be added the trope that 'equity will not tolerate clogs or fetters on the equity of redemption'. In its early formulations, this principle meant that a mortgagee was not allowed to obtain, through an agreement made contemporaneously with the mortgage, any advantages under the mortgage other than the recovery of principal, interest and costs. In the 1902 Canadian decision in *Stephen v. Black,* equity's position was described as follows:

> [A] mortgage creditor shall not be permitted to obtain, by or through any agreement made contemporaneously with the mortgage, any advantage beyond principal, interest and costs, and in such cases, equity will let a man [sic] loose from his agreement, or even against his agreement, admit him to redeem a mortgage. Whatever his security may be, whether land, chattels, bond, note or covenant, the moment it appears that it is a security, the party cannot recover any more in equity than his debt, interests and costs, unless, of course, under some subsequent arrangement made between the parties.[33]

At its inception the rule against clogs served as a means of curbing usurious practices. It was based on the recognition that the return on the loan could be covertly augmented by appending collateral advantages to a mortgage. The rule against clogs is now premised on the view that a mortgage is a security device, no more and no less. It is concerned with impediments imposed on the right of a borrower to regain the land in the state that it was in when the loan was given. In effect, the rule deals with the reverse situation to that of the disguised mortgage. Here, one looks within the body of the mortgage for other hidden arrangements that are not mortgage-like, and that detract from the rights normally enjoyed by a mortgagor. The rule provides protection for consumers by taking the right to acquire collateral advantages outside of the legitimate ambit of the mortgage arrangement.

The quoted statement from *Stephen v. Black*[34] suggests that there is no room at all for the existence of any collateral benefits in a mortgage; that is no longer so. In recent times, disputes over 'clogs' have arisen in relation to agreements that seek to control the commercial dealings of the mortgagor. Some of the English case law on point has involved mortgage deals between brewing companies and the landlords of pubs, under which a publican-mortgagor might also agree to purchase beer from a supplier-mortgagee. In Canada, similar tying agreements are sometimes found between large gasoline companies and the owners of local

---

33 *Stephen v. Black* (1902) Cout.S.C. 217, at 247-8 (*per* Davies J.). See also *Jennings v. Ward* (1705) 2 Vern. 520, 23 E.R. 935, and the strict test in *Bradley v. Carritt,* [1903] A.C. 253, [1900-3] All E.R.Rep. 633 (H.L.).

34 *Supra*, note 33.

service stations. The current view[35] is that these collateral advantages will be found to be invalid unless (i) the mortgagee has acted unfairly, oppressively or unconscionably; (ii) the agreement acts as a penalty clogging the equity of redemption; or (iii) the agreed terms are otherwise inconsistent with contractual or equitable rights to redeem. It is now accepted that an agreement for a tied house or service station does not necessarily trigger any of these concerns. Moreover, if conditions are truly independent of the mortgage, these collateral rights may validly continue in operation after the stated time for redemption has passed.[36] In any event, there is another potential evil associated with bargains of this type. An agreement that is in 'restraint of trade' is itself subject to judicial scrutiny and potential invalidity, whether or not it happens to impose a clog on the equity of redemption.[37]

It is enshrined doctrine that a mortgage cannot be rendered irredeemable. Put another way, a mortgagee cannot contract out of the right to redeem. Again, this is designed to give integrity to the idea that a mortgage is a mere security device. Accordingly, a mortgagee cannot obtain, as part of the mortgage, the right to buy the property outright, because this would amount to a power to terminate the mortgagor's rights prematurely, thus eradicating the right to redeem.[38] Actually, the parties to a mortgage *can* decide that the land is to be sold to the lender, but to accomplish this a truly independent bargain must be struck.[39]

(d)   alienation of the mortgagor's and mortgagee's interests

The equity of redemption is an alienable interest.[40] When a home is mortgaged it is the equity of redemption that is the subject of any subsequent sale of

---

35 See *G. & C. Kreglinger v. New Patagonia Meat & Cold Storage Co.*, [1914] A.C. 25, [1911-13] All E.R.Rep. 970 (H.L.). See also *Kosiur v. Kushinski*, [1949] 2 W.W.R. 24, [1949] 3 D.L.R. 493 (Alta.C.A.); *Niagara Resorts Inc. v. 1086868 Ontario Ltd.* (1999) 24 R.P.R. (3d) 138 (Ont.Gen.Div.) additional reasons at (July 8, 1999) Doc. 98-CL-3123 (S.C.J.)

36 *G. & C. Kreglinger v. New Patagonia Meat & Cold Storage Co.*, supra, note 35.

37 See generally M.J. Trebilcock, *The Common Law of Restraint of Trade: A Legal and Economic Analysis* (Toronto: Carswell, 1986). See also *Stephens v. Gulf Oil Canada Ltd.* (1975) 11 O.R. (2d) 129, 25 C.P.R. (2d) 64, 65 D.L.R. (3d) 193 (C.A.) leave to appeal to S.C.C. refused (1976) 11 O.R. (2d) 129n (S.C.C.). In Ontario, it has been recommended that the rules against clogs be abolished, except in the case of "protected borrowers" (including homeowners). Others would be left to rely on remedies under the general law (such as the law of unconscionability), and the common law of restraint of trade: see further Ontario Law Reform Commission, *Report on the Law of Mortgages* (Toronto: A.G. (Ont.), 1987) at 28*ff*. The concept of the protected borrower is described in the Report at ch. 4, *passim*.

38 See, *e.g.*, *Hoar v. Mills (No. 2)*, [1935] 1 W.W.R. 433 (Sask.C.A.) and the authorities reviewed in that judgment.

39 See, *e.g.*, *400091 British Columbia Ltd. v. Copper Beach Estates Ltd.* (1992) 25 R.P.R. (2d) 189 (B.C.S.C.); *Young v. Kinnis* (1953) 61 Man.R. 374, 11 W.W.R. (N.S.) 436, [1954] 3 D.L.R. 381 (Q.B.). See also *Moore v. Texaco Canada Ltd.*, [1965] 2 O.R. 253, 50 D.L.R. (2d) 300 (H.C.). Additionally, the right to redeem cannot be postponed in a way that renders it illusory: see *Fairclough v. Swan Brewery Co.*, [1912] A.C. 565, [1911-13] All E.R.Rep. 397 (P.C.) for an explanation and a rare application of this idea. *Cf. Knightsbridge Estates Trust, Ltd. v. Byrne*, [1939] Ch. 441, [1938] 4 All E.R. 618 (C.A.) affirmed [1940] A.C. 613, [1940] 2 All E.R. 401 (H.L.); *Clark v. Supertest Petroleum Corp.*, [1958] O.R. 474, 14 D.L.R. (2d) 454 (H.C.).

40 *Petranik v. Dale*, supra, note 17.

the property. Of course, at common law, the mortgagor cannot escape the liability under the mortgage simply by selling the property; the obligation to repay the loan survives as a matter of general contract law. At the same time, the new owner may agree to assume the existing mortgage and to make payments under that mortgage as part of the purchase price. A properly drafted 'assumption' agreement would contain a promise by the assignee to indemnify the vendor if the original mortgagor (the vendor) is sued on the promise to pay.[41]

Under the common law, an assumption by the purchaser does not create a privity relationship between the assignee of the mortgagor and the original mortgagee, though this could of course be arranged if those parties decided to strike a new agreement. Furthermore, a right of indemnity will be implied as a matter of construction in favour of the original mortgagor.[42] Some jurisdictions, such as Alberta,[43] go further, by (i) providing an automatic right of indemnity, and (ii) presumptively deeming privity to exist between the purchaser and the original mortgagee.[44] As a result of item (ii), if there is a default, the mortgagee can sue the new owner directly.[45]

We saw in the context of leasehold transfers that the landlord often tries to control the tenant's ability to alienate rights under the lease.[46] Likewise, the mortgagee may wish to regulate transfers by the mortgagor. Hence, a mortgage may provide that on the sale of Blackacre the remaining payments become immediately payable; they are 'due on sale'. Some due-on-sale clauses are triggered only if the mortgagee does not consent to the transfer. Uncertainty has arisen as to whether due-on-sale clauses are valid: do they create unacceptable restraints on alienation?[47] The bulk of the Canadian cases on this issue have upheld the validity of these clauses.[48] However, in *Royal Bank v. Freeborn* the Court stayed an action of foreclosure based on the breach of a clause under which the mortgagee had to consent to a proposed sale. The power that the clause gave to the bank was

---

41 See generally J.T. Robertson, "Neither a Borrower Nor a Lender Be: The Problem With Sales of Real Property Subject to Existing Mortgages" (1989) 38 U.N.B.L.J. 31.

42 See *Williston v. Lawson* (1891) 19 S.C.R. 673, at 678; *Thompson v. Wilkes* (1856) 5 Gr. 594 (U.C.Ch.D.). But see T.G. Feeney "Mortgages – Implied Covenant by the Purchaser of Mortgaged Land to Indemnify the Mortgagor – Statutory Action by the Mortgagee Against the Purchaser" (1964) 42 Can.B.Rev. 157.

43 *Land Titles Act*, R.S.A. 1980, c. L-5, sub. 62(1). See further E. Mirth, "Mortgage Renewals in Alberta" (1985) 23 Alta.L.Rev. 405; Alberta Law Reform Institute, *Mortgage Remedies in Alberta* (Edmonton: A.L.R.I., 1994) at 56*ff.*

44 See also *Mortgages Act*, R.S.O. 1990, c. M.40, sub. 20(2). See further *Malaviya v. Lankin* (1985) 53 O.R. (2d) 1, 38 R.P.R. 97, 23 D.L.R. (4th) 245 (C.A.).

45 This is subject to the rules governing the ability to bring an action on the personal covenant: see Part 4(b), *infra*.

46 See Part 3(b), Chapter 8.

47 Recall the discussion of restraints on alienation in Part 3(e), Chapter 7.

48 See, *e.g.*, *Canada Permanent Trust Co. v. King's Bridge Apartments Ltd.* (1984) 48 Nfld. & P.E.I.R. 345, 8 D.L.R. (4th) 152 (Nfld.C.A.); *Weeks v. Rosocha* (1983) 41 O.R. (2d) 787, 28 R.P.R. 126 (C.A.). See also *C.M.H.C. v. Hongkong Bank of Canada*, [1993] 1 S.C.R. 167, 100 D.L.R. (4th) 40, 6 Alta.L.R. (3d) 337. But see *Re Bahnsen and Hazelwood* (1960) 23 D.L.R. (2d) 76, [1960] O.W.N. 155 (C.A.).

likened to that wielded by a feudal lord. Reflecting on the impact of *Quia Emptores* of 1290,[49] it was observed that,

> [i]mmediate lords similar to those in the 13th century no longer exist, at least under the land titles system, in Alberta. But in effect a great majority of the homes which have been built in Alberta during the past 25 years are held in the service of another kind of lord, that is to say, the holder of the mortgage on the home whether the mortgagee be a mortgage company, a bank, a trust company, an insurance company, Central Mortgage and Housing Corporation or the Alberta Housing Authority.[50]

One argument against validity is that an owner will not sell if it is known that the full debt burden will have to be immediately satisfied. And it is obvious that if the mortgagor can advertise the fact that her home is encumbered with a mortgage at 7%, at a time when new mortgages are being offered on the market at 12%, her property will appear more attractive to potential buyers. A due-on-sale clause destroys this benefit. If the clause is valid, the sale allows the mortgagee to bring the (cheaper) mortgage to an abrupt end.

Does this mean that due-on-sale clauses are objectionable? The fact that the benefit of a low mortgage rate cannot be passed on to a purchaser is not invariably going to be fatal to a sale. While it would be desirable for a would-be vendor to be able to say that the property includes a low mortgage rate, it is erroneous to treat this as one of the advantages of that property if that mortgage contains, in addition to a lucrative interest rate, a due-on-sale provision. The interest charge might have been initially set at a lower rate with a view to the due-on-sale clause.[51]

The mortgagee also has an interest that can be transferred: the right to enforce the loan. At common law, the right to sue on the debt, a chose in action, is not assignable. Equity, on the other hand, permits these transfers. One means of overcoming the impediment at law is for the old mortgagee to give a power of attorney to the new one. If there is a breach, the new mortgagee can sue on the debt in the name of the old, using the power of attorney as the authority for doing so. This is no longer necessary, now that a legal assignment is possible by virtue of statute.[52]

---

49 *Quia Emptores Terrarum, 1290*, 18 Edw. 1, c. 3. See Part 2(a), Chapter 2.

50 *Royal Bank v. Freeborn* (1974) 22 Alta.L.R. (2d) 279, 39 A.R. 380 (S.C.) at 285 Alta.L.R. (*per* Turcotte L.J.S.C.).

51 The arguments are more thoroughly rehearsed in *Mortgage Remedies in Alberta, supra*, note 43, at 85*ff*, where American developments and authorities as well as the few relevant Canadian cases on point are discussed. See also E.J. Murdock, "The Due-On-Sale Controversy: Beneficial Effects of the Garn-St. Germain Depository Institution Act of 1982", 1984 Duke L.J. 121. The Ontario Law Reform Commission recommended against the introduction of a general statutory prohibition on due-on-sale clauses: *Report on the Law of Mortgages, supra*, note 37, at 87. But the Commission also recommended that the borrower have the right to pay off the loan, on a sale, where the mortgage contains a due-on-sale clause. See also *ibid.*, at 87-9, concerning recommendations about the validity of due-on-encumbrance and due-on-negotiation clauses.

52 See, *e.g.*, *Judicature Act*, R.S.A. 1980, c. J-1, s. 21.

4.   AN OUTLINE OF REMEDIES AND RELATED MATTERS[53]

(a)   introduction

There are five main remedies ordinarily available to the mortgagee once default has occurred. In some jurisdictions, or in a specific mortgage relationship, these may not all be available; so much depends on the mortgage itself and the idiosyncrasies of the laws of each jurisdiction. The main remedies are as follows. The mortgagee may: (a) bring an action against the mortgagor on the personal covenant; (b) take possession; (c) appoint a receiver; (d) foreclose; or (e) sell the land. These may be supplemented by additional protections, such as a collateral guarantee or a chattel mortgage. Sometimes suing the mortgagor on the personal covenant can be of value, but often the lender is in the predicament of having to take enforcement action against the land because the borrower's pockets are empty. Repossession and the appointment of a receiver can be useful as temporary measures, but of the five principal remedies, it is sale and foreclosure – going after the "the money or the mud"[54] that often provide the best means of realizing on the security.

(b)   the personal covenant

The umbrella term 'personal covenant' can be used to refer to the set of contractual promises made by the mortgagor.[55] The possible range of terms is quite broad. Various standard covenants fall in and out of vogue, and economic variables – downturns, upturns, *etc.* – affect the conventions that are adopted or discarded. Additionally, there are usually vast differences between mortgages of commercial properties and those geared toward home purchases.

Within the array of personal covenants the key term is the promise to repay the loan. In establishing the payment schedule, the convention in Canada is to 'blend' together the obligations to pay the principal and interest into a series of monthly payments of a fixed sum, the first payment being due one month after the money is advanced to the borrower. The ratio of these two components changes incrementally with each payment. As the months pass, the amount of interest paid decreases, while the amount directed toward paying off the capital increases.

The quantum of the monthly payments depends on the size of the loan and the selected period of 'amortization'. This term describes the time required to pay off the debt (including interest) were the blended payments to run their full course. This period may be different from the actual intended length of the mortgage contract. The typical duration in Canada these days for residential mortgages ranges from six months to five years, but the payments might be based on a much longer amortization period (such as 25 years).

---

53 See generally J.E. Roach, *The Canadian Law of Mortgages of Land* (Toronto: Butterworths, 1993).

54 *Mortgage Remedies in Alberta, supra*, note 43, at 24.

55 Including, for example, a promise not to commit waste: see *Parisian Fashions Ltd. v. Petrus* (1996) 46 Alta.L.R. (3d) 159, 6 R.P.R. (3d) 219 (Q.B.).

A simple example can be used to demonstrate these ideas. A three-year mortgage of $100,000.00 at an interest rate of 8% per annum, amortized over 25 years, results in a blended monthly payment of $763.00.[56] The first payment that would be made under this mortgage would be composed of about $666.00 in interest and $97.00 of principal. The last payment (of $763.00) would be composed of about $56.00 in interest and $707.00 principal. Only a dent (of a few thousand dollars) would be made in the amount owing after three years. If this arrangement continued over the full period of amortization, the total amount repaid would be $228,000.00, of which $128,000.00 would be interest.

Default on a mortgage does not usually occur in isolation. Obviously, during periods of depression and recession, foreclosure epidemics often break out. Indeed, mortgage defaults serve as measures of economic prosperity and pathology. Added to the problems precipitated by a poor economic climate are the personal calamities that can befall one, such as failed business ventures and family breakdown. In the midst of such things, a law suit and judgment on the personal promise to pay is a daunting prospect for many homeowners.

Some provinces have responded to these harsh realities by imposing restrictions on the ability of a lender to sue on the personal debt. In Alberta, as a general rule, no action lies on the personal covenant against a private individual.[57] The immunity was introduced during the depression by the Social Credit Party in order to protect farmers and others from having to endure monumental personal liability at a time when land values had plummeted. It was a natural by-product of the irrepressible hostility that Social Credit, under the leadership of William Aberhart, held for the commercial banks doing business in the Province.[58] This bar has remained in force and was extended when the fall in oil prices prompted a recession in the 1980s.[59] However, it is not universal: for instance, corporations and guarantors are not covered. Loans under the *Canada Mortgage and Housing Corporation Act* are also outside the scope of the Alberta protections.[60]

---

56 Similar calculations are more fully set out in D. King, "Mathematics for All" (1983) 127 Sol.J. 820.

57 *Law of Property Act*, R.S.A. 1980, c. L-8, paras. 41(1)(a) and (b). The complicated state of the law surrounding the basic idea of the immunity from suit in Alberta is explained in *Mortgage Remedies in Alberta*, supra, note 43, at 42*ff*.

58 See further J.J. Barr, *The Dynasty: The Rise and Fall of the Social Credit in Alberta* (Toronto: McClelland & Stewart, 1974) at ch. 6, *passim*.

59 The exemption now applies to an individual who takes an assignment of a corporate mortgage, provided that the land is used by that person or the family as a *bona fide* residence: s. 43.4 [as am.]. See further *Alberta Mortgage & Housing Corp. v. Ciereszko* (1987) 50 Alta.L.R. (2d) 289, [1987] 3 W.W.R. 513, 36 D.L.R. (4th) 666 (C.A.) additional reasons at (1987) 54 Alta.L.R. (2d) 191, [1987] 6 W.W.R. 191, 43 D.L.R. (4th) 319 (C.A.) leave to appeal to S.C.C. refused [1987] 4 W.W.R. lxvi (S.C.C.). See also *Paramount Life Insurance Co. v. Torgerson Development Corp. (Alberta) Ltd.* (1988) 58 Alta.L.R. (2d) 13, 48 R.P.R. 136, [1988] 3 W.W.R. 685 (C.A.); *Canadian Imperial Bank of Commerce v. Ohlson* (1996) 180 A.R. 248 (Q.B.) reversed (1997) 57 Alta.L.R. (3d) 213, [1998] 6 W.W.R. 115, 154 D.L.R. (4th) 33 (C.A.). As to Saskatchewan, see further P. Devonshire, "The Mortgagor's Liability on the Personal Covenant: *National Trust Co. v. Mead*" (1991) 55 Sask.L.Rev. 429.

60 A contentious question, not definitively decided, is whether mortgages granted to the Crown are subject to the immunity from liability on the personal covenant: see the thorough discussion of this issue in *Mortgage Remedies in Alberta*, supra, note 43, at 48*ff*.

(c)   taking possession[61] or appointing a receiver

Under a classic common law mortgage, the lender, as holder of the legal fee simple, is entitled to possession of the premises, even "before the ink is dry on the mortgage",[62] unless that right is given up (expressly or impliedly) under the mortgage.[63] Typically, there is a re-letting of the lands, or an attornment clause under which the mortgagor is declared to be a tenant of the mortgagee.[64] The mortgage usually also provides that the mortgagee is entitled to possession if the mortgagor is in default.[65] The right to take possession is not an inherent part of a *charge* over land, because under a charge no estate is acquired by the mortgagee.[66] This same limitation has been applied to an equitable mortgagee.[67] In these latter two situations an order for possession may be sought if the mortgage does not contain such a right.

The issue of what amounts to sufficient possession-taking by a mortgagee can sometimes be a difficult one.[68] As we saw in Chapter 4, possession is a rather ductile term. It seems that when the property is being occupied by tenants of the defaulting mortgagor, the collection of rents by the mortgagee alone will not normally serve as proof of an assumption of possession. It must be shown that the power to manage the property has been taken out of the hands of the mortgagor.[69] Of course, a mortgagee cannot oust tenants of the mortgagor who acquired their leasehold before the mortgage; those tenants have priority. But the converse

---

61 See generally R.A. Pearce, "Keeping a Mortgagee Out of Possession", [1979] C.L.J. 257; R.J. Smith, "The Mortgagee's Right to Possession: The Modern Law", [1979] Conv. 266; P. Butt, *Land Law,* 3rd ed. (Sydney: Law Book Co., 1996) at 573*ff.*

62 *Four-Maids Ltd. v. Dudley Marshall (Properties) Ltd.*, [1957] Ch. 317, [1957] 2 All E.R. 35, at 320 Ch. (*per* Harman J.).

63 *Doe d. Mowat v. Smith* (1851) 8 U.C.Q.B. 139.

64 Attornment clauses are invalid in Alberta, except for mortgages (a) given to the Farm Credit Corporation; (b) under the *National Housing Act* [R.S.C. 1985, c. N-11]; or (c) given in relation to business premises: *Law of Property Act*, R.S.A. 1980, c. L-8, ss. 35-7.

65 It has been said that in Ontario it is "the almost invariable practice to provide in the mortgage that the borrower will have possession of the secured property until default with respect to either payment of the debt or the performance of another contractual obligation": *Report on the Law of Mortgages, supra,* note 37, at 211. In some jurisdictions the right of the lender to assume possession is limited to protect some mortgagors (such as homeowners): in Alberta, see *Co-operative Centre Credit Union Ltd. v. Greba* (1984) 32 Alta.L.R. (2d) 389, [1984] 5 W.W.R. 481, 10 D.L.R. (4th) 449 (C.A.). See also *Mortgages Act*, R.S.O. 1990, c. M.40, Part V [as am.].

66 *Hebert v. George,* [1933] 3 W.W.R. 399, [1933] 4 D.L.R. 658 (Alta.C.A.); *Co-operative Centre Credit Union Ltd. v. Greba, supra,* note 65. In Ontario, see *Land Registration Reform Act,* R.S.O. 1990, c. L.4. sub. 6(3).

67 See, *e.g., Royal Bank v. Nicholson* (1980) 28 O.R. (2d) 377, 110 D.L.R. (3d) 763 (H.C.). The correctness of this treatment of the equitable mortgage is questioned in H.W.R. Wade, "An Equitable Mortgagee's Right to Possession" (1955) 71 L.Q.R. 204.

68 See generally *Shantz v. Hallman* (1927) 60 O.L.R. 543, [1927] 3 D.L.R. 658 (C.A.) affirmed on other grounds (*sub nom. Modern Realty Co. v. Shantz*), [1928] S.C.R. 213, [1928] 2 D.L.R. 705.

69 See *Noyes v. Pollock* (1886) 32 Ch. 53 (C.A.). See also *Municipal Savings & Loan Corp. v. Sharp* (1996) 6 R.P.R. (3d) 207 (Ont.Gen.Div.). The mortgagee was found to be in possession in *Unican Development Corp. Ltd. v. Settlers Savings & Mortgage Corp.* (1984) 30 Alta.L.R. (2d) 66, 51 A.R. 178 (Q.B.).

is also true: at common law a lease granted after a mortgage is subordinate to that mortgage.[70] This means that when a mortgagee takes possession a lease granted by the mortgagor subsequent to the mortgage can be terminated. For this reason, some provinces explicitly provide protection against the possibility of an eviction of the tenants of the mortgagor.[71] Even absent a protection of that kind, if a tenant remains in possession and pays rent to the mortgagee a new lease may be implied.[72]

The mortgagee is entitled to apply the rents and profits that are received to pay down the indebtedness. Needless to say, that is normally the reason for taking over the property. Also, the costs of necessary repairs can be recouped.[73] Reimbursement for lasting improvements can be made if these are reasonable[74] (such as when they are designed to put the property into a sellable state), as long as these added costs do not "make it utterly impossible [for] the mortgagor ever to redeem".[75] I am surprised that the law allows this much (apparent) scope to the lender. I can understand why the law would want a mortgagee who repairs or acts with the consent of the mortgagor to be reimbursed. I can even appreciate that on a sale of improved property, account would have to be made for the increased sale value attributable to the improvements. But by the same token, to allow a claim based on improvements, however reasonable and long-lasting, seems to permit a unilateral increase in the mortgage debt, and invites action by the lender that undermines the personhood interests of the borrower in relation to the property.[76]

With possession comes responsibility.[77] Obligations to make repairs and to refrain from committing waste apply once the mortgagee has taken possession[78] but not beforehand.[79] And an occupation rent may be payable to the borrower

---

70 See *Kelvedon Holdings Ltd. v. Papandreou* (1996) 44 Alta. L.R. (3d) 378, 5 R.P.R. (3d) 294 (Q.B.).

71 See, *e.g.*, *Mortgages Amendment Act, 1991*, S.O. 1991, vol. 2, c. 6, s. 2.

72 See, *e.g.*, *Goodyear Canada Inc. v. Burnhamthorpe Square Inc.* (1998) 41 O.R. (3d) 321, 21 R.P.R. (3d) 1, 166 D.L.R. (4th) 625 (C.A.) leave to appeal to S.C.C. refused (1999) 243 N.R. 400 (note) (S.C.C.).

73 See *Romanes v. Herns* (1875) 22 Gr. 469 (Ont.Ch.D.).

74 "[T]he courts will not hesitate to order reimbursement of the mortgagee's expenses when the improvements are reasonable and enhance the value of the property": Roach, *supra*, note 53, at 228.

75 *Sandon v. Hooper* (1843) 6 Beav. 246, 49 E.R. 820, at 821 E.R. (*per* Lord Langdale). See also *Shepard v. Jones* (1882) 21 Ch.D. 469 (C.A.).

76 These personhood interests seem to have been relevant in *Kerby v. Kerby* (1856) 5 Gr. 587 (U.C.Ch.D.) where a claim for compensation failed.

77 See generally *Merriam v. Cronk* (1874) 21 Gr. 60 (Ont. Ch.D.); S. Valo, "Possession" in Law Society of Upper Canada, *Mortgage Rights and Remedies* (Toronto: L.S.U.C., 1982).

78 See *Sandon v. Hooper* (1843) 6 Beav. 246, 49 E.R. 820, affirmed (1844) 14 L.J.Ch. 120. *Cf.* R.E. Megarry & H.W.R. Wade, *The Law of Real Property*, 5th ed. (London: Stevens & Sons, 1984) at 944.

79 And no liability attaches if the property is demolished by a municipal authority at a time when the mortgagor could have assumed possession: *Royal Bank of Canada v. Quality Construction Ltd.* (1997) 156 Sask.R. 125, [1998] 4 W.W.R. 162 (Q.B.). See also *AIB Finance Ltd. v. Debtors*, [1998] 2 All E.R. 929 (C.A.).

(which is credited against the debt).[80] Moreover, the mortgagee has to be thoughtful about how the land is used to generate income. The early authorities speak of the mortgagee being liable for "gross default, mismanagement, or fraud",[81] though modern Canadian decisions refer instead to a general requirement of prudence:

> Looking at the matter afresh and without the benefit of precedent, the basic rule is that a mortgagee in possession must act as a prudent owner and protect the equity of redemption. An owner with sufficient money to pay the interest on the second mortgage or, alternatively, to effect repairs, might well decide that the interest should be paid and the repairs put over to another day; otherwise there is a risk of loss of possession of the property. From the mortgagee's vantage point, there is an increased exposure to loss if the debt is increased by adding interest on unpaid interest. There may be a benefit in allocating the money to repairs, but it seems reasonable that the choice should be that of the mortgagee in possession.[82]

The mortgagee's failure to obtain a proper rent for the premises may amount to conduct that falls short of the standard of prudence. However, this level of care is tempered somewhat by the fact that the mortgagor also assumes a measure of responsibility: if the mortgagor knows that the property can yield a higher rent than that proposed by the mortgagee, there is a duty to advise the mortgagee accordingly.[83]

The appointment of a receiver is designed to serve the same end as the assumption of possession.[84] The right to make an appointment may be contained in the mortgage; otherwise, an order must be sought. The judicial power to appoint a receiver is the product of equity, and by statute this power has generally been extended to legal mortgages.[85] The court has a discretion to appoint a receiver;[86] however, where the property is income-producing the request for a receiver is quite likely to be treated favourably.[87]

(d)   foreclosure[88] (and redemption)

The idea behind foreclosure can be understood by recalling the structure of the mortgage at common law. As we have seen, in the seventeenth century this

---

80 See *Lambert v. MacKenzie*, [1949] O.W.N. 758, [1950] 1 D.L.R. 178 (C.A.); *Re Allen's Danforth Theatre* (1925) 7 C.B.R. 87, 29 O.W.N. 73, [1925] 4 D.L.R. 556 (S.C.).

81 *Merriam v. Cronk, supra*, note 77, at 63 (*per* Blake V.C., quoting *Fisher on Mortgages*).

82 *Capsule Investments Ltd. v. Heck* (1993) 103 D.L.R. (4th) 556, 12 O.R. (3d) 225 (C.A.) at 562-3 D.L.R. (*per* Carthy J.A.) affirming (1990) 72 O.R. (2d) 481, 10 R.P.R. (2d) 281 (Gen.Div.) leave to appeal to S.C.C. refused (1993) 14 O.R. (3d) xv (S.C.C.). But see the analysis of the mortgagor's duties when exercising a power of sale, in the text accompanying notes 109 to 116, *infra*.

83 See *Re Allen's Danforth Theatre, supra*, note 80. Other details of the mortgagor's responsibilities are reviewed in *Capsule Investments Ltd. v. Heck, supra*, note 82.

84 As to the general obligations of the receiver, see the text accompanying notes 109 to 116, *infra*.

85 See further *Associated Mortgage Investors v. Roseburgh*, [1925] 3 W.W.R. 505 (Alta.S.C.).

86 See generally *National Trust Co. v. Yellowvest Holdings Ltd.* (1979) 24 O.R. (2d) 11, 98 D.L.R. (3d) 189 (H.C.).

87 See the criteria discussed in *Citibank Canada v. Calgary Auto Centre Ltd.* (1989) 75 C.B.R. (N.S.) 74, 98 A.R. 250, 58 D.L.R. (4th) 447 (Q.B.).

88 From a purely conceptual perspective, 'foreclosure' is an inapt way to describe the perfecting of a security under a land titles charge. Nevertheless, the statutory procedures available for

took the form of a grant in fee simple to the mortgagee that was subject to a proviso for reconveyance once the debt was repaid. The failure to do so meant that the mortgagor's rights to the property were terminated. The potential for hardship that such a stern rule invited eventually aroused the interest of the Chancery. In response, equitable principles emerged that allowed for a redemption of the property even after the due date (the 'law day') had come and gone. However, some limit had to be imposed on this ability to redeem. The mortgagee was entitled to expect that at some stage the security could be realized to the exclusion of the original owner. This was, after all, the very purpose of the security component of the loan; equity was quite prepared to acknowledge this reality. A procedure for terminating – foreclosing – the mortgagor's equity of redemption was thus developed.

The specifics of foreclosure vary quite a bit across the country, though some common themes can be seen. For one thing, the process tends to be cumbersome, and foreclosure actions are often long drawn-out affairs. Generally, the right to commence the foreclosure process arises once the contractual right to redeem is lost to the mortgagor by virtue of a breach of the mortgage. The mortgagee may then seek an order of foreclosure as long as the default continues. The mortgagor is given a wide window of opportunity to redeem, or, alternatively, to transform the proceedings from a foreclosure action into one of sale. In most jurisdictions an order *nisi* of foreclosure is first granted, and this typically establishes the remaining period of redemption and calls for an accounting of the indebtedness (including costs) to be undertaken. In some jurisdictions, the standard order *nisi* may also provide that the property is to be offered for sale. A final order of foreclosure may then issue when the mortgage remains unredeemed (or unsold) for the stated period.[89]

Despite outward appearances, a final order of foreclosure does not put the mortgagor's interest past the point of no return; even at this juncture an application may be launched to set aside or stay the order.[90] The maxim 'once a mortgage always a mortgage' has great staying-power.[91] The survival of the right to redeem has been explained on the basis that even by obtaining the final order the mortgagee does not take the property in place of the debt. The order merely authorizes that this can be done, such as through a private sale.[92]

The basic principles concerning whether or not to open up a final order should sound familiar.[93] It has been said, for instance, that a court is "always ready

---

these charges resemble the conventional action for foreclosure and the differences are largely nominal: see further *Colonial Investment & Loan Co. v. King* (1902) 5 Terr.L.R. 371 (N.W.T.S.C.).

89 Immediate foreclosure is sometimes possible in Alberta: see further F.C.R. Price & M.J. Trussler, *Mortgage Actions in Alberta* (Calgary: Carswell, 1985) at 142*ff.*

90 In Alberta, see *Judicature Act*, R.S.A. 1980, c. J-1, s. 18.

91 See further *Petranik v. Dale*, [1977] 2 S.C.R. 959, 69 D.L.R. (3d) 411.

92 See *Davidson v. Sharpe* (1920) 60 S.C.R. 72, [1920] 1 W.W.R. 888, 52 D.L.R. 186.

93 See the review of the Canadian authorities in J.T. Robertson, "The Folly of Foreclosure Absolute and the Problem of Unjust Enrichment" (1988) 23 U.B.C.L.Rev. 301, at 307*ff.* See also *Marriott & Dunn, Practice in Mortgage Remedies in Ontario*, 5th ed., G.W. Dunn & W.S. Gray, eds. (Toronto: Carswell, 1991) at paras. 15.12 to 15.14.

to hear a meritorious application for relief against a foreclosure, and will open it whenever good and substantial reasons for such a course are [shown]".[94] However, it has also been offered that a final order should be re-opened "cautiously and only under circumstances of severe hardship to the mortgagor".[95] The factors that typically affect a court of equity in granting relief are relevant here. A delay by the mortgagor must normally be explained. Furthermore, equity will not act in vain: there must be a reasonable prospect that the debt will be paid.[96] The fact that the property is worth significantly more than the mortgage, or that it is of special value to the mortgagor, are relevant factors, but these are not always going to be controlling.[97] If it is not possible to return the mortgagee to the position that existed prior to foreclosure, this may be a telling consideration.[98] And equity will protect a *bona fide* purchaser for value of the legal interest who acquired the property without notice of the mortgagor's foreclosed equitable interest.[99]

The action of foreclosure may affect not only the owner of the land, but also other interest-holders. Imagine a situation in which there are three mortgages on a property. Assume also that the mortgagor defaults under the second mortgage only and that the second mortgagee elects to foreclose. If this action is carried to completion it would have the effect of extinguishing the right to redeem that mortgage. It would also destroy the third mortgage as an interest in land.[100] Foreclosure operates downwards to destroy the equity of redemption and any interests founded on that equity. Conversely, in the scenario set out above, the first mortgage is entirely unscathed by the process, and any new title issuing from the foreclosure of the second mortgage would still be subject to the first. It would not even be necessary for the first mortgagee to be made a party to the foreclosure proceedings.[101] In addition, the third mortgagee would be able to prevent the effects of the foreclosure by paying the amount owing to the second mortgagee, thereby redeeming that mortgage and stepping into the shoes of that mortgagee. In summary, a time-honoured adage of mortgage law reads: redeem up, foreclose down.

---

94 *Dovercourt Land Building & Savings Co. v. Dunvegan Heights Land Co.* (1920) 47 O.L.R. 105 (Chambers) at 108 (*per* Meredith C.J.C.P.). See, *e.g.*, *Platt v. Ashbridge* (1865) 12 Gr. 105 (U.C.Ch.D.). The leading early English authority is *Campbell v. Holyland* (1877) 7 Ch.D. 166.

95 *Canadian Deposit Insurance Corp. v. Greymac Mortgage Corp.* (1991) 2 O.R. (3d) 446 (Gen.Div.) at 453 (*per* Chadwick J.) affirmed (1991) 4 O.R. (3d) 608 (C.A.).

96 *Dand v. MacKenzie*, [1944] O.W.N. 535 (H.C.).

97 See, *e.g.*, *Miles v. Cameron* (1883) 9 P.R. 502 (Ont. Master). The fact that the mortgagor had a substantial equity in the property was pivotal in the decision to re-open a final order in *355498 B.C. Ltd. v. Namu Properties Ltd.* (1999) 171 D.L.R. (4th) 513, 63 B.C.L.R. (3d) 138 (C.A.).

98 But see *Greisman v. Rosenberg* (1918) 13 O.W.N. 382 (H.C.).

99 See further *Alexanian v. Dolinski*, [1968] S.C.R. 473, 67 D.L.R. (2d) 646; *Quill Lake Savings & Credit Union Ltd. v. Luczak*, [1976] 3 W.W.R. 721, 67 D.L.R. (3d) 168 (Sask.Q.B.) affirmed [1976] 5 W.W.R. 597, 69 D.L.R. (3d) 158 (C.A.). To prevent the property from passing to a *bona fide* purchaser for value without notice, a mortgagor endeavouring to re-open the order should register a *lis pendens* on title, as was done in *Pacific Savings & Mortgage Corp. v. Can-Corp. Development Ltd.* (1982) 37 B.C.L.R. 42, [1982] 4 W.W.R. 239, 135 D.L.R. (3d) 623 (C.A.).

100 But see *Wasyl Holdings Ltd. v. Allarie* (1981) 31 A.R. 275 (Q.B.).

101 *Union Trust Co. v. Duplat* (1908) 7 W.L.R. 459 (Sask.T.D.).

(e)   sale[102]

It is the right of sale of the mortgaged lands that, in the end, is often the mechanism that winds up being used to obtain the money due under a mortgage in default. The other rights of the mortgagee are best understood as ancillary to sale. The taking of possession or the appointment of a receiver may be useful as interim measures, and the resumption of possession can allow a sale of the property with vacant possession. Bringing foreclosure proceedings is, functionally, only a preliminary step for the institutional lender, leading ultimately to a sale to liquidate the property.

Foreclosure is a blunt instrument – it is bound either to over- or under-compensate the lender. For this reason the ability of a court to order a sale in lieu of foreclosure was introduced into English law in the 1850s.[103] Just as with foreclosure, the rules for court-ordered sales are somewhat different across Canada. However, the essence of all the schemes is that there is a judicial power either to pursue a judicial sale or to convert a foreclosure action into one allowing for sale, frequently with foreclosure as a backstop if the attempt to sell fails.

Special procedures have been developed in Alberta. In foreclosure proceedings the long-standing practice has been to grant a 'Rice order'.[104] It works this way: the land is first offered for sale by tender. The mortgagee does not normally bid. If no acceptable tender is received the mortgagee can then present a proposal to the court to purchase the property, based on an appraisal. If this offer is regarded as reasonable it is usually endorsed, subject to the condition that the other interested parties are given a period of time (such as two months) to produce a better offer. If this does not happen, the mortgagee's proposal is either accepted or is made subject to a further application. This standard approach has been modified somewhat in recent years. It is now possible to obtain an order allowing the mortgagee to purchase the land without offering the property for sale, if a Rice order, or some variation, would likely be futile. Flexibility is now the order of the day.[105]

The right to sell can be so advantageous that it is sometimes inserted as a term of the mortgage. The ability of the mortgagee to sell off the mortgagor's equity has withstood the challenge that this amounts to a clog on the equity of redemption, at least as long as it is conditioned (as it invariably is) on the default of the mortgagor.[106] In Alberta, this extra-judicial power of sale has been severely

---

102 See further J.A. Carfagnini, "Sale of Property" in F. Bennett, ed., *Bennett on Power of Sale* (Toronto: Carswell, 1997) 159.

103 *Chancery Procedure Amendment Act, 1851*, 14 & 15 Vict., c. 86.

104 See *Trusts & Guarantee Co. v. Rice* (1924) 20 Alta.L.R. 444, [1924] 2 W.W.R. 691, [1924] 3 D.L.R. 352 (C.A.).

105 See *Canada Permanent Trust Co. v. King Art Developments Ltd.* (1984) 32 Alta.L.R. (2d) 1, [1984] 4 W.W.R. 587, 12 D.L.R. (4th) 161 (C.A.) at 645 W.W.R. (*per* Laycraft J.A.). As to the question of the proper price at which the mortgagee should be allowed to purchase the property, see F.C.R. Price, "*Mfr. Life Ins. Co. v. Doan Dev. Corp.*; Rice Orders – A Missed Opportunity" (1989) 65 Alta.L.R. (2d) 50.

106 See also *Ferris v. Nowitskey* (1951) 3 W.W.R. (N.S.) 49, [1952] 1 D.L.R. 721 (Alta.T.D.) affirmed 3 W.W.R. (N.S.) 702, [1952] 1 D.L.R. 754 (C.A.).

limited.[107] In other jurisdictions, such as Ontario, it is commonly invoked, and in that province a contractual power of sale is implied under statute.[108]

The position of the mortgagee seeking a sale is analogous to that of the mortgagee in possession, who, as we saw briefly, must obey a code of conduct when in occupation.[109] I also see the mortgage sale situation as giving rise, potentially at least, to a tragedy-of-the-commons problem.[110] The mortgagee seeking a sale, though motivated by self-interest, is taking action that can affect others. Any proceeds of sale beyond those that are needed to pay off the debt (and any allowable expenses) belong to the mortgagor and the subsequent encumbrancers. Some responsibility must therefore be assumed by the lender to see to it that the other parties with a stake in the sale are not neglected. For those persons, the income from the sale will represent all that remains of their interests.

Therefore, as in the tragedy parable, one finds a number of people with an interest in some form of common property. If a sale is agreed at a price well below what the property should have fetched on the open market this creates losses for all those with an interest in the lands. Yet, if the mortgagee has at least managed to dispose of the property at a price equivalent to his or her own indebtedness, the lost sale value is borne only by the others. Phrased another way, all of the benefits of the sale are hoarded entirely by the selling mortgagee. Therefore, if there are no controls placed on how the sale is conducted there is a risk that the mortgagee with carriage of the sale will not take into account the other affected parties: why bother, especially if this would entail delay, inconvenience, or additional expense?

To motivate the mortgagee to act fairly a number of obligations are imposed. However, the duties assumed remain somewhat ill-defined in Canada. We do know that the mortgagee becomes a bare trustee for any surplus money received, and that the proceeds of sale must be accounted for "fully, promptly, and accurately".[111] In conducting the sale the mortgagee is not a trustee, strictly speaking, but must nevertheless act in good faith. As a general matter that mortgagee is not permitted to purchase the property,[112] and must not "fraudulently, or wilfully, or recklessly sacrifice the property of the mortgagor".[113] Moreover, the applicable duties may be affected by statute or the mortgage.

---

107 See *Co-operative Centre Credit Union Ltd. v. Greba* (1984) 32 Alta.L.R. (2d) 389, 33 R.P.R. 71, 10 D.L.R. (4th) 449 (C.A.).

108 See *Mortgages Act*, R.S.O. 1990, c. M.40, s. 24. The original statutory implication was introduced in *Lord Cranworth's Act, 1860* , 23 & 24 Vict., c. 145. See the discussion in Ontario Law Reform Commission, *Report on the Law of Mortgages* (Toronto: A.G. (Ont.), 1987) at ch. 8, *passim*. Since mortgages in Ontario normally include an express power of sale, the implied power is of little practical consequence: J.E. Roach, *The Canadian Law of Mortgages of Land* (Markham, Ont.: Butterworths, 1993) at 132-3.

109 See Part 4(c), *supra*.

110 See Part 3(b)(ii), Chapter 1.

111 *Beatty v. O'Connor* (1884) 5 O.R. 747 (Ch.D.) at 748 (*per* Boyd C.).

112 See, *e.g.*, *Cummings v. Semerad* (1908) 2 Alta.L.R. 82, 8 W.L.R. 644 (S.C., Chambers). *Cf. London & British North America Co. v. Haigh* (1921) 15 Sask.L.R. 71, [1922] 1 W.W.R. 172, 62 D.L.R. 592 (Chambers).

113 *Kennedy v. De Trafford*, [1896] 1 Ch. 762 (C.A.) at 772 (*per* Lindley L.J.) affirmed [1897]

So much is clear. Many Canadian courts go further than this, by demanding, all else being equal, that a level of prudence or diligence be present.[114] Opposing this position is the view, recently reiterated by the Privy Council, that the tort of negligence has no role to play when equitable principles are involved, and that the duty, properly understood, is one of good faith.[115] Yet, even here it was acknowledged by the Board that once a sale is undertaken, an obligation arises to take reasonable care to obtain a proper price. In this way, the apparently discrete ideas of good faith and due diligence (whatever the latter concept's juridical source) converge.[116] In addition, Canadian cases can be found which support the right of a mortgagee to elect the time of sale;[117] others deny that the lender has that much discretion.[118] In any event, the principles of good faith and diligence do not apply to a sale made after a final order of foreclosure. By that time the foreclosing party is the owner of the land,[119] so there is no longer a duty owed to others, and there is no requirement to account for any notional surplus.

A.C. 180 (H.L.) quoted in *Aldrich v. Canada Permanent Loan & Savings Co.* (1897) 24 O.A.R. 193 (C.A.) at 195.

114 For instance, MacLennan J.A. in *Aldrich, ibid.*, went on to say: "Recklessly means carelessly, negligently, and if there be negligence and want of proper care and precaution and if that is followed by a sacrifice of the interest of the mortgagor, then according to all the authorities, the mortgagee is answerable for the loss and must make it good". See also *Prentice v. Consolidated Bank* (1886) 13 O.A.R. 69 (C.A.); *McHugh v. Union Bank of Canada*, [1913] A.C. 299, 3 W.W.R. 1052, 10 D.L.R. 562 (P.C.) (which deals with a chattel mortgage). See further the review of Canadian authorities in J.E. Roach, *The Canadian Law of Mortgages of Land, supra*, note 108, at 130ff. The English standard bearer for this point of view has for the last 30 years been *Cuckmere Brick Co. Ltd. v. Mutual Finance Ltd.*, [1971] Ch. 949, [1971] 2 All E.R. 633 (C.A.). Cf. *J. & W. Investments Ltd. v. Black* (1963) 38 D.L.R. (2d) 251, 41 W.W.R. 577 (B.C.C.A.).

115 *Downsview Nominees Ltd. v. First City Corp. Ltd.*, [1993] A.C. 295, 148 N.R. 47 (P.C.); *Yorkshire Bank Plc. v. Hall*, [1999] 1 W.L.R. 1713 (C.A.). See also P. Butt, *Land Law*, 3rd ed. (Sydney: Law Book Co., 1996) at 600ff. The *Downsview* case is referred to with apparent approval in *Levy-Russell Ltd. v. Tecmotiv Inc.* (1994) 13 B.L.R. (2d) 1, 54 C.P.R. (3d) 161, [1994] O.J. No. 650 (Gen.Div.).

116 See *Medforth v. Blake*, [1999] 3 W.L.R. 922, [1999] 3 All E.R. 97 (C.A.). Although the case deals with receivers, it is clear from the judgment that the reasoning is treated as applicable to mortgagees exercising a power of sale. See also *Banque Nationale du Canada v. Desrosiers* (1996) 167 N.B.R. (2d) 241, 427 A.P.R. 241 (C.A.) which does not cite the *Downsview* case, *supra*, note 115. Should mortgagees be treated as fiduciaries *qua* mortgagors in default? Perhaps so: see P. Devonshire, "The Mortgagee as Fiduciary: Comparative Perspectives on an Emerging Doctrine" in P. Jackson & D.C. Wilde, eds., *The Reform of Property Law* (Aldershot, Eng.: Ashgate Dartmouth, 1997) 264.

117 See, *e.g.*, *Rhonmont Properties Ltd. v. Canadian Imperial Bank of Commerce*, [1999] O.J. No. 2775 (S.C.J.); *Canada Trustco Mortgage Co. v. Simon* (1997) 36 O.T.C. 52, [1997] O.J. No. 3110 (Gen.Div.).

118 See *Canada Trustco Mortgage Co. v. Windsor Painting Contractors Ltd.* (1991) 22 R.P.R. (2d) 222 (Ont.Gen.Div.), which quotes *Cuckmere, supra*, note 114, but goes on to hold that the mortgagee in possession must act prudently in deciding *when* to sell.

119 See *Municipal Savings & Loan Corp. v. Wilson* (1981) 127 D.L.R. (3d) 127, 20 R.P.R. 188 (Ont.C.A.).

(f)   the interrelationship of remedies

The battery of remedies available to a mortgagee is impressive, even if some are more useful than others in practice. How do they mesh together? There is no obstacle to the mortgagee relying on any or all possible remedies contemporaneously. Accordingly, to take a clear example, it is possible to obtain sale of the property, while retaining the right to sue on the personal covenant for any portion of the debt not recovered through the sale.

While all of the remedies may be pursued, following one course of action can wind up precluding others. The lender may go into possession while requesting the appointment of a receiver, but as both are directed at siphoning off income generated by the property, they seem mutually exclusive.[120] Of course, both are impossible after a sale of the property. Obtaining an order of foreclosure has the most dramatic effect of all. After a sale, the amount of continuing indebtedness can be easily reckoned, so it makes sense to allow the personal action, even if the mortgagee is the purchaser.[121] However, the amount of the remaining indebtedness is uncertain after foreclosure, because at that stage the borrower has only the mud, but no money. Consequently, it would be unfair to allow the mortgagee to sue on the covenant for the money still owing. What amount could a court possibly award? Accordingly, at common law such a suit on the personal covenant is tenable only if the mortgagor is once again given the opportunity to redeem.[122] In some jurisdictions this type of action has been removed. In Alberta, for example, the final order of foreclosure extinguishes liability under the personal covenant.[123]

(g)   relief from acceleration, etc.

As a general matter the ability of the mortgagee to continue on a campaign of enforcement is predicated on the ongoing default of the mortgagor. That mortgagor might be able to gain a respite by paying the arrears, plus the costs associated with the default, thereby restoring the debt to good standing. However, mortgages frequently provide that on default the entire indebtedness becomes due, or is 'accelerated'. With the full debt thundering down on the mortgagor the ability to rectify the deficiency is obviously going to be impeded. One response would be for the borrower to refinance, that is, to obtain a second loan to pay off the first. Judicial relief from acceleration may also be available. For instance, the governing provision in Alberta provides that a court shall[124] grant relief from the

---

120 See *North American Trust Co. v. Consumers' Gas Co.* (1997) 34 O.R. (3d) 35, 10 R.P.R. (3d) 1, 147 D.L.R. (4th) 645 (C.A.).

121 See *Canada Permanent Trust Co. v. King Art Developments Ltd.*, *supra*, note 105.

122 See *Dashwood v. Blythway* (1729) 1 Eq.Cas.Ab. 317, 21 E.R. 1072; *Royal Bank v. McLeod* (1919) 27 B.C.R. 376, [1919] 3 W.W.R. 544, 48 D.L.R. 500 (C.A.). See generally *Mutual Life Assurance Co. v. Douglas* (1918) 57 S.C.R. 243, [1918] 3 W.W.R. 529, 44 D.L.R. 115.

123 Under Alberta law, an order of foreclosure "operates as full satisfaction of the debt secured by the mortgage or encumbrance": *Law of Property Act*, R.S.A. 1980, c. L-8, para. 44(1)(a). See also Law Reform Commission of British Columbia, *Report on Mortgages: Judicial Sales and Deficiency Claims* (Vancouver: L.R.C.B.C.,1991); Roach, *supra*, note 108, at 168*ff.*

124 The language has a mandatory tone about it, and intentionally so, according to *Kolacz v. Munzel*, [1971] 5 W.W.R. 757 (Alta.T.D.) at 759.

consequences of a breach when the mortgagor remedies the breach or pays all arrears owing, together with any lawfully incurred expenses.[125]

Accelerating the payment of the entire amount owing can be a two-edged sword. Indeed, there may be times when the mortgagor is quite content to see the mortgagee resort to this remedy. If it so happens that interest rates are declining, and alternative cheaper financing is available, mortgagors may intentionally default in the hope that the mortgagee will seek to accelerate the indebtedness. The mortgagor is then served up a chance to redeem. And, once the mortgagee has truly demanded full payment, there is no turning back; the mortgagor is entitled to redeem.[126]

5.   TO THE AID OF THE CONSUMER

(a)   generally

Throughout this chapter we have seen the ways that equity assists the mortgagor. A look at the broader picture reveals that the specifics of mortgage law represent one part of a spectrum of protections that are available to those who assume obligations to repay a loan, whether secured or unsecured. The usurious nature of lending adds a further dimension to the policies that have influenced the regulation of loans secured by a mortgage.[127] Exacting an interest payment as part of a loan transaction is no longer regarded as wrongful, and indeed anyone holding an interest-bearing bank account is engaging in the practice. Even so, an element of circumspection still attends this type of commercial activity. This has prompted legislative measures aimed at providing protection to consumers against (i) loan sharking;[128] (ii) other types of unconscionable transactions;[129] and, more generally, (iii) the unappreciated consequences of loan agreements. This latter concern has prompted the imposition of obligations on lenders to disclose certain terms of the loan to the borrower.[130] These measures are a patchwork of federal and provincial laws that are designed to supplement the protections available under the general law of contract.

---

125 See further *Law of Property Act*, R.S.A. 1980, c. L-8, sub. 39(1).

126 *Fort McMurray Housing Inc. v. Sun Communities Alberta Ltd. Partnership* (1998) 58 Alta.L.R. (3d) 58, 15 R.P.R. (3d) 149, [1998] 6 W.W.R. 750 (Q.B.). *Cf. Central Trust Co. v. Dunne* (1984) 49 Nfld. & P.E.I.R. 28, 145 A.P.R. 28 (Nfld.C.A.).

127 Early usury control laws in Canada are reviewed in M.A. Waldron, *The Law of Interest in Canada* (Toronto: Carswell, 1992) at 5*ff.*

128 *Criminal Code*, R.S.C. 1985, c. C-46, s. 347. The Code criminalizes loans at an interest rate of more than 60% per annum. The origins and ambit of this provision are discussed in Waldron, *supra*, note 127, at 60-72.

129 See, *e.g.*, *Unconscionable Transactions Act*, R.S.A. 1980, c. U-2. See also *Canadian Imperial Bank of Commerce v. Ohlson* (1997) 57 Alta.L.R. (3d) 213, [1998] 6 W.W.R. 115, 154 D.L.R. (4th) 33 (C.A.).

130 See further R.H. Bowes, "Annual Percentage Rate Disclosure in Canadian Cost of Credit Disclosure Laws" (1997) 29 Can.Bus.L.J. 183.

(b)   the Canada Interest Act

Central to the regime governing fairness in mortgage lending is the *Canada Interest Act*.[131] The Act does not attempt to fix a general maximum rate of interest.[132] Instead, it is designed mainly to promote full disclosure of the liability for interest assumed by a borrower. The Act provides that when interest is to be paid, a rate of 5% is set unless otherwise specified.[133] When the mortgage debt is to be repaid through blended payments of principal and interest, there is no liability for interest unless the mortgage contains a statement showing the principal owing and the interest charged, calculated yearly or half-yearly and not in advance.[134] When the interest contained in that statement is less than the amount contained elsewhere in the mortgage, only the lesser amount can be charged.[135]

Section 8 of the Act imposes a substantive restriction on the ability of a mortgagee to receive an interest bonus, or impose fines or penalties. This protection is similar to one found in equity.[136] The section provides as follows:

> 8(1) No fine, penalty or rate of interest shall be stipulated for, taken, reserved or exacted on any arrears of principal or interest secured by mortgage on real property, that has the effect of increasing the charge on the arrears beyond the rate of interest payable on principal money not in arrears.

> (2) Nothing in this section has the effect of prohibiting a contract for the payment of interest on arrears of interest or principal at any rate not greater than the rate payable on principal money not in arrears.

Under what is called a 'closed' mortgage, the borrower is not entitled to pay off the principal sum totally before the maturity date of the mortgage has arrived. However, it is a common practice for a closed mortgage to allow the mortgagor the right to terminate the mortgage early by providing adequate notice, and paying an additional interest charge, normally amounting to three or six months worth of interest. These terms do not violate section 8 because they are designed to provide some compensation for the lender who has agreed to accept such a payment instead of demanding the interest that would otherwise accrue over the full term of the loan.[137] Moreover, section 8 is not infringed by an acceleration clause that calls for all money owing to be immediately payable in the event of a

---

131 R.S.C. 1985, c. I-15 [as am.].

132 In fact, subject to other controls, the right to set mortgage rates is declared in s. 2.

133 S. 3. The meaning given to this provision is more fully explained in Waldron, *supra*, note 127, at 80*ff*.

134 S. 7. See further M.A. Waldron, "The Federal Interest Act: It Sure is Broke, But is it Worth Fixin'?" (1997) 29 Can.Bus.L.J. 161, at 169*ff*.

135 S. 7. An analysis of the jurisprudence under (the old) s. 6, and s. 7 of the *Canada Interest Act* can be found in M.A. Waldron, "Sections 6 and 7 of the Canada Interest Act: Curiouser and Curiouser" (1984) 62 Can.B.Rev. 146. See also s. 10, and the analysis of that provision in *Royal Trust Co. v. Potash*, [1986] 2 S.C.R. 351, 41 R.P.R. 197, 31 D.L.R. (4th) 321, and M.A. Waldron, "Section 10 of the Interest Act: All the King's Men" (1988) 13 Can.Bus. L.J. 468.

136 The equitable position is summarized Butt, *supra*, note 115, at 547*ff*.

137 *O'Shanter Development Co. v. Gentra Canada Investments Inc.* (1995) 25 O.R. (3d) 188, 47 R.P.R. (2d) 24 (Div.Ct.).

default. What the section does preclude is the lumbering of an additional interest charge that comes into play on default.[138] To provide that the rate of interest is 10% while the loan is in good standing, but 12% on default, contravenes the section.

The neat question has always been this: is a mortgage that allows a *reduced* rate of interest for *timely payment* contrary to the statute? In other words, is this equivalent, in substance, to a penalty for tardiness? Assume, for example, that the mortgage requires a rate of interest of 10% per annum, but allows for a rebate (say of 1%) if all payments are made on time. One mode of analysis, with a long pedigree,[139] suggests that in the case of default the 10% is due, as agreed, and that therefore no penalty is being imposed. The contrary position, which also enjoys judicial support, and which seems more consonant with the real substance of the transaction, recognizes that this arrangement produces a higher rate of interest when there is a default than when there is not, which is the very mischief at which section 8 is directed.[140]

6. OTHER TYPES OF SECURITY ARRANGEMENTS

(a) pledges, charges, liens

The term 'security' refers to an arrangement under which a creditor can obtain a right over an object of property that is exercisable in some way in the event that an obligation is not fulfilled by the debtor. The mortgage of land is the best example. However, the brief outline of the history of the mortgage showed that there are other security forms that can be created. One is the *pledge* which, generally, involves a loan secured by the lender taking possession of an object, such as when goods are left with a pawnbroker. Another is the *charge*, which imposes an encumbrance on the property but which does not otherwise involve a transfer of title to the holder of the security. As we have seen, in Alberta a registered mortgage of land is regarded as a charge.[141]

Another commonly found type of security is the *lien*, which is an embracing concept with legal, equitable, contractual, and statutory forms.[142] The common

---

138 See, *e.g.*, *Mascan Corp. v. March Investments Inc.* (1988) 57 Alta.L.R. (2d) 237, 89 A.R. 1 (Q.B.); *Dickson v. Bluestein* (1990) 2 O.R. (3d) 131, 16 R.P.R. (2d) 29 (Gen.Div.). A claim for compound interest on default was held not to violate the Act in *C.I.B.C. Mortgage Corp. v. Duguay* (1991) 49 C.P.C. (2d) 129 (B.C. Master).

139 See, *e.g.*, *Strode v. Parker* (1694) 2 Vern. 315, 23 E.R. 804. See further A.C. Meredith, ''A Nicety in the Law of Mortgages'' (1916) 32 L.Q.R. 420.

140 See, *e.g.*, *Re Weirdale Investments Ltd. and Canadian Imperial Bank of Commerce* (1981) 32 O.R. (2d) 183, 121 D.L.R. (3d) 150 (H.C.). See also *Industrial Life Management Co. v. Kings Mount Holdings Ltd.* (1988) 26 B.C.L.R. (2d) 246 (C.A.). *Cf. North West Life Assurance Co. of Canada v. Kings Mount Holdings Ltd.* (1987) 15 B.C.L.R. (2d) 376 (C.A.). See also the analysis in *Patrician Land Corp. v. Dillingham Construction Ltd.* (1985) 37 Alta.L.R. (2d) 193, 36 R.P.R. 136, [1985] 4 W.W.R. 468 (C.A.). See generally Waldron, *supra*, note 127, at 85*ff*, where the authorities are reviewed.

141 See Part 2, *supra*.

142 See generally Alberta Law Reform Institute, *Report on Liens* (Edmonton: A.L.R.I., 1992); A.P. Bell, *The Modern Law of Personal Property in England and Ireland* (London: Butterworths, 1989) ch. 6.

law recognized that it was often appropriate to allow creditors to retain possession of an object as a way of providing security for the payment of money owing. For example, innkeepers, common carriers, sea carriers, and salvors are afforded such liens by the common law. Further, an artificer who improves the goods (other than by mere repair or maintenance[143]) enjoys a lien for the authorized work that has been performed. Liens can also arise as a matter of trade usage,[144] through an express contractual term, or under statute.[145]

The liens recognized by the common law are 'particular', relating to the very goods for which a service has been rendered. 'General' liens, which can arise under contract, trade usage or statute, permit a lien to be imposed over other property of the debtor. Normally, a lien over personalty arises when the creditor takes possession,[146] and as a general rule, it survives only as long as that possession is retained.[147] The possessory lien arising by operation of the common law allows the debtor to hold the goods hostage until the amount owing is paid.[148] But there is no inherent right to sell the items. A power of sale can be inserted to bolster a contractual lien; is implicit in some liens arising through trade usage;[149] or may be conferred by statute. Equity can impose both liens and charges as part of its available stock of remedies. For example, on the sale of real property an equitable vendor's lien will be implied for the outstanding indebtedness of the full purchase price, and the existence of this security right is not dependent on the vendor retaining possession.[150] A purchaser of real estate holds a lien to protect money that has been laid down as a deposit.[151] Under statute,[152] a builder's lien (sometimes called a mechanic's lien) is available to secure payments for improvements or repairs made to land.[153] The rationale here is, quite simply, that "the land which

---

143 See, *e.g.*, *Hatton v. Car Maintenance Co.*, [1915] 1 Ch. 621, [1911-13] All E.R.Rep. 890.

144 For example, the solicitor's lien is said to have arisen in this way: see *Cowell v. Simpson* (1809) 16 Ves. 275, 33 E.R. 989.

145 See, *e.g.*, *Livery Stable Keepers Act*, R.S.A. 1980, c. L-20.

146 Some statutory liens are non-possessory: see, *e.g.*, *Garagemen's Lien Act*, R.S.A. 1980, c. G-1. Under this Act, the lien must be registered to be effective. In 1991, 12,604 liens were registered in Alberta: *Report on Liens*, *supra*, note 142, at 13. Compare the situation in Prince Edward Island, reviewed in *McGowan Motors Ltd. (Receivership) v. Hughes (J. Gary) Inc.* (1999) 174 Nfld. & P.E.I.R. 194, 533 A.P.R. 194, 45 B.L.R. (2d) 188 (P.E.I.C.A.).

147 See, *e.g.*, *Re Lehner* (1985) 4 P.P.S.A.C. 254, 38 Sask.R. 95 (Q.B.). But see *J.H. Early Motor Co. v. Siekawitch*, [1931] 3 W.W.R. 521 (Sask.C.A.).

148 See, *e.g.*, *Possessory Liens Act*, R.S.A. 1980, c. P-13.

149 See, *e.g.*, *Jones v. Davidson Partners Ltd.* (1981) 31 O.R. (2d) 494, 1 P.P.S.A.C. 242, 121 D.L.R. (3d) 127 (H.C.) where it was said that a stockbroker's lien carries with it a power of sale.

150 See, *e.g.*, *Silaschi v. 1054473 Ontario Ltd.* (1998) 20 R.P.R. (3d) 320 (Ont.Gen.Div.). See also *Laidlaw v. Vaughan-Rhys* (1911) 44 S.C.R. 458 leave to appeal refused (1911) 44 S.C.R. ix (P.C.).

151 See *Whitbread & Co. v. Watt*, [1902] 1 Ch. 835 (C.A.).

152 Builder's liens are not tenable at common law: *Johnson v. Crew* (1836) 5 U.C.Q.B. (o.s.) 200.

153 See, *e.g.*, *Builders' Lien Act*, R.S.A. 1980, c. B-12. See further D.N. Macklem & D.I. Bristow, *Construction Builders' and Mechanics' Liens in Canada*, 6th ed. (Looseleaf, Carswell, 1990).

receives the benefit [should] bear the burden".[154] Like the vendor's lien, a person holding a builder's lien does not need to assume possession.

(b)   other forms of personal property security[155]

There are a host of other ways in which commercial and consumer transactions concerning personal property can involve a secured element.[156] A *chattel mortgage* can be given under which legal title is held by the lender as security (as in a land mortgage). Property may be sold by means of a *conditional sales agreement*: here, title does not pass until the full purchase price is paid.[157] This is similar to a device popular in England (but much less so here), the *hire-purchase agreement*. Under that type of agreement goods are hired by a lessee who is given an option to purchase the goods (usually for a nominal amount) at the end of the hiring term. If the rental payments are not made the lessor can repossess the goods.

A creditor may hold a security known as a *floating charge*. This instrument does not immediately attach to specific assets. Rather it hovers over designated goods until default or some other event occurs (such as the debtor ceasing to carry on business), at which time the charge crystallizes and fixes on the available assets. The floating charge is an ideal device to use to obtain security interests over goods that form part of a borrower's inventory.[158] Another commonly used form of security involves the lender taking an *assignment of book debts* from the borrower. Under this method the lender obtains a right to enforce the accounts receivable of the person to whom funds have been advanced by that lender.

(c)   modern personal property security law

The general law governing secured interests in personalty has been described as "conceptually inconsistent, administratively inefficient and unnecessarily complex".[159] The devices listed above generate discrete legal issues and may be governed by different registration requirements and enforcement rules. The modern approach, now the predominant one in Canada, is to collect these diverse

---

154 *Scratch v. Anderson* (1909) 11 Alta.L.R. 55, [1917] 1 W.W.R. 1340, 33 D.L.R. 620 (C.A.) at 1342 W.W.R. (*per* Harvey J.) affirmed (*sub nom. Limoges v. Scratch*) (1910) 44 S.C.R. 86.

155 A detailed analysis of this topic is beyond the scope of this introductory work. For further reading, see R.H. McLaren, *Personal Property Security: An Introductory Analysis*, 5th ed. (Toronto: Carswell, 1992); R.C.C. Cuming & R.J. Wood, *Alberta Personal Property Security Act Handbook*, 4th ed. (Toronto: Carswell, 1998); R.J. Wood, ed. *An Introduction to the Personal Property Security Act of Alberta* (Edmonton: Alta.L.Rev., 1990).

156 The efficiency arguments underlying secured transactions are assessed in J.J. White, "Efficiency Justifications for Personal Property Security", 37 Vand.L.Rev. 473 (1984).

157 In England, the courts have recognized a security interest created by a 'reservation of title' clause, sometimes referred to as a 'Romalpa' clause, after the leading authority endorsing its validity: see *Aluminium Industrie Vaassen B.V. v. Romalpa Aluminium Ltd.*, [1976] 1 W.L.R. 676, [1976] 2 All E.R. 552 (C.A.) at 557. As to the general nature of such a clause, see Bell, *supra*, note 142, at 202*ff*.

158 See further R.J. Wood, "The Floating Charge in Canada" (1989) 27 Alta.L.Rev. 191.

159 R.C.C. Cuming, "The Scope of the Alberta Personal Property Security Act" in *An Introduction to the Personal Property Security Act of Alberta, supra*, note 155, at 15.

forms of security within a single system, one designed to provide a generic form of security interest to be governed by a uniform code.[160]

For example, the Alberta *Personal Property Security Act* applies:

(a) to every transaction that in substance creates a security interest, without regard to its form and without regard to the person who has title to the collateral, and

(b) without limiting the generality of clause (a), [the Act also applies] to a chattel mortgage, conditional sale, floating charge, pledge, trust indenture, trust receipt, assignment, consignment, lease, trust, and transfer of chattel paper where they secure payment or performance of an obligation.[161]

For transactions caught within this wide net there is a common mode of registration. The new laws endeavour to respond to current commercial reality, abolishing the obsolete trappings of nineteenth century English commercial practice, and replacing these with a system that is supposed to meet the contemporary needs of consumers and lenders in this country. The purpose of the reforms is to promote efficiency by reducing the costs inherent in an uncertain system. However, it has to be said that the Canadian developments do not (yet) fully reach this goal: certain security transactions under federal law are not covered;[162] some provinces have not opted for these reforms; and there is not complete symmetry among the P.P.S.A. statutes presently in force in Canada.[163]

---

160 The Canadian laws are based principally on Article 9 of the American Law Institute's *Uniform Commercial Code*. See generally B. Clark, *The Law of Secured Transactions under the Uniform Commercial Code*, 2nd ed. (Boston: Warren, Gorman & Lamont, 1988).

161 *Personal Property Security Act*, S.A. 1988, c. P-4.05, paras. 3(1)(a) and (b).

162 See *Bank Act*, S.C. 1991, c. 46, s. 427.

163 J.S. Ziegel, "The New Personal Property Regimes: Have We Gone Too Far?" in *An Introduction to the Personal Property Security Act of Alberta, supra*, note 155, 191, at 192.

12

PRIORITIES AND REGISTRATION

It is a maxim, that those to whom everybody allows the
second place have undoubted title to the first.

Jonathan Swift

1. INTRODUCTION

This chapter examines the basic rules and policies governing priorities and
registration. The need to rank competing interests emerges naturally in a property
regime that stresses the relativity of title and allows an unlimited number of
interests to be created over the same tract of land. The rules considered below are
those that are used to assess the strengths and weaknesses of claims and to place
these entitlements in order. The significance of the relative ordering of interests
should already be appreciated. In Chapter 4 the law of finders was used to
demonstrate that ownership is a relational concept. In Chapter 11 we saw how
the priority of mortgages will affect the foreclosure process and determine which
secured creditors will prevail over others.

Systems of registration are sometimes thought of as providing a thin procedural veneer that covers the substantive law of property. This is a fairly apt
description because the rules here presuppose existing entitlements and seek to
determine only how these stand in relation to each other. At this stage in the text,
now that basic substantive interests have been presented, this procedural overlay
is described. At the same time, we will see that registration and priority regimes
can actually affect rights – in a substantial way – by postponing some interests
and thereby advancing others.

The composition of the rules of priority is influenced partially by considerations of fairness, stemming from the idea that 'first in time is first in right'.[1] Yet
other values are also encased in the law. In the introductory chapter it was
suggested that a principal aim of property doctrine is to facilitate private dealings
and that one of the means of doing so is to reduce the costs of property transactions.[2] The more complete the relevant information, and the more accessible this
is to the parties, the greater the likelihood that effective and informed bargaining
will take place. Furthering efficient negotiations, or, more generally, minimizing
transaction costs, is a central aim of registration systems.[3]

All sales, whether of goods or land, involve some element of risk. In a typical
house purchase there are a number of concerns that have to be addressed: Is the

---

1 See Part 3(g), Chapter 1.
2 See Part 4(b), Chapter 1.
3 See further J.T. Janczyk, "An Economic Analysis of the Land Titles System for Transferring
  Real Property", 6 J.Leg.Stud. 213 (1977).

structure sound? Are the walls filled with some toxic form of insulation? Do the neighbours like to listen to acid rock?[4] Some of these worries can be dealt with by doing a physical inspection or making a few discreet inquiries. Likewise, various questions about the legal state of affairs are normally addressed: Does the seller actually own the property? Are there any encumbrances? The rules presented here are concerned with the ways in which the legal risks, and the costs associated with them, are spread.

The basic idea of risk allocation can be succinctly explained. A centuries-old principle of property law is captured by the phrase *nemo dat quod non habet*, which means – one cannot give that which one does not have. The maxim states a seller cannot confer a greater title than that which he or she holds. When this rule applies the buyer must determine if the seller can confer good title; the buyer assumes this risk. Consider, for example, the sale of a chattel from B to C. If shortly after this sale, A appears on the scene with a superior right to the property, C will lose the item to A.[5] C may have a right to sue B for damages, but B's claim to the object, her right *in rem*, is gone. In short, the security of title of the prior owner (A) is protected by the *nemo dat* rule. Therefore, the buyer must proceed with caution, by making inquiries about the seller or by attempting to trace the root of title; this, in turn, generates transaction costs.

The *nemo dat* rule is so sensible that it would not seem to require a Latin brocard. The key to understanding its significance lies in the fact that this obvious tenet of fairness is subject to a number of exceptions: there *are* times when one can confer more than one actually owns! These exceptions exist because the law occasionally places facility of transfer ahead of the security of title of a prior owner.[6] A legal system might provide, for instance, that if C buys property from B, innocently unaware of A's superior claim, C will prevail.[7] In sum, the rules that are examined below seek to respond to issues of justice and efficiency. They are aimed at preventing wrongful dealings, while also attempting to spread the risks in an efficient and fair way.

To the practising solicitor involved in real estate work, a sound familiarity with the rules of land registration is of the utmost importance. The first stage in that process is to understand the rudiments, and accordingly this concluding chapter, in line with the others, paints a broad brush picture of the major issues and policies. Models will be used to describe the various approaches found in common law Canada, with the law of Alberta furnishing the main examples. This

---

4 Or, is the attic infested with bats? See *Kirby v. Walker*, [1998] O.J. No. 1095 (Gen.Div.).

5 This conclusion is subject to the possibility that A's claim is statute-barred: see Part 3, Chapter 4.

6 See further *Bishopgate Motor Finance Corp. v. Transport Brakes Ltd.*, [1949] 1 K.B. 322, [1949] 1 All E.R. 37 (C.A.) at 336-7 K.B. (*per* Denning L.J., as he then was): "In the development of our law, two principles have striven for mastery. The first is for the protection of property: no one can give a better title than [s(he)] . . . possesses. The second is for the protection of commercial transactions: the person who takes in good faith and for value without notice should get a good title. The first principle has held sway for a long time, but it has been modified by the common law itself and by statute so as to meet the needs of our own times."

7 See further G.H.L. Fridman, *The Sale of Goods in Canada*, 3rd ed. (Toronto: Carswell, 1986) ch. 6, "Sales Without Title", *passim*.

allows the primary questions of policy to be confronted. It must be remembered, however, that the resolution of these issues differs across the country.[8]

2.   AN OVERVIEW OF PRIORITIES AT COMMON LAW AND IN EQUITY

(a)   introduction

Registration serves two related functions: it determines the ordering of rights, and it assists a vendor in demonstrating a valid title on sale. There is no general system of registration under the common law. Instead, a labyrinth of priority rules developed, and facets of these rules remain applicable in some Canadian jurisdictions for land and personalty. Moreover, reviewing the features of the old rules can help explain the impact of the reforms introduced to modify and replace them.

(b)   priorities

Underlying the common law priority rules is the importance of possession as proof of title. Absent other probative evidence, the law protects the competing claimant who is able to show prior possession. This basic point makes sense of the curious ritual described earlier as 'livery of seisin'.[9] In the absence of a registration system, livery provided a palpable manifestation of the transfer of ownership, alerting the community "in a most public way".[10] While livery of seisin has been replaced by the use of paper as a means of exchanging rights of ownership, the transfer of possession still performs a notification function for many personal property transactions.

The rules for the ranking of interests vary depending on whether the competing rights are equitable or legal in nature. That being so, there are four basic factual permutations that can arise. One may have to determine the relative rights of two claimants when: (i) there are two legal interests; (ii) an equitable interest is followed by a legal one; (iii) a legal interest is followed by an equitable one; or (iv) there are two equitable interests.

When two legal interests are involved, priority is based on chronology. The person who is first in time is preferred by the law (*qui prior est tempore, potior est jure*). Therefore, a purported sale of Blackacre by B to C, when title was properly in A, gave C nothing. Here, the *nemo dat* rule governs. The rule allows

---

8   "It is disconcerting to recognize the diversity which characterizes the Canadian legislation in this area of the law": A.H. Oosterhoff & W.B. Rayner, *Anger & Honsberger Law of Real Property*, 2nd ed. (Aurora, Ont.: Canada Law Book, 1985) vol. 2, at 1606. For an earlier gasp of despair, see J.E. Hogg, "Uniformity in Registration of Title Law" (1917) 37 Can.L.T. 374, at 376: "[a] great opportunity has been lost, and the disadvantages of legislation being carried out in a haphazard manner by different legislatures, though the principles underlying it and the objects to be attained are substantially the same, will be clearly seen by some observations on the different systems of registration of title now in force in Canada." But see the reform proposals in Part 6(a), *infra*.

9   See Part 5(a), Chapter 4.

10   T.F.T. Plucknett, *A Concise History of the Common Law*, 5th ed. (London: Butterworth & Co., 1956) at 611.

A to rest comfortably, knowing that no such transaction could destroy or affect the state of title. This rule shouts 'caveat emptor' (buyer beware). Accordingly, C must make sure that B has some worthwhile title to give. C must also be alive to the possibility that some other legal interest affects B's title. If prior to the sale to C, A had been granted a lease, legally perfect in all respects, that right would bind C. Notice would be irrelevant.

When the prior interest is equitable and the subsequent one is legal, the legal claim will sometimes prevail. Equitable rules are not so strongly tied to chronology, though this element can be a significant factor. Equity acts on the conscience of the relevant parties; that is why a *bona fide* purchaser for value of the legal title who buys land without notice of an equitable interest will not be bound by that interest. The good faith purchaser has what we would now call a 'clear conscience', and the presence of such a person can alter the ordering of rights. Assume, for instance, that A, the owner of the legal fee simple of Blackacre, agrees to sell to B. They sign a contract by virtue of which B acquires an equitable interest in the land. Following this, A receives a much more lucrative offer from C, to whom the property is then sold, thereby 'gazumping' the first purchaser, B. Assume finally that there is eventually a conveyance of the legal title to C, who remains unaware of the prior deal. Equity would probably grant C priority, as a *bona fide* purchaser of the legal title taking without notice of the purely equitable interest of B. While B can maintain an action for damages against A, there is no recourse against C to recover the realty. The corollary of this is that if C is *not* a good faith purchaser, B should be given priority.

The '*bona fide* purchaser[11] for value without notice' is treated as the "polar star"[12] of equity, especially in disputes of this type. However, in order to be able to claim this status the full constellation of factors must exist. The element of good faith embraces the absence of notice, but also has a broader connotation. Fraud in the acquisition of that legal interest will destroy this element even if there was no knowledge of the prior equitable right. In short, the requirement of good faith is no more than an application of the maxim 'those who come to equity must come with clean hands'. To be a good faith purchaser, one must not have the grime of unfairness under one's fingernails.

Another maxim underscores the requirement that the subsequent owner must be a purchaser for value: generally speaking, 'equity will not assist a volunteer'. A donee of property might well be disappointed by the discovery that the gift received is less valuable than expected (*i.e.*, because it belongs to someone else), but this will not prompt equitable protection. To qualify as a purchaser, some value, even if below the full market value, must be received, in money or money's worth,[13] and it must actually be provided.[14] One might argue that even a nominal payment might be taken to be sufficient, since this at least provides a bright line

11 This includes a mortgagee, or a tenant; anyone who acquires a legal interest in the property by purchase.

12 *Stanhope v. Verney* (1761) 2 Eden 81, at 85, 28 E.R. 826, at 828 (*per* the Lord Chancellor).

13 The long-standing English authority on point is *Bassett v. Nosworthy* (1673) Rep.temp.Finch 102, 23 E.R. 55. See also *Bondy v. Fox* (1869) 29 U.C.Q.B. 64 (Full Ct.).

14 See *Thomas v. Thomas* (1939) 14 M.P.R. 76, [1939] 4 D.L.R. 202 (N.B.C.A.).

rule as to when the requirement is met. At the same time, it is hard to look at a transaction in which land is sold for $1.00, and not view this as, in substance, a gift.[15] That seems to be the correct treatment based on the older English authorities, and I believe that were a Canadian court to be confronted with such an issue today, it would regard the transfer as gratuitous.[16] Moreover, the sale of property at an inordinately low price might itself be a sign of fraud, which on its own would deny the *bona fide* status of the buyer.

The absence of notice of the rival equitable right at the time the consideration is paid is essential if the legal owner is to enjoy priority. In equity, notice may be (i) actual; (ii) imputed; or (iii) constructive. *Actual notice* means a real knowledge of the circumstances.[17] The reading of the relevant document is the paradigm form. The test of actual notice is a stringent one: it appears that an examination of document X, which refers to document Y, does not normally amount to actual notice of document Y.[18] In addition, knowing that a party is in possession of the property is not generally treated as actual notice of the interest under which that possession is enjoyed.[19] Information conveyed by rumour is also not adequate.

Imputed notice is that which is attributed to a principal through an agent.[20] One is put on *constructive* notice of facts or circumstances that ought to have been appreciated or understood. This is a legal fiction[21] that is designed to promote care on the part of a buyer. In the sale of land, constructive notice may be found when a purchaser would likely have become aware of a relevant fact had all of the normal inquiries been conducted. The chief consideration in determining whether notice should be deemed to exist is whether a prudent person should have made the necessary inquiries in view of the known circumstances. Therefore, constructive notice may be found when some information is available to the purchaser who either deliberately avoids conducting a further investigation or neglects to do so. While knowledge that there is a person in possession is not enough to count as actual notice, it is normally sufficient to impel a purchaser to determine the basis upon which this possession is being enjoyed, and the failure

---

15 See T.W. Mapp, *Torrens' Elusive Title* (Edmonton: Alta.L.Rev., 1978) at 21. See also G.V. La Forest, "The History and Place of the Registry Act in New Brunswick Land Law" (1970) 20 U.N.B.L.J 1, at 7: "I suggest that a nominal consideration might not be enough, for the disproportion between the price and the value of the thing may be so great as to be evidence of fraud". In support of that view, see *Wilkinson v. Conklin* (1860) 10 U.C.C.P. 211.

16 *Cf. 1224948 Ontario Ltd. v. 448332 Ontario Ltd.* (1998) 22 R.P.R. (3d) 200 (Ont.Gen.Div.) at 243, relying on *Carson v. McMahon* (1940) 15 M.P.R. 109, [1940] 4 D.L.R. 249 (N.B.C.A.). See also the reforms discussed in Part 6(a), *infra*.

17 See *Harrington v. Spring Creek Cheese Manufacturing Co.* (1904) 7 O.L.R. 319 (C.A.).

18 *Foster v. Beall* (1868) 15 Gr. 244 (Ont.Ch.D.). See especially *Re Hoback Investments Ltd. and Loblaws Ltd.* (1981) 32 O.R. (2d) 95, 17 R.P.R. 127, 120 D.L.R. (3d) 682 (H.C.) which reviews the authorities. See also *Canadian Imperial Bank of Commerce v. Rockway Holdings Ltd.* (1996) 29 O.R. (3d) 350, 3 R.P.R. (3d) 174 (Gen.Div.) affirmed (1998) 108 O.A.C. 231 (C.A.) and critiqued in J.W. Lem, Annotation (1996) 3 R.P.R. (3d) 174, especially at 178-9.

19 *Grey v. Ball* (1876) 23 Gr. 390 (Ont.Ch.D.).

20 However, no imputation is made if the agent acquires this knowledge while attempting to defraud the principal.

21 "[T]he doctrine is a dangerous one. It is contrary to the truth": *English & Scottish Mercantile Investment Co. v. Brunton*, [1892] 2 Q.B. 700 (C.A.) at 708 (*per* Lord Esher).

to do so will typically lead to a finding that there was constructive notice of that interest.[22]

When a legal interest is followed by an equitable interest, the prior (legal) right will not normally be affected. First in time is first in right, or, as it is sometimes put: 'where the equities are equal, the law will prevail'. However, it is within the realm of possibility that some conduct on the part of the prior holder may preclude that person from asserting a better title, and warrant a postponement of the legal interest in favour of the later equitable one. That might occur, for example, when the holder of legal title has been a party to fraud in the creation of the equitable interest, is guilty of gross negligence affecting that subsequent interest,[23] or has acted in some other way that estops the holder of the earlier legal interest from insisting that the normal ordering should govern. Indeed, all of this postponing conduct can be thought of as being founded on the idea of estoppel.[24] For example, the holder of a first (and legal) mortgage who leads a second (equitable) mortgagee to believe that the debt under the first encumbrance has been paid off, may find that this conduct confers priority on a second mortgagee who advances money based on those representations.

If the contest involves two equitable interests the position is this: when the equities are otherwise equal, the first in time prevails. Therefore, the order in which the interests are acquired governs unless there is a reason that induces equity to rearrange these rights. In fact, it is best to treat the chronological ordering as the default position, "the ground of preference last resorted to",[25] to be applied if, at the end of the day, other circumstances do not suggest that another result would be the fairest. In this determination equity examines the cleanliness of the hands of the parties to the transactions in search of the best equity, looking at all of the relevant conduct, even that which occurs after the creation of the second interest.[26]

The fact that the second party is a *bona fide* purchaser for value without notice is an important factor, naturally, but it is not necessarily the controlling element when both interests are equitable. If all else is equal, I do not think that the innocence of the second party will normally be enough to reverse the order.

---

22 See further *Hunt v. Luck*, [1902] 1 Ch. 428, [1900-3] All E.R.Rep. 295 (C.A.).

23 See *Tyrell v. Mills*, [1924] 3 W.W.R. 387 (B.C.Co.Ct.) where, seemingly, gross negligence was regarded as postponing conduct. In *Northern Counties of England Fire Insurance Co. v. Whipp* (1884) 26 Ch.D. 482 (C.A.) an early and important authority, it was said that gross negligence can be relevant as an indication of fraud. This viewpoint implies that gross negligence on its own would not justify a postponement of a prior legal right. See also S. Hepburn, *Principles of Property Law* (Sydney: Cavendish Pr., 1998) at 164, where it is suggested that a modern court might adopt a more flexible standard, under which a lack of prudence, in all of the circumstances, would be considered sufficient.

24 See also P. Butt, *Land Law*, 3rd ed. (Sydney: Law Book Co., 1996) at 657.

25 *Rice v. Rice* (1854) 2 Drew 73, at 78, 61 E.R. 646, at 648 (*per* Kindersley V.C.). See also *McDougall v. McKay* (1922) 64 S.C.R. 1, [1922] 3 W.W.R. 191, 68 D.L.R. 245. See further P. Watts, "The Loss of Equitable Priority Through Negligent Omission – Kindersley V-C's Heresy" (1998) 18 N.Z.U.L.Rev. 46.

26 *Australian Guarantee Corp. (N.Z.) Ltd. v. C.F.C. Commercial Finance Ltd.*, [1995] 1 N.Z.L.R. 129 (C.A.).

However, to act fraudulently, or to cause the subsequent party to believe that the first interest is not effective or will not be enforced, will usually amount to postponing conduct to the detriment of the prior equitable holder. Negligent conduct by the holder of that prior right can also prompt a postponement of the prior right.[27]

The holder of a 'mere equity' may find that this interest is the most vulnerable of all equitable rights. Therefore, it is more likely to be given a subordinate ranking, for example, when the subsequent interest is given to a *bona fide* purchaser.[28] In general, a mere equity is a right that falls short of a full-bodied equitable interest in land.[29] It is a form of equitable right that is "ancillary to or dependent upon"[30] some other property interest. Included under this rubric are rights to: set aside a transaction on the ground of fraud, undue influence or mistake; open a final order of foreclosure; or seek equitable rectification of a flawed transfer. It has been suggested that the common denominator is that these mere equities "involve an attempt to capture an interest that in whole or in part is held by someone else".[31]

(c) proving good title

Assume that P wishes to buy Blackacre from V in a locale in which no registration system exists. Assume also that the priority rules just described are in force. Any potential purchaser would worry about V's title, the existence of prior encumbrances, *etc.* Inquiries may be made by P, and a warranty of title included in the sale, but an element of uncertainty and chance would remain. At common law, to provide some comfort, the vendor was obliged to demonstrate a good and sufficient chain of title. The best chain would be one that could be traced back to the first Crown grant, but of course tracking the title over an extended period of time would be an arduous task (especially in England). Instead, a good chain of title linking back 60 years was required at common law, unless there was agreement on some different period. As there was no general government registry that could serve as a repository for title deeds, it was necessary for these to be kept by the vendor. To alleviate some of the inconvenience that would result, a practice developed of requiring the vendor to prepare an abstract that would outline the interests affecting the title and show a good chain of title, as plotted

---

27 This does not need to amount to gross negligence: see the brief discussion in *National Provincial Bank of England v. Jackson* (1886) 33 Ch.D. 1 (C.A.) at 12-3.

28 See *Double Bay Newspapers Pty. Ltd. v. A.W. Holdings Pty. Ltd.* (1997) 42 N.S.W.L.R. 409 (Eq.Div.).

29 R.E. Megarry & H.W.R. Wade, *The Law of Real Property*, 5th ed. (London: Stevens & Sons, 1984) at 146.

30 *National Provincial Bank Ltd. v. Ainsworth*, [1965] A.C. 1175, [1965] 2 All E.R. 472 (H.L.) at 1238 A.C. (*per* Lord Upjohn). Not all 'mere equities' will have this quality, and a "mere 'equity' naked and alone is incapable of binding successors in title even with notice; it is personal to the parties": *ibid.*

31 See A.P. Bell, *The Modern Law of Personal Property in England and Ireland* (London: Butterworths, 1989) at 522. A detailed analysis is undertaken in A.R. Everton, " 'Equitable Interests' and 'Equities' – In Search of a Pattern", [1976] Conv. 209. See also Hepburn, *supra*, note 23, at 185*ff*, and the references cited there.

from an earlier transfer document onward. A period of time was allowed for the purchaser to examine the abstract and raise objections about perceived problems or to make requisitions intended to satisfy any elements of doubt that might have arisen as to the correct state of title.

The key to this process was the identification of an earlier transfer document that could be used to trace ownership into the hands of the present vendor. To qualify as a good root of title, such a document must (a) identify the land adequately; (b) show a disposition of the whole legal and equitable interests to be transferred; and (c) provide nothing that would cast doubt on the validity of the title.[32] However, even if such a document existed, and a good title was shown for the requisite period on the basis of it, this did not foreclose the possibility of a valid rival claimant emerging afterward. For example, the document chosen to support the chain may itself have been forged, and at common law this would not prevent the real owner from coming out of the woodwork and asserting a claim to have the land back.[33] In essence, this approach to title searching is still followed in parts of England, though the standard period for the proving of a good chain has been whittled down to 15 years. As will be seen below, the need to demonstrate a sufficient chain of title still prevails, in a modified form, in those jurisdictions in which systems of 'deeds registration' are found.[34]

3.   THE ADVENT OF REGISTRATION

(a)   introduction

The first general legislation concerning registration emerged as a by-product of the *Statute of Uses*.[35] As we have seen, prior to the Statute the ceremony of livery of seisin was the means used for transferring the legal title to freehold property. Thereafter, the Statute could be used to transfer legal title from the feoffee to uses to the *cestui que use*.[36] One common way of doing so was by way of a 'bargain and sale', which raised an equity in the purchaser that was then executed under the Statute. In consequence, legal title was transferred without livery of seisin. This result, though an incidental product of the *Statute of Uses*, was anticipated. Accordingly, a comprehensive registration system was designed to accompany the Statute. That effort did not succeed; in 1535 the *Statute of*

---

32 This description is based on the oft-cited authority, T.C. Williams, *The Law of Vendor and Purchaser*, 4th ed. (London: Sweet & Maxwell, 1936) at 123-4. See also E.D. Armour, *A Treatise on the Investigation of Titles to Real Estate in Ontario*, 2nd ed. (Aurora, Ont.: Canada Law Book, 1894) at 28*ff*.

33 Some protection against this calamity was (is) provided by the law of adverse possession, for even if the vendor is shown to have had no proper paper title, a possessory title might have accrued so as to extinguish the rights of some unknown (earlier) claimant. That is one of the stated reasons for the existence of the law of adverse possession: it serves to quiet titles and facilitate transfers. See generally Part 3(b), Chapter 4. Other factors undermining the validity of a transfer are outlined in Mapp, *supra*, note 15, at 8*ff*.

34 See Part 3(b), *infra*.

35 *An Act Concerning Uses and Wills, 1535*, 27 Hen. 8, c. 10.

36 See Part 3(f), Chapter 6.

Enrolments[37] was enacted instead. That Statute provides that a bargain and sale would not be effective to pass the legal estate unless it was enrolled in one of the King's courts. That requirement was soon circumvented by the employment of conveyancing techniques that were not caught by the registration requirements; as a result, the system for enrolments fell into disuse.

In the centuries that followed there were a number of unsuccessful attempts in England to introduce some other form of general registration system.[38] These sundry failures were probably due, in part, to the monumental effort needed to bring the cluttered titles throughout England under a new regime. Another factor, and one that has impeded development up until the modern era, was resistance from the legal profession.[39] Legislation allowing for registration in Yorkshire and Middlesex was eventually introduced in the eighteenth century. After other limited experiments, the *Land Transfer Act* was implemented in 1897.[40] It mandated registration only in London. The current English law, introduced in 1925,[41] establishes a system of title registration. However, not all land in England has been brought under this statute. For unregistered land, the "wearisome and intricate task"[42] of examining the title deeds held by the owner to prove a good title survives as the main feature of conveyancing, though there is provision for registering some charges against the name of an estate owner.[43] The conversion of unregistered land over to the 1925 Act was initially thought to be a 30-year project, but it is ongoing.[44] Estimates are that 80% of real property in England and Wales is now registered land.[45]

Canadian law reformers did not wait for these English developments. Registration was introduced in various parts of the country beginning in the mid-eighteenth century.[46] The federal government introduced a comprehensive system for the Northwest Territories in 1886, which later formed the basis of the land titles systems on the Prairies. Speaking in broad terms, two models have been tried in Canada: deeds registration and title registration

---

37 *An Act Concerning Enrolments and Contracts of Lands and Tenements, 1535*, 27 Hen. 8, c. 16.
38 See the brief review in E. Jenks, *Modern Land Law* (1899, reprinted, *Scientia Verlag und Antiquariat*, 1979) at 443*ff*, and R.R.A. Walker, "The Genesis of Land Registration in England" (1939) 55 L.Q.R. 547.
39 See B. Abel-Smith & R. Stevens, *Lawyers and the Courts* (London: Heinemann, 1967) at 196-206.
40 *Land Transfer Act, 1897*, 60 & 61 Vict., c. 65.
41 *Land Registration Act, 1925*, 15 & 16 Geo. 5, c. 21.
42 *Williams & Glyn's Bank Ltd. v. Boland*, [1981] A.C. 487, [1980] 2 All E.R. 408 (H.L.) at 511 A.C. (*per* Lord Scarman).
43 See *Land Charges Act, 1972*, c. 61.
44 See further H.W. Wilkinson, "I Have a Dream", [1993] Conv. 101.
45 Law Commission & H.M. Land Registry, *Land Registration for the Twenty-First Century: A Consultative Document* (London: H.M.S.O., 1998) at 4.
46 It appears that the first registry system was introduced, by Imperial Ordinance, in Nova Scotia in 1752: see J.E. Roach, *The Canadian Law of Mortgages of Land* (Markham, Ont.: Butterworths, 1993) at 364-5. See also S.N.S. 1759, c. 2; S.N.S. 1760, c. 4. In Ontario, see *Registry Act*, 35 Geo. 3, c. 5. Early Ontario practice and the statutory evolution of Ontario law is discussed in T.G. Youdan, "The Length of a Title Search in Ontario" (1986) 64 Can.B.Rev. 507.

(b)   deeds registration

Under a deeds registration statute an attempt is made to create a record and repository of all documents pertaining to a given parcel. Instead of having the deeds held by the owner, these become a matter of public record; accordingly, registration can serve as notice to the world. The private practice of assembling an abstract is replaced by the compilation of a government record, so that the work of the vendor is significantly reduced. Still, registration has nothing what-soever to do with the extrinsic or intrinsic validity of the instruments that are noted on the register: the substantive value of a deed rests on its validity under the general law of property (and contract, *etc.*). So, for example, a document infected with fraud is not in any way cured or validated by registration.

Deeds registration systems may be classified as (i) race (to register); (ii) notice; or (iii) race-notice.[47] These models establish different criteria for deter-mining how competing rights will be ordered. An illustration should demonstrate the different approaches: Assume that O, the owner of Blackacre, mortgages the property to A, but for some reason this mortgage is not registered. Next, a second mortgage is granted to B. Later, B registers this mortgage; throughout, B was fully aware of the prior security interest given to A.

Under a *race* system, it is generally the order of registration that determines the priorities. The order in which the transactions actually occur is generally irrelevant; and so is notice (outside of the register itself). Under a pure race system, B, having registered first, gains priority over A. A *notice* system, as its name suggests, is concerned with ascertaining whether a subsequent transaction was undertaken with notice of a prior one; this is central to the determination of how interests will be ranked. Of course, the register is regarded as a perfectly good means of giving notice, but the real question is whether there existed sufficient notice at the time of the subsequent transaction. (Whether that notice may be actual, constructive, or imputed, depends on whatever a given system allows.) A person without notice takes free of the prior interest, even without the need to register. In the sample problem, A would prevail over B, since B had notice.[48] A *race-notice* statute accords priority to a party who acquires a subsequent interest without notice of a previous one, and registers before that prior interest is placed on title. If either one of these elements is missing, the first interest will prevail. In the example above, A would enjoy priority over B.

The race-notice approach seems the most common of the three forms. Fur-thermore, although some statutes seem to establish race systems, courts have sometimes read these quite differently, adding a notice gloss. Consider for ex-ample, the current Newfoundland provision:

---

47 See further T. Mattis, "Recording Acts: Anachronistic Reliance", 25 Real Prop., Prob. & Tr.J. 17 (1990).

48 An example of such a system is the informal register referred to in *C.I.B.C. Mortgage Corp. v. Quassa*, [1996] N.W.T.J. No.17 (S.C.).

An instrument . . . not proved and registered, and a mortgage by deposit of deeds without writing, shall be judged fraudulent and void both at law and in equity, as against a subsequent purchaser or mortgagee for valuable consideration who first registers his or her instrument . . .[49]

Despite this language, it has been held that notice of an unregistered interest at the time of a second transaction is enough to preserve the priority of that prior interest.[50] The reasoning is that the point of the statute is to protect innocent purchasers. That goal is fully satisfied if the second party is aware of the prior right.

Ontario's Act illustrates a race-notice approach that differs somewhat from the model described above.[51] In Ontario, the law provides that an instrument affecting land is to be regarded as "fraudulent and void against any subsequent purchaser for valuable consideration without actual notice" unless that prior instrument is registered first.[52] This creates a race-notice rule as defined above. Furthermore, the Act provides that prior registration by B would prevail over A, unless before registration B gains actual knowledge of A's rights.[53] In other words, B must (i) be unaware of a prior interest at the time of purchase; (ii) remain unaware until registration; and (iii) register first. For these purposes, notice may be actual or imputed.[54] Under such systems the registration of a deed is treated as "equivalent to actual notice".[55] I find this language misleading because the party deemed to be notified may not, in fact, have examined the register. To avoid confusion it might be better to speak of 'notice by registration' as being adequate to protect an interest endorsed on the register.

As I have suggested, none of the three forms of deeds registration purports to guarantee the authenticity of anything that is registered. Registration is a ministerial act only: the validity of any document remains open to challenge. As a result, a historical search to show a good chain of title is still necessary. Under current Ontario law,[56] a 40-year search is required, though a longer period must be used if there has been no conveyance (other than a mortgage) noted on title during the preceding 40 years. It is no longer necessary to start with a good root of title as defined by the common law. Moreover, proof of title during the appropriate period has a cleansing effect on claims existing beforehand. Putting cases

---

49 *Registration of Deeds Act*, R.S.N. 1990, c. R-10, s. 10.

50 See further *Fortis Trust Corp. v. Caribou Investment & Loan Co.* (1997) 16 R.P.R. (3d) 24, 159 Nfld. & P.E.I.R. 91, 492 A.P.R. 91 (Nfld.C.A.); *Recon Ltd. v. Curtis* (1996) 142 Nfld. & P.E.I.R. 276, 445 A.P.R. 276 (Nfld.T.D.). See also J. Howell, "The Doctrine of Notice: An Historical Perspective", [1997] Conv. 431.

51 See further M. Neave, "Conveyancing Under the Ontario Registry Act: An Analysis of the Priority Provisions and Some Suggestions for Reform" (1977) 55 Can.B.Rev. 500.

52 *Registry Act*, R.S.O. 1990, c. R.20, sub. 70(1). See also *Ross v. Hunter* (1882) 7 S.C.R. 289; *Duguay v. Kenney* (1989) 101 N.B.R. (2d) 157, 254 A.P.R. 157 (Q.B.); *Hoback Investments Ltd. v. Loblaws Ltd.*, *supra*, note 18.

53 S. 71.

54 Concerning imputed notice, see, *e.g.*, *Green v. Stevenson* (1905) 9 O.L.R. 671 (Div.Ct.). *Cf. Durbin v. Monserat Investments Ltd.* (1978) 20 O.R. (2d) 181, 5 R.P.R. 15, 87 D.L.R. (3d) 593 (C.A.).

55 *Rooker v. Hoofstetter* (1896) 26 S.C.R. 41, at 46 (*per* Gwynne J.).

56 *Registry Act*, R.S.O. 1990, c. R.20, Part III ("Investigation of Titles").

of fraud to one side, as a general rule earlier claims will be extinguished if they are not sufficiently noted on the register during the 40-year period.[57]

Current Ontario law deviates from conventional deeds registration principles in another way. It is now possible to seek certification of title under the *Registry Act*, and once obtained this creates an element of conclusiveness for the title. Additionally, a party deprived of a right by virtue of the certification process can apply for compensation from a government fund.[58] These elements resemble features commonly found in systems of title registration, as we will see immediately below.[59]

(c)   title registration

The modern system of land titles registration found in force in western Canada[60] can be traced to the pioneering work of Robert Torrens and the implementation of the first Torrens title registration system in South Australia in 1858. Torrens's model was inspired by the principles of registration found in the law regulating merchant shipping, the land systems in the Hanseatic towns (such as Hamburg),[61] recommendations made by the English Real Property Commissioners, and, so it has been maintained, the recording methods used in England for copyhold tenure.[62] The conventional view is that the move for reform was driven by Torrens's strong antipathy toward the complexity of the received English law

---

57 S. 113. The first version of this provision was first introduced in Ontario in the *Investigation of Titles Act, 1929*, S.O. 1929, c. 41. See generally Youdan, *supra*, note 46, at 514*ff*, for an analysis of the 1929 Act, and the modern version. See also *Marketable Titles Act*, S.N.S. 1995-6, c. 9, applied in *Penny v. Hartling* (1999) 25 R.P.R. (3d) 283, 177 N.S.R. (2d) 378, 542 A.P.R. 378 (S.C.).

58 *Certification of Titles Act*, R.S.O. 1990, c. C.6. It has been suggested that the Act has fallen into disuse. The procedures for obtaining a certificate are similar to those required for bringing land under the land titles system, an approach that is preferred: B.J. Reiter *et al.*, eds., *Real Estate Law*, 4th ed. (Toronto: Emond Montgomery, 1992) at 464. A limited right of compensation is conferred under Part IV of the *Registry Act*, R.S.O. 1990, c. R.20.

59 The law in Ontario is described in the text above with a serene simplicity that obscures the raging debate that erupted over the operation of Part III of the *Registry Act* following the introduction of amendments in 1981. The Ontario Court of Appeal, in its efforts to explain the meaning of the law, created a bit of a mess: see *Ontario Hydro v. Tkach* (1992) 10 O.R. (3d) 257, 28 R.P.R. (2d) 1, 95 D.L.R. (4th) 18 (C.A.); *National Sewer Pipe Ltd. v. Azova Investments* (1993) 14 O.R. (3d) 385, 105 D.L.R. (4th) 12, 34 R.P.R. (2d) 1 (C.A.); *Camrich Developments Inc. v. Ontario Hydro* (1993) 14 O.R. (3d) 410, 105 D.L.R. (4th) 1, 34 R.P.R. (2d) 27 (C.A.); *Fire v. Longtin* (1994) 17 O.R. (3d) 418, 112 D.L.R. (4th) 34, 38 R.P.R. (2d) 1 (C.A.). The Court of Appeal decision in *Longtin* was affirmed in its entirety by the Supreme Court of Canada (*Fire v. Longtin*, [1995] 4 S.C.R. 3, 48 R.P.R. (2d) 1, 128 D.L.R. (4th) 767) and so it is now the leading authority on the operation of Part III. See further B. Bucknall *et al.*, "Title Searching Under the Ontario Registry Act After *Fire v. Longtin*: A Consensus Position" (1996) 1 R.P.R. (3d) 173, and the references cited there.

60 In general, land titles predominates in western Canada, and deeds registration in Ontario and the Maritimes. In Manitoba and Ontario both systems can be found, with 'deeds' land being converted over time to 'land titles' land. Efforts have been made in the Maritimes to do the same. On this latter point, see generally R.T.J. Stein, "Implementation of Enacted Title by Registration Legislation in the Maritimes" (1987) 10 Dal.L.J. 125.

61 Butt, *supra*, note 24, at 687.

62 See Walker, *supra*, note 38, at 548.

of conveyancing. The laborious process of rummaging through a collection of title deeds represented everything that Torrens despised about the English practice of law. His mission, therefore, was to create a registration procedure that would be simple, efficient and inexpensive. Recently, a new theory has emerged that suggests that the motivation for the introduction of a comprehensive land titles system was to provide a means of obliterating Aboriginal claims to lands in South Australia.[63]

Even if in today's world controversies over land registration seem too tepid to make the blood boil, Torrens's plan was, in its day in South Australia, a *cause célèbre* and the subject of passionate debate.[64] The reforms were met with stiff resistance from lawyers,[65] who had a vested interest in maintaining the occult of conveyancing.[66] Yet, the proposed scheme enjoyed widespread popular support. Robert Torrens was elected to the legislature on the strength of his plan, resigning later so that he could become the first Registrar-General for the Colony of South Australia.

The South Australian statute suffered teething problems and had to be significantly amended within a year of its enactment.[67] Despite these initial difficulties, other Australian colonies soon adopted the system. The new system also attracted attention elsewhere. Before the end of the nineteenth century it had been adopted in western Canada and in a few, but only a few, American states.[68] Torrens's influence continues; these days throughout eastern Europe.

4.   THE CARDINAL ELEMENTS OF TORRENS TITLE[69]

The main goals of Torrens title are to create a system that facilitates transfers, allows for simplicity, and reduces the costs of conveyancing. In the pursuit of these ends the system sacrifices to some extent the security of title enjoyed by an owner at common law. As we will soon see, one effect of the Torrens approach is to create a mile-wide exception to the principle *nemo dat quod non habet.*

---

63 S. Ainger, "Aboriginal Trailblazer Uncovers 'Extraordinary Conspiracy' ", Sydney Alumni Gazette (June, 1991) at 18.

64 "In Australia the great mass of people are, or confidently look forward to [becoming], landed proprietors. In Australia, therefore, thorough land reform is essentially the people's question": R.R. Torrens' Election Speech, as reported in *The South Australian Register*, February 2, 1857, and quoted in D.J. Whalan, *The Torrens System in Australia* (Sydney: Law Book Co., 1982) at 7, n. 22.

65 Whalan, *ibid.*, at 5.

66 See P. Moerlin Fox, "The Story Behind the Torrens System" (1950) 23 A.L.J. 489.

67 See D. Pike, "Introduction of the Real Property Act in South Australia" (1961) 1 Adelaide L.Rev. 169; D.J. Whalan, "Immediate Success of Registration of Title to Land in Australasia and Early Failures in England" (1967) 2 N.Z.U.L.Rev. 416; W.N. Harrison, "The Transformation of Torrens's System into the Torrens System" (1961-4) 4 U.Qd.L.J. 125.

68 See further J. Dukeminier & J. Krier, eds., *Property*, 4th ed. (New York: Aspen Law, 1998) at 720-2; J.L. McCormack, "Torrens and Recording: Land Title Assurance in the Computer Age", 18 Wm. Mitchell L.Rev. 61 (1992).

69 See generally T.W. Mapp, *Torrens' Elusive Title* (Edmonton: Alta.L.Rev., 1978); I.L. Head, "The Torrens System in Alberta: A Dream in Operation" (1957) 35 Can.B.Rev. 1; Whalan, *supra*, note 64.

Instead of protecting the current holder of the legal estate at all costs, the Torrens system sometimes favours an innocent purchaser. In other words, the risk of a sale transaction, which is borne so heavily by the purchaser under the common law rules, is now shifted (partially) onto the lap of a current owner. However, an assurance fund is supposed to provide a safety net by providing monetary compensation when the system wrongfully and irreversibly divests an owner.

Under Torrens the register is supposed to be everything. This means that one should (in theory anyway) be able to examine an abstract of title for a specific parcel of land and see listed there all of the interests in land that pertain to that parcel. The register is said to be a *mirror* of all rights in relation to that land. (Since a mirror actually reverses the image being reflected, I would prefer to say that the register is a 'photo'; but 'mirror' is well-entrenched as the metaphor.) The failure to register a property interest alters the priorities that would otherwise govern that entitlement. A person registering without proper notice of a prior interest can claim priority over it.

The Torrens system also attempts to certify titles. It seeks to minimize the need to second-guess the government records as to the validity of the rights listed on the register. So, when the register shows O as the owner of Blackacre, there should be no need, as there is under a deeds system or at common law, to look behind this record and determine if O had acquired the property from someone who had a right to sell (and so on), or to ascertain if the prior documentation is free of defects. In other words, under Torrens a *curtain* is supposed to be brought down on these past dealings.[70] This principle lies at the heart of the concept of 'indefeasibility' that is so pivotal to the Torrens system. This idea is more fully explained below.[71]

The keystone provision of the Alberta statute reflects the dominance of the register:

> The owner of land in whose name a certificate of title has been granted shall, except in case of fraud wherein he has participated or colluded, hold it, subject (in addition to the incidents implied by virtue of this Act) to the encumbrances, liens, estates and interests that are endorsed on the certificate of title, absolutely free from all other encumbrances, liens, estates, or interests whatsoever except the estate and interest of an owner claiming the same land under a prior certificate of title granted under this Act or granted under any law heretofore in force and relating to title to real property.[72]

Under Torrens the interposition of the state is crucial. While at common law conveyancing was fundamentally a private matter, here it is the state that confers title through registration, and it is the state that warrants (in some measure) the ownership rights of the seller. As alluded to above, an integral element of Torrens title regimes is the insurance (or *net*) principle. If it is the government's responsibility to issue title, and if it purports to convey an indefeasible title, it is to be

---

70 The tags 'mirror' and 'curtain', now in common usage, have been attributed to T.B.F. Ruoff, "An Englishman Looks at the Torrens System: I" (1952) 26 A.L.J. 118.

71 See Part 5, *infra*.

72 *Land Titles Act*, R.S.A. 1980, c. L-5, sub. 64(1) [as am.].

expected that some mistakes will result. After all, we live in a world where fraud occurs, and where governmental bureaucracies are administered by civil servants. The owner who is deprived of the property is expected to make a claim against the fund for errors resulting from fraud, mistake or maladministration.[73]

The aims and virtues of the Torrens system were applauded over a century ago in the British Columbia case of *Re Shotbolt*:[74]

Some of the good results of the adoption of this system are:

1. The title to real property has been greatly simplified, without radical changes in the general law.

2. Stability to title, with safety to purchasers and mortgagees, has been secured.

3. The ownership of property, either in town or country, is [shown] by the register at a glance, and whether encumbered or not.

4. It increases the saleable value of property.

5. It enables both vendors and purchasers to accurately ascertain the expenses of carrying out any sale or transfer.

6. It protects trust estates and beneficiaries.

7. It prevents frauds and protects purchasers and mortgagees from those misrepresentations common in all countries among a certain class of legal practitioners and land agents.

8. It has secured the chief advantages of the old system of the registration of deeds (of which notice is the most important principle), and has operated so as to almost entirely dispense with the investigation of prior title.

9. Loans on mortgages are effected and transfers of the fee are made with . . . ease.

10. After a certificate of indefeasible title under the Act is obtained, no retrospective investigation is necessary.

11. A transfer in the form of the Act of all or any clearly identified part of the land held by such indefeasible title, conveys to and entitles the transferee to be registered as the owner of a similarly indefeasible fee simple in the land so transferred.

Lamentably, departures from the Torrens paradigm have diminished some of these attributes; and this list does not address the potential harms to owners that Torrens invites. First, we will soon see that some interests not on title can hover as invisible clouds, binding even purchasers without notice: the system tolerates the presence of various 'overriding interests' that need not be registered. Second, obtaining registration as the owner of Blackacre does not invariably mean that one can be completely confident that past defects in earlier dealings cannot return to haunt; this too will be examined later on. Third, the new owner, even if described as holding an unchallengeable title, cannot be certain that a *subsequent* error will not lead to defeasance, since the Torrens system might work to vest title (wrongfully perhaps) in some other person, who then may be able to claim an indefeasible title of the same type. Fourth, the insurance fund will not always provide compensation merely because a loss has occurred.[75] Finally, an important

---

73 See further *Land Titles Act*, R.S.A. 1980, c. L-5, ss. 154-172 [as am.].

74 (1888) 1 B.C.R. 337 (S.C.) at 348-9 (*per* Crease J.).

75 See, *e.g.*, *Barty v. Kerr & Registrar of Northern Alberta Land Registration Dist.* (1975) 8 Alta.L.R. (2d) 275 (Dist.Ct.).

claim of advocates of Torrens title is that it is less expensive for consumers. When one compares the tasks associated with closing a land deal under the common law or deeds systems, this seems a likely result. However, it has been suggested that the costs of conveyancing are not as dependent on the system in force as they are to the existence of a viable market for conveyancing services. On this view, competition in the conveyancing industry is the main variable of cost-reduction.[76]

5.   INDEFEASIBILITY AND ITS QUALIFICATIONS

(a)   the nature of indefeasibility

"Indefeasibility is the heart of the Torrens system."[77] However, as we will see, this concept is qualified in major ways.

A title is indefeasible when it cannot be vitiated by some antecedent act that might undermine the validity of current rights. In theory, therefore, state registration provides a safe harbour from any defects in title for the party declared by the register to be the owner of Blackacre. The idea of indefeasibility involves the lowering of a curtain on past transactions.

There is a pivotal question under all Torrens systems concerning the moment at which an impeachable title becomes indefeasible: when does the curtain fall? Two basic approaches are possible and both are supportable on policy grounds. Under the first, indefeasibility is described as being *immediate*; under the second it is *deferred*.[78] Courts have wavered on which approach to take, though the preponderant view in Torrens jurisdictions today is that immediate indefeasibility is the rule.[79]

The difference between these two approaches can be explained with the aid of the following hypothetical. Imagine that A purchases Blackacre from someone

---

76 See B. Reiter *et al.*, eds., *Real Estate Law*, 3rd ed. (Toronto: Emond Montgomery, 1986) at 534.

77 *Re Cartlidge and Granville Savings & Mortgage Corp.* (1987) 44 Man.R. (2d) 252, [1987] 2 W.W.R. 673, 34 D.L.R. (4th) 161 (C.A.) at 172 D.L.R. (*per* Philip J.A.).

78 See generally M. Neave, "Indefeasibility of Title in the Canadian Context" (1976) 26 U.T.L.J. 173.

79 See, *e.g.*, *Hermanson v. Martin* (1986) 52 Sask.R. 164, [1987] 1 W.W.R. 439, 33 D.L.R. (4th) 12 (C.A.) additional reasons at [1987] 4 W.W.R. 94, 59 Sask.R. 95 (C.A.) applying the leading commonwealth authority of *Frazer v. Walker*, [1967] 1 A.C. 569, [1967] 1 All E.R. 649 (P.C.). See further G.W. Hinde, Note, (1968) 46 Can.B.Rev. 304; W. Taylor, "Scotching *Frazer v. Walker*" (1970) 44 A.L.J. 248; J. Lee, "Case Comment: *Registrar of Regina Land Registration District v. Hermanson et al.*" (1988) 52 Sask.L.Rev. 303. In Alberta, the issue of whether *Frazer v. Walker* should be adopted has not been definitively resolved. A report for discussion released by the Alberta Law Reform Institute has opined that immediate indefeasibility is probably the law in Alberta: *Towards a New Alberta Land Titles Act* (Edmonton: A.L.R.I., 1990) at 16. But see *Beneficial Realty Ltd. v. Sun Bae* (1996) 182 A.R. 356 (Master). The leading Commonwealth authority on deferred indefeasibility is *Gibbs v. Messer*, [1891] A.C. 248 (P.C.). Not that long ago the courts in the Australian State of Victoria vacillated on this point, though the latest authorities have opted for immediate indefeasibility: see generally G. The, "Deferred Indefeasibility of Title in Victoria?" (1991) 17 Monash U.L.Rev. 77, and J. Shultz, "Judicial Acceptance of Immediate Indefeasibility in Victoria" (1993) 19 Monash U.L.Rev. 326. See also *Horvath v. Commonwealth Bank of Australia*, [1999] 1 V.R. 643 (C.A.) which applied *Frazer v. Walker*.

claiming to be O, the owner of the property. In fact the vendor is not the real O, but rather what law texts call a 'rogue' (R). Assume that R has forged O's signature but that when the transfer documents are tendered for registration, the registrar is satisfied that this is a legitimate transaction. A is then registered as the new owner of the property. Some time later A agrees to sell the property to B. Before this transfer is registered on title the earlier sham is uncovered and the real O tries to have the register rectified by the cancellation of A's title. Can this be done?

If the governing principle is one of immediate indefeasibility, the opportunity for rectification was lost on the registration of the transfer in A's name. At that time A became immediately entitled to the indefeasibility protections of Torrens. The deferred rule would require that A's interest be sold to and registered in favour of B before the title is rendered indefeasible (in this hypothetical).

Which of these two approaches applies in a given jurisdiction depends, of course, on the language of the governing statute. The immediate approach is faithful to the wording of the Alberta provision quoted above,[80] though in other parts of the Act there are a few mixed signals; the statute does not definitively resolve the controversy.[81] The thinking behind immediate indefeasibility is that in the absence of fraud on the purchaser's part (as is assumed here), a good title should issue once A is registered. This reduces the need for A to undertake inquiries at the time of sale. In accordance with the Torrens ethos, facility of transfer is promoted even though the security of O's title is sacrificed in the process. O must turn to the assurance fund for compensation.

The rationale of deferred indefeasibility is based on significance of detrimental reliance *on the register*. The assumption is that the purpose of Torrens is to allow one to rely on the register and that no errors in the registered title should prejudice a buyer. In this example there was initially no error in the title: O was the owner. Both the purchaser and the registrar were not relying solely on the accuracy of the title, but also on the apparent identity of the rogue. And it was concerning this latter element – outside of the register – that the fatal error was made. The mistake that both the registrar and the purchaser made was in failing to detect the forgery. The deferred rule places an onus on the purchaser to determine if the transfer instrument is a genuine one; a purchaser who fails to do so must pay the consequences. By comparison, on the subsequent sale from A to B, B would be relying on the tainted registration. In this sale there would be no forgery: B would be taking title directly from the registered owner, A. The argument, therefore, is that indefeasibility is deferred until this second dealing, when it is the register itself that contains the lie. The same result should obtain if the rogue managed to secure title in his or her name and then transferred this interest to an innocent purchaser.[82]

---

80 See the text accompanying note 72, *supra*.
81 See ss. 158, 160 and 173.
82 *De Lichtbuer v. Dupmeier*, [1941] 3 W.W.R. 64 (Sask.K.B.).

(b)   the impact of fraud

The Torrens system creates an exception to the rule *nemo dat quod non habet* by allowing title to pass wrongfully out of the hands of the true owner through the incorrect registration of a defective transfer. This, no doubt, raises the potential for unscrupulous dealings. However, it has always been a tenet of the Torrens system that a purchaser contaminated with fraud does not acquire an indefeasible title. If the land thereafter passes to a good faith purchaser, the earlier element of fraud cannot then work to upset this second purchaser's rights. But until then the title of the fraudulent party is vulnerable to challenge, and this is so under both the immediate and deferred theories of indefeasibility.

The courts have resisted providing closed and specific definitions of fraud, preferring instead to be "free to deal with it in whatever form it may present itself".[83] At its nucleus, fraud involves a dishonest dealing leading to deprivation, and this embraces acts or omissions (where there is a legal or equitable duty imposed) that produce an undue or unconscionable injury or advantage.[84] The fraud must result in either the loss of an interest currently on title, or the gaining of priority over some unregistered document. Acts of fraud perpetrated by the purchaser are obviously caught. So are dishonest dealings by some other person that are known to the purchaser. When it is clear to all that the putative vendor has no title whatsoever to give, fraud is committed by both that vendor and the purchaser.[85]

A person who unwittingly accepts and tenders for registration a forged transfer is not acting fraudulently; knowledge of the forgery, as I have just mentioned, is another matter altogether. There may be cases where the purchaser has got wind that something might be awry. The question then becomes whether the failure to resolve this uncertainty, once the purchaser has been put on notice, is enough to count as fraud. The general position is that the failure to uncover fraud, when reasonable inquiries would have done so, is not itself fraudulent, but the failure to make inquiries *once suspicions are aroused* will usually suffice.[86] To use criminal law terminology, the difference here is that which exists between objective negligence (which is not Torrens fraud) and wilful blindness (which is).

Let us dilute the level of knowledge in another way. Consider these facts, which are loosely based on the case of *Holt Renfrew & Co. v. Henry Singer Ltd.*[87]

---

83 *Independent Lumber Co. v. Gardiner* (1910) 3 Sask.L.R. 140, 13 W.L.R. 548 (S.C. *in banco*) at 143-4 Sask.L.R. (*per* Lamont J.).

84 *Ibid.* at 144, quoting *Kerr on Fraud and Mistake*, at 1.

85 These circumstances normally occur as a prelude to a (fraudulent) registration, but they may occur afterwards, such as in the case of a subsequent repudiation of an unregistered interest to which the purchaser had agreed to be bound: see, *e.g., Bahr v. Nicolay (No. 2)* (1988) 164 C.L.R. 604, 78 A.L.R. 1 (Aust.H.C.). See also *Lyus v. Prowsa Developments Ltd.*, [1982] 1 W.L.R. 1044, [1982] 2 All E.R. 953, 44 P. & C.R. 213 (Ch.D.). It was seen earlier that this type of undertaking may give rise to a constructive trust: see Part 7, Chapter 8. *Cf. Maurice Demers Transport Ltd. v. Fountain Tire Distributors (Edmonton) Ltd.*, [1974] 1 W.W.R. 348, 42 D.L.R. (3d) 412 (Alta.C.A.).

86 *Assets Co. v. Mere Roihi*, [1905] A.C. 176 (P.C.) at 210.

87 (1982) 20 Alta.L.R. (2d) 97, [1982] 4 W.W.R. 481, 135 D.L.R. (3d) 391 (C.A.) leave to appeal

P is interested in purchasing prime commercial space in Edmonton, and so starts negotiations with the owner of the freehold. It comes to the attention of P that the current tenant (T) has not registered the lease under which it enjoys possession. P is aware of this and has actually seen a copy of T's lease. In the face of this knowledge, P purchases the property, registers, and then claims a priority over T. The following question arises: is knowledge of a valid but unregistered interest enough to constitute fraud for the purpose of Torrens? If it is, then actual knowledge outside of the register is as good as registration, with the result that the comprehensiveness of the system is reduced. On the other hand, if this is not sufficient to invoke the exception to indefeasibility, then the system permits, even facilitates, a form of sharp practice that the law should not tolerate, let alone encourage.

Some statutes explicitly provide that notice, without more, is not to be equated with fraud.[88] The question then becomes what counts as 'more' for these purposes, an issue that arose in *Holt Renfrew*.[89] The solicitor for the purchaser (P above) advised the vendor (V) that "with respect to the matter of the existing tenant (T), we do not believe that situation would be a deterrent to our client's interest".[90] However, P advised its solicitor that P was not interested in buying the land if T's lease was still on foot. Later, an offer was made to buy the property, subject only to those encumbrances noted on title. After some further negotiations a similar offer was accepted. P promptly registered a caveat[91] protecting the agreement for sale and, having done so, claimed that it was not bound by T's unregistered leasehold interest.

A minority of the Alberta Court of Appeal found this to be fraud under the *Land Titles Act*. Adopting orthodox contract principles, they held that P had a duty to advise V that the original position concerning P's willingness to accept the lease had changed. It was further found by the minority that P knew that V would sell the freehold only if the sale was subject to the lease, so the failure to correct the (honestly made) statement amounted to fraud. It did not matter that P's solicitor believed that he owed a duty to his client that mandated his continued silence. A majority of the Court concluded that there was no fraud. They endorsed the proposition that fraud requires more than mere knowledge that there is an unregistered interest. Importantly, they seem also to have accepted (along with

---

to S.C.C. refused (1982) 22 Alta.L.R. (2d) xxxvi (note) (S.C.C.). See also *Hackworth v. Baker*, [1936] 1 W.W.R. 321 (Sask.C.A.) leave to appeal to P.C. refused [1936] 2 W.W.R. 622 (Sask. C.A.).

88 See, *e.g.*, *Land Titles Act*, R.S.A. 1980, c. L-5, s. 195 [as am]. In Ontario, actual notice of unregistered interests will suffice to bind a subsequent party: *Dominion Stores v. United Trust Co.*, [1977] 2 S.C.R. 915, 1 R.P.R. 1, 71 D.L.R. (3d) 72, questioned in A.H. Oosterhoff & W.B. Rayner, *Anger & Honsberger Law of Real Property*, 2nd ed. (Aurora, Ont.: Canada Law Book, 1985) vol. 2, at 1611*ff*. See also the dissenting judgment of Laskin C.J. in *Dominion Stores*. *Cf. Randvest Inc. v. 741298 Ontario Ltd.* (1996) 30 O.R. (3d) 473, 5 R.P.R. (3d) 198, 139 D.L.R. (4th) 321 (Gen.Div.). See further M. Neave, "The Concept of Notice and the Ontario Land Titles Act" (1976) 54 Can.B.Rev. 132.

89 *Supra*, note 87.

90 *Ibid.*, 20 Alta.L.R. (2d) at 104.

91 See Part 5(e), *infra*.

the minority) that knowing that registration will defeat the prior interest is also not equivalent to fraud: some further element of dishonesty had to be brought home to the purchaser. The majority found none here. It was not shown that P's representations were relied on by V, or that the offers were cleverly drafted so as to mislead. Perhaps most importantly, the last offers to purchase showed that the purchaser (P) intended to be bound only by the *registered* encumbrances.[92] Had V's solicitor been paying sufficient attention, this would have been noticed.

The case of *Alberta v. McCulloch*[93] invites comparisons with *Holt Renfrew*. A had purchased Blackacre subject to a caveat (protecting a right of repurchase) in favour of the Alberta Ministry of Forestry, Lands and Wildlife. Owing to a mistake the caveat was cancelled by the Land Titles Office. A, realizing this, contacted a Forestry official and inquired as to why that had been done. It appeared to the official to have been an inadvertent error, and it was suggested that the matter would be investigated. Shortly afterwards, and without contacting the department, A transferred his interest in Blackacre to A Ltd., a company owned solely by A and his wife. It was claimed that this was done for tax reasons and to raise money to repay a loan.

In *McCulloch* the purchaser was found to have been one step over the line demarcating fraud under Alberta Torrens law. The trial judge acknowledged the conventional position that "knowledge of the unregistered interest, by itself, does not constitute fraud". He added that "[f]or there to be fraud, the knowledge must be used for an unjust or inequitable purpose".[94] Such a purpose was found in this case: it was concluded that the transaction was designed, in part, to defeat the unregistered interest. This holding was affirmed on appeal. In a concise memorandum of judgment, the Court of Appeal said this:

> In cases of this sort usually the transferor and transferee dealt at arm's length, and so the intent of the transferor is then irrelevant. Here, the transferor controlled the transferee numbered company . . . We have no doubt that the acts of the transferor were fraud in the narrow and strict sense and that the two parties shared that intent. This is therefore a case where the transferee had far more than mere knowledge.[95]

The reasoning in *McCulloch* comes close to equating knowledge with fraud. The outcome suggests that even if actual notice of a prior unprotected right is not enough, knowing of the legal effect of a subsequent transfer on that prior right may still suffice. That position is hard to reconcile with *Holt Renfrew* (which was not cited by either court in *McCulloch*), where the purchaser, while obviously not in league with the vendor, was quite aware of the legal impact that the sale and registration would have on the unregistered lease. Moreover, in *Holt Renfrew* it was possible to conclude, as the minority did, that the purchaser lulled the vendor

---

92 The purchaser lost anyway, because the Court of Appeal found that the caveat was fatally defective and therefore of no effect.

93 *Alberta (Minister of Forestry, Lands & Wildlife) v. McCulloch* (1991) 78 Alta.L.R. (2d) 375, [1991] 3 W.W.R. 662, 116 A.R. 261 (Q.B.) affirmed (1991) 83 Alta.L.R. (2d) 156, [1992] 1 W.W.R. 747 (C.A.).

94 *Ibid.*, [1991] 3 W.W.R., at 669 (*per* Sinclair J.).

95 *Supra*, note 93, [1992] 1 W.W.R., at 747 (*per* Côté J.A.).

into thinking that the current lease was of no concern, and this might be viewed as unacceptable behaviour. And the race to register the caveat once the freehold was purchased showed that the purchaser in *Holt Renfrew* was well aware of the effect that a proper caveat would have on the priority accorded to the unregistered lease. In *McCulloch* the purchaser did at least advise the prior interest holder of the loss of their caveat protection.

The Court of Appeal in *McCulloch* seems to be intimating that it was lifting the corporate veil and, hence, treating the transfer to the company as a sham; yet the Court stopped short of saying so explicitly. Perhaps the case can be accepted on the basis that the transfer contravened (arguably) the vendor's contract with the Province. These facts were known to the purchaser, obviously, and so the transfer might be seen as fraudulent because the transferee was inducing a breach of contract. Nothing precisely of this kind occurred in *Holt Renfrew*.

(c)   personal rights

Even in jurisdictions that have embraced the principle of immediate inde-feasibility, the transferee's title may still be affected by claims that exist between the transferor and the transferee. Personal (or *in personam*) rights remain available and may lead to the return of the property to the transferring party. Personal claims relate to some right of action that exists between the parties locked in a dispute, the result of which can lead to a change in the state of title. (Hence, it might be best to label these *inter se* (not *in personam*) situations.) For instance, a right of rectification based on error in the transfer document, a claim for rescission based on mutual mistake, and other rights of termination under contract law (assuming there is a contract), can serve as a basis for the vitiation of the deal.[96]

A more controversial argument has been advanced that, when C takes a transfer on which B has forged the signature of A (the true owner), A may have a restitutionary *in personam* claim against C, provided that C ought to have detected the forgery. If that line of reasoning – yet untried in Canada – holds water, its effect under an immediate indefeasibility system can be significant. We know that absent this proposition, C would acquire an indefeasible title, and need not take the slightest precaution in detecting the forgery. Absent fraud by the purchaser, C enjoys the status of a *bona fide* purchaser. Add the chance of a restitutionary action by A, and C will be liable if C should have known of the facts that give rise to that action. This constructive notice does not relate to a pre-existing but unregistered interest (which is the type of deemed notice that Torrens statutes discount), but rather to notice of facts that would support imposing a fresh obligation on C.[97]

The upshot of accepting that *in personam* rights exist in the above example is that a purchaser would be required to make some normal inquiries as to whether a forgery has occurred. From a policy point of view this is not an unfortunate

---

96 See further P. Butt, *Land Law*, 3rd ed. (Sydney: Law Book Co., 1996) at 751*ff*.

97 See R. Chambers, "Indefeasible Title as a Bar to a Claim for Restitution", [1998] Rest.L.Rev. 126. Chambers's basic position is endorsed in J. Moore, "Equity, Restitution, and In Personam Claims under the Torrens System: Part Two" (1999) 73 A.L.J. 712.

result. On the other hand, the downside is that permitting the infusion of a type of constructive notice renders a determination of the ultimate validity of a tainted transaction far less certain. Torrens title statutes are, as we know, designed to produce ownership rules that have finely tapered edges, even if this means that sometimes only rough justice is achieved.

(d)   overriding interests

In a perfect Torrens world the register would be a true reflection of all interests affecting a parcel of land. This, again, is the mirror principle. The first South Australian statute was faithful to this objective; however, not long afterwards exceptions were introduced. Probably all Torrens statutes allow some rights to remain outside the system, and yet be binding on subsequent purchasers. In Alberta, the principal list of these overriding interests is as follows:[98]

> (a) any subsisting reservations or exceptions, including royalties, contained in the original grant of the land from the Crown,
>
> (b) all unpaid taxes, including irrigation and drainage district rates,
>
> (c) any public highway or right of way or other public easement, howsoever created, on, over or in respect of the land,[99]
>
> (d) any subsisting lease or agreement for a lease for a period not exceeding 3 years, if there has been actual occupation of the land under the lease or agreement,
>
> . . .
>
> (f) any right of expropriation that may by statute be vested in any person or corporation or Her Majesty, and
>
> (g) any right of way or other easement granted or acquired under any Act or law in force in Alberta.

The rights vested in the state ((a)-(c) and (f)) can be tolerated as unregistered interests given the costs (to the public) and the inconvenience that would result from the need to register all such claims.[100] The exemption for short-term leases (item (d)) seems to be based on pragmatism. It would be rather excessive to require that all leases, however short their duration, be registered. These are, by definition, only a minor fetter, and they can often be discovered by a simple inquiry, or through an inspection of the premises. The protection of private easements defies explanation and the absence of a sound policy basis has prompted a restriction of this protection: item (g) is treated as covering only statutory and implied easements, but not express ones.[101]

---

98 *Land Titles Act*, R.S.A. 1980, c. L-5, sub. 65(1) [as am.].

99 See further *Foothills Municipal District No. 31 v. Stockwell* (1985) 41 Alta.L.R. (2d) 184, 39 R.P.R. 82, [1986] 1 W.W.R. 668 (C.A.).

100 Utility arrears now appear to be covered here: see *Municipal Government Act*, R.S.A. 1980, c. 26.1, s. 553 [as am.].

101 *Petro-Canada Inc. v. Shaganappi Village Shopping Centre Ltd.* (1990) 76 Alta.L.R. (2d) 162, 14 R.P.R. (2d) 127, [1991] 1 W.W.R. 169 (C.A.). See further B.H. Ziff, "A Matter of Overriding Interest: Unregistered Easements Under Alberta's Land Titles System" (1991) 29 Alta.L.Rev. 718. Implied easements are discussed in Parts 4(b) and (c), Chapter 10. Perhaps easements arising through estoppel fall within para. 65(1)(g).

This statutory list is not an exhaustive accounting, because it is possible for overriding interests to arise under other legislation. Even the common law can create rights or interests that are, from a functional perspective, just like overriding interests. For instance, a parcel of land may be subject to natural rights, such as the right of support.[102] These rights do not need to be registered on title to bind new owners of Blackacre.[103] Additionally, in the analysis below I will argue that Aboriginal land rights, including those created through the recognition rules of the common law, seem also to fall within the category of overriding interests.

(e)   caveats

'Registration' giving rise to the issuance of a Torrens-guaranteed title is available only for a defined (albeit large) set of interests. These typically include freehold estates, leases, and charges; the list varies with each statute. There is an obvious need to allow all tenable rights to appear on title, so that the mirror can reflect each and every entitlement that might pertain to a parcel. The primary means of providing protection for rights that are not amenable to registration in the strict sense is through the filing (or 'recording') of a caveat.

A caveat is a warning. It preserves the *status quo*, recording the presence of some interest in land. A caveat cannot create new rights.[104] Originally, the caveat was designed to provide interim protection for interests that would later be registered. In some jurisdictions it remains a temporary measure, and serves to "freeze the title situation on the register until a claimant of an interest [can] take legal steps to protect the claim".[105] Under the current Alberta system it is widely used as a means of recording interests, including those that cannot be registered. Generally, to be protectable by a caveat, the right claimed must be an interest in land.[106]

In what way does the filing of a caveat affect priorities? Different solutions are possible. A land titles system can incorporate the priority rules created at common law and in equity to determine the ranking of a caveated interest.[107] Or, the statute may provide that the filing of a caveat has the same effect on priority as does the registration of an instrument.[108] This latter approach means, in general,

---

102 See Part 4(b), Chapter 3.

103 See further *Jennings v. Sylvania Waters Pty. Ltd.*, [1972] 2 N.S.W.L.R. 4 (S.C.) at 11-2.

104 See *Royal Bank v. Banque d'Hochelaga* (1914) 8 Alta.L.R. 125, 7 W.W.R. 817, 19 D.L.R. 19 (C.A.).

105 Alberta Law Reform Institute, *Towards a New Alberta Land Titles Act* (Edmonton: A.L.R.I., 1990) at 7.

106 See, *e.g.*, *Land Titles Act*, R.S.A. 1980, c. L-5, s. 130 [as am.]. See, *e.g.*, *Iverson Heating Ltd. v. Canadian Imperial Bank of Commerce* (1983) 43 A.R. 142 (Q.B.). See also D.J. Purich, "The Caveat: An Uncertain Instrument In An Exact System" (1982-3) 47 Sask.L.Rev. 353; Mapp, *supra*, note 69, at 144, suggests that mere equities can be protected by caveat. This makes sense.

107 This is the case in New South Wales: see *Double Bay Newspapers Pty. Ltd. v. A.W. Holdings Pty. Ltd.* (1997) 42 N.S.W.L.R. 409 (Eq.Div.).

108 See, *e.g.*, *Land Titles Act*, R.S.A. 1980, c. L-5, ss. 145, 195 [as am.]. See *White Resource Management Ltd. v. Durish*, [1995] 1 S.C.R. 633, 26 Alta.L.R. (3d) 153, 121 D.L.R. (4th) 577, critiqued in W.H. Hurlbut, "Case Comment: Effect of *White Resource Management v. Durish*"

that a caveat protects a *bona fide* purchaser for value from interests not on title[109] (except those that qualify as overriding interests). In other words, under this approach caveated interests are treated more or less in the same way as if they had been noted on a race system form of deeds registration. Registration equals notice.

(f)   the place of Aboriginal land entitlements

With the emergence of a growing body of law concerning Aboriginal land rights, questions have arisen concerning the status of those interests within the existing land registration systems. In some instances Bands have attempted to file a caveat to record the existence of an Aboriginal right, or to file a *lis pendens*, which serves to declare that the land is the subject of litigation. The unique nature of Aboriginal title (the Supreme Court has said that it is a *sui generis* interest[110]) has spawned uncertainty as to whether it is possible to record Aboriginal claims under the existing land titles statutes.

So far the courts have rejected these attempts to record. In 1977, the Supreme Court of Canada decided that the land titles rules then in force in the Northwest Territories did not allow for the filing of a caveat on unpatented land; on this basis a caveat concerning an Aboriginal land claim would be of no effect.[111] Subsequent cases have also denied validity of a recording, on a host of grounds. In one case, the right to file a caveat was rejected because the plaintiff Band was asserting that the land in issue was within a federal reserve. If this claim were to succeed at trial the lack of registration under provincial law would pose no bar to the recovery of those lands, because the federal Crown would not be bound by the operation of the provincial land titles regime.[112] That type of reasoning has been applied to Aboriginal land claims that are not dependent on proof that the land is a reserve.[113] The right to file a caveat was refused in one decision because the interest claimed under the caveat (a right to hunt) was not found to be an interest in land.[114] In another case it was said that, because Aboriginal title is inalienable except through surrender to the Crown, this form of holding was incompatible with Torrens systems, which are designed to promote transferability.[115]

(1996) 34 Alta.L.Rev. 449. The case deals primarily with the effect of a lapse of a caveat on the determination of priorities.

109 See *Stephens v. Bannan* (1913) 6 Alta.L.R. 418, 14 D.L.R. 333 (C.A.); *Royal Bank v. Banque d'Hochelaga, supra,* note 104.

110 See Part 3(b)(i), Chapter 2.

111 *Paulette v. The Queen,* [1977] 2 S.C.R. 628, [1977] 1 W.W.R. 321, 72 D.L.R. (3d) 161.

112 *Lac La Ronge Indian Band v. Beckman* (1990) 70 D.L.R. (4th) 193, [1990] 4 W.W.R. 211 (Sask.C.A.).

113 *Chippewas of Kettle & Stony Point v. Canada (Attorney General)* (1994) 17 O.R. (3d) 831, 27 C.P.C. (3d) 322, [1994] 4 C.N.L.R. 34 (Gen.Div.).

114 *James Smith Indian Band v. Saskatchewan (Master of Titles)* (1995) 131 Sask.R. 60, [1995] 6 W.W.R. 158, 123 D.L.R. (4th) 280 (C.A.) leave to appeal to S.C.C. refused: [1995] S.C.C.A. 274. The majority in *James Smith Indian Band* left open the possibility that some Aboriginal interests might be compatible with land titles registration and would therefore fall within the system. Wakeling J.A. doubted this proposition. See further P. Babie, "Is Native Title Capable of Supporting a Torrens Caveat?" (1995) 20 Melb.U.L.Rev. 588.

115 *Uukw v. The Queen in Right of British Columbia,* [1987] 6 W.W.R. 240, 16 B.C.L.R. (2d)

While the upshot of these holdings is to put Aboriginal claimants on the outside of the land titles systems looking in, I do not think that this is problematic. This is especially so for claims in which the land in issue was patented by the Crown and put into circulation.[116] Following the original grant, many of the parcels have passed in and out of the hands of countless purchasers. There having been no record of the Aboriginal interest on title for most of this period, a *bona fide* purchaser for value who wished to rely on the Torrens system would presumably argue that the lands have been acquired free from the Aboriginal right. To put it another way, the curtain principle would protect the purchaser from having to accept the pre-existing Aboriginal claim. And if the basic rule of indefeasibility applies in this situation, then the private owners would be absolutely right: their titles would be free and clear. It would be simply too late to place a caveat on the titles to protect the Aboriginal right.

Therefore, except perhaps in the case where the disputed land is still in the hands of the Crown, nothing is lost simply because a caveat cannot be placed on the register. It is better for a Band to adopt the stance that the registration of ownership under Torrens is irrelevant to the continued validity of Aboriginal title.[117] The cases that hold that native land rights fall outside of the purview of the land registration system because those rights might undermine the register are saying, in effect, that Aboriginal rights are overriding interests. My advice would be to steer clear of the land titles system for fear that any attempt to invoke part of the system by filing a caveat or *lis pendens* might persuade a court to find that other parts of the Torrens scheme – specifically the principle of indefeasibility – should also be applied. (Of course, such a holding would be questionable: I doubt that a *provincial* land titles system can extinguish Aboriginal rights.)

(g) gratuitous transfers

A person who receives an interest by way of gift may be in no better position under a land titles system than under the general law. Equity will not assist a volunteer; that is the position in Alberta, and it appears to be the majority view under the Torrens statutes now in operation.[118] In consequence, registration in the name of a donee does nothing to affect the claims of prior owners. In effect, a

---

145, 37 D.L.R. (4th) 408 (C.A.) leave to appeal to S.C.C. refused [1987] 6 W.W.R. 240n (S.C.C.).

116 This was not the case in *Uukw v. The Queen in Right of British Columbia, ibid.,* where the claim was against Crown land. Likewise, one of the claims in *Lac La Ronge Indian Band, supra,* note 112, related to unpatented lands. Of course, in these cases the law concerning whether a caveat can be filed, by anyone, against Crown land, may preclude the filing of a caveat designed to protect Aboriginal title: see *Paulette v. The Queen, supra,* note 111.

117 It might be argued in reply that the issuance of the original letters patent to the land by the Crown works to extinguish Aboriginal title, but that is another matter: see Part 3(b)(iii), Chapter 2.

118 See *Kaup v. Imperial Oil Ltd.,* [1962] S.C.R. 170, 37 W.W.R. 193, 32 D.L.R. (2d) 38; *Passburg Petroleums Ltd. v. Landstrom Developments Ltd.* (1984) 30 Alta.L.R. (2d) 379, [1984] 4 W.W.R. 14, 8 D.L.R. (4th) 363 (C.A.) leave to appeal to S.C.C. refused (1984) 54 A.R. 160n (S.C.C.). But see *Anger & Honsberger Law of Real Property, supra,* note 88, vol. 2, at 1616; R. Carter, "Does Indefeasibility Protect the Title of a Volunteer? A Comment on *Matkowski v. Matkowski Estate* and *Matkowski and Sim v. Sim*" (1984-5) 49 Sask.L.Rev. 329.

donee can acquire no better title than that held by the donor. This rule can produce hardship in instances where a donee has made improvements on the land. There is a separate remedy that can be invoked in that eventuality, which is applicable whether or not one is a volunteer.[119]

(h) substantive validity

An interest is not validated in all respects by registration. The fact that a title is certified, or an easement is recorded[120] or protected by caveat, is no guarantee of complete substantive validity, no matter how many times these interests have changed hands over the years. It will be recalled that there are four elements of an easement at common law.[121] An easement may be noted on title, but this by no means certifies that these four prerequisites have been met. Terms which are void for uncertainty remain so even after registration. A term that contravenes the rule against perpetuities cannot logically be perfected by registration. Likewise, the registration of a charge does not place a stamp of juridical approval on every clause in that security instrument:

> The Torrens system does not make valid that which is invalid. Registration of a mortgage at Land Titles does not overcome a term which is void for uncertainty. Registration at Land Titles is not designed to affect that which is within the four corners of a contract, or designed to have an effect on the interpretation of a contract or of any of its terms. The interpretation of a contract is a matter of law, not registration.[122]

(i) misdescription and prior certificate of title

Under some Torrens systems the curtain will not be drawn to prevent an assertion that the land has been misdescribed in a certificate of title, even one issued to a *bona fide* purchaser for value. This means that boundary errors that result in too much or too little land being contained in the certificate of title can later be rectified.[123] Additionally, a purchaser deriving title from the uncancelled prior certificate of title will apparently retain the priority accorded to this earlier transaction.[124] Concerns over these possibilities can be allayed by a historical search to determine whether the 'top title' is a correct reflection of entitlements.[125]

---

119 See, *e.g.*, *Law of Property Act*, R.S.A. 1980, c. L-8, s. 60, referred to in Part 3(a), Chapter 3.

120 S. 70 of the Alberta Act directs the registrar to record a memorandum on title noting an easement or other incorporeal interests.

121 See Part 2, Chapter 10.

122 *Northland Bank v. Munzel Properties Ltd.*, [1985] A.J. No. 291 (Master) at para. 61 (*per* Master Funduk). See also *Travinto Nominees Pty. Ltd. v. Vlattas* (1973) 129 C.L.R. 1 (Aust.H.C.) at 17. *Cf. Consolidated Development Pty. Ltd. v. Holt* (1986) 6 N.S.W.L.R. 607 (Eq.Div.).

123 See further *Edwards v. Duborg* (1982) 22 Alta.L.R. (2d) 63, [1982] 6 W.W.R. 128 (Q.B.), additional reasons at (1982) 31 Alta.L.R. (2d) 96, [1983] 6 W.W.R. 672 (Q.B.) affirmed without reasons (C.A.).

124 See further *Canadian Pacific Railway Ltd. v. Turta*, [1954] S.C.R. 427, 12 W.W.R. (N.S.) 97, [1954] 3 D.L.R. 1. This decision, a classic in Canadian law, contains a compendium of principles relating to the Alberta *Land Titles Act*.

125 See further I.L. Head, "The Torrens System in Alberta: A Dream in Operation" (1957) 35 Can.B.Rev. 1, at 12*ff*.

In those Torrens jurisdictions in which adverse possession is possible, proof of possession for the requisite limitation period may result in the quieting of titles when a defect concerning a misdescription or a prior certificate is at issue. By relying on the law of adverse possession the true owner is saying 'while the Torrens certificate may be in error, I have nonetheless run out the clock over the lands in question against any alleged prior owner'.[126]

6. REFORM IDEAS

(a) improving land titles[127]

In the mid-nineteenth century, Robert Torrens called for reform on a grand scale. In his view the regime then in place "could not be patched or mended: the very foundation was rotten".[128] As we know, he was able to replace the old ways with the system that now bears his name. In 1990, the Joint Land Titles Committee, a group composed of representatives from the Council of Maritime Premiers and the other common law provinces and territories, published a draft *Model Land Recording and Registration Act* for real property.[129] The Canadian Torrens statutes are looking frayed after a century of use, but the Joint Committee chose not to discard them altogether. Rather, their reforms are designed to patch and mend. If these proposals become law, many of the uncertainties and anomalies emerging out of more than a century of jurisprudence would be removed. Moreover, if the reforms are adopted across the country, there will be inter provincial harmony in this area of the law for the first time.[130]

The Model Act would retain the distinction between title registration (proper) and interest recording (*i.e.*, what is now called the filing of caveats). Registration can give rise to indefeasibility; a recording affects only priorities. On the matter of the time at which indefeasibility is conferred, the Model Act adopts a middle ground between the immediate and deferred approaches. The general rule would be that deferred indefeasibility would apply to registered interests. If fraud in transaction #1 is discovered before the land is registered as part of transaction #2, title would normally be restored to the true owner on the view that this is generally going to be the least intrusive measure. The purchaser (in #1) who is deprived of a registered interest by the operation of the deferred rule would be able to seek compensation from the land titles assurance fund. That is new.[131] Moreover, a court would be empowered to grant immediate indefeasibility in favour of the

---

126 See further Part 3, Chapter 4.

127 Queensland has recently reformed its Torrens statute: see generally P. Butt, "A New Era in Torrens Title in Queensland: The Land Title Act 1994" (1994) 68 A.L.J. 675.

128 Robert Torrens, quoted in D.J. Whalan, *The Torrens System in Australia* (Sydney: Law Book Co, 1982) at 21.

129 Joint Land Titles Committee, *Renovating the Foundation: Proposals for a Model Land Recording and Registration Act for the Provinces and Territories of Canada* (Edmonton: A.L.R.I., 1990). See also Alberta Law Reform Institute, *Proposals for a Land Recording and Registration Act for Alberta* (Edmonton: A.L.R.I., 1993).

130 Recall the lament in note 8, *supra*.

131 See also New South Wales Law Reform Commission, *Torrens Title: Compensation for Loss* (Sydney: N.S.W.L.R.C., 1996).

first purchaser when it would be just and equitable to do so having regard to: (i) the nature of the ownership and the use of the property by the parties; (ii) the circumstances of the invalid transaction; (iii) the special characteristics of the property and its appeal to the parties;[132] (iv) the willingness of a party to receive compensation; (v) the ease of determining the proper quantum of an award; and (vi) any other relevant circumstance.[133] Volunteers would be protected by the deferred indefeasibility rule for registered instruments, but not for recorded interests. In addition, the distinguishing feature of a purchase for value would be clarified. The general rule is that any consideration sufficient to support a contract will do.[134]

Under the Model Act, the fuzzy edges of fraud would be sharpened, especially with regard to the line between notice and fraud. The doctrine of constructive notice would remain inapplicable. In accordance with the prevailing view, actual notice of an unrecorded or unregistered interest would not amount to fraud, and one would be entitled to assume (unless one knows better) that the proposed transfer is authorized by the owner of that unprotected interest.

Under the proposals the number of standard overriding interests would be reduced to these: (i) reservations or exceptions in the original grant of fee simple, inserted expressly or by virtue of statute; (ii) municipal tax liens; and (iii) leases of less than three years, if there is actual occupation that could have been discovered through a reasonable investigation of the property.[135] In the case of two conflicting registers (a rare problem), priority would be based on possession. If this test does not resolve the dispute, preference will be given to a holder who has given value, or to one taking from a person giving value. When this is not decisive, it would be necessary to review the chain of title to see who has the earliest derived claim.[136] Once a determination is made, compensation would become available to the subordinated party. A misdescription of boundaries would not be treated as a separate exception to the indefeasibility principle.

We still do not know whether this Model Act will be adopted across the country. It has received favourable reviews from abroad.[137] More significant is the fact that it has been implemented in parts of Alberta. In Chapter 5 mention was made of the Métis land systems that have been established in eight communities in the Province.[138] Within these settlements various land interests have been

---

132 This is an explicit recognition of the personhood theory of private property: see Part 3(e), Chapter 1.

133 S. 5(6).5.

134 Para. 1.1(w). See also subparas. 1.1(w)(i)-(iii).

135 Specified 'utility interests' might also be protected here; this is an optional feature of the Model Act: see para. 6.1(d). Additional overriding interests may be added expressly under another statute: para. 6.1(e).

136 S. 5(8).

137 See, e.g., E. Toomey, "Fraud and Forgery in the 1990's: Can *Frazer v. Walker* Survive the Strain?", presented at the Australasian Law Teachers Association Conference, Hobart, Tasmania, September, 1994 [copy on file at the University of Alberta]; L.A. McCrimmon, "Protection of Equitable Interests Under the Torrens System: Polishing the Mirror of Title" (1994) 20 Monash U.L.Rev. 300.

138 See Part 7, Chapter 5.

conferred. A registry has been established under the system, and the governing land titles law is based closely on the *Model Land Recording and Registration Act*.[139]

(b)   title insurance

In the United States private title insurance is widely available as a means of protecting a purchaser or lender against the dangers of acquiring an imperfect title. In the past few years the use of title insurance has grown considerably in Canada, especially in Ontario.[140] There are now a handful of title insurance companies in that Province, including one (TitlePlus) which operates under the auspices of the Law Society of Upper Canada. Along with this development, 'closing centres' have been established to provide an array of real estate services. Even in jurisdictions such as Alberta, where Torrens title is designed to facilitate transfer, title insurance companies offer policies that purport to complement the land titles protections. There is a gap to be filled: the assurance fund under current Torrens law is available for the deprived owner, while title insurance is designed to protect a purchaser who acquires a title that does not turn out to be indefeasible.

The use of insurance policy in relation to land sales reminds us that property registration rules are fundamentally about the allocation of *risk*, a point made at the beginning of this chapter. Risk spreading is, of course, the province of insurance. The kinds of coverage that are available vary widely, but they commonly involve protection against defects in title, or in title documents, lack of valid access to the subject parcel, and the right to reimbursement for legal expenses associated with a law suit brought in relation to the insured risks. Through the inclusion of special endorsements, the standard coverage can be augmented. Of course, like all insurance contracts – in which the big print giveth and the small print taketh away – there are typically numerous exclusions, exemptions and limitations. These qualifications seem to make the stated advantages of insurance systems (that is, that they are cheap, efficient and effective) sound very much like the grandiose claims that are occasionally made by proponents of Torrens statutes. As we have seen throughout this chapter, many of the touted benefits of Torrens title are not fully realized.

---

139 See further C.E. Bell, *Alberta's Metis Settlements Legislation: An Overview of Ownership and Management of Settlement Lands* (Regina: Canadian Plains Research Centre, 1994) ch. 4.

140 See further B.A. McKenna, ed., *Title Insurance: A Guide to Regulation, Coverage and Claims Process in Ontario* (Toronto: C.C.H. Can.Ltd., 1999).

INDEX